# PROJECT

# Project

This is not a course in theoretical philosophy, nor is it concerned with precise terminology in connection with origins. It is concerned only with Atonement, or the correction of perception. The means of the Atonement is forgiveness. The structure of "individual consciousness" is essentially irrelevant, because it is a concept representing the "original error" or the "original sin." To study the error itself does not lead to correction, if you are indeed to succeed in overlooking the error. And it is just this process of overlooking at which the course aims

All terms are potentially controversial, and those who seek controversy will find it. Yet those who seek clarification will find it as well. They must, however, be willing to overlook controversy, recognizing that it is a defence against truth in the form of a delaying manoeuvre.

Theological-considerations as such are necessarily controversial, since they depend on belief and can therefore be accepted or rejected. A universal theology is impossible, but a universal experience is not only possible but necessary. It is this experience toward which the course is directed. Here alone consistency becomes possible, because here alone uncertainty ends.

This course remains within the ego framework, where it is needed. It is not concerned with what is beyond all error because it is planned only to set the direction towards it. Therefore, it uses words, which are symbolic, and cannot express what lies beyond symbols. It is always the ego that questions because it is only the ego that doubts. The course merely gives another Answer, once a question has been raised. However, this Answer does not attempt to resort to inventiveness or ingenuity. These are attributes of the ego. The course is simple. It has one function and one goal. Only in that does it remain wholly consistent because only that can be consistent.

The ego will demand many answers this course does not give. It does not recognize as questions the mere form of a question to which an answer is impossible. The ego may ask, "How did the impossible occur?", "to what did the impossible happen?", and may ask in many forms. Yet there is no answer; only an experience. Seek only this, and do not let theology delay you.

You will notice that the emphasis on structural issues in the course is brief and early. Afterwards and soon it drops away to make way for the central teaching. Since you have asked for clarification, however, these are some of the terms that are used: The term "mind" is used to represent the activating agent of spirit, supplying its creative energy. When the term is capitalized it refers to God or Christ (i.e. the Mind of God or the Mind of Christ).

Spirit is the thought of God which he created like himself. The unified Spirit is God's one Son, or Christ. In this world, because the mind is split, the Sons of God appear to be separate. Nor do their minds seem to be joined. In this illusory state the concept of an "individual mind" seems to be meaningful. It is therefore described in the course as if it has two parts; spirit and ego. Spirit is the part that is still in contact with God through the Holy Spirit, Who abides in this part but sees the other part as well. The term "soul" is not used except in direct Biblical quotations because of its highly controversial nature. It would, however, be an equivalent of "spirit," with the understanding that being of God it is eternal and was never born.

The other part of the mind is entirely illusory and makes only illusions. Spirit retains the potential for creating, but its Will which is God's, seems to be imprisoned while the mind is not unified. Creation continues unabated because that is the Will of God. This will is always unified, and therefore has no meaning in this world. It has no opposite and no degrees. The mind can be right or wrong, depending on the voice to which it listens. "Right-mindedness" listens to the Holy Spirit, forgives the world, and through Christ's vision sees the real world in its place. This is the final vision, the last perception, the condition in which God takes the final step Himself. Here time and illusions end together. "Wrong-mindedness" listens to the ego and makes illusions; perceiving sin and justifying anger, and seeing guilt, disease and death as real. Both this world and the real world are illusions, because right-mindedness merely overlooks, or forgives what never happened. Therefore it is not the "One-mindedness" of the Christ Mind, Whose Will is one with God's.

In this world the only remaining freedom is the freedom of choice; always between two choices or two voices. Will is not involved in perception at any level and has nothing to do with choice. Consciousness is the receptive mechanism, receiving messages from above or below; from the Holy Spirit or the ego. Consciousness has levels and awareness can shift quite dramatically, but it cannot transcend the perceptual realm. At its highest it becomes aware of the real world and can be trained to do so increasingly. Yet the very fact that it has levels and can be trained demonstrates that consciousness cannot reach knowledge.

Illusions will not last. Their death is sure, and this alone is certain in their world. It is the ego's world because of this. What is the ego? But a dream of what you really are. A thought you are apart from your Creator and a wish to be what He created not. It is a thing of madness, not reality at all. A name for namelessness is all it is. A symbol of impossibility; a choice for options that do not exist. We call it that to help us understand that it is nothing but an ancient thought that what is made has immortality. But what could come of this except a dream which like all dreams could only die?

What is the ego? Nothingness, but in a form that seems like something. In a world of form the ego cannot be denied, for it alone seems real. How could God's Son as He created him abide in form or in a world of form? Who asks you to define the ego and explain how it arose can be but he who thinks it real, and seeks by definition to ensure that its illusive nature is concealed behind the words that seem to make it so. There is no definition for a lie that serves to make it true. Nor can there be a truth that lies conceal effectively. The ego's unreality is not denied by words nor is its meaning clear because its nature seems to have a form. Who can define the undefinable? And yet there is an answer even here. We cannot really make a definition for what the ego is, but we can say what it is not and this is shown to us with perfect clarity. It is from this that we deduce all that the ego is. Look at its opposite and you can see the only answer that is meaningful.

The ego's opposite in every way, – in origin, effect and consequence we call a miracle. And here we find all that is not the ego in the world. Here is the ego's opposite and here alone we look on what the ego was. For here we see all that it seemed to do, and cause and its effects must still be one. Where there was darkness now we see the light. What was the ego? What the darkness was. Where was the ego? Where the darkness was. What is it now and where can it be found? Nothing and nowhere. Now the light has come. Its opposite has gone without a trace. Where evil was there now is holiness. What is the ego? What the evil was. Where is the ego? In an evil dream that but seemed real while you were dreaming it. Where there was crucifixion stands God's Son. What is the ego? Who has need to ask? Where is the ego? Who has need to seek for an illusion now the dreams are gone? What is a miracle?

A dream as well. But look at all the aspects of this dream, and you will never question any more. Look at the kindly world you see stretch forth before you as you walk in gentleness. Look at the helpers all along the way you travel, happy in the hope of Heaven and the certainty of peace. And look an instant, too, on what you left behind at last and finally passed by. This was the ego – all the cruel hate, the need for vengeance and the cries of pain, the fear of dying and the urge to kill, the brotherless illusion and the self that seemed alone in all the universe.

This terrible mistake about yourself the miracle corrects as gently as a loving mother sings her child to rest. Is not a song like this what you would hear? Would it not answer all you thought to ask, and even make the question meaningless? Your questions have no answer, being made to still God's Voice, Which asks of everyone one question only: "Are you ready yet to help Me save the world?" Ask this instead of what the ego is, and you will see a sudden brightness cover up the world the ego made. No miracle is now withheld from anyone. The world is saved from what you thought it was.

And what it is, is wholly uncondemned and wholly pure. The miracle forgives; the ego damns. Neither need be defined except by this. Yet could a definition be more sure or more in line with what salvation asks? Problem and answer lie together here and having met at last the choice is clear. Who chooses hell when it is recognized? And who would not go on a little while when it is given him to understand the way is short and Heaven is his goal?

Forgiveness is for God and toward God but not of Him. It is impossible to think of anything He created that could need forgiveness. Forgiveness, then, is an illusion, but because of its purpose, which is the Holy Spirit's, it has one difference. Unlike all other illusions, it leads away from error and not towards it. Forgiveness might be called a kind of happy fiction; a way in which the unknowing can bridge the gap between their perception and the truth. They cannot go directly from perception to knowledge because they do not think it is their will to do so. This makes God appear to be an enemy instead of what He really is. And it is just this insane perception that makes them unwilling merely to rise up and to return to Him in peace.

And so they need an illusion of Help because they are helpless; a Thought of peace because they are in conflict. God knows what His Son needs before he asks. He is not at all concerned with form but having given the content it is His Will that it be understood. And that suffices. The form adapts itself to need; the content is unchanging, as eternal as its Creator. The Face of Christ has to be seen before the memory of God can return. The reason is obvious. Seeing the Face of Christ is perception. No one can look on knowledge. But the Face of Christ is the great symbol of forgiveness. It is salvation. It is the symbol of the real world. Whoever looks on this no longer sees the world. He is as near to Heaven as possible outside the gate. Yet from this gate it is no more than just a step inside. It is the final step. And this we leave to God. It is a symbol, too, but as the symbol of His Will alone it cannot be divided. And so the Unity that it reflects becomes His Will. It is the only thing still in the world in part, and yet the bridge to Heaven.

God's Will is all there is. We can but go from nothingness to everything; from hell to Heaven. Is this a journey? No, not in truth, for truth goes nowhere. But illusions shift from place to place; from time to time. The final step is also but a shift. As a perception it is partly unreal. And yet this part will vanish. What remains is peace eternal and the Will of God. There are no wishes now, for wishes change. Even the wished-for can become unwelcome. That must be so, because the ego cannot be at peace. But Will is constant, as the gift of God. And what He gives is always like Himself.

This is the purpose of the Face of Christ. It is the gift of God to save His Son. But look on this and you have been forgiven. How lovely does the world become in just that single instant when you see the truth about yourself reflected there. Now you are sinless and behold your sinlessness. Now you are holy and perceive it so. And now the mind returns to its Creator; the joining of the Father and the Son; the Unity of unities that stands behind all joining but still beyond them all. God is not seen but only understood. His Son is not attacked but recognized.

The world you see is an illusion of a world. God did not create it, for what He creates must be eternal as Himself. Yet there is nothing in the world you see that will endure forever. Some things will last in time a little while longer than others. But the time will come when all things visible will have an end. The body's eyes are therefore not the means by which the real world can be seen, for the illusions that they look upon must lead to more illusions (of reality). And so they do. For everything they see not only will not last but lends itself to thoughts of sin and guilt. While everything that God created is forever without sin and therefore is forever without guilt. Knowledge is not the remedy for false perception since, being another level, they can never meet. The one correction possible for false perception must be true perception. It will not endure. But for the time it lasts, it comes to heal. For true perception is a remedy with many names.

Forgiveness, salvation, Atonement, true perception, all are one. They are as one beginning with the end to lead to Oneness far beyond themselves. True perception is the means by which the world is saved from sin, for sin does not exist. And it is this that true perception sees.

The world stands like a block before Christ's face. But true perception looks on it as nothing more than just a fragile veil, so easily dispelled that it can last no longer than an instant. It is seen at last for only what it is. And now it cannot fail to disappear, for now there is an empty place made clean and ready. Where destruction was perceived the face of Christ appears, and in that instant is the world forgot, with time forever ended as the world spins into nothingness from where it came.

A world forgiven cannot last. It was the home of bodies. But forgiveness looks past bodies. This is its holiness; this is how it heals. The world of bodies is the world of sin, for only if there is a body is sin possible. From sin comes guilt as surely as forgiveness takes all guilt away. And once all guilt is gone what more remains to keep a separated world in place? For place has gone as well along with time. Only the body makes the world seem real, for being separate it could not remain where separation is impossible. Forgiveness proves it is impossible because it sees it not. And what you then will overlook will not be understandable to you, just as its opposite was once your certainty; just as its presence once had been your certainty.

This is the shift that true perception brings: what was projected out is seen within and there forgiveness lets it disappear. For there the altar to the Son is set, and there his Father is remembered. Here are all illusions brought to truth and laid upon the altar. What is seen outside must lie beyond forgiveness, for it seems to be forever sinful. Where is hope while sin is seen as outside? What remedy can guilt expect? But seen within your mind, guilt and forgiveness for an instant lie together, side by side, upon one altar. There at last are sickness and its single remedy joined in one healing brightness. God has come to claim His Own. Forgiveness is complete.

And now God's knowledge, changeless, certain, pure and wholly understandable, enters its Kingdom. Gone is perception, false and true alike. Gone is forgiveness, for its task is done. And gone are bodies in the blazing light upon the altar to the Son of God. God knows it is His Own as it is his. And here They join, for here the face of Christ has shone away time's final instant, and now is the last perception of the world without a purpose and without a cause. For where God's memory has come at last there is no journey, no belief in sin, no walls, no bodies, and the grim appeal of guilt and death is there snuffed out forever.

O my brothers, if you only knew the peace that will envelop you and hold you safe and pure and lovely in the Mind of God, you could but rush to meet Him where His altar is. Hallowed your Name and His, for they are joined here in this holy place. Here He leans down to lift you back to Him, out of illusions into holiness; out of the world and into eternity; out of all fear and given back to Love.

There is no need for help to enter Heaven, for you never left. But there is need for help beyond yourself as you (are) circumscribed by false beliefs of your Identity, Which God alone established in reality. Helpers are given you in many forms, although upon the altar They are one. Beyond each one, there is a Thought of God, and this will never change. But they have names which differ for a time, for time needs symbols, being itself unreal. Their names are legion, but we will not go beyond the names the course itself employs. God does not help because He knows no need. But He creates all Helpers of His Son while he believes his fantasies are true. Thank God for them, for they will lead you home.

The Name of Jesus is the name of one who was a man but saw the face of Christ in all his brothers and remembered God. So he became identified with Christ, a man no longer but at one with God. The man was an illusion, for he seemed to be a separate being, walking by himself, within a body that appeared to hold his self from Self, as all illusions do. Yet who can save unless he sees illusions, and then identifies them as what they are? Jesus remains a Saviour because he saw the false without accepting it as true. And Christ needed his form that He might appear to men and save them from their own illusions

In his complete identification with the Christ, the perfect Son of God, His one creation and His happiness, forever like Himself and one with Him— Jesus became what all of us must be. He led the way for us to follow him. He leads us back to God because he saw the road before him, and he followed it. He made a clean distinction, still obscure to us, between the false and true. He offered us all a final demonstration it is impossible to kill God's Son; nor can his life in any way be changed by sin and evil, malice, fear or death. And therefore all your sins have been forgiven you because they carried no effects at all. And so they were but dreams. Arise with him who showed you this because you owe him this who shared your dreams that they might be dispelled. And shares them still to be at one with you.

Is he the Christ? O yes, along with you. His little life on earth was not enough to teach the mighty lesson that he learned for all of us. He will remain with you to lead you from the hell you made to God. And when you join your will with his your sight will be his vision for the eyes of Christ are shared. Walking with him is just as natural as walking with a brother whom you knew since you were born, for such indeed he is. Some bitter idols have been made of him who would be only brother to the world. Forgive him your illusions and behold how dear a brother he would be to you. For he will set your mind at rest at last and carry it with you unto your God.

Is he God's only Helper? No indeed. For Christ takes many forms with different names until their oneness can be recognized. But Jesus is for you the bearer of Christ's single message of the Love of God. You need no other. It is possible to read his words and benefit from them without accepting him into your life. Yet he would help you yet a little more if you will share your pains and joys with him and leave them both to find the peace of God. Yet still it is his lesson most of all that he would have you learn, and it is this: "There is no death because the Son of God is like his Father. Nothing you can do can change Eternal Love. Forget y our dreams of sin and guilt and come with me instead to share the resurrection of God's Son. And bring with you all those whom He has sent to you to care for as I care for you."

Jesus is the manifestation of the Holy Spirit, whom he called down upon the earth after he ascended into Heaven, or became completely identified with the Christ, the Son of God as He created him. The Holy Spirit, being a creation of the One Creator, creating with him and in His likeness or Spirit, is eternal and has never changed. He was "called down upon the earth" in the sense that it was now possible to accept Him and to hear His Voice. His is the Voice for God and has therefore taken form.

This form is not his reality Which God alone knows along with Christ, His real Son, Who is part of Him. The Holy Spirit is described throughout the course as giving us the answer to the separation and bringing the plan of the Atonement to us, establishing our particular part in it, and showing us exactly what it is. He has established Jesus as the leader in carrying out this plan, since he was the first to complete his own part perfectly. All power in Heaven and earth is therefore given him, and he will share it with you when you have completed yours. The Atonement principle was given to the Holy Spirit long before Jesus set it in motion.

The Holy Spirit is described as the remaining communication link between God and His separated sons. In order to fulfil this special function the Holy Spirit has assumed a dual function; He knows because He is part of God. He perceives because He was sent to save humanity. He is the great correction principle; the bringer of true perception, the inherent power of the vision of Christ. He is the light in which the forgiven world is perceived; in which the face of Christ alone is seen. He never forgets the Creator or His Creation. He never forgets the Son of God. He never forgets you. And He brings the Love of your Father to you in an eternal shining that will never be obliterated because God has put it there.

The Holy Spirit abides in the part of your mind that is part of the Christ Mind. He represents your Self and your Creator, Who are One. He speaks for God and also for you, being joined with both. And therefore it is He Who proves them one. He seems to be a Voice, for in that form He speaks God's Word to you. He seems to be a Guide through a far country, for you need that form of help. He seems to be whatever meets the needs you think you have. But He is not deceived when you perceive your self entrapped in needs you do not have. It is from these He would deliver you. It is from these that He would make you safe.

You are His manifestation in this world. Your Brother calls to you to be His Voice along with him. Alone he cannot be the Helper of God's Son, for he alone is functionless. But joined with you he is the shining saviour of the world, whose part in its redemption you have made complete. He offers thanks to you as well as him, for you arose with him when he began to save the world. And you will be with him when time is over, and no trace remains of dreams of spite in which you dance to death's thin melody. For in its place the hymn to God is heard a little while. And then the voice is gone, no longer to take form but to return to the eternal formlessness of God.

This is a course in miracles. It is a required course. Only the time you take it is voluntary. Free will does not mean that you can establish the curriculum. It means only that you may elect what you want to take at a given time. The course does not aim at teaching the meaning of love, for that is beyond what can be taught. It does aim, however, at removing the blocks to the awareness of love's Presence,

Which is your natural inheritance. The opposite of love is fear, but what is all-encompassing can have no opposite. This course can therefore be summed up very simply in this way:

Nothing real can be threatened.
Nothing unreal exists.
Herein lies the Peace of
God. Principles of miracles

1. There is no order of difficulty among miracles. One is not "harder" or "bigger" than another. They are all the same. All expressions of love are maximal.
2. Miracles as such do not matter. The only thing that matters is their Source, Which is far beyond human evaluation
3. Miracles occur naturally as expressions of love. The real miracle is the love that inspires them. In this sense, everything that comes from love is a miracle.
4. All miracles mean life, and God is the Giver of life. His Voice will direct you very specifically. You will be told all you need to know.
5. Miracles are habits and should be involuntary. They should not be under conscious control. Consciously selected miracles can be misguided.
6. Miracles are natural. When they do not occur something has gone wrong.
7. Miracles are everyone's right, but purification is necessary first.
8. Miracles are healing because they supply a lack in that they are performed by those who temporarily have more for those who temporarily have less.
9. Miracles are a kind of exchange. Like all expressions of love, which are always miraculous in the true sense, the exchange reverses the physical laws. They bring more love both to the giver and the receiver.
10. The use of miracles as spectacles to induce belief is wrong; or, better, is a misunderstanding of their purpose. They are really used for and by believers.

11. Prayer is the medium of miracles. Prayer is the natural communication of the created with the Creator. Through prayer love is received, and through miracles love is expressed.
12. Miracles are thoughts. Thoughts can represent lower-order or higher order reality. This is the basic distinction between intellectualizing and thinking. One makes the physical and the other creates the spiritual, and we believe in what we make or create.
13. Miracles are both beginnings and endings. They thus alter the temporal order. They are always affirmations of rebirth, which seem to go back, but really go forward. They undo the past in the present, and thus release the future.
14. Miracles bear witness to truth. They are convincing because they arise from conviction. Without conviction they deteriorate into magic, which is mindless, and therefore destructive; or rather, the uncreative use of mind.
15. Each day should be devoted to miracles. The purpose of time is to enable man to learn to use it constructively. Time is thus a teaching device, and a means to an end. It will cease when it is no longer useful in facilitating learning.
16. Miracles are teaching devices for demonstrating that it is more blessed to give than to receive. They simultaneously increase the strength of the giver and supply strength to the receiver.
17. Miracles are the transcendence of the body. They are sudden shifts into invisibility, away from a sense of lower-order reality. That is why they heal.
18. A miracle is a service. It is the maximal service one individual can render another. It is a way of loving your neighbour as yourself. The doer recognizes his own and his neighbour's inestimable worth simultaneously.
19. Miracles make minds one in God. They depend on cooperation, because the Sonship is the sum of all the Souls God created. Miracles therefore rest on the laws of eternity, not of time.
20. Miracles reawaken the awareness that the Spirit, not the body, is the altar of truth. This is the recognition that leads to the healing power of the miracle.
21. Miracles are natural expressions of total forgiveness. Through miracles, man accepts God's forgiveness by extending it to others.
22. Miracles are associated with fear only because of the fallacious belief that darkness can hide. Man believes that what he cannot see does not exist, and his physical eyes cannot see in the dark.

This is a very primitive solution and has led to a denial of the Spiritual eye.

* The escape from darkness involves two stages:
   A. The recognition that darkness cannot hide. This step usually entails fear.
   B. The recognition that there is nothing you want to hide, even if you could. This step brings escape from fear.
   C. The term "Spiritual eye" is later replaced by the Holy Spirit and the physical eye becomes the ego. The emphasis on the two ways of seeing, however, remains throughout.

23. Miracles rearrange perception and place the levels of perception in true perspective. This heals at all levels, because sickness comes from confusing the levels. When you have become willing to hide nothing, you will not only be willing to enter into communion but will also understand peace and joy. Your commitment is not yet total, and that is why you still have more to learn than to teach. When your equilibrium stabilizes, you will be able to teach as much as you learn, which will give you the proper balance. Meanwhile, remember that no effort is wasted, for unless you remember this, you cannot avail yourselves of my efforts, which are limitless. Only eternity is real. Why not use the illusion of time constructively?

    Miracles enable man to heal the sick and raise the dead because he made sickness and death himself and can abolish both. You are a miracle, capable of creating in the likeness of your Creator. Everything else is only your own nightmare and does not exist. Only the Creations of Light are real.

24. Miracles are part of an interlocking chain of forgiveness which, when completed, is the Atonement. This process works all the time, and in all the dimensions of time.
    I am in charge of the process of Atonement, which I undertook to begin. When you offer a miracle unto any of my brothers, you do it unto yourself and me. The reason you come before me is that I do not need miracles for my own Atonement, but I stand at the end in case you fail temporarily. The purpose of my part in the Atonement is the cancelling out of all lacks of love which men could not otherwise correct. The word "sin" should be changed to "lack of love," because "sin" is a man-made word with threat connotations which he made up himself. No real

threat is involved anywhere. Nothing is gained by frightening yourselves, and it is very destructive to do so.

25. Miracles represent freedom from fear. "Atoning" really means "undoing." The undoing of fear is an essential part of the Atonement value of miracles.

    The purpose of the Atonement is to restore everything to you; or rather, to restore it to your awareness. You were given everything when you were created, just as everyone was. When you have been restored to the recognition of your original state, you naturally become part of the Atonement yourself. As you share my inability to tolerate lack of love in yourself and others, you must join the Great Crusade to correct it. The slogan for the Crusade is "Listen, learn, and do;" – Listen to my voice, learn to undo error, and do something to correct it.

    The power to work miracles belongs to you. I will provide the opportunities to do them, but you must be ready and willing, since you are already able. Doing them will bring conviction in the ability, since conviction really comes through accomplishment. The ability is the potential; the achievement is its expression; and the atonement is the purpose.

26. A miracle is a universal blessing from God through me to all my brothers. It is the privilege of the forgiven to forgive.

    The disciples were specifically told to be physicians of the Lord and to heal others. They were also told to heal themselves and were promised that I would never leave them or forsake them. Atonement is the natural profession of the Children of God, because they have professed me. "Heaven and earth shall pass away" simply means that they will not continue to exist as separate states. My word, which is the Resurrection and the Light, shall not pass away because Light is eternal. you are the work of God, and His work is wholly lovable and wholly loving. This is how a man must think of himself in his heart, because this is what he is.

27. Miracles are a means of organizing different levels of consciousness. Miracles come from the below or subconscious level. Revelations come from the above or superconscious level. The conscious level is in between and reacts to either sub- or superconscious impulses in varying ratios. Consciousness is the level which engages in the world and is capable of responding to both. Having no impulses from itself, and being primarily a mechanism for inducing response, it can be very wrong.

Revelation induces complete but temporary suspension of doubt and fear. It represents the original form of communication between God and His Souls, involving an extremely personal sense of closeness to Creation, which man tries to find in physical relationships. Physical closeness can not achieve this. The subconscious impulses properly induce miracles, which are genuinely interpersonal, and result in real closeness to others. This can be misunderstood by a personally wilful consciousness as impulses toward physical gratification.

Revelation unites Souls directly with God. Miracles unite minds directly with each other. Neither emanates from consciousness, but both are experiences there. This is essential, since consciousness is the state which induces action, though it does not inspire it. Man is free to believe what he chooses, and what he does attests to what he believes. The deeper levels of the subconscious always contain the impulse to miracles, but man is free to fill its more superficial levels, which are closer to consciousness, with the impulses of this world, and to identify himself with them. This results in denying himself access to the miracle level underneath. In his actions, then, his relationships also become superficial, and miracle-inspired relating becomes impossible.

28. Miracles are a way of earning release from fear. Revelation induces a state in which fear has already been abolished. Miracles are thus a means, and revelation is an end. Miracles do not depend on revelation; they induce it. Revelation is intensely personal and cannot actually be translated into conscious content at all. That is why any attempt to describe it in words is usually incomprehensible. Revelation induces only experience. Miracles, on the other hand, induce action. Miracles are more useful now, because of their interpersonal nature. In this phase of learning, working miracles is more important because freedom from fear cannot be thrust upon you.

29. Miracles praise God through men. They praise God by honouring His Creations, affirming their perfection. They heal because they deny body identification and affirm Soul-identification. By perceiving the Spirit, they adjust the levels and see them in proper alignment. This places the Spirit at the centre, where Souls can communicate directly.

30. Miracles should inspire gratitude, not awe. Man should thank God for what he really is. The Children of God are very holy, and the miracle honours their holiness. God's Creations never lose their holiness, although it can be hidden. The miracle uncovers it and brings it into the light where it belongs. Holiness can never be really hidden in darkness, but man can deceive himself about it. This illusion makes him fearful, because he knows in his heart it IS an illusion, and he exerts enormous efforts to establish its reality. The miracle sets reality where it belongs. Eternal reality belongs only to the Soul, and the miracle acknowledges only the truth. It thus dispels man's illusions about himself and puts him in communion with himself and God.

31. Christ inspires all miracles, which are really intercessions. They intercede for man's holiness and make his perceptions holy. By placing him beyond the physical laws, they raise him into the sphere of celestial order. In this order, man is perfect.

    The Soul never loses its communion with God. Only the mind needs Atonement. The miracle joins in the Atonement of Christ by placing the mind in the service of the Spirit. This establishes the proper function of the mind and corrects its errors.

32. Miracles honour man because he is lovable. They dispel illusions about him and perceive the Light in him. They thus atone for his errors by freeing him from his own nightmares. They release him from a prison in which he has imprisoned himself, and by freeing his mind from illusions, they restore his sanity. Man's mind can be possessed by illusions, but his Spirit is eternally free. If a mind perceives without love it perceives an empty shell and is unaware of the Spirit within it. But the Atonement restores the Soul to its proper place. The mind that serves the Spirit is invulnerable.

33. Miracles restore the mind to its fullness. By atoning for lack, they establish perfect protection. The strength of the Soul leaves no room for intrusions. The forgiven are filled with the Soul, and they forgive in return. It is the duty of the released to release their brothers.

    The forgiven are the means of Atonement. Those released by Christ must join in releasing their brothers, for this is the Plan of the Atonement. Miracles are the way in which minds which serve the Spirit unite with Christ for the salvation, or release, of all God's Creations.

34. Miracles are expressions of love, but it does not follow that they will always have observable effects. I am the only one who can

perform miracles indiscriminately, because I am the Atonement. You have a role in the Atonement, which I will dictate to you. Ask me which miracles you should perform. This spares you exhaustion, because you will act under direct communication.

35. Christ-controlled miracles are part of the Atonement, but Christ-guidance is personal. The impersonal nature of miracles is an essential ingredient, because this enables me to control their distribution. Christ-guidance leads to the highly personal experience of Revelation. This is why it involves personal choice. A guide does not control, but he does direct, leaving the following up to you. "Lead us not into temptation" means "guide us out of our own errors." "Take up thy cross and follow me" means "recognize your errors and choose to abandon them by following my guidance."

Remember that error cannot really threaten truth, which can always withstand it. Only the error is really vulnerable. You are free to establish your kingdom where you see fit, but the right choice is inevitable if you remember this: –

"The Soul is in a state of grace forever. Man's reality is only his Soul. Therefore, man is in a state of grace forever."

Atonement undoes all errors in this respect, and thus uproots the real source of fear. Whenever God's reassurances are experienced as threat, it is always because you are defending misplaced and misdirected loyalty. That is what projection always involves. Error is lack of love. When man projects this onto others, he does imprison them, but only to the extent that he reinforces errors they have already made.

This makes them vulnerable to the distortions of others, since their own perception of themselves is distorted. The miracle worker can only bless, and thus undoes their distortions, and frees them from prison.

37. Miracles are examples of right thinking. Reality contact at all levels becomes strong and accurate, thus permitting correct delineation of intra – and interpersonal boundaries. As a result, the doer's perceptions are aligned with truth as God created it.

38. A miracle is a correction factor introduced into false thinking by me. It acts as a catalyst, shaking up erroneous perception, and reorganizing it properly. This places man under the Atonement principle, where his perception is healed. Until this has occurred, revelation of the Divine order is impossible.

39. The Spiritual eye is the mechanism of miracles because what It perceives is true. It perceives both the Creations of God and the creations of man. Among the creations of man, It can also separate the true from the false by Its ability to perceive totally, rather than selectively. It thus becomes the proper instrument for reality testing, which always involves the necessary distinction between the false and the true.

40. The miracle dissolves error because the Spiritual eye identifies error as false, or unreal. This is the same as saying that by perceiving light, darkness automatically disappears.

   Darkness is lack of light, as sin is lack of love. It has no unique properties of its own. It is an example of the "scarcity" fallacy, from which only error can proceed. Truth is always abundant. Those who perceive and acknowledge that they have everything have no need for driven behaviour of any kind.

41. The miracle acknowledges all men as your brothers and mine. It is a way of perceiving the universal mark of God in them. The specialness of God's Sons does not stem from exclusion, but from inclusion. All my brothers are special. If they believe they are deprived of anything, their perception becomes distorted. When this occurs, the whole family of God, or the Sonship, is impaired in its relationships. Ultimately, every member of the family of God must return. The miracle calls him to return, because it blesses and honours him even though he may be absent in spirit

   > "God is not mocked" is not a warning, but a reassurance on this point. God would be mocked if any of His Creations lacked holiness.

The Creation is whole, and the mark of wholeness is holiness.

42. Wholeness is the perceptual content of miracles. It thus corrects, or atones for, the faulty perception of lack anywhere.

Here we begin to make the fundamental distinction between miracles and projection. The stimulus must precede the response and will also determine the kind of response that is evoked. Behaviour is response, so that the question "response to what?" becomes crucial. Since stimuli are identified through perception, you first perceive the stimulus and then behave accordingly. It follows, then, that:

> "As ye perceive, So shall ye behave."

The Golden Rule asks you to behave toward others as you would have them behave toward you. This means that the perception of both must be accurate. The Golden Rule is the rule for appropriate behaviour. You cannot behave appropriately unless you perceive accurately, because appropriate behaviour depends on lack of level confusion. The presence of level confusion always results in variable reality testing, and therefore in variability in behavioural appropriateness. Since you and your neighbour are equal members of the same family, as you perceive both, so you will behave toward both. The way to perceive for Golden Rule behaviour is to look out from the perception of your own holiness and perceive the holiness of others.

The emptiness engendered by fear should be replaced by love, because love and its absence are in the same dimension, and correction cannot be undertaken except within a dimension. Otherwise, there has been a confusion of levels. Death is a human affirmation of a belief in "fate," or level confusion. That is why the Bible says, "There is no death," and why I demonstrated that death does not exist. I came to fulfil the law by reinterpreting it. The law itself, if properly understood, offers only protection to man. It is those who have not yet "changed their minds" who entered the "hellfire" concept into it.

I assure you that I will witness for anyone who lets me, and to whatever extent he permits it. your witnessing demonstrates your belief, and thus strengthens it. Those who witness for me are expressing, through their miracles, that they have abandoned the belief in deprivation in-favour of the abundance they have learned belongs to them.

43. A major contribution of miracles is their strength in releasing man from his misplaced sense of isolation, deprivation and lack. Miracles are affirmations of Sonship, which is a state of completion and abundance. Whatever is true and real is eternal and cannot change or be changed. The Soul is therefore unalterable because it is already perfect, but the mind can elect the level it chooses to serve. The only limit which is put on its choice is that it cannot serve two masters. The mind, if it elects to do so, becomes a medium by which the Soul creates along the line of its own Creation. If it does not freely elect to do so, it retains its creative potential but places itself under tyrannous rather than genuinely authoritative control. As a result it imprisons, because such are the dictates of tyrants. To change your mind means to place it at the disposal of true authority. The miracle is thus a sign that the mind has chosen to be led by

Christ in His service. The abundance of Christ is the natural result of choosing to follow Him. All shallow roots must be uprooted, because they are not deep enough to sustain you. The illusion that shallow roots can be deepened, and thus made to hold, is one of the distortions on which the reversal of the Golden Rule rests. As these false underpinnings are given up, the equilibrium is temporarily experienced as unstable. However, the fact is that nothing is less stable than an orientation that is upside down. Nor can anything which holds it that way be really conducive to greater stability.

44. Miracles arise from a miraculous state of mind. By being one, this state of mind goes out to anyone, even without the awareness of the miracle worker himself. The impersonal nature of miracles is because the Atonement itself is one, uniting all creations with their Creator.

45. The miracle is an expression of an inner awareness of Christ, and the acceptance of His Atonement. The mind is then in a state of grace, and naturally becomes gracious, both to the Host within and the stranger without. By bringing in the stranger, he becomes your brother.

46. A miracle is never lost. It touches many people you do not even know, and sometimes produces undreamed of changes in forces of which you are not even aware. That is not your concern. The miracle will always bless you.

    The miracles you are not of your own state of grace, but the action aspect of the miracle should be Christ-controlled because of His complete awareness of the Whole Plan. The impersonal nature of miracle-mindedness ensures your grace, but only Christ is in a position to know where grace can be bestowed.

47. Miracle-mindedness means miracle-readiness. Readiness means that you should always keep your perceptions straight, so that you will always be ready, willing and able. These are the essentials for "listen, learn and do." You must be ready to listen, willing to learn, and able to do. Only the last is involuntary, because it is the application of miracles which must be Christ-controlled. The other two, which are the voluntary aspects of miracle mindedness, are up to you.

48. Awe is an inappropriate response to miracles. Revelation is literally unspeakable because it is an experience of unspeakable love. Awe should be reserved for revelation, to which it is perfectly and correctly applicable. It is not appropriate for miracles because a state of awe is worshipful. It implies that

one of a lesser order stands before a greater one. This is the case only when a Soul stands before its Creator. Souls are perfect creations, and experience awe only in the Presence of the Creator of perfection.

The miracle, on the other hand, is a sign of love among equals. Equals cannot be in awe of one another because awe implies inequality. It is therefore an inappropriate reaction to me. An elder brother is entitled to respect for his greater experience, and a reasonable amount of obedience for his greater wisdom. He is also entitled to love because he is a brother, and also to devotion if he is devoted. It is only my devotion that entitles me to yours. There is nothing about me that you cannot attain. I have nothing that does not come from God. The main difference between us as yet is that I have nothing else. This leaves me in a state of true holiness, which is only a potential in you.

"No man cometh unto the Father but by me" is among the most misunderstood statements in the Bible. It does not mean that I am in any way separate or different from you except in time, which does not really exist at all. Actually, the quotation is more meaningful if it is considered on a vertical rather than a horizontal axis. Regarded along the vertical, man stands below me and I stand below God. In the process of "rising up," I am higher. This is because, without me, the distance between God and man would be too great for you to encompass.

I bridge the distance as an elder brother to man on the one hand, and as a Son of God on the other. My devotion to my brothers has placed me in charge of the Sonship, which I can render complete only to the extent to which I can share it. This may appear to contradict the statement "I and my Father are one," but there are still separate parts in the statement, in recognition that the Father is greater. (The original statement was "are of one kind"). The Holy Spirit is the Bringer of Revelations. Revelations are indirectly inspired by me, because I am close to the Holy Spirit, and alert to the revelation-readiness of my brothers. I can thus bring down to them more than they can draw down to themselves.

49. The Holy Spirit is the Highest Communication Medium. Miracles do not involve this type of communication because they are temporary communication devices. When man returns to his original form of communication with God, the need for miracles is over. The Holy Spirit mediates higher to lower

communication, keeping the direct channel from God to man open for revelation. Revelation is not reciprocal. It is always from God to man. The miracle is reciprocal because it involves equality.

50. The miracle is a learning device which lessens the need for time. In the longitudinal or horizontal plane, the recognition of the true equality of all the members of the Sonship appears to involve almost endless time. However, the sudden shifts from horizontal to vertical perception which the miracle entails introduces an interval from which the doer and the receiver both emerge much farther along in time than they would otherwise have been.

The miracle thus has the unique property of shortening time by rendering the space of time it occupies unnecessary. There is no relationship between the time a miracle takes and the time it covers. It substitutes for learning that might have taken thousands of years. It does this by the underlying recognition of perfect equality and holiness between the doer and the receiver on which the miracle rests.

We said before that the miracle abolishes time. It does this by a process of collapsing it, and thus abolishing certain intervals within it. It does this, however, within the larger temporal sequence. It establishes an out-of-pattern time interval which is not under the usual laws of time. Only in this sense is it timeless. By collapsing time it literally saves time, much as daylight saving time does. It rearranges the distribution of light.

51. The miracle is the only device which man has at his immediate disposal for controlling time. Only revelation Transends time, having nothing to do with time at all. The miracle is much like the body, in that both are learning aids which aim at facilitating a state in which they are unnecessary. When the Soul's original state of direct communication is reached, neither the body nor the miracle serves any purpose. While he believes he is in a body, however, man can choose between loveless and miraculous channels of expression. He can make an empty shell, but he cannot express nothing at all. He can wait, delay, paralyse himself, reduce his creativity to almost nothing, and even introduce a developmental arrest or even a regression. But he cannot abolish his creativity. He can destroy his medium of communication, but not his potential.

Man was not created by his own free will alone. Only what he creates is his to decide. The basic decision of the miracle-minded is not to wait on time any longer than is necessary. Time can waste as well as be wasted. The miracle-worker, therefore, accepts the time-control factor gladly, because he recognizes that every collapse of time brings all men closer to the ultimate release from time, in which the Son and the Father are one.

Equality does not imply homogeneity now. When everyone recognizes that he has everything, individual contributions to the Sonship will no longer be necessary. When the Atonement has been completed, all talents will be shared by all the Sons of God. God is not partial. All His children have His total love, and all his gifts are freely given to everyone alike. "Except ye become as little children" means that, unless you fully recognize your complete dependence on God, you cannot know the real power of the Son in his true relationship with the Father.

You who want peace can find it only by complete forgiveness. You never really wanted peace before, so there was no point in being told how to achieve it. No learning is acquired by anyone unless he wants to learn it and believes in some way that he needs it. While the concept of lack does not exist in the Creation of God, it is very apparent in the creations of man. It is, in fact, the essential difference. A need implies lack by definition. It involves the recognition that you would be better off in a state which is somehow different from the one you are in.

Until the "separation," which is a better term than the "fall," nothing was lacking. This meant that man had no needs at all. If he had not deprived himself, he would never have experienced them. After the separation, needs became the most powerful source of motivation for human action. All behaviour is essentially motivated by needs, but behaviour itself is not a Divine attribute. The body is the mechanism for behaviour. The belief that he could be better off is the reason why man has this mechanism at his disposal.

Each one acts according to the particular hierarchy of needs he establishes for himself. His hierarchy, in turn, depends on his perception of what he IS; that is, what he lacks. A sense of separation from God is the only lack he really needs to correct. This sense of separation would never have occurred if he had not distorted his perception of truth, and thus perceived himself as lacking. The concept of any sort of need hierarchy arose because, having made this fundamental error, he had already fragmented himself into levels with different needs. As he integrates he becomes one, and his needs become one accordingly.

Unified need produces unified action because it produces a lack of ambivalence. The concept of a need hierarchy, a corollary to the original error that man can be separated from God, requires correction at its own level, before the error of perceiving levels at all can be corrected. Man cannot behave effectively while he operates at split levels. However, while he does, correction must be introduced from the bottom up. This is because he now operates in space, where concepts such as "up" and "down" are meaningful. Ultimately, space is as meaningless as time. The concept is really one of space-time belief.

The physical world exists only because man can use it to correct his unbelief, which placed him in it originally. He can never control the effects of fear himself because he made fear and believes in what he made. In attitude, then, though not in content, he resembles his own Creator who has perfect faith in His creations because He created them. Belief in a creation produces its existence. That is why a man can believe in what no-one else thinks is true. It is true for him because it was made by him.

Every aspect of fear proceeds from upside-down perception. The more truly creative devote their efforts to correcting perceptual distortions. The neurotic devotes his to compromise. The psychotic tries to escape by establishing the certain truth of his own errors. It is most difficult to free him by ordinary means, because he is more consistent in his own denial of truth. The miracle, however, makes no such distinctions. It corrects errors because they are errors. Thus, the next point to remember about miracles is:

52. The miracle makes no distinction among degrees of misperception. It is a device for perception-correction, effective quite apart from either the degree or the direction of the error. This is its true indiscriminateness.

Christ-controlled miracles are selective only in the sense that they are directed towards those who can use them for themselves. Since this makes it inevitable that they will extend them to others, a strong chain of Atonement is welded. However, Christ control takes no account at all of the magnitude of the miracle itself, because the concept of size exists in a plane that is itself unreal. Since the miracle aims at restoring the awareness of reality it would hardly be useful if it were bound by the laws which govern the error it aims to correct. Only man makes this kind of mistake. It is an example of the foolish consistency which his own false beliefs have engendered.

The power and strength of man's creative will must be understood before the real meaning of denial can be appreciated and relinquished. It is not mere negation. It is a positive miscreation. While the miscreation is necessarily believed in by its maker, it does not exist at all at the level of true creation.

53.    The miracle compares what man has made with the higher-level creation, accepting what is in accord as true and rejecting the discordant as false. All aspects of fear are untrue because they do not exist at the higher creative levels, and therefore do not exist at all. To whatever extent a man is willing to submit his beliefs to this test, to that extent are his perceptions corrected.

In sorting out the false from the true, the miracle proceeds along the following lines;

"If perfect love casts out fear, and if fear
exists, then there is not perfect love."
but
"Only perfect love really exists. If there is fear,
it creates a state which does not exist."

Believe this, and you will be free. Only God can establish this solution and this faith is His gift. You are involved in unconscious distortions which are producing a dense cover over miracle impulses, and which make it hard for them to reach consciousness. The nature of any interpersonal relationship is limited or defined by what you want it to do. Relating is a way of achieving an outcome. The danger of defences lies in their propensity for holding misperceptions rigidly in place. All actions which stem from reverse thinking are literally the behavioural expressions of those who know not what they do. A rigid orientation can be extremely reliable, even if it is upside-down. In fact, the more consistently upside-down it is, the more reliable it is.

However, validity is still the ultimate goal, which reliability can only serve. Hostility, triumph, vengeance, self-debasement, and all kinds of expressions of lack of love are often very clearly seen in the fantasies which accompany them. But it is a profound error to imagine that because these fantasies are so frequent, or occur so reliably, that this implies validity. Remember that while validity implies reliability, the relationship is not reversible. You can be wholly reliable and entirely wrong. While a reliable instrument does measure something, what use is it unless you discover what the "something" is? This course, then, will concentrate on validity, and let reliability fall naturally into place.

The confusion of miracle impulses with physical impulses is a major source of perceptual distortion because it induces, rather than straightens out, the basic level confusion which underlies the perception of all those who seek happiness with the instruments of this world. Inappropriate physical impulses (or misdirected miracle impulses) result in conscious guilt if expressed and depression if denied. All real pleasure comes from doing God's Will. This is because not doing it is a denial of self. Denial of error results in projection. Correction of error brings release. "Lead us not into temptation" means "do not let us deceive ourselves into believing that we can relate in peace to God or to our brothers with anything external."

Child of God, you were created to create the good, the beautiful, and the holy. Do not lose sight of this. The love of God, for a little while, must still be expressed through one body to another because the real vision is still so dim. Everyone can use his body best by enlarging man's perception, so he can see the real vision. This vision is invisible to the physical eye. The ultimate purpose of the body is to render itself unnecessary. Learning to do this is the only real reason for its creation.

Fantasies of any kind are distorted forms of thinking because they always involve twisting perception into unreality. Fantasy is a debased form of vision. Vision and revelation are closely related, while fantasy and projection are more closely associated because both attempt to control external reality according to false internal needs. Twist reality in any way, and you are perceiving destructively. Reality was lost through usurpation, which in turn produced tyranny. I told you that you are now restored to your former role in the plan of Atonement, but you must still choose freely to devote yourselves to the greater restoration. As long as a single slave remains to walk the earth, your release is not complete. complete restoration of the Sonship is the only true goal of the miracle-minded.

No fantasies are true. They are distortions of perception, by definition. They are a means of making false associations and obtaining pleasure from them. Man can do this only because he is creative. But although he can perceive false associations, he can never make them real except to himself. Man believes in what he creates. If he creates miracles, he will be equally strong in his belief in them. The strength of HIS conviction will then sustain the belief of the miracle receiver. And fantasies become totally unnecessary as the wholly satisfying nature of reality becomes apparent to both. This section deals with a fundamental misuse of knowledge, referred to in the Bible as the cause of the "fall," or separation. There are some definitions which I asked you to take from the dictionary which will be helpful here. They are somewhat unusual, since they are not the first definitions which are given. Nevertheless, the fact that each of them does appear in the dictionary should be reassuring.

> Project (verb): to extend forward or out.
> Project (noun): a plan in the mind. World: a natural grand division.

We will refer later to projection as related to both mental health and mental illness. We have already observed that man can create an empty shell, but he cannot create nothing at all. This emptiness provides the screen for the misuse of projection.

The Garden of Eden, which is described as a literal garden in the Bible, was not an actual garden at all. It was merely a mental state of complete need-lack. Even in the literal account, it is noteworthy that the pre-separation state was essentially one in which man needed nothing. The "tree of knowledge" is also an overly literal figure. These concepts need to be clarified before the real meaning of the separation, or the "detour into fear," can be fully understood.

To "project," as defined above, is a fundamental attribute of God, which He gave to His Son. In the Creation, God projected His Creative Ability from Himself to the Souls He created, and He also imbued them with the same loving will to create. The Soul has not only been fully created, but has also been created perfect. There is no emptiness in it. Because of its likeness to its Creator, it is creative. No Child of God can lose this ability because it is inherent in what he is, but he can use it inappropriately. Whenever projection is used inappropriately, it always implies that some emptiness or lack exists, and that it is in man's ability to put his own ideas there instead of truth.

If you consider carefully what this entails, the following will become quite apparent:

First, the assumption is implicit that what God created can be changed by the mind of man.

Second, the concept that what is perfect can be rendered imperfect, or wanting, is accepted.

Third, the belief that man can distort the Creations of God, including himself, is accepted.

Fourth, the idea that, since man can create himself, the direction of his own creation is up to Him is implied.

These related distortions represent a picture of what actually occurred in the separation. None of this existed before, nor does it actually exist now. The world was made as "a natural grand division," or a projecting outward of God. That is why everything that He created is like Him. Projection, as undertaken by God, is very similar to the kind of inner radiance which the Children of the Father inherit from Him. It is important to note that the term "project outward" necessarily implies that the real source of projection is internal. This is as true of the Son as of the Father.

The world, in the original connotation of the term, included both the proper Creation of man by God and the proper creation by man in his right mind. The latter required the endowment of man by God with free will, because all loving creation is freely given. Nothing in these statements implies any sort of level involvement, or, in fact, anything except one continuous line of creation, in which all aspects are of the same order.

When the "lies of the serpent" were introduced, they were specifically called "lies" because they are not true. When man listened, all he heard was untruth. He does not have to continue to believe what is not true unless he chooses to do so. All of his miscreations can literally disappear in "the twinkling of an eye," because they are merely visual misperceptions. Man's Spiritual eye can sleep, but a sleeping eye can still see. What is seen in dreams seems to be very real. The Bible mentions that "a deep sleep fell upon Adam," and nowhere is there any reference to his waking up.

The history of man in the world as he sees it has not yet been marked by any genuine or comprehensive reawakening or rebirth. This is impossible as long as man projects in the spirit of miscreation. It still remains within him, however, to project as God projected His Own Spirit to him. In reality, this is his only choice, because his free will was given him for his own joy in creating the perfect.

All fear is ultimately reducible to the basic misperception that man has the ability to usurp the power of God. It can only be emphasized that he neither can nor has been able to do this. In this fact lies the real justification for his escape from fear. The escape is brought about by his acceptance of the Atonement, which places him in a position to realize that his own errors never really occurred. When the "deep sleep" fell upon Adam, he was in a condition to experience nightmares because he was asleep. If a light is suddenly turned on while someone is dreaming a fearful dream, he may initially interpret the light itself as a part of his own dream and be afraid of it. However, when he awakens, the light is correctly perceived as the release from the dream, which is no longer accorded reality.

It is quite apparent that this release does not depend on the kind of "knowledge" which is nothing more than deceiving lies. The knowledge which illuminates rather than obscures is the knowledge which not only sets you free, but which also shows you clearly that you are free. Whatever lies you may believe are of no concern to the miracle, which can heal any of them with equal ease. It makes no distinctions among misperceptions. Its sole concern is to distinguish between truth on the one hand, and all kinds of errors on the other. Some miracles may seem to be of greater magnitude than others. But remember the first point in this course; that there is no order of difficulty in miracles.

In reality, you are perfectly unaffected by all expressions of lack of love. These can be either from yourself and others, or from yourself to others, or from others to you. Peace is an attribute in you. You cannot find it outside. All mental illness is some form of external searching. Mental health is inner peace. It enables you to remain unshaken by lack of love from without, and capable, through your own miracles, of correcting the external conditions which proceed from lack of love in others.

When you are afraid of anything, you are acknowledging its power to hurt you. Remember that where your heart is, there is your treasure also. This means that you believe in what you value. If you are afraid, you are valuing wrongly. Human understanding will inevitably value wrongly, and, by endowing all human thoughts with equal power, will inevitably destroy peace. That is why the Bible speaks of "The peace of God which passeth (human) understanding." This peace is totally incapable of being shaken by human errors of any kind. It denies the ability of anything which is not of God to affect you in any way.

This is the proper use of denial. It is not used to hide anything, but to correct error. It brings all error into the light, and since error and darkness are the same, it corrects error automatically. True denial is a powerful protective device. You can and should deny any belief that error can hurt you. This kind of denial is not a concealment device, but a correction device. The "right mind" of the mentally healthy depends on it.

You can do anything I ask. I have asked you to perform miracles, and have made it clear that miracles are natural, corrective, healing, and universal. There is nothing good they cannot do, but they cannot be performed in the spirit of doubt.

God and the Souls He created are completely dependent on each other. The creation of the Soul has already been perfectly accomplished, but the creation by Souls has not. God created Souls so He could depend on them because He created them perfectly. He gave them His peace so they could not be shaken, and would be unable to be deceived. Whenever you are afraid, you are deceived.

Your mind is not serving the Soul. This literally starves the Soul by denying its daily bread. God offers only mercy. Your words should reflect only mercy because that is what you have received, and that is what you should give.

Justice is a temporary expedient, or an attempt to teach man the meaning of mercy. Its judgmental side arises only because man is capable of injustice, if that is what his mind creates. You are afraid of God's Will because you have used your own will, which He created in the likeness of His Own, to miscreate. What you do not realize is that the mind can miscreate only when it is not free. An imprisoned mind is not free, by definition. It is possessed, or held back, by itself. Its will is therefore limited and is not free to assert itself. The real meaning of "are of one kind," which was mentioned before, is "are of one mind or will." When the Will of the Sonship and the Father are One, their perfect accord is Heaven.

Denial of error is a powerful defence of truth. You will note that we have been shifting the emphasis from the negative to the positive use of denial. As we have already stated, denial is not a purely negative device; it results in positive miscreation. That is the way the mentally ill do employ it. But remember a very early thought of your own; – "Never underestimate the power of denial." In the service of the "right mind," the denial of error frees the mind and re-establishes the freedom of the will. When the will is really free, it cannot miscreate because it recognizes only truth.

False projection arises out of false denial, not out of its proper use. My own role in the Atonement is one of true projection; I can project to you the affirmation of truth. If you project error to me, or to yourself, you are interfering with the process. My use of projection, which can also be yours, is not based on faulty denial. It does involve, however, the very powerful use of the denial of errors. The miracle worker is one who accepts my kind of denial and projection, unites his own inherent abilities to deny and project with mine, and imposes them back on himself and others. This establishes the total lack of threat anywhere. Together we can then work for the real time of peace, which is eternal.

The improper use of defences is quite widely recognized, but their proper use has not been sufficiently understood as yet. They can indeed create man's perception, both of himself and of the world.

They can distort or correct, depending on what you use them for. Denial should be directed only to error, and projection should be reserved only for truth. You should truly give as you have truly received. The Golden Rule can work effectively only on this basis.

Intellectualisation is a term which stems from the mind-brain confusion. "Rightmindedness" is the device which defends the right mind, and gives it control over the body. "Intellectualisation" implies a split, while "right-mindedness" involves healing.

Withdrawal is properly employed in the service of withdrawing from the meaningless. It is not a device for escape, but for consolidation. There is only one mind.

Dissociation is quite similar. You should split off or dissociate yourself from error, but only in defence of integration.

Detachment is essentially a weaker form of dissociation. Flight can be undertaken in whatever direction you choose but note that the concept itself implies flight from something. Flight from error is perfectly appropriate.

Distantiation can be properly used as a way of putting distance between yourself and what you should fly from.

Regression is an effort to return to your own original state. It can thus be utilized to restore, rather than to go back to the less mature.

Sublimation should be a redirection of effort to the sublime. There are many other so-called "dynamic" concepts which are profound errors due essentially to the misuse of defences. Among them is the concept of different levels of aspiration, which actually result from level confusion. However, the main point to be understood from this section is that you can defend truth as well as error, and, in fact, much better.

The means are easier to clarify after the value of the goal itself is firmly established. Everyone defends his own treasure. You do not have to tell him to do so, because he will do it automatically. The real questions still remain. What do you treasure, and how much do you treasure it? Once you have learned to consider these two questions, and to bring them into all your actions as the true criteria for behaviour, I will have little difficulty in clarifying the means. You have not learned to be consistent about this as yet. I have therefore concentrated on showing you that the means are available whenever you ask. You can, however, save a lot of time if you do not extend this step unduly. The correct focus will shorten it immeasurably.

The Atonement is the only defence which cannot be used destructively. That is because, while everyone must eventually join it, it is not a device which was generated by man. The Atonement principle was in effect long before the Atonement itself began. The principle was love, and the Atonement itself was an act of love. Acts were not necessary before the separation, because the time-space belief did not exist. It was only after the separation that the defence of Atonement, and the necessary conditions for its fulfilment, were planned.

It became increasingly apparent that all of the defences which man can choose to use constructively or destructively were not enough to save him. It was therefore decided that he needed a defence which was so splendid that he could not misuse it, although he could refuse it. His choice could not, however, turn it into a weapon of attack, which is the inherent characteristic of all other defences. The Atonement thus becomes the only defence which is not a two-edged sword.

The Atonement actually began long before the crucifixion. Many Souls offered their efforts on behalf of the separated ones, but they could not withstand the strength of the attack and had to be brought back. Angels came, too, but their protection did not suffice, because the separated ones were not interested in peace. They had already split their minds, and were bent on further dividing, rather than reintegrating. The levels they introduced into their minds turned against each other, and they established differences, divisions, cleavages, dispersions, and all the other concepts related to the increasing splits which they produced.

Not being in their right minds, they turned their defences from protection to assault, and acted literally insanely. It was essential to introduce a split-proof device which could be used only to heal, if it were used at all. The Atonement was built into the space-time belief in order to set a limit on the need for the belief, and ultimately to make learning complete. The Atonement is the final lesson.

Learning itself, like the classrooms in which it occurs, is temporary. The ability to learn has no value when change of understanding is no longer necessary. The eternally creative have nothing to learn. Only after the separation was it necessary to direct the creative forces to learning, because changed behaviour had become mandatory.

Men can learn to improve their behaviour and can also learn to become better and better learners. This serves to bring them into closer and closer accord with the Sonship, but the Sonship Itself is a perfect Creation, and perfection is not a matter of degree. Only while there are different degrees is learning meaningful. The "evolution" of man is merely a process by which he proceeds from one degree to the next. He corrects his previous missteps by stepping forward. This represents a process which is actually incomprehensible in temporal terms, because he returns as he goes forward.

The Atonement is the device by which he can free himself from the past as he goes ahead. It undoes his past errors, thus making it unnecessary for him to keep retracing his steps without advancing to his return. In this sense the Atonement saves time, but, like the miracle which serves it, does not abolish it. As long as there is need for Atonement there is need for time. But the Atonement, as a completed plan, does have a unique relationship to time. Until the Atonement is finished, its various phases will proceed in time, but the whole Atonement stands at time's end. At this point, the bridge of the return has been built.

The Atonement is a total commitment. You still think this is associated with loss. This is the same mistake all the separated ones make, in one way or another. They cannot believe that a defence which cannot attack is the best defence. This is what is meant by "the meek shall inherit the earth." They will literally take it over because of their strength. A two-way defence is inherently weak precisely because it has two edges and can turn against the self very unexpectedly. This tendency cannot be controlled except by miracles.

The miracle turns the defence of Atonement to the protection of the inner self, which, as it becomes more and more secure, assumes its natural talent of protecting others. The inner self knows itself as both a brother and a Son. You know that when defences are disrupted there is a period of real disorientation, accompanied by fear, guilt, and usually vacillations between anxiety and depression.

This course is different in that defences are not being disrupted but reinterpreted, even though you may experience it as the same thing. In the reinterpretation of defences, only their use for attack is lost. Since this means they can be used only one way, they become much stronger and much more dependable. They no longer oppose the Atonement, but greatly facilitate it.

The Atonement can only be accepted within you. You have perceived it largely as external thus far, and that is why your experience of it has been minimal. The reinterpretation of defences is essential in releasing the inner light. Since the separation, man's defences have been used almost entirely to defend himself against the Atonement, and thus maintain the separation. They themselves generally see this as a need to protect the body. The many body fantasies with which men's minds are engaged arise from the distorted belief that the body can be used as a means for attaining "atonement."

Perceiving the body as a temple is only the first step in correcting this kind of distortion. It alters part of the misperception, but not all of it. It does recognize, however, that the concept of Atonement in physical terms is not appropriate. However, the next step is to realize that a temple is not a building at all. Its real holiness lies in the inner altar, around which the building is built. The inappropriate emphasis men have put on beautiful church buildings is a sign of their fear of Atonement, and their unwillingness to reach the altar itself. The real beauty of the temple cannot be seen with the physical eye. The Spiritual eye, on the other hand, cannot see the building at all because It has perfect sight. It can, however, see the altar with perfect clarity.

For perfect effectiveness, the Atonement belongs at the centre of the inner altar, where it undoes the separation and restores the wholeness of the mind. Before the separation the mind was invulnerable to fear, because fear did not exist. Both the separation and the fear are miscreations of the mind, which must be undone. This is what is meant by "the restoration of the temple." It does not mean the restoration of the building, but the opening of the altar to receive the Atonement. This heals the separation, and places within man the one defence against all separation mind-errors which can make him perfectly invulnerable. Within man the one defence against all separation mind-errors which can make him perfectly invulnerable.

The acceptance of the Atonement by everyone is only a matter of time. In fact, both time and matter were created for this purpose. This appears to contradict free will because of the inevitability of the final decision. If you review the idea carefully, however, you will realize that this is not true. Everything is limited in some way by the manner of its creation. Free will can temporize and is capable of enormous procrastination. But it cannot depart entirely from its Creator, Who set the limits on its ability to miscreate by virtue of its own real purpose.

The misuse of will engenders a situation which, in the extreme, becomes altogether intolerable. Pain thresholds can be high, but they are not limitless. Eventually everyone begins to recognize, however dimly, that there must be a better way. As this recognition becomes more firmly established, it becomes a perceptual turning-point. This ultimately reawakens the Spiritual eye, simultaneously weakening the investment in physical sight. The alternating investment in the two types or levels of perception is usually experienced as conflict for a long time and can become very acute. But the outcome is as certain as God.

The Spiritual eye literally cannot see error and merely looks for Atonement. All the solutions which the physical eyes seek dissolve in Its sight. The Spiritual eye, which looks within, recognizes immediately that the altar has been defiled, and needs to be repaired and protected. Perfectly aware of the right defence, It passes over all others, looking past error to truth. Because of the real strength of its vision, It pulls the will into Its service and impels the mind to concur. This re-establishes the true power of the will and makes it increasingly unable to tolerate delay. The mind then realizes with increasing certainty that delay is only a way of increasing unnecessary pain which it need not tolerate at all. The pain threshold drops accordingly, and the mind becomes increasingly sensitive to what it would once have regarded as very minor intrusions of discomfort.

The Children of God are entitled to perfect comfort, which comes from a sense of perfect trust. Until they achieve this, they waste themselves and their true creative powers on useless attempts to make themselves more comfortable by inappropriate means. But the real means is already provided and does not involve any effort at all on their part. Their egocentricity usually misperceives this as personally insulting, an interpretation which obviously arises from their misperception of themselves. Egocentricity and communion cannot coexist. Even the terms are contradictory.

The Atonement is the only gift that is worthy of being offered to the altar of God. This is because of the inestimable value of the altar itself. It was created perfect and is entirely worthy of receiving perfection. God is lonely without His Souls and they are lonely without Him. Men must learn to perceive the world as a means of healing the separation. The Atonement is the guarantee that they will ultimately succeed.

The emphasis will now be on healing. The miracle is the means, the Atonement is the principle, and healing is the result. Those who speak of "a miracle of healing" are combining two orders of reality inappropriately. Healing is not a miracle. The Atonement, or the final miracle, is a remedy, while any type of healing is a result. The kind of error to which atonement is applied is irrelevant. Essentially, all healing is the release from fear. To undertake this, you cannot be fearful yourself. You do not understand healing because of your own fear.

A major step in the Atonement plan is to undo error at all levels. Illness, which is really "not-right-mindedness," is the result of level confusion in the sense that it always entails the belief that what is amiss in one level can adversely affect another. We have constantly referred to miracles as the means of correcting level confusion, and all mistakes must be corrected at the level on which they occur. Only the mind is capable of error. The body can act erroneously, but this is only because it is responding to mis-thought. The body cannot create, and the belief that it can, a fundamental error, produces all physical symptoms.

All physical illness represents a belief in magic. The whole distortion which created magic rests on the belief that there is a creative ability in matter which the mind cannot control. This error can take two forms; it can be believed that the mind can miscreate in the body, or that the body can miscreate in the mind. If it is understood that the mind, which is the only level of creation, cannot create beyond itself, neither type of confusion need occur.

The reason only the mind can create is more obvious than may be immediately apparent. The Soul has been created. The body is a learning device for the mind. Learning devices are not lessons in themselves. Their purpose is merely to facilitate the thinking of the learner. The most that a faulty use of a learning device can do is to fail to facilitate learning. It has no power in itself to introduce actual learning errors.

The body, if properly understood, shares the invulnerability of the Atonement to two-edged application. This is not because the body is a miracle, but because it is not inherently open to misinterpretation. The body is merely a fact in human experience. Its abilities can be, and frequently are, over evaluated. However, it is almost impossible to deny its existence. Those who do so are engaging in a particularly unworthy form of denial. The term "unworthy" here implies simply that it is not necessary to protect the mind by denying the unmindful. If one denies this unfortunate aspect of the mind's power, one is also denying the power itself.

All material means which man accepts as remedies for bodily ills are merely restatements of magic principles. It was the first level of the error to believe that the body created its own illness. It is a second misstep to attempt to heal it through non-creative agents. It does not follow, however, that the use of these very weak corrective devices are evil. Sometimes the illness has a sufficiently great hold over a mind to render a person inaccessible to Atonement. In this case it may be wise to utilize a compromise approach to mind and body, in which something from the outside is temporarily given healing belief.

This is because the last thing that can help the non-rightminded, or the sick, is an increase in fear. They are already in a fear weakened state. If they are inappropriately exposed to an "undiluted" miracle, they may be precipitated into panic. This is particularly likely to occur when upside-down perception has induced the belief that miracles are frightening.

The value of the Atonement does not lie in the manner in which it is expressed. In fact, if it is truly used, it will inevitably be expressed in whatever way is most helpful to the receiver. This means that a miracle, to attain its full efficacy, must be expressed in a language which the recipient can understand without fear. It does not follow, by any means, that this is the highest level of communication of which he is capable. It does mean, however, that it is the highest level of communication of which he is capable now. The whole aim of the miracle is to raise the level of communication, not to impose regression in the improper sense upon it.

Before miracle workers are ready to undertake their function in this world, it is essential that they fully understand the fear of release. Otherwise, they may unwittingly foster the belief that release is imprisonment, a belief that is very prevalent. This misperception arose from the underlying misbelief that harm can be limited to the body. This was because of the much greater fear that the mind can hurt itself. Neither error is really meaningful, because the miscreations of the mind do not really exist. This recognition is a far better protective device than any form of level confusion because it introduces correction at the level of the error.

It is essential to remember that only the mind can create. Implicit in this is the corollary that correction belongs at the thought level. To repeat an earlier statement and to extend it somewhat, the Soul is already perfect, and therefore does not require correction. The body does not really exist except as a learning device for the mind. This learning device is not subject to errors of its own because it was created but is not creating. It should be obvious, then, that correcting the creator, or inducing it to give up its miscreations, is the only application of creative ability which is truly meaningful.

Magic is essentially mindless, or the miscreative use of the mind. Physical medications are forms of "spells." Those who are afraid to use the mind to heal should not attempt to do so. The very fact that they are afraid has made them vulnerable to miscreation. They are therefore likely to misunderstand any healing they might induce, and, because egocentricity and fear usually occur together, may be unable to accept the real Source of the healing. Under these conditions, it is safer for them to rely temporary on physical healing devices, because they cannot misperceive them as their own creations. As long as their sense of vulnerability persists, they should be preserved from even attempting miracles.

We have already said that the miracle is an expression of miracle-mindedness. Miracle-mindedness merely means rightmindedness in the sense that we are now using it. The rightminded neither exalt nor depreciate the mind of the miracle worker or the miracle receiver. However, as a creative act, the miracle need not await the right-mindedness of the receiver. In fact, its purpose is to restore him to his right mind. It is essential, however, that the miracle worker be in his right mind, or he will be unable to re-establish right-mindedness in someone else.

The healer who relies on his own readiness is endangering his understanding. He is perfectly safe as long as he is completely unconcerned about His readiness but maintains a consistent trust in mine. If your miracle working propensities are not functioning properly, it is always because fear has intruded on your right-mindedness and has literally upset it (or turned it upside-down). All forms of not-rightmindedness are the result of refusal to accept the Atonement for yourself. If the miracle worker does accept it, he places himself in a position to recognize that those who need to be healed are simply those who have not realized that right-mindedness is healing.

The sole responsibility of the miracle worker is to accept the Atonement for himself. This means that he recognizes that mind is the only creative level, and that its errors are healed by the Atonement. Once he accepts this, his mind can only heal. By denying his mind any destructive potential, and reinstating its purely constructive powers, he has placed himself in a position where he can undo the level confusion of others. The message he then gives to others is the truth that their minds are similarly constructive, and that their miscreations cannot hurt them. By affirming this, the miracle worker releases the mind from over evaluating its own learning device (the body) and restores the mind to its true position as the learner.

It should be emphasized again that the body does not learn, any more than it creates. As a learning device it merely follows the learner, but if it is falsely endowed with self-initiative, it becomes a serious obstruction to the very learning it should facilitate. Only the mind is capable of illumination. The Soul is already illuminated, and the body in itself is too dense. The mind, however, can bring its illumination to the body by recognizing that density is the opposite of intelligence, and therefore unamenable to independent learning. It is, however, easily brought into alignment with a mind which has learned to look beyond density toward light.

Corrective learning always begins with the awakening of the Spiritual eye, and the turning away from the belief in physical sight. The reason this so often entails fear is because man is afraid of what his Spiritual eye will see. We said before that the Spiritual eye cannot see error, and is capable only of looking beyond it to the defence of Atonement. There is no doubt that the Spiritual eye does produce extreme discomfort by what It sees. Yet what man forgets is that the discomfort is not the final outcome of Its perception. When the Spiritual eye is permitted to look upon the defilement of the altar, it also looks immediately toward the Atonement.

Nothing the Spiritual eye perceives can induce fear. Everything that results from accurate spiritual awareness is merely channelized toward correction. Discomfort is aroused only to bring the need for correction forcibly into awareness. What the physical eye sees is not corrective, nor can it be corrected by any device which can be seen physically. As long as a man believes in what his physical sight tells him, all his corrective behaviour will be misdirected. The real vision is obscured because man cannot endure to see his own defiled altar. But since the altar has been defiled, his state becomes doubly dangerous unless it is perceived.

The fear of healing arises, in the end, from an unwillingness to accept the unequivocal fact that healing is necessary. Man is not willing to look on what he has done to himself. Healing is an ability lent to man after the separation, before which it was completely unnecessary. Like all aspects of the space-time belief, healing ability is temporary. However, as long as time persists, healing is needed as a means for human protection. This is because healing rests on charity, and charity is a way of perceiving the perfection of another even if he cannot perceive it himself.

Most of the loftier concepts of which man is capable now are time dependent. Charity is really a weaker reflection of a much more powerful love-encompassment which is far beyond any form of charity that man can conceive of as yet. Charity is essential to right-mindedness in the limited sense in which right-mindedness can now be attained. Charity is a way of looking at another as if he had already gone far beyond his actual accomplishments in time. Since his own thinking is faulty he cannot see the Atonement for himself, or he would have no need for charity. The charity which is accorded him is both an acknowledgment that he IS weak and a recognition that he could be stronger.

The way in which both of these perceptions are stated clearly implies their dependence on time, making it quite apparent that charity lies within the human limitations, though toward its higher levels. We said before that only revelation transcends time. The miracle, as an expression of true human charity, can only shorten time at most. It must be understood, however, that whenever a man offers a miracle to another, he is shortening the suffering of both. This introduces a correction into the whole record which corrects retroactively as well as progressively.

You believe that "being afraid" is involuntary; something beyond your control. Yet I have told you several times that only constructive acts should be involuntary. We have said that Christ-control can take over everything that does not matter, while Christ-guidance can direct everything that does, if you so choose. Fear cannot be Christ-controlled, but it can be self-controlled. It prevents me from controlling it. The correction is therefore a matter of your will, because its presence shows that you have raised the unimportant to a higher level than it warrants. You have thus brought it under your will, where it does not belong. This means that you feel responsible for it. The level confusion here is obvious.

The reason I cannot control fear for you is that you are attempting to raise to the mind level the proper content of lower-order reality. I do not foster level confusion, but you can choose to correct it. You would not tolerate insane behaviour on your part, and would hardly advance the excuse that you could not help it. Why should you tolerate insane thinking? There is a confusion here which you would do well to look at clearly. You believe that you are responsible for what you do, but not for what you think. The truth is that you are responsible for what you think because it is only at this level that you can exercise choice.

What you do comes from what you think. You cannot separate yourself from the truth by "giving" autonomy to behaviour. This is controlled by me automatically, as soon as you place what you think under my guidance. Whenever you are afraid, it is a sure sign that you have allowed your mind to miscreate or have not allowed me to guide it. It is pointless to believe that controlling the outcome of mis-thought can result in healing. When you are fearful you have willed wrongly. This is why you feel responsible for it. You must change your mind, not your behaviour, and this is a matter of will.

You do not need guidance except at the mind level. Correction belongs only at the level where creation is possible. The term does not mean anything at the symptom level, where it cannot work. The correction of fear is your responsibility. When you ask for release from fear, you are implying that it is not. You should ask, instead, for help in the conditions which have brought the fear about. These conditions always entail a separated mind willingness. At that level, you can help it. You are much too tolerant of mind wandering, thus passively condoning its miscreations. The particular result does not matter, but the fundamental error does. The correction is always the same. Before you will to do anything, ask me if your will is in accord with mine. If you are sure that it is, there will be no fear.

Fear is always a sign of strain, which arises whenever the will to do conflicts with what you do. This situation arises in two ways;

1. You can will to do conflicting things, either simultaneously or successively. This produces conflicted behaviour, which is intolerable to yourself because the part of the will that wants to do something else is outraged.
2. You can behave as you think you should, but without entirely willing to do so. This produces consistent behaviour but entails great strain within the self. In both cases, the will and the behaviour are out of accord, resulting in a situation in which you are doing what you do not will. This arouses a sense of coercion, which usually produces rage. The rage then invades the mind, and projection in the wrong sense is likely to follow. Depression or anxiety is virtually certain.

Remember that whenever there is fear, it is because you have not made up your mind. Your will is split, and your behaviour inevitably becomes erratic. Correcting at the behavioural level can shift the error from the first to the second type of strain described above but will not obliterate the fear. It is possible to reach a state in which you bring your will under my guidance without much conscious effort, but this implies habit patterns which you have not developed dependably as yet. God cannot ask more than you will. The strength to do comes from your own undivided will to do. There is no strain in doing God's Will as soon as you recognize that it is also your own.

The lesson here is quite simple, but particularly apt to be overlooked. I will therefore repeat it, urging you to listen. Only your mind can produce fear. It does so whenever it is conflicted in what it wills, thus producing inevitable strain because willing and doing become discordant. This cannot be corrected by better doing, but it can be corrected by higher willing.

The first corrective step is know first that this is an expression of fear. Then say to yourself that you must somehow have willed not to love or the fear which arises from behaviour-will conflict could not have arisen, then the whole process is nothing more than a series of pragmatic steps in the larger process of accepting the Atonement as the remedy. These steps can be summarized as follows:

1. Know first that this is fear.
2. Fear arises from lack of love.
3. The only remedy for lack of love is perfect love.
4. Perfect love is the Atonement.

We have emphasized that the miracle, or the expression of Atonement is always a sign of real respect from the worthy to the worthy. This worth is re-established by the Atonement. It is obvious, then, that when you are afraid you have placed yourself in a position where you need Atonement, because you have done something loveless, having willed without love. This is precisely the situation for which the Atonement was offered. The need for the remedy inspired its creation. As long as you recognize only the need for the remedy, you will remain fearful. However, as soon as you remedy it, you have also abolished the fear. This is how true healing occurs.

Everyone experiences fear, and no-one enjoys it. Yet it would take very little right-thinking to realize why fear occurs. Very few people appreciate the real power of the mind, and no-one remains fully aware of it all the time. However, if anyone hopes to spare himself from fear, there are some things he must realize, and realize fully. The mind is a very powerful creator and it never loses its creative force. It never sleeps. Every instant it is creating, and always as you will. Many of your ordinary expressions reflect this. For example, when you say, "Don't give it a thought," you imply that if you do not think about something, it will have no effect on you. And this is true enough.

On the other hand, many other expressions clearly illustrate the prevailing lack of awareness of thought-power. For example, you say, "Just an idle thought," and mean that the thought has no effect. You also speak of some actions as "thoughtless," implying that if the person had thought, he would not behave as he did. While expressions like "think big" give some recognition to the power of thought, they still come nowhere near the truth.

You do not expect to grow when you say it, because you do not really think that you will.

It is hard to recognize that thought and belief combine into a power surge that can literally move mountains. It appears at first glance that to believe such power about yourself is merely arrogant, but that is not the real reason why you do not believe it. People prefer to believe that their thoughts cannot exert real control because they are literally afraid of them. Many psychotherapists attempt to help people who are afraid, say, of their death wishes by depreciating the power of the wish. They even try to "free" the patient by persuading him that he can think whatever he wants without any real effect at all.

There is a real dilemma here which only the truly right-minded can escape. Death wishes do not kill in the physical sense, but they do kill spiritual awareness. All destructive thinking is dangerous. Given a death wish, a man has no choice except to act upon the thought or behave contrary to it. He thus chooses only between homicide and fear. The other possibility is that he depreciates the power of his thought. This is the usual psychoanalytic approach. It does allay guilt, but at the cost of rendering thinking impotent. If you believe that what you think is ineffectual you may cease to be overly afraid of it, but you are hardly likely to respect it.

The world is full of examples of how man has depreciated himself because he is afraid of his own thoughts. In some forms of insanity thoughts are glorified, but this is only because the underlying depreciation was too effective for tolerance. The truth is that there are no "idle" thoughts. All thinking produces form at some level. The reason people are afraid of ESP and so often react against it is because they know that thoughts can hurt them. Their own thoughts have made them vulnerable.

You who constantly complain about fear still persist in creating it. I told you before that you cannot ask me to release you from fear because I know it does not exist, but you do not. If I merely intervened between your thoughts and their results, I would be tampering with a basic law of cause and effect, the most fundamental law there is in this world. I would hardly help if I depreciated the power of your own thinking. This would be in direct opposition to the purpose of this course. It is much more helpful to remind you that you do not guard your thoughts carefully except for a small part of the day, and somewhat inconsistently even then. You may feel at this point that it would take a miracle to enable you to do this, which is perfectly true.

Men are not used to miraculous thinking, but they can be trained to think that way. All miracle workers need that kind of training. I cannot let them leave their minds unguarded or they will not be able to help me. Miracle working entails a full realization of the power of thought, and real avoidance of miscreation. Otherwise a miracle will be necessary to set the mind itself straight, a circular process which would hardly foster the time collapse for which the miracle was intended. Nor would it induce the healthy respect for true cause and effect which every miracle worker must have.

Both miracles and fear come from thoughts, and if you were not free to choose one, you would also not be free to choose the other. By choosing the miracle you have rejected fear. You have been afraid of God, of me, of yourselves, and of practically everyone you know at one time or another. This is because you have misperceived or miscreated us and believe in what you have made. You would never have done this if you were not afraid of your own thoughts. The vulnerable are essentially miscreators because they misperceive creation.

You persist in believing that, when you do not consciously watch your mind, it is unmindful. It is time, however, to consider the whole world of the unconscious or "unwatched" mind. This may well frighten you because it is the source of fear. The unwatched mind is responsible for the whole content of the unconscious which lies above the miracle level. All psychoanalytic theorists have made some contribution in this connection, but none of them has seen it in its true entirety. They have all made one common error in that they attempted to uncover unconscious content. You cannot understand unconscious activity in these terms because "content" is applicable only to the more superficial unconscious levels, to which the individual himself contributes. This is the level at which he can readily introduce fear, and usually does.

When man miscreates he is in pain. The cause and effect principle here is temporarily a real expeditor. Actually, "Cause" is a term properly belonging to God, and "Effect," which should also be capitalized, is His Son. This entails a set of Cause and Effect relationships which are totally different from those which man introduced into his own miscreations. The fundamental opponents in the real basic conflict are Creation and miscreation. All Fear is implicit in the second, just as all love is inherent in the first. Because of this difference, the basic conflict is one between love and fear.

It has already been said that man believes he cannot control fear because he himself created it. His belief in it seems to render it out of his control by definition. Yet any attempt to resolve the basic conflict through the concept of mastery of fear is meaningless. In fact, it asserts the power of fear by the simple assumption that it need be mastered. The essential resolution rests entirely on the mastery of love. In the interim, the sense of conflict is inevitable, since man has placed himself in a strangely illogical position. He believes in the power of what does not exist.

Two concepts which cannot coexist are "nothing" and "everything." To whatever extent one is believed in, the other has been denied. In the conflict fear is really nothing, and love is everything. This is because whenever light enters darkness, the darkness is abolished. What man believes is true for him. In this sense the separation has occurred, and to deny this is merely to misuse denial. However, to concentrate on error is merely a further misuse of defences. The true corrective procedure is to recognize error temporarily, but only as an indication that immediate correction is mandatory. This establishes a state of mind in which the Atonement can be accepted without delay.

It should be emphasized, however, that ultimately there is no compromise possible between everything and nothing. Time is essentially a device by which all compromise in this respect can be given up. It seems to be abolished by degrees because time itself involves a concept of intervals which do not really exist. The faulty use of creation made this necessary as a corrective device. "And God so loved the world that He gave His only begotten Son that whosoever believeth on Him shall not perish, but have eternal life" needs only one slight correction to be entirely meaningful in this context. It should read, "He gave it to His only begotten Son."

It should especially be noted that God has only one Son. If all the Souls God created are His Sons, then every Soul must be an integral part of the whole Sonship. You do not find the concept that the whole is greater than its parts difficult to understand. You should, therefore, not have too much trouble in understanding this. The Sonship in its Oneness does transcend the sum of its parts. However, this is obscured as long as any of its parts are missing. That is why the conflict cannot ultimately be resolved until all the parts of the Sonship have returned. Only then can the meaning of wholeness, in the true sense, be fully understood.

Any part of the Sonship can believe in error or incompleteness, if he so elects. However, if he does so, he is believing in the existence of nothingness. The correction of this error is the Atonement. We have already briefly spoken about readiness, but there are some additional points which might be helpful here. Readiness is nothing more than the prerequisite for accomplishment. The two should not be confused. As soon as a state of readiness occurs, there is usually some will to accomplish, but this is by no means necessarily undivided. The state does not imply more than a potential for a shift of will.

Confidence cannot develop fully until mastery has been accomplished. We have already attempted to correct the fundamental error that fear can be mastered and have emphasized that only love can be mastered. You have attested only to your readiness. Mastery of love involved a much more complete confidence than either of you has attained. However, the readiness at least is an indication that you believe this is possible. That is only the beginning of confidence. In case this be misunderstood to imply that an enormous amount of time will be necessary between readiness and mastery, let me remind you that time and space are under my control.

One of the chief ways in which man can correct his magic miracle confusion is to remember that he did not create himself. He is apt to forget this when he becomes egocentric, and this places him in a position where the belief in magic in some form is virtually inevitable. His will to create was given him by his own Creator, Who was expressing the same Will in His Creation. Since creative ability rests in the mind, everything that man creates is necessarily a matter of will. It also follows that whatever he creates is real in his own sight, but not necessarily in the Sight of God. This basic distinction leads us directly into the real meaning The Last

Judgment is one of the greatest threat concepts in man's perception. This is only because he does not understand it. Judgment is not an essential attribute of God. Man brought judgment into being only because of the separation. After the separation, however, there was a place for judgment as one of the many learning devices which had to be built into the overall plan. Just as the separation occurred over many millions of years, the Last Judgment will extend over a similarly long period, and perhaps an even longer one. Its length depends, however, on the effectiveness of the present speed-up.

We have frequently noted that the miracle is a device for shortening but not abolishing time. If a sufficient number of people become truly miracle-minded quickly, the shortening process can be almost immeasurable. It is essential, however, that these individuals free themselves from fear sooner than would ordinarily be the case, because they must emerge from the conflict if they are to bring peace to other minds.

The Last Judgment is generally thought of as a procedure undertaken by God. Actually it will be undertaken by man, with my help. It is a Final Healing, rather than a meting out of punishment, however much man may think that punishment is deserved. Punishment is a concept in total opposition to right-mindedness. The aim of the Last Judgment is to restore right-mindedness to man.

The Last Judgment might be called a process of right evaluation. It simply means that finally all men will come to understand what is worthy and what is not. After this, their ability to choose can be directed reasonably. Until this distinction is made, however, the vacillations between free and imprisoned will cannot but continue. The first step toward freedom must entail a sorting out of the false from the true. This is a process of division only in the constructive sense and reflects the true meaning of the Apocalypse. Man will ultimately look upon his own creations and will to preserve only what is good, just as God Himself looked upon what he had created and knew that it was good.

At this point, the will can begin to look with love on its own creations because of their great worthiness. The mind will inevitably disown its miscreations which, without the mind's belief, will no longer exist. The term "Last Judgement" is frightening not only because it has been falsely projected onto God, but also because of the association of "last" with death. This is an outstanding example of upside down perception. Actually, if the meaning of the Last Judgement is objectively examined, it is quite apparent that it is really the doorway to life.

No-one who lives in fear is really alive. His own last judgement cannot be directed toward himself because he is not his own creation. He can, however, apply it meaningfully and at any time to everything he has created, and retain in his memory only what is good. This is what his right-mindedness cannot but dictate. The purpose of time is solely to "give him time" to achieve this judgement. It is his own perfect judgement of his own creations. When everything he retains is loveable, there IS no reason for fear to remain with him. This is his part in the Atonement.

This is a course in mind training. All learning involves attention and study at some level. Some of the later parts of the course rest too heavily on these earlier sections not to require their study. You will also need them for preparation. Without this, you may become much too fearful when the unexpected does occur to make constructive use of it. However, as you study these earlier sections, you will begin to see some of their implications, which will be amplified considerably later on.

The reason a solid foundation is necessary is because of the confusion between fear and awe to which we have already referred, and which so many people hold. You will remember that we said that awe is inappropriate in connection with the Sons of God because you should not experience awe in the presence of your equals. However, it was also emphasized that awe is a proper reaction in the presence of your Creator. I have been careful to clarify my own role in the Atonement, without either over- or understating it. I have also tried to do the same in connection with yours. I have stressed that awe is not an appropriate reaction to me because of my inherent equality.

Some of the later steps in this course, however, do involve a more direct approach to God Himself. It would be most unwise to start on these steps without careful preparation, or awe will be confused with fear, and the experience will be more traumatic than beatific. Healing is of God in the end. The means are being carefully explained to you. Revelation may occasionally reveal the end to you, but to reach it the means are needed.

1. The miracle abolishes the need for lower-order concerns. Since it is an out-of-pattern time interval, the ordinary considerations of time and space do not apply. When you perform a miracle, I will arrange both time and space to adjust to it.
2. Clear distinction between what has been created and what is being created is essential. All forms of correction (or healing) rest on this fundamental correction in level perception.
3. Another way of stating the above point is; – Never confuse right with wrong-mindedness. Responding to any form of miscreation with anything expect a desire to heal (or a miracle) is an expression of this confusion.
4. The miracle is always a denial of this error and an affirmation of the truth. Only right-mindedness can create in a way that has any real effect. Pragmatically, what has no real effect has no real existence. Its effect, then, is emptiness. Being without

substantial content, it lends itself to projection in the improper sense.
5. The level-adjustment power of the miracle induces the right perception for healing. Until this has occurred healing cannot be understood. Forgiveness is an empty gesture unless it entails correction. Without this, it is essentially judgmental rather than healing.
6. Miraculous forgiveness is only correction. It has no element of judgment at all. "Father forgive them for they know not what they do" in no way evaluates what they do. It is strictly limited to an appeal to God to heal their minds. There is no reference to the outcome of their misthought. That does not matter.
7. The Biblical injunction "Be of one mind" is the statement for revelation-readiness. My own injunction "Do this in remembrance of me" is the request for cooperation from miracle-workers. It should be noted that the two statements are not in the same order of reality. The latter involves a time awareness, since to remember implies recalling the past in the present. Time is under my direction, but Timelessness belongs to God alone. In time we exist for and with each other. In Timelessness we coexist with God.

There is another point which must be perfectly clear before any residual fear which may still be associated with miracles becomes entirely groundless. The crucifixion did not establish the Atonement. The Resurrection did. This is a point which many very sincere Christians have misunderstood. No-one who is free of the scarcity-error could possibly make this mistake. If the crucifixion is seen from an upside-down point of view, it does appear as if God permitted, and even encouraged, one of his Sons to suffer because he was good. Many ministers preach this every day.

This particularly unfortunate interpretation, which arose out of the combined mis projections of a large number of my would-be followers, has led many people to be bitterly afraid of God. This particularly anti-religious concept enters into many religions, and this is neither by chance nor by coincidence. Yet the real Christian would have to pause and ask, "How could this be?" Is it likely that God Himself would be capable of the kind of thinking which His own words have clearly stated is unworthy of man?

The best defence, as always, is not to attack another's position, but rather to protect the truth. It is unwise to accept any concept, if you have to turn a whole frame of reference around in order to justify it. This procedure is painful in its minor applications, and genuinely tragic on a mass basis.

Persecution is a frequent result, undertaken to justify the terrible misperception that God Himself persecuted His Own Son on behalf of salvation. The very words are meaningless.

It has been particularly difficult to overcome this because, although the error itself is no harder to overcome than any other error, men were unwilling to give this one up because of its prominent "escape" value. In milder forms, a parent says, "This hurts me more than it hurts you," and feels exonerated in beating a child. Can you believe that the Father really thinks this way? It is so essential that all such thinking be dispelled that we must be very sure that nothing of this kind remains in your mind. I was not punished because you were bad. The wholly benign lesson the Atonement teaches is lost if it is tainted with this kind of distortion in any form.

"Vengeance is Mine sayeth the Lord" is a strictly karmic viewpoint. It is a real misperception of truth, by which man assigns his own "evil" past to God. The "evil conscience" from the past has nothing to do with God. He did not create it and He does not maintain it. God does not believe in karmic retribution. His Divine Mind does not create that way. He does not hold the evil deeds of a man even against himself. Is it likely, then, that He would hold against anyone the evil that another did?

Be very sure that you recognize how utterly impossible this assumption really is, and how entirely it arises from misprojection. This kind of error is responsible for a host of related errors, including the belief that God rejected man, and forced him out of the Garden of Eden. It is also responsible for the fact that you may believe, from time to time, that I am misdirecting you. I have made every effort to use words that are almost impossible to distort, but man is very inventive when it comes to twisting symbols around.

God Himself is not symbolic; He is fact. The Atonement, too, is totally without symbolism. It is perfectly clear because it exists in light. Only man's attempts to shroud it in darkness have made it inaccessible to the unwilling and ambiguous to the partly willing.

The Atonement itself radiates nothing but truth. It therefore epitomizes harmlessness and sheds only blessing. It could not do this if it arose from anything but perfect innocence. Innocence is wisdom because it is unaware of evil, which does not exist. It is, however, perfectly aware of everything that is true.

The Resurrection demonstrated that nothing can destroy truth. Good can withstand any form of evil because light abolishes all forms of darkness. The Atonement is thus the perfect lesson. It is the final demonstration that all of the other lessons which I taught are true. Man is released from all errors if he believes in this. The deductive approach to teaching accepts the generalization which is applicable to all single instances, rather than building up the generalization after analysing numerous single instances separately. If you can accept the one generalization now, there will be no need to learn from many smaller lessons.

Nothing can prevail against a Son of God who commends his Spirit into the hands of his Father. By doing this, the mind awakens from its sleep and remembers its Creator. All sense of separation disappears, and level confusion vanishes. The Son of God is part of the Holy Trinity, but the Trinity Itself is one. There is no confusion within its levels because they are of One Mind and One Will. This Single Purpose creates perfect integration and establishes the peace of God. Yet this Vision can be perceived only by the truly innocent.

Because their hearts are pure, the innocent defend true perception instead of defending themselves against it. Understanding the lesson of the Atonement, they are without the will to attack, and therefore they see truly. This is what the Bible means when it says

"When He shall appear (or be perceived) we shall be like Him, for we shall see Him as He is."

Sacrifice is a notion totally unknown to God. It arises solely from fear. This is particularly unfortunate because frightened people are apt to be vicious. Sacrificing another in any way is a clear-cut violation of God's Own injunction that man should be merciful even as his Father in Heaven. It has been hard for many Christians to realize that this commandment (or assignment) also applies to themselves. Good teachers never terrorize their students. To terrorize is to attack, and this results in rejection of what the teacher offers. The result is learning failure.

I have been correctly referred to as "The Lamb of God who taketh away the sins of the world." Those who represent the lamb as bloodstained, an all-too-widespread error, do not understand the meaning of the symbol. Correctly understood, it is a very simple parable which merely speaks of my innocence. The lion and the lamb lying down together refers to the fact that strength and innocence are not in conflict, but naturally live in peace. "Blessed are the pure in heart for they shall see God" is another way of saying the same thing.

There has been some human controversy about the nature of seeing in relation to the integrative powers of the brain. Correctly understood, the issue revolves around the question of whether the body or the mind can see (or understand). This is not really open to question at all. The body is not capable of understanding, and only the mind can perceive anything. A pure mind knows the truth, and this is its strength. It cannot attack the body because it recognizes exactly what the body is. This is what "a sane mind in a sane body" really means. It does not confuse destruction with innocence because it associates innocence with strength, not with weakness.

Innocence is incapable of sacrificing anything, because the innocent mind has everything and strives only to protect its wholeness. This is why it cannot misproject. It can only honour man, because honour is the natural greeting of the truly loved to others who are like them. The lamb taketh away the sins of the world only in the sense that the state of innocence, or grace, is one in which the meaning of the Atonement is perfectly apparent. The innocence of God is the true state of mind of His Son. In this state, man's mind does see God in the sense that he sees Him as He is, and realizes that the Atonement, not sacrifice, is the only appropriate gift to His Own altar, where nothing except true perfection belongs. The understanding of the innocent is truth. That is why their altars are truly radiant.

We have repeatedly stated that the basic concepts referred to in this course are not matters of degree. Certain fundamental concepts cannot be meaningfully understood in terms of coexisting polarities. It is impossible to conceive of light and darkness, or everything and nothing, as joint possibilities. They are all true or all false. It is essential that you realize that behaviour is erratic until a firm commitment to one or the other is made.

A firm commitment to darkness or nothingness is impossible. No-one has ever lived who has not experienced some light and some thing. This makes everyone really unable to deny truth totally, even if he generally deceives himself in this connection. That is why those who live largely in darkness and emptiness never find any lasting solace. Innocence is not a partial attribute. It is not a real defence until it is total. When it is partial, it is characterized by the same erratic nature that holds for other two-edged defences. The partly innocent are apt to be quite stupid at times. It is not until their innocence becomes a genuine viewpoint which is universal in its application that it becomes wisdom. Innocent (or true) perception means that you never misperceive and always see truly. More simply, it means that you never see what does not really exist. When you lack confidence in what someone will do, you are attesting to your belief that he is not in his right mind. This is hardly a miracle-based frame of reference. It also has the disastrous effect of denying the creative power of the miracle.

The miracle perceives everything as it is. If nothing but the truth exists, (and this is really a redundant statement because what is not true can not exist), right-minded seeing cannot see anything but perfection. We have said many times that only what God creates, or what man creates with the same will, has any real existence. This, then, is all the innocent can see. They do not suffer from the distortions of the separated ones. The way to correct all such distortions is to withdraw your faith from them and invest it only in what is true.

You cannot validate the invalid. I would suggest that you voluntarily give up all such attempts, because they can only be frantic. If you are willing to validate what is true in everything you perceive, you will make it true for you. Truth overcomes all error. This means that if you perceive truly, you are cancelling out misperceptions in yourself and in others simultaneously. Because you see them as they are, you offer them your own validation of their truth. This is the healing which the miracle actively fosters.

We have been emphasizing perception and have said very little about cognition as yet, because you are confused about the difference between them. The reason we have dealt so little with cognition is because you must get your perceptions straightened out before you can know anything. To know is to be certain. Uncertainty merely means that you do not know. Knowledge is power because it is certain, and certainty is strength. Perception is merely temporary. It is an attribute of the space-time belief and is therefore subject to fear or love. Misperceptions produce fear, and true perceptions produce love. Neither produces certainty, because all perception varies. That is why it is not knowledge.

True perception is the basis for knowledge but knowing is the affirmation of truth. All your difficulties ultimately stem from the fact that you do not recognize or know yourselves, each other, or God. To recognize means to "know again," implying that you knew before. You can see in many ways, because perception involves different interpretations, and this means that it is not whole. The miracle is a way of perceiving, not of knowing. It is the right answer to a question, and you do not ask questions at all when you know.

Questioning illusions is the first step in undoing them. The miracle, or the "right answer," corrects them. Since perceptions change, their dependence on time is obvious. They are subject to transitory states, and this necessarily implies variability. How you perceive at any given time determines what you do, and action must occur in time. Knowledge is timeless because certainty is not questionable. You know when you have ceased to ask questions.

The questioning mind perceives itself in time, and therefore looks for future answers. The unquestioning mind is closed because it believes the future and present will be the same. This establishes an unchanged state, or stasis. It is usually an attempt to counteract an underlying fear that the future will be worse than the present, and this fear inhibits the tendency to question at all.

Visions are the natural perception of the Spiritual eye, but they are still corrections. The Spiritual eye is symbolic, and therefore not a device for knowing. It is, however, a means of right perception, which brings it into the proper domain of the miracle. Properly speaking, "a vision of God" is a miracle rather than a revelation. The fact that perception is involved at all removes the experience from the realm of knowledge. That is why visions do not last.

The Bible instructs you to "know yourself," or be certain. Certainty is always of God. When you love someone, you have perceived him as he is, and this makes it possible for you to know him. However, it is not until you recognize him that you can know him. While you ask questions about God, you are clearly implying that you do not know Him. Certainty does not require action. When you say that you are acting on the basis of knowledge, you are really confusing perception and cognition. Knowledge brings the mental strength for creative thinking but not for right doing. Perception, miracles and doing are closely related. Knowledge is the result of revelation and induces only thought. Perception involves the body even in its most spiritualized form. Knowledge comes from the altar within and is timeless because it is certain. To perceive the truth is not the same as knowing it.

If you attack error in one another, you will hurt yourself. You cannot recognize each other when you attack. Attack is always made on a stranger. You are making him a stranger by misperceiving him, so that you cannot know him. It is because you have made him a stranger that you are afraid of him. Perceive him correctly so that you can know him. Right perception is necessary before God can communicate directly to His own altars, which He has established in His Sons. There He can communicate His certainty, and His knowledge will bring peace Without question.

God is not a stranger to His Sons, and His Sons are not strangers to each other. Knowledge preceded both perception and time and will ultimately replace them. That is the real meaning of the Biblical description of God as "Alpha and Omega, the Beginning and the End." It also explains the quotation, "Before Abraham was I am." Perception can and must be stabilized, but knowledge IS stable. "Fear God and keep his commandments" should read "Know God and accept His certainty." There are no strangers in His Creation. To create as He created, you can create only what you Know and accept as yours. God knows His Children with perfect certainty. He created them by knowing them. He recognized them perfectly. When they do not recognize each other, they do not recognize him.

The abilities man now possesses are only shadows of his real strengths. All of his functions are equivocal and open to question or doubt. This is because he is not certain how he will use them. He is therefore incapable of knowledge, being uncertain. He is also incapable of knowledge because he can perceive lovelessly. He cannot create surely because his perception deceives. Perception did not exist until the separation had introduced degrees, aspects and intervals. The Soul has no levels, and all conflict arises from the concept of levels. Only the Levels of the Trinity are capable of Unity. The levels which man created by the separation cannot but conflict. This is because they are essentially meaningless to each other.

Freud realized this perfectly, and that is why he conceived the different levels in his view of the psyche as forever irreconcilable. They were conflict-prone by definition because they wanted different things and obeyed different principles. In our picture of the psyche, there is an unconscious level which properly consists only of the miracle ability and which should be under my direction. There is also a conscious level, which perceives or is aware of impulses from both the unconscious and the superconscious. Consciousness is thus the level of perception, but not of knowledge. Again, to perceive is not to know.

Consciousness was the first split that man introduced into himself. He became a perceiver, rather than a creator in the true sense. Consciousness is correctly identified as the domain of the ego. The ego is a man-made attempt to perceive himself as he wished to be, rather than as he is. This is an example of the created-creator confusion we have spoken of before. Yet man can only know himself as he is because that is all he can be sure of. Everything else is open to question.

The ego is the questioning compartment in the post-separation psyche which man created for himself. It is capable of asking valid questions but not of perceiving valid answers, because these are cognitive and cannot be perceived. The endless speculation about the meaning of mind has led to considerable confusion because the mind is confused. Only One-Mindedness is without confusion. A separated or divided mind must be confused; it is uncertain by definition. It has to be in conflict because it is out of accord with itself.

Intrapersonal conflict arises from the same basis as interpersonal conflict. One part of the psyche perceives another part as on a different level and does not understand it. This makes the parts strangers to each other, without recognition. This is the essence of the fear-prone condition, in which attack is always possible. Man has every reason to feel afraid, as he perceives himself. This is why he cannot escape from fear until he knows that he did not and could not create himself. He can never make his misperceptions valid. His creation is beyond his own error, and that is why he must eventually choose to heal the separation.

Right-mindedness is not to be confused with the knowing mind because it is applicable only to right perception. You can be rightminded or wrong-minded, and even this is subject to degrees, a fact which clearly demonstrates a lack of association with knowledge. The term "right-mindedness" is properly used as the correction for "wrongmindedness," and applies to the state of mind which induces accurate perception. It is miraculous because it heals misperception, and this is indeed a miracle in view of how man perceives himself.

Perception always involves some misuse of will because it involves the mind in areas of uncertainty. The mind is very active because it has will-power. When it willed the separation, it willed to perceive. Until then, it willed only to know. Afterwards it willed ambiguously, and the only way out of ambiguity is clear perception. The mind returns to its proper function only when it wills to know. This places it in the Soul's service, where perception is meaningless. The superconscious is the level of the mind which wills this.

The mind chose to divide itself when it willed to create both its own level and the ability to perceive, but it could not entirely separate itself from the Soul because it is from the Soul that it derives its whole power to create. Even in miscreation will is affirming its source, or it would merely cease to be. This is impossible because it is part of the Soul, which God created and which is therefore eternal.

The ability to perceive made the body possible because you must perceive something, and with something. This is why perception involves an exchange or translation, which knowledge does not need. The interpretive function of perception, actually a distorted form of creation, then permitted man to interpret the body as himself, which, though depressing, was an attempt to escape from the conflict he had induced. The superconscious, which knows, could not be reconciled with this loss of power because it is incapable of darkness. This is why it became almost inaccessible to the mind and entirely inaccessible to the body.

Thereafter, the superconscious was perceived as a threat, because light does abolish darkness merely by establishing the fact that it is not there. The truth will always overcome error in this sense. This is not an active process of destruction at all. We have already emphasized that knowledge does not do anything. It can be perceive as an attacker, but it cannot attack. What man perceives as its attack is merely his own vague recognition of the fact that it can always be remembered, never having been destroyed.

God and the Souls He created remain in surety, and therefore know that no miscreation exists. Truth cannot deal with unwilling error, because it does not will to be blocked out. I was a man who remembered the Soul and its knowledge, and as a man, I did not attempt to counteract error with knowledge so much as to correct error from the bottom up. I demonstrated both the powerlessness of the body and the power of the mind. By uniting my will with that of my Creator, I naturally remembered the Soul and its own real purpose.

I cannot unite your will with God's for you, but I can erase all misperceptions from your mind if you will bring it under my guidance. only your misperceptions stand in your own way. Without them your choice is certain. Sane perception induces sane choosing. The Atonement was an act based on true perception. I cannot choose for you, but I can help you make your own right choice. "Many are called but few are chosen" should read, "all are called but few choose to listen. Therefore, they do not choose right."

The "chosen ones" are merely those who choose right sooner. This is the real meaning of the celestial speed-up. Strong wills can do this now, and you will find rest for your Souls. God knows you only in peace, and this is your reality.

We said before that the abilities which man possesses are only shadows of his real strengths, and that the intrusion of the ability to perceive, which is inherently judgemental, was introduced only after the separation. No-one has been sure of anything since. You will also remember, however, that I made it clear that the Resurrection was the means for the return to knowledge, which was accomplished by the union of my will with the Father's. We can now make a distinction which will greatly facilitate clarity in our subsequent statements.

Since the separation, the words "create" and "make" have been greatly confused. When you make something, you make it out of a sense of lack or need. Anything that is made is made for a specific purpose and has no true generalizable. When you make something to fill a perceived lack, which is obviously why you would want to make anything, you are tacitly implying that you believe in separation. Knowing, as we have frequently observed, does not lead to doing at all.

The confusion between your own creation and what you create is so profound that it has become literally impossible for you to know anything. Knowledge is always stable, and it is quite evident that human beings are not. Nevertheless, they are perfectly stable as God created them. In this sense, when their behaviour is unstable they are disagree with God's Idea of the Creation. Man can do this if he chooses, but he would hardly want to do it if he were in his right mind. The problem that bothers you most is the fundamental question which man continually asks of himself, but which cannot properly be directed to himself at all. He keeps asking himself what he IS. This implies that the answer is not only one which he knows but is also one which is up to him to supply.

Man cannot perceive himself correctly. He has no image. The word "image" is always perception-related, and not a product of learning. Images are symbolic and stand for something else. The current emphasis on "changing your image" merely recognizes the power of perception, but it also implies that there is nothing to know. Knowing is not open to interpretation. It is possible to "interpret" meaning, but this is always open to error because it refers to the perception of meaning. Such wholly needless complexities are the result of man's attempt to regard himself as both separated and unseparated at the same time. It is impossible to undertake a confusion as fundamental as this without engaging in further confusion.

Methodologically man's mind has been very creative, but, as always occurs when method and content are separated, it has not been utilized for anything but an attempt to escape a fundamental and entirely inescapable impasse. This kind of thinking cannot result in a creative outcome, although it has resulted in considerable ingenuity. It is noteworthy, however, that this ingenuity has almost totally divorced him from knowledge. Knowledge does not require ingenuity. When we say, "the truth shall set you free," we mean that all this kind of thinking is a waste of time, but that you are free of the need to engage in it if you are willing to let it go.

Prayer is a way of asking for something. Prayer is the medium of miracles, but the only meaningful prayer is for forgiveness, because those who have been forgiven have everything. Once forgiveness has been accepted, prayer in the usual sense becomes utterly meaningless. Essentially, a prayer for forgiveness is nothing more than a request that we may be able to recognize something we already have. In electing to perceive instead of to know, man placed himself in a position where he could resemble his Father only by miraculously perceiving. He has lost the knowledge that he himself is a miracle. Miraculous creation was his Source, and also his real function.

"God created man in his Own image and likeness" is correct in meaning, but the words are open to considerable misinterpretation. This is avoided, however, if "image" is understood to mean "thought" and "likeness" is taken as "of a like quality." God did create the Soul in His Own Thought, and of a quality like to His Own. There is nothing else. Perception, on the other hand, is impossible without a belief in "more" and "less." Perception at every level involves selectivity and is incapable of organization without it. In all types of perception there is a continual process of accepting and rejecting, or organizing and reorganizing, of shifting and changing focus. Evaluation is an essential part of perception because judgements must be made for selection.

What happens to perceptions if there are no judgements and there is nothing but perfect equality? Perception becomes impossible. Truth can only be known. All of it is equally true and knowing any part of it is to know all of it. Only perception involves partial awareness. Knowledge transcends all the laws which govern perception because partial knowledge is impossible. It is all One and has no separate parts. You who are really one with it need but know yourself, and your knowledge is complete. To know God's Miracle is to know Him.

Forgiveness is the healing of the perception of separation. Correct perception of each other is necessary, because minds have willed to see themselves as separate. Each Soul knows God completely. That is the miraculous power of the Soul. The fact that each One has this power completely is a fact that is entirely alien to human thinking, in which if anyone has everything, there is nothing left. God's Miracles are as total as His Thoughts because they are His Thoughts.

As long as perception lasts prayer has a place. Since perception rests on lack, those who perceive have not totally accepted the Atonement and given themselves over to truth. Perception is a separated state, and a perceiver does need healing. Communion, not prayer, is the natural state of those who know. God and His Miracles are inseparable. How beautiful indeed are the Thoughts of God Who live in His Light! Your worth is beyond perception because it is beyond doubt. Do not perceive yourself in different lights. Know yourself in the One Light where the miracle that is you is perfectly clear.

We have already discussed the Last Judgement in some though insufficient detail. After the Last Judgement there will be no more. This is symbolic only in the sense that everyone is much better off without judgement. When the Bible says "Judge not that ye be not judged" it merely means that if you judge the reality of others at all, you will be unable to avoid judging your own. The choice to judge rather than to know was the cause of the loss of peace. Judgement is the process on which perception, but not cognition, rests. We have discussed this before in terms of the selectivity of perception, pointing out that evaluation is its obvious prerequisite.

Judgement always involves rejection. It is not an ability which emphasizes only the positive aspects of what is judged, whether it be in or out of the self. However, what has been perceived and rejected, – or judged and found wanting, – remains in the unconscious because it has been perceived. One of the illusions from which man suffers is the belief that what he judged against has no effect. This cannot be true unless he also believes that what he judged against does not exist. He evidently does not believe this, or he would not have judged against it. It does not matter, in the end, whether you judge right or wrong. Either way, you are placing your belief in the unreal. This cannot be avoided in any type of judgment, because it implies the belief that reality is yours to choose from.

You have no idea of the tremendous release and deep peace that comes from meeting yourselves and your brothers totally without judgment. When you recognize what you and your brothers are, you will realize that judging them in any way is without meaning. In fact, their meaning is lost to you precisely because you are judging them. All uncertainty comes from a totally fallacious belief that you are under the coercion of judgment. You do not need judgment to organize your life, and you certainly do not need it to organize yourselves. In the presence of knowledge all judgment is automatically suspended, and this is the process which enables recognition to replace perception.

Man is very fearful of everything he has perceived but has refused to accept. He believes that, because he has refused to accept it, he has lost control over it. This is why he sees it in nightmares, or in pleasant disguises in what seem to be his happier dreams. Nothing that you have refused to accept can be brought into awareness. It does not follow that it is dangerous, but it does follow that you have made it dangerous.

When you feel tired, it is merely because you have judged yourself as capable of being tired. When you laugh at someone, it is because you have judged him as debased. When you laugh at yourself you are singularly likely to laugh at others, if only because you cannot tolerate the idea of being more debased than they are. All of this does make you feel tired because it is essentially disheartening. You are not really capable of being tired, but you are very capable of wearying yourselves. The strain of constant judgment is virtually intolerable. It is a curious thing that any ability which is so debilitating should be so deeply cherished.

Yet, if you wish to be the author of reality, which is totally impossible anyway, you will insist on holding on to judgment. You will also use the term with considerable fear, believing that judgment will someday be used against you. To whatever extent it is used against you, it is due only to your belief in its efficacy as a weapon of defence for your own authority. The issue of authority is really a question of authorship. When an individual has an "authority problem," it is always because he believes he is the author of himself, projects his delusion onto others, and then perceives the situation as one in which people are literally fighting him for his authorship. This is the fundamental error of all those who believe they have usurped the power of God.

The belief is very frightening to them, but hardly troubles God. He is, however, eager to undo it, not to punish His children, but only because He knows that it makes them unhappy. Souls were given their true Authorship, but men preferred to be anonymous when they chose to separate themselves from their Author. The word "authority" has been one of their most fearful symbols ever since. Authority has been used for great cruelty because, being uncertain of their true Authorship, men believe that their creation was anonymous. This has left them in a position where it sounds meaningful to consider the possibility that they must have created themselves.

The dispute over authorship has left such uncertainty in the minds of men that some have even doubted whether they really exist at all. Despite the apparent contradiction in this position, it is in one sense more tenable than the view that they created themselves. At least it acknowledges the fact that some true authorship is necessary for existence.

Only those who give over all desire to reject can know that their own rejection is impossible. You have not usurped the power of God, but you have lost it. Fortunately, when you lose something, it does not mean that the "something" has gone. It merely means that you do not know where it is. Existence does not depend on your ability to identify it, nor even to place it. It is perfectly possible to look on reality without judgment, and merely know that it is there.

Peace is a natural heritage of the Soul. Everyone is free to refuse to accept his inheritance, but he is not free to establish what his inheritance is. The problem which everyone must decide is the fundamental question of authorship. All fear comes ultimately and sometimes by way of very devious routes, from the denial of Authorship. The offense is never to God, but only to those who deny Him. To deny His Authorship is to deny themselves the reason for their own peace, so that they see themselves only in pieces. This strange perception IS the authority problem.

There is no man who does not feel that he is imprisoned in some way. If this is the result of his own free will, he must regard his will as if it were not free, or the obviously circular reasoning involved in his position would be quite apparent. Free will must lead to freedom. Judgment always imprisons, because it separates segments of reality according to the highly unstable scales of desire. Wishes are not facts by definition. To wish is to imply that willing is not sufficient. Yet no-one believes that what is wished is as real as what is willed.

Instead of "Seek ye first the Kingdom of Heaven" say, "will ye first the Kingdom of Heaven," and you have said, "I know what I am, and I will to accept my own inheritance." Every system of thought must have a starting point. It begins with either a making or a creating, a difference which we have discussed already. Their resemblance lies in their power as foundations. Their difference lies in what rests upon them. Both are cornerstones for systems of belief by which men live. It is a mistake to believe that a thought system which is based on lies is weak. Nothing made by a child of God is without power. It is essential to realize this, because otherwise you will not understand why you have so much trouble with this course and will be unable to escape from the prisons which you have made for yourselves.

You cannot resolve the authority problem by depreciating the power of your minds. To do so is to deceive yourself, and this will hurt you because you know the strength of the mind. You also know that you cannot weaken it, any more than you can weaken God. The "devil" is a frightening concept because he is thought of as extremely powerful and extremely active. He is perceived as a force in combat with God, battling Him for possession of the Souls He created. He deceives by lies, and builds kingdoms of his own, in which everything is in direct opposition to God. Yet he attracts men rather than repels them, and they are seen as willing to "sell" him their Souls in return for gifts they recognise are of no real worth.

This makes absolutely no sense. The whole picture is one in which man acts in a way he himself realizes is self-destructive, but which he does not choose to correct, and therefore perceives the cause as beyond his control. We have discussed the fall, or separation, before, but its meaning must be clearly understood without symbols. The separation is not symbolic. It is an order of reality, or a system of thought that is real enough in time, though not in eternity. All beliefs are real to the believe.

The fruit of only one tree was "forbidden" to man in his symbolic garden. But God could not have forbidden it, or it could not have been eaten. If God knows His children, and I assure you that He does, would He have put them in a position where their own destruction was possible? The "tree" which was forbidden was named the "tree of knowledge." Yet God created knowledge and gave it freely to His creations. The symbolism here has been given many interpretations, but you may be sure that any interpretation which sees either God or His creations as capable of destroying their own purpose is in error.

Eating of the fruit of the tree of knowledge is a symbolic expression for incorporating into the self the ability for self-creating. This is the only sense in which God and His Souls are not co-creators. The belief that they are is implicit in the "self-concept," a concept now made acceptable by its weakness, and explained by a tendency of the self to create an image of itself. Its fear aspect is often ascribed to fear of retaliation by a "father figure," a particularly curious idea in view of the fact that no-one uses the term to refer to the physical father. It refers to an image of a father in relation to an image of the self.

Images are perceived, not known. Knowledge cannot deceive, but perception can. Man can perceive himself as self-creating, but he cannot do more than believe it. He cannot make it true. And, as we said before, when you finally perceive correctly, you can only be glad that you cannot. But until then, the belief that you can is the central foundation stone in your thought system, and all your defences are used to attack ideas which might bring it to light. You still believe you are images of your own creation. Your minds are split with your Souls on this point, and there is no resolution while you believe the one thing that is literally inconceivable. That is why you cannot create and are filled with fear about what you make.

The mind can make the belief in separation very real and very fearful, and this belief is the "devil." It is powerful, active, destructive, and clearly in opposition to God because it literally denies His Fatherhood. Never underestimate the power of this denial. Look at your lives and see what the devil has made. But know that this making will surely dissolve in the light of truth, because its foundation is a lie.

Your creation by God is the only foundation which cannot be shaken because the light is in it. Your starting point is truth, and you must return to this beginning. Much has been perceived since then, but nothing else has happened. That is why your Souls are still in peace, even though your minds are in conflict. You have not yet gone back far enough, and that is why you become so fearful. As you approach the beginning, you feel the fear of the destruction of your thought system upon you, as if it were the fear of death. There is no death, but there is a belief in death.

The Bible says that the branch that bears no fruit will be cut off and will wither away. Be glad! The light will shine from the true Foundation of Life, and your own thought system will stand corrected. It cannot stand otherwise. You who fear salvation are willing death. Life and death, light and darkness, knowledge and perception are irreconcilable. To believe that they can be reconciled is to believe that God and man cannot. Only the Oneness of knowledge is conflictless. Your kingdom is not of this world because it was given you from beyond this world. Only in this world is the idea of an authority problem meaningful. The world is not left by death but by truth, and truth can be known by all those for whom the Kingdom was created, and for whom it waits.

The Bible says that you should go with a brother twice as far as he asks. It certainly does not suggest that you set him back on his journey. Devotion to a brother cannot set you back, either. It can lead only to mutual progress. The result of genuine devotion is inspiration, a word which, properly understood, is the opposite of fatigue. To be fatigued is to be dis-spirited, but to be inspired is to be in the spirit. To be egocentric is to be dispirited, but to be self-centred in the right sense is to be inspired, or in the Soul. The truly inspired are enlightened and cannot abide in darkness.

You can speak from the Soul or from the ego, precisely as you choose. If you speak from the Soul, you have chosen "to be still and know that I am God." These words are inspired because they come from knowledge. If you speak from the ego, you are disclaiming knowledge instead of affirming it, and are thus dispiriting yourself. Do not embark on foolish journeys, because they are indeed in vain. The ego may desire them, but the Soul cannot embark on them because it is forever unwilling to depart from its Foundation.

The journey to the cross should be the last foolish journey for every mind. Do not dwell upon it but dismiss it as accomplished. If you can accept it as your own last foolish journey, you are also free to join my Resurrection. Human living has indeed been needlessly wasted in a repetition compulsion. It re-enacts the separation, the loss of power, the foolish journey of the ego in an attempt at reparation and finally, the crucifixion of the body, or death.

Repetition compulsions can be endless unless they are given up by an act of will. Do not make the pathetic human error of "clinging to the old rugged cross." The only message of the crucifixion was that we can overcome the cross. Unless you do so, you are free to crucify yourself as often as you choose. But this is not the Gospel I intended to offer you. We have another journey to undertake, and if you will read these lessons carefully, they will help to prepare you to undertake it.

We have spoken of many different human symptoms, and at this level there is almost endless variation. There is, however, only one cause of all of them. The authority problem is "the root of all evil." Money is but one of its many reflections and is a reasonably representative example of the kind of thinking which stems from it. The idea of buying and selling implies precisely the kind of exchange that the Soul cannot understand at all, because its Supply is always abundant, and all its demands are fully met.

Every symptom which the ego has made involves a contradiction in terms. This is because the mind is split between the ego and the Soul, so that whatever the ego makes is incomplete and contradictory. This untenable position is the result of the authority problem which, because it accepts the one inconceivable thought as its premise, can only produce ideas which are inconceivable. The term "profess" is used quite frequently in the Bible. To profess is to identify with an idea and offer the idea to others to be their own. The idea does not lessen; it becomes stronger.

A good teacher clarifies his own ideas and strengthens them by teaching them. Teacher and pupil are alike in the learning process. They are in the same order of learning, and unless they share their lessons, they will lack conviction. A good teacher must believe in the ideas which he professes, but he must meet another condition; he must also believe in the students to whom he offers his ideas. Many stand guard over their ideas because they want to protect their thought systems as they are, and learning means change. Change is always fearful to the separated ones, because they cannot conceive of it as a change towards healing the separation. They always perceive it as a change towards further separation, because the separation was their first experience of change.

You believe that, if you allow no change to enter into your ego, your Soul will find peace. This profound confusion is possible only if one maintains that the same thought system can stand on two foundations. Nothing can reach the Soul from the ego, and nothing from the Soul can strengthen the ego, or reduce the conflict within it. The ego is a contradiction. Man's self and God's Self are in opposition. They are opposed in creation, in will, and in outcome. They are fundamentally irreconcilable because the Soul cannot perceive and the ego cannot know. They are therefore not in communication and can never be in communication. Nevertheless, the ego can learn because its maker can be misguided but cannot make the totally lifeless out of the life-given. The Soul need not be taught, but the ego must.

The ultimate reason why learning is perceived as frightening is because learning does lead to the relinquishment (not destruction) of the ego to the Light of the Soul. This is the change the ego must fear because it does not share my charity. My lesson was like yours, and because I learned it I can teach it. I never attack your egos, but I do try to teach you how their thought system arose. When I remind you of your true creation, your egos cannot but respond with fear.

Teaching and learning are your greatest strengths now because you must change your mind and help others change theirs. It is pointless to refuse to tolerate change because you believe you can demonstrate that, by doing so, the separation has not occurred. The dreamer who doubts the reality of his dream while he is still dreaming is not really healing the level-split. You have rests upon it. This is very real to you. You cannot undo this by doing nothing and not changing.

If you are willing to renounce the role of guardian of your thought system and open it to me, I will correct it very gently and lead you home. Every good teacher hopes to give his students so much of his own thinking that they will one day no longer need him. This is the one real goal of the parent, teacher and therapist. This goal will not be achieved by those who believe that they will lose their child or pupil or patient if they succeed. It is impossible to convince the ego of this because it goes against all of its own laws. But remember that laws are set up to protect the continuity of the system in which the lawmaker believes.

It is natural enough for the ego to try to protect itself, once you have made it, but it is not natural for you to want to obey its laws unless you believe in them. The ego cannot make this choice because of the nature of its origin. You can because of the nature of yours. Egos can clash in any situation, but Souls cannot clash at all. If you perceive a teacher as merely a "larger ego," you will be afraid, because to enlarge an ego is to increase separation anxiety. I will teach with you and live with you if you will think with me, but my goal will always be to absolve you finally from the need for a teacher.

This is the opposite of the ego-oriented teacher's goal. He is concerned with the effect of his ego on other egos, and therefore interprets their interaction as a means of ego preservation. I would not be able to devote myself to teaching if I believed this, and you will not be a devoted teacher as long as you maintain it. I am constantly being perceived as a teacher either to be exalted or rejected, but I do not accept either perception for myself.

Your worth is not established by your teaching or your learning. Your worth was established by God. As long as you dispute this everything you do will be fearful, particularly any situation which lends itself to the "superiority-inferiority" fallacy. Teachers must be patient and repeat their lessons until they are learned. I am willing to do this because I have no right to set your learning limits for you. Once again, – nothing you do or think or wish or make is necessary to establish your worth. This point is not debatable except in delusions. Your ego is never at stake because God did not create it. Your Soul is never at stake because He did. Any confusion on this point is a delusion and no form of devotion is possible as long as this delusion lasts.

The ego tries to exploit all situations into forms of praise for itself in order to overcome its doubts. It will be doubtful forever, or rather, as long as you believe in it. You who made it cannot trust it because you know it is not real. The only sane solution is not to try to change reality, which is indeed a fearful attempt, but to see it as it is. You are part of reality, which stands unchanged beyond the reach of your ego, but within easy reach of your Soul. When you are afraid, be still and know that God is real and you are His beloved Son in whom He is well pleased. Do not let your ego dispute this, because the ego cannot know what is as far beyond its reach as you are.

God is not the author of fear. You are. You have chosen, therefore, to create unlike Him, and you have made fear for yourselves. You are not at peace because you are not fulfilling your function. God gave you a very lofty responsibility which you are not meeting. You know this, and you are afraid. In fact, your egos have chosen to be afraid instead of meeting it. When you awaken, you will not be able to understand this because it is literally incredible. Do not believe the incredible now. Any attempt to increase its believableness is merely to postpone the inevitable.

The word "inevitable" is fearful to the ego, but joyous to the Soul. God is inevitable, and you cannot avoid Him any more than He can avoid you. The ego is afraid of the Soul's joy because, once you have experienced it, you will withdraw all protection from the ego, and become totally without the investment in fear. Your investment is great now because fear is a witness to the separation, and your ego rejoices when you witness to it. Leave it behind! Do not listen to it, and do not preserve it. Listen only to God, Who is as incapable of deception as are the Souls He created.

Release yourselves and release others. Do not present a false and unworthy picture of yourself to others, and do not accept such a picture of them yourselves. The ego has built a shabby and unsheltering home for you because it cannot build otherwise. Do not try to make this impoverished house stand. Its weakness is your strength. Only God could make a home that is worthy of His creations, who have chosen to leave it empty by their own dispossession. Yet His home will stand forever and is ready for you when you choose to enter it. Of this you can be wholly certain. God is as incapable of creating the perishable as the ego is of making the eternal.

Of your egos you can do nothing to save yourselves or others, but of your Souls you can do everything for the salvation of both. Humility is a lesson for the ego, not for the Soul. The Soul is beyond humility because it recognizes its radiance, and gladly sheds its light everywhere. The meek shall inherit the earth because their egos are humble, and this gives them better perception. The Kingdom of Heaven is the right of the Soul, whose beauty and dignity are far beyond doubt, beyond perception, and stand forever as the mark of the Love of God for His creations, who are wholly worthy of Him and only of Him. Nothing else is sufficiently worthy to be a gift for a creation of God Himself.

I will substitute for your ego if you wish, but never for your Soul. A father can safely leave a child with an elder brother who has shown himself responsible, but this involves no confusion about the child's origin. The brother can protect the child's body and his ego, which are very closely related, but he does not confuse himself with the father because he does this, although the child may. I can be entrusted with your body and your ego simply because this enables you not to be concerned with them and lets me teach you their unimportance. I could not understand their importance to you if I had not once been tempted to believe in them myself.

Let us undertake to learn this lesson together, so we can be free of them together. I need devoted teachers who share my aim of healing the mind. The Soul is far beyond the need of your protection or mine. Remember this:

"In this world you need not have tribulation because I have overcome the world."

That is why you should be of good cheer.

You have asked lately how the mind could ever have made the ego. This is a perfectly reasonable question; in fact, the best question you could ask. There is, however, no point in giving an historical answer because the past does not matter in human terms, and history would not exist if the same errors were not being repeated in the present. Abstract thought applies to knowledge because knowledge is completely impersonal, and examples are irrelevant to its understanding.

Perception, however, is always specific, and therefore quite concrete. Each man makes one ego for himself, although it is subject to enormous variation because of its instability, and one for everyone he perceives, which is equally variable. Their interaction is a process which literally alters both, because they were not made either by or with the unalterable. It is particularly important to realize that this alteration can and does occur as readily when the interaction takes place in the mind as when it involves physical presence. Thinking about another ego is as effective in changing relative perception as is physical interaction. There could be no better example of the fact that the ego is an idea, though not a reality-based thought.

Your own present state is a good example of how the mind made the ego. You do have knowledge at times, but when you throw it away it is as if you never had it. This wilfulness is so apparent that one need only perceive it to see that it does happen. If it can occur that way in the present, why is it surprising that it occurred that way in the past? Psychology rests on the principle of the continuity of behaviour. Surprise is a reasonable response to the unfamiliar, but hardly to something that has occurred with such persistence. I am using your present state of how the mind can work, provided you fully recognize that it need not work that way. Why are you surprised that something happened in the dim past when it is so clearly happening right now?

You forget the love that animals have for their own offspring, and the need they feel to protect them. This is because they regard them as part of themselves. No-one disowns something he regards as a very real part of himself. Man reacts to his ego much as God does to His Souls; – with love, protection and great charity. The reaction of man to the self he made is not at all surprising. In fact it duplicates, in many ways, how he will one day react to his real creations, which are as timeless as he is. The question is not how man responds to his ego, but what he believes he is.

Belief is an ego function, and as long as your origin is open to belief at all, you are regarding it from an ego viewpoint. When teaching is no longer necessary, you will merely know God. Belief that there is another way is the loftiest idea of which ego thinking is capable. That is because it contains a hint of recognition that the ego is not the self. Undermining the ego's thought system must be perceived as painful, even though this is anything but true. Babies scream in rage if you take away a knife or a scissors, even though they may well harm themselves if you do not. The speed-up has placed you in the same position.

You are not prepared, and in this sense, you are babies. You have no sense of real self-preservation, and are very likely to decide that you need precisely what would hurt you most. Whether you know it now or not, however, you have willed to cooperate in a concerted and very commendable effort to become both harmless and helpful, two attributes which must go together. Your attitudes, even toward this, are necessarily conflicted because all attitudes are ego-based. This will not last. Be patient awhile and remember that the outcome is as certain as God.

Only those who have a real and lasting sense of abundance can be truly charitable. This is quite obvious when you consider the concepts involved. To the ego, to give anything implies that you will do without it. When you associate giving with sacrifice, then, you give only because you believe that you are somehow getting something better, so that you can do without the thing you give. "Giving to get" is an inescapable law of the ego, which always evaluates itself in relation to other egos, and is therefore continually preoccupied with the scarcity principle which gave rise to it. This is the meaning of Freud's "reality principle," since Freud thought of the ego as very weak and deprived, capable of functioning only as a thing in need.

The "reality principle" of the ego is not real at all. The ego is forced to perceive the "reality" of other egos because it cannot establish the reality of itself. In fact, its whole perception of other egos as real is only an attempt to convince itself that it is real. "Self-esteem," in ego terms, means nothing more than that the ego has deluded itself into accepting its reality, and is therefore temporarily less predatory. This "self-esteem" is always vulnerable to stress, a term which actually refers to a condition in which the delusion of the ego's reality is threatened. This produces either ego deflation or ego inflation, resulting in either withdrawal or attack.

The ego literally lives by comparisons. This means that equality is beyond its grasp, and charity becomes impossible. The ego never gives out of abundance, because it was made as a substitute for it. That is why the concept of "getting" arose in the ego's thought system. All appetites are "getting" mechanisms, representing the ego's need to confirm itself. This is as true of bodily appetites as it is of the so-called "higher" ego needs. Bodily appetites are not physical in origin. The ego regards the body as its home and does try to satisfy itself through the body, but the idea that this is possible is a decision of the ego, which is completely confused about what is really possible. This accounts for its erratic nature.

The ego believes it is completely on its own, which is merely another way of describing how it originated. This is such a fearful state that it can only turn to other egos and try to unite with them in a feeble attempt at identification or attack them in an equally feeble show of strength. It is not free, however, to consider the validity of the premise itself because this premise is its foundation. The ego is the belief of the mind that it is completely on its own. Its ceaseless attempts to gain the Soul's acknowledgment, and thus to establish its own existence, are utterly useless.

The Soul in its knowledge is unaware of the ego. It does not attack it; it merely cannot conceive of it at all. While the ego is equally unaware of the Soul, it does perceive itself as rejected by "something" which is greater than itself. This is why self-esteem in ego terms must be a delusion. The creations of God do not create myths, although the creative efforts of man can turn to mythology. It can do so, however, only under one condition; what man then makes is no longer creative. Myths are entirely perceptions and are so ambiguous in form and so characteristically good and evil in nature that the most benevolent of them is not without fearful components, if only by innuendo.

Myths and magic are closely associated in that myths are usually related to the ego origins, and magic to the powers which the ego ascribes to itself. Every mythological system includes some account of "the creation," and associates this with its particular perception of magic. The "battle for survival" is nothing more than the ego's struggle to preserve itself and its interpretation of its own beginning. This beginning is always associated with physical birth, because no-one maintains that the ego existed before that point in time. The religiously ego-oriented believe that the Soul existed before and will continue to exist afterwards, after a temporary lapse in ego life. Some actually believe that the Soul will be punished for this lapse, even though in reality, it could not possibly know anything about it.

The term "salvation" does not apply to the Soul, which is not in danger, and does not need to be salvaged. Salvation is nothing more than "right-mindedness," which is not the One-Mindedness of the Soul, but which must be accomplished before the One-Mindedness can be restored. Right-mindedness dictates the next step automatically because right perception is uniformly without attack, so that wrongmindedness is obliterated. The ego cannot survive without judgment and is laid aside accordingly. The mind then has only one direction in which it can move. The direction which the mind will take is always automatic, because it cannot but be dictated by the thought system to which the mind adheres.

Every thought system has internal consistency, and this provides the basis for the continuity of behaviour. However, this is a matter of reliability, and not validity. "Reliable behaviour" is a meaningful perception, as far as ego thinking goes. However, "valid behaviour" is an expression which is inherently contradictory, because validity is an end and behaviour is a means. These cannot be combined logically because, when an end has been attained, the means for its attainment are no longer meaningful.

A hypothesis is either false or true, to be accepted or rejected accordingly. If it is shown to be true it becomes a fact, after which no one attempts to evaluate it unless its status as fact is questioned. Every idea to which the ego has accorded the status of fact is questionable, because facts are in the realm of knowledge.

Confusing realms of discourse is a thinking error which philosophers have recognized for centuries. Psychologists are generally quite deficient in this respect, as are many theologians. Data from one realm of discourse do not mean anything in another because they can be understood only within the thought system of which they are a part. That is why psychologists are concentrating increasingly on the ego, in an attempt to unify their clearly unrelated data. It need hardly be said that an attempt to relate the unrelated cannot succeed.

The more recent ecological emphases are but another ingenious way of trying to impose order on chaos. We have already credited the ego with considerable ingenuity, though not with creativeness. It should, however, be remembered that inventiveness is really wasted effort, even in its most ingenious forms. We do not have to explain anything. This is why we need not trouble ourselves with inventiveness. The highly specific nature of invention is not worthy of the abstract creativity of God's creations.

You have never understood what "the Kingdom of Heaven is within you" means. The reason you have not understood it is because it is not understandable to the ego, which interprets it as if something outside is inside, and this does not mean anything. The word "within" is unnecessary. The Kingdom of Heaven is you. What else but you did the Creator create, and what else but you is His Kingdom? This is the whole message of the Atonement, a message, which, in its totality, transcends the sum of its parts. Christmas is not a time; it is a state of mind. The Christ Mind wills from the Soul, not from the ego, and the Christ Mind is yours.

You, too, have a kingdom which your Soul created. It has not ceased to create because your ego has set you on the road of perception. Your Soul's creations are no more fatherless than you are. Your ego and your Soul will never be co-creators, but your Soul and your Creator will always be. Be confident that your creations are as safe as you are.

> "The Kingdom is perfectly united and perfectly protected, and the ego will not prevail against it, – Amen."

That was written in that form because it is a good thing to use as a kind of a prayer in moments of temptation. It is a Declaration of Independence. You will find it very helpful if you understand it fully. In its characteristically upside-down way, the ego has taken the impulses from the superconscious and perceives them as if they arise in the unconscious. The ego judges what is to be accepted, and the impulses from the superconscious are unacceptable to it because they clearly point to the nonexistence of the ego itself. The ego therefore experiences threat, and not only censors but also reinterprets the data. However, as Freud correctly pointed out, what you have repressed can retain a very active life beyond your awareness.

Repression thus operates to conceal not only the baser impulses but also the most lofty ones from awareness because both are threatening to the ego and, being concerned primarily with its own preservation in the face of threat, the ego perceives them as the same. The threat-value of the lofty is actually much greater to the ego because the pull of God Himself can hardly be equated with the pull of human appetites. By perceiving them as the same, the ego attempts to save itself from being swept away, as it would surely be in the presence of knowledge.

The upper level of the unconscious thus contains the Call of God as well as the call of the body. That is why the basic conflict between love and fear is unconscious; the ego cannot tolerate either and represses both by resorting to inhibition. Society depends on inhibiting the latter, but salvation depends on dis inhibiting the former. The reason you need my help is because you have repressed your own Guide, and therefore need guidance. My role is to separate the true from the false in your unconscious, so it can break through the barriers the ego has set up, and shine into your minds. Against our united strength the ego cannot prevail.

It should be apparent to you by now why the ego regards the Soul as its "enemy." The ego arose from the separation, and its continued existence depends on your continuing belief in the separation. Having reduced the Soul impulses to the unconscious, the ego has to offer you some sort of reward for maintaining this belief. All it can offer is a sense of temporary existence, which begins with its own beginning and ends with its own ending. It tells you this life is your existence because it is its own. Against this sense of temporary existence the Soul offers you the knowledge of permanence and unshakable being. No-one who has experienced the revelation of this can ever fully believe in the ego again.

How can its meagre offering to you prevail against the glorious gift of God?

You who identify with your egos cannot believe that God loves you. you do not love what you have made, and what you made does not love you. Being made out of the denial of the Father, the ego has no allegiance to its own maker. You cannot conceive of the real relationship which exists between God and His Souls because of the hatred you have for the self you have made. You project onto your own idea of yourself the will to separate, which conflicts with the love you feel for what you made because you made it. No human love is without this ambivalence, and since no ego has experienced love without ambivalence, the concept is beyond its understanding.

Love will enter immediately into any mind which truly wants it, but it must want it truly. This means that it wants it without ambivalence, and this kind of wanting is wholly without the ego's "drive to get." There is a kind of experience which is so different from anything the ego can offer that you will never recover. The word "recover" is used quite literally here, – you will never be able to cover or hide again. It is necessary to repeat here that your belief in darkness and in hiding is why the Light cannot enter. The Bible gives many references to the immeasurable gifts which are for you, but for which you must ask. This is not a condition as the ego sets conditions. It is the glorious condition of what you are.

No force except your own will is strong enough or worthy enough to guide you. In this you are as free as God and must remain so forever. You can never be bound except in honour, and that is always voluntary. Let us ask the Father in my name to keep you mindful of His Love for you and yours for Him. He has never failed to answer this request because it asks only for what He has already willed. Those who call truly are always answered. Thou shalt have no other gods before Him because there are none.

It has never really entered your mind to give up every idea you ever had that opposes knowledge. You retain thousands of little scraps of meanness which prevent the Holy One from entering. Light cannot penetrate through the walls you make to block it, and it is forever unwilling to destroy what you have made. No-one can see through a wall, but I can step around it. Watch your minds for the scraps of meanness, or you will be unable to ask me to do so. I can help you only as our Father created us. I will love you and honour you and maintain complete respect for what you have made, but I will neither honour it nor love it unless it is true.

I will never forsake you, any more than God will, but I must wait as long as you choose to forsake yourself. Because I wait in love and not in impatience you will surely ask me truly. I will come in response to a single unequivocal call. Watch carefully and see what it is you are really asking for. Be very honest with yourself about this, for we must hide nothing from each other. If you will really try to do this, you have taken the first step toward preparing your mind for the Holy One to enter. We will prepare for this together, for once He has come you will be ready to help me make other minds ready for Him. How long will you deny Him His Kingdom?

In your own unconscious, deeply repressed by the ego, is the declaration of your release. God had given you everything. This is the one fact that means the ego does not exist, and which therefore makes it profoundly afraid. In the ego's language, remember, "to have" and "to be" are different, but they are identical to the Soul. The Soul knows that you both have everything and are everything. Any distinction in this respect is meaningful only when the idea of "getting," which implies a lack, has already been accepted. That is why we made no distinction before between having the Kingdom of God and being the Kingdom of God.

The calm being of God's Kingdom, which in your sane mind is perfectly conscious, is ruthlessly banished from the part of the mind which the ego rules. The ego is desperate because it opposes literally invincible odds, whether you are asleep or awake. Consider how much vigilance you have been willing to exert to protect your ego, and how little you have been willing to expend to protect your higher mind. Who but the insane would undertake to believe what is not true, and then protect this belief at the cost of truth?

If you cannot hear the Voice of God, it is because you do not choose to listen. The fact that you do listen to the voice of your ego is demonstrated by your attitudes, your feelings and your behaviour. Your attitudes are obviously conflicted, your feelings have a narrow range on the negative side but are never purely joyous, and your behaviour is either strained or unpredictable. Yet this is what you want. This is what you are fighting to keep and what you are vigilant to save. Your minds are filled with schemes to save the face of your egos, and you do not seek the Face of God. The glass in which the ego seeks to see its face is dark indeed. How can it maintain the trick of its existence except with mirrors? But where you look to find yourself is up to you.

We have said that you cannot change your mind by changing your behaviour, but we have also said, and many times before, that you can change your mind. When your mood tells you that you have chosen wrongly, and this is so whenever you are not joyous, then know this need not be. In every case you have thought wrongly about some Soul that God created and are perceiving images your ego makes in a darkened glass. Think honestly what you have thought that God would not have thought, and what you have not thought that God would have you think. Search sincerely for what you have done and left undone accordingly, and then change your minds to think with God's.

This may seem hard to you, but it is much easier than trying to think against it. Your mind is one with God's. Denying this and thinking otherwise has held your ego together but has literally split your mind. As a loving brother, I am deeply concerned with your mind, and urge you to follow my example as you look at yourselves and at each other and see in both the glorious creations of a glorious Father.

When you are sad, know that this need not be. Depression always arises ultimately from a sense of being deprived of something you want and do not have. Know you are deprived of nothing except by your own decisions, and then decide otherwise.

When you are anxious, know that all anxiety comes from the capriciousness of the ego, and need not be. You can be as vigilant against the ego's dictates as for them.

When you feel guilty, know that the ego has indeed violated the laws of God, but you have not. Leave the sins of the ego to me. That is what Atonement is for. But until you change your mind about those your ego has hurt the Atonement cannot release you. As long as you feel guilty your ego is in command because only the ego can experience guilt. this need not be.

Watch your mind for the temptations of the ego, and do not be deceived by it. Know it offers you nothing. When you have given up this voluntary dispiriting, you will see how your mind can focus and rise above fatigue and heal. Yet you are not sufficiently vigilant against the demands of the ego to disengage yourself. This need not be.

The habit of engaging with God and His creations is easily made if you actively refuse to let your minds slip away. The problem is not one of concentration; it is the belief that no-one, including yourself, is worth consistent effort. Side with me consistently against this deception, and do not permit this shabby belief to pull you back. The disheartened are useless to themselves and to me, but only the ego can be disheartened. Have you really considered how many opportunities you have to gladden yourselves, and how many of them you have refused? There is no limit to the power of a Son of God, but he himself can limit the expression of his power as much as he chooses.

Your mind and mine can unite in shining your ego away and releasing the strength of God into everything you think and will and do. Do not settle for anything less than this and refuse to accept anything but this as your goal. Watch your minds carefully for any beliefs that hinder its accomplishment, and step away from them. Judge how well you have done this by your own feelings, for this is the one right use of judgment. Judgment, like any other defence, can be used to attack or protect, to hurt or to heal. The ego should be brought to your judgment and found wanting there. Without your own allegiance, protection and love, it cannot exist. Judge your ego truly and you must withdraw allegiance, protection and love from it.

You are mirrors of truth in which God Himself shines in perfect Light. To the ego's dark glass you need but say, "I will not look there because I know these images are not true." Then let the Holy One shine on you in peace, knowing that this and only this must be. His Mind shone on you in your creation and brought your mind into being. His Mind still shines on you and must shine through you. Your ego cannot prevent Him from shining on you, but it can prevent you from letting Him shine through you.

The first coming of Christ is just another name for the creation, for Christ is the Son of God. The second coming of Christ means nothing more than the end of the ego's rule over part of the minds of men, and the healing of the mind. I was created like you in the first, and I have called you to join with me in the second. If you will think over your lives you will see how carefully the preparations were made. I am in charge of the Second Coming, and my judgment, which is used only for protection, cannot be wrong because it never attacks. Yours is so distorted that you believe I was mistaken in choosing you. I assure you this is a mistake of your egos. Do not mistake it for humility.

Your egos are trying to convince you that they are real and I am not, because if I am real, I am no more real than you are. That knowledge, and I assure you that it is knowledge, means that Christ must come into your minds and heal them. Although I am not attacking your egos, I am working with your higher mind whether you are asleep or awake, just as your ego does with your lower mind. I am your vigilance in this because you are too confused to recognize your own hope. I was not mistaken. Your minds will elect to join with mine, and together we are invincible.

You will yet come together in my name and your sanity will be restored. I raised the dead by knowing that life is an eternal attribute of everything that the living God created. Why do you believe it is harder for me to inspire the dispirited, or to stabilize the unstable? I do not believe that there is an order of difficulty in miracles; you do. I have called, and you will answer. I know that miracles are natural because they are expressions of love. My calling you is as natural as your answer, and as inevitable.

All things work together for good. There are no exceptions except in the ego's judgment. Control is a central factor in what the ego permits into consciousness, and one to which it devotes its maximum vigilance. This is not the way a balanced mind holds together. Its control is unconscious. The ego is further off balance by keeping its primary motivation unconscious and raising control rather than sensible judgment to predominance. The ego has every reason to do this, according to the thought system which gave rise to it, and which it serves. Sane judgment would inevitably judge against the ego and must be obliterated by the ego in the interest of its self-preservation.

A major source of the ego's off-balanced state is its lack of discrimination between impulses from God and from the body. Any thought system which makes this confusion must be insane. Yet this demented state is essential to the ego, which judges only in terms of threat or non-threat to itself. In one sense the ego's fear of the idea of God is at least logical, since this idea does dispel the ego. Fear of dissolution from the Higher Source, then, makes some sense in ego-terms. But fear of the body, with which the ego identifies so closely, is more blatantly senseless.

The body is the ego's home by its own election. It is the only identification with which the ego feels safe because the body's vulnerability is its own best argument that you cannot be of God. This is the belief that the ego sponsors eagerly. Yet the ego hates the body because it does not accept the idea that the body is good enough to be its home. Here is where the mind becomes actually dazed. Being told by the ego that it is really part of the body and that the body is its protector, the mind is also constantly informed that the body cannot protect it. This, of course, is not only accurate but perfectly obvious.

Therefore the mind asks, "Where can I go for protection?" to which the ego replies, "Turn to me." The mind, and not without cause, reminds the ego that it has itself insisted that it is identified with the body, so there is no point in turning to it for protection. The ego has no real answer to this because there is none, but it does have a typical solution. It obliterates the question from the mind's awareness. Once unconscious, the question can and does produce uneasiness, but it cannot be answered because it cannot be asked. This is the question which must be asked: "Where am I to go for protection?" Even the insane ask it unconsciously, but it requires real sanity to ask it consciously.

When the Bible says, "Seek and ye shall find," it does not mean that you should seek blindly and desperately for something you would not recognize. Meaningful seeking is consciously undertaken, consciously organized, and consciously directed. The goal must be formulated clearly and kept in mind. As a teacher with some experience, let me remind you that learning and wanting to learn are inseparable. All learners learn best when they believe that what they are trying to learn is of value to them. However, values in this world are hierarchical, and not everything you may want to learn has lasting value.

Indeed, many of the things you want to learn are chosen because their value will not last. The ego thinks it is an advantage not to commit itself to anything that is eternal because the eternal must come from God. Eternalness is the one function which the ego has tried to develop but has systematically failed. It may surprise you to learn that had the ego wished to do so it could have made the eternal because, as a product of the mind, it is endowed with the power of its own creator. However, the decision to do this, rather than the ability to do it, is what the ego cannot tolerate. That is because the decision, from which the ability would naturally develop, would necessarily involve accurate perception, a state of clarity which the ego, fearful of being judged truly, must avoid.

The results of this dilemma are peculiar, but no more so than the dilemma itself. The ego has reacted characteristically here as elsewhere because mental illness, which is always a form of ego involvement, is not a matter of reliability as much as of validity. The ego compromises with the issue of the eternal, just as it does with all issues that touch on the real question in any way. By compromising in connection with all tangential questions, it hopes to hide the real question and keep it out of mind. The ego's characteristic busyness with nonessentials is for precisely that purpose.

Consider the alchemist's age-old attempts to turn base metal into gold. The one question which the alchemist did not permit himself to ask was, "what for?" He could not ask this, because it would immediately become apparent that there was no sense in his efforts even if he succeeded. If gold became more plentiful its value would decrease, and his own purpose would be defeated. The ego has countenanced some strange compromises with the idea of the eternal, making many odd attempts to relate the concept to the unimportant, in an effort to satisfy the mind without jeopardizing itself. Thus, it has permitted minds to devote themselves to the possibility of perpetual motion but not to perpetual thoughts.

Ideational preoccupations with problems set up to be incapable of solution are also favourite ego devices for impeding the strong-willed from making real learning progress. The problems of squaring the circle and carrying pi to infinity are good examples. A more recent ego attempt is particularly noteworthy. The idea of preserving the body by suspension, thus giving it the kind of limited immortality which the ego can tolerate, is among its more recent appeals to the mind. It is noticeable, however, that in all these diversionary tactics, the one question which is never asked by those who pursue them is,
"What for?"

This is the question which you must learn to ask, in connection with everything your mind wishes to undertake. What is the purpose? Whatever it is, you cannot doubt that it will channelize your efforts automatically. When you make a decision of purpose, then, you have made a decision about your future effort, a decision which will remain in effect unless you change the decision.

Psychologists are in a good position to realize that the ego is capable of making and accepting as real some very distorted associations. The confusion of sex with aggression, and the resulting behaviour which is perceived as the same for both, serves as an example. This is "understandable" to the psychologist and does not produce surprise. The lack of surprise, however, is not a sign of understanding. It is a symptom of the psychologist's ability to accept as reasonable a compromise which is clearly senseless; to attribute it to the mental illness of the patient, rather than his own, and to limit his questions about both the patient and himself to the trivial.

Such relatively minor confusions of the ego are not among its more profound misassociations, although they do reflect them. Your egos have been blocking the more important questions which your minds should ask. You do not understand a patient while you yourselves are willing to limit the questions you raise about his mind, because you are also accepting these limits for yours. This makes you unable to heal him and yourselves. Be always unwilling to adapt to any situation in which miracle-mindedness is unthinkable. That state in itself is enough to demonstrate that the perception is wrong.

It cannot be emphasized too often that correcting perception is merely a temporary expedient. It is necessary to do so only because misperception is a block to knowledge, while accurate perception is a stepping-stone towards it. The whole value of right perception lies in the inevitable judgment which it entails that it is unnecessary. This removes the block entirely. You may ask how this is possible as long as you appear to be living in this world, and since this is a sensible question, it has a sensible answer. You must be careful, however, that you really understand the question. What IS the "you" who are living in this world?

Immortality is a constant state. It is as true now as it ever was or ever will be, because it implies no change at all. It is not a continuum, nor is it understood by being compared to an opposite. Knowledge never involves comparisons. That is its essential difference from everything else the mind can grasp. "A little knowledge" is not dangerous except to the ego. Vaguely it senses threat and being unable to realize that "a little knowledge" is a meaningless phrase since "all" and "a little" in this context are the same, the ego decides that since "all" is impossible, the fear does not lie there. "A little," however, is a scarcity concept, and this the ego understands well. "A little," then, is perceived as the real threat.

The essential thing to remember is that the ego does not recognize the real source of its perceived threat, and if you associate yourself with the ego, you do not perceive the whole situation as it is. Only your allegiance to it gives the ego any power over you. We have spoken of the ego as if it were a separate thing acting on its own. This was necessary to persuade you that you cannot dismiss it lightly and must realize how much of your thinking is ego-directed. We cannot safely let it go at that, however, or you will regard yourselves as necessarily conflicted as long as you are here, or more properly, as long as you believe that you are here.
    The ego is nothing more than a part of your belief about yourselves. Your other life has continued without interruption and has been and always will be totally unaffected by your attempts to disassociate. The ratio of repression and dissociation varies with the individual ego-illusion, but dissociation is always involved, or you would not believe that you are here. In learning to escape from the illusions you have made, your great debt to each other is something you must never forget. It is exactly the same debt that you owe to me. Whenever you react egotistically towards each other, you are throwing away the graciousness of your indebtedness, and the holy perception it would produce.
    The term "holy" can be used here because, as you learn how much you are indebted to the whole Sonship, which includes me, you come as close to knowledge as perception ever can. The gap is then so small that knowledge can easily flow across it and obliterate it forever. You have very little trust in me as yet, but it will increase as you turn more and more often to me instead of your egos for guidance. The results will convince you increasingly that your choice in turning to me is the only sane one you can make. No-one who has learned from experience that one choice brings peace and joy, while another brings chaos and disaster, needs much conditioning.
    The ego cannot withstand the conditioning process because the process itself demonstrates that there is another way. Conditioning by rewards has always been more effective than conditioning by pain because pain is an ego-illusion and can never induce more than a temporary effect. The rewards of God, however, are immediately recognized as eternal. Since this recognition is made by you and not the ego, the recognition itself establishes that you and your ego can not be identical. You may believe that you have already accepted the difference, but you are by no means convinced as yet. The very fact that you are preoccupied with the idea of escaping from the ego shows this.

You cannot escape from the ego by humbling it or controlling it or punishing it. Remember that the ego and the Soul do not know each other. The separated mind cannot maintain the separation except by dissociating. Having done this, it utilizes repression against all truly natural impulses, not because the ego is a separate thing, but because you want to believe that you are. The ego is a device for maintaining this belief, but it is still only your willingness to use the device that enables it to endure.

My trust in you is greater than yours in me at the moment, but it will not always be that way. Your mission is very simple. You have been chosen to live so as to demonstrate that you are not an ego. I repeat that I do not choose God's channels wrongly. The Holy One shares my trust, and always approves my Atonement decisions because my will is never out of accord with His. I have told you before that I am in charge of the whole Atonement. This is only because I completed my part in it as a man and can now complete it through other men. My chosen receiving and sending channels cannot fail because I will lend them my strength as long as theirs is wanting.

I will go with you to the Holy One, and through my perception he can bridge the little gap. Your gratitude to each other is the only gift I want. I will bring it to God for you, knowing that to know your brother is to know God. A little knowledge is an all-encompassing thing. If you are grateful to each other, you are grateful to God for what He created. Through your gratitude you can come to know each other, and one moment of real recognition makes all men your brothers, because they are all of your Father. Love does not conquer all things, but it does set all things right. Because you are all the Kingdom of God, I can lead you back to your own creations, which you do not yet know. What has been dissociated is still there.

As you come closer to a brother you do approach me, and as you withdraw from him, I become distant to you. Your giant step forward was to insist on a "collaborative venture." This does not go against the true spirit of meditation; it is inherent in it. Meditation is a collaborative venture with God. It can not be undertaken successfully by those who disengage themselves from the Sonship, because they are disengaging themselves from me. God will come to you only as you will give Him to your brothers.
Learn first of them, and you will be ready to hear God as you hear them.

That is because the function of love is one.

How can you teach someone the value of something he has deliberately thrown away? He must have thrown it away because he did not value it. You can only show him how miserable he is without it, and bring it near very slowly, so he can learn how his misery lessens as he approaches it. This conditions him to associate his misery with its absence, and to associate the opposite of misery with its presence. It gradually becomes desirable, as he changes his mind about its worth. I am conditioning you to associate misery with the ego and joy with the Soul. You have conditioned yourselves the other way around. A far greater reward, however, will break through any conditioning, if it is repeatedly offered whenever the old habit pattern is broken. You are still free to choose, but can you really want the rewards of the ego in the presence of the rewards of God?

It should be clear by now that, while the content of any particular ego-illusion does not matter, it is usually more helpful to correct it in a specific context. Ego-illusions are quite specific, although they frequently change, and although the mind is naturally abstract. The mind nevertheless becomes concrete voluntarily as soon as it splits. However, only part of it splits, so only part of it is concrete. The concrete part is the same part that believes in the ego because the ego depends on the specific. It is the part that believes your existence means you are separate.

Everything the ego perceives is a separate whole, without the relationships that imply being. The ego is thus against communication, except in so far as it is utilized to establish separateness rather than to abolish it. The communication system of the ego is based on its own thought system, as is everything else it dictates. Its communication is controlled by its need to protect itself, and it will disrupt communication when it experiences threat. While this is always so, individual egos perceive different kinds of threat, which are quite specific in their own judgment. For example, although all forms of perceived demands may be classified, or judged, by the ego as coercive communication which must be disrupted, the response of breaking communication will nevertheless be to a specific person or persons.

The specificity of the ego's thinking, then, results in a spurious kind of generalization which is really not abstract at all. It will respond in certain specific ways to all stimuli which it perceives as related. In contrast, the Soul reacts in the same way to everything it knows is true and does not respond at all to anything else. Nor does it make any attempt to establish what is true. It knows that what is true is everything that God created. It is in complete and direct communication with every aspect of creation because it is in complete and direct communication with its Creator.

This communication is the Will of God. Creation and communication are synonymous. God created every mind by communicating His Mind to it, thus establishing it forever as a channel for the reception of His Mind and Will. Since only beings of a like order can truly communicate, His creations naturally communicate with Him and like Him. This communication is perfectly abstract in that its quality is universal in application, and not subject to any judgement, any exception, or any alteration. God created you by this and for this. The mind can distort its function, but it cannot endow itself with functions it was not given. That is why the mind cannot totally lose the ability to communicate, even though it may refuse to utilize it on behalf of being.

Existence as well as being rests on communication. Existence, however, is specific in how, what, and with whom communication is judged to be worth undertaking. Being is completely without these distinctions. It is a state in which the mind IS in communication with everything that is real, including the Soul. To whatever extent you permit this state to be curtailed, you are limiting your sense of your own reality, which becomes total only by your recognizing all reality in the glorious context of its real relationship to you. This is your reality. Do not desecrate it or recoil from it. It is your real home, your real temple, and your real Self.

God, Who encompasses all being, nevertheless created beings who have everything individually, but who want to share it to increase their joy. Nothing that is real can be increased except by sharing. That is why God Himself created you. Divine Abstraction takes joy in application, and that is what creation means. "How," "what" and "to whom" are irrelevant because real creation gives everything, since it can create only like itself. Remember that in being there is no difference between "having" and "being," as there is in existence. In the state of being, the mind gives everything always.

The Bible repeatedly states that you should praise God. This hardly means that you should tell Him how wonderful He is. He has no ego with which to accept such thanks, and no perception with which to judge such offerings. But unless you take your part in the creation, His joy is not complete because yours is incomplete. And this He does know. He knows it in His own Being and Its experience of His Son's experience. The constant going out of His Love is blocked when His channels are closed, and He is lonely when the minds He created do not communicate fully with Him.

God has kept your kingdom for you, but He cannot share His joy with you until you know it with your whole mind. Even revelation is not enough, because it is communication from God. It is not enough until it is shared. God does not need revelation returned to Him, which would clearly be impossible, but He does want revelation brought to others. This cannot be done with the actual revelation because its content cannot be expressed, and it is intensely personal to the mind which receives it. It can, however, still be returned by that mind through its attitudes to other minds which the knowledge from the revelation brings.

God is praised whenever any mind learns to be wholly helpful. This is impossible without being wholly harmless because the two beliefs coexist. The truly helpful are invulnerable because they are not protecting their egos, so that nothing can hurt them. Their helpfulness is their praise of God, and He will return their praise of Him because they are like Him, and they can rejoice together. God goes out to them and through them, and there is great joy throughout the Kingdom. Every mind that is changed adds to this joy with its own individual willingness to share in it. The truly helpful are God's miracle workers, whom I direct until we are all united in the joy of the Kingdom. I will direct you to wherever you can be truly helpful, and to whoever can follow my guidance through you.

Every mind which is split needs rehabilitation. The medical orientation to rehabilitation emphasizes the body, while the vocational orientation stresses the ego. The "team" approach generally leads more to confusion than to anything else because it is too often misused as a way of exerting the ego's domination over other egos, rather than as a real experiment in the cooperation of minds. Rehabilitation as a movement is an improvement over the overt neglect of those in need of help, but it is often little more than a painful attempt on the part of the halt to lead the blind.

The ego is likely to fear broken bodies because it cannot tolerate them. The ego cannot tolerate ego weakness either without ambivalence because it is afraid of its own weakness as well as the weakness of its chosen home. When it is threatened, the ego blocks your natural impulse to help, placing you under the strain of divided will. You may then be tempted to withdraw to allow your ego to recover and to gain enough strength to be helpful again on a basis limited enough not to threaten your ego, but too limited to give you joy. Those with broken bodies are often looked down on by the ego because of its belief that nothing but a perfect body is worthy as its own temple.

A mind that recoils from a hurt body is in great need of rehabilitation itself. All symptoms of hurt need true helpfulness, and whenever they are met with this, the mind that so meets them heals itself. Rehabilitation is an attitude of praising God as He Himself knows praise. He offers praise to you, and you must offer it to others. The chief handicaps of the clinicians lie in their attitudes to those whom their egos perceive as weakened and damaged. By these evaluations, they have weakened and damaged their own helpfulness, and have thus set their own rehabilitation back.

Rehabilitation is not concerned either with the ego's fight for control, or its need to avoid and withdraw. You can do much on behalf of your own rehabilitation and that of others if, in a situation calling for healing, you think of it this way:

"I am here only to be truly helpful.

I am here to represent Christ, Who sent me.

I do not have to worry about what to say or what to do because He Who sent me will direct me.

I am content to be wherever He wishes, knowing He goes there with me. I will be healed as I let Him teach me to heal."

To heal is to make happy. I have told you before to think how many opportunities you have to gladden yourselves, and how many you have refused. This is exactly the same as telling you that you have refused to heal yourselves. The light that belongs to you is the light of joy. Radiance is not associated with sorrow. Depression is often contagious, but although it may affect those who come in contact with it, they do not yield to the influence whole-heartedly. But joy calls forth an integrated willingness to share in it, and thus promotes the mind's natural impulse to respond as one.

Those who attempt to heal without being wholly joyous themselves call forth different kinds of responses at the same time, and thus deprive others of the joy of responding whole-heartedly. To be whole-hearted, you must be happy. If fear and love cannot coexist, and if it is impossible to be wholly fearful and remain alive, then the only possible whole state is that of love. There is no difference between love and joy. Therefore, the only possible whole state is the wholly joyous. To heal or to make joyous is therefore the same as to integrate and to make one. That is why it makes no difference to what part or by what part of the Sonship the healing is done. Every part benefits, and benefits equally.

You are being blessed by every beneficent thought of any of your brothers anywhere. You should want to bless them in return, out of gratitude. You do not have to know them individually, or they you. The light is so strong that it radiates throughout the Sonship and returns thanks to the Father for radiating His joy upon it. Only God's holy children are worthy to be channels of His beautiful joy, because only they are beautiful enough to hold it by sharing it. It is impossible for a Child of God to love his neighbour Except as himself. That is why the healer's prayer is:

"Let me know this brother as I know myself"

Healing is an act of thought by which two minds perceive their oneness and become glad. This gladness calls to every part of the Sonship to rejoice with them and lets God Himself go out into them and through them. Only the healed mind can experience revelation with lasting effect because revelation is an experience of pure joy. If you do not choose to be wholly joyous, your mind cannot have what it does not choose to be. Remember that the Soul knows no difference between "being" and "having." The higher mind thinks according to the laws which the Soul obeys, and therefore honours only the laws of God. To Him, getting is meaningless and giving is all. Having everything, the Soul holds everything by giving it, and thus creates as the Father created.

If you think about it, you will see that, while this kind of thinking is totally alien to having things, even to the lower mind it is quite comprehensible in connection with ideas. If you share a physical possession, you do divide its ownership. If you share an idea, however, you do not lessen it. All of it is still yours, although all of it has been given away. Further, if the person to whom you give it accepts it as His, he reinforces it in your mind, and thus increases it. If you can accept the concept that the world is one of ideas, the whole belief in the false association which the ego makes between giving and losing is gone.

Let us start our process of re-awakening with just a few simple concepts:

> "Thoughts increase by being given away.
> The more who believe in them, the stronger they become.
> everything is an idea.
> How, then, is it possible that giving and losing can be meaningfully associated?"

This is the invitation to the Holy Spirit. I told you that I could reach up and bring the Holy Spirit down to you, but I can bring Him to you only at your own invitation. The Holy Spirit is nothing more than your own right mind. He was also mine. The Bible says, "May the mind be in you that was also in Christ Jesus," and uses this as a blessing. It is the blessing of miracle-mindedness. It asks that you may think as I thought, joining with me in Christ-thinking.

The Holy Spirit is the only part of the Holy Trinity which is symbolic. He is referred to in the Bible as the Healer, the Comforter, and the Guide. He is also described as something "separate," apart from the Father and from the Son. I myself said, "If I go I will send you another comforter, and He will abide with you." The Holy Spirit is a difficult concept to grasp precisely because it is symbolic, and therefore open to many different interpretations. As a man and as one of God's creations, my right thinking, which came from the Universal Inspiration which is the Holy Spirit, taught me first and foremost that this Inspiration is for all. I could not have It myself without knowing this.

The word "know" is proper in this context, because the Holy Inspiration is so close to knowledge that It calls it forth; or better, allows it to come. We have spoken before of the higher, or the "true" perception, which is so close to truth that God Himself can flow across the little gap. Knowledge is always ready to flow everywhere, but it cannot oppose.

Therefore, you can obstruct it, although you can never lose it. The Holy Spirit is the Christ Mind Which senses the knowledge that lies beyond perception. It came into being with the separation as a protection, inspiring the beginning of the Atonement at the same time. Before that, there was no need for healing, and no-one was comfortless.

God honoured even the miscreations of His Children because they had made them, but He also blessed them with a way of thinking that could raise their perceptions until they became so lofty that they could reach almost back to Him. The Holy Spirit is the Mind of the Atonement. It represents a state of mind that comes close enough to One-Mindedness that transfer to it is at last possible. Transfer depends on common elements in the old learning and the new situation to which it is transferred. Perception is not knowledge, but it can be transferred to knowledge, or cross over into it. It might even be more helpful here to use the literal meaning of "carried" over, since the last step is taken by God.

The Holy Spirit, the shared Inspiration of all the Sonship, induces a kind of perception in which many elements are like those in the Kingdom of Heaven itself.

First, its universality is perfectly clear, and no-one who receives it could ever believe for one instant that sharing it involves anything but gain.

Second, it is incapable of attack, and is therefore truly open. This means that, although it does not engender knowledge, it does not obstruct it in any way. There is a point at which sufficient quantitative changes produce real qualitative differences. The next point requires real understanding because it is the point at which the shift occurs:

Finally, it points the way beyond the healing which it brings and leads the mind beyond its own integration into the paths of creation. Healing is not creating; it is reparation. The Holy Spiritpromotes healing by looking beyond it, to what the Children of God were before healing was needed and will be when they have been healed. This alteration of the time sequence should be quite familiar because it is very similar to the shift in time perception which the miracle introduces. The Holy Spirit is the motivation for miracle-mindedness; the will to heal the separation by letting it go. This will is in you because God placed it in your mind, and although you can keep it asleep, you cannot obliterate it.

God Himself keeps this will alive by transmitting it from His Mind to yours as long as there is time. It is partly His and partly yours. The miracle itself is just this fusion or union of will between Father and Son. The Holy Spirit is the spirit of joy. He is the Call to return with which God blessed the minds of His separated Sons. This is the vocation of the mind. The mind had no calling until the separation because, before that, it had only being and would not have understood the call to right thinking. The Holy Spirit was God's Answer to the separation, the means by which the Atonement could repair until the whole mind returned to creating.

The Atonement and the separation began at the same time. When man made the ego, God placed in him the call to joy. This call is so strong that the ego always dissolves at its sound. That is why you can choose to listen to two voices within you. One you made yourself, and that one is not of God. But the other is given you by God Who asks you only to listen to it. The Holy Spirit is in you in a very literal sense. His is the Voice that calls you back to where you were before and will be again.

It is possible, even in this world, to hear only that voice and no other. It takes effort and great willingness to learn. It is the final lesson that I learned, and God's Sons are as equal as learners as they are as Souls. The Voice of the Holy Spirit is the call to Atonement, or the restoration of the integrity of the mind. When the Atonement is complete and the whole Sonship is healed, there will be no call to return, but what God creates is eternal. The Holy Spirit will remain with the Sons of God, to bless their creations, and keep them in the light of joy.

You are the Kingdom of Heaven, but you have let the belief in darkness enter your minds, and so you need a new light. The Holy Spirit is the radiance that you must let banish the idea of darkness. His is the glory before which dissociation falls away, and the Kingdom of Heaven breaks through into its own. Before the separation you did not need guidance. You knew as you will know again, but as you do not know now. God does not guide because he can share only perfect knowledge. Guidance is evaluative because it implies that there is a right way and also a wrong way, one to be chosen and the other to be avoided. By choosing one, you give up the other.

This is a conflict state. It means that knowledge has been lost because knowledge is sure. God is not in you in a literal sense; you are part of Him. When you chose to leave Him, He gave you a Voice to speak for Him because He could no longer share His knowledge with you without hindrance. Direct communication was broken because you had made another voice through another will. The Holy Spirit calls you both to remember and to forget. You have chosen to be in a state of opposition, in which opposites are possible. As a result, there are choices which you must make. In the holy state, the will is free in the sense that its creative power is unlimited, but choice itself is meaningless.

Freedom to choose is the same power as freedom to create, but its application is different. Choosing means divided will. The Holy Spirit is one way of choosing. This way is in you because there is also another way. God did not leave His Children comfortless, even though they chose to leave Him. The voice they put in their minds was not the voice of His Will, for which the Holy Spirit speaks. The call to return is stronger than the call to depart, but it speaks in a different way.

The Voice of the Holy Spirit does not command because it is incapable of arrogance. It does not demand because it does not seek control. It does not overcome because it does not attack. It merely reminds. It is compelling only because of what it reminds you of. It brings to your mind the other way, remaining quiet even in the midst of the turmoil you have made for yourselves. The Voice for God is always quiet because it speaks of peace. Yet peace is stronger than war because It heals. War is division, not increase. No-one gains from strife.

"What profiteth it a man if he gain the whole world and lose his own Soul?" That means that if he listens to the wrong voice, he has lost sight of his Soul. He cannot lose it, but he an not know it. It is therefore lost to him until he chooses right. The Holy Spirit is your Guide in choosing. He is the part of your mind which always speaks for the right choice because He speaks for God. He is your remaining communication with God, which you can interrupt but cannot destroy.

The Holy Spirit is the way in which God's Will can be done on earth as it is in Heaven. Both Heaven and earth are in you because the call of both is in your will, and therefore in your mind. The Voice for God comes from your own altars to Him. These altars are not things; they are devotions. Yet you have other devotions now. Your divided devotion has given you the two voices, and you must choose at which altar you will to serve. The call you answer now is an evaluation because it is a decision. The decision itself is very simple. It is made on the basis of which call is worth more to you.

My mind will always be like yours because we were created as equals. It was only my decision that gave me all power in Heaven and earth. My only gift to you is to help you make the same decision for yourself. The will for this decision is the will to share it because the decision itself IS the decision to share. It is made by giving and is therefore the one act of mind that resembles true creation. You understand the role of "models" in the learning process, and the importance of the models you value and choose to follow in determining what you will to learn. I am your model for decision. By deciding for God I showed you that this decision can be made, and that you can make it.

I promised you that the mind that made the decision for me is also in you, and that you can let it change you just as it changed me. This mind is unequivocal because it hears only one voice and answers in only one way. You are the light of the world with me. Rest does not come from sleeping but from waking. The Holy Spirit is the call to awake and be glad. The world is very tired because it is the idea of weariness. Our task is the joyous one of waking it to the Call for God. Everyone will answer the Call of the Holy Spirit, or the Sonship cannot be as one. What better vocation could there be for any part of the Kingdom than to restore it to the perfect integration that can make it whole?

Hear only this through the Holy Spirit within you and teach your brothers to listen as I am teaching you. When you are tempted by the wrong voice, call on me to remind you how to heal by sharing my decision and making it stronger. As we share this goal we increase its power to attract the whole Sonship, and to bring it back into the Oneness in which it was created. Remember that "yoke" means "join together" and "burden" means message. Let us reconsider the Biblical statement "my yoke is easy and my burden light" in this way; let us join together, for my message is Light.

I came into your minds because you had grown vaguely aware of the fact that there is another way, or another Voice. Having given this invitation to the Holy Spirit, I could come to provide the model for how to think. Psychology has become the study of behaviour, but no-one denies the basic law that behaviour is a response to motivation, and motivation is will. I have enjoined you to behave as I behaved, but we must respond to the same mind to do this. This mind is the Holy Spirit, Whose will is for God always. He teaches you how to keep me as the model for your thought, and to behave like me as a result.

The power of our joint motivation is beyond belief but not beyond accomplishment. What we can accomplish together has no limits because the Call for God is the call to the unlimited. Child of God, my message is for you, to hear and give away as you answer the Holy Spirit within you.

The way to learn to know your brother is by perceiving the Holy Spirit in him. We have already said that the Holy Spirit is the bridge or thought-transfer of perception to knowledge, so we can use the terms as if they were related because, in His mind, they are. The relationship must be in His mind because, unless it were, the separation between the two ways of thinking would not be open to healing. He is part of the Holy Trinity because His mind is partly yours and also partly God's. This needs clarification, not in statement since we have said it before, but in experience.

The Holy Spirit is the idea of healing. Being thought, the idea gains as it is shared. Being the Call for God, it is also the idea of God. Since you are part of God, it is also the idea of yourself, as well as of all the parts of God. The idea of the Holy Spirit shares the property of other ideas because it follows the laws of the Universe of which it is a part. Therefore, it is strengthened by being given away. It increases in you as you give it to your brothers. Since thoughts do not have to be conscious to exist, your brother does not have to be aware of the Holy Spirit, either in himself or in you, for this miracle to occur.

Your brother may have dissociated the Call for God, just as you have. The dissociation is healed in both of you as you become aware of the Call for God in him, and thus acknowledge its being. There are two ways of seeing your brother which are diametrically opposed to each other. They must both be in your mind because you are the perceiver. They must also be in his because you are perceiving him. See him through the Holy Spirit in his mind, and you will recognize Him in yours. What you acknowledge in your brother you are acknowledging in yourself, and what you share you strengthen.

The Voice of the Holy Spirit is weak in you. That is why you must share it. It must be increased in strength before you can hear it. It is impossible to hear it in yourself while it is so weak in your own mind. It is not weak in itself, but it is limited by your unwillingness to hear it. Will itself is an idea? And is therefore strengthened by being shared. If you make the mistake of looking for the Holy Spirit in yourself alone, your meditations will frighten you because, by adopting the ego's viewpoint, you are undertaking an ego-alien journey with the ego as guide. This is bound to produce fear.

Delay is of the ego because time is its concept. Delay is obviously a time idea. Both time and delay are meaningless in eternity. We have said before that the Holy Spirit is God's answer to the ego. Everything of which the Holy Spirit reminds you is in direct opposition to the ego's notions because true and false perceptions are themselves opposed. The Holy Spirit has the task of undoing what the ego has made. He undoes it in the same realm of discourse in which the ego itself operates, or the mind would be unable to understand the change.

We have repeatedly emphasized that one level of the mind is not understandable to another. So it is with the ego and the Soul; with time and eternity. Eternity is an idea of God, so the Soul understands it perfectly. Time is a belief of the ego, so the lower mind, which IS the ego's domain, accepts it without question. The only aspect of time which is really eternal is now. That is what we really mean when we say that "now is the only time." The literal nature of this statement does not mean anything to the ego, which interprets it, at best, to mean "don't worry about the future." That is not what it really means at all.

The Holy Spirit is the Mediator between the interpretations of the ego and the knowledge of the Soul. His ability to deal with symbols enables Him to work against the ego's beliefs in its own language. His equal ability to look beyond symbols into eternity also enables Him to understand the laws of God, for which He speaks. He can thus perform the function of reinterpreting what the ego makes, not by destruction, but by understanding. Understanding is light, and light leads to knowledge. The Holy Spirit is in light because He is in you who are light, but you yourselves do not know this. It is therefore the task of the Holy Spirit to reinterpret you on behalf of God.

You cannot understand yourselves alone. This is because you have no meaning apart from your rightful place in the Sonship, and the rightful place of the Sonship in God. This is your life, your eternity and yourself. It is of this that the Holy Spirit reminds you. It is this that the Holy Spirit sees. This vision invariably frightens the ego because it is so calm. Peace is the ego's greatest enemy because, according to its interpretation of reality, war is the guarantee of its survival. The ego becomes strong in strife. If you believe there is strife, you will react viciously because the idea of danger has entered your mind. The idea itself is an appeal to the ego.

The Holy Spirit is as vigilant as the ego to the call of danger, opposing it with His strength just as the ego welcomes it with all its might. The Holy Spirit counters this welcome by welcoming peace. Peace and eternity are as closely related as are time and war. Perception as well as knowledge derives meaning from relationships. Those which you accept are the foundations of your beliefs. The separation is merely another term for a split mind. It was not an act, but a thought. Therefore, the idea of separation can be given away, just as the idea of unity can. Either way, the idea will be strengthened in the mind of the giver.

The ego is the symbol of separation, just as the Holy Spirit is the symbol of peace. What you perceive in others you are strengthening in yourself. You let your mind misperceive, but the Holy Spirit lets your mind reinterpret its own misperceptions. The Holy Spirit is the perfect teacher. He uses only what your minds already understand to teach you that you do not understand it. The Holy Spirit can deal with an unwilling learner without going counter to his will because part of his will is still for God. Despite the ego's attempts to conceal this part it is still much stronger than the ego, even though the ego does not recognize it.

The Holy Spirit recognizes it perfectly because it is His own dwelling place, or the place in the mind where He is at home.

You are at home there, too, because it is a place of peace and peace is of God. You who are part of God are not at home except in His peace. If peace is eternal, you are at home only in eternity. The ego made the world as it perceives it, but the Holy Spirit, the re-interpreter of what the ego made, sees it only as a teaching device for bringing you home. The Holy Spirit must perceive time and re-interpret it into the timeless. The mind must be led into eternity through time because, having made time, it is capable of perceiving its opposite.

The Holy Spirit must work through opposites because He must work with and for a mind that is in opposition. Correct and learn and be open to learning. You have not made truth, but truth can still set you free. Look as the Holy Spirit looks and understand as He understands. His understanding looks back to God in remembrance of me. He is in Holy Communion always, and He is part of you. He is your Guide to salvation because He holds the remembrance of things past and to come. He holds this gladness gently in your minds, asking only that you increase it in His name by sharing it to increase His joy in you.

You must have noticed how often I have used your own ideas to help you. You have learned to be a loving, wise and very understanding therapist except for yourself. That exception has given you more than perception for others because of what you saw in them, but less than knowledge of your real relationships to them because you did not accept them as part of you. Understanding is beyond perception because it introduces meaning. It is, however, below knowledge, even though it can grow towards it. It is possible, with great effort, to understand someone else to some extent and to be quite helpful to him, but the effort is misdirected. The misdirection is quite apparent; it is directed away from you.

This does not mean that it is lost to you, but it does mean that you are not aware of it. I have saved all your kindnesses and every loving thought you have had. I have purified them of the errors which hid their light and have kept them for you in their own perfect radiance. They are beyond destruction and beyond guilt. They came from the Holy Spirit within you, and we know what God creates is eternal. What fear has hidden still is part of you.

Joining the Atonement, which I have repeatedly asked you to do, is always a way out of fear. This does not mean that you can safely fail to acknowledge anything that is true. However, the Holy Spirit will not fail to help you re-interpret everything that you perceive as fearful and teach you that only what is loving is true. Truth is beyond your ability to destroy, but entirely within your grasp. It belongs to you because you created it. It is yours because it is a part of you, just as you are part of God because He created you.

The Atonement is the guarantee of the safety of the Kingdom. Nothing good is lost because it comes from the Holy Spirit, the Voice for creation. Nothing that is not good was ever created. And therefore, cannot be protected. What the ego makes it keeps to itself, and so it is without strength. Its unshared existence does not die; it was merely never born. Real birth is not a beginning; it is a continuing. Everything that can continue has been born, but it can increase as you are willing to return the part of your mind that needs healing to the higher part, and thus render your creating undivided.

As a therapist, you yourself tell your patients that the real difference between neurotic and "healthy" guilt feelings is that neurotic guilt feelings do not help anyone. This distinction is wise though incomplete. Let us make the distinction a little sharper now. Neurotic guilt feelings are a device of the ego for "atoning" without sharing, and for asking pardon without change. The ego never calls for real Atonement, and cannot tolerate forgiveness, which is change.

Your concept of "healthy guilt feelings" has merit, but without the concept of the Atonement it lacks the healing potential it holds. You made the distinction in terms of feelings which led to a decision not to repeat the error, which is only part of healing. Your concept lacked the idea of undoing it. What you were really advocating, then, was adopting a policy of sharing without a real foundation. I have come to give you the foundation, so your own thoughts can make you really free. You have carried the burden of the ideas you did not share and which were therefore too weak to increase, but you did not recognize how to undo their existence because you had made them.

You cannot cancel out your past errors alone. They will not disappear from your mind without remedy. The remedy is not of your making, any more than you are. The Atonement cannot be understood except as a pure act of sharing. That is what is meant when we said it is possible, even in this world, to listen to one voice. If you are part of God and the Sonship is one, you cannot be limited to the "self" the ego sees. Every loving thought held in any part of the Sonship belongs to every part. It is shared because it is loving. Sharing is God's way of creating, and also yours. Your ego can keep you in exile from the Kingdom, but in the Kingdom itself it has no power.

You have become willing to receive my messages as I give them without interference by the ego, so we can clarify an earlier point. We said that you will one day teach as much as you learn, and that will keep you in balance. The time is now because you have let it be now. You cannot learn except by teaching. I heard one voice because I had learned that learning is attained by teaching. I understood that I could not atone for myself alone. Listening to one voice means the will to share the voice in order to hear it yourself. The mind that was in me is still irresistibly drawn to every mind created by God because God's Wholeness is the wholeness of His Son.

Turning the other cheek does not mean that you should submit to violence without protest. It means that you cannot be hurt, and do not want to show your brother anything except your wholeness. Show him that he cannot hurt you and hold nothing against him, or you hold it against yourself. Teaching is done in many ways, – by formal means, by guidance, and above all by example, ideas, and the awareness that to share them is to strengthen them. The union of the Sonship is its protection. The ego cannot prevail against the Kingdom because it is united, and the ego fades away and is undone in the presence of the attraction of the parts of the Sonship which hear the call of the Holy Spirit to be as One.

I cannot forget my need to teach what I have learned, which arose in me because I learned it. I call upon you to teach what you have learned because, by so doing, you can depend on it. Make it dependable in my name because my name is the name of God's Son. What I learned I give you freely, and the mind which was in me rejoices as you choose to hear it. The Holy Spirit atones in all of us by undoing, and thus lifts the burden you have placed in your mind. By following Him, He leads you back to God where you belong, and how can you find this way except by taking your brother with you?

My part in the Atonement is not complete until you join it and give it away. As you teach, so shall you learn. I will never leave you or forsake you, because to forsake you would be to forsake myself and God who created me. You will forsake yourselves and God if you forsake any of your brothers. You are more than your brother's keeper. In fact, you do not want to keep him. You must learn to see him as he is and know that he belongs to God as you do. How could you treat your brother better than by rendering unto God the things which are God's?

Ideas do not leave the mind which thought them to have a separate being, nor do separate thoughts conflict with one another in space because they do not occupy space at all. However, human ideas can conflict in content because they occur at different levels and include opposite thoughts at the same level. It is impossible to share opposing thoughts. The Holy Spirit does not let you forsake your brothers. Therefore, you can really share only the parts of your thoughts which are of Him, and which He also keeps for you. And of such is the Kingdom of Heaven. All the rest remains with you until He has re-interpreted them in the light of the Kingdom, making them, too, worthy of being shared. When they have been sufficiently purified He lets you give them away. The will to share them is their purification.

The Atonement gives you the power of a healed mind, but the power to create is of God. Therefore, those who have been forgiven must devote themselves first to healing because, having received the idea of healing, they must give it to hold it. The full power of creation cannot be expressed as long as any of God's ideas with hold it from the Kingdom. The joint will of all the Sonship is the only creator that can create like the Father, because only the complete can think completely, and the thinking of God lacks nothing. Everything you think that is not through the Holy Spirit is lacking.

How can you who are so holy suffer? All your past, except its beauty, is gone, and nothing is left except a blessing. You can indeed depart in peace because I have loved you as I loved myself. You go with my blessing and for my blessing. Hold it and share it, that it may always be ours. I place the peace of God in your heart and in your hands, to hold and share. The heart is pure to hold it and the hands are strong to give it. We cannot lose. My judgment is as strong as the wisdom of God, in Whose Heart and Hands we have our being. His quiet children are His Blessed Sons. The Thoughts of God are with you.

Perhaps some of our concepts will become clearer and more personally, meaningful if the ego's use of guilt is clarified. The ego has a purpose, just as the Holy Spirit has. The ego's purpose is fear, because only the fearful can be egotistic. The ego's logic is as impeccable as that of the Holy Spirit because your mind has all the means at its disposal to side with Heaven or earth, as it elects. But again, let us remember that both are in you. In Heaven there is no guilt because the Kingdom is attained through the Atonement, which releases you to create. The word "create" is appropriate here because, once what you have made is undone by the Holy Spirit, the blessed residue is restored, and therefore continues in creation.

What is truly blessed is incapable of giving rise to guilt and must give rise to joy. This makes it invulnerable to the ego because its peace is unassailable. It is invulnerable to disruption because it is whole. Guilt is always disruptive. Anything that engenders fear is divisive because it obeys the law of division. If the ego is the symbol of the separation, it is also the symbol of guilt. Guilt is more than merely not of God. It is the symbol of the attack on God. This is a totally meaningless concept except to the ego, but do not underestimate the power of the ego's belief in it. This is the belief from which all guilt really stems.

The ego is the part of the mind which believes in division. How can part of God detach itself without believing it is attacking Him? We spoke before of the authority problem as involving the concept of usurping God's power. The ego believes that this is what you did because it believes it is you. It follows, then, that if you identify with the ego, you must perceive yourself as guilty. Whenever you respond to your ego you will experience guilt, and you will fear punishment. The ego is quite literally a fearful thought.

However ridiculous the idea of attacking God may be to the sane mind, never forget that the ego is not sane. It represents a delusional system, and it speaks for it. Listening to the ego's voice means that you believe it is possible to attack God. You believe that a part of Him has been torn away by you. The classic picture of fear of retaliation from without then follows because the severity of the guilt is so acute that it must be projected. Although Freud was wrong about the basic conflict itself, he was very accurate in describing its effects.

Whatever you accept into your mind has reality for you. It is, however, only your accepting of it that makes it real. If you enthrone the ego in it, the fact that you have accepted it or allowed it to enter makes it your reality. This is because the mind, as God created it, is capable of creating reality. We said before that you must learn to think with God. To think with Him is to think like Him. This engenders joy, not guilt, because it is natural. Guilt is a sure sign that your thinking is unnatural. Perverted thinking will always be attended with guilt because it is the belief in sin.

The ego does not perceive sin as a lack of love. It perceives sin as a positive act of assault. This is an interpretation which is necessary to the ego's survival because, as soon as you regard sin as a lack, you will automatically attempt to remedy the situation. And you will succeed. The ego regards this as doom, but you must learn to regard it as freedom. The guiltless mind cannot suffer. Being sane, it heals the body because it has been healed. The sane mind cannot conceive of illness because it cannot conceive of attacking anyone or anything.

We said before that illness is a form of magic. It might be better to say that it is a form of magical solution. The ego believes that by punishing itself it will mitigate the punishment of God. Yet even in this it is arrogant. It attributes to God a punishing intent, and then takes over this intent as its own prerogative. It tries to usurp all the functions of God as it perceives them because it recognizes that only total allegiance can be trusted.

The ego cannot oppose the laws of God any more than you can, but it can interpret them according to what it wants, just as you can. That is why the question, "What do you want?" must be answered. You are answering it every minute and every second, and each moment of decision is a judgment which is anything but ineffectual. Its effects will follow automatically until the decision is changed. This is repeated here because you have not learned it. But again, your decision can be unmade as well as made. Remember, though, that the alternatives are unalterable.

The Holy Spirit, like the ego, is a decision. Together they constitute all the alternatives which the mind can accept and obey. The ego and the Holy Spirit are the only choices open to you. God created one, and so you cannot eradicate it. You made the other, and so you can. Only what God creates is irreversible and unchangeable. What you have made can always be changed because, when you do not think like God, you are not really thinking at all. Delusional ideas are not real thoughts, although you can believe in them. But you are wrong.

The function of thought comes from God and is in God. As part of His Thought, you cannot think apart from Him.

Irrational thought is a thought disorder. God Himself orders your thought because your thought was created by Him. Guilt feelings are always a sign that you do not know this. They also show that you believe you can think apart from God and want to. Every thought disorder is attended by guilt at its inception and maintained by guilt in its continuance. Guilt is inescapable for those who believe they order their own thought and must therefore obey its orders. This makes them feel responsible for their mind errors, without recognizing that, by accepting this responsibility, they are really reacting irresponsibly. If the sole responsibility of the miracle worker is to accept the Atonement for himself, and I assure you that it is, then the responsibility for what is atoned for cannot be yours.

The dilemma cannot be resolved except by accepting the solution of undoing. You would be responsible for the effects of all your wrong thinking if it could not be undone. The purpose of the Atonement is to save the past in purified form only. If you accept the remedy for a thought disorder, and a remedy whose efficacy is beyond doubt, how can its symptoms remain? You have reason to question the validity of symptom cure, but on-one believes that the symptoms can remain if the underlying cause is removed.

The continuing will to remain separated is the only possible reason for continuing guilt feelings. We have said this before, but we did not emphasize the destructive results of this decision at that time. Any decision of the mind will affect both behaviour and experience. What you will, you expect. This is not delusional. Your mind does create your future, and it can turn it back to full creation at any minute, if it accepts the atonement first. It will also turn back to full creation the instant it has done so. Having given up its thought disorder, the proper ordering of thought becomes quite apparent.

God in His knowledge is not waiting, but His Kingdom is bereft while you wait. All the Sons of God are waiting for your return, just as you are waiting for theirs. Delay does not matter in eternity, but it is tragic in time. You have elected to be in time rather than eternity and have therefore changed your belief in your status. Yet your election is both free and alterable. You do not belong in time. Your place is only in eternity, where God Himself placed you forever.

Guilt feelings are the preservers of time. They induce fears of future retaliation or abandonment, and thus ensure that the future will remain like the past. This is the ego's continuity and gives it a false sense of security through the belief that you cannot escape from it. But you can and must. God offers you the continuity of eternity in exchange.

When you choose to make this exchange, you will simultaneously exchange guilt for joy, viciousness for love, and pain for peace. My role is only to unchain your will and make it free. Your ego cannot accept this freedom and will oppose your free decision at every possible moment and in every possible way. And as its maker you recognize what it can do because you gave it the power to do it.

The mind does indeed know its power, because the mind does indeed know God. Remember the Kingdom always and remember that you who are part of the Kingdom cannot be lost. The mind that was in me is in you, for God creates with perfect fairness. Let the Holy Spirit remind you always of His fairness and let me teach you how to share it with your brothers. How else can the chance to claim it for yourself be given you? What you do not understand is that the two voices speak for different interpretations of the same thing simultaneously, or almost simultaneously, for the ego always speaks first. Alternate interpretations were unnecessary until the first one was made and speaking itself was unnecessary before the ego was made.

The ego speaks in judgment and the Holy Spirit reverses its decisions, much as the Supreme Court has the power to reverse the lower courts' decisions about the laws of this world. The ego's decisions are always wrong because they are based on a complete fallacy which they were made to uphold. Nothing the ego perceives is interpreted correctly. Not only does it cite Scripture for its purpose, but it even interprets Scripture as a witness for itself. The Bible is a fearful thing to the ego because of its prejudiced judgment. Perceiving it as fearful, it interprets it fearfully. Having made you afraid, you do not appeal to the Higher Court because you believe its judgment would be against you.

We need cite only a few examples to see how the ego's interpretations have misled you. A favorited ego quotation is "As ye sow, so shall ye reap." Another is "Vengeance is mine, sayeth the Lord." Still another is "I will visit the sins of the father unto the third and fourth generation," and also "The wicked shall perish. "There are many others, but if you will let the Holy Spirit re-interpret these in His own light, they will suffice.

"As ye sow, so shall ye reap" merely means that what you believe to be worth cultivating you will cultivate in yourself. Your judgement of what is worthy makes it worthy for you. "Vengeance is mine, sayeth the Lord" is easily explained if you remember that ideas increase only by being shared. This quotation therefore emphasizes the fact that vengeance cannot be shared. Give it therefore to the Holy Spirit, Who will undo it in you because it does not belong in your mind, which is part of God.

"I will visit the sins of the fathers unto the third and fourth generation," as interpreted by the ego, is particularly vicious. It is used, in fact, as an attempt to guarantee its survival beyond itself. Actually, all the quotation means is that the Holy Spirit, in later generations, retains the power to interpret correctly what former generations have thought, and thus release their thoughts from the ability to produce fear anywhere in the Sonship. "The wicked shall perish" is merely a statement of fact, if the word "perish" is properly understood. Every loveless thought must be undone. Even the word "undone" is fearful to the ego, which interprets "I am undone" as "I am destroyed."

The ego will not be destroyed because it is part of your thought, but because it is uncreative, and therefore unsharing, it will be re-interpreted entirely, to release you from fear. The part of your thought which you have given to the ego will merely return to the Kingdom where your whole mind belongs. The ego is a form of arrest, but arrest is merely delay. It does not involve the concept of punishment, although the ego welcomes that interpretation. You can delay the completion of the Kingdom, but you cannot introduce the concept of assault into it.

When I said, "I am come as a light into the world," I surely came to share the light with you. Remember the symbolic reference we made before to the ego's dark glass, and remember also that we said," Do not look there." It is still true that "where you look to find yourself is up to you." The Higher Court will not condemn you. It will merely dismiss the case against you. There can be no case against a Child of God, and every witness to guilt in God's creations is bearing false witness to God Himself.

Appeal everything you believe gladly to God's Own Higher Court because it speaks for Him, and therefore speaks truly. It will dismiss the case against you however carefully you have built it. The case may be foolproof, but it is not God-proof. The Voice for God will not hear it at all because He can only witness truly. His verdict will always be "Thine is the Kingdom" because He was given you to remind you of what you are.

Your patience with each other is your patience with yourselves. Is not a Child of God worth patience? I have shown you infinite patience because my will is that of our Father, from Whom I learned of infinite patience. His Voice was in me as it is in you, speaking for patience towards the Sonship in the Name of its Creator. What you need to learn now is that only infinite patience can produce immediate effects. This is the way in which time is exchanged for eternity. Infinite patience calls upon infinite love, and by producing results now it renders time unnecessary.

To say that time is temporary is merely redundant. We have repeatedly said that time is a learning device which will be abolished when it is no longer useful. The Holy Spirit, Who speaks for God in time, also knows that time is meaningless. He reminds you of this in every passing moment of time because it is His special function to return you to eternity and remain to bless your creations there. He is the only blessing you can truly give because He is so truly blessed, and because He has been given you so freely by God, you must give Him as you received Him. The idea of "set" is among the better psychological concepts. Actually, it is used quite frequently in the Bible and also in this course under many different terms. For example

"God will keep him in perfect peace whose mind is stayed (or set) on Him,"

a statement which means that God's peace is set in the Holy Spirit because it is fixed on God. It is also fixed in you. You, then, are fixed in the peace of God. The concept of "Fixation" is also a very helpful one which Freud understood perfectly. Unfortunately, he lost his understanding because he was afraid, and, as you know all too well, fear is incompatible with good judgment. Fear distorts thinking, and therefore disorders thought.

Freud's system of thought was extremely ingenious because Freud was extremely ingenious, and a mind must endow its thoughts with its own attributes. This is its inherent strength, although it may misuse its power. Freud lost much of the potential value of his thought system because he did not include himself in it. This is a dissociated state because the thinker cuts himself off from his thoughts. Freud's thought was so conflicted that he could not have retained his sanity as he saw it without dissociation. That is why the many contradictions which are quite apparent in his thinking became increasingly less apparent to him. A man who knows what fixation really means and yet does not yield to it is terribly afraid.

Fixation is the pull of God, on Whom your mind is fixed because of the Holy Spirit's irrevocable set. "Irrevocable" means "cannot be called back or redirected." The irrevocable nature of the Holy Spirit's set is the basis for His Unequivocal Voice. The Holy Spirit never changes His mind. Clarity of thought cannot occur under conditions of vacillation. Unless a mind is fixed in its purpose it is not clear. Clarity literally means the state of light, and enlightenment is understanding. Enlightenment stands under perception because you have denied it as the real foundation of thought. This is the basis for all delusional systems.

The concept of fixation, as Freud saw it, has a number of learning advantages. First, it recognizes that man can be fixated at a point in development which does not accord with a point in time. This clearly could have been a means toward real release from the time belief had Freud pursued it with an open mind. Freud, however, suffered all his life from refusal to allow eternity to dawn upon his mind and enlighten it truly. As a result, he overlooked now entirely, and merely saw the continuity of past and future.

Second, although Freud misinterpreted what the Holy Spirit told him, or better, reminded him of, he was too honest to deny more than was necessary to keep his fear in tolerable bounds as he perceived the situation. Therefore, he emphasized that the point in development at which the mind is fixated is more real to itself than the external reality with which it disagrees. This, again, could have been a powerful release mechanism had Freud not decided to involve it in a strong defence system because he perceived it as an attack.

Third, although Freud interpreted fixation as involving irrevocable "danger points" to which the mind could always regress, the concept can also be interpreted as an irrevocable call to sanity which the mind cannot lose. Freud himself could not accept this interpretation, but throughout his thought system, the "threat" of fixation remained, and could never be eliminated by any living human being. Essentially, this was the basis of Freud's pessimism, personally as well as theoretically. He tried every means his very inventive mind could devise to set up a form of therapy which could enable the mind to escape from fixation forever, even though he knew this was impossible.

This knowledge plagued Freud's belief in his own thought system at every turn because he was both an honest man and a healer. He was therefore only partially insane and was unable to relinquish the hope of release even though he could not cope with it. The reason for this amount of detail is because you are in the same position. You were eternally fixated on God in your creation, and the pull of this fixation is so strong that you will never overcome it. The reason is perfectly clear. The fixation is on a level so high that it cannot be surmounted. You are always being pulled back to your Creator because you belong to Him.

Do you really believe you can make a voice that can drown out His? Do you really believe that you can devise a thought system which can separate you from His? Do you really believe that you can plan for your safety and joy better than He can? You need be neither careful nor careless; you need merely cast your cares upon Him because He careth for you. You are His care because He loves you. His Voice reminds you always that all hope is yours because of His care. You cannot choose to escape His care because that is not His Will, but you can choose to accept His care and use the infinite power of His care for all those He created by it.

There have been many healers who did not heal themselves. They have not moved mountains by their faith because their faith was not whole. Some of them have healed the sick at times, but they have not raised the dead. Unless the healer heals himself, he does not believe that there is no order of difficulty in miracles. He has not learned that every mind God created is equally worthy of being healed because god created it whole. You are merely asked to return to God the mind as he created it. He asks you only for what He gave, knowing that this giving will heal you. Sanity is wholeness, and the sanity of your brothers is yours.

Why should you listen to the endless insane calls which you think are made upon you when you know the Voice of God Himself is in you? God commended His Spirit to you and asks that you commend yours to Him. He wills to keep it in perfect peace because you are of one mind and Spirit with Him. Excluding yourself from the Atonement is the ego's last-ditch defence of its own existence. It reflects both the ego's need to separate, and your willingness to side with its separateness. This willingness means that you do not want to be healed.

But the time is now. You have not been asked to work out the plan of salvation yourselves because, as I told you before, the remedy is not of your making. God Himself gave you the perfect correction for everything you have made which is not in accord with His Holy Will. I have made His plan perfectly explicit to you and have also told you of your part in His plan, and how urgent it is that you fulfil it. There is time for delay, but there need not be. God weeps at the "sacrifice" of His Children who believe they are lost to Him.

I have already told you that whenever you are not wholly joyous it is because you have reacted with a lack of love to some Soul which God created. Perceiving this as "sin," you become defensive because expect attack. The decision to react in this way, however, is yours, and can therefore be undone. It cannot be undone by repentance in the usual sense, because this implies guilt. If you allow yourself to feel guilty you will re-enforce the error rather than allow it to be undone for you.

Decisions cannot be difficult. This is obvious if you realize that you must already have made a decision not to be wholly joyous if that is how you feel. Therefore, the first step in the undoing is to recognize that you actively decided wrongly but can as actively decide otherwise. Be very firm with yourselves in this and keep yourselves fully aware of the fact that the undoing process, which does not come from you, is nevertheless within you because God placed it there. Your part is merely to return your thinking to the point at which the error was made and give it over to the Atonement in peace. Say to yourselves the following as sincerely as you can, remembering that the Holy Spirit will respond fully to your slightest invitation:

"I must have decided wrongly because I am not at peace. I made the decision myself, but I can also decide otherwise. I will to decide otherwise because I want to be at peace.

I do not feel guilty because the Holy Spirit will undo all the consequences of my wrong decision if I will let him, I will to let Him by allowing Him to decide for God for Me."

The relationship of anger to attack is obvious, but the inevitable association of anger and fear is not always so clear. Anger always involves projection of separation, which must ultimately be accepted as entirely one's own responsibility. Anger cannot occur unless you believe that you have been attacked; that your attack was justified; and that you are in no way responsible.

Given these three wholly irrational premises, the equally irrational conclusion that a brother is worthy of attack rather than of love follows. What can be expected from insane premises except an insane conclusion? The way to undo an insane conclusion is to consider the sanity of the premises on which it rests. You cannot be attacked; attack have no justification; and you are responsible for what you believe. You have been asked to take me as your model for learning, since an extreme example is a particularly helpful learning device. Everyone teaches and teaches all the time. This is a responsibility which he inevitably assumes the moment he accepts any premise at all, and no-one can organize his life without any thought system. Once he has developed a thought system of any kind, he lives by it and teaches it.

You have been chosen to teach the Atonement precisely because you have been extreme examples of allegiance to your thought systems, and therefore have developed the capacity for allegiance. It has indeed been misplaced, but it is a form of faith, which you yourselves have been willing to redirect. You cannot doubt the strength of your devotion, when you consider how faithfully you have observed it. It was quite evident that you had already developed the ability to follow a better model, if you could accept it.

For teaching purposes, let us consider the crucifixion again. We have not dwelt on it before, because of its fearful connotations. The only emphasis we laid upon it was that it was not a form of punishment. Nothing, however, can be really explained in negative terms only. There is a positive interpretation of the crucifixion which is wholly devoid of fear, and therefore wholly benign in what it teaches, if it is properly understood. The crucifixion is nothing more than an extreme example. Its value, like the value of any teaching device, lies solely in the kind of learning it facilitates. It can be, and has been, misunderstood. This is only because the fearful are apt to perceive fearfully.

I have already told you that you can always call on me to share my decision and thus make it stronger. I also told you that the crucifixion was the last foolish journey that the Sonship need take, and that it should mean release from fear to anyone who understands it. While we emphasized only the resurrection before, the purpose of the crucifixion and how it actually led to the resurrection was not clarified at that time. Nevertheless, it has a definite contribution to make to your own lives, and if you will consider it without fear, it will help you understand your own role as teachers.

You have reacted for years as if you were being crucified. This is a marked tendency of the separated ones, who always refuse to consider what they have done to themselves. Projection means anger, anger fosters assault, and assault promotes fear. The real meaning of the crucifixion lies in the apparent intensity of the assault of some of the Sons of God upon another. This, of course, is impossible, and must be fully understood as an impossibility. In fact, unless it is fully understood as only that, I cannot serve as a real model for learning.

Assault can ultimately be made only on the body. There is little doubt that one body can assault another and can even destroy it. Yet if destruction itself is impossible, then anything that is destructible cannot be real. Therefore, its destruction does not justify anger. To the extent to which you believe that it does, you must be accepting false premises and teaching them to others. The message which the crucifixion was intended to teach was that it is not necessary to perceive any form of assault in persecution because you cannot be persecuted. If you respond with anger you must be equating yourself with the destructible and are therefore regarding yourself insanely.

I have made it perfectly clear that I am like you and you are like me, but our fundamental equality can be demonstrated only through joint decision. You are free to perceive yourselves as persecuted if you choose. You might remember, however, when you do choose to react that way, that I was persecuted as the world judges, and did not share this evaluation for myself. And because I did not share it I did not strengthen it. I therefore offered a different interpretation of attack, and one which I do want to share with you. If you will believe it, you will help me to teach it.

We have said before, "As you teach so shall you learn." If you react as if you are persecuted, you are teaching persecution. This is not a lesson which the Sons of God should want to teach if they are to realize their own salvation. Rather teach your own perfect immunity, which IS the truth in you, and know that it cannot be assailed. Do not protect it yourselves, or you have believed that it is assailable. You are not asked to be crucified, which was part of my own teaching contribution. You are merely asked to follow my example in the face of much less extreme temptations to misperceive, and not to accept them falsely as justifications for anger.

There can be no justification for the unjustifiable. Do not believe there is, and do not teach that there is. Remember always that what you believe, you will teach. Believe with me, and we will become equal as teachers. your resurrection is your re-awakening. I am the model for rebirth but rebirth itself is merely the dawning on your minds of what is already in them. God placed it there Himself, and so it is true forever. I believed in it, and therefore made it forever true for me. Help me to teach it to our brothers in the name of the Kingdom of God, but first believe that it is true for you, or you will teach amiss.

My brothers slept during the so-called "agony" in the garden, but I could not be angry with them because I had learned I could not be abandoned. Peter swore he would never deny me, but he did so three times. He did offer to defend me with the sword, which I naturally refused, not being at all in need of bodily protection. I am sorry when my brothers do not share my decision to hear only one voice, because it weakens them as teachers and as learners. Yet I know that they cannot really betray themselves or me, and that it is still on them that I must build my church.

There is no choice in this because only you can be the foundation of God's church. A church is where an altar is, and the presence of the altar is what makes it a church. Any church which does not inspire love has a hidden altar which is not serving the purpose for which God intended it. I must find His church on you because you who accept me as a model are literally my disciples. Disciples are followers, but if the model they follow has chosen to save them pain in all respects, they are probably unwise not to follow him.

I elected, both for your sake and mine, to demonstrate that the most outrageous assault, as judged by the ego, did not matter. As the world judges these things, but not as God knows them, I was betrayed, abandoned, beaten, torn, and finally killed. It was perfectly clear that this was only because of the projection of others, because I had not harmed anyone and had healed many. We are still equal as learners, even though we need not have equal experiences. The Holy Spirit is glad when you can learn enough from mine to be re-awakened by them. That was their only purpose, and that is the only way in which I can be perceived as the Way, the Truth and the Light.

When you hear only one voice you are never called on to sacrifice. On the contrary, by enabling yourselves to hear the Holy Spirit in others, you can learn from their experiences and gain from them without experiencing them yourselves. That is because the Holy Spirit is one, and anyone who listens is inevitably led to demonstrate His way for all. You are not persecuted, nor was I. You are not asked to repeat my experiences because the Holy Spirit, whom we share, makes this unnecessary. To use my experiences constructively, however, you must still follow my example in how to perceive them.

My brothers and yours are constantly engaged in justifying the unjustifiable. My one lesson, which I must teach as I learned, is that no perception which is out of accord with the judgement of the Holy Spirit can be justified. I undertook to show this was true in a very extreme case merely because it would serve as a good teaching aid to those whose temptations to give in to anger and assault would not be so extreme. I will, with God, that none of His Sons should suffer.

Remember that the Holy Spirit is the communication link between God the Father and His Separated Sons. If you will listen to His Voice, you will know that you cannot either hurt or be hurt, and that many need your blessing to help them hear this for themselves. When you perceive only this need in them, and do not respond to any other, you will have learned of me, and will be as eager to share your learning as I am. The crucifixion cannot be shared because it is the symbol of projection, but the resurrection is the symbol of sharing because the re-awakening of every Son of God is necessary to enable the Sonship to know its wholeness. Only this is knowledge.

The message of the crucifixion is perfectly clear:
"Teach only love, for that is what you are."

If you interpret the crucifixion in any other way, you are using it as a weapon for assault rather than as the call for peace for which it was intended. The Apostles often misunderstood it, and always for the same reason that makes anyone misunderstand anything. Their own imperfect love made them vulnerable to projection, and out of their own fear they spoke of the "wrath of God" as His retaliatory weapon. Nor could they speak of the crucifixion entirely without anger because their own sense of guilt had made them angry.

There are two glaring examples of upside-down thinking in the New Testament, whose whole gospel is only the message of love. These are not like the several slips into impatience which I made. I had learned the Atonement prayer, which I also came to teach, too well to engage in upside-down thinking myself. If the Apostles had not felt guilty they never could have quoted me as saying, "I come not to bring peace but a sword." This is clearly the exact opposite of everything I taught.

Nor could they have described my reactions to Judas as they did if they had really understood me. They would have realized I could not have said, "Betrayest thou the Son of Man with a kiss?" unless I believed in betrayal. The whole message of the crucifixion was simply that I did not. The "punishment" which I am said to have called forth upon Judas was a similar reversal. Judas was my brother and a Son of God, as much a part of the Sonship as myself. Was it likely that I would condemn him when I was ready to demonstrate that condemnation is impossible?

I am very grateful to the Apostles for their teaching and fully aware of the extent of their devotion to me. Nevertheless, as you read their teachings, remember that I told them myself that there was much they would understand later because they were not wholly ready to follow me at the time. I emphasize this only because I do not want you to allow any fear to enter into the thought system toward which I am guiding you. I do not call for martyrs, but for teachers. No-one is "punished" for sins, and the Sons of God are not sinners.

Any concept of "punishment" involves the projection of blame, and re-enforces the idea that blame is justified. The behaviour that results is a lesson in blame, just as all behaviour teaches the beliefs which motivate it. The crucifixion was a complex of behaviours arising out of clearly opposed thought systems. As such, it was the perfect symbol of conflict between the ego and the Son of God. The conflict is just as real now, and its lessons, too, have equal reality when they are learned. I do not need gratitude any more than I needed protection, but you need to develop your weakened ability to be grateful, or you cannot appreciate God. He does not need your appreciation, but you do.

You cannot love what you do not appreciate, and fear makes appreciation impossible. Whenever you are afraid of what you are you do not appreciate it and will therefore reject it. As a result, you will teach rejection. The power of the Sons of God is operating all the time because they were created as creators. Their influence on each other is without limit and must be used for their joint salvation. Each one must learn to teach that all forms of rejection are utterly meaningless. The separation is the notion of rejection. As long as you teach this, you still believe it. This is not as God thinks, and you must think as He thinks if you are to know Him again.

Any split in will must involve a rejection of part of it, and this is the belief in separation. The wholeness of God, which is His peace, cannot be appreciated except by a whole mind, which recognizes the wholeness of God's creation, and by this recognition, knows its Creator. Exclusion and separation are synonymous, as are separation and dissociation. We have said before that the separation was and is dissociation, and also that, once it had occurred, projection became its main defence, or the device that keeps it going. The reason, however, may not be as clear as you think.

In the ego's use of projection, to which we are obviously referring, what you project you disown, and therefore do not believe is yours. You are excluding yourself by the very statement you are making that you are different from the one on whom you project. Since you have also judged against what you project, you continue to attack it because you have already attacked it by projecting it. By doing this unconsciously, you try to keep the fact that you must have attacked yourself first out of awareness, and thus imagine that you have made yourself safe.

Projection will always hurt you. It re-enforces your belief in your own split mind, and its only purpose is to keep the separation going. It is solely a device of the ego to make you feel different from your brothers and separated from them. The ego justifies this on the wholly spurious grounds that it makes you seem "better" than they are, thus obscuring your equality with them still further. Projection and attack are inevitably related because projection is always a means of justifying attack. Anger without projection is impossible.

The ego uses projection only to distort your perception both of yourself and your brothers. The process begins by excluding something that exists in you which you do not want and leads directly to excluding you from your brothers. We have learned, however, that there is another use of projection. Every ability of the ego has a better counterpart because its abilities are directed by the mind, which has a better Voice. The Holy Spirit as well as the ego utilizes projection, but since their goals are opposed, so is the result.

The Holy Spirit begins by perceiving you as perfect. Knowing this perfection is shared, He recognizes it in others, thus strengthening it in both. Instead of anger this arouses love for both because it establishes inclusion. Perceiving equality, the Holy Spirit perceives equal needs. This invites Atonement automatically because Atonement is the one need which, in this world, is universal. To perceive yourself this way is the only way in which you can find happiness in the world. That is because it is the acknowledgement that you are not in this world, for the world is unhappy.

How else can you find joy in a joyless place except by realizing that you are not there? You cannot be anywhere that God did not put you, and God created you as part of Him. That is both where you are and what you are. It is completely unalterable. It is total inclusion. You cannot change it now or ever. It is forever true. It is not a belief, but a fact. Anything that God created is as true as He is. Its truth lies only in its perfect inclusion in Him Who alone is perfect. To deny this in any way is to deny yourself and Him, since it is impossible to accept one without the other.

The perfect equality of the Holy Spirit's perception is the counterpart of the perfect equality of God's knowing. The ego's perception has no counterpart in God, but the Holy Spirit remains the bridge between perception and knowledge. By enabling you to use perception in a way that parallels knowledge, you will ultimately meet it and know it. The ego would prefer to believe that this meeting is impossible, yet it is your perception which the Holy Spirit guides. You might remember that the human eye perceives parallel lines as if they meet in the distance, which is the same as in the future, if time and space are one dimension. Your perception will end where it began. Everything meets in God because everything was created by Him and in Him.

God created His Sons by extending His thought and retaining the extensions of His thought in His mind. All His thoughts are thus perfectly united within themselves and with each other because they were created neither partially nor in part. The Holy Spirit enables you to perceive this wholeness now. You can no more pray for yourselves alone than you can find joy for yourself alone. Prayer is the re-statement of inclusion, directed by the Holy Spirit under the laws of God. God created you to create. You cannot extend His Kingdom until you know of its wholeness.

Thoughts begin in the mind of the thinker, from which they extend outward. This is as true of God's Thinking as it is of yours. Because your minds are split, you can also perceive as well as think. Yet perception cannot escape from the basic laws of mind. You perceive from your mind and extend your perceptions outward. Although perception of any kind is unnecessary, you made it, and the Holy Spirit can therefore use it well. He can inspire perception and lead it toward God by making it parallel to God's way of thinking and thus guarantee their ultimate meeting. This convergence seems to be far in the future only because your mind is not in perfect alignment with the idea and therefore does not want it now.

The Holy Spirit uses time, but does not believe in it. Coming from God He uses everything for good, but He does not believe in what is not true. Since the Holy Spirit is in your minds, your minds must also be able to believe only what is true. The Holy Spirit can speak only for this because he speaks for God. He tells you to return your whole mind to God because it has never left him. If it has never left Him you need only perceive it as it is to be returned. The full awareness of the Atonement, then, is the recognition that the separation never occurred. The ego cannot prevail against this because it is an explicit statement that the ego never occurred.

The ego can accept the idea that return is necessary because it can so easily make the idea seem so difficult. Yet the Holy Spirit tells you that even return is unnecessary because what never happened cannot involve any problem. It does not follow, however, that you cannot make the idea of return necessary and difficult. It is surely clear, however, that the perfect need nothing, and cannot experience perfection as a difficult accomplishment because that is what they are.

This is the way in which you must perceive God's creations, bringing all your perceptions into the one parallel line which the Holy Spirit sees. This line is the direct line of communication with God, and lets your mind converge with his. There is no conflict anywhere in this perception because it means that all perception is guided by the Holy Spirit, whose mind is fixed on God. Only the Holy Spirit can resolve conflict because only the Holy Spirit is conflict-free. He perceives only what is true in your mind and extends outward only to what is true in other minds.

The difference between the ego's use of projection and projection as the Holy Spirit uses it is very simple. The ego projects to exclude, and therefore to deceive. The Holy Spirit projects by recognizing himself in every mind, and thus perceives them as one. Nothing conflicts in this perception because what the Holy Spirit perceives is the same. Wherever He looks He sees Himself, and because He is united, He offers the whole Kingdom always. This is the one message God gave to Him, and for which He must speak because that is what He is. The peace of God lies in that message, and so the peace of God lies in you.

The great peace of the Kingdom shines in your mind forever, but it must shine outward to make you aware of it. The Holy Spirit was given you with perfect impartiality, and only by perceiving Him impartially can you perceive Him at all. The ego is legion, but the Holy Spirit is One. No darkness abides anywhere in the Kingdom, but your part is only to allow no darkness to abide in your own mind. This alignment with Light is unlimited because it is in alignment with the Light of the world. Each of us is the Light of the world, and by joining our minds in this Light, we proclaim the Kingdom of God together and as one.

We have used many words as synonymous which are not ordinarily regarded as the same. We began with having and being, and more recently have used others. Hearing and being are examples, to which we can also add teaching and being, learning and being, and, above all, projecting and being. This is because, as we have said before, every idea begins in the mind of the thinker and extends outward. Therefore, what extends from the mind is still in it, and from what it extends it knows itself. That is its natural talent. The word "knows" is correct here, even though the ego does not know, and is not concerned with being at all.

The Holy Spirit still holds knowledge safe through His impartial perception. By attacking nothing, He presents no barrier at all to the communication of God. Thus, being is never threatened. Your Godlike mind can never be defiled. The ego never was and never will be part of it, but through the ego you can hear and teach and learn what is not true. From this, which you have made, you have taught yourselves to believe that you are not what you are. You cannot teach what you have not learned and what you teach you strengthen in yourselves because you are sharing it. Every lesson you teach, you are learning.

That is why you must teach only one lesson. If you are to be conflict-free yourselves, you must learn only from the Holy Spirit, and teach only by Him. You are only love, but when you denied this you made what you are something you must learn. We said before that the message of the crucifixion was "Teach only love, for that is what you are. " This is the one lesson which is perfectly unified because it is the only lesson which is one. Only by teaching it can you learn it. "As you teach so will you learn. " If that is true and it is true indeed, you must never forget that what you teach is teaching you. What you project you believe.

The only real safety lies in projecting only the Holy Spirit, because as you see His gentleness in others, your own mind perceives itself as totally harmless. Once it can accept this fully, it does not see the need to protect itself. The protection of God then dawns upon it, assuring it that it is perfectly safe forever. The perfectly safe are wholly benign. They bless because they know they are blessed. Without anxiety the mind is wholly kind, and because it projects beneficence, it is beneficent.

Safety is the complete relinquishment of attack. No compromise is possible in this. Teach attack in any form, and you have to learned it and it will hurt you. Yet your learning is not immortal, and you can unlearn it by not teaching it. Since you cannot not teach, your salvation lies in teaching the exact opposite of everything the ego believes. This is how you will learn the truth that will set you free and keep you so as others learn it of you. The only way to have peace is to teach peace. By learning it through projection, it becomes a part of what you know because you cannot teach what you have dissociated. Only thus can you win back the knowledge that you threw away. An idea which you share you must have. It awakens in you through the conviction of teaching. Remember that if teaching is being and learning is being, teaching is learning. Everything you teach you are learning. Teach only love, and learn that love is yours, and you are love.

Remember that the Holy Spirit is the answer, not the question. The ego always speaks first because it is capricious and does not mean its maker well. That is because it believes, and correctly, that its maker may withdraw his support from it at any moment. If it meant you well it would be glad, as the Holy Spirit will be glad when He has brought you home, and you no longer need His guidance. The ego does not regard itself as part of you. Herein lies its primary perceptual error, the foundation of its whole thought system.

When God created you, He made you part of Him. That is why attack within the Kingdom is impossible. You made the ego without love, and so it does not love you. You could not remain within the Kingdom without love, and since the Kingdom is love, you believe that you are without it. This enables the ego to regard itself as separate and outside its maker, thus speaking for the part of your mind that believes you are separate and outside the Mind of God. The ego, then, raised the first question that was ever asked, but one which it can never answer. That question, – "What are you?" – was the beginning of doubt.

The ego has never answered any questions since, although it has raised a great many. The most inventive activities of the ego have never done more than obscure the question because you have the answer, and the ego is afraid of you. You cannot understand the conflict until you fully understand one basic fact that the ego does not know. The Holy Spirit does not speak first, but he always answers. Everyone has called upon Him for help at one time or another and in one way or another and has been answered. Since the Holy Spirit answers truly, He answers for all time, which means that everyone has the answer now.

The ego cannot hear the Holy Spirit, but it does believe that part of the same mind that made it is against it. It interprets this as a justification for attacking its maker. It believes that the best defence is attack and wants you to believe it. Unless you do believe it you will not side with it and the ego feels badly in need of allies, though not of brothers. Perceiving something alien to itself in your mind, the ego turns to the body, not the mind, as its ally because the body is not part of you. This makes the body the ego's friend. It is an alliance frankly based on separation. If you side with this alliance you will be afraid, because you are siding with an alliance of fear.

The ego and the body conspire against your minds, and because the ego realizes that its "enemy" can end them both merely by knowing they are not part of him, they join in the attack together. This is perhaps the strangest perception of all, if you consider what it really involves. The ego, which is not real, attempts to persuade the mind, which is real, that the mind is its own learning device, and that the learning device is more real than IT is. No-one in his right mind could possibly believe this, and no-one in his right mind does believe it.

Hear, then, the one answer of the Holy Spirit to all the questions which the ego raises. You are a Child of God, a priceless part of His Kingdom, which He created as part of Him. Nothing else exists and only this is real. You have chosen a sleep in which you have had bad dreams, but the sleep is not real, and God calls you to awake. There will be nothing left of your dream when you hear Him because you will be awake. Your dreams have contained many of the ego's symbols, and they have confused you. Yet that was only because you were asleep and did not know. When you awake you will see the truth around you and in you and you will no longer believe in dreams because they will have no reality for you.

Yet the Kingdom and all that you have created there will have great reality for you because they are beautiful and true. In the Kingdom, where you are and what you are is perfectly certain. There is no doubt there because the first question was never asked. Having finally been wholly answered, it has never been. Being alone lives in the Kingdom, where everything lives in God without question. The time that was spent on questioning in the dream has given way to creation and to its eternity.

You are as certain as God because you are as true as He is, but what was once quite certain in your minds has become only the ability for certainty. The introduction of abilities into being was the beginning of uncertainty because abilities are potentials, not accomplishments. Your abilities are totally useless in the presence of God's accomplishments, and also of yours. Accomplishments are results which have been achieved. When they are perfect, abilities are meaningless. It is curious that the perfect must now be perfected. In fact, it is impossible. You must remember, however, that when you put yourselves in an impossible situation, you believed that the impossible was possible.

Abilities must be developed, or you cannot use them. This is not true of anything that God created, but it is the kindest solution possible to what you have made. In an impossible situation you can develop your abilities to the point where they can get you out of it. You have a Guide to how to develop them, but you have no commander except yourself. This leaves you in charge of the Kingdom, with both a Guide to find it and a means to keep it. You have a model to follow who will strengthen your command, and never detract from it in any way. You therefore retain the central place in your perceived enslavement, a fact which itself demonstrates that you are not enslaved.

You are in an impossible situation only because you thought it was possible to be in one. You would be in an impossible situation if God showed you your perfection and proved to you that you were wrong. This would demonstrate that the perfect were inadequate to bring themselves to the awareness of their perfection, and thus side with the belief that those who have everything need help and are therefore helpless. This is the kind of "reasoning" which the ego engages in, but God, who knows that His creations are perfect, does not insult them. This would be as impossible as the ego's notion that it has insulted him.

That is why the Holy Spirit never commands. To command is to assume inequality, which the Holy Spirit demonstrates does not exist. Fidelity to premises is a law of mind, and everything God created is faithful to His laws. Fidelity to other laws is also possible, however, not because the laws are true, but because you made them. What would be gained if God proved to you that you have thought insanely? Can God lose His own certainty? We have frequently stated that what you teach you are. Would you have God teach you that you have sinned? If He confronted the self you made with the truth He created for you, what could you be but afraid? You would doubt your sanity, which is the one thing in which you can find the sanity He gave you.

God does not teach. To teach is to imply a lack which God knows is not there. God is not conflicted. Teaching aims at change, but God created only the changeless. The separation was not a loss of perfection but a failure in communication. A harsh and strident form of communication arose as the ego's voice. It could not shatter the peace of God, but it could shatter yours. God did not blot it out, because to eradicate it would be to attack it. Being questioned, He did not question. He merely gave the Answer. His Answer is your Teacher.

"To have, give all to all"

Like any good teacher, the Holy Spirit does know more than you do now, but He teaches only to make you equal with Him. This is because you had already taught wrongly, having believed what was not true. You did not believe in your own perfection. Could God teach you that you had made a split mind, when He knows your mind only as whole? What God does know is that His communication channels are not open to Him, so that He cannot impart His joy and know that His Children are wholly joyous. This is an ongoing process, not in time, but in eternity. God's extending outward, though not His completeness, is blocked when the Sonship does not communicate with Him as one. So, He thought,

"My Children sleep and must be awakened."

How can you wake children better and more kindly than by a gentle Voice that will not frighten them, but will merely remind them that the night is over and the Light has come? You do not inform them that the nightmares which frightened them so badly were not real because children believe in magic. You merely reassure them that they are safe now. Then you train them to recognize the difference between sleeping and waking, so that they will understand they need not be afraid of dreams. Then, when bad dreams come, they will call on the light themselves to dispel them.

A wise teacher teaches through approach, not avoidance. He does not emphasize what you must avoid to escape from harm so much as what you need to learn to have joy. This is true even of the world's teachers. Consider the confusion a child would experience if he were told "Do not do this because it might hurt you and make you unsafe, but if you do that you will escape from harm and be safe, and then you will not be afraid. "All of this could be included in only three words: "Do only that!" This simple statement is perfectly clear, easily understood, and very easily remembered.

The Holy Spirit never itemizes errors because He does not frighten children, and those who lack wisdom are children. Yet He always answers their call, and His dependability makes them more certain. Children do confuse fantasy and reality, and they are frightened because they do not know the difference. The Holy Spirit makes no distinction among dreams. He merely shines them away.

His Light is always the call to awake, whatever you have been dreaming. Nothing lasting lies in dreams, and the Holy Spirit, shining with the Light from God Himself, speaks only for what lasts forever.

When your body and your ego and your dreams are gone, you will know that you will last forever. Many think this is accomplished through death, but nothing is accomplished through death because death is nothing. Everything is accomplished through life, and life is of the mind and in the Mind. The body neither lives nor dies because it cannot contain you who are life. If we share the same mind, you can overcome death because I did. Death is an attempt to resolve conflict by not willing at all. Like any other impossible solution which the ego attempts, it will not work.

God did not make the body because it is destructible, and therefore not of the Kingdom. The body is the symbol of what you think you are. It is clearly a separation device, and therefore does not exist. The Holy Spirit, as always, takes what you have made and translates it into a learning device for you. Again, as always, He reinterprets what the ego uses as an argument for separation into a demonstration against it. If the mind can heal the body but the body cannot heal the mind, then the mind must be stronger. Every miracle demonstrates this.

We have said that the Holy Spirit is the motivation for miracles. This is because He always tells you that only the mind is real since only the mind can be shared. The body is separate, and therefore cannot be part of you. To be of one mind is meaningful, but to be of one body is meaningless. By the laws of mind, then, the body is meaningless. To the Holy Spirit there is no order of difficulty in miracles. This is familiar enough to you by now, but it has not yet become believable. Therefore, you do not understand it and cannot use it.

We have too much to accomplish on behalf of the Kingdom to let this crucial concept slip away. It is a real foundation stone of the thought system I teach and want you to teach. You cannot perform miracles without believing it because it is a belief in perfect equality. Only one equal gift can be offered to the equal Sons of God, and that is full appreciation. Nothing more and nothing less. Without a range an order of difficulty is meaningless, and there must be no range in what you offer to each other.

The Holy Spirit, who leads to God, translates communication into being, just as He ultimately translates perception into knowledge. The ego uses the body for attack, for pleasure, and for pride. The insanity of this perception makes it a fearful one indeed. The Holy Spirit sees the body only as a means of communication, and because communicating is sharing, it becomes communion. You might argue that fear as well as love can be communicated, and therefore can be shared. Yet this is not so real as it sounds. Those who communicate fear are promoting attack and attack always breaks communication, making it impossible. Egos do join together in temporary allegiance, but always for what each one can get separately. The Holy Spirit communicates only what each one can give to all. He never takes anything back because He wants you to keep it. Therefore, His teaching begins with the lesson:

"To have, give all to all"

This is a very preliminary step, and the only one you must take for yourself. It is not even necessary that you complete the step yourself, but it is necessary that you turn in that direction. Having chosen to go that way, you place yourself in charge of the journey, where you and only you must remain. This step appears to exacerbate conflict rather than resolve it because it is the beginning step in reversing your perception and turning it right-side up. This conflicts with the upside-down perception which you have not yet abandoned, or the change in direction would not have been necessary. Some people remain at this step for a very long time, experiencing very acute conflict.

At this point many try to accept the conflict, rather than take the next step towards its resolution. Having taken the first step, however, they will be helped. Once they have chosen what they cannot complete alone, they are no longer alone.

## "To Have Peace, Teach Peace to Learn It"

All the separated ones have a basic fear of retaliation and abandonment. This is because they believe in attack and rejection, so this is what they perceive and teach and learn. These insane concepts are clearly the result of their own dissociation and projection. What you teach you are, but it is quite apparent that you can teach wrongly, and therefore teach yourselves wrong. Many thought that I was attacking them, even though it was quite apparent that I was not. An insane learner learns strange lessons.

What you must understand is that, when you do not share a thought system, you are weakening it. Those who believe in it therefore perceive this as an attack on them. This is because everyone identifies himself with his thought system, and every thought system centres on what you believe you are. If the centre of the thought system is true, only truth extends from it. But if a lie is at its centre, only deception proceeds from it. All good teachers realize that only fundamental change will last, but they do not begin at that level. Strengthening motivation for change is their first and foremost goal. It is also their last and final one.

Increasing motivation for change in the learner is all that a teacher need do to guarantee change. This is because a change in motivation is a change of mind, and this will inevitably produce fundamental change because the mind is fundamental. The first step in the reversal or undoing process, then, is the undoing of the getting concept. Accordingly, the Holy Spirit's first lesson was "To have, give all to all." We said that this is apt to increase conflict temporarily and we can clarify this still further now.

At this point, the equality of "having" and "being" is not yet perceived. Until it is, "having" appears to be the opposite of being. "Therefore, the first lesson seems to contain a contradiction, since it is being learned by a conflicted mind. This means conflicting motivation, and so the lesson cannot be learned consistently as yet. Further, the mind of the learner projects its own split and thus does not perceive consistent minds in others, making him suspicious of their motivation. This is the real reason why, in many respects, the first lesson is the hardest to learn. Still strongly aware of the ego in himself, and responding primarily to the ego in others, he is being taught to react to both as if what he does believe is not true.

Upside-down as always, the ego perceives the first lesson as insane. In fact, this is its only alternative here, since the other one, which would be much less acceptable to it, would obviously be that is insane. The ego's judgement, then, is predetermined by what it is though no more so than is any other product of thought. The fundamental change will still occur with the change of mind in the thinker. Meanwhile, the increasing clarity of the Holy Spirit's Voice makes it impossible for the learner not to listen. For a time, then, he is receiving conflicting messages, and accepting both. This is the classic "double bind" in communication.

The way out of conflict between two opposing thought systems is clearly to choose one and relinquish the other. If you identify with your thought system, and you cannot escape this and if you accept two thought systems which are in complete disagreement, peace of mind is impossible. If you teach both, which you will surely do as long as you accept both, you are teaching conflict and learning it. Yet you do want peace, or you would not have called upon the Voice for peace to help you. His lesson is not insane; the conflict is.

There can be no conflict between sanity and insanity. Only one is true, and therefore only one is real. The ego tries to persuade you that it is up to you to decide which voice is true, but the Holy Spirit teaches you that truth was created by God, and your decision cannot change it. As you begin to realize the quiet power of the Holy Spirit's Voice and its perfect consistency, it must dawn on your minds that you are trying to undo a decision which was made irrevocably for you. That is why we suggested before that there was help in reminding yourselves to allow the Holy Spirit to decide for God for you. You are not asked to make insane decisions, although you are free to think you are. It must, however, be insane to believe that it is up to you to decide what God's creations are. The Holy Spirit perceives the conflict exactly as it is. Therefore, His second lesson is:

"To have peace, teach peace to learn it"

This is still a preliminary step, since "having" and "being" are still not equated. It is, however, more advanced than the first step, which is really only a thought reversal. The second step is a positive affirmation of what you want. This, then, is a step in the direction out of conflict, since it means that alternatives have been considered, and one has been chosen as more desirable.

Nevertheless, the evaluation "more desirable" still implies that the desirable has degrees. Therefore, although this step is essential for the ultimate decision, it is clearly not the final one. It is clear, at this point, that the lack of order of difficulty in miracles has not yet been accepted, because nothing is difficult that is wholly desired. To desire wholly is to create and creating cannot be difficult if God Himself created you as a creator. The second step, then, is still perceptual, although it is a giant step toward the unified perception which parallels God's knowing.

As you take this step and hold this direction, will be pushing toward the centre of your thought system, where the fundamental change will occur. You are only beginning this step now, but you have started on this way by realizing that only one way is possible. You do not yet realize this consistently and so your progress is intermittent, but the second step is easier than the first because it follows. The very fact that you have accepted that is a demonstration of your growing awareness that the Holy Spirit will lead you on.

"Be Vigilant Only for God and His Kingdom "

For your own salvation you must be critical, since your salvation is critical to the whole Sonship. We said before that the Holy Spirit is evaluative and must be. Yet His evaluation does not extend beyond you, or you would share it. In your mind, and your mind only, He sorts out the true from the false and teaches you to judge every thought that you allow to enter your mind in the light of what God put there. Whatever is in accord with this light He retains, to strengthen the Kingdom in you. What is partly in accord with truth He accepts and purifies. But what is out of accord entirely He rejects by judging against. This is how He keeps the Kingdom perfectly consistent and perfectly unified.

What you must remember, however, is that what the Holy Spirit rejects the ego accepts. This is because they are in fundamental disagreement about everything, being in fundamental disagreement about what you are. The ego's beliefs on this crucial issue vary, and that is why it promotes different moods. The Holy Spirit never varies on this point and so the one mood He engenders is joy. He protects it by rejecting everything that does not foster joy and so He alone can keep you wholly joyous.

The Holy Spirit does not teach your mind to be critical of other minds because He does not want you to teach errors and learn them yourselves. He would hardly be consistent if He allowed you to strengthen what you must learn to avoid. In the mind of the thinker, then, He is judgemental, but only in order to unify the mind so it can perceive without judgement. This enables the mind to teach without judgement, and therefore to learn to be without judgement. The undoing is necessary only in your mind, so that you cannot project falsely. God Himself has established what you can project with perfect safety. Therefore, the Holy Spirit's third lesson is:

"Be vigilant only for God and HIS Kingdom"

This is a major step toward fundamental change. Yet it is still a lesson in thought reversal, since it implies that there is something you must be vigilant against. It has advanced far from the first lesson which was primarily a reversal, and also from the second which was essentially the identification of what is more desirable. this step, which follows from the second as the second follows from the first, emphasizes the dichotomy between the desirable and the undesirable. It therefore makes the ultimate choice inevitable.

While the first step seems to increase conflict and the second step still entails it to some extent, this one calls for Consistent effort against it. We said already that you can be as vigilant against the ego as for it. This lesson teaches not only that you can be, but that you must be. It does not concern itself with order of difficulty, but with clear-cut priority for vigilance. This step is unequivocal in that it teaches there must be no exceptions, although it does not deny that the temptation to make exceptions will occur. Here, then, your consistency is called on despite chaos. Yet chaos and consistency cannot coexist for long, since they are mutually exclusive.

As long as you must be vigilant against anything, however, you are not recognizing this mutual exclusiveness, and are holding the belief that you can choose either one. By teaching what to choose, the Holy Spirit will ultimately be able to teach you that you need not choose at all. This will finally liberate your will from choice and direct it towards creation within the Kingdom. Choosing through the Holy Spirit will lead you to the Kingdom. You create by what you are, but this is what you must learn. The way to learn it is inherent in the third step, which brings together the lessons implied in the others, and goes beyond them towards real integration.

If you allow yourselves to have in your minds only what God put there, you are acknowledging your mind as God created it. Therefore, you are accepting it as it is. Since it is whole, you are teaching peace because you believe in it. The final step will still be taken for you by God, but by the third step, the Holy Spirit has prepared you for God. He is getting you ready for the translation of having into being by the very nature of the steps you must take with Him.

You learn first that having rests on giving and not on getting. Next you learn that you learn what you teach and that you want to learn peace. This is the condition for identifying with the Kingdom, since it is the condition of the Kingdom. You have believed that you are without the Kingdom and have therefore excluded yourself from it in your belief. It is therefore essential to teach you that you must be included and that the belief that you are not is the only thing that you must exclude.

The third step is thus one of protection for your minds, allowing you to identify only with the centre, where God placed the altar to Himself. We have already said that altars are beliefs, but God and His creations are beyond belief because they are beyond question. The Voice for God speaks only for belief beyond question, which is the preparation for being without question. As long as belief in God and His Kingdom is assailed by any doubts in your minds, His perfect accomplishment is not apparent to you. This is why you must be vigilant on god's behalf. The ego speaks against His creation and therefore does engender doubt. You cannot go beyond belief until you believe fully. Transfer, which is extension, is a measure of learning because it is its measurable result. This, however, does not mean that what it transfers to is measurable.

On the contrary, unless it transfers to the whole Sonship, which is immeasurable because it was created by the Immeasurable, the learning itself must be incomplete. To teach the whole Sonship without exception demonstrates that you perceive its wholeness and have learned that it is one. Now you must be vigilant to hold its oneness in your minds because, if you let doubt enter, you will lose awareness of its wholeness and will be unable to teach it. The wholeness of the Kingdom does not depend on your perception, but your awareness of its wholeness does. It is only your awareness which needs protection, since your being cannot be assailed.

Yet a real sense of being cannot be yours while you are doubtful of what you are. This is why vigilance is essential. Doubts about being must not enter your mind, or you cannot know what you are with certainty. Certainty is of God for you. Vigilance is not necessary for truth, but it is necessary against illusions. Truth is without illusions, and therefore within the Kingdom. Everything outside the Kingdom is illusion, but you must learn to accept truth because you threw it away. You therefore saw yourself as if you were without it. By making another kingdom which you valued, you did not keep only the Kingdom of God in your minds, and thus placed part of your mind outside it. What you have made has thus divided your will and given you a sick mind which must be healed.

Your vigilance against this sickness is the way to heal it. Once your mind is healed, it radiates health and thereby teach healing. This establishes you as a teacher who teaches like me. Vigilance was required of me as much as of you but remember that those who will to teach the same thing must be in agreement about what they believe.

The third step, then, is a statement of what you want to believe and entails a willingness to relinquish everything else. I told you that you were just beginning the second step, but I also told you that the third one follows it. The Holy Spirit will enable you to go on, if you follow Him. Your vigilance is the sign that you want Him to guide you. Vigilance does require effort, but only to teach you that effort itself is unnecessary. You have exerted great effort to preserve what you made because it was not true. Therefore, you must now turn your effort against it. Only this can cancel out the need for effort and call upon the being which you both have and are.

This recognition is wholly without effort, since it is already true and needs no protection. It is in the perfect safety of God. Therefore, inclusion is total and creation is without limit. The creative power of both God and His creations is limitless, but they are not in reciprocal relationship. You do communicate fully with God, as He does with you. This is an ongoing process in which you share, and because you share it, you are inspired to create like God. Yet in creation you are not in reciprocal relation to God, since He created you, but you did not create Him. We have already said that only in this respect your creative power differs from His. Even in this world there is a parallel. Parents give birth to children, but children do not give birth to parents. They do, however, give birth to their children and thus give birth as their parents do.

If you created God and He created you, the Kingdom could not increase through its own creative thought. Creation would therefore be limited, and you would not be co-creators with God. As God's creative thought proceeds from Him to you, so must your creative thought proceed from you to your creations. Only in this way can all creative power extend outward. God's accomplishments are not yours. But yours are like His. He created the Sonship, and you increase it. You have the power to add to the Kingdom, but not to add to the creator of the Kingdom. You claim this power when you become vigilant only for God and His Kingdom. By accepting this power as yours, you have learned to be what you are.

Your creations belong in you, as you belong in God. You are part of God, as your sons are part of His Sons. To create is to love. Love extends outward simply because it cannot be contained. Being limitless, it does not stop. It creates forever, but not in time. God's creations have always been, because he has always been. Your creations have always been, because you can create only as God creates. Eternity is yours because He created you eternal.

The ego demands reciprocal rights, because it is competitive rather than loving. It is always willing to make a "deal," but it cannot understand that to be like another means that no deals are possible. To gain you must give, not bargain. To bargain is to limit giving, and this is not God's Will. To will with God is to create like Him. God does not limit His gifts in any way. You are His gifts, and so your gifts must be like His. Your gifts to the Kingdom must be like His Gifts to you.

I gave only love to the Kingdom because I believed that was what I was. What you believe you are determines your gifts, and if God created you by extending Himself as you, you can only extend yourself as He did. Only joy increases forever, since joy and eternity are inseparable. God extends outward beyond limits and beyond time, and you, who are co-creators with Him, extend His Kingdom forever and beyond limit. Eternity is the indelible stamp of creation. The eternal are in peace and joy forever.

To think like God is to share His certainty of what you are, and to create like Him is to share the perfect love He shares with you. To this the Holy Spirit leads you, that your joy may be complete because the Kingdom of God is whole. We have said that the last step in the re-awakening of knowledge is taken by God. This is true, but it is hard to explain in words, because words are symbols, and nothing that is true needs to be explained.

However, the Holy Spirit has the task of translating the useless into the useful, the meaningless into the meaningful, and the temporary into the timeless. He can, therefore, tell you something about this last step, although this one you must know yourself, since by it you know what you are. This is your being.

God does not take steps because His accomplishments are not gradual. He does not teach because His creations are changeless. He does nothing last because He created first and for always. It must be understood that the word "first "as applied to Him is not a time concept. He is first in the sense that He is the first in the Holy Trinity Itself. He is the Prime Creator because He created His cocreators. Because He did, time applies neither to Him nor to what He created. The "last step" that God will take was therefore true in the beginning, is true now and will be true forever.

What is timeless is always there because it's being is eternally changeless. It does not change by increase because it was forever created to increase. If you perceive it as not increasing, you do not know what it is. You also do not know what created it, or Who he is. God does not reveal this to you because it was never hidden. His Light was never obscured because it is His Will to share it. How can what is fully shared be withheld and then revealed?

To heal is the only kind of thinking in this world that resembles the Thought of God, and because of the elements which they share, can transfer to it. When a brother perceives himself as sick, he is perceiving himself as not whole and therefore in need. If you, too, see him this way, you are seeing him as if he were absent from the Kingdom or separated from it, thus making the Kingdom itself obscure to both of you. Sickness and separation are not of God, but the Kingdom is. If you obscure the Kingdom, you are perceiving what is not of god.

To heal, then, is to correct perception in your brother and yourself by sharing the Holy Spirit with him. This places you both within the Kingdom and restores its wholeness in your minds. This parallels creation because it unifies by increasing and integrates by extending. What you project you believe. This is an immutable law of the mind in this world as well as in the Kingdom. However, the content is different in this world, because the thoughts it governs are very different from the thoughts in the Kingdom. Laws must be adapted to circumstances, if they are to maintain order.

The outstanding characteristic of the laws of mind as they operate in this world is that by obeying them – and I assure you that you must obey them - you can arrive at diametrically opposed results. This is because the laws have adapted to the circumstances of this world, in which diametrically opposed outcomes are believed in. The laws of mind govern thoughts, and you do respond to two conflicting voices. You have heard many arguments on behalf of "the freedoms," which would indeed have been freedom if man had not chosen to fight for them. That is why they perceive "the freedoms" as many, instead of as one. Yet the argument that underlies the defence of freedom is perfectly valid. Because it is true it should not be fought for, but it should be sided with.

Those who are against freedom believe that its outcome will hurt them, which cannot be true. But those who are for freedom, even if they are misguided in how to defend it, are siding with the one thing in this world which is true. Whenever anyone can listen fairly to both sides of any issue, he will make the right decision. This is because he has the answer. Conflict can seem to be interpersonal, but it must be intrapersonal first.

The term "intrapersonal" is an ego term, because "personal" implies "of one person," and not of others. "Interpersonal" has a similar error, in that it refers to something that exists among different or separate people. When we spoke before of the extremely personal nature of revelation, we followed this statement immediately with a description of the inevitable outcomes of the revelation in terms of sharing. A person conceives of himself as separate largely because he perceives of himself as bounded by a body. Only if he perceives himself as a mind can this be overcome. Then he is free to use terms like "intramental" and "intermental" without seeing them as different or conflicting because minds can be in perfect accord.

Outside the Kingdom, the law which prevails inside it is adapted to "what you project you believe". "This is its teaching form, since outside the Kingdom teaching is mandatory because learning is essential. This form of the law clearly implies that you will learn what you are from what you have projected onto others, and therefore believe they are. In the Kingdom there is no teaching or learning because there is no belief. There is only certainty. God and His Sons, in the surety of being, know that what you project you are. That form of the law is not adapted at all, being the Law of Creation. God Himself created the law by creating by it. And His Sons, who create like Him, follow it gladly, knowing that the increase of the Kingdom depends on it, just as their own creation did.

Laws must be communicated if they are to be helpful. In effect, they must be translated for those who speak a different language. Nevertheless, a good translator, although he must alter the form of what he translates, never changes the meaning. In fact, his whole purpose is to change the form so that the original meaning is retained. The Holy Spirit is the translator of the Laws of God to those who do not understand them. You could not do this yourselves because conflicted minds cannot be faithful to one meaning and will therefore change the meaning to preserve the form.

The Holy Spirit's purpose in translating is naturally exactly the opposite. He translates only to preserve the original meaning in all respects and in all languages. Therefore, He opposes differences in form as meaningful, emphasizing always that these differences do not matter. The meaning of His message is always the same, and only the meaning matters. God's Law of Creation in perfect form does not involve the use of truth to convince His Sons of truth. The extension of truth, which is the Law of the Kingdom, rests only on the knowledge of what truth is. This is your inheritance and requires no learning at all, but when you disinherited yourselves, you became learners.

No-one questions the intimate connection of learning and memory. Learning is impossible without memory since it cannot be consistent unless it is remembered. That is why the Holy Spirit is a lesson in remembering. We said before that He teaches remembering and forgetting, but the forgetting aspect is only to make the remembering consistent. You forget to remember better.

You will not understand His translations while you listen to two ways of perceiving them. Therefore, you must forget, or relinquish, one to understand the other. This is the only way you can learn consistency, so that you can finally be consistent. What can the perfect consistency of the Kingdom mean to the confused? It is apparent that confusion interferes with meaning, and therefore prevents the learner from appreciating it. There is no confusion in the Kingdom, because there is only one meaning. This meaning comes from God and is God. Because it is also you, you share it and extend it as your Creator did. This needs no translation because it is perfectly understood, but it does need extension because it means extension. Communication is perfectly direct and perfectly united. It is totally without strain because nothing discordant ever enters. That is why it is the Kingdom of God. It belongs to Him and is therefore like Him. That is its reality, and nothing can assail it.

To heal is to liberate totally. We once said there is no order of difficulty in miracles because they are all maximal expressions of love. This has no range at all. The non-maximal only appears to have a range. This is because it seems to be meaningful to measure it from the maximum and identify its position by how much it is not there. Actually, this does not mean anything. It is like negative numbers in that the concept can be used theoretically, but it has no application practically. It is true that if you put three apples on the table and then take them away, the three apples are not there. But it is not true that the able is now minus three apples. If there is nothing on the table, it does not matter what was there in terms of amount. The "nothing" is neither greater nor less because of what is absent.

That is why "all" and "nothing" are dichotomous, without a range. This is perfectly clear in considering psychological tests of maximal performance. You cannot interpret the results at all unless you assume either maximal motivation or no motivation at all. Only in these two conditions can you validly compare responses, and you must assume the former because, if the latter were true, the subject would not do anything. Given variable motivation he will do something, but you cannot understand what it is.

The results of such tests are evaluated relatively assuming maximal motivation, but this is because we are dealing with abilities, where degree of development is meaningful. This does not mean that what the ability is used for is necessarily either limited or divided. Yet one thing is certain; abilities are potentials for learning, and you will apply them to what you want to learn. Learning is effort, and effort means will. We have used the term "abilities" in the plural because abilities began with the ego, which perceived them as potentials for excelling. This is how the ego still perceives them and uses them.

The ego does not want to teach everyone all it has learned, because that would defeat its purpose. Therefore, it does not really learn at all. The Holy Spirit teaches you to use what the ego has made to teach the opposite of what the ego has learned. The kind of learning is as irrelevant as is the particular ability which was applied to the learning. You could not have a better example of the Holy Spirit's unified purpose than this course. The Holy Spirit has taken very diversified areas of your learning and has applied them to a unified curriculum. The fact that this was not the ego's reason for learning is totally irrelevant.

You made the effort to learn and the Holy Spirit has a unified goal for all effort. He adapts the ego's potentials for excelling to potentials for equalizing. This makes them useless for the ego's purpose, but very useful for His. If different abilities are applied long enough to one goal, the abilities themselves become unified. This is because they are channelized in one direction, or in one way. Ultimately, then, they all contribute to one result, and by so doing, their similarity rather than their differences is emphasized. You can excel in many different ways, but you can equalize in one way only. Equality is not a variable state by definition.

That is why you will be able to perform all aspects of your work with ease when you have learned this course. To the ego there appears to be no connection because the ego is discontinuous. Yet the Holy Spirit teaches one lesson and applies it to all individuals in all situations. Being conflict-free, He maximizes all efforts and all results. By teaching the power of the Kingdom of God Himself, He teaches you that all power is yours. Its application does not matter. It is always maximal. Your vigilance does not establish it as yours, but it does enable you to use it always and in all ways.

When I said, "I am with you always," I meant it literally. I am not absent to anyone, in any situation. Because I am always with you, you are the Way and the Truth and the Light. You did not make this power any more than I did. It was created to be shared, and therefore cannot be meaningfully perceived as belonging to anyone at the expense of another. Such a perception makes it meaningless by eliminating or overlooking its real and only meaning.

God's meaning waits in the Kingdom because that is where He placed it. It does not wait in time. It merely rests in the Kingdom because it belongs there, as You do. How can you, who are God's meaning, perceive yourselves as absent from it? You can see yourselves as separated from your meaning only by experiencing yourself as unreal. This is why the ego is insane; it teaches that you are not what you are. This is so contradictory that it is clearly impossible. It is therefore a lesson which you cannot really learn, and therefore, cannot really teach. Yet you are always teaching. You must, therefore, be teaching something else as well, even though the ego does not know what it is.

The ego, then, is always being undone, and does suspect your motives. Your mind cannot be unified in allegiance to the ego, because the mind does not belong to it. Yet what is "treacherous" to the ego is faithful to peace. The ego's "enemy" is therefore your friend. We said before that the ego's friend is not part of you, since the ego perceives itself as at war, and therefore in need of allies

You, who are not at war, must look for brothers and recognize all whom you see as brothers, because only equals are at peace.

Because God's equal Sons have everything, they cannot compete. Yet if they perceive any of their brothers as anything other than their perfect equals, the idea of competition has entered their minds. Do not underestimate your need to be vigilant against this idea, because all your conflicts come from it. It is the belief that conflicting interests are possible and therefore you have accepted the impossible as true. How is that different from saying that you are perceiving yourself as unreal?

To be in the Kingdom is merely to focus your full attention on it. As long as you believe that you can attend to what is not true, you are accepting conflict as your choice. Is it really a choice? It seems to be but seeming and reality are hardly the same. You who are the Kingdom are not concerned with seeming. Reality is yours because you are reality. This is how having and being are ultimately reconciled, not in the Kingdom, but in your minds. The altar there is the only reality. The altar is perfectly clear in thought because it is a reflection of perfect Thought. It sees only brothers because it sees only in its own Light.

God has lit your minds Himself and keeps your minds lit by His Light because His Light is what your minds are. This is totally beyond question and when you questioned it, you were answered. The answer merely undoes the question by establishing the fact that to question reality is to question meaninglessly. That is why the Holy Spirit never questions. His sole function is to undo the questionable and thus lead to certainty. The certain are perfectly calm because they are not in doubt. They do not raise questions because nothing questionable enters their minds. This holds them in perfect serenity because this is what they share, knowing what they are.

As has so often been said, healing is both an art and a science. It is an art because it depends on inspiration in the sense that we have already used the term. Inspiration is the opposite of dispiriting, and therefore means to make joyous. The dispirited are depressed because they believe that they are literally "without the Spirit," which is an illusion. You do not put the Spirit in them by inspiring them because that would be magic, and therefore would not be real healing. You do, however, recognize the Spirit that is already there, and thereby reawaken it. This is why the healer is part of the resurrection and the life. The Spirit is not asleep in the minds of the sick, but the part of the mind that can perceive it and be glad is.

Healing is also a science because it obeys the laws of God, Whose laws are true. because they are true they are perfectly dependable, and therefore universal in application. The real aim of science is neither prediction nor control, but only understanding. This is because it does not establish the laws it seeks; cannot discover them through prediction; and has no control over them at all. Science is nothing more than an approach to what already is. Like inspiration it can be misunderstood as magic and will be whenever it is undertaken as separate from what already is and perceived as a means for establishing it. To believe this is possible is to believe you can do it. This can only be the voice of the ego. Truth can only be recognized and need only be recognized.

Inspiration is of the Spirit, and certainty is of God according to His laws. Both, therefore, come from the same Source, since inspiration comes from the Voice for God and certainty comes from the laws of God. Healing does not come directly from God, Who knows His creations as perfectly whole. Yet healing is still of God because it proceeds from His Voice and from His laws. It is their result, in a state of mind which does not know Him. The state is unknown to Him and therefore does not exist, but those who sleep are stupefied, or better, unaware. Because they are unaware, they do not know.

The Holy Spirit must work through you to teach you He is in you. This is an intermediary step toward the knowledge that you are in God because you are part of Him. The miracles which the Holy Spirit inspires can have no order of difficulty because every part of creation is of one order. This is God's will and yours. The laws of God establish this, and the Holy Spirit reminds you of it. When you heal, you are remembering the laws of God and forgetting the laws of the ego. We said before that forgetting is merely a way of remembering better. It is therefore not the opposite of remembering, when it is properly perceived. Perceived improperly, it induces a perception of conflict with something else, as all incorrect perception does. Properly perceived, it can be used as a way out of conflict, as all proper perception can.

All abilities, then should be given over to the Holy Spirit who knows how to use them properly. He can use them only for healing because He knows you only as whole. By healing you learn of wholeness, and by learning of wholeness you learn to remember God. You have forgotten Him, but the Holy Spirit still knows that your forgetting must be translated into a way of remembering and not perceived as a separate ability which opposes an opposite. That is the way in which the ego tries to use all abilities, since its goal is always to make you believe that you are in opposition.

The ego's goal is as unified as the Holy Spirit's and it is because of this that their goals can never be reconciled in any way or to any extent. The ego always seeks to divide and separate. The Holy Spirit always seeks to unify and heal. As you heal you are healed because the Holy Spirit sees no order of healing. Healing is the way to undo the belief in differences, being the only way of perceiving the Sonship without this belief. This perception is therefore in accord with the laws of God even in a state of mind which is out of accord with His. The strength of right perception is so great that it brings the mind into accord with His because it yields to His pull, which is in all of you.

To oppose the pull or the Will of God is not an ability but a real delusion. The ego believes that it has this ability and can offer it to you as a gift. You do not wait it. It is not a gift. It is nothing at all. God has given you a gift which you both have and are. When you do not use it, you do not know you have it. By not knowing this, you do not know what you are. Healing, then, is a way of approaching knowledge by thinking in accordance with the laws of God and recognizing their universality. Without this recognition, you have made the laws themselves meaningless to you. Yet the laws are not meaningless since all meaning is contained by them and in them.

Seek ye first the Kingdom of Heaven because that is where the laws of God operate truly, and they can operate only truly, since they are the laws of Truth. But seek this only because you can find nothing else. There is nothing else. God is all in all in a very literal sense. All being is in Him who is all being. You are therefore in Him since your being is His. Healing is a way of forgetting the sense of danger the ego has induced in you by not recognizing its existence in your brothers. This strengthens the Holy Spirit in both of you because it is a refusal to acknowledge fear. Love needs only this invitation. It comes freely to all the Sonship, being what the Sonship is.

By your awakening to it, you are merely forgetting what you are not. This enables you to remember what you are healing and the changelessness of mind. The body is nothing more than a framework for developing abilities. It is therefore a means for developing potentials, which is quite apart from what the potential is used for. That is a decision. The effects of the egos' decision in this matter are so apparent that they need no elaboration here, but the Holy Spirit's decision to use the body only for communication has such a direct connection with healing that it does need clarification.

The unhealed healer obviously does not understand his own vocation. Only minds communicate. Since the ego cannot obliterate the impulse to communicate because it is also the impulse to create, the ego can only teach you that the body can both communicate and create, and therefore does not need the mind. The ego thus tries to teach you that the body can act like the mind and is therefore self-sufficient. Yet we have learned that behaviour is not the level for either teaching or learning. This must be so, since you can act in accordance with what you do not believe. To do this, however, will weaken you as teachers and learners because, as has been repeatedly emphasized, you teach what you do believe. An inconsistent lesson will be poorly taught and poorly learned. If you teach both sickness and healing you are both a poor teacher and a poor learner.

Healing is the one ability which everyone can develop and must develop, if he is to be healed. Healing is the Holy Spirit's form of communication, and the only one He knows. He recognizes no other because he does not accept the ego's confusion of mind and body. Minds can communicate, but they cannot hurt. The body in the service of the ego can hurt other bodies, but this cannot occur unless the body has already been confused with the mind. This fact, too, can be used either for healing or for magic, but you must remember that magic is always the belief that healing is harmful.

This is its totally insane premise and so it proceeds accordingly. Healing only strengthens. Magic always tries to weaken. Healing perceives nothing in the healer that everyone else does not share with him. Magic always sees something "special" in the healer, which he believes he can offer as a gift to someone who does not have it. He may believe that the gift comes from God to Him, but it is quite evident that he does not understand God if he thinks he has something that others lack. You might well ask, then, why some healing can result from this kind of thinking and there is a reason for this:

However, misguided the "magical healer" may be, he is also trying to help. He is conflicted and unstable, but at times he is offering something to the Sonship, and the only thing the Sonship can accept is healing. When the so-called "healing" works, then, the impulse to help and to be helped have coincided. This is coincidental, because the healer may not be experiencing himself as truly helpful at the time, but the belief that he is, in the mind of another, helps him.

The Holy Spirit does not work by chance and healing that is of Him always works. Unless the healer always heals by Him, the results will vary. Yet healing itself is consistence, since only consistence is conflict-free and only the conflict-free are whole. By accepting exceptions and acknowledging that he can sometimes heal and sometimes not, the healer is obviously accepting inconsistency. He is therefore in conflict and teaching conflict. Can anything of God not be for all and for always?

Love is incapable of any exceptions. Only if there is fear does the idea of exceptions seem to be meaningful. Exceptions are fearful because they are made by fear. The "fearful healer" is a contradiction in terms and is therefore a concept which only a conflicted mind could possibly perceive as meaningful. Fear does not gladden. Healing does. Fear always makes exceptions. Healing never does. Fear produces dissociation because it induces separation. Healing always produces harmony because it proceeds from integration.

Healing is predictable because it can be counted on. Everything that is of God can be counted on, because everything of God is wholly real. Healing can be counted on because it is inspired by His Voice and is in accord with His laws. Yet if healing is consistence, it cannot be inconsistently understood. Understanding means consistence because God means consistence. Since that is his meaning, it is also yours. Your meaning cannot be out of accord with His because your whole meaning, and you're only meaning, comes from His and is like His. God cannot be out of accord with himself, and you cannot be out of accord with Him. You cannot separate yourself from your Creator, Who created you by sharing His being with you.

The unhealed healer wants gratitude from his brothers, but he is not grateful to them. This is because he thinks he is giving something to them and is not receiving something equally desirable in return. His teaching is limited because he is learning so little. His healing lesson is limited by his own ingratitude, which is a lesson in sickness.

Learning is constant, and so vital in its power for change that a Son of God can recognize his power in one instant and change the world in the next. That is because, by changing His mind, he has changed the most powerful device that was ever created for change.

This in no way contradicts the changelessness of mind as God created it, but you think that you have changed it as long as you learn through the ego. This does place you in a position of needing to learn a lesson which seems contradictory; – you must learn to change your mind about your mind. Only by this can you learn that it is changeless. When you heal, that is exactly what you are learning. You are recognizing the changeless mind in your brother by realizing that he could not have changed his mind. That is how you perceive the Holy Spirit in him. It is only the Holy Spirit in him that never changes His mind. He himself must think he can, or he would not perceive himself as sick. He therefore does not know what his self is.

If you see only the changeless in him, you have not really changed him at all. By changing your mind about his for him, you help him undo the change his ego thinks it has made in him. As you can hear two voices, so you can see in two ways. One way shows you an image, or better, an idol, which you may worship out of fear, but which you will never love. The other shows you only truth, which you will love because you will understand it. Understanding is appreciating, because what you understand you can identify with, and by making it part of you, you have accepted it with love.

That is how God Himself created you; in understanding, in appreciation and in love. The ego is totally unable to understand this because it does not understand what it makes; it does not appreciate it, and it does not love it. It incorporates to take away. It literally believes that every time it deprives someone of something, it has increased. We have spoken often of the increase of the Kingdom by your creations, which can only be created as you were. The whole glory and perfect joy that is the Kingdom lies in you to give. Do you not want to give it?

You cannot forget the Father because I am with you, and I cannot forget Him. To forget me is to forget yourself and Him who created you. Our brothers are forgetful. That is why they need your remembrance of me, and Him who created me. Through this remembrance you can change their minds about themselves, as I can change yours. Your minds are so powerful a light that you can look into theirs and enlighten them, as I can enlighten yours.

I do not want to share my body in communion because that is to share nothing. Yet I do want to share my mind with you because we are of one Mind and that mind is ours.

See only this mind everywhere, because only this is everywhere and in everything. It is everything because it encompasses all things within itself. Blessed are you who perceive only this, because you perceive only what is true. Come therefore unto me and learn of the truth in you. The Mind we share is shared by all our brothers, and as we see them truly, they will be healed. Let your mind shine with mine upon their minds, and by our gratitude to them, make them aware of the light in them.

This light will shine back upon you and on the whole Sonship because this is your proper gift to God. He will accept it and give it to the Sonship because it is acceptable to Him, and therefore to His Sons. This is the true communion of the Spirit Who sees the altar of God in everyone, and by bringing it to your appreciation, calls upon you to love God and His creations. You can appreciate the Sonship only as one. This is part of the law of creation, and therefore governs all thought.

Although you can love the Sonship only as one, you can perceive it as fragmented. It is impossible, however, for you to see something in part of it that you will not attribute to all of it. That is why attack is never discrete, and why attack must be relinquished entirely. If it is not relinquished entirely, it is not relinquished at all. Fear and love are equally reciprocal. They make or create depending on whether the ego or the Holy Spirit begets or inspires them, but they will return to the mind of the thinker, and they will affect his total perception. That includes his perception of God, of His creations, and of his own. He will not appreciate any of them if he regards them fearfully. He will appreciate all of them if he regards them with love.

The mind that accepts attack cannot love. That is because it believes that it can destroy love, and therefore does not understand what love is. If it does not understand what love is, it cannot perceive itself as loving. This loses the awareness of being; induces feelings of unreality; and results in utter confusion. Your own thinking has done this because of its power, but your own thinking can also save you from this because its power is not of your making. Your ability to direct your thinking as you will is part of its power. If you do not believe you can do this, you have denied the power of your thought, and thus rendered it powerless in your belief.

The ingeniousness of the ego to preserve itself is enormous, but it stems from the power of the mind which the ego denies. This means that the ego attacks what is preserving it, and this must be a source of extreme anxiety. That is why the ego never knows what it is doing. It is perfectly logical, but clearly insane. The ego draws upon the one source which is totally inimical to its existence for its existence. Fearful of perceiving the power of this source, it is forced to depreciate it. This threatens its own existence, a state which it finds intolerable.

Remaining logical but still insane, the ego resolves this completely insane dilemma in a completely insane way. It does not perceive its existence as threatened by projecting the threat onto you and perceiving your being as non-existent. This ensures its continuance, if you side with it, by guaranteeing that you will not know your own safety. The ego cannot afford to know anything. Knowledge is total, and the ego does not believe in totality. This unbelief is its origin, and while the ego does not love you, it is faithful to its own antecedents, begetting as it was begotten.

Mind always reproduces as it was produced. Produced by fear, the ego reproduces fear. This is its allegiance, and this allegiance makes it treacherous to love because you are love. Love is your power, which the ego must deny. It must also deny everything which this power gives you because it gives you everything. No-one who has everything wants the ego. Its own maker, then, does not want it. Rejection is therefore the only decision which the ego could possibly encounter, if the mind which made it knew itself. And if it recognized any part of the Sonship it would know itself.

The ego therefore opposes all appreciation, all recognition, all sane perception and all knowledge. It perceives their threat as total because it senses the fact that all commitments the mind makes are total. Forced, therefore, to detach itself from you who are mind, it is willing to attach itself to anything else. But there is nothing else. It does not follow that the mind cannot make illusions, but it does follow that, if it makes illusions, it will believe in them, because that is how it made them.

The Holy Spirit undoes illusions without attacking them merely because He cannot perceive them at all. They therefore do not exist for Him. He resolves the apparent conflict which they engender by perceiving conflict as meaningless. We said before that the Holy Spirit perceives the conflict exactly as it is, and it is meaningless.

The Holy Spirit does not want you to understand conflict; He wants you to realize that because conflict is meaningless, it cannot be understood. We have already said that understanding brings appreciation, and appreciation brings love. Nothing else can be understood because nothing else is real and therefore nothing else has meaning.

If you will keep in mind what the Holy Spirit offers you, you cannot be vigilant for anything but God and His Kingdom. The only reason you find this difficult is because you think there IS something else. Belief does not require vigilance unless it is conflicted. If it is, there are conflicting components within it which have engendered a state of war, and vigilance therefore has become essential. Vigilance has no place at all in peace. It is necessary against beliefs which are not true, and would never have been called upon by the Holy Spirit if you had not believed the untrue. You cannot deny that when you believe something, you have made it true for you.

When you believe what God does not know, your thought seems to contradict His, and this makes it appear as if you are attacking Him. We have repeatedly emphasized that the ego does believe it can attack God and tries to persuade you that you have done this. If the mind cannot attack, the ego proceeds perfectly logically to the position that you cannot be mind. By not seeing you as you are, it can see itself as it wants to be. Aware of its weakness the ego wants your allegiance, but not as you really are. The ego therefore wants to engage your mind in its own delusional system because otherwise the light of your understanding would dispel it.

The ego wants no part of truth because the truth is that the ego is not true. If truth is total the untrue cannot exist. Commitment to either must be total, since they cannot co-exist in your minds without splitting them. If they cannot co-exist in peace, and if you want peace, you must give up the idea of conflict entirely and for all time. While you believe that two totally contradictory thought systems share truth, your need for vigilance is apparent. Your minds are dividing their allegiance between two kingdoms, and you are totally committed to neither.

Your identification with the Kingdom is totally beyond question except by you, when you are thinking insanely. What you are is not established by your perception and is not influenced by it at all. All perceived problems in identification at any level are not problems of fact. They are problems of understanding, since they mean that you believe what you can understand is up to you to decide. The ego believes this totally, being fully committed to it.

It is not true. The ego therefore is totally committed to untruth, perceiving in total contradiction to the Holy Spirit and to the knowledge of God. You can be perceived with meaning only by the Holy Spirit because your being is the knowledge of God. Any belief that you accept which is apart from this will obscure God's Voice in you and will therefore obscure God to you. Unless you perceive His creation truly you cannot know the Creator, since God and His creation are not separate. The Oneness of the Creator and the creation is your wholeness, your sanity and your limitless power. This limitless power is God's gift to you because it is what you are. If you dissociate your mind from it, you are perceiving the most powerful force in the universe as if it were weak because you do not believe you are part of it.

Perceived without your part in it, God's creation is perceived as weak, and those who see themselves as weakened do attack. The attack must be blind, however, because there is nothing to attack. Therefore, they make up images, perceive them as unworthy, and attack them for their unworthiness. That is all the world of the ego is. Nothing, it has no meaning. It does not exist. Do not try to understand it because, if you do, you are believing that it can be understood, and is therefore capable of being appreciated and loved. That would justify it, and it cannot be justified. You cannot make the meaningless meaningful. This can only be an insane attempt.

Allowing insanity to enter your minds means that you have not judged sanity as wholly desirable. If you want something else you will make something else, but because it is something else it will attack your thought system and divide your allegiance. You cannot create in this divided state, and you must be vigilant against this divided state because only peace can be extended. Your divided minds are blocking the extension of the Kingdom and its extension is your joy. If you do not extend the Kingdom, you are not thinking with your Creator and creating as He created.

In this depressing state the Holy Spirit reminds you gently that you are sad because you are not fulfilling your function as co-creators with God and are therefore depriving yourselves of joy. This is not God's Will, but yours. If your will is out of accord with God's, you are willing without meaning. Yet because God's Will is unchangeable, no real conflict of will is possible. This is the Holy Spirit's perfectly consistent teaching.

Creation, not separation, is your will because it is God's, and nothing that opposes this means anything at all. Being a perfect accomplishment, the Sonship can only accomplish perfectly, extending the joy in which it was created, and identifying itself with both its Creator and its creations, knowing they are One.

Whenever you deny a blessing to a brother you will feel deprived. This is because denial is as total as love. It is as impossible to deny part of the Sonship as it is to love it in part. Nor is it possible to love it totally at times. You cannot be totally committed sometimes. Remember a very early lesson; – "Never underestimate the power of denial." It has no power in itself, but you can give it the power of your mind, whose power is without limit of any kind. If you use it to deny reality, reality is gone for you. Reality cannot be partly appreciated.

That is why denying any part of it means you have lost awareness of all of it. That is the negative side of the law, as it operates in this world. Yet denial is a defence, and so it is as capable of being used positively as it is of being used destructively. Used negatively it will be destructive because it will be used for attack, but in the service of the Holy Spirit, the law requires you to recognize only part of reality to appreciate all of it. Mind is too powerful to be subject to exclusion. You will never be able to exclude yourself from what you project.

When a brother acts insanely, he is offering you an opportunity to bless him. His need is yours. You need the blessing you can offer him. There is no way for you to have it except by giving it. This is the law of God, and it has no exceptions. What you deny you lack, not because it is lacking, but because you have denied it in another, and are therefore not aware of it in you. Every response you make is determined by what you think you are, and what you want to be \what you think you are. Therefore, what you want to be determines every response you make.

You do not need God's blessing, since that you have forever, but you do need yours. The picture you see of yourselves is deprived, unloving and very vulnerable. You cannot love this. Yet you can very easily escape from it, or better, leave it behind. You are not there, and that is not you. Do not see this picture in anyone, or you have accepted it as you. All illusions about the Sonship are dispelled together, as they were made together. Teach no-one that he is what you would not want to be. Your brother is the mirror in which you will see the image of yourself, as long as perception lasts.

And perception will last until the Sonship knows itself as whole. You made perception, and it must last as long as you want it. Illusions are investments. They will last as long as you value them. Values are relative, but they are powerful because they are mental judgements. The only way to dispel illusions is to withdraw all investment from them and they will have no life for you because you have put them out of your mind. While you include them in it, you are giving life to them. Except there is nothing there to receive your gift.

The gift of life is yours to give, because it was given you. You are unaware of your gift because you do not give it. You cannot make nothing live, since it cannot be enlivened. Therefore, you are not extending the gift you both have and are, and so you do not know your being. All confusion comes from not extending life, since that is not the will of your Creator. You can do nothing apart from Him, and you do, do nothing apart from Him. Keep His way to remember yourselves, and teach His way, lest you forget yourselves. Give only honour to the Sons of the Living God and count yourselves among them gladly.

Only honour is a fitting gift for those whom God Himself created worthy of honour, and whom He honours. Give them the appreciation which God accords them always, because they are His Beloved Sons in whom He is well pleased. You cannot be apart from them because you are not apart from Him. Rest in His Love and protect your rest by loving. But love everything He created, of which you are a part, or you cannot learn of His peace, and accept His gift for yourself and as yourself. You cannot know your own perfection until you have honoured all those who were created like you.

One Child of God is the only teacher sufficiently worthy to teach another. One Teacher is in all your minds, and He teaches the same lesson to all. He always teaches you the inestimable worth of every Son of God, teaching it with infinite patience born of the infinite Love for which he speaks. Every attack is a call for His patience since only His patience can translate attack into blessing. Those who attack do not know they are blessed. They attack because they believe they are deprived. Give, therefore, of your abundance, and teach your brothers theirs. Do not share their delusions of scarcity, or you will perceive yourself as lacking.

Attack could never promote attack unless you perceived it as a means of depriving you of something you want. Yet you cannot lose anything unless you did not value it, and therefore did not want it. This makes you feel deprived of it, and by projecting your own rejection, you believe that others are taking it from you. One must be fearful, if he believes that his brother is attacking him to tear the Kingdom of Heaven from him. This is the ultimate basis for all of the ego's projection.

Being the part of your mind, which does not believe it is responsible for itself, and being without allegiance to God, the ego is incapable of trust. Projecting its insane belief that you have been treacherous to your Creator, it believes that your brothers, who are as incapable of this as you are, are out to take God from you. Whenever a brother attacks another, this is what he believes. Projection always sees your will in others. If you will to separate yourself from God, that is what you will think others are doing to you.

You are the Will of God. Do not accept anything else as your will, or you are denying what you are. Deny this and you will attack, believing you have been attacked. But see the Love of God in you, and you will see It everywhere because it is everywhere. See His abundance in everyone, and you will know that you are in Him with them. They are part of you, as you are part of God. You are as lonely without understanding this as God Himself is lonely when His Sons do not know Him. The peace of God is understanding this. There is only one way out of the world's thinking, just as there was only one way into it. Understand totally by understanding totally.

Perceive any part of the ego's thought system as wholly insane, wholly delusional and wholly undesirable, and you have correctly evaluated all of it. This correction enables you to perceive any part of creation as wholly real, wholly perfect, and wholly desirable. Wanting this only, you will have this only, and giving this only, you will be only this. The gifts you offer to the ego are always experienced as sacrifices, but the gifts you offer to the Kingdom are gifts to you. They will always be treasured by God because they belong to His beloved Sons, who belong to Him. All power and glory are yours because the Kingdom is His.

We once said that without projection there can be no anger, but it is also true that without projection there can be no love. Projection is a fundamental law of the mind, and therefore one which always operates. It is the law by which you create and were created. It is the law which unifies the Kingdom and keeps it in the Mind of God. To the ego, the law is perceived as a way of getting rid of something it does not want.

To the Holy Spirit, it is the fundamental law of sharing by which you give what you value in order to keep it in your own mind. Projection, to the Holy Spirit, is the law of extension. To the ego, it is the law of deprivation. It therefore produces abundance or scarcity, depending on how you choose to apply it. This choice is up to you, but it is not up to you to decide whether or not you will utilize projection. Every mind must project because that is how it lives, and every mind is life. The ego's use of projection must be fully understood before its inevitable association between projection and anger can be finally undone.

The ego always tries to preserve conflict. It is very ingenious in devising ways which seem to diminish conflict because it does not want you to find conflict so intolerable that you will insist on giving it up. Therefore, the ego tries to persuade you that it can free you of conflict, lest you give the ego up and free yourself.

The ego, using its own warped version of the laws of God, utilizes the power of the mind only to defeat the mind's real purpose. It projects conflict from your mind to others minds, in an attempt to persuade you that you have gotten rid of it. This has several fallacies which may not be so apparent.

Strictly speaking, conflict cannot be projected precisely because it cannot be fully shared. Any attempt to keep part of it and get rid of another part does not really mean anything. Remember that a conflicted teacher is a poor teacher and a poor learner. His lessons are confused, and their transfer value is severely limited by his confusion. A second fallacy is the idea that you can get rid of something you do not want by giving it away. Giving it is how you keep it. The belief that by giving it out you have excluded it from within is a complete distortion of the power of extension.

That is why those who project from the ego are vigilant for their own safety. They are afraid that their projections will return and hurt them. They do believe they have blotted their projections from their own minds, but they also believe their projections are trying to creep back into them. That is because the projections have not left their minds, and this, in turn, forces them to engage in compulsive activity in order not to recognize this. You cannot perpetuate an illusion about another without perpetuating it about yourself. There is no way out of this because it is impossible to fragment the mind.

To fragment is to break into pieces, and mind cannot attack or be attacked. The belief that it can, a fallacy which the ego always makes, underlies its whole use of projection. It does not understand what mind is, and therefore does not understand what you are.

Yet its existence is dependent on your mind because the ego is your belief. The ego is therefore a confusion in identification which never had a consistent model, and never developed consistently. It is the distorted product of the misapplication of the laws of God, by distorted minds which are misusing their own power.

Do not be afraid of the ego. It does depend on your mind, and as you made it by believing in it, so you can dispel it by withdrawing belief from it. Do not project the responsibility for your belief in it onto anyone else, or you will preserve the belief. When you are willing to accept sole responsibility for the ego's existence yourself you will have laid aside all anger and all attack, because they come from an attempt to project responsibility for your own errors. But having accepted the errors as yours, do not keep them. Give them over quickly to the Holy Spirit to be undone completely, so that all their effects will vanish from your minds and from the Sonship as a whole.

The Holy Spirit will teach you to perceive beyond belief because truth is beyond belief, and His perception is true. The ego can be completely forgotten at any time because it was always a belief that is totally incredible. No-one can keep a belief he has judged to be unbelievable. The more you learn about the ego, the more you realize that it cannot be believed. The incredible cannot be understood because it is unbelievable. The utter meaninglessness of all perception that comes from the unbelievable must be apparent, but it is not recognised as beyond belief because it was made by belief.

The whole purpose of this course is to teach you that the ego is unbelievable and will forever be unbelievable. You who made the ego by believing the unbelievable cannot make this judgement alone. By accepting the Atonement for yourself, you are deciding against the belief that you can be alone, thus dispelling the idea of separation, and affirming your true identification with the whole Kingdom as literally part of you. This identification is as beyond doubt as it is beyond belief. Your wholeness has no limits because being is in infinity.

Only you can limit your creative power, but God wills to release it. He no more wills you to deprive yourself of your creations than He wills to deprive Himself of His. Do not withhold your gifts to the Sonship, or you withhold yourself from God. Selfishness is of the ego, but self-fullness is of the Soul because that is how God created it. The Holy Spirit is the part of the mind that lies between the ego and the Soul, mediating between them always in favour of the Soul.

To the ego this is partiality and it therefore responds as if it were the part that is being sided against. To the Soul this is truth, because it knows its fullness, and cannot conceive of any part from which it is excluded.

The Soul knows that the consciousness of all its brothers is included in its own, as it is included in God. The power of the whole Sonship and of its Creator is therefore the Soul's own fullness, rendering its creations equally whole and equal in perfection. The ego cannot prevail against a totality which includes God, and any totality must include God. Everything He created is given all His power because it is part of Him and shares His Being with Him. Creating is the opposite of loss, as blessing is the opposite of sacrifice. Being must be extended. That is how it retains the knowledge of itself.

The Soul yearns to share its being as its Creator did. Created by sharing, its will is to create. It does not wish to contain God but to extend His Being. The extension of God's Being is the Soul's only function. Its fullness cannot be contained, any more than can the fullness of its Creator. Fullness is extension. The ego's whole thought system blocks extension, and thus blocks your only function. It therefore blocks your joy, and that is why you perceive yourselves as unfulfilled. Unless you create you are unfulfilled, but God does not know of unfulfillment, and therefore you must create. You may not know your own creations, but this can no more interfere with their reality than your unawareness of your Soul can interfere with its being.

The Kingdom is forever extending because it is in the Mind of God. You do not know your joy because you do not know your own self-fullness. Exclude any part of the Kingdom from yourself, and you are not whole. A split mind cannot perceive its fullness and needs the miracle of its wholeness to dawn upon it and heal it. This reawakens the wholeness in it and restores it to the Kingdom because of its acceptance of wholeness. The full appreciation of its self-fullness makes selfishness impossible and extension inevitable. That is why there is perfect peace in the Kingdom. Every Soul is fulfilling its function, and only complete fulfilment is peace.

Insanity appears to add to reality, but no-one would claim that what it adds is true. Insanity is therefore the non-extension of truth, which blocks joy because it blocks creation, and thus blocks self-fulfilment. The unfulfilled must be depressed because their self-fullness is unknown to them. Your creations are protected for you because the Holy Spirit, who is in your mind, knows of them and can bring them into your awareness whenever you will let Him.

They are there as part of your own being because your fulfilment includes them. The creations of every Son of God are yours since every creation belongs to everyone, being created for the Sonship as a whole.

You have not failed to add to the inheritance of the Sons of God and thus have not failed to secure it for yourselves. If it was the Will of God to give it to you, He gave it forever. If it was His Will that you have it forever, He gave you the means for keeping it, and you have done so. Disobeying God's Will is meaningful only to the insane. In truth it is impossible. Your self-fullness is as boundless as God's. Like His, it extends forever and in perfect peace. Its radiance is so intense that it creates in perfect joy, and only the whole can be born of its wholeness.

Be confident that you have never lost your identity and the extensions which maintain it in wholeness and peace. Miracles are an expression of this confidence. They are reflections both of your own proper identification with your brothers, and of your own awareness that your identification IS maintained by extension. The miracle is a lesson in total perception. By including any part of totality in the lesson, you have included the whole. You have said that, when you write of the Kingdom and your creations which belong in it, you are describing what you do not know. That is true in a sense, but no more true than your failure to acknowledge the whole result of the ego's premises. The Kingdom is the result of premises, just as this world is.

You have carried the ego's reasoning to its logical conclusion, which is total confusion about everything. Yet you do not really believe this, or you could not possibly maintain it. If you really saw this result, you could not want it. The only reason why you could possibly want any part of it is because you do not see the whole of it. You are willing to look at the ego's premises, but not at their logical outcome. Is it not possible that you have done the same thing with the premises of God?

Your creations are the logical outcome of His premises. His thinking has established them for you. They are therefore there, exactly where they belong. They belong in your mind as part of your identification with His, but your state of mind and your recognition of what is in your mind depends, at any given moment, on what you believe about your mind. Whatever these beliefs may be, they are the premises which will determine what you accept into your mind. It is surely clear that you can both accept into your mind what is not really there and deny what is.

Neither of these possibilities requires further elaboration here, but both are clearly indefensible, even if you elect to defend them.

Yet the function which God Himself gave your minds through His you may deny, but you cannot prevent. It is the logical outcome of what you are. The ability to see a logical outcome depends on the willingness to see it, but its truth has nothing to do with your willingness at all. Truth is God's Will. Share His Will, and you share what He knows. Deny His Will as yours, and you are denying His Kingdom and yours. The Holy Spirit will direct you only so as to avoid pain. The undoing of pain must obviously avoid pain. Surely no-one would object to this goal if he recognises it. The problem is not whether what the Holy Spirit says is true, but whether you want to listen to what He says.

You no more recognize what is painful than you know what is joyful, and are, in fact, very apt to confuse the two. The Holy Spirit's main function is to teach you to tell them apart. However strange it may seem that this is necessary, it obviously is. The reason is equally obvious. What is joyful to you is painful to the ego, and as long as you are in doubt about what you are, you will be confused about joy and pain. This confusion is the cause of the whole idea of sacrifice. Obey the Holy Spirit and you will be giving up the ego. But you will be sacrificing nothing. On the contrary, you will be gaining everything If you believed this, there would be no conflict.

That is why you need to demonstrate the obvious to yourselves. It is not obvious to you. You believe that doing the opposite of God's Will can be better for you. You also believe that it is possible to do the opposite of God's Will. Therefore, you believe that an impossible choice is open to you, and one which is both very fearful and very desirable. Yet God Wills. He does not wish. Your will is as powerful as His because it is His. The ego's wishes do not mean anything, because the ego wishes for the impossible. You can wish for the impossible, but you can will only with God. This is the ego's weakness and your strength.

The Holy Spirit always sides with you and with your strength. As long as you avoid His guidance in any way, you want to be weak. Yet weakness is frightening. What else, then, can this decision mean except that you want to be fearful? The Holy Spirit never asks for sacrifice, but the ego always does. When you are confused about this very clear distinction in motivation, it can only be due to projection. Projection of this kind is a confusion in motivation and given this confusion, trust becomes impossible.

No-one obeys gladly a guide he does not trust, but this does not mean that the guide is untrustworthy. In this case, it always means that the follower is. However, this, too, is merely a matter of his own belief. Believing that he can betray, he believes that everything can betray Him. Yet this is only because he has elected to follow false guidance. Unable to follow this guidance without fear, he associates fear with guidance, and refuses to follow any guidance at all. The Holy Spirit is perfectly trustworthy, as you are. God Himself trusts you, and therefore your trustworthiness is beyond question. It will always remain beyond question, however much you may question it.

We said before that you are the Will of God. His Will is not an idle wish, and your identification with His Will is not optional since it is what you are. Sharing His Will with me is not really open to choose, though it may seem to be. The whole separation lies in this fallacy. The only way out of the fallacy is to decide that you do not have to decide anything. Everything has been given you by God's decision. That is His Will and you cannot undo it. Even the relinquishment of your false decision-making prerogative, which the ego guards so jealously, is not accomplished by your wish. It was accomplished for you by the Will of God, Who has not left you comfortless. His Voice will teach you how to distinguish between pain and joy and will lead you out of the confusion which you have made. There is no confusion in the mind of a Son of God, whose will must be the Will of the Father because the Father's Will is His Son.

Miracles are in accord with the Will of God, Whose Will you do not know, because you are confused about what you will. This means that you are confused about what you are. If you are God's Will and do not accept His Will, you are denying joy. The miracle is therefore a lesson in what joy is. Being a lesson in sharing, it is a lesson in love, which is joy. Every miracle is thus a lesson in truth, and by offering truth you are learning the difference between pain and joy.

The Holy Spirit will always guide you truly, because your joy is His. This is His Will for everyone, because He speaks for the Kingdom of God, which is joy. Following Him is therefore the easiest thing in the world, and the only thing that is easy, because it is not of the world, and is therefore natural. The world goes against your nature, being out of accord with God's laws. The world perceives orders of difficulty in everything. This is because the ego perceives nothing as wholly desirable.

By demonstrating to yourselves that there is no order of difficulty in miracles, you will convince yourselves that in your natural state, there is no difficulty because it is a state of grace.

Grace is the natural state of every Son of God. When he is not in a state of grace, he is out of his natural environment and does not function well. Everything he does becomes a strain, because he was not created for the environment that he has made. He therefore cannot adapt to it, nor can he adapt it to Him. There is no point in trying. A Son of God is happy only when he knows he is with God. That is the only environment in which he will not experience strain, because that is where he belongs. It is also the only environment that is worthy of him, because his own worth is beyond anything he can make.

Consider the kingdom you have made and judge its worth fairly. Is it worthy to be a home for a Child of God? Does it protect his peace, and shine love upon him? Does it keep his heart untouched by fear, and allow him to give always, without any sense of loss? Does it teach him that this giving is his joy, and that God Himself thanks him for his giving? That is the only environment in which you can be happy. You cannot make it, any more than you can make yourselves. It has been created for you, as you were created for it. God watches over His Children and denies them nothing. Yet when they deny Him they do not know this, because they deny.

You who could give the Love of God to everything you see and touch and remember are literally denying Heaven to yourselves. I call upon you again to remember that I have chosen you to teach the Kingdom to the Kingdom. There are no exceptions to this lesson because the lack of exceptions IS the lesson. Every Son who returns to the Kingdom with this lesson in his heart has healed the Sonship and given thanks to God. Everyone who learns this lesson has become the perfect teacher because he has learned it of the Holy Spirit, who wants to teach him everything He knows. When a mind has only light, it knows only light. Its own radiance shines all around it, and extends out into the darkness of other minds, transforming them into majesty.

The Majesty of God is there, for you to recognize and appreciate and know. Perceiving the Majesty of God as your brother is to accept your own inheritance. God gives only equally. If you recognize His gift in anyone else, you have acknowledged what He has given you. Nothing is so easy to perceive as truth. This is the perception which is immediate, clear and natural. You have trained yourselves not to see it, and this has been very difficult for you.

Out of your natural environment you may well ask "What is truth?" since truth is the environment by which and for which you were created.

You do not know yourselves because you do not you're your Creator. You do not know your creations because you do not know your brothers, who created them with you. We said before that only the whole Sonship is worthy to be co-creator with God because only the whole Sonship can create like Him. Whenever you heal a brother by recognizing his worth, you are acknowledging His power to create and yours. He cannot have lost what you recognize, and you must have the glory you see in him. He is a cocreator with God with you. Deny His creative power, and you are denying yours and that of god who created you. You cannot deny part of truth. You do not know your creations because you do not know their creator. You do not know yourselves because you do not know yours.

Your creations cannot establish your reality, any more than you can establish God's. But you can know both. Being is known by sharing. Because God shared His Being with you, you can know Him. But you must also know all He created, to know what they have shared. Without your Father, you will not know your fatherhood. The Kingdom of God includes all His Sons and their children, who are like the Sons as they are like the Father. Know, then, the Sons of God, and you will know all creation. You are hampered in your progress by your demands to know what you do not know. This is actually a way of holding on to deprivation. You cannot reasonably object to following instructions in a course for knowing on the grounds that you do not know. The need for the course is implicit in your objection. Knowledge is not the motivation for learning this course. Peace is. As the prerequisite for knowledge, peace must be learned. This is only because those who are in conflict are not peaceful, and peace is the condition of knowledge, because it is the condition of the Kingdom.

Knowledge will be restored when you meet its conditions. This is not a bargain made by God, Who makes no bargains. It is merely the result of your misuse of His laws on behalf of a will that is not His. Knowledge is His Will. If you are opposing His Will, how can you have knowledge? I have told you what knowledge offers you, but it is clear that you do not regard this as wholly desirable. If you did, you would hardly be willing to throw it away so readily, when the ego asks for your allegiance. The distraction of the ego seems to interfere with your learning, but the ego has no power to distract you, unless you give it the power. The ego's voice is a hallucination.

You cannot expect it to say "I am not real." Hallucinations are inaccurate perceptions of reality. Yet you are not asked to dispel them alone. You are merely asked to evaluate them in terms of their results to you. If you do not want them on the basis of loss of peace, they will be removed from your mind for you. Every response to the ego is a call to war, and war does deprive you of peace. Yet in this war there is no opponent. THIS is the reinterpretation of reality which you must make to secure peace, and the only one you need ever make.

Those whom you perceive as opponents are part of your peace, which you are giving up by attacking them. How can you have what you give up? You share to have, but you do not give it up yourself. When you give up peace, you are excluding yourself from it. This is a condition which is so alien to the Kingdom that you cannot understand the state which prevails within it. Your past learning must have taught you the wrong things, simply because it has not made you happy. On this basis alone, its value should be questioned.

If learning aims at change, and that is always its purpose, are you satisfied with the changes your learning has brought you? Dissatisfaction with learning outcomes must be a sign of learning failure, since it means that you did not get what you want. The curriculum of the Atonement is the opposite of the curriculum you have established for yourselves, but so is its outcome. If the outcome of yours has made you unhappy, and if you want a different one, a change in the curriculum is obviously necessary.

The first change that must be introduced is a change in direction. A meaningful curriculum cannot be inconsistent. If it is planned by two teachers, each believing in diametrically opposed ideas, it cannot be integrated. If it is carried out by these two teachers simultaneously, each one merely interferes with the other. This leads to fluctuation, but not to change. The volatile has no direction. They cannot choose one, because they cannot relinquish the other even if the other does not exist. Their conflicted curriculum teaches them all directions exist and gives them no rationale for choice.

The total senselessness of such a curriculum must be fully recognized before a real change in direction becomes possible. You cannot learn simultaneously from two teachers who are in total disagreement about everything. Their joint curriculum presents an impossible learning task. They are teaching you entirely different things in entirely different ways, which might be possible, except for the crucial fact that both are Teaching you about yourself.

Your reality is unaffected by both, but if you listen to both, your mind will be split about what your reality is.

There is a rationale for choice. Only one Teacher knows what your reality is. If learning that is the purpose of the curriculum, you must learn it of Him. The ego does not know what it is trying to teach. It is trying to teach you what you are without knowing it. The ego is expert only in confusion. It does not understand anything else. As a teacher, then, it is totally confused and totally confusing. Even if you could disregard the Holy Spirit entirely, which is quite impossible, you could learn nothing from the ego because the ego knows nothing.

Is there any possible reason for choosing a teacher such as this? Does the total disregard of anything it teaches make anything but sense? Is this the teacher to whom a Son of God should turn to find himself? The ego has never given you a sensible answer to anything. Simply on the grounds of your own experience with the ego's teaching, should not this alone disqualify it as your future teacher? Yet the ego has done more harm to your learning than this alone. Learning is joyful if it leads you along your natural path and facilitates the development of what you have. When you are taught against your nature, however, you will lose by your learning because your learning will imprison you. Your will is in your nature, and therefore cannot go against it.

The ego cannot teach you anything as long as your will is free because you will not listen to it. It is not your will to be imprisoned because your will is free. That is why the ego is the denial of free will. It is never God Who coerces you because He shares His Will with you. His Voice teaches only His Will, but that is not the Holy Spirit's lesson because that is what you are. The lesson is that your will and God's cannot be out of accord because they are one. This is the undoing of everything the ego tries to teach. It is not, then, only the direction of the curriculum which must be unconflicted, but also the content.

The ego wants to teach you that you want to oppose God's Will. This unnatural lesson cannot be learned, but the attempt to learn it is a violation of your own freedom and makes you afraid of your will because it is free. The Holy Spirit opposes any imprisoning of the will of a Son of God, knowing that the will of the Son is the Father's. The Holy Spirit leads you steadily along the path of freedom, teaching you how to disregard, or look beyond, everything that would hold you back.

We said before that the Holy Spirit teaches you the difference between pain and joy. That is the same as saying that He teaches you the difference between imprisonment and freedom. You cannot make this distinction without Him. That is because you have taught yourself that imprisonment IS freedom. Believing them to be the same, how can you tell them apart? Can you ask the part of your mind that taught you to believe they are the same to teach you the difference between them?

The Holy Spirit's teaching takes only one direction and has only one goal. His direction is freedom and His goal is God. Yet he cannot conceive of God without you because it is not God's Will to be without you. When you have learned that your will is God's, you could no more will to be without Him than He could will to be without you. This is freedom, and this is joy. Deny yourself this and you are denying God His Kingdom because He created you for this. When we said, "All power and glory are yours because the Kingdom is His," this is what we meant:

The Will of God is without limit, and all power and glory lie within it. It is boundless in strength and in love and in peace. It has no boundaries because Its extension is unlimited, and It encompasses all things because It created all things. By creating all things, it made them part of Itself. You are the Will of God because this is how you were created. Because your Creator creates only like Himself, you are like Him. You are part of Him Who is all power and glory and are therefore as unlimited as He is.

To what else except all power and glory can the Holy Spirit appeal to restore God's Kingdom? His appeal, then, is merely to what the Kingdom is, and for its own acknowledgment of what it is. When you acknowledge this, you bring the acknowledgment automatically to everyone because you have acknowledged everyone. By your recognition you awaken theirs and through theirs yours is extended. Awakening runs easily and gladly through the Kingdom, in answer to the Call of God. This is the natural response of every Son of God to the Voice of his Creator, because it is the Voice for His creations and for HIS own extension.

Glory be to God in the highest, and to you because He has so willed it. Ask and it shall be given you because it has already been given. Ask for light and learn that you are light. If you want understanding and enlightenment you will learn it, because your will to learn it is your decision to listen to the Teacher Who knows of light and can therefore teach it to you. There is no limit on your learning because there is no limit on your minds. There is no limit on His will to teach because He was created to teach.

Knowing His function perfectly He wills to fulfil it perfectly, because that is His joy and yours.

To fulfil the Will of God perfectly is the only joy and peace that can be fully known because it is the only function that can be fully experienced. When this is accomplished, then, there is no other experience. Yet the wish for other experience will block its accomplishment because God's Will cannot be forced upon you, being an experience of total willingness. The Holy Spirit knows how to teach this, but you do not. That is why you need Him and why God gave Him to you. Only His teaching will release your will to God's, uniting it with His power and glory, and establishing them as yours. You share them as God shares them because this is the natural outcome of their being.

The Will of the Father and of the Son are One together by their extension. Their extension is the result of their Oneness, holding their unity together by extending their joint will. This is perfect creation by the perfectly created in union with the Perfect Creator. The Father must give fatherhood to His Son because His own Fatherhood must be extended outward. You who belong in God have the holy function of extending His Fatherhood by placing no limits upon it. Let the Holy Spirit teach you how to do this, for you will know what it means of God Himself.

When you meet anyone, remember it is a holy encounter. As you see him you will see yourself. As you treat him you will treat yourself. As you think of him you will think of yourself. Never forget this, for in him you will find yourself or lose sight of yourself. Whenever two Sons of God meet, they are given another chance at salvation. Do not leave anyone without giving salvation to him and receiving it yourself. For I am always there with you, in remembrance of you.

The goal of the curriculum, regardless of the teacher you choose, is know thyself. There is nothing else to learn. Everyone is looking for himself, and for the power and glory he thinks he has lost. Whenever you are with anyone, you have another opportunity to find them. Your power and glory are in him because they are yours. The ego tries to find them in yourself because it does not know where to look. The Holy Spirit teaches you that, if you look only at yourself, you cannot find yourself because that is not what you are.

Whenever you are with a brother, you are learning what you are because you are teaching what you are. He will respond either with pain or with joy, depending on which teacher you are following. He will be imprisoned or released according to your decision, and so will you. Never forget your responsibility to him because it is your responsibility to yourself. Give him His place in the Kingdom, and you will have yours. The Kingdom cannot be found alone, and you who are the Kingdom cannot find yourselves alone.

To achieve the goal of the curriculum, then, you cannot listen to the ego. Its purpose is to defeat its own goal. The ego does not know this because it does not know anything. But you can know this, and you will know it if you are willing to look at what the ego has made of you. This is your responsibility because, once you have really done this, you will accept the Atonement for yourself. What other choice could you make? Having made this choice, you will begin to learn and understand why you have believed that, when you met someone else, you had thought that he was someone else. And every holy encounter in which you enter fully will teach you this is not so.

You can encounter only part of yourself because you are part of God, who is everything. His power and glory are everywhere, and you cannot be excluded from them. The ego teaches that your strength is in you alone. The Holy Spirit teaches that all strength is in God and therefore in you. God wills no one suffers. He does not will anyone to suffer for a wrong decision, including you. That is why He has given you the means for undoing it. Through His power and glory all your wrong decisions are undone completely releasing you and your brothers from everything imprisoning thought any part of the Sonship has accepted. Wrong decisions have no power because they are not true. The imprisonment which they seem to produce is no more true than they are.

Power and glory belong to God alone. So do you. God gives whatever belongs to Him because He gives of Himself, and everything belongs to Him. Giving of your self is the function He gave you. Fulfilling it perfectly will teach you what you have of Him, and this will teach you what you are in Him. You cannot be powerless to do this because this is your power. Glory is God's gift to you because that is what he is. See this glory everywhere to learn what you are.

If God's Will for you is complete peace and joy, unless you experience only this you must be refusing to acknowledge His Will. His Will does not vacilate, being changeless forever.

When you are not at peace, it can only be because you do not believe you are in Him. Yet He is all in all. His peace is complete, and you must be included in it. His laws govern you because they govern everything. You cannot exempt yourself from His laws, although you can disobey them. Yet if you do, and only if you do, you will feel lonely and helpless because you are denying yourself everything.

I am come as a light into a world that does deny itself everything. It does this simply by dissociating itself from everything. It is therefore an illusion of isolation, maintained by fear of the same loneliness which is its illusion. I have told you that I am with you always, even to the end of the world. That is why I am the light of the world. If I am with you in the loneliness of the world the loneliness is gone. You cannot maintain the illusion of loneliness if you are not alone. My purpose, then, is to overcome the world. I do not attack it, but my light must dispel it because of what it is.

Light does not attack darkness, but it does shine it away. If my light goes with you everywhere, you shine it away with me. The light becomes ours, and you cannot abide in darkness any more than darkness can abide wherever you go. The remembrance of me is the remembrance of yourself and of Him Who sent me to you. You were in darkness until God's Will was done completely by any part of the Sonship. When this was done, it was perfectly accomplished by all. How else could it be perfectly accomplished? My mission was simply to unite the will of the Sonship with the Will of the Father by being aware of the Father's Will myself. This is the awareness I came to give you, and your problem in accepting it is the problem of this world. Dispelling it is salvation, and in this sense I am the salvation of the world.

The world must despise and reject me because the world is the belief that love is impossible. Your reactions to me are the reactions of the world to God. If you will accept the fact that I am with you, you are denying the world and accepting God. My will is His, and your will to hear me is the decision to hear His Voice and abide in His Will. As God sent me to you, so will I send you to others. And I will go to them with you, so we can teach them peace and union.

Do you not think the world needs peace as much as you do? Do you not want to give it to the world as much as you want to receive it? For unless you do, you will not receive it. If you will to have it of me, you must give it. Rehabilitation does not come from anyone else. You can have guidance from without, but you must be accepting it from within.

The guidance must be what you want, or it will be meaningless to you. That is why rehabilitation is a collaborative venture.

I can tell you what to do, but this will not help you unless you collaborate by believing that I know what to do. Only then will your mind choose to follow me. Without your will you cannot be rehabilitated. Motivation to be healed is the crucial factor in rehabilitation. Without this, you are deciding against healing and your veto of my will for you makes healing impossible. If healing is our joint will, unless our wills are joined you cannot be healed. This is obvious when you consider what healing is for. Healing is the way in which the separation is overcome. Separation is overcome by union. It cannot be overcome by separating.

The will to unite must be unequivocal, or the will itself is divided or not whole. Your will is the means by which you determine your own condition because will is the mechanism of decision. It is the power by which you separate or join, and experience pain or joy accordingly. My will cannot overcome yours, because yours is as powerful as mine. If it were not so, the Sons of God would be unequal. All things are possible through our joint will, but my will alone cannot help you. Your will is as free as mine, and God Himself would not go against it. I cannot will what God does not will. I can offer you my will to make yours invincible by this sharing, but I cannot oppose yours without competing with it, and thereby violating God's Will for you.

Nothing God created can oppose your will, as nothing God created can oppose His. God gave your will its power, which I can only acknowledge in honour of His. If you want to be like me I will help you, knowing that we are alike. If you want to be different, I will wait until you change your mind. I can teach you, but only you can choose to listen to my teaching. How else can it be, if God's Kingdom is freedom? Freedom cannot be learned by tyranny of any kind, and the perfect equality of all God's Sons cannot be recognized through the dominion of one will over another. God's Sons are equal in will, all being the Will of their Father. This is the only lesson I came to teach, knowing that it is true.

When your will is not mine, it is not our Father's. This means that you have imprisoned yours and have not let it be free. Of yourselves you can do nothing, because of yourselves you are nothing. I am nothing without the Father, and you are nothing without me because, by denying the Father, you deny yourself. I will always remember you, and in my remembrance of you lies your remembrance of yourself.

In our remembrance of each other lies our remembrance of God. And in this remembrance lies your freedom because your freedom is in Him. Join, then, with me in praise of Him and you whom He created. This is our gift of gratitude to Him, which He will share with all His creations, to whom He gives equally whatever is acceptable to Him. Because it is acceptable to Him it is the gift of freedom, which is His Will for all His Sons. By offering freedom you will be free.

Freedom is the only gift you can offer to God's Sons, being an acknowledge of what they are and what He is. Freedom is creation because it is love. What you seek to imprison you do not love. Therefore, when you seek to imprison anyone, including yourself, you do not love him, and you cannot identify with him. When you imprison yourself, you are losing sight of your true identification with me and with the Father. Your identification is with the Father and with the Son. It cannot be with one and not the other. If you are part of one, you must be part of the other because they are One.

The Holy Trinity is holy because It is One. If you exclude yourself from this union, you are perceiving the Holy Trinity as separated. You must be included in It, because It is everything. Unless you take your place in It and fulfil your function as part of It, It is as bereft as you are. No part of It can be imprisoned if Its truth is to be known. Can you be separated from your identification and be at peace? Dissociation is not a solution; it is a delusion. The delusional believe that truth will assail them, and so they do not see it because they prefer the delusion. Judging truth as something they do not want, they perceive deception and block knowledge.

Help them by offering them your unified will on their behalf, as I am offering you mine on yours. Alone we can do nothing, but together, our wills fuse into something whose power is far beyond the power of its separate parts. By not being separate, the Will of God is established in ours and as ours. This Will is invincible because it is undivided. The undivided will of the Sonship is the perfect creator, being wholly in the likeness of God, Whose Will it is. You cannot be exempt from it, if you are to understand what it is and what you are. By separating your will from mine, you are exempting yourself from the Will of God which is yourself.

Yet to heal is still to make whole. Therefore, to heal is to unite with those who are like you because perceiving this likeness is to recognize the Father. If your perfection is in Him and only in Him, how can you know it without recognizing Him? The recognition of God is the recognition of yourself.

There is no separation of God and His creation. You will learn this as you learn that there is no separation of your will and mine. Let the Love of God shine upon you by your acceptance of me. My reality is yours and His. By joining your will with mine you are signifying your awareness that the Will of God is one.

God's Oneness and ours are not separate because His Oneness encompasses ours. To join with me is to restore His power to you because we are sharing it. I offer you only the recognition of His power in you, but in that lies all truth. As we unite, we unite with Him. Glory be to the union of God and His Holy Sons! All glory lies in them because they are united. The miracles we do bear witness to the Will of the Father for His Son, and to our joy in uniting with His Will for us.

When you unite with me, you are uniting without the ego because I have renounced the ego in myself and therefore cannot unite with yours. Our union is therefore the way to renounce the ego in yourself. The truth in both of us is beyond the ego. By willing that, you have gone beyond it toward truth. Our success in transcending the ego is guaranteed by God, and I can share this confidence for both of us and all of us. I bring God's peace back to all His children because I received it of Him for us all. Nothing can prevail against our united wills because nothing can prevail against God's. Would you know the Will of God for you? Ask it of me who knows it for you, and you will find it. I will deny you nothing, as God denies me nothing.

Ours is simply the journey back to God, Who is our home. Whenever fear intrudes anywhere along the road to peace, it is always because the ego has attempted to join the journey with us and cannot do so. Sensing defeat and angered by it, the ego regards itself as rejected and becomes retaliative. You are invulnerable to its retaliation because I am with you. On this journey you have chosen me as your companion instead of the ego. Do not try to hold on to both, or you will try to go in different directions, and will lose the way.

The ego's way is not mine, but it is also not yours. The Holy Spirit has one direction for all minds, and the one He taught me is yours. Let us not lose sight of His direction through illusions, for only illusions of another direction can obscure the one for which God's Voice speaks in all of us. Never accord the ego the power to interfere with the journey because it has none, since the journey is the way to what is true. Leave all deception behind and reach beyond all attempts of the ego to hold you back. I go before you because I am beyond the ego.

Reach, therefore, for my hand because you want to transcend the ego. My will, will never be wanting, and if you want to share it, you will. I give it willingly and gladly because I need you as much as you need me.

We are the joint will of the Sonship, whose wholeness is for all. We begin the journey back by setting out together and gather in our brothers as we continue together. Every gain in our strength is offered for all, so they, too, can lay aside their weakness and add their strength to us. God's welcome waits for us all, and He will welcome us as I am welcoming you. Forget not the Kingdom of God for anything the world has to offer. The world can add nothing to the power and the glory of God and His Holy Sons, but it can blind the Sons to the Father if they behold it. You cannot behold the world and know God. Only one is true.

I am come to tell you that the choice of which is true is not yours. If it were, you would have destroyed yourselves. Yet God did not will the destruction of His creations, having created them for eternity. His Will has saved you, not from yourselves but from your illusions of yourselves. He has saved you for yourselves. Let us glorify Him Whom the world denies, for over His Kingdom it has no power. No-one created by God can find joy in anything except the eternal. That is not because he is deprive of anything else, but because nothing else is worthy of him. What God and His Sons create is eternal and in this and this only is their joy.

Listen to the story of the prodigal son and learn what God's treasure is and yours: This son of a loving father left his home and thought he squandered everything for nothing of any value, although he did not know its worthlessness at the time. He was ashamed to return to his father, because he thought he had hurt him. Yet when he came home, the father welcomed him with joy because only the son himself was his father's treasure. He wanted nothing else.

God wants only His Son because His Son is His only treasure. You want your creations as He wants His. Your creations are your gift to the Holy Trinity, created in gratitude for your creation. They do not leave you any more than you have left your Creator, but they extend your creation as God extended Himself to you. Can the creations of God Himself take joy in what is not real? And what is real except the creations of God and those which are created like His? Your creations love you as your Soul loves your Father for the gift of creation. There is no other gift which is eternal, and therefore there is no other gift which is true.

How, then, can you accept anything else or give anything else, and expect joy in return? And what else but joy would you want? You made neither yourself nor your function. You made only the decision to be unworthy of both. Yet you could not make yourself unworthy, because you are the treasure of God. What He values is valuable. There can be no question of its worth because its value lies in God's sharing Himself with it and establishing its value forever.

Your function is to add to God's treasure by creating yours. His Will to you is His Will for you. He would not withhold creation from you because His joy is in it. You cannot find joy except as God does. His joy lay in creating you and He extends His Fatherhood to you so that you can extend yourself as He did. You do not understand this because you do not understand Him. No-one who does not know his function can understand it and no one can know his function unless he knows who he is. Creation is the Will of God. His Will created you to create. Your will was not created separate from His and so it wills as he wills.

An "unwilling will" does not mean anything, being a contradiction in terms which actually leaves nothing. When you think you are unwilling to will with God, you are not thinking. God's Will is thought. It cannot be contradicted by thought. God does not contradict himself, and His Sons, who are like Him, cannot contradict themselves or Him. Yet their thought is so powerful that they can even imprison the minds of God's Sons, if they choose. This choice does make the Son's function unknown to Him, but never to his Creator. And because it is not unknown to his Creator, it is forever knowable to him.

There is no question but one you should ever ask of yourself: –"Do I want to know my Father's Will for me?"

He will not hide it. He has revealed it to me because I asked it of Him and learned of what He had already given. Our function is to function together because, apart from each other, we cannot function at all. The whole power of God's Son lies in all of us, but not in any of us alone. God would not have us be alone because He does not will to be alone. That is why He created His Son and gave him the power to create with Him.

Our creations are as holy as we are, and we are the Sons of God Himself, and therefore as holy as He is. Through our creations we extend our love, and thus increase the joy of the Holy Trinity. You do not understand this for a very simple reason. You who are God's own treasure do not regard yourselves as valuable. Given this belief, you cannot understand anything.

I share with God the knowledge of the value He puts upon you. My devotion to you is of Him, being born of my knowledge of myself and Him. We cannot be separated. Whom God has joined cannot be separated, and God has joined all His Sons with Himself. Can you be separated from your life and your being?

The journey to God is merely the reawakening of the knowledge of where you are always, and what you are forever. It is a journey without distance to a goal that has never changed. Truth can only be experienced. It cannot be described, and it cannot be explained. I can make you aware of the conditions of truth, but the experience is of God. Together we can meet its conditions, but truth will dawn upon you of itself.

What God has willed for you is yours. He has given His Will to His treasure, whose treasure It is. Your heart lies where your treasure is, as His does. You who are beloved of God are wholly blessed. Learn this of me and free the holy will of all those who are as blessed as you are.

Attack is always physical. When attack in any form enters your mind, you are equating yourself with a body. This is the ego's interpretation of the body. You do not have to attack physically to accept this interpretation. You are accepting it simply by the belief that attack can get you something you want. If you did not believe this, the idea of attack would have no appeal for you. When you equate yourself with a body you will always experience depression. When a Child of God thinks of himself in this way he is belittling himself and seeing his brothers as similarly belittled. Since he can find himself only in them, he has cut himself off from salvation.

Remember that the Holy Spirit interprets the body only as a means of communication. Being the communication link between God and His Separated Sons, the Holy Spirit interprets everything you have made in the light of what He is. The ego separated through the body. The Holy Spirit reaches through it to others. You do not perceive your brothers as the Holy Spirit does because you do not interpret their bodies and yours solely as a means of joining their minds and uniting them with yours and mine. This interpretation of the body will change your mind entirely about its value. Of itself it has none.

If you use the body for attack, it is harmful to you. If you use it only to reach the minds of those who believe they are bodies and teach them through the body that this is not so, you will begin to understand the power of the mind that is in both of you. If you use the body for this and only for this, you cannot use it for attack.

In the service of uniting, it becomes a beautiful lesson in communion, which has value until communion is. This is God's way of making unlimited what you have limited. The Holy Spirit does not see the body as you do because He knows the only reality anything can have is the service it can render God on behalf of the function He has given it.

Communication ends separation. Attack promotes it. The body is beautiful or ugly, holy or savage, helpful or harmful, according to the use to which it is put. And in the body of another you will see the use to which you have put yours. If the body becomes for you a means which you give to the Holy Spirit to use on behalf of union of the Sonship, you will not see anything physical except as what it is. Use it for truth, and you will see it truly. misuse it, and you will misunderstand it because you have already done so by misusing it. Interpret anything apart from the Holy Spirit, and you will mistrust it. This will lead you to hatred and attack and loss of peace.

Yet all loss comes only from your own misunderstanding. Loss of any kind is impossible. When you look upon a brother as physical entity, His power and glory are lost to you, and so are yours. You have attacked him, but you must have attacked yourself first. Do not see him this way for your own salvation, which must bring him His. Do not allow him to belittle himself in your mind, but give him freedom from his belief in littleness, and thus escape from yours. As part of you, He is holy. As part of me, you are. To communicate with part of God Himself is to reach beyond the Kingdom to its Creator, through His Voice Which He has established as part of you.

Rejoice, then, that of yourselves you can do nothing. You are not of yourselves. He of Whom you are has willed your power and glory for you, with which you can perfectly accomplish His holy Will for you, when you so will it yourself. He has not withdrawn His gifts from you, but you have withdrawn them from Him. Let no Son of God remain hidden for His Name's sake, because His Name is yours.

Remember that the Bible says, "The Word (or thought) was made flesh." Strictly speaking this is impossible, since it seems to involve the translation of one order of reality into another. Different orders of reality merely appear to exist, just as different orders of miracles do. Thought cannot be made into flesh except by belief, since thought is not physical. Yet thought is communication, for which the body can be used.

This is the only natural use to which it can be put. To use the body unnaturally is to lose sight of the Holy Spirit's purpose, and thus to confuse the goal of His curriculum.

There is nothing so frustrating to a learner as to be placed in a curriculum which he cannot learn. His sense of adequacy suffers, and he must become depressed. Being faced with an impossible learning situation, regardless of why it is impossible, is the most depressing thing in the world. In fact, it is ultimately why the world is depressing. The Holy Spirit's curriculum is never depressing because it is a curriculum of joy. Whenever the reaction to learning is depression, it is only because the goal of the curriculum has been lost sight of.

In the world, not even the body is perceived as whole. Its purpose is seen as fragmented into many functions which bear little or no relationship to each other, so that it appears to be ruled by chaos. Guided by the ego, it is. Guided by the Holy Spirit, it is not. It becomes only a means by which the part of the mind you have separated from your Soul can reach beyond its distortions and return to the Soul. The ego's temple thus becomes the temple of the Holy Spirit, where devotion to Him replaces devotion to the ego. In this sense the body does become a temple to God, because His Voice abides in it by directing the use to which it is put.

Healing is the result of using the body solely for communication. Since this is natural, it heals by making whole, which is also natural. All mind is whole and the belief that part of it is physical, or not mind, is a fragmented (or sick) interpretation. Mind cannot be made physical, but it can be made manifest through the physical if it uses the body to go beyond itself. By reaching out, the mind extends itself. It does not stop at the body, for if it does, it is blocked in its purpose. A mind which has been blocked has allowed itself to be vulnerable to attack because it has turned against itself.

The removal of the blocks, then, is the only way to guarantee help and healing. Help and healing are the normal expressions of a mind which is working through the body, but not in it. If the mind believes the body is its goal, it will distort its perception of the body, and by blocking its own extension beyond it, will induce illness by fostering separation. Perceiving the body as a separate entity cannot but foster illness, because it is not true. A medium of communication will lose its usefulness if it is used for anything else.

To use a medium of communication as a medium of attack is an obvious confusion in purpose. To communicate is to join, and to attack is to separate. How can you do both simultaneously with the same thing, and not suffer?

Perception of the body can be unified only by one purpose. This releases the mind from the temptation to see the body in many lights and gives it over entirely to the One Light in which it can be really understood at all. To confuse a learning device with a curriculum goal is a fundamental confusion. Learning can hardly be arrested at its own aids with hope of understanding either the aids or the learning's real purpose. Learning must lead beyond the body to the re-establishment of the power of the mind in it. This can be accomplished only if the mind extends to other minds and does not arrest itself in its extension.

The arrest of the mind's extension is the cause of all illness because only extension is the mind's function. The opposite of joy is depression. When your learning promotes depression instead of joy, you cannot be listening to God's joyous Teacher, and you must be learning amiss. To see a body as anything except a means of pure extension is to limit your mind and hurt yourself. Health is therefore nothing more than united purpose. If the body is brought under the purpose of the mind, the body becomes whole because the mind's purpose is one. Attack can only be an assumed purpose of the body, because apart from the mind the body has no purpose at all.

You are not limited by the body, and thought cannot be made flesh. Yet mind can be manifested through the body if it goes beyond it and does not interpret it as limitation. Whenever you see another as limited to or by the body, you are imposing this limit on yourself. Are you willing to accept this, when your whole purpose for learning should be to escape from limitations? To conceive of the body as a means of attack of any kind and to entertain even the possibility that joy could possibly result, is a clear-cut indication of a poor learner. He has accepted a learning goal in obvious contradiction to the unified purpose of the curriculum and is interfering with his ability to accept its purpose as his own.

Joy is unified purpose, and unified purpose is only God's. When yours is unified, it is His. Interfere with His purpose and you need salvation. You have condemned yourself, but condemnation is not of God. Therefore, it is not true. No more are any of the result of your condemnation. When you see a brother as a body, you are condemning him because you have condemned yourself. Yet if all condemnation is unreal and it must be unreal since it is a form of attack then it can have no results.

Do not allow yourselves to suffer from the results of what is not true. Free your minds from the belief that this is possible. In its complete impossibility, and your full awareness of its complete impossibility, lie your only hope for release.

But what other hope would you want? Freedom from illusions lies only in not believing them. There is no attack, but there is unlimited communication, and therefore unlimited power and wholeness. The power of wholeness is extension. Do not arrest your thought in this world and you will open your mind to creation in God.

Attitudes toward the body are attitudes toward attack. The ego's definitions of everything are childish and always based on what it believes a thing is for. This is because it is incapable of true generalizations and equates what it sees with the function it ascribes to it. It does not equate it with what it is. To the ego, the body is to attack with. Equating you with the body, it teaches that you are to attack with because this is what it believes. The body, then, is not the source of its own health. The body's condition lies solely in your interpretation of its function.

The reason why definitions in terms of function are inferior is that they may well be inaccurate. Functions are part of being since they arise from it, but the relationship is not reciprocal. The whole does define the part, but the part does not define the whole. This is as true of knowledge as it is of perception. The reason to know in part is to know entirely is because of the fundamental difference between knowledge and perception. In perception the whole is built up of parts, which can separate and reassemble in different constellations. Knowledge never changes, so its constellation is permanent. The only areas in which part-whole relationships have any meaning are those in which change is possible. There is no difference between the whole and the part where change is impossible.

The body exists in a world which seems to contain two voices which are fighting for its possession. In this perceived constellation, the body is regarded as capable of shifting its control from one to the other, making the concept of both health and sickness possible. The ego makes a fundamental confusion between means and ends as it always does. Regarding the body as an end, the ego has no real use for it because it is not an end. You must have noticed an outstanding characteristic of every end that the ego has accepted as its own. When you have achieved it, it has not satisfied you. This is why the ego is forced to shift from one end to another without ceasing, so that you will continue to hope that it can yet offer you something.

It has been particularly difficult to overcome the ego's belief in the body as an end because this is synonymous with the belief in attack as an end. The ego has a real investment in sickness.

If you are sick, how can you object to the ego's firm belief that you are not invulnerable? This is a particularly appealing argument from the ego's point of view because it obscures the obvious attack which underlies the sickness. If you accepted this and also decided against attack, you could not give this false witness to the ego's stand.

It is hard to perceive sickness as a false witness, because you do not realize that it is entirely out of keeping with what you want. This witness, then, appears to be innocent and trustworthy because you have not seriously cross-examined him. If you did, you would not consider sickness such a strong witness on behalf of the ego's views. A more honest statement would be as follows: Those who want the ego are predisposed to defend it. Therefore, their choice of witnesses should be suspect from the beginning. The ego does not call upon witnesses who would disagree with its case, nor does the Holy Spirit. We have said that judgement is the function of the Holy Spirit, and one which He is perfectly equipped to fulfil. The ego, as a judge, gives anything but an impartial judgement. When the ego calls on a witness, it has already made the witness an ally.

It is still true that the body has no function of itself because it is not an end. The ego, however, establishes it as an end because, as such, it will lose its true function. This is the purpose of everything the ego does. Its sole aim is to lose sight of the function of everything. A sick body does not make any sense. It could not make sense because sickness is not what the body is for. Sickness is meaningful only if the two basic premises on which the ego's interpretation of the body rests are true. Specifically, these are that the body is for attack, and that you are a body. Without these premises, sickness is completely inconceivable.

Sickness is a way of demonstrating that you can be hurt. It is a witness to your frailty, your vulnerability and your extreme need to depend on external guidance. The ego uses this as its best argument for your need for its guidance. It dictates endless prescriptions for avoiding catastrophic outcomes. The Holy Spirit, perfectly aware of the same data, does not bother to analyse them at all. If the data are meaningless there is no point in considering them. The function of truth is to collect data which are true. There is no point in trying to make sense out of meaningless data. Any way you handle them results in nothing. The more complicated the results become, the harder it may be to recognize their nothingness, but it is not necessary to examine all possible outcomes to which premises give rise to judge them truly.

A learning device is not a teacher. It cannot tell you how you feel. You do not know how you feel because you have accepting the ego's confusion, and you think that a learning device can tell you how you feel. Sickness is merely another example of your insistence on asking the guidance of a teacher who does not know the answer. The ego is incapable of knowing how you feel. When we said that the ego does not know anything, we said the one thing about the ego that is wholly true. But there is a corollary; if knowledge is being and the ego has no knowledge, then the ego has no being.

You might well ask how the voice of something which does not exist can be so insistent. Have you seriously considered the distorting power of something you want, even if it is not true? You have had many instances of how what you want can distort what you see and hear. No-one can doubt the ego's skill in building up false cases. Nor can anyone doubt your willingness to listen until you will not to tolerate anything except truth. When you lay the ego aside, it will be gone. The Holy Spirit's Voice is as loud as your willingness to listen. It cannot be louder without violating your will, which the Holy Spirit seeks to free, but never to command.

The Holy Spirit teaches you to use your body only to reach your brothers, so He can teach His message through you. This will heal them and therefore heal you. Everything used in accordance with its function as the Holy Spirit sees it cannot be sick. Everything used otherwise is. Do not allow the body to be a mirror of a split mind. Do not let it be an image of your own perception of littleness. Do not let it reflect your will to attack. Health is the natural state of anything whose interpretation is left to the Holy Spirit, Who perceives no attack on anything. Health is the result of relinquishing all attempts to use the body lovelessly. Health is the beginning of the proper perspective on life under the guidance of the one Teacher Who knows what life is, being the Voice for Life Itself.

We once said that the Holy Spirit is the answer. He is the Answer to everything, because He knows what the answer to everything is. The ego does not know what a real question is, although it asks an endless number. Yet you can learn this as you learn to question the value of the ego, and thus establish your ability to evaluate its questions. When the ego tempts you to sickness, do not ask the Holy Spirit to heal the body, for this would merely be to accept the ego's belief that the body is the proper aim for healing. Ask, rather, that the Holy Spirit teach you the right perception of the body, for perception alone can be distorted. Only perception can be sick, because only perception can be wrong.

Wrong perception is distorted willing, which wants things to be as they are not. The reality of everything is totally harmless, because total harmlessness is the condition of its reality. It is also the condition of your awareness of its reality. You do not have to seek reality. It will seek you and find you, when you meet its conditions. Its conditions are part of what it is. And this part only is up to you. The rest is of Itself. You need do so little, because it is so powerful that your little part will bring the whole to you. Accept, then, your little part and let the whole be yours.

Wholeness heals because it is of the mind. All forms of sickness, even unto death, are physical expressions of the fear of awakening. They are attempts to reinforce unconciousness out of fear of consciousness. This is a pathetic way of trying not to know by rendering the faculties for knowing ineffectual. "rest in peace" is a blessing for the living, not the dead, because rest comes from waking, not from sleeping. Sleep is withdrawing; waking is joining. Dreams are illusion of joining, taking on the ego's distortions about what joining means if you are sleeping under its guidance. Yet the Holy Spirit, too, has use for sleep, and can use dreams on behalf of waking, if you will let Him.

How you wake is the sign of how you have used sleep. To whom did you give it? Under which teacher did you place it? Whenever you wake dispiritedly, it was not of the Holy Spirit. Only when you awaken joyously have you utilized sleep according to the Holy Spirit's purpose. You can indeed be "drugged by sleep," but this is always because you have misused it on behalf of sickness. Sleep is no more a form of death than death is a form of unconsciousness.

Unconsciousness is impossible. You can rest in peace only because you are awake. Healing is release from the fear of waking and the substitution of the will to wake. The will to wake is the will to love, since all healing involves replacing fear with love. The Holy Spirit cannot distinguish among degrees of error, for if He taught that one form of sickness is more serious than another, He would be teaching that one error can be more real than another. His function is to distinguish only between the false and the true, replacing the false with the true.

The ego, which always weakens the will, wants to separate the body from the mind. This is an attempt to destroy it, yet the ego actually believes that it is protecting it. This is because the ego believes that mind is dangerous, and that to make mindless is to heal. But to make mindless is impossible, since it would mean to make nothing out of what God created. The ego despise weakness, even though it makes every effort to induce it. The ego wants only what it hates. To the ego this is perfectly sensible. Believing in the power of attack, the ego wants attack.

You have surely begun to realize that this is a very practical course, which means exactly what it says. So, does the Bible, if it is properly understood. There has been a marked tendency on the part of many of the Bible's followers, and also its translators, to be entirely literal about fear and its effects, but not about love and its results. Thus, "hellfire" means "burning," but raising the dead becomes allegorical. Actually, it is particular the references to the outcomes of love which should be taken literally because the Bible is about love, being about God.

The Bible enjoins you to be perfect, to heal all errors, to take no thought of the body as separate, and to accomplish all things in my name. This is not my name alone, for ours is a shared identification. The Name of God's Son is one, and you are enjoined to do the works of love because we share this oneness. Our minds are whole because they are one. If you are sick you are withdrawing from me. Yet you cannot withdraw from me alone. You can only withdraw from yourself and me.

I would not ask you to do the things you cannot do, and it is impossible that I could do things you cannot do. Given this, and given this quite literally, there can be nothing which prevents you from doing exactly what I ask, and everything which argues for your doing it. I give you no limits because God lays none upon you. When you limit yourself, we are not of one mind, and that is sickness. Yet sickness is not of the body, but of the mind. All forms of dysfunction are merely signs that the mind has split and does not accept a unified purpose.

The unification of purpose, then, is the Holy Spirit's only way of healing. This is because it is the only level at which healing means anything. The re-establishing of meaning in a chaotic thought system is the only way to heal it. We have said that your task is only to meet the conditions for meaning, since meaning itself is of God. Yet your return to meaning is essential to His because your meaning is part of His. Your healing, then, is part of His health since it is part of His Wholeness. He cannot lose this, but you cannot know it. Yet it is still His Will for you, and His Will must stand forever and in all things.

Fear of the Will of God is one of the strangest beliefs that the human mind has ever made. This could not possibly have occurred unless the mind were already profoundly split, making it possible for the mind to be afraid of what it really is.

It is apparent that reality cannot "threaten" anything except illusions, since reality can only uphold truth. The very fact that the Will of God, which is what you are, is perceived as fearful to you demonstrates that you are afraid of what you are. It is not, then, the Will of God of which you are afraid, but yours. Your will is not the ego's and that is why the ego is against you. What seems to be the fear of God is really only the fear of your own reality.

It is impossible to learn anything consistently in a state of panic. If the purpose of this course is to help you learn what you are and if you have already decided that what you are is fearful, then it must follow that you will not learn this course. Yet you might remember that the reason for the course is that you do not know who you are. If you do not know your reality, how would you know whether it is fearful or not?

The association of truth and fear, which would be highly artificial at most, is particularly inappropriate in the minds of those who do not know what truth is. All that this kind of association means is that you are arbitrarily endowing something quite beyond your awareness with something you do not want. It is evident, then, that you are judging something of which you are totally unaware. You have set this strange situation up so that it is completely impossible to escape from it without a Guide Who does know what your reality is. The purpose of this Guide is merely to remind you of what you want. He is not attempting to force an alien will upon you. He is merely making every possible effort, within the limits you impose on Him, to re-establish your own will in your consciousness.

You have imprisoned your will in your unconscious, where it remains available but cannot help you. When we said that the Holy Spirit's function is to sort out the true from the false in your unconscious, we meant that He has the power to look into what you have hidden and perceive the Will of God there. His perception of this Will can make it real to you because He is in your mind, and therefore He is your reality. If, then, His perception of your mind brings its reality to you, He is teaching you what you are.

The only source of fear in this whole process can only be what you think you lose. Yet it is only what the Holy Spirit sees that you can possibly have. We have emphasized many times that the Holy Spirit will never call upon you to sacrifice anything. But if you ask the sacrifice of reality of yourself, the Holy Spirit must remind you that this is not God's Will because it is not yours. There is no difference between your will and God's. If you did not have split minds, you would recognize that willing is salvation because it is communication. It is impossible to communicate in alien tongues.

You and your Creator can communicate through creation because that, and only that, is your joint Will.

Divided wills do not communicate because they speak for different things to the same mind. This loses the ability to communicate simply because confused communication does not mean anything. A message cannot be said to be communicated unless it makes sense. How sensible can your messages be when you ask for what you do not want? Yet as long as you are afraid of your will, this is precisely what you will ask for. You may insist that the Holy Spirit does not answer you, but it might be wiser to consider the kind of asker you are.

You do not ask only for what you want. This is solely because you are afraid you might receive it, and you would. That is really why you persist in asking the teacher who could not possibly teach you your will. Of him you can never learn it, and this gives you the illusion of safety. Yet you cannot be safe from truth, but only in it. Reality is the only safety. Your will is your salvation because it is the same as God's. The separation is nothing more than the belief that it is different.

No mind can believe that its will is stronger than God's. If, then, a mind believes that its will is different from His, it can only decide either that there is no God or that God's will is fearful. The former accounts for the atheist and the latter for the martyr. Martyrdom takes many forms, the category including all doctrines which hold that God demands sacrifices of any kind. Either basic type of insane decision will induce panic because the atheist believes he is alone and the martyr believes that God is crucifying him. Both really fear abandonment and retaliation, but the atheist is more reactive against abandonment and the martyr against retaliation.

The atheist maintains that God has left him, but he does not care. He will, however, become very fearful and hence very angry, If anyone suggests that God has not left him. The martyr, on the other hand, is more aware of guilt, and believing that punishment is inevitable, attempts to teach himself to like it. The truth is, very simply, that no-one wants either abandonment or retaliation. Many people seek both, but it is still true that they do not want them. Can you ask the Holy Spirit for "gifts" such as these, and actually expect to receive them? He cannot make you want something you do not want. When you ask the Universal Giver for what you do not want, you are asking for what cannot be given because it was never created. It was never created because it was never your will for you.

Ultimately everyone must remember the Will of God, because ultimately everyone must recognize himself. This recognition is the recognition that his will and God's are one. In the presence of truth there are no unbelievers and no sacrifices. In the security of reality, fear is totally meaningless. To deny what is can only seem to be fearful. Fear cannot be real without a cause, and God is the only Cause. God is Love, and you do want Him. This is your will. Ask for this and you will be answered because you will be asking only for what belongs to you.

When you ask the Holy Spirit for what would hurt you, He cannot answer because nothing can hurt you, and so you are asking for nothing. Any desire which stems from the ego is a desire for nothing, and to ask for it is not a request. It is merely a denial in the from of a request. The Holy Spirit is not concerned with form at all, being aware only of meaning. The ego cannot ask the Holy Spirit for anything because there is complete communication failure between them. Yet you can ask for everything of the Holy Spirit because your requests are real, being of your will. Would the Holy Spirit deny the Will of God? And could He fail to recognize it in His Sons?

The energy which you withdraw from creation you expend on fear. This is not because your energy is limited, but because you have limited it. You do not recognize the enormous waste of energy which you expend in denying truth. What would you say of someone who persisted in attempting the impossible, believing that to achieve it is success? The belief that you must have the impossible in order to be happy is totally at variance with the principle of creation. God could not will that happiness depends on what you could never have.

The fact that God is Love does not require belief, but it does require acceptance. It is indeed possible for you to deny facts, although it is impossible for you to change them. If you hold your hands over your eyes, you will not see because you are interfering with the laws of seeing. If you deny love, you will not know it because your cooperation is the law of its being. You cannot change laws you did not make, and the laws of happiness were created for you, not by you.

Attempts of any kind to deny what is are fearful, and if they are strong, they will induce panic. Willing against reality, though impossible, can be made into a very persistent goal even though you do not want it. But consider the result of this strange decision. You are devoting your mind to what you do not want. How real can this devotion be? If you do not want it, it was never created. If it was never created, it is nothing. Can you really devote yourself to nothing?

God in His devotion to you created you devoted to everything. and gave you what you are devoted to. Otherwise, you would not have been created perfect. Reality is everything and therefore you have everything because you are real. You cannot make the unreal because the absence of reality is fearful, and fear cannot be created. As long as you believe that fear is possible, you will not create. Opposing orders of reality make reality meaningless and reality is meaning.

Remember, then, that God's Will is already possible, and nothing else will ever be. This is the simple acceptance of reality because only this is real. You cannot distort reality and know what it is. And if you do distort reality, you will experience anxiety, depression and ultimately panic because you are trying to make yourself unreal. When you feel these things, do not try to look beyond yourself for truth, for truth can only be within you. Say, therefore:

> "Christ is in me and where He is God must be, for Christ is part of Him."

Everyone who has ever tried to use prayer to request something has experienced what appears to be failure. This is not only true in connection with specific things which might be harmful, but also in connection with requests which are strictly in line with this course. The latter, in particular, might be incorrectly interpreted as "proof" that the course does not mean what it says. You must remember, however, that the course does state, and repeatedly, that its purpose is the escape from fear.

Let us suppose, then, that what you request of the Holy Spirit is what you really want, but you are still afraid of it. Should this be the case, your attainment of it would no longer be what you want, even if it is. This accounts for why certain specific forms of healing are not achieved, even though the state of healing is. It frequently happens that an individual asks for physical healing because he is fearful of bodily harm. At the same time, however, if he were healed physically, the threat to his thought system would be considerably more fearful to him than its physical expression. In this case he is not really asking for release from fear, but for the removal of a symptom which he has selected. This request is, therefore, not for healing at all.

The Bible emphasizes that all prayers are answered, and this must be true if no effort is wasted. The very fact that one has asked the Holy Spirit for anything will ensure a response. Yet it is equally certain that no response given by the Holy Spirit will ever be one which would increase fear. It is possible that His answer will not be heard at all. It is impossible, however, that it will be lost. There are many answers which you have already received but have not yet heard. I assure you that they are waiting for you. It is indeed true that no effort is wasted.

If you would know your prayers are answered, never doubt a Son of God. Do not question him and do not confound him, for your faith in him is your faith in yourself. If you would know God and His Answer, believe in me whose faith in you cannot be shaken. Can you ask of the Holy Spirit truly, and doubt your brother? Believe his words are true because of the truth which is in him. You will unite with the truth in him, and his words will be true. As you hear Him you will hear me. Listening to truth is the only way you can hear it now and finally know it.

The message your brother gives you is up to you. What does he say to you? What would you have him say? Your decision about him determines the message you receive. Remember that the Holy Spirit is in him, and His Voice speaks to you through him. What can so holy a brother tell you except truth? But are you listening to it? Your brother may not know who he is, but there is a light in his mind which does know. This light can shine into yours, making His words true and making you able to hear them. His words are the Holy Spirit's answer to you. Is your faith in him strong enough to let you hear?

Salvation is of your brother. The Holy Spirit extends from your mind to his and answers you. You cannot hear the Voice for God in yourself alone because you are not alone. And His answer is only for what you are. You will not know the trust I have in you unless you extend it. You will not trust the guidance of the Holy Spirit or believe that it is for you unless you hear it in others. It must be for your brother because it is for you. Would God have created a Voice for you alone? Could you hear His answer except as He answers all of God's Sons? Hear of your brother what you would have me hear of you, for you would not want me to be deceived.

I love you for the truth in you, as God does. Your deceptions may deceive you, but they cannot deceive me. Knowing what you are, I cannot doubt you. I hear only the Holy Spirit in you, Who speaks to me through you.

If you would hear me, hear my brothers in whom God's Voice speaks. The answer to all prayers lies in them. You will be answered as you hear the answer in everyone. Do not listen to anything else or you will not hear truth.

Believe in your brothers because I believe in you, and you will learn that my belief in you is justified. Believe in me by believing in them, for the sake of what God gave them. They will answer you, if you learn to ask truth of them. Do not ask for blessings without blessing them, for only in this way can you learn how blessed you are. By following this way, you are looking for the truth in you. This is not going beyond yourself but toward yourself. Hear only God's Answer in His Sons, and you are answered.

To disbelieve is to side against, or to attack. To believe is to accept, and to side with. To believe is not to be credulous, but to accept and appreciate. What you do not believe you do not appreciate, and you cannot be grateful for what you do not value. There is a price you will pay for judgement because judgement is the setting of a price. And as you set it you will pay it.

If paying is equated with getting, you will set the price low but demand a high return. You will have forgotten, however, that your return is in proportion to your judgement of worth. If paying is associated with giving, it cannot be perceived as loss, and the reciprocal relationship of giving and receiving will be recognized. The price will then be set high because of the value of the return. The price for getting is to lose sight of value, making it inevitable that you will not value what you receive. Valuing it little, you will not appreciate it and will not want it.

Never forget, then, that you have set the value on what you receive, and have priced it by what you give. To believe that it is possible to get much for little is to believe that you can bargain with God. God's laws are always fair and perfectly consistent. By giving you receive. But to receive is to accept, not to get. It is impossible not to have, but it is possible not to know you have. The recognition of having is the willingness for giving and only by this willingness can you recognize what you have. What you give is therefore the value you put on what you have, being the exact measure of the value you put upon it. And this, in turn, is the measure of how much you want it.

You can ask of the Holy Spirit, then, only by giving to Him, and you can give to Him only where you see Him. If you see Him in everyone, consider how much you will be asking of Him, and how much you will receive. He will deny you nothing because you have denied Him nothing, and so you can share everything. This is the way, and the only way, to have His answer because His answer is all you can ask for and want. Say, then, to everyone,

> "Because I will to know myself, I see you as God's Son and my brother."

The alertness of the ego to the errors which other egos make is not the kind of vigilance the Holy Spirit would have you maintain. Egos are critical in terms of the kind of "sense" they stand for. They understand this kind of sense, because it is sensible to them. To the Holy Spirit, it makes no sense at all. To the ego, it is kind and right and good to point out errors and "correct" them. This makes perfect sense to the ego, which is totally unaware of what errors are and what correction is.

Errors are of the ego, and correction of errors of any kind lies solely in the relinquishment of the ego. When you correct a brother, you are telling him that he is wrong. He may be making no sense at the time, and it is certain that, if he is speaking from the ego, he will be making no sense. But your task is still to tell him he is right. You do not tell him this verbally, if he is speaking foolishly, because he needs correction at another level, since his error is at another level. he is still right, because he is a Son of God. His ego is always wrong, no matter what it says or does.

If you point out the errors of your brother's ego, you must be seeing through yours, because the Holy Spirit does not perceive his errors. This must be true if there is no communication at all between the ego and the Holy Spirit. The ego makes no sense, and the Holy Spirit does not attempt to understand anything that arises from it. Since He does not understand it, He does not judge it, knowing that nothing it engenders means anything.

When you react at all to errors, you are not listening to the Holy Spirit. He has merely disregarded them, and if you attend to them, you are not hearing Him. If you do not hear Him, you are listening to your ego, and making as little sense as the brother whose errors you perceive. This cannot be correction. Yet it is more than merely lack of correction for him. It is the giving up of correction in yourself.

When a brother behaves insanely, you can heal him only by perceiving the sanity in him. If you perceive his errors and accept them, you are accepting yours. If you want to give yours over to the Holy Spirit, you must do this with his.

Unless this becomes the one way in which you handle all errors, you cannot understand how all errors are undone. How is this different from telling you that what you teach you learn? Your brother is as right as you are, and if you think he is wrong you are condemning yourself.

You cannot correct yourself. Is it possible, then, for you to correct another? Yet you can see him truly because it is possible for you to see yourself truly. It is not up to you to change him, but merely to accept him as he is. His errors do not come from the truth that is in him, and only this truth is yours. His errors cannot change this and can have no effect at all on the truth in you. To perceive errors in anyone, and to react to them as if they were real, is to make them real to you. You will not escape paying the price for this, not because you are being punished for it, but because you are following the wrong guide, and will lose your way.

Your brother's errors are not of him, any more than yours are of you. Accept his errors as real, and you have attacked yourself. If you would find your way and keep it see only truth beside you, for you walk together. The Holy Spirit in you forgives all things in you and in your brother. His errors are forgiven with yours. Atonement is no more separate than love. Atonement cannot be separate because it comes from love. Any attempt you make to correct a brother means that you believe correction by you is possible, and this can only be the arrogance of the ego. Correction is of God, Who does not know of arrogance. The Holy Spirit forgives everything because God created everything.

Do not undertake His function or you will forget yours. Accept only the function of healing in time because that is what time is for. God gave you the function to create in eternity. You do not need to learn this, but you do need to learn to want this, and for this all learning was made. This is the Holy Spirit's good use of an ability which you do not need, but which you have made. Give it to Him! You do not know how to use it. He will teach you how to see yourself without condemnation by learning how to look on everything without it. Condemnation will then not be real to you and all your errors will be forgiven.

Atonement is for all because it is the way to undo the belief that anything is for you alone. To forgive is to overlook. Look, then, beyond error, and do not let your perception rest upon it, for you will believe what your perception holds. Accept as true only what your brother is, if you would know yourself. Perceive what he is not, and you cannot know what you are because you see him falsely. Remember always that your identity is shared, and that its sharing is its reality.

You have a part to play in the Atonement, but the plan of the Atonement is beyond you. You do not know how to overlook errors, or you would not make them. It would merely be further error to think either that you do not make them, or that you can correct them without a Guide to correction. And if you do not follow this Guide, your errors will not be corrected. The plan is not yours because of your limited ideas of what you are. This limitation is where all errors arise. The way to undo them, therefore, is not of you but for you.

The Atonement is a lesson in sharing, which is given you because you have forgotten how to do it. The Holy Spirit merely reminds you of what is your natural ability. By reinterpreting the ability to attack, which you did make, into the ability to share, He translates what you have made into what God created. If you would accomplish this through Him, you cannot look on your abilities through the eyes of the ego, or you will judge them as it does. All their harmfulness lies in its judgement. All their helpfulness lies in the judgement of the Holy Spirit.

The ego, too, has a plan of forgiveness because you are asking for one, though not of the right teacher. The ego's plan, of course, makes no sense and will not work. By following it you will merely place yourself in an impossible situation, to which the ego always leads you. The ego's plan is to have you see error clearly first, and then overlook it. Yet how can you overlook what you have made real? By seeing it clearly you have made it real and cannot overlook it.

This is where the ego is forced to appeal to "mysteries," and begins to insist that you must accept the meaningless to save yourself. Many have tried to do this in my name, forgetting that my words make perfect sense because they come from God. They are as sensible now as they ever were because they speak of ideas which are eternal. Forgiveness that is learned of me does not use fear to undo fear. Nor does it make real the unreal and then destroy it.

Forgiveness through the Holy Spirit lies simply in looking beyond error from the beginning, and thus keeping it unreal for you. Do not let any belief in its realness enter your minds at all, or you will also believe that you must undo what you have made in order to be forgiven. What has no effect does not exist, and to the Holy Spirit the effects of error are totally non-existent. By steadily and consistently cancelling out all its effects, everywhere and in all respects, He teaches that the ego does not exist, and proves it. Follow His teaching in forgiveness, then, because forgiveness is His function, and He knows how to fulfil it perfectly. That is what we meant when we once said that miracles are natural, and when they do not occur something has gone wrong.

Miracles are merely the sign of your willingness to follow the Holy Spirit's plan of salvation, in recognition of the fact that you do not know what it is. His work is not your function, and unless you accept this, you cannot learn what your function is. The confusion of functions is so typical of the ego that you should be quite familiar with it by now. The ego believes that all functions belong to it, even though it has no idea what they are. This is more than mere confusion. It is a particularly dangerous combination of grandiosity and confusion which makes it likely that the ego will attack anyone and anything for no reason at all. This is exactly what the ego does. It is totally unpredictable in its responses because it has no idea of what it perceives.

If one has no idea of what is happening, how appropriately can you expect him to react? You might still ask yourself, regardless of how you can account for the reactions, whether they place the ego in a very sound position as the guide for yours. It seems absurd to have to emphasize repeatedly that the ego's qualifications as a guide are singularly unfortunate, and that it is a remarkably poor choice as a teacher of salvation. Yet this question, ridiculous as it seems, is really the crucial issue in the whole separation fantasy. Anyone who elects a totally insane guide must be totally insane himself.

It is not true that you do not know the guide is insane. You know it because I know it, and you have judged it by the same standard as I have. The ego literally lives on borrowed time, and its days are numbered. Do not fear the Last Judgement, but welcome it and do not wait, for the ego's time is borrowed from your eternity. This is the Second Coming, which was made for you as the First was created. The Second Coming is merely the return of sense. Can this possibly be fearful?

What can be fearful but fantasy, and no-one turns to fantasy unless he despairs of finding satisfaction in reality. Yet it is certain that he will never find satisfaction in fantasy, so that his only hope is to change his mind about reality. Only if the decision that reality is fearful is wrong can God be right. And I assure you that God is right. Be glad, then, that you have been wrong, but this was only because you did not know who you were. Had you remembered, you could no more have been wrong than God can. The impossible can happen only in fantasy. When you search for reality in fantasies you will not find it. The symbols of fantasy are of the ego, and of these you will find many. But do not look for meaning in them. They have no more meaning than the fantasies into which they are woven.

Fairy tales can be pleasant or fearful, pretty or ugly, but no-one calls them true. Children may believe them, and so, for a while, the tales are true for them. Yet when reality dawns the fantasies are gone. Reality has not gone in the meanwhile. The Second Coming is the awareness of reality, not its return. Behold, my children, reality is here. It belongs to you and me and God and is perfectly satisfying to all of us. Only this awareness heals, because it is the awareness of truth. The ego's plan for forgiveness is far more widely used than God's. This is because it is undertaken by unhealed healers and is therefore of the ego. Let us consider the unhealed healer more carefully now. By definition, he is trying to give what he has not received. If he is a theologian, he may begin with the premise, "I am a miserable sinner and so are you." If he is a psychotherapist, he is more likely to start with the equally incredible idea that He really believes in attack and so does the patient, but it does not matter in either case.

We have repeatedly stated that beliefs of the ego cannot be shared, and this is why they are unreal. How, then, can "uncovering" them make them real? Every healer who searches fantasies for truth must be unhealed because he does not know where to look for truth, and therefore does not have the answer to the problem of healing. There is an advantage to bringing nightmares into awareness, but only to teach that they are not real, and that anything they contain is meaningless. The unhealed healer cannot do this because he does not believe it.

All unhealed healers follow the ego's plan for forgiveness in one form or another. If they are theologians, they are likely to condemn themselves, teach condemnation, and advocate a very fearful solution. Projecting condemnation onto God, they make Him appear retaliative and fear His retribution.

What they have done is merely to identify with the ego, and by perceiving clearly what it does, condemn themselves because of this profound confusion. It is understandable that there has been a revolt against this concept, but to revolt against it is still to believe in it. The form of the revolt, then, is different, but not the content.

The newer forms of the ego's plan are as unhelpful as the older ones, because form does not matter to the Holy Spirit, and therefore does not matter at all. According to the newer forms of the ego's plan, the therapist interprets the ego's symbols in the nightmare, and then uses them to prove that the nightmare is real. Having made it real, he then attempts to dispel its effects by depreciating the importance of the dreamer. This would be a healing approach if the dreamer were properly identified as unreal. Yet if the dreamer is equated with the mind, the mind's corrective power through the Holy Spirit is denied.

It is noteworthy that this is a contradiction even in the ego's terms, and one which it usually does note, even in its confusion. If the way to counteract fear is to reduce the importance of the fearer, how can this build ego strength? These perfectly self-evident inconsistencies account for why, except in certain stylized verbal accounts, no-one can explain what happens in psychotherapy. Nothing real does. Nothing real has happened to the unhealed healer and he learns from his own teaching.

Because His ego is involved, it always attempts to gain some support from the situation. Seeking to get something for himself the unhealed healer does not know how to give, and consequently cannot share. He cannot correct because he is not working correctively. He believes that it is up to him to teach the patient what is real, but he does not know it himself. What, then, should happen? When God said, "Let there be light" there was light. Can you find light by analysing darkness as the psychotherapist does, or like the theologian by acknowledging darkness in yourself and looking for a distant light to remove it while emphasizing the distance?

Healing is not mysterious. Nothing will occur unless you understand it since light is understanding. A "miserable sinner" cannot be healed without magic, nor can an "unimportant mind" esteem itself without magic. Both forms of the ego's approach, then, must arrive at an impasse, the characteristic "impossible situation' to which the ego always leads. It can be helpful to point out to a patient where he is heading, but the point is lost unless he can change his direction. The therapist cannot do this for him, but he also cannot do this for himself.

The only meaningful contribution the therapist can make is to present an example of one whose direction has been changed for him, and who no longer believes in nightmares of any kind. The light in His mind will therefore answer the questioner, who must decide with God that there is light because he sees it. And by His acknowledgment the therapist knows it is there. That is how perception ultimately is translated into knowledge. The miracle worker begins by perceiving light and translates His perception into sureness by continually extending it and accepting its acknowledgment. Its effects assure him it is there.

The therapist does not heal; he lets healing be. He can point to darkness, but he cannot bring light of himself, for light is not of him. Yet, being for him, it must also be for his patient. The Holy Spirit is the only Therapist. He makes healing perfectly clear in any situation in which he is the Guide. The human therapist can only let Him fulfil His function. He needs no help for this. He will tell you exactly what to do to help anyone He sends to you for help, and will speak to him through you, if you do not interfere. Remember that you are choosing a guide for helping, and the wrong choice will not help. But remember also that the right one will. Trust Him, for help is His function and He is of God.

As you awaken other minds to the Holy Spirit through Him, and not yourself, you will understand that you are not obeying the laws of this world, but that the laws you are obeying work. "The good is what works" is a sound though insufficient statement. Only the good can work. Nothing else works at all. This course is a guide to behaviour. Being a very direct and very simple learning situation, it provides the Guide Who tells you what to do. If you do it, you will see that it works. Its results are more convincing than its words. They will convince you that the words are true. By following the right Guide, you will learn the simplest of all lessons:

"By their fruits ye shall know them,
and they shall know themselves"

How can you become increasingly aware of the Holy Spirit in you except by His effects? You cannot see Him with your eyes, nor hear Him with your ears. How, then, can you perceive Him at all? If you inspire joy, and others react to you with joy, even though you are not experiencing joy yourself, there must be something in you that is capable of producing it. If it is in you and can produce joy, and if you see that it does produce joy in others, you must be dissociating it in yourself.

It seems to you that the Holy Spirit does not produce joy consistently in you only because you do not consistently arouse joy in others. Their reactions to you are your evaluations of His consistency. When you are inconsistent you will not always give rise to joy, and so you will not always recognise His consistency. What you offer to your brother you offer to Him, because He cannot go beyond your offering in His giving. This is not because He limits His giving, but simply because you have limited your receiving. The will to receive is the will to accept.

If your brothers are part of you, will you accept them? Only they can teach you what you are, and your learning is the result of what you taught them. What you call upon in them you call upon in yourself. And as you call upon it in them it becomes real to you. God has but one Son, knowing them all as one. Only God Himself is more than they, but they are not less than He is. Would you know what this means? If what you do to my brother you do to me, and if you do everything for yourself because we are part of you, everything we do belongs to you as well. Every Soul God created is part of you and shares His glory with you. His Glory belongs to Him, but it is equally yours. You cannot, then, be less glorious than He is.

God is more than you only because He created you, but not even this would He keep from you. Therefore, you can create as He did, and your dissociation will not alter this. Neither God's Light nor yours is dimmed because you do not see. Because the Sonship must create as one, you remember creation whenever you recognize part of creation. Each part you remember adds to your wholeness because each part is whole. Wholeness is indivisible, but you cannot learn of your wholeness until you see it everywhere. You can know yourself only as God knows His Son, for knowledge is shared with God. When you awake in Him you will know your magnitude by accepting His limitlessness as yours, but meanwhile you will judge it as you judge your brothers' and will accept it as you accept theirs.

You are not yet awake, but you can learn how to awaken. Very simply the Holy Spirit teaches you to awaken others. As you see them waken you will learn what waking means, and because you have willed to wake them, their gratitude and their appreciation of what you have given them will teach you its value. They will become the witnesses to your reality, as you were created witnesses to God's. Yet when the Sonship comes together and accepts its oneness, it will be known by its creations, who witness to its reality as the Son does to the Father.

Miracles have no place in eternity because they are reparative. Yet while you still need healing, your miracles are the only witnesses to your reality which you can recognise. You cannot perform a miracle for yourself because miracles are a way of giving acceptance and receiving it. In time the giving comes first, though they are simultaneous in eternity, where they cannot be separated. When you have learned that they are the same, the need for time is over.

Eternity is one time, its only dimension being "always". This cannot mean anything to you, however, until you remember God's open arms and finally know His open Mind. Like Him, you are "always" in His Mind and with a mind like His. In your open mind are your creations, in perfect communication born of perfect understanding. Could you but accept one of them, you would not want anything the world has to offer. Everything else would be totally meaningless. God's meaning is incomplete without you, and you are incomplete without your creations. Accept your brother in this world and accept nothing else, for in him you will find your creations because he created them with you. You will never know that you are co-creator with God until you learn that your brother is a co-creator with you.

God's Will is your salvation. Would He not have given you the means to find it? If He wills you to have it, He must have made it possible and very easy to obtain it. Your brothers are everywhere. You do not have to seek far for salvation. Every minute and every second gives you a chance to save yourself. Do not lose these chances, not because they will not return, but because delay of joy is needless. God wills you perfect happiness now. Is it possible that this is not also your will? And is it possible that this is not also the will of your brothers?

Consider, then, that in this joint will you are all united, and in this only. There will be disagreement on anything else, but not on this. This, then, is where peace abides. And you abide in peace when you so decide. Yet you cannot abide in peace unless you accept the Atonement because the Atonement is the way to peace. The reason is very simple, and so obvious that it is often overlooked. That is because the ego is afraid of the obvious, since obviousness is the essential characteristic of reality. Yet you cannot overlook it unless you are not looking.

It is perfectly obvious that, if the Holy Spirit looks with love on all He perceives, He looks with love on you. His evaluation of you is based on His knowledge of what you are and so He evaluates you truly. And this evaluation must be in your mind because He is. The ego is also in your mind because you have accepted it there. Its evaluation of you, however, is the exact opposite of the Holy Spirit's because the ego does not love you. It is unaware of what you are, and wholly mistrustful of everything it perceives because its own perceptions are so shifting. The ego is therefore capable of suspiciousness at best and viciousness at worst. That is its range. It cannot exceed it because of its uncertainty. And it can never go beyond it because it can never be certain.

You, then, have two conflicting evaluations of yourself in your minds and they cannot both be true. You do not yet realize how completely different these evaluations are because you do not understand how lofty the Holy Spirit's perception of you really is. He is not deceived by anything you do because he never forgets what you are. The ego is deceived by everything you do, even when you respond to the Holy Spirit, because at such times its confusion increases. The ego is, therefore, particularly likely to attack you when you react lovingly because it has evaluated you as unloving, and you are going against its judgement.

The ego will begin to attack your motives as soon as they become clearly out of accord with its perception of you. This is when it will shift abruptly from suspiciousness to viciousness, since its uncertainty is increased. Yet it is surely pointless to attack in return. What can this mean except that you are agreeing with the ego's evaluation of what you are? If you are willing to see yourself as unloving, you will not be happy. You are condemning yourself and must therefore regard yourself as inadequate. Would you look to the ego to help you escape from a sense of inadequacy it has produced, and must maintain for its existence? Can you escape from its evaluation of you by using its methods for keeping this picture intact?

You cannot evaluate an insane belief system from within it. Its own range precludes this. You can only go beyond it, look back from a point where sanity exists, and see the contrast. Only by this contrast can insanity be judged as insane. With the grandeur of God in you, you have chosen to be little and to lament your littleness. Within the system which dictated this choice the lament is inevitable. Your littleness is taken for granted there, and you do not ask, "Who granted it?" The question is meaningless within the ego's thought system because it opens the whole thought system to question.

We said before that the ego does not know what a real question is. Lack of knowledge of any kind is always associated with unwillingness to know and produces a total lack of knowledge simply because knowledge is total. Not to question your littleness, therefore, is to deny all knowledge and keep the ego's whole thought system intact. You cannot retain part of a thought system because it can be questioned only at its foundation. And this must be questioned from beyond it because within it its foundation does stand. The Holy Spirit judges against the reality of the ego's thought system merely because He knows its foundation is not true. Therefore, nothing that arises from it means anything. The Holy Spirit judges every belief you hold in terms of where it comes from. If it comes from God, He knows it to be true. If it does not, He knows that it is meaningless. Whenever you question your value, say:

"God Himself is incomplete without me."

Remember this when the ego speaks, and you will not hear it. The truth about you is so lofty that nothing unworthy of God is worthy of you. Choose, then, what you want in these terms, and accept nothing that you would not offer to God as wholly fitting for Him, for you do not want anything else. Return your part of Him, and He will give you all of Himself in exchange for your return of what belongs to Him and renders Him complete.

Grandeur is of God, and only of Him. Therefore, it is in you. Whenever you become aware of it, however dimly, you abandon the ego automatically because, in the presence of the grandeur of God, the meaninglessness of the ego becomes perfectly apparent. Though it does not understand this, the ego believes that its "enemy" has struck and attempts to offer gifts to induce you to return to its "protection." self-inflation of the ego is its alternative to the grandeur of God. Which will you choose?

Grandiosity is always a cover for despair. It is without hope because it is not real. It is an attempt to counteract your littleness, based on the belief that the littleness is real. Without this belief grandiosity is meaningless, and you could not possibly want it. The essence of grandiosity is competitiveness, because it always involves attack. It is a delusional attempt to outdo, but not to undo. We said before that the ego vacillates between suspiciousness and viciousness. It remains suspicious as long as you despair of yourself. It shifts to viciousness whenever you will not tolerate self-abasement and seek relief. Then it offers you the illusion of attack as a solution.

The ego does not know the difference between grandeur and grandiosity because it does not know the difference between miracle impulses and ego-alien beliefs of its own. We once said that the ego is aware of threat, but does not make distinctions between two entirely different kinds of threat to its existence. Its own profound sense of vulnerability renders it incapable of judgement except in terms of attack. When it experiences threat, its only decision is whether to attack now, or to withdraw to attack later. If you accept its offer of grandiosity, it will attack immediately. If you do not, it will wait.

The ego is immobilized in the presence of God's grandeur because His grandeur establishes your freedom. Even the faintest hint of your reality literally drives the ego from your mind because of complete lack of investment in it. Grandeur is totally without illusions, and because it is real, it is compellingly convincing. Yet the conviction of reality will not remain with you unless you do not allow the ego to attack it. The ego will make every effort to recover and mobilize its energies against your release. It will tell you that you are insane and argue that grandeur cannot be a real part of you because of the littleness in which it believes.

Yet your grandeur is not delusional because you did not make it. You have made grandiosity and are afraid of it because it is a form of attack, but your grandeur is of God, Who created it out of His Love. From your grandeur you can only bless because your grandeur is your abundance. By blessing you hold it in your minds, protecting it from illusions and keeping yourself in the Mind of God. Remember always that you cannot be anywhere except in the Mind of God. When you forget this, you will despair, and you will attack.

The ego depends solely on your willingness to tolerate it. If you are willing to look upon your grandeur you cannot despair, and therefore you cannot want the ego. Your grandeur is God's answer to the ego because it is true. Littleness and grandeur cannot co-exist, nor is it possible for them to alternate in your awareness. Littleness and grandiosity can and must alternate in your awareness since both are untrue and are therefore on the same level. Being the level of shift it is experienced as shifting, and extremes are its essential characteristic.

Truth and littleness are denials of each other because grandeur is truth. Truth does not vacillate; it is always true. When grandeur slips away from you, you have replaced it with something you have made. Perhaps it is the belief in littleness; perhaps it is the belief in grandiosity. Yet it must be insane because it is not true. Your grandeur will never deceive you, but your illusions always will.

Illusions are deceptions. You cannot triumph, but you are exalted. And in your exalted state you seek others like you and rejoice with them.

It is easy to distinguish grandeur from grandiosity because love is returned, but pride is not. Pride will not produce miracles, and therefore will deprive you of your true witnesses to your reality. Truth is not obscure nor hidden, but its obviousness to you lies in the joy you bring to its witnesses, who show it to you. They attest to your grandeur, but they cannot attest to pride because pride is not shared. God wants you to behold what He created because it is His joy.

Can your grandeur be arrogant when God Himself witnesses to it? And what can be real that has no witnesses? What good can come of it? And if no good can come of it, the Holy Spirit cannot use it. What He cannot transform to the Will of God does not exist at all. Grandiosity is delusional because it is used to replace your grandeur. Yet what God has created cannot be replaced. God is incomplete without you because His grandeur is total, and you cannot be missing from it.

You are altogether irreplaceable in the Mind of God. No-one else can fill your part of It and while you leave your part of It empty, your eternal place merely waits for your return. God, through His Voice, reminds you of It, and God Himself keeps your extensions safe within it. Yet you do not know them until you return to them. You cannot replace the Kingdom, and you cannot replace yourself. God, who knows your value, would not have it so, and so it is not so. Your value is in God's Mind, and therefore not in yours alone. To accept yourself as God created you cannot be arrogance because it is the denial of arrogance. To accept your littleness is arrogant because it means that you believe your evaluation of yourself is truer than God's.

Yet if truth is indivisible your evaluation of yourself must be God's. You did not establish your value, and it needs no defence. Nothing can attack it or prevail over it. It does not vary. It merely is. Ask the Holy Spirit what it is, and He will tell you, but do not be afraid of His answer, for it comes from God. It is an exalted answer because of its Source, but the Source is true and so is Its answer.

Listen and do not question what you hear, for God does not deceive. He would have you replace the ego's belief in littleness with His own exalted answer to the question of your being, so that you can cease to question it and know it for what it is.

Nothing beyond yourself can make you fearful or loving because nothing is beyond you. Time and eternity are both in your minds and will conflict until you perceive time solely as a means to regain eternity. You cannot do this as long as you believe that anything which happens to you is caused by factors outside yourself. You must learn that time is solely at your disposal, and that nothing in the world can take this responsibility from you. You can violate God's laws in your imagination, but you cannot escape from them. They were established for your protection and are as inviolate as your safety.

God created nothing beside you and nothing beside you exists, for you are part of Him. What except Him can exist? Nothing beyond Him can happen because nothing except Him is real. Your creations add to Him as you do, but nothing is added that is different because everything has always been. What can upset you except the ephemeral, and how can the ephemeral be real if you are God's only creation and He created you eternal? Your holy will establish everything that happens to you. Every response you make to everything you perceive is up to you because your will determines your perception of it.

God does not change His Mind about you, for He is not uncertain of himself. And what He knows can be known because He does not know only for Himself. He created you for Himself, but He gave you the power to create for yourself so you could be like him. That is why your will is holy. Can anything exceed the Love of God? Can anything, then, exceed your will? Nothing can reach you from beyond it because, being in God, you encompass everything. Believe this, and you will realize how much is up to you. When anything threatens your peace of mind, ask yourself, "Has God changed His Mind about me?" then accept His decision, for it is indeed changeless, and refuse to change your mind about yourself. God will never decide against you, or He would be deciding against Himself.

The reason you do not know your creations is simply that you would decide against them as long as your minds are split, and to attack what you have created is impossible. But remember that it is as impossible for God. The law of creation is that you love your creations as yourself because they are part of you. Everything that was created is therefore perfectly safe because the laws of God protect it by His Love. Any part of your mind that does not know this has banished itself from knowledge because it has not met its conditions.

Who could have done this but you? Recognize this gladly, for in this recognition lies the realization that your banishment is not of God, and therefore does not exist. You are at home in God, dreaming of exile, but perfectly capable of awakening to reality. Is it your will to do so? You know, from your own experience, that what you see in dreams you think is real as long as you are asleep. Yet the instant you waken you know that everything that seemed to happen did not happen at all. You do not think this mysterious, even though all the laws of what you awakened to were violated while you slept. Is it not possible that you merely shifted from one dream to another, without really wakening?

Would you bother to reconcile what happened in conflicting dreams, or would you dismiss both together if you discovered that reality is in accord with neither? You do not remember being awake. When you hear the Holy Spirit you merely feel better because loving seems possible to you, but you do not remember yet that it once was so. And it is in this remembering that you will know it can be so again. What is possible has not yet been accomplished. Yet what has once been is so now, if it is eternal. When you remember, you will know what you remember is eternal, and therefore is now.

You will remember everything the instant you desire it wholly, for if to desire wholly is to create, you will have willed away the separation, returning your mind simultaneously to your Creator and your creations. Knowing them you will have no wish to sleep, but only the will to waken and be glad. Dreams will be impossible because you will want only truth and being at last your will it will be yours.

Unless you know something, you cannot dissociate it. Knowledge therefore precedes dissociation, and dissociation is nothing more than a decision to forget. What has been forgotten then appears to be fearful, but only because the dissociation was an attack on truth. You are fearful because you have forgotten. And you have replaced your knowledge by an awareness of dreams because you are afraid of your dissociation, not of what you have dissociated. Even in this world's therapy, when dissociated material is accepted it ceases to be fearful, for the laws of mind always hold.

Yet to give up the dissociation of reality brings more than merely lack of fear. In this decision lie joy and peace and the glory of creation. Offer the Holy Spirit only your will to remember, for He retains the knowledge of God and of yourself for you, waiting for your acceptance.

Give up gladly everything that would stand in the way of your remembering, for God is in your memory, and His Voice will tell you that you are part of Him when you are willing to remember Him and know your own reality again. Let nothing in this world delay your remembering of Him, for in this remembering is the knowledge of yourself.

To remember is merely to restore to your mind what is already there. You do not make what you remember; you merely accept again what has been made but was rejected. The ability to accept truth in this world is the perceptual counterpart of creating in the Kingdom. God will do His part if you will do yours, and His return in exchange for yours is the exchange of knowledge for perception. nothing is beyond His Will for you. But signify your will to remember Him and behold! He will give you everything but for the asking.

When you attack you are denying yourself. You are specifically teaching yourself that you are not what you are. Your denial of reality precludes the acceptance of God's gift because you have accepted something else in its place. If you understand that the misuse of defences always constitutes an attack on truth and truth is God, you will realize why this is always fearful. If you further recognize that you are part of God, you will understand why it is that you always attack yourself first.

If you realized the complete havoc this makes of your peace of mind, you could not make such an insane decision. You make it only because you still believe that it can get you something you want. It follows, then, that you want something other than peace of mind, but you have not considered what it must be. Yet the logical outcome of your decision is perfectly clear, if you will look at it. By deciding against your reality, you have made yourself vigilant against God and His Kingdom. And it is this vigilance that makes you afraid to remember Him.

You have not attacked God and you do love Him. Can you change your reality? No-one can will to destroy himself. When you think you are attacking yourself, it is a sure sign that you hate what you think you are. And this, and only this, can be attacked by you. What you think you are can be hateful and what this strange image makes you do can be very destructive. Yet the destruction is no more real than the image, although those who make idols do worship them. The idols are nothing, but their worshippers are the Sons of God in sickness.

God would have them released from their sickness and returned to His Mind. He will not limit your power to help them because He has given it to you.

Do not be afraid of it because it is your salvation. What Comforter can there be for the sick Children of God except His power through you? Remember that it does not matter where in the Sonship He is accepted. He is always accepted for all, and when your mind receives Him the remembrance of Him awakens throughout the Sonship. Heal your brothers simply by accepting God for them.

Your minds are not separate, and God has only one channel for healing because He has but one Son. His remaining communication link with all His Children joins them together and them to Him. To be aware of this is to heal them because it is the awareness that no one is separate, and so no-one is sick. To believe that a Son of God can be sick is to believe that part of God can suffer. Love cannot suffer because it cannot attack. The remembrance of love therefore brings invulnerability with it.

Do not side with sickness in the presence of a Son of God even if He believes in it, for your acceptance of God in him acknowledgement the Love of God which he has forgotten. Your recognition of him as part of God teaches him the truth about himself, which He is denying. Would you strengthen his denial of God, and thus lose sight of yourself? Or would you remind him of his wholeness, and remember your Creator with him? To believe a Son of God is sick is to worship the same idol he does. God created love, not idolatry. All forms of idolatry are caricatures of creation, taught by sick minds which are too divided to know that creation shares power and never usurps it. Sickness is idolatry because it is the belief that power can be taken from you. Yet this is impossible because you are part of God, Who is all power.

A sick god must be an idol, made in the image of what its maker thinks He is. And that is exactly what the ego does perceive in a Son of God; a sick god, self-created, self-sufficient, very vicious, and very vulnerable. Is this the idol you would worship? Is this the image you would be vigilant to save? Look calmly at the logical conclusion of the ego's thought system, and judge whether its offering is really what you want, for this IS what it offers you. To obtain this you are willing to attack the Divinity of your brothers, and thus lose sight of yours. And you are willing to keep it hidden and to protect this idol, which you think will save you from the dangers which the idol itself stands for, but which do not exist.

There are no idolaters in the Kingdom, but there is great appreciation for every Soul which God created because of the calm knowledge that each one is part of Him. God's Son knows no idols, but he does know His Father.

Health in this world is the counterpart of value in Heaven. It is not my merit that I contribute to you but my love, for you do not value yourselves. When you do not value yourself you become sick, but my value of you can heal you because the value of God's Son is one. When I said, "My peace I give unto you," I meant it. Peace came from God through me to you. It was for you although you did not ask.

When a brother is sick it is because he is not asking for peace, and therefore does not know he has it. The acceptance of peace is the denial of illusion, and sickness is an illusion. Yet every Son of God has the power to deny illusions anywhere in the Kingdom merely by denying them completely in himself. I can heal you because I know you. I know your value for you, and it is this value that makes you whole. A whole mind is not idolatrous and does not know of conflicting laws. I will heal you merely because I have only one message and it is true. Your faith in it will make you whole when you have faith in me.

I do not bring God's message with deception and you will learn this as you learn that you always receive as much as you accept. You could accept peace now for everyone you meet and offer them perfect freedom from all illusions because you heard. But have no other gods before Him, or you will not hear. God is not jealous of the gods you make, but you are. You would save them and serve them because you believe that they made you. You think they are your father because you are projecting onto them the fearful fact that you made them to replace God. Yet when they seem to speak to you remember that nothing can replace God, and whatever replacements you have attempted are nothing.

Very simply, then, you may believe you are afraid of nothingness, but you are really afraid of nothing. And in that awareness, you are healed. You will hear the god you listen to. You made the god of sickness, and by making him, you made yourself able to hear him. Yet you did not create him because he is not the Will of the Father. He is therefore not eternal and will be unmade for you the instant you signify your willingness to accept only the eternal. If God has but one Son, there is but one God. You share reality with Him because reality is not divided. To accept other gods before Him is to place other images before yourself.

You do not realize how much you listen to your gods and how vigilant you are on their behalf. Yet they exist only because you honour them. Place honour where it is due, and peace will be yours. It is your inheritance from your real Father. You cannot make your Father and the father you made did not make you.

Honour is not due to illusions, for to honour them is to honour nothing. Yet fear is not due them either, for nothing cannot be fearful. You have chosen to fear love because of its perfect harmlessness, and because of this fear, you have been willing to give up your own perfect helpfulness and your own perfect Help.

Only at the altar of God will you find peace. And this altar is in you because God put it there. His Voice still calls you to return, and He will be heard when you place no other gods before Him. You can give up the god of sickness for your brothers; in fact, you would have to do so if you give him up for yourself. For if you see him anywhere, you have accepted him. And if you accept him, you will bow down and worship him, because he was made as God's replacement. He is the belief that you can choose which god is real. Although it is perfectly clear that this has nothing to do with reality, it is equally clear that it has everything to do with reality as you perceive it.

All magic is a form of reconciling the irreconcilable. All religion is the recognition that the irreconcilable cannot be reconciled. Sickness and perfection are irreconcilable. If God created you perfect, you are perfect. If you believe you can be sick, you have placed other gods before Him. God is not at war with the god of sickness you made, but you are. He is the symbol of willing against God, and you are afraid of him because he cannot be reconciled with God's Will. If you attack him, you will make him real to you. But if you refuse to worship him in whatever form he may appear to you and wherever you think you see him, he will disappear into the nothingness out of which he was made.

Reality can dawn only on an unclouded mind. It is always there to be accepted, but its acceptance depends on your willingness to have it. To know reality must involve the willingness to judge unreality for what it is. This is the right use of selective perception. To overlook nothingness is merely to judge it correctly, and because of your ability to evaluate it truly, to let it go. Knowledge cannot dawn on a mind full of illusions, because truth and illusions are irreconcilable. Truth is whole and cannot be known by part of a mind.

The Sonship cannot be perceived as partly sick because to perceive it that way is not to perceive it at all. If the Sonship is one, it is one in all respects. Oneness cannot be divided. If you perceive other gods your mind is split, and you will not be able to limit the split because the split is the sign that you have removed part of your mind from God's Will, and this means it is out of control. To be out of control is to be out of reason, and the mind does become unreasonable without reason. This is merely a matter of definition. By defining the mind wrongly, you perceive it as functioning wrongly.

God's laws will keep your minds at peace because peace is His Will, and His laws are established to uphold it. His are the laws of freedom, but yours are the laws of bondage. Since freedom and bondage are irreconcilable, their laws cannot be understood together. The laws of God work only for your good, and there are no other laws beside His. Everything else is merely lawless, and therefore chaotic. Yet God Himself has protected everything He created by His laws. Therefore, everything that is not under them does not exist. "Laws of chaos" are meaningless by definition.

Creation is perfectly lawful, and the chaotic is without meaning because it is without God. You have given your peace to the gods you made, but they are not there to take it from you, and you are not able to give it to them.

You are not free to give up freedom, but only to deny it. You cannot do what God did not intend because what He did not intend does not happen. Your gods do not bring chaos; you are endowing them with chaos and accepting it of them. All this has never been. Nothing but the laws of God have ever operated and nothing except His Will, will ever be. You were created through His laws and by His Will, and the manner of your creation established you as creators. What you have made is so unworthy of you that you could hardly want it if you were willing to see it as it is. You will see nothing at all. And your vision will automatically look beyond it to what is in you and all around you. Reality cannot break through the obstructions you interpose, but it will envelop you completely when you let them go.

When you have experienced the protection of God the making of idols becomes inconceivable. There are no strange images in the Mind of God, and what is not in His Mind cannot be in yours because you are of one Mind, and that Mind belongs to Him. It is yours because it belongs to Him, for ownership is sharing to Him. And if it is so for Him, it is so for you. His definitions are His laws, for by them He established the universe as what it is. No false gods you attempt to interpose between yourself and your reality affect truth at all. Peace is yours because God created you. And He created nothing else.

The miracle is the act of a Son of God who has laid aside all false gods, and who calls on his brothers to do likewise. It is an act of faith because it is the recognition that his brother can do it. It is a call to the Holy Spirit in his mind, a call to Him which is strengthened by this joining. Because the miracle worker has heard Him he strengthens His Voice in a sick brother by weakening his belief in sickness, which he does not share. The power of one mind can shine into another because all the lamps of God were lit by the same spark. It is everywhere, and it is eternal.

In many only the spark remains, for the great rays are obscured. Yet God has kept the spark alive so that the rays can never be completely forgotten. If you but see the little spark you will learn of the greater light, for the rays are there unseen. Perceiving the spark will heal but knowing the light will create. Yet in the returning the little light must be acknowledged first, for the separation was a descent from magnitude to littleness. But the spark is still as pure as the great light because it is the remaining call of creation. Put all your faith in it, and God Himself will answer you.

The rituals of the god of sickness are strange and very demanding. Joy is never permitted, for depression is the sign of allegiance to him. Depression means that you have foresworn God. Men are afraid of blasphemy, but they do not know what it means. They do not realize that to deny God is to deny their own identity, and in this sense the wages of sin is death. The sense is very literal; denial of Life perceives its opposite, as all forms of denial replace what is with what is not. No-one can really do this, but that you can think you can and believe you have is beyond dispute.

Do not forget, however, that to deny God will inevitably result in projection, and you will believe that others and not yourself have done this to you. You will receive the message you give because it is the message you want. You may believe that you judge your brothers by the messages they give you, but you have judged them by the message you give to them. Do not attribute your denial of joy to them, or you cannot see the spark in them that could bring joy to you. It is the denial of the spark that brings depression, and whenever you see your brothers without it, you are denying God.

Allegiance to the denial of God is the ego's religion. The god of sickness obviously demands the denial of health because health is in direct opposition to its own survival. But consider what this means to you. Unless you are sick you cannot keep the gods, you made, for only in sickness could you possibly want them. Blasphemy, then, is self-destructive, not God-destructive. It means that you are willing not to know yourself in order to be sick. This is the offering which your god demands because, having made him out of your insanity, he is an insane idea. He has many forms, but although he may seem like many different things he is but one idea; – the denial of God.

Sickness and death entered the mind of God's Son against His Will. The "attack on God" made His Son think he was fatherless, and out of his depression he made the god of depression. This was his alternative to joy because he would not accept the fact that, although he was a creator, he had been created. Yet the Son is helpless without the Father, who alone is his Help. We said before that of yourselves you can do nothing, but you are not of yourselves. If you were, what you have made would be true, and you could never escape.

It is because you did not make yourselves that you need be troubled by nothing. Your gods are nothing because your Father did not create them. You cannot make creators who are unlike your Creator any more than He could have created a Son who was unlike Him. If creation is sharing it cannot create what is unlike itself. It can share only what it is. Depression is isolation, and so it could not have been created.

Son of God, you have not sinned, but you have been much mistaken. Yet this can be corrected, and God will help you, knowing that you could not sin against Him. You denied Him because you loved Him, knowing that, if you recognised your love for Him you could not deny Him. Your denial of Him therefore means that you love Him, and that you know He loves you. Remember that what you deny you must have known. And if you accept denial, you can accept its undoing.

Your Father has not denied you. He does not retaliate, but He does call to you to return. When you think He has not answered your call, you have not answered His. He calls to you from every part of the Sonship because of His Love for His Son. If you hear His message He has answered you, and you will learn of Him if you hear aright. The Love of God is in everything He created, for His Son is everywhere. Look with peace upon your brothers, and God will come rushing into your heart in gratitude for your gift to Him.

Do not look to the god of sickness for healing but only to the God of love, for healing is the acknowledgement of Him. When you acknowledge Him, you will know that He has never ceased to acknowledge you, and that in His acknowledgment of you lies your Being. You are not sick and you cannot die. But you can confuse yourself with things that do. Remember, though, that to do this is blasphemy, for it means that you are looking without love on God and His creation, from which he cannot be separated. Only the eternal can be loved, for love does not die. What is of God is His forever, and you are of God. Would He allow Himself to suffer? And would He offer His Son anything that is not acceptable to Him?

If you will accept yourself as God created you, you will be incapable of suffering. Yet to do this, you must acknowledge Him as your Creator. This is not because you will be punished otherwise. It is merely because your acknowledgment of your Father is the acknowledgment of yourself as you are. Your Father created you wholly without sin, wholly without pain, and wholly without suffering of any kind. If you deny Him you bring sin, pain and suffering into your own mind because of the power He gave it. Your mind is capable of creating worlds, but it can also deny what it creates because it is free.

You do not realize how much you have denied yourself, and how much God, in His Love, would not have it so. Yet He would not interfere with you because He would not know His Son if he were not free. To interfere with you would be to attack Himself and God is not insane. When you denied Him, you were insane. Would you have Him share your insanity? God will never cease to love His Son and His Son will never cease to love Him. That was the condition of His Son's creation, fixed forever in the Mind of God. To know that is sanity. To deny it is insanity. God gave Himself to you in your creation, and His gifts are eternal. Would you deny yourself to Him?

Out of your gifts to Him the Kingdom will be restored to His Son. His Son removed himself from His gift by refusing to accept what had been created for him, and what he himself had created in the Name of his Father. Heaven waits for his return, for it was created as the dwelling place of God's Son. You are not at home anywhere else, or in any other condition. Do not deny yourself the joy which was created for you for the misery you have made for yourselves. God has given you the means for undoing what you have made. Listen, and you will learn what you are.

If God knows His Children as wholly sinless, it is blasphemous to perceive them as guilty. If God knows His Children as wholly without pain, it is blasphemous to perceive suffering anywhere. If God knows His children to be wholly joyous, it is blasphemous to feel depressed. All of these illusions and the many other forms which blasphemy may take, are refusals to accept creation as it is. If God created His Son perfect, that is how you must learn to see him to learn of his reality. And as part of the Sonship, that is how you must see yourself to learn of yours.

Do not perceive anything God did not create, or you are denying Him. His is the only Fatherhood, and it is yours only because He has given it to you. Your gifts to yourself are meaningless, but your gifts to your creations are like His because they are given in His Name.

That is why your creations are as real as His. Yet the real

Fatherhood must be acknowledged if the real Son is to be known. You believe that the sick things which you have made are your real creations because you believe that the sick images you perceive are the Sons of God.

Only if you accept the Fatherhood of God will you have anything because His Fatherhood gave you everything. That is why to deny Him is to deny yourself. Arrogance is the denial of love because love shares, and arrogance withholds. As long as both appear to you to be desirable, the concept of choice, which is not of God, will remain with you. While this is not true in eternity, it is true in time, so that, while time lasts in your minds, there will be choices. Time itself was your choice.

If you would remember eternity, you must learn to look only on the eternal. If you allow yourselves to become preoccupied with the temporal, you are living in time. As always, your choice is determined by what you value. Time and eternity cannot both be real because they contradict each other. If you will accept only what is timeless as real, you will begin to understand eternity, and make it yours.

Either God or the ego is insane. If you will examine the evidence on both sides fairly, you will realize that this must be true. Neither God nor the ego proposes a partial thought system. Each is internally consistent, but they are diametrically opposed in all respects, so that partial allegiance is impossible. Remember, too, that their results are as different as their foundations, and their fundamentally irreconcilable natures cannot be reconciled by your vacillations. Nothing alive is fatherless, for life is creation. Therefore, your decision is always an answer to the question, "Who is my father?" And you will be faithful to the father you choose.

Yet what would you say to someone who really believed this question involves conflict? If you made the ego, how can the ego have made you? The authority problem remains the only source of perceived conflict, because the ego was made out of the wish of God's Son to father Him. The ego, then, is nothing more than a delusional system, in which you made your own father. Make no mistake about this. It sounds insane when it is stated with perfect honesty, but the ego never looks upon what it does with perfect honesty. Yet that is its insane premise, which is carefully hidden in the dark cornerstone of its thought system. And either the ego, which you made, is your father, or its whole thought system will not stand.

You have made by projection, but God has created by extension. The cornerstone of God's creation is you, for His thought system is light. Remember the rays that are there unseen.

The more you approach the centre of His thought system, the clearer the light becomes. The closer you come to the ego's thought system, the darker and more obscure becomes the way. Yet even the little spark in your mind is enough to lighten it. Bring this light fearlessly with you and hold it up to the foundation of the ego's thought system bravely. Be willing to judge it with perfect honesty. Open the dark cornerstone of terror on which it rests and bring it out into the light.

There you will see that it rests on meaninglessness, and that everything of which you have been afraid was based on nothing. My brother, you are part of God and part of me. When you have at last looked at the ego's foundation without shrinking, you will also have looked upon ours. I come to you from our Father to offer you everything again. Do not refuse it in order to keep a dark cornerstone hidden, for its protection will not save you. I give you the lamp and I will go with you. You will not take this journey alone. I will lead you to your true Father, Who hath need of you, as I have. Will you not answer the call of love with joy?

You have learned your need of healing. Would you bring anything else to the Sonship, recognizing your need of healing for yourself? For in this lies the beginning of knowledge; the foundation on which God will help you build again the thought system which you share with Him. Not one stone you place upon it but will be blessed by Him, for you will be restoring the holy dwelling place of His Son, where He wills His Son to be and where he is. In whatever part of the mind of God's Son you restore this reality, you restore it to yourself. For you dwell in the Mind of God with your brother, for God Himself did not will to be alone.

To be alone is to be separated from infinity, but how can this be if infinity has no end? No-one can be beyond the limitless because what has no limits must be everywhere. There are no beginnings and no endings in God, whose universe is Himself. Can you exclude yourself from the universe, or from God Who is the universe? I and my Father are one with you, for you are part of us. Do you really believe that part of God can be missing or lost to Him? If you were not part of God, His Will would not be unified. Is this conceivable? Can part of His Mind contain nothing? If your place in His Mind cannot be filled by anyone except you, and your filling it was your creation, without you there would be an empty place in God's Mind.

Extension cannot be blocked, and it has no voids. It continues forever, however much it is denied. Your denial of its reality arrests it in time, but not in eternity. That is why your creations have not ceased to be extended, and why so much is waiting for your return.

Waiting is possible only in time, but time has no meaning. You who made delay can leave time behind simply by recognizing that neither beginnings nor endings were created by the Eternal, Who placed no limits on His creation, nor upon those who create like Him. You do not know this simply because you have tried to limit what He created, and so you believe that all creation is limited.

How, then, could you know your creations, having denied infinity? The laws of the universe do not permit contradiction. What holds for God holds for you. If you believe you are absent from God, you will believe that He is absent from you.

Infinity is meaningless without you, and you are meaningless without God. There is no end to God and His Son, for we are the universe. God is not incomplete, and He is not childless. Because He did not will to be alone, He created a Son like Himself. Do not deny Him His Son, for your unwillingness to accept His Fatherhood has denied you yours. See His creations as His Son, for yours were created in honour of Him. The universe of love does not stop because you do not see it and your closed eyes have not lost the ability to see. Look upon the glory of His creation, and you will learn what God has kept for you.

God had given you a place in His Mind which is yours forever. Yet you could keep it only by giving it, as it was given you. Could you be alone there, if it was given you because God did not will to be alone? God's Mind cannot be lessened. It can only be increased, and everything He creates has the function of creating. Love does not limit, and what it creates is not limited. To give without limit is God's Will for you because only this can bring you the joy which is His, and which He wills to share with you. Your love is as boundless as His because it is His.

Could any part of God be without His Love, and could any part of His Love be contained? God is your heritage because His one gift is Himself. How can you give except like Him, if you would know His gift to you? Give, then, without limit and without end, to learn how much He has given you. Your ability to accept Him depends on your willingness to give as He gives. Your fatherhood and your Father are One. God willed to create, and your will is His. It follows, then, that you will to create, since your will follows from His. And being an extension of His Will, yours must be the same.

Yet what you will you do not know. This is not strange when you realize that to deny is to "not know." God's Will is that you are His Son. By denying this you denied your own will, and therefore do not know what it is. The reason you must ask what God's Will is in everything is merely because It is yours.

You do not know what it is, but the Holy Spirit remembers it for you. Ask Him, therefore, what God's Will is for you, and He will tell you yours. It cannot be too often repeated that you do not know it. Whenever what the Holy Spirit tells you appears to be coercive, it is only because you do not recognise your own will.

The projection of the ego makes it appear as if God's Will is outside yourself, and therefore not yours. In this interpretation, it is possible for God's Will and yours to conflict. God, then, may seem to demand of you what you do not want to give, and thus deprive you of what you want. Would God, Who wants only your will, be capable of this? Your will is His Life, which He has given to you. Even in time you cannot live apart from Him, for sleep is not death. What He created can sleep, but it cannot die. Immortality is His Will for His Son, and His Son's will for himself. God's Son cannot will death for himself because His Father is Life, and His Son is like Him. Creation is your will because it is His.

You cannot be happy unless you do what you will truly, and you cannot change this because it is immutable. It is immutable by God's Will and yours, for otherwise His Will would not have been extended. You are afraid to know God's Will because you believe it is not yours. This belief is your whole sickness and your whole fear.

Every symptom of sickness and fear arises here because this is the belief that makes you want not to know. Believing this, you hide in darkness, denying that the Light is in you.

You are asked to trust the Holy Spirit only because He speaks for you. He is the Voice for God, but never forget that God did not will to be alone. He shares His Will with you; He does not thrust It upon you. Always remember that what He gives He holds, so that nothing He gives can contradict Him. You who share His Life must share it to know it, for sharing is knowing. Blessed are you who learn that to hear the Will of your Father is to know your own. For it is your will to be like Him, Whose Will it is that it be so. God's Will is that His Son be one, and united with Him in His Oneness. That is why healing is the beginning of the recognition that your will is His.

If sickness is separation, the will to heal and be healed is the first step toward recognizing what you truly want. Every attack is a step away from this, and every healing thought brings it closer. The Son of God has both Father and Son because he is both Father and Son. To unite having and being is only to unite your will with His, for He wills you Himself. And you will yourself to Him because, in your perfect understanding of Him, you know there is, but One Will.

Yet when you attack any part of God and His Kingdom, your understanding is not perfect and what you will is therefore lost to you.

Healing thus becomes a lesson in understanding and the more you practice it, the better teacher and learner you become. If you have denied truth, what better witnesses to its reality could you have than those who have been healed by it? But be sure to count yourself among them, for in your willingness to join them is your healing accomplished. Every miracle which you accomplish speaks to you of the Fatherhood of God. Every healing thought which you accept, either from your brother or in your own mind, teaches you that you are God's Son. In every hurtful thought you hold, wherever you perceive it, lies the denial of God's Fatherhood and your Sonship.

And denial is as total as love. You cannot deny part of yourself, because the remainder will seem to be unintegrated, and therefore without meaning. And being without meaning to you, you will not understand it. To deny meaning must be to fail to understand. You can heal only yourself, for only God's Son needs healing. He needs it because he does not understand himself, and therefore knows not what he does. Having forgotten his will, he does not know what he wants.

Healing is a sign that he wants to make whole. And this willingness opens his own ears to the Voice of the Holy Spirit, whose message is wholeness. He will enable you to go far beyond the healing you would undertake, for beside your small willingness to make whole He will lay His Own complete Will and make yours whole. What can the Son of God not accomplish with the Fatherhood of God in him? And yet the invitation must come from you, for you have surely learned that whom you invite as your guest will abide with you.

The Holy Spirit cannot speak to an unwelcoming host because He will not be heard. The Eternal Guest remains, but His Voice grows faint in alien company. He needs your protection, but only because your care is a sign that you want Him. Think like Him ever so slightly, and the little spark becomes a blazing light that fills your mind so that He becomes your only Guest. Whenever you ask the ego to enter, you lessen His welcome. He will remain, but you have allied yourself against Him. Whatever journey you choose to take, He will go with you, waiting. You can safely trust His patience, for He cannot leave a part of God. Yet you need far more than patience.

You will never rest until you know your function and fulfil it, for only in this can your will and your Father's be wholly joined. To have Him is to be like Him, and He has given Himself to you. You who have God must be as God, for His function became yours with His gift. Invite this knowledge back into your minds and let nothing that will obscure it enter. The Guest Whom God sent you will teach you how to do this, if you but recognize the little spark and are willing to let it grow. Your willingness need not be perfect because His is. If you will merely offer Him a little place, He will lighten it so much that you will gladly extend it. And by this extending, you will begin to remember creation.

Would you be hostage to the ego or host to God? You will accept only whom you invite. You are free to determine who shall be your guest, and how long he shall remain with you. Yet this is not real freedom, for it still depends on how you see it. The Holy Spirit is there although He cannot help you without your invitation, and the ego is nothing whether you invite it in or not. Real freedom depends on welcoming reality, and of your guests only He is real. Know, then, who abides with you merely by recognizing what is there already, and do not be satisfied with imaginary comforters, for the Comforter of God is in you.

When you are weary, remember you have hurt yourself. Your Comforter will rest you, but you cannot. You do not know how, for if you did you could never have grown weary. Unless you have hurt yourselves, you could never suffer in any way, for that is not God's Will for His Son. Pain is not of Him, for He knows no attack and His peace surrounds you silently. God is very quiet, for there is no conflict in Him. Conflict is the root of all evil, for being blind it does not see whom it attacks. Yet it always attacks the Son of God, and the Son of God is you.

God's Son is indeed in need of comfort, for he knows not what he does, believing his will is not his own. The Kingdom is his, and yet he wanders homelessly. At home in God he is lonely, and amid all his brothers he is friendless. Would God let this be real if He did not will to be alone Himself? And if your will is His, it cannot be true of you because it is not true of Him. Oh, my children, if you knew what God wills for you your joy would be complete! And what He wills has happened, for it was always true.

When the light comes, and you have said, "God's Will is mine," you will see such beauty that you will know it is not of you. Out of your joy you will create beauty in His name, for your joy could no more be contained than His.

The bleak little world will vanish into nothingness, and your heart will be so filled with joy that it will leap into Heaven and into the Presence of God. I cannot tell you what this will be like, for your hearts are not ready. Yet I can tell you, and remind you often, that what God wills for Himself He wills for you, and what He wills for you is yours.

The way is not hard, but it is very different. Yours is the way of pain, of which God knows nothing. That way is hard indeed, and very lonely. Fear and grief are your guests, and they go with you and abide with you on the way. But the dark journey is not the way of God's Son. Walk in light and do not see the dark companions, for they are not fit companions for the Son of God, who was created of Light and in Light. The Great Light always surrounds you and shines out from you. How can you see the dark companions in a Light such as this? If you see them it is only because you are denying the Light. But deny them instead, for the Light is here and the way is clear.

God hides nothing from His Son, even though His Son would hide himself. Yet the Son of God cannot hide his glory, for God wills him to be glorious, and gave him the Light that shines in him. You will never lose your way for God leads you. When you wander you but undertake a journey which is not real. The dark companions, the dark way, are all illusions. Turn toward the Light, for the little spark in you is part of a Light so great that It can sweep you out of all darkness forever. For your Father is your creator, and you are like Him.

The Children of Light cannot abide in darkness, for darkness is not in them. Do not be deceived by the dark comforters, and never let them enter the mind of God's Son, for they have no place in His temple. When you are tempted to deny Him, remember that there are no other gods that you can place before Him, and accept His Will for you in peace. For you cannot accept it otherwise. Only God's Comforter can comfort you. In the quiet of His temple, He waits to give you the peace that is yours. Give His peace that you may enter the temple and find it waiting for you. But be holy in the Presence of God, or you will not know that you are there. For what is unlike God cannot enter His Mind because it was not His Thought, and therefore does not belong to Him. And your minds must be as pure as His, if you would know what belongs to you.

Guard carefully His temple, for He Himself dwells there, and abides in peace. You cannot enter God's Presence with the dark companions beside you, but you also cannot enter alone. All your brothers must enter with you, for until you have accepted them you cannot enter. For you cannot understand Wholeness unless you are whole, and no part of the Son can be excluded if he would know the Wholeness of his Father. In your mind you can accept the whole Sonship and bless it with the Light your Father gave it. Then you will be worthy to dwell in the temple with Him because it is your will not to be alone. God blessed His Son forever. If you will bless him in time, you will be in eternity. Time cannot separate you from God if you use it on behalf of the eternal.

Never forget that the Sonship is your salvation for the Sonship is your Soul. As God's creation it is yours and belonging to you it is His. Your Soul does not need salvation, but your mind needs to learn what salvation is. You are not saved from anything, but you are saved for glory. Glory is your inheritance, given your Soul by its Creator that you might extend it. Yet if you hate part of your own Soul all your understanding is lost, because you are looking on what God created as yourself without love. And since what He created is part of Him, you are denying Him His place in His own altar.

Could you try to make God homeless and know that you are at home? Can the Son deny the Father without believing that the Father has denied Him? God's laws hold only for your protection, and they never hold in vain. What you experience when you deny your Father is still for your protection, for the power of your will cannot be lessened without the intervention of God against it, and any limitation on your power is not the Will of God. Therefore, look only to the power that God gave to save you, remembering that it is yours because it is His, and join with your brothers in His peace.

The peace of your Soul lies in its limitlessness. Limit the peace you share, and your own Soul must be unknown to you. Every altar to God is part of your Soul because the Light He created is One with Him. Would you cut off a brother from the Light that is yours? You would not do so if you realized that you can only darken your own mind. As you bring Him back, so will your mind return. That is the law of God, for the protection of the wholeness of His Son. Only you can deprive yourself of anything. Do not oppose this realization, for it is truly the beginning of the dawn of light. Remember also that the denial of this simple fact takes many forms, and these you must learn to recognize, and to oppose steadfastly and without exception.

This is a crucial step in the re-awakening. The beginning phases of this reversal are often quite painful, for as blame is withdrawn from without there is a strong tendency to harbor within. It is difficult, at first, to realize that this is exactly the same thing, for there is no distinction between within and without. If your brothers are part of you and you blame them for your deprivation, you are blaming yourself. And you cannot blame yourself without blaming them. That is why blame must be undone, not re-allocated. Lay it to yourself and you cannot know yourself, for only the ego blames at all. Self-blame is therefore ego identification, and as strong as an ego defence as blaming others you cannot enter God's presence if you attack His Son. When His Son lifts his voice in praise of his Creator, he will hear the Voice of his Father. Yet the Creator cannot be praised without His Son, for their glory is shared, and they are glorified together.

Christ is at God's altar, waiting to welcome His Son. But come wholly without condemnation, for otherwise you will believe that the door is barred, and you cannot enter. The door is not barred, and it is impossible for you to be unable to enter the place where God would have you be. But love yourself with the Love of Christ, for so does your Father love you. You can refuse to enter, but you cannot bar the door which Christ holds open. Come unto me who holds it open for you, for while I live it cannot be shut, and I live forever. God is my life and yours, and nothing is denied by God to His Son.

God's altar Christ waits for the restoration of Himself in you. God knows His Son as wholly blameless as Himself, and He is approached through the appreciation of His Son. Christ waits for your acceptance of Him as yourself, and of His Wholeness as yours. For Christ is the Son of God who lives in his Creator and shines with His glory. Christ is the extension of the Love and the Loveliness of God, as perfect as his Creator, and at peace with Him.

Blessed is the Son of God, whose radiance is of his Father, and whose glory he wills to share as his Father shares it with him. There is no condemnation in the Son for there is no condemnation in the Father. Sharing the perfect Love of the Father the Son must share what belongs to Him, for otherwise he will not know the Father or the Son. Peace be unto you who rest in God and in whom the whole Sonship rests.

No-one can escape from illusions unless he looks at them, for not looking is the way they are protected. There is no need to shrink from illusions, for they cannot be dangerous. We are ready to look more closely at the ego's thought system because, together, we have the lamp that will dispel it, and since you realize you do not want it you must be ready. Let us be very calm in doing this, for we are merely looking honestly for truth. The "dynamics" of the ego will be our lesson for a while, for we must look first at this to look beyond it since you have made it real. We will undo this error quietly together and then look beyond it to truth.

What is healing but the removal of all that stands in the way of knowledge? And how else can one dispel illusions except by looking at them directly, without protecting them? Be not afraid, therefore, for what you will be looking at is the source of fear, but you have surely learned by now that fear is not real. We have accepted the fact already that its effects can be dispelled merely by denying their reality. The next step is obviously to recognize that what has no effects does not exist. Laws do not operate in a vacuum, and what leads to nothing has not happened. If reality is recognized by its Extension, what extends to nothing cannot be real. Do not be afraid, then, to look upon fear, for it cannot be seen.

Clarity undoes confusion by definition, and to look upon darkness through light must dispel it. Let us begin this lesson in "ego dynamics" by understanding that the term itself does not mean anything. In fact, it contains exactly the contradiction in terms which makes it meaningless. "Dynamics" implies the power to do something, and the whole separation fallacy lies in the belief that the ego has the power to do anything. The ego is fearful to you because you believe this. Yet the truth is very simple; all power of God. What is not of Him has no power to do anything. When we look at the ego, then, we are not considering dynamics, but delusions.

We can surely regard a delusional system without fear, for it cannot have any effects if its source is not true. Fear becomes more obviously inappropriate if one recognizes the ego's goal, which is so clearly senseless that any effort exerted on its behalf is necessarily expended on nothing. The ego's goal is quite explicitly ego autonomy. From the beginning, then, its purpose is to be separate, sufficient unto itself, and independent of any power except its own. This is why it is the symbol of separation.

Every idea has a purpose, and its purpose is always the natural extension of what it is. Everything that stems from the ego is the natural outcome of its central belief, and the way to undo its results is merely to recognize that their source is not natural, being out of accord with your true nature. We once said that to will contrary to God is wishful thinking, and not real willing. His Will is One because the extension of His Will cannot be unlike Itself. The real conflict you experience, then, is between the ego's idle wishes and the Will of God, Which you share. Can this be a real conflict?

Yours is the independence of creation, not of autonomy. Your whole creative function lies in your complete dependence on God, Whose function He shares with you. By His willingness to share it, He became as dependent on you as you are on Him. Do not ascribe the ego's arrogance to Him Who wills not to be independent of you. He has included you in His Autonomy. Can you believe that autonomy is meaningful apart from Him? The belief in ego autonomy is costing you the knowledge of your dependence on God in which freedom lies. The ego sees all dependency as threatening and has twisted even your longing for God into a means of establishing itself. But do not be deceived by its interpretation of your conflict.

The ego always attacks on behalf of separation. Believing it has the power to do this it does nothing else, because its goal of autonomy is nothing else. The ego is totally confused about reality, but it does not lose sight of its goal. It is much more vigilant than you are because it is perfectly certain of its purpose. You are confused because you do not know yours.

What you must learn to recognize is that the last thing the ego wishes you to realize is that you are afraid of it. For if the ego gives rise to fear it is diminishing your independence and weakening your power. Yet its one claim to your allegiance is that it can give power to you. Without this belief you would not listen to it at all. How, then, can its existence continue if you realize that, by accepting it, you are belittling yourself and depriving yourself of power?

The ego can and does allow you to regard yourself as supercilious, unbelieving, "light-hearted", distant, emotionally shallow, callous, uninvolved, and even desperate, but not really afraid. Minimizing fear, but not its undoing, is the ego's constant effort, and is indeed the skill at which it is very ingenious. How can it preach separation without upholding it through fear, and would you listen to it if you recognized this is what it is doing?

Your recognition that whatever seems to separate you from God is only fear, regardless of the form it takes and quite apart from how the ego wants you to experience it, is therefore the basic ego threat. Its dream of autonomy is shaken to its foundation by this awareness.

For though you may countenance a false idea of independence, you will not accept the cost of fear if you recognize it. Yet this is the cost, and the ego cannot minimize it. For if you overlook love you are overlooking yourself, and you must fear unreality because you have denied yourself. By believing that you have successfully attacked truth, you are believing that attack has power. Very simply, then, you have become afraid of yourself. And no-one wills to learn what he believes would destroy him.

If the ego's goal of autonomy could be accomplished God's purpose could be defeated, and this is impossible. Only by learning what fear is can you finally learn to distinguish the possible from the impossible and the false from the true. According to the ego's teaching, Its goal can be accomplished, and God's purpose cannot. According to the Holy Spirit's teaching, only God's purpose is accomplishment and it is already accomplished.

God is as dependent on you as you are on Him because His autonomy encompasses yours and is therefore incomplete without it. You can only establish your autonomy by identifying with Him and fulfilling your function as it exists in truth.

The ego believes that to accomplish its goal is happiness. But it is given you to know that God's function is yours, and happiness cannot be found apart from your joint will. Recognize only that the ego's goal, which you have pursued quite diligently, has merely brought you fear, and it becomes difficult to maintain that fear is happiness.

Upheld by fear, this is what the ego would have you believe. Yet God's Son is not insane and cannot believe it. Let him but recognise it, and he will not accept it. For only the insane would choose fear in place of love, and only the insane could believe that love can be gained by attack. But the sane know that only attack could produce fear, from which the Love of God completely protects them.

The ego analyses; the Holy Spirit accepts. The appreciation of wholeness comes only through acceptance, for to analyse means to separate out. The attempt to understand totality by breaking it up is clearly the characteristically contradictory approach of the ego to everything. Never forget that the ego believes that power, understanding and truth lie in separation, and to establish this belief it must attack. Unaware that the belief cannot be established, and obsessed with the conviction that separation is salvation, the ego attacks everything it perceives by breaking it up into small and disconnected parts, without meaningful relationships, and thus without meaning.

The ego will always substitute chaos for meaning, for if separation is salvation, harmony is threat. The ego's interpretation of the laws of perception are, and would have to be, the exact opposite of the Holy Spirit's. The ego focuses on errors and overlooks truth. It makes real every mistake it perceives, and with characteristically circular reasoning concludes that because of the mistake, consistent truth must be meaningless. The next step, then, is obvious. If consistent truth is meaningless, inconsistency must be true if truth has meaning. Holding error clearly in mind, and protecting what it has made real, the ego proceeds to the next step in its thought system; that error is real, and truth is error.

The ego makes no attempt to understand this, and it is clearly not understandable, but the ego does make every attempt to demonstrate it, and this it does constantly. Analysing to attack meaning, the ego does succeed in overlooking it, and is left with a series of fragmented perceptions which it unifies on behalf of itself. This, then, becomes the universe it perceives. And it is this universe which, in turn, becomes its demonstration of its own reality.

Do not underestimate the appeal of the ego's demonstrations to those who would listen. Selective perception chooses its witnesses carefully, and its witnesses are consistent. The case for insanity is strong to the insane. For reasoning ends at its beginning, and no thought system transcends its source. Yet reasoning without meaning cannot demonstrate anything, and those who are convinced by it must be deluded. Can the ego teach truly when it overlooks truth? Can it perceive what it has denied? Its witnesses do attest to its denial, but hardly to what it has denied! The ego looks straight at the Father and does not see Him, for it has denied His Son.

Would you remember the Father? Accept His Son and you will remember Him. Nothing can demonstrate that His Son is unworthy, for nothing can prove that a lie is true. What you see of His Son through the eyes of the ego is a demonstration that His Son does not exist, yet where the Son is the Father must be. Accept what God does not deny, and He will demonstrate its truth. The witnesses for God stand in His Light and behold what He created.

Their silence is the sign that they have beheld God's Son, and in the Presence of Christ they need demonstrate nothing, for Christ speaks to them of Himself and of His Father. They are silent because Christ speaks to them, and it is His words that they speak.

Every brother you meet becomes a witness for Christ or for the ego, depending on what you perceive in him. Everyone convinces you of what you want to perceive, and of the reality of the kingdom you have chosen for your vigilance. Everything you perceive is a witness to the thought system you want to be true. Every brother has the power to release you if you will be free. You cannot accept false witness of Him unless you have evoked false witnesses against him.

If He speaks not of Christ to you, you spoke not of Christ to him. You hear but your own voice, and if Christ speaks through you, you will hear Him.

It is impossible not to believe what you see, but it is equally impossible to see what you do not believe. Perceptions are built up on the basis of experience, and experience leads to beliefs. It is not until beliefs are fixed that perceptions stabilize. In effect, then, what you believe you do see. That is what I meant when I said, "Blessed are ye who have not seen and still believe," for those who believe in the resurrection will see it. The resurrection is the complete triumph of Christ over the ego, not by attack, but by transcendence. For Christ does rise above the ego and all its works and ascends to the Father and His Kingdom.

Would you join in the resurrection or the crucifixion? Would you condemn your brothers or free them? Would you transcend your prison and ascend to the Father? For these questions are all the same and are answered together. There has been much confusion about what perception means, because the same word is used both for awareness and for the interpretation of awareness. Yet you cannot be aware without interpretation, and what you perceive is your interpretation. This course is perfectly clear. You do not see it clearly because you are interpreting against it, and therefore do not believe it. And if belief determines perception, you do not perceive what it means and therefore do not accept it.

Yet different experiences lead to different beliefs, and experience teaches. I am leading you to a new kind of experience which you will become less and less willing to deny. Learning of Christ is easy, for to perceive with Him involves no strain at all. HIS perceptions are your natural awareness, and it is only distortions which you introduce that tire you.

Let the Christ in you interpret for you, and do not try to limit what you see by narrow little beliefs which are unworthy of God's Son. For until Christ comes into His Own, the Son of God will see himself as fatherless.

I am your resurrection and your life. You live in me because you live in God. And everyone lives in you, as you live in everyone. Can you, then, perceive unworthiness in a brother and not perceive it in yourself? And can you perceive it in yourself and not perceive it in God? Believe in the resurrection because it has been accomplished, and it has been accomplished in you. This is as true now as it will ever be, for the resurrection is the Will of God, Which knows no time and no exceptions. But make no exceptions yourself, or you will not perceive what has been accomplished for you. For we ascend unto the Father together, as it was in the beginning, is now, and ever shall be, for such is the nature of God's Son as His Father created him.

Do not underestimate the power of the devotion of God's Son, nor the power of the god he worships over him. For he places himself at the altar of his god, whether it be the god he made or the God Who created him. That is why his slavery is as complete as his freedom, for he will obey only the god he accepts. The god of the crucifixion demands that he crucify, and his worshippers obey. In his name they crucify themselves, believing that the power of the Son of God is born of sacrifice and pain. The God of the resurrection demands nothing, for He does not will to take away. He does not require obedience, for obedience implies submission. He would only have you learn your own will and follow it, not in the spirit of sacrifice and submission, but in the gladness of freedom.

Resurrection must compel your allegiance gladly because it is the symbol of joy. Its whole compelling power lies in the fact that it represents what you want to be. The freedom to leave behind everything that hurts you and humbles you and frightens you cannot be thrust upon you, but it can be offered you through the grace of God. And you can accept it by His grace, for God is gracious to His Son, accepting him without question as His Own. Who, then, is your own? The Father has given you all that is His, and He Himself is yours with them. Guard them in their resurrection, for otherwise you will not awake in God, safely surrounded by what is yours forever.

You will not find peace until you have removed the nails from the hands of God's Son and taken the last thorn from his forehead. The Love of God surrounds His Son whom the god of the crucifixion condemns. Teach not that I died in vain. Teach rather that I did not die by demonstrating that I live in you.

For the undoing of the crucifixion of God's Son is the work of the redemption, in which everyone has a part of equal value. God does not judge His blameless Son. Having given himself to him, how could it be otherwise?

You have nailed yourself to a cross and placed a crown of thorns upon your own head. Yet you cannot crucify God's Son, for the Will of God cannot die. His Son has been redeemed from his own crucifixion, and you cannot assign to death whom God has given eternal life. The dream of crucifixion still lies heavy on your eyes, but what you see in dreams is not reality. While you perceive the Son of God as crucified you are asleep. And as long as you believe that you can crucify him you are only having nightmares. You who are beginning to wake are still aware of dreams and have not yet forgotten them. The forgetting of dreams and the awareness of Christ comes with the awakening of others to share your redemption.

You will awaken to your own call, for the Call to awake is within you. If I live in you, you are awake. Yet you must see the works I do through you, or you will not perceive that I have done them unto you. Do not set limits on what you believe I can do through you, or you will not accept what I can do for you. For it is done already, and unless you give all that you have received, you will not know that your Redeemer liveth and that you have awakened with Him.

Redemption is recognized only by sharing it. God's Son is saved. Bring only this awareness to the Sonship, and you will have a part in the redemption as valuable as mine. For your part must be like mine if you learn it of me. If you believe that yours is limited, you are limiting mine. There is no order of difficulty in miracles because all of God's Sons are of equal value, and their equality is their Oneness. The whole power of God is in every part of Him, and nothing contradictory to His Will is either great or small. What does not exist has no size and no measure. To God all things are possible. And to Christ it is given to be like the Father.

The world as you perceive it cannot have been created by the Father, for the world is not as you see it. God created only the eternal, and everything you see is perishable. Therefore, there must be another world which you do not see. The Bible speaks of a new Heaven and a new earth, yet this cannot be literally true, for the eternal are not re-created. To perceive anew is merely to perceive again, implying that before, or in the interval, you were not perceiving at all. What, then, is the world that awaits your perception when you see it?

Every loving thought that the Son of God ever had is eternal. Those which his mind perceived in this world are the world's only reality. They are still perceptions because he still believes that he is separate. Yet they are eternal because they are loving. And being loving, they are like the Father, and therefore cannot die. The real world can actually be perceived. All that is necessary is a willingness to perceive nothing else. For if you perceive both good and evil, you are accepting both the false and the true and making no distinction between them.

The ego sees some good, but never only good. That is why its perceptions are so variable. It does not reject goodness entirely for that you could not accept, but it always adds something that is not real to the real, thus confusing illusion and reality.

For perceptions cannot be partly true. If you believe in truth and illusion you cannot tell which is true. To establish your personal autonomy, you tried to create unlike your Father, believing what you made to be capable of being unlike Him. Yet everything in what you have made that is true is like Him. Only this is the real world and perceiving only this will lead you to the real Heaven because it will make you capable of understanding it.

The perception of goodness is not knowledge, but the denial of the opposite of goodness enables you to perceive a condition in which opposites do not exist. And this is the condition of knowledge. without this awareness you have not met its conditions, and until you do you will not know that it is yours already. You have made many ideas which you have placed between yourselves and your Creator, and these beliefs are the world as you perceive it. Truth is not absent here, but it is obscure. You do not know the difference between what you have made and what God created, and so you do not know the difference between what you have made and what you have created.

To believe that you can perceive the real world is to believe that you can know yourself. You can know God because it is His Will to be known. The real world is all that the Holy Spirit has saved for you out of what you have made, and to perceive only this is salvation because it is the recognition that reality is only what is true. This is a very simple course. Perhaps you do not feel that a course which, in the end, teaches nothing more than that only reality is true is necessary. But do you believe it? When you have perceived the real world, you will recognize that you did not believe it. Yet the swiftness with which your new and only real perception will be translated into knowledge will leave you only an instant to realize that this judgement is true.

And then everything you made will be forgotten, the good and bad, the false and the true. For as Heaven and earth become one, even the real world will vanish from your sight. The end of the world is not its destruction but its translation into Heaven. The reinterpretation of the world is the transfer of all perception to knowledge. The Bible tells you to become as little children. Little children recognize that they do not understand what they perceive, and so they ask what it means. Do not make the mistake of believing that you understand what you perceive, for its meaning is lost to you. Yet the Holy Spirit has saved its meaning for you, and if you will let Him interpret it for you, He will restore what you have thrown away. As long as you think you know its meaning, you will see no need to ask it of Him.

You do not know the meaning of anything you perceive. Not one thought you hold is wholly true. The recognition of this is your firm beginning. You are not misguided; you have accepted no guide at all. Instruction in perception is your great need, for you understand nothing. Recognize this but do not accept it, for understanding is your inheritance. Perceptions are learned, and you are not without a Teacher. Yet your willingness to learn of Him depends on your willingness to question everything you have learned of yourself, for you who have learned amiss should not be your own teachers.

No-one can withhold truth except from himself. Yet God will not refuse the answer He gave you. Ask, then, for what is yours but which you did not make, and do not defend yourself against truth. you made the problem which God has answered. Ask yourselves, therefore, but one simple question,

"Do I want the problem or do I want the answer?"

Decide for the answer and you will have it, for you will see it as it is, and it is yours already. You complain that this course is not sufficiently specific for you to understand it and use it. Yet it has been very specific, and you have not done what it specifically advocates. This is not a course in the play of ideas, but in their practical application. Nothing could be more specific than to be told very clearly that if you ask you will receive. The Holy Spirit will answer every specific problem as long as you believe that problems are specific. His answer is both many and one, as long as you believe that the One is many. Realize that you are afraid of His specificity, for fear of what you think it will demand of you. Yet only by asking will you learn that nothing that is of God demands anything of you. God gives; He does not take.

You are refusing to ask because you believe that asking is taking, and you do not perceive it as sharing. The Holy Spirit will give you only what is yours and will take nothing in return. For what is yours is everything, and you share it with God. This is its reality. Would the Holy Spirit, Who wills only to restore, be capable of misinterpreting the question you must ask to learn His answer?

You have heard the answer, but you have misunderstood the question. You have believed that to ask for guidance of the Holy Spirit is to ask for deprivation. Little children of God, you do not understand your Father. You believe in a world that takes because you believe that you can get by taking. And by that perception you have lost sight of the real world. You are afraid of the world as you see it, but the real world is still yours for the asking. Do not deny it to yourself, for it can only free you. Nothing of God will enslave His Son, whom He created free and whose freedom is protected by His Being.

Blessed are you who will ask the truth of God without fear, for only thus can you learn that His answer IS the release from fear. Beautiful Child of God, you are asking only for what I promised you. Do you believe I would deceive you? The Kingdom of Heaven is within you. Believe that the truth is in me, for I know that it is in you. God's Sons have nothing which they do not share. Ask for truth of any Son of God, and you have asked it of me. No-one of us but has the answer in him, to give to anyone who asks it of him. Ask anything of God's Son and His Father will answer you, for Christ is not deceived in His Father and His Father is not deceived in Him.

Do not, then, be deceived in your brother, and see only his loving thoughts as his reality, for by denying that his mind is split you will heal yours. Accept him as his Father accepts him and heal him unto Christ, for Christ is his healing and yours. Christ is the Son of God Who is in no way separate from His Father, Whose every thought is as loving as the Thought of His Father by which He was created. Be not deceived in God's Son, for thereby you must be deceived in yourself. And being deceived in yourself you are deceived in your Father, in Whom no deceit is possible.

In the real world there is no sickness, for there is no separation and no division. Only loving thoughts are recognized, and because no-one is without your help the Help of God goes with you everywhere. As you become willing to accept this Help by asking for it, you will give it because you want it. Nothing will be beyond your healing power because nothing will be denied your simple request. What problems will not disappear in the presence of God's answer?

Ask, then, to learn of the reality of your brother because this is what you will perceive in him, and you will see your beauty reflected in him.

Do not accept your brother's variable perception of himself, for his split mind is yours, and you will not accept your healing without his. For you share the real world as you share Heaven, and his healing is yours. To love yourself is to heal yourself, and you cannot perceive part of you as sick and achieve your own goal. Brother, we heal together as we live together and love together. Be not deceived in God's Son, for he is one with himself and One with his Father. Love him who is beloved of His Father, and you will learn of the Father's Love for you.

If you perceive offense in a brother pluck the offense from your mind, for you are offended by Christ, and are deceived in Him. heal in Christ and be not offended by Him, for there is no offense in Him. If what you perceive offends you, you are offended in yourself and are condemning God's Son whom God condemneth not. Let the Holy Spirit remove all offense of God's Son against himself and perceive no-one but through His guidance, for He would save you from all condemnation. Accept His healing power and use it for all He sends you, for He wills to heal the Son of God in whom He is not deceived.

Children perceive terrifying ghosts and monsters and dragons and they are terrified. Yet if they ask someone they trust for the real meaning of what they perceive and are willing to let their interpretations go in favour of reality, their fear goes with them. When a child is helped to translate his "ghost" into a curtain, his "monster" into a shadow and his "dragon" into a dream he is no longer afraid and laughs happily at his own fear. You, my children, are afraid of your brothers and of your Father and of yourself. But you are merely deceived in them.

Ask what they are of the Teacher of Reality, and hearing His answer, you too will laugh at your fears and replace them with peace. For fear lies not in reality, but in the minds of children who do not understand reality. It is only their lack of understanding which frightens them, and when they learn to perceive truly they are not afraid. And because of this they will ask for truth again when they are frightened. It is not the reality of your brothers or your Father or yourself which frightens you. You do not know what they are, and so you perceive them as ghosts and monsters and dragons. Ask of their reality from the One Who knows it, and He will tell you what they are. You do not understand them and because you are deceived by what you see, you need reality to dispel your fears.

Would you not exchange your fears for truth if the exchange is yours for the asking? For if God is not deceived in you, you can be deceived only in yourself. Yet you can learn the truth of yourself of the Holy Spirit, Who will teach you that, as part of God, deceit in you is impossible. When you perceive yourself without deceit, you will accept the real world in place of the false one you have made. And then your Father will lean down to you and take the last step for you by raising you unto Himself.

You have been told not to make error real, and the way to do this is very simple. If you want to believe in error, you would have to make it real, because it is not true. But truth is real in its own right, and to believe in truth, you do not have to do anything. Understand that you do not respond to stimuli, but to stimuli as you interpret them. Your interpretation thus becomes the justification for the response. That is why analyzing the motives of others is hazardous to you. If you decide that someone is really trying to attack you or desert you or enslave you, you will respond as if he had actually done so, because you have made his error real to you. To interpret error is to give it power, and having done this, you will overlook truth.

The analysis of ego-motivation is very complicated, very obscuring, and never without the risk of your own ego involvement. The whole process represents a clear cut attempt to demonstrate your own ability to understand what you perceive. This is shown by the fact that you react to your interpretations as if they were correct, and control your reactions behaviourally, but not emotionally. This is quite evidently a mental split, in which you have attacked the integrity of your mind and pitted one level within it against another.

There is but one interpretation of all motivation that makes any sense. And because it is the Holy Spirit's judgement, it requires no effort at all on your part. Every loving thought is true. Everything else is an appeal for healing and help. That is what it is, regardless of the form it takes. Can anyone be justified in responding with anger to a plea for help? No response can be appropriate except the willingness to give it to him, for this and only this is what he is asking for. Offer him anything else and you are assuming the right to attack his reality by interpreting it as you see fit.

Perhaps the danger of this to your own mind is not yet fully apparent to you, but this by no means signifies that it is not perfectly clear. If you maintain that an appeal for help is something else you will react to something else, and your response will be inappropriate to reality as it is, but not to your perception of it. This is poor reality testing by definition.

There is nothing to prevent you from recognizing all calls for help as exactly what they are except your own perceived need to attack. It is only this that makes you willing to engage in endless "battles" with reality, in which you deny the reality of the need for healing by making id unreal. You would not do this except for your unwillingness to perceive reality, which you withhold from yourself.

It is surely good advice to tell you not to judge what you do not understand. No-one with a personal investment is a reliable witness, for truth to him has become what he wants it to be. If you are unwilling to perceive an appeal for help as what it is, it is because you are unwilling to give help and to receive it. The analysis of the ego's "real" motivation is the modern equivalent of the inquisition, for in both a brother's errors are "uncovered" and he is then attacked for his own good. What can this be but projection? For his errors lay in the minds of his interpreters, for which they punished him.

Whenever you fail to recognize a call for help you are refusing help. Would you maintain that you do not need it? Yet this is what you are maintaining when you refuse to recognize a brother's appeal, for only by answering his appeal can you be helped. Deny him your help and you will not perceive God's answer to you.

The Holy Spirit does not need your help in interpreting motivation, but you do need His. Only appreciation is an appropriate response to your brother. Gratitude is due him for both his loving thoughts and his appeals for help, for both are capable of bringing love into your awareness if you perceive them truly. And all your sense of strain comes from your attempts not to do just this. How simple, then, is God's plan for salvation. There is but one response to reality, for reality evokes no conflict at all. There is but one Teacher of reality, Who understands what it is. He does not change His Mind about reality because reality does not change.

Although your interpretations of reality are meaningless in your divided state, His remain consistently true. He gives them to you because they are for you. Do not attempt to "help" a brother in your way, for you cannot help yourselves. But hear his call for the help of God, and you will recognize your own need for the Father.

Your interpretations of your brother's need is your interpretation of yours. By giving help you are asking for it, and if you perceive but one need in yourself you will be healed. For you will recognize God's answer as you want it to be, and if you want it in truth it will be truly yours. Every appeal you answer in the Name of Christ brings the remembrance of your Father closer to your awareness. For the sake of your need, then, hear every call for help as what it is, so God can answer you.

By applying the Holy Spirit's interpretation of the reactions of others more and more consistently, you will gain an increasing awareness that His criteria are equally applicable to you. For to recognize fear is not enough to escape from it, although the recognition is necessary to demonstrate the need for escape. The Holy Spirit must still translate into truth. If you were left with the fear, having recognized it, you would have taken a step away from reality, not towards it. Yet we have repeatedly emphasized the need to recognize fear and face it without disguise as a crucial step in the undoing of the ego. Consider how well the Holy Spirit's interpretation of the motives of others will serve you then.

Having taught you to accept only loving thoughts in others and to regard everything else as an appeal for help, He has taught you that fear is an appeal for help. This is what recognizing it really means. If you do not protect it, He will re-interpret it. That is the ultimate value to you in learning to perceive attack as a call for love. We have learned surely that fear and attack are inevitably associated. If only attack produces fear and if you see attack as the call for help that it is, the unreality of fear must dawn upon you. For fear is a call for love, in unconscious recognition of what has been denied.

Fear is a symptom of your deep sense of loss. If when you perceive it in others you learn to supply the loss, the basic cause of fear is removed. Thereby you teach yourself that fear does not exist in you, for you have in yourself the means for removing it and have demonstrated this by giving it. Fear and love are the only emotions of which you are capable. One is false for it was made out of denial denial depends on the real belief in what is denied for its own existence.

By interpreting fear correctly as a positive affirmation of the underlying belief it masks, you are undermining its perceived usefulness by rendering it useless. Defences which do not work at all are automatically discarded. If you raise what fear conceals to clear-cut, unequivocal predominance, fear becomes meaningless. You have denied its power to conceal love, which was its only purpose. The mask which you have drawn across the face of love has disappeared.

If you would look upon love, which is the world's reality, how could you do better than to recognize, in every defence against it, the underlying appeal for it? And how could you better learn of its reality than by answering the appeal for it by giving it? The Holy Spirit's interpretation of fear does dispel it, for the awareness of truth cannot be denied.

Thus does the Holy Spirit replace fear with love and translate error into truth. And thus will you learn of Him how to replace your dream of separation with the fact of unity. For the separation is only the denial of union, and correctly interpreted, attests to your eternal knowledge that union is true.

Miracles are merely the translation of denial into truth. If to love oneself is to heal oneself, those who are sick do not love themselves. Therefore, they are asking for the love that would heal them, but which they are denying to themselves. If they knew the truth about themselves they could not be sick. The task of the miracle-worker thus becomes to deny the denial of truth. The sick must heal themselves, for the truth is in them. Yet, having obscured it, the light in another mind must shine into theirs because that light is theirs.

The light in them shines as brightly regardless of the density of the fog that obscures it. If you give no power to the fog to obscure the light it has none, for it has power only because the Son of God gave power to it. He must himself withdraw that power, remembering that all power is of God. You can remember this for all the sonship.

Do not allow your brother not to remember, for his forgetfulness is yours. But your remembering is His, for God cannot be remembered alone. This is what you have forgotten. To perceive the healing of your brother as the healing of yourself is thus the way to remember God. For you forgot your brothers with Him, and God's answer to your forgetting is but the way to remember.

Perceive in sickness but another call for love and offer your brother what he believes he cannot offer himself. Whatever the sickness, there is but one remedy. You will be made whole as you make whole, for to perceive in sickness the appeal for health is to recognize in hatred the call for love. And to give a brother what he really wants is to offer it unto yourself, for your Father wills you to know your brother as yourself. Answer His call for love and yours is answered. Healing is the love of Christ for His Father and for Himself.

Remember what we said about the frightening perceptions of little children, which terrify them because they do not understand them. If they ask for enlightenment and accept it their fears vanish, but if they hide their nightmares they will keep them. It is easy to help an uncertain child, for he recognizes that he does not know what his perceptions mean. Yet you believe that you do know. Little children, you are hiding your heads under the covers of the heavy blankets you have laid upon yourselves.

You are hiding your nightmares in the darkness of your own certainty and refusing to open your eyes and look at them.

Let us not save nightmares, for they are not fitting offerings for Christ, and so they are not fit gifts for you. Take off the covers and look at what you are afraid of. Only the anticipation will frighten you, for the reality of nothingness cannot be frightening. Let us not delay this, for your dream of hatred will not leave you without help, and help is here. Learn to be quiet in the midst of turmoil, for quietness is the end of strife and this is the journey to peace. Look straight at every image that rises to delay you, for the goal is inevitable because it is eternal. The goal of love is but your right and it belongs to you despite your preference.

You still want what God wills, and no nightmare can defeat a Child of God in his purpose. For your purpose was given you by God, and you must accomplish it because it is His Will. Awake and remember your purpose, for it is your will to do so. What has been accomplished for you must be yours. Do not let your hatred stand in the way of love, for nothing can withstand the love of Christ for His Father, or His Father's Love for Him.

A little while and you will see me, for I am not hidden because you are hiding. I will awaken you as surely as I awakened myself, for I awoke for you. In my resurrection is your release. Our mission is to escape crucifixion, not redemption. Trust in my help for I did not walk alone, and I will walk with you as our Father walked with me. Did you not know that I walked with Him in peace? And does not that mean that peace goes with us on the journey?

There is no fear in perfect love. We will but be making perfect to you what is already perfect in you. You do not fear the unknown but the known. You will not fail in your mission because I failed not in mine. Give me but a little trust in the name of the complete trust I have in you, and we will easily accomplish the goal of perfection together. For perfection is and cannot be denied. To deny the denial of perfection is not so difficult as the denial of truth, and what we can accomplish together must be believed when you see it as accomplished.

You who have tried to banish love have not succeeded, but you who choose to banish fear will succeed. The Lord is with you, but you know it not. Yet your Redeemer liveth, and abideth in you in the peace out of which He was created. Would you not exchange this awareness for the awareness of your fear? When we have overcome fear, not by hiding it, not by minimizing it, not by denying its full import in any way, this is what you will really see.

You cannot lay aside the obstacle to real vision without looking upon it, for to lay aside means to judge against. If you will look the Holy Spirit will judge and will judge truly. He cannot shine away what you keep hidden, for you have not offered it to Him, and He cannot take it from you.

We are therefore embarking on an organized, well-structured and carefully planned program aimed at learning how to offer to the Holy Spirit everything you do not want. He knows what to do with it. You do not know how to use what He knows. Whatever is revealed to Him that is not of God is gone. Yet you must reveal it to yourself in perfect willingness, for otherwise His knowledge remains useless to you. Surely He will not fail to help you, since help is His only purpose. Do you not have greater reason for fearing the world as you perceive it than for looking at the cause of fear, and letting it go forever?

I once asked if you were willing to sell all you have and give to the poor and follow me. This is what I meant: If you had no investment in anything in this world, you could teach the poor where their treasure is. The poor are merely those who have invested wrongly, and they are poor indeed! Because they are in need it is given you to help them, since you are among them. Consider how perfectly your lesson would be learned if you were unwilling to share their poverty. For poverty is lack, and there is but one lack since there is but one need.

Suppose a brother insists on having you do something you think you do not want to do. The very fact of his insistence should tell you that he believes salvation lies in it. If you insist on refusing and experience a quick response of opposition, you are believing that your salvation lies in not doing it. You, then, are making the same mistake that he is, and are making his error real to both of you. Insistence means investment, and what you invest in is always related to your notion of salvation. The question is always two-fold; first, what is to be saved, and second, how can it be saved?

Whenever you become angry with a brother, for whatever reason, you are believing that the ego is to be saved and to be saved by attack. If he attacks you are agreeing with this belief, and if you attack you are reinforcing it. Remember that those who attack are poor. Their poverty asks for gifts, not for further impoverishment. You who could help them are surely acting destructively if you accept their poverty as yours. If you had not invested as they had, it would never occur to you to overlook their need.

Recognize what does not matter and if your brothers ask you for something "outrageous", do it because it does not matter. Refuse, and your opposition establishes that it does matter to you. It is only you, therefore, who have made the request outrageous, for nothing can be asked of you, and every request of a brother is for you. Why would you insist in denying him? For to do so is to deny yourself and impoverish both. He is asking for salvation, as you are. Poverty is of the ego, and never of God. No "outrageous" request can be made of one who recognizes what is valuable and wants to accept nothing else.

Salvation is for the mind, and it is attained through peace. This is the only thing that can be saved and the only way to save it. Any response other than love arises from a confusion about the "what" and the "how" of salvation, and this is the only answer. Never lose sight of this, and never allow yourself to believe, even for an instant, that there I another answer. For you will surely place yourself among the poor, who do not understand that they dwell in abundance and that salvation is come.

To identify with the ego is to attack yourself and make yourself poor. That is why everyone who identifies with the ego feels deprived. What he experiences then is depression or anger, but what he did is to exchange his self-love for self-hate, making him afraid of himself. He does not realize this. Even if he is fully aware of anxiety he does not perceive its source as his own ego identification, and he always tries to handle it by making some sort of insane "arrangement" with the world. He always perceives this world as outside himself, for this is crucial to his adjustment. He does not realize that he makes this world, for there is no world outside of him.

If only the loving thoughts of God's Son are the world's reality, the real world must be in his mind. His insane thoughts, too, must be in his mind, but an internal conflict of this magnitude he cannot tolerate. A split mind is endangered, and the recognition that it encompasses completely opposed thoughts within itself is intolerable. Therefore the mind projects the split, not the reality.

Everything you perceive as the outside world is merely your attempt to maintain your ego identification, for everyone believes that identification is salvation. Yet consider what has happened, for thoughts do have consequences to the thinker.

You are at odds with the world as you perceive it because you think it is antagonistic to you. This is a necessary consequence of what you have done. You have projected outward what is antagonistic to what is inward, and therefore you would have to perceive it this way. That is why you must realize that your hatred is in your mind and not outside it before you can get rid of it; and why you must get rid of it before you can perceive the world as it really is.

We once said that God so loved the world that He gave it to His only-begotten Son. God does love the real world, and those who perceive its reality cannot see the world of death. For death is not of the real world, in which everything is eternal. God gave you the real world in exchange for the one you made out of your split mind, and which is the symbol of death. For if you could really separate yourselves from the Mind of God you would die, and the world you perceive is a world of separation.

You were willing to accept even death to deny your Father. Yet He would not have it so, and so it is not so. You still could not will against Him, and that is why you have no control over the world you made. It is not a world of will because it is governed by the desire to be unlike Him, and this desire is not will. The world you made is therefore totally chaotic, governed by arbitrary and senseless "laws", and without meaning of any kind. For it was made out of what you do not want, projected from your mind because you were afraid of it.

Yet this world is only in the mind of its maker, along with his real salvation. Do not believe it is outside of yourself, for only by recognizing where it is will you gain control over it. For you do have control over your mind, since the mind is the mechanism of decision. If you will recognize that all attack which you perceive is in your own mind and nowhere else, you will at last have placed its source, and where it began it must end. For in this same place also lies salvation. The altar of God where Christ abideth is there.

You have defiled the altar but not the world. Yet Christ has placed the Atonement on the altar for you. Bring your perceptions of the world to this altar, for it is the altar to truth. There you will see your vision changed, and there you will learn to see truly. From this place, where God and His Son dwell in peace and where you are welcome, you will look out in peace and behold the world truly. Yet to find the place, you must relinquish your investment in the world as you have projected it, allowing the Holy Spirit to project the real world to you from the altar of God.

The ego is certain that love is dangerous, and this is always its central teaching. It never puts it this way; on the contrary, everyone who believes that the ego is salvation is intensely engaged in the search for love. Yet the ego, though encouraging the search very actively, makes one proviso; do not find it. Its dictates, then, can be summed up simply as: "Seek and do not find." This is the one promise the ego holds out to you, and the one promise it will keep.

For the ego pursues its goal with fanatic insistence, and its reality testing, though severely impaired, is completely consistent. The search which the ego undertakes is therefore bound to be defeated. And since it also teaches that it is your identification, its guidance leads you to a journey which must end in perceived self defeat. For the ego cannot love, and in its frantic search for love, it is seeking what it is afraid to find. The search is inevitable because the ego is part of your mind, and because of its source, the ego is not wholly split off, or it could not be believed at all. For it is your mind that believes in it, and gives existence to it. Yet it is also your mind that has the power to deny the ego's existence, and you will surely do so when you realize exactly what the journey is on which the ego sets you.

It is surely obvious that no-one wants to find what would utterly defeat him. Being unable to love, the ego would be totally inadequate in love's presence, for it could not respond at all. You would have to abandon the ego's guidance, for it would be quite apparent that it had not taught you the response pattern you need. The ego will therefore distort love, and teach you that love calls forth the responses which the ego can teach. Follow its teaching, then, and you will search for love, but will not recognise it.

Do you realize that the ego must set you on a journey which cannot but lead to a sense of futility and depression? To seek and not to find is hardly joyous. Is this the promise you would keep? The Holy Spirit offers you another promise, and one that will lead to joy. For His promise is always, "Seek and you will find," and under His guidance you cannot be defeated. His is the journey to accomplishment, and the goal He sets before you He will give you.

For He will never deceive God's Son, whom He loves with the Love of the Father. You will undertake a journey because you are not at home in this world. And you will search for your home whether you know where it is or not. If you believe it is outside yourself the search will be futile, for you will be seeking it where it is not. You do not know how to look within yourself, for you do not believe your home is there. Yet the Holy Spirit knows it for you, and He will guide you to your home because that is His mission.

As He fulfils His mission He will teach you yours, for your mission is the same as His. By guiding your brothers home you are but following Him.

Behold the Guide your Father gave you that you might learn you have eternal life. For death is not your Father's Will nor yours, and whatever is true is the Will of the Father. You pay no price for life for that was given you, but you do pay a price for death, and a very heavy one. If death is your treasure, you will sell everything else to purchase it. And you will believe that you have purchased it because you have sold everything else. Yet you cannot sell the Kingdom of Heaven. Your inheritance can neither be bought nor sold. There can be no disinherited parts of the Sonship, for God is whole, and all his extensions are like Him.

The Atonement was not the price of our wholeness, but it was the price of your awareness of your wholeness. For what you chose to "sell" had to be kept for you, since you could not "buy" it back. Yet you must invest in it, not with money, but with your spirit. For Spirit is will and will is the "price" of the Kingdom. Your inheritance awaits only the recognition that you have been redeemed. The Holy Spirit guides you into life eternal, but you must relinquish your investment in death, or you will not see life though it is all around you.

Only love is strong because it is undivided. The strong do not attack because they see no need to do so. Before the idea of attack can enter your mind you must have perceived yourself as weak. Because you had attacked yourself and believed that the attack was effective, you behold yourself as weakened. No longer perceiving yourself and all your brothers as equal, and regarding yourself as weaker, you attempt to "equalize" the situation you have made. You use attack to do so because you believe that attack was successful in weakening you.

That is why the recognition of your own invulnerability is so important in the restoration of your sanity. For if you accept your invulnerability, you are recognizing that attack has no effect. Although you have attacked yourself, and very brutally, you will demonstrate that nothing happened. Therefore, by attacking you have not done anything. Once you realize this there is no longer any sense in attack, for it manifestly does not work, and cannot protect you. Yet the recognition of your invulnerability has more than negative value. If your attacks on yourself have failed to weaken you, you are still strong. You therefore have no need to "equalize" the situation to establish your strength.

You will never realize the utter uselessness of attack except by recognizing that your attack on yourself had no effects. For others do react to attack if they perceive it, and if you are trying to attack them you will be unable to avoid interpreting this as reinforcement. The only place where you can cancel out all reinforcement is in yourself. For you are always the first point of your attack, and if this has never been it has no consequences.

The Holy Spirit's love is your strength, for yours is divided and therefore not real. You could not trust your own love when you have attacked it. You cannot learn of perfect love with a split mind because a split mind has made itself a poor learner. You tried to make the separation eternal because you wanted to retain the characteristics of creation with your own content. Yet creation is not of you, and poor learners need special teaching. You have learning handicaps in a very literal sense.

There are areas in your learning skills which are so impaired that you can progress only under constant, clear-cut direction, provided by a Teacher Who can transcend your limited resources. He becomes your Resource, because of yourself you cannot learn. The learning situation in which you placed yourself is impossible, and in this situation, you clearly require a special Teacher and a special curriculum. Poor learners are not good choices for teachers, either for themselves or for anyone else. You would hardly turn to them to establish the curriculum by which they can escape from their limitations. If they understood what is beyond them they would not be handicapped.

You do not know the meaning of love, and that is your handicap. Do not attempt to teach yourselves what you do not understand, and do not try to set up curriculum goals where yours have clearly failed. Your learning goal has been not to learn, and this cannot lead to successful learning. You cannot transfer what you have not learned, and the impairment of the ability to generalize is a crucial learning failure. Would you ask those who have failed to learn what learning aids are for? They do not know. For if they could interpret the aids correctly they would have learned from them.

We have said that the ego's rule is, "Seek and do not find." Translated into curricular terms, this is the same as saying, "Try to learn but do not succeed." The result of this curriculum goal is obvious. Every legitimate teaching aid, every real instruction, and every sensible guide to learning will be misinterpreted. For they are all for learning facilitation, which this strange curriculum goal is against. If you are trying to learn how not to learn, and are using the aim of teaching to defeat itself, what can you expect but confusion? The curriculum does not make sense.

This kind of "learning" has so weakened your mind that you cannot love, for the curriculum you have chosen is against love, and amounts to a course in how to attack yourself. A necessary minor, supplementing this major curriculum goal, is learning how not to overcome the split which made this goal believable. And you cannot overcome it, for all your learning is on its behalf. Yet your will speaks against your learning as your learning speaks against your will, and so you fight against learning and succeed, for that is your will. But you do not realize, even yet, that there is something you do will to learn, and that you can learn it because it is your will to do so.

You who have tried to learn what you do not will should take heart, for although the curriculum you set yourself is depressing indeed, it is merely ridiculous, if you look at it. Is it possible that the way to achieve a goal is not to attain it? Resign now as your own teachers. This resignation will not lead to depression. It is merely the result of an honest appraisal of what you have taught yourselves, and of the learning outcomes which have resulted. Under the proper learning conditions, which you can neither provide nor understand, you will become excellent learners and teachers. But it is not so yet, and will not be so until the whole learning situation, as you have set it up, is reversed.

Your learning potential, properly understood, is limitless because it will lead you to God. You can teach the way to Him and learn it, if you follow the Teacher Who knows it, and His curriculum for learning it. The curriculum is totally unambiguous because the goal is not divided, and the means and the end are in complete accord. You need offer only undivided attention. Everything else will be given you. For it is your will to learn aright, and nothing can oppose the will of God's Son. His learning is as unlimited as He is.

The ego is trying to teach you how to gain the whole world and lose your own Soul. The Holy Spirit teaches that you cannot lose your Soul and there is no gain in the world, for of itself it profits nothing. To invest in something without profit is surely to impoverish yourself, and the overhead is high. Not only is there no profit in the investment, but the cost to you is enormous. For this investment costs you the world's reality by denying yours and gives you nothing in return. You cannot sell your Soul, but you can sell your awareness of it. You cannot perceive your Soul, but you will not know it while you perceive anything else as more valuable.

The Holy Spirit is your strength because He perceives nothing but your Soul as you. He is perfectly aware that you do not know yourselves, and perfectly aware of how to teach you what you are. because He loves you, He will gladly teach you what He loves, for He wills to share it. Remembering you always, He cannot let you forget your worth. For the Father never ceases to remind Him of His Son, and He never ceases to remind His Son of the Father. God is in your memory because of Him. You chose to forget your Father but you did not will to do so, and therefore you can decide otherwise. As it was my decision, so is it yours.

You do not want the world. The only thing of value in it is whatever part of it you look upon with love. This gives it the only reality it will ever have. Its value is not in itself, but yours is in you. As self-value comes from self-extension, so does the perception of self-value come from the projection of loving thoughts outward. Make the world real unto yourself, for the real world is the gift of the Holy Spirit, and so it belongs to you.

Correction is for all who cannot see. To open the eyes of the blind is the Holy Spirit's mission, for He knows that they have not lost their vision, but merely sleep. He would awaken them from the sleep of forgetting to the remembering of God. Christ's eyes are open, and He will look upon whatever you see with love if you accept His vision as yours.

The Holy Spirit keeps the vision of Christ for every Son of God who sleeps. In His sight the Son of God is perfect, and He longs to share His vision with you. He will show you the real world because God gave you Heaven. Through Him your Father calls His Son to remember. The awakening of His Son begins with his investment in the real world, and by this he will learn to re-invest in himself. For reality is one with the Father and the Son, and the Holy Spirit blesses the real world in Their Name.

When you have seen this real world, as you will surely do, you will remember us. Yet you must learn the cost of sleeping, and refuse to pay it. Only then will you decide to awaken. And then the real world will spring to your sight, for Christ has never slept. He is waiting to be seen, for He has never lost sight of you. He looks quietly on the real world, which He would share with you because He knows of the Father's Love for Him. And knowing this, He would give you what is yours. In perfect peace He waits for you at His Father's altar, holding out the Father's Love to you in the quiet light of the Holy Spirit's blessing. For the Holy Spirit will lead everyone home to his Father, where Christ waits as his Self.

Every Child of God is one in Christ, for his Being is in Christ as Christ's is in God. Christ's love for you is His love for His Father, which He knows because He knows His Father's Love for Him. When the Holy Spirit has at last led you to Christ at the altar to His Father, perception fuses into knowledge because perception has become so holy that its transfer to holiness is merely its natural extension. Love transfers to love without any interference, for the situations are identical. As you perceive more and more common elements in all situations, the transfer of your training under the Holy Spirit's guidance increases and becomes generalized.

Gradually you learn to apply it to everyone and everything, for its applicability is universal. When this has been accomplished, perception and knowledge have become so similar that they share the unification of the laws of God.

What is one cannot be perceived as separate, and the denial of the separation is the re-instatement of knowledge. At the altar of God, the holy perception of God's Son becomes so enlightened that light streams into it, and the Spirit of God's Son shines in the Mind of the Father and becomes One with It. Very gently does God shine upon Himself, loving the extension of Himself which is His Son. The world has no purpose as it blends into the Purpose of God. For the real world has slipped quietly into Heaven, where everything eternal in it has always been. There the Redeemer and the redeemed join in perfect love of God and of each other. Heaven is your home and being in God it must also be in you.

Miracles demonstrate that learning has occurred under the right guidance, for learning is invisible, and what has been learned can be recognized only by its results. Its generalization is demonstrated as you use it in more and more situations. You will recognize that you have learned there is no order of difficulty in miracles when you have applied them to all situations. There is no situation to which miracles do not apply and by applying them to all situations you will gain the real world. For in this holy perception you will be made whole, and the Atonement will radiate from your acceptance of it for yourself to everyone the Holy Spirit sends you for your blessing. In every Child of God His blessing lies, and in your blessing of the Children of God is His blessing to you.

Everyone in the world must play his part in the redemption of the world, to recognize that the world has been redeemed. You cannot see the invisible. Yet if you see its effects you know it must be there. By perceiving what it does, you recognize its being. And by what it does, you learn what it is.

You cannot see your abilities, but you gain confidence in their existence as they enable you to act and the results of your actions you can see.

The Holy Spirit is invisible, but you can see the results of His Presence, and through them you will learn that He is there. What He enables you to do is clearly not of this world, for miracles violate every law of reality as this world judges it. Every law of time and space, of magnitude and mass, of prediction and control is transcended, for what the Holy Spirit enables you to do is clearly beyond all of them. Perceiving His results, you will understand where He must be, and finally know what He is.

You cannot see the Holy Spirit, but you can see His manifestations. And unless you do, you will not realize He is there. Miracles are His witnesses and speak for his Presence. What you cannot see becomes real to you only through the witnesses who speak for it. For you can be aware of what you cannot see, and it can become compellingly real to you as its presence becomes manifest through you. Do the Holy Spirit's work, for you share in His function. As your function in Heaven is creation, so your function on earth is healing. God shares His function with you in Heaven, and the Holy Spirit shares His with you on earth.

As long as you believe you have two functions, so long will you need correction. For this belief is the destruction of peace, a goal in direct opposition to the Holy Spirit's purpose. You see what you expect, and you expect what you invite. Your perception is the result of your invitation, coming to you as you sent for it. Whose manifestations would you see? Of whose presence would you be convinced? For you will believe in what you manifest, and as you look out so will you see in. Two ways of looking at the world are in your mind, and your perception will reflect the guidance you chose.

I am the manifestation of the Holy Spirit, and when you see me it will be because you have invited Him. For He will send you His witnesses if you will but look upon them. Remember always that you see what you seek, for what you seek you will find. The ego finds what it seeks, and only that. It does not find love, for that is not what it is seeking. Yet seeking and finding are the same, and if you seek for two goals you will find them, but you will recognise neither.

For you will think they are the same because you want them both. The mind always strives for integration, and if it is split and wants to keep the split, it will believe it has one goal by making it one. We said before that what you project is up to you, but it is not up to you whether to project, for projection is a law of mind. Perception is projection, and you look in before you look out.

As you look in you choose the guide for seeing, and then you look out and behold his witnesses. This is why you find what you seek. What you want in yourself you will make manifest by projection, and you will accept it from the world because you put it there by wanting it.

When you think you are projecting what you do not want, it is still because you do want it. This leads directly to dissociation, for it represents the acceptance of two goals, each perceived in a different place, separated from each other because you made them different. The mind then sees a divided world outside itself, but not within. This gives it an illusion of integrity and enables it to believe that it is pursuing one goal. As long as you perceive the world as split, you are not healed. For to be healed is to pursue one goal because you have accepted only one and want but one.

When you want only love you will see nothing else. The contradictory nature of the witnesses you perceive is merely the reflection of your conflicting invitations. You have looked upon your minds and accepted opposition there, having sought it there. But do not then believe that the witnesses for opposition are true, for they attest only to your decision about reality, returning to you the message you gave them. Love is recognized by its messengers. If you make love manifest, its messengers will come to you because you invited them.

The power of decision is your one remaining freedom as a prisoner of this world. You can decide to see it right. What you made of it is not its reality, for its reality is only what you gave it. You cannot really give anything but love to anyone or anything, nor can you really receive anything else from them. If you think you have received anything else, it is because you have looked within and thought you saw the power to give something else within yourself. It was only this decision that determined what you found, for it was the decision of what you sought

You are afraid of me because you looked within and are afraid of what you saw. Yet you could not have seen reality, for the reality of your mind is the loveliest of God's creations. Coming only from God, its power and grandeur could only bring you peace if you really looked upon it. If you are afraid, it is because you saw something that it is not there. Yet in that same place you could have looked upon me and all your brothers, in the perfect safety of the Mind Which created us. For we are there in the peace of the Father, who wills to project His peace through you.

When you have accepted your mission to project peace you will find it, for by making it manifest you will see it. Its holy witnesses will surround you because you called upon them and they will come to you. I have heard your call and I have answered it, but you will not look upon me nor hear the answer which you sought. That is because you do not yet want only that. Yet as I become more real to you, you will learn that you do want only that.

And you will see me as you look within, and we will look upon the world as God created it together. Through the eyes of Christ only the real world exists and can be seen. As you decide so will you see. And all that you see but witnesses to your decision. When you look within and see me, it will be because you have decided to manifest truth. And as you manifest it you will see it both without and within, for you will see it without because you saw it first within.

Everything you behold without is a judgement of what you beheld within. If it is your judgement it will be wrong, for judgement is not your function. If it is the judgement of the Holy Spirit it will be right, for judgement is His function. You share His function only by judging as He does, reserving no judgement at all unto yourselves. For you will judge against yourselves, but He will judge for you.

Remember, then, that whenever you look without and react unfavourably to what you see, you have judged yourself unworthy and have condemned yourself to death. The death penalty is the ego's ultimate goal, for it fully believes that you are a criminal, as deserving of death as God knows you are deserving of life. The death penalty never leaves the ego's mind, for that is what it always reserves for you in the end. Wanting to kill you as the final expression of its feeling for you, it lets you live but to await death. It will torment you while you live, but its hatred is not satisfied until you die. For your destruction is the one end toward which it works, and the only end with which it will be satisfied.

The ego is not a traitor to God to Whom treachery is impossible, but it is a traitor to you who believe you have been treacherous to your Father. That is why the undoing of guilt is an essential part of the Holy Spirit's teaching. For as long as you feel guilty you are listening to the voice of the ego, which tells you that you have been treacherous to God and therefore deserve death. You will think that death comes from God and not from the ego because, by confusing yourself with the ego, you believe that you want death. And from what you want God does not save you.

When you are tempted to yield to the desire for death. Remember that I did not die. You will realize that this is true when you look within and see me. Would I have overcome death for myself alone? And would eternal life have been given me of the Father unless he had also given it to you? When you learn to make me manifest you will never see death. For you will have looked upon the deathless in yourself, and you will see only the eternal as you look out upon a world that cannot die.

Do you really believe that you can kill the Son of God? The Father has hidden His Son safely within Himself and kept him far away from your destructive thoughts, but you know neither the Father nor the Son because of them. You attack the real world every day and every hour and every minute, and yet you are surprised that you cannot see it. If you seek love in order to attack it you will never find it. For if love is sharing, how can you find it except through itself? Offer it and it will come to you because it is drawn to itself. But offer attack and it will remain hidden, for it can live only in peace.

God's Son is as safe as his Father, for the Son knows his Father's protection and cannot fear. His Father's Love holds him in perfect peace, and needing nothing, he asks for nothing. Yet he is far from you whose Self he is, for you chose to attack him, and he disappeared from your sight into his Father. He did not change, but you did. For a split mind and all its works were not created by the Father and could not live in the knowledge of Him.

When you made what is not true visible, what is true became invisible. Yet it cannot be invisible in itself for the Holy Spirit sees it with perfect clarity. It is invisible to you because you are looking at something else. Yet it is no more up to you to decide what is visible and what is invisible than it is up to you to decide what reality is. What can be seen is what the Holy Spirit sees. The definition of reality is God's, not yours. He created it, and He knows what it is. You who knew have forgotten, and unless He had given you a way to remember you would have condemned yourselves to oblivion.

Because of your Father's Love you can never forget Him, for no-one can forget what God Himself placed in his memory. You can deny it, but you cannot lose it. A Voice will answer every question you ask, and a Vision will correct the perception of everything you see. For what you have made invisible is the only truth, and what you have not heard is the only answer. God would reunite you with yourself and did not abandon you in your seeming distress. You are waiting only for Him and do not know it.

Yet His memory shines in your minds and cannot be obliterated. It is no more past than future, being forever always.

You have but to ask for this memory and you will remember. Yet the memory of God cannot shine in a mind which has made it invisible and wants to keep it so. For the memory of God can dawn only in a mind that wills to remember, and that has relinquished the insane desire to control reality. You who cannot even control yourselves should hardly aspire to control the universe. But look upon what you have made of it and rejoice that it is not so. Son of God, be not content with nothing! What is not real cannot be seen and has no value. God could not offer His Son what has no value, nor could His Son receive it. You were redeemed the instant you thought you had deserted Him.

Everything you made has never been and is invisible because the Holy Spirit does not see it. Yet what He does see is yours to behold, and through His vision your perception is healed. You have made the invisible the only truth that this world holds. Valuing nothing, you have sought nothing and found nothing. By making nothing real to you, you have seen it. But it is not there. And Christ is invisible to you because of what you have made visible to yourselves. Yet it does not matter how much distance you have tried to interpose between your awareness and truth. God's Son can be seen because his vision is shared. The Holy Spirit looks upon him and sees nothing else in you. What is invisible to you is perfect in His sight and encompasses all of it. He has remembered you because He forgot not the Father.

You looked upon the unreal and found despair. Yet by seeking the unreal, what else could you find? The unreal world is a thing of despair, for it can never be. And you who share God's Being with Him could never be content without reality. What God did not give you has no power over you and the attraction of love for love remains irresistible. For it is the function of love to unite all things unto itself, and to hold all things together by extending its wholeness.

The real world was given you by God in loving exchange for the world you made and which you see. But take it from the hand of Christ and look upon it. Its reality will make everything else invisible, for beholding it is total perception. And as you look upon it, you will remember that it was always so. Nothingness will become invisible, for you will at last have seen truly. Redeemed perception is easily translated into knowledge, for only perception is capable of error, and perception has never been. Being corrected it gives place to knowledge, which is forever the only reality.

The Atonement is but the way back to what was never lost. Your Father could not cease to love His Son.

If you did not feel guilty you could not attack, for condemnation is the root of attack. It is the judgement of one mind by another as unworthy of love and deserving of punishment. But herein lies the split. For the mind that judges perceive itself as separate from the mind being judged, believing that by punishing another it will escape punishment. All this is but the delusional attempt of the mind to deny itself and escape the penalty of denial. It is not an attempt to relinquish denial, but to hold on to it. For it is guilt that has obscured the Father to you, and it is guilt that has driven you insane.

The acceptance of guilt into the mind of God's Son was the beginning of the separation, as the acceptance of the Atonement is its end. The world you see is the delusional system of those made mad by guilt. Look carefully at this world, and you will realize that this is so. For this world is the symbol of punishment, and all the laws which seem to govern it are the laws of death. Children are born into it through pain and in pain. Their growth is attended by suffering, and they learn of sorrow and separation and death. Their minds are trapped in their brain, and its powers decline if their bodies are hurt. They seem to love, yet they desert and are deserted. They appear to lose what they love, perhaps the most insane belief of all. And their bodies wither and gasp and are laid in the ground and seem to be no more. Not one of them but has thought that God is cruel.

If this were the real world God would be cruel. For no father could subject his children to this as the price of salvation and BE loving. Love does not kill to save. If it did, attack would be salvation, and this is the ego's interpretation, not God's. Only the world of guilt could demand this, for only the guilty could conceive of it. Adam's "sin" could have touched none of you had you not believed that it was the Father who drove him out of paradise. For in that belief the knowledge of the Father was lost, since only those who do not understand Him could believe it.

This world is a picture of the crucifixion of God's Son. And until you realize that God's Son cannot be crucified, this is the world you will see. Yet you will not realize this until you accept the eternal fact that God's Son is not guilty. He deserves only love because he has given only love. He cannot be condemned because he has never condemned. The Atonement is the final lesson he need learn, for it teaches him that, never having sinned, he has no need of salvation.

Long ago we said that the Holy Spirit shares the goal of all good teachers, whose ultimate aim is to make themselves unnecessary by teaching their pupils all they know. The Holy Spirit wills only this, for sharing the Father's Love for His Son, He wills to remove all guilt from his mind that he may remember his Father in peace. For peace and guilt are antithetical, and the Father can be remembered only in peace. Love and guilt cannot coexist, and to accept one is to deny the other. Guilt hides Christ from your sight, for it is the denial of the blamelessness of God's Son.

In this strange world which you have made, the Son of God has sinned. How could you see him, then? By making him invisible, the world of retribution rose in the black cloud of guilt which you accepted, and you hold it dear. For the blamelessness of Christ is the proof that the ego never was and can never be. Without guilt the ego has no life, and God's Son is without guilt. As you look upon yourselves and judge what you do honestly, as you have been asked to do, you may be tempted to wonder how you can be guiltless. Yet consider this:

You are not guiltless in time, but in eternity. You have "sinned" in the past, but there is no past. Always has no direction. Time seems to go in one direction, but when you reach its end it will roll up like a long carpet which has spread along the past behind you and will disappear. As long as you believe the Son of God is guilty you will walk along this carpet, believing that it leads to death. And the journey will seem long and cruel and senseless, for so it IS.

The journey which the Son of God has set himself is foolish indeed, but the journey on which his Father sets him is one of release and joy. The Father is not cruel, and His Son cannot hurt himself. The retaliation he fears and which he sees will never touch him, for although he believes in it the Holy Spirit knows it is not true. The Holy Spirit stands at the end of time, where you must be because He is with you. He has always undone everything unworthy of the Son of God, for such was His mission, given Him by God. And what God gives has always been.

You will see me as you learn the Son of God is guiltless. He has always sought his guiltlessness, and he has found it. For everyone is seeking to escape from the prison he has made, and the way to find release is not denied him. Being in him, he has found it. When he finds it is only a matter of time, and time is but an illusion. For the Son of God is guiltless now, and the brightness of his purity shines untouched forever in God's Mind. God's Son will always be as he was created. Deny your world and judge him not, for his eternal guiltlessness is in the Mind of his Father and protects him forever.

When you have accepted the Atonement for yourselves, you will realize that there is no guilt in God's Son. And only as you look upon him as guiltless can you understand his oneness. For the idea of guilt brings a belief in condemnation of one by another, projecting separation in place of unity. You can condemn only yourself, and by so doing you cannot know that you are God's Son. You have denied the condition of his Being, which is his perfect blamelessness. Out of Love he was created, and in Love he abides. Goodness and mercy have always followed him, for he has always extended the Love of his Father.

As you perceive the holy companions who travel with you, you will realize that there is no journey, but only an awakening. The Son of God, who sleepeth not, has kept faith with his Father for you. There is no road to travel on, and no time to travel through. For God waits not for His Son in time, being forever unwilling to be without him. And so it has always been. Let the holiness of God's Son shine away the cloud of guilt that darkens your mind, and by accepting his purity as yours, learn of him that it is yours.

You are invulnerable because you are guiltless. You can hold on to the past only through guilt. For guilt establishes that you will be punished for what you have done, and thus depends on one dimensional time, proceeding from past to future. No-one who believes this can understand what always means. And therefore guilt must deprive you of the appreciation of eternity. You are immortal because you are eternal, and always must be now. Guilt, then, is a way of holding past and future in your minds to ensure the ego's continuity. For if what has been will be punished, the ego's continuity is guaranteed. Yet the guarantee of your continuity is God's, not the ego's. And immortality is the opposite of time, for time passes away, while immortality is constant.

Accepting the Atonement teaches you what immortality is, for by accepting your guiltlessness you learn that the past has never been, and so the future is needless. The future, in time, is always associated with expiation, and only guilt could induce a sense of need for expiation. Accepting the guiltlessness of the Son of God as yours is therefore God's way of reminding you of His Son, and what he is in truth. God has never condemned His Son and being guiltless he is eternal.

You cannot dispel guilt by making it real and then atoning for it. This is the ego's plan, which it offers instead of dispelling it. The ego believes in atonement through attack, being fully committed to the insane notion that attack is salvation.

And you who cherish guilt must also believe it, for how else but by identifying with the ego could you hold dear what you do not want?

The ego teaches you to attack yourself because you are guilty, and this must increase the guilt, for guilt is the result of attack. In the ego's teaching, then, there is no escape from guilt. For attack makes guilt real, and if it is real there is no way to overcome it. The Holy Spirit dispels it simply through the calm recognition that it has never been. As He looks upon the guiltless Son of God, He knows this is true. And being true for you, you cannot attack yourself, for without guilt attack is impossible. You, then, are saved because God's Son is guiltless. And being wholly pure, you are invulnerable.

The ultimate purpose of projection as the ego uses it is always to get rid of guilt. Yet, characteristically, the ego attempts to get rid of guilt from its viewpoint only, for much as the ego wants to retain guilt, you find it intolerable, since guilt stands in the way of your remembering God, Whose pull is so strong that you cannot resist it. On this issue, then, the deepest split of all occurs, for if you are to retain guilt, as the ego insists, you cannot be you. Only by persuading you that it is you could the ego possibly induce you to project guilt, and thereby keep it in your mind.

Yet consider how strange a solution the ego's arrangement is. You project guilt to get rid of it, but you are actually merely concealing it. You do experience guilt feelings, but you have no idea why. On the contrary, you associate them with a weird assortment of ego ideals, which the ego claims you have failed. Yet you have no idea that you are failing the Son of God by seeing him as guilty. Believing you are no longer you, you do not realize that you are failing yourself.

The darkest of your hidden cornerstones holds your belief in guilt from your awareness. For in that dark and secret place is the realization that you have betrayed God's Son by condemning him to death. You do not even suspect this murderous but insane idea lies hidden there, for the ego's destructive urge is so intense that nothing short of the crucifixion of God's Son can ultimately satisfy it. It does not know who the Son of God is, because it is blind. Yet let it perceive guiltlessness anywhere, and it will try to destroy it, because it is afraid.

Much of the ego's strange behaviour is directly attributable to its definition of guilt. To the ego, the guiltless are guilty. Those who do not attack are its "enemies", because, by not valuing its interpretation of salvation, they are in an excellent position to let it go.

They have approached the darkest and deepest cornerstone in the ego's foundation and while the ego can withstand your raising all else to question, it guards this one secret with its life, for its existence does depend on keeping this secret. So it is this secret that we must look upon calmly, for the ego cannot protect you against truth, and in its presence the ego is dispelled.

In the calm light of truth, let us recognize that you believe you have crucified God's Son. You have not admitted to this "terrible" secret because you still wish to crucify him if you could find him. Yet the wish has hidden him from you because it is very fearful, and you are afraid to find him. You have handled this wish to kill yourself by not knowing who you are and identifying with something else. You have projected guilt blindly and indiscriminately, but you have not uncovered its source. For the ego does want to kill you, and if you identify with it you must believe its goal is yours.

We once said that the crucifixion is the symbol of the ego. When it was confronted with the real guiltlessness of God's Son it did attempt to kill him and the reason it gave was that guiltlessness is blasphemous to God. To the ego the ego is god, and guiltlessness must be interpreted as the final guilt which fully justifies murder. You do not yet understand that all your fear of this course stems ultimately from this interpretation, but if you will consider your reactions to it, you will become increasingly convinced that this is so.

This course has explicitly stated that its goal for you is happiness and peace. Yet you are afraid of it. You have been told again and again that it will make you free, yet you react as if it is trying to imprison you. Most of the time you dismiss it, but you do not dismiss the ego's thought system. You have seem its results and you still lack faith in it. You must, then, believe that by not learning the course you are protecting yourself. And you do not realize that it is only your guiltlessness which can protect you.

The Atonement has always been interpreted as the release from guilt, and this is correct if it is understood. Yet even when I have interpreted it for you, you have rejected it and have not accepted it for yourself. You have recognized the futility of the ego and its offerings, but though you do not want the ego you do not look upon the alternative with gladness. You are afraid of redemption, and you believe it will kill you. Make no mistake about the depth of your fear. For you believe that, in the presence of truth, you will turn on yourself and destroy yourself.

Little children, this is not so. Your "guilty secret" is nothing, and if you will but bring it to the light the Light will dispel it. And then no dark cloud will remain between you and the remembrance of your Father, for you will remember His guiltless Son, who did not die because he is immortal. And you will see that you were redeemed with him and have never been separated from him. In this understanding lies your remembering, for it is the recognition of love without fear. There will be great joy in Heaven on your homecoming, and the joy will be yours. For the redeemed son of man is the guiltless Son of God, and to recognize him is your redemption.

You may wonder why it is so crucial that you look upon your hatred and realize its full extent. You may also think that it would be easy enough for the Holy Spirit to show it to you and dispel it without the need for you to raise it to awareness yourself. Yet there is one more complication which you have interposed between yourself and the Atonement which you do not yet realize. We have said that no-one will countenance fear if he recognizes it. Yet in your disordered state, you are not afraid of fear. You do not like it, but it is not your desire to attack which really frightens you. You are not seriously disturbed by your hostility. You keep it hidden because you are more afraid of what it covers.

You could look even upon the ego's darkest cornerstone without fear if you did not believe that, without the ego, you would find within yourself something you fear even more. You are not afraid of crucifixion. Your real terror is of redemption. Under the ego's dark foundation is the memory of God, and it is of this that you are really afraid. For this memory would instantly restore you to your proper place, and it is this place that you have sought to leave.

Your fear of attack is nothing compared to your fear of love. You would be willing to look even upon your savage wish to kill God's Son if you did not believe that it saves you from love. For this wish caused the separation. You have protected it because you do not want the separation healed, and you realize that, by removing the dark cloud that obscures it, your love for your Father would impel you to answer his call and leap into Heaven. You believe that attack is salvation to prevent you from this. For still deeper than the ego's foundation, and much stronger than it will ever be, is your intense and burning love of God, and His for you. This is what you really want to hide.

In honesty, is it not harder for you to say "I love" than "I hate"? You associate love with weakness and hatred with strength and your own real power seems to you as your real weakness. For you could not control your joyous response to the call of love if you heard it, and the whole world you think you control would vanish.

The Holy Spirit, then, seems to be attacking your fortress, for you would shut out God, and He does not will to be excluded.

You have built your whole insane belief system because you think you would be helpless in God's Presence and you would save yourself from His Love because you think It would crush you into nothingness. You are afraid It would sweep you away from yourself and make you little. For you believe that magnitude lies in defiance, and that attack is grandeur. You think you have made a world which God would destroy; and by loving Him, which you do, you would throw this world away, which you would. Therefore, you have used the world to cover your love, and the deeper you go into the blackness of the ego's foundation, the closer you come to the Love that is hidden there and it is this that frightens you.

You can accept insanity because you made it, but you cannot accept love because you did not. You would rather be slaves of the crucifixion than Sons of God in redemption. For your individual death is more valued than your living oneness, and what is given you is not so dear as what you made. You are more afraid of God than of the ego, and love cannot enter where it is not welcome. But hatred can, for it enters of its will and cares not for yours.

The reason you must look upon your delusions and not keep them hidden is that they do not rest on their own foundation. In concealment they appear to do so, and thus they seem to be selfsustained. This is the fundamental illusion on which they rest. For beneath them, and concealed as long as they are hidden, is the loving mind that thought it made them in anger and the pain in this mind is so apparent, when it is uncovered, that its need of healing cannot be denied. Not all the tricks and games you offer it can heal it, for here is the real crucifixion of God's Son.

And yet he is not crucified. Here is both his pain and his healing, for the Holy Spirit's vision is merciful and His remedy is quick. Do not hide suffering from His sight but bring it gladly to Him. Lay before His eternal sanity all your hurt and let Him heal you. Do not leave any spot of pain hidden from His light and search your minds carefully for any thoughts which you may fear to uncover. For He will heal every little though which you have kept to hurt you, and cleanse it of its littleness, restoring it to the magnitude of God.

Beneath all your grandiosity, which you hold so dear, is your real call for help. For you call for love to your Father as your Father calls you to Himself. In that place which you have hidden you will only to unite with the Father, in loving remembrance of Him.

You will find this place of truth as you see it in your brothers, for though they may deceive themselves, like you they long for the grandeur that is in them. And perceiving it you will welcome it, and it will be yours. For grandeur is the right of God's Son, and no illusions can satisfy him or save him from what he is. Only his love is real, and he will be content only with his reality.

Save him from his illusions that you may accept the magnitude of your Father in peace and joy. But exempt no-one from your love, or you will be hiding a dark place in your mind where the Holy Spirit is not welcome. And you will exempt yourself from His healing power, for by not offering total love you will not be healed completely. Healing must be as complete as fear, for love cannot enter where there is one spot of fear to mar its welcome.

You who prefer specialness to sanity could not obtain it in your right minds. You were at peace until you asked for special favour. And God did not give it, for the request was alien to Him, and you could not ask this of a Father Who truly loved His Son. Therefore, you made of Him an unloving father, demanding of Him what only such a father could give. And the peace of God's Son was shattered, for he no longer understood his Father. He feared what he had made, but still more did he fear his real father, having attacked his own glorious equality with Him.

In peace he needed nothing and asked for nothing. In war he demands everything and found nothing. For how could the gentleness of love respond to his demands except by departing in peace and returning to the Father? If the Son did not wish to remain in peace, he could not remain at all. For a darkened mind cannot live in the light and it must seek a place of darkness where it can believe it is where it is not. God did not allow this to happen. Yet you demanded that it happen and therefore believed that it was so.

To "single out" is to "make alone," and thus make lonely. God did not do this to you. Could He set you apart, knowing that your peace lies in His oneness? He denied you only your request for pain, for suffering is not of His creation. Having given you creation, He could not take it from you. He could but answer your insane request with a sane answer which would abide with you in your insanity. For His answer is the reference point beyond illusions, from which you can look back on them and see them as insane. But seek this place and you will find it, for love is in you and will lead you there.

Now the reason why you are afraid of this course should be apparent. For this is a course on love because it is about you. You have been told that your function in this world is healing, and your function in Heaven is creating. The ego teaches that your function on earth is destruction, and that you have no function at all in Heaven. It would thus destroy you here and bury you here, leaving you no inheritance except the dust out of which it thinks you were made. As long as it is reasonably satisfied with you, as its reasoning goes, it offers you oblivion. When it becomes overtly savage, it offers you hell.

Yet neither oblivion nor hell is as unacceptable to you as Heaven. For your definition of Heaven is hell and oblivion, and the real Heaven is the greatest threat you think you could experience. For hell and oblivion are ideas which you made up, and you are bent on demonstrating their reality to establish yours. If their reality is questioned, you believe that yours is. For you believe that attack is your reality, and that your destruction is the final proof that you were right.

Under the circumstances, would it not be more desirable to have been wrong, even apart from the fact that you were wrong? While it could perhaps be argued that death suggests there was life, no-one would claim that it proves there is life. Even the past life which death might indicate could only have been futile if it must come to this and needs this to prove that it was. You question Heaven, but you do not question this. You could heal and be healed if you did question it. And even though you know not Heaven, might it not be more desirable than death? You have been as selective in your questioning as in your perception. An open mind is more honest than this.

The ego has a very strange notion of time, and it is with this notion that your questioning might well begin. The ego invests heavily in the past, and in the end believes that the past is the only aspect of time that is meaningful. You will remember that we said its emphasis on guilt enables it to ensure its continuity by making the future like the past, and thus avoiding the present. By the notion of paying for the past in the future the past becomes the determiner of the future, making them continuous without an intervening present. For the ego uses the present only as a brief transition to the future, in which it brings the past to the future by interpreting the present in past terms.

Now has no meaning to the ego. The present merely reminds it of past hurts, and it reacts to the present as if it were the past. The ego cannot tolerate release from the past and although the past is no more, the ego tries to preserve its image by responding as if it were present. Thus it dictates reactions to those you meet now from a past reference point, obscuring their present reality. In effect, if you follow the ego's dictates, you will react to your brothers as though they were someone else, and this will surely prevent you from perceiving them as they are. And you will receive messages from them out of your own past because, by making it real in the present, you are forbidding yourself to let it go. You thus deny yourself the message of release that every brother offers you now.

The shadowy figures from the past are precisely what you must escape. For they are not real and have no hold over you unless you bring them with you. They carry the spots of pain in your minds, directing you to attack in the present in retaliation for a past that is no more. And this decision is one of future pain. Unless you learn that past pain is delusional, you are choosing a future of illusions and losing the endless opportunities which you could find for release in the present. The ego would preserve your nightmares and prevent you from awakening and understanding that they are past.

Would you recognise a holy encounter if you are merely perceiving it as a meeting with your own past? For you are meeting no-one and the sharing of salvation which makes the encounter holy, is excluded from your sight. The Holy Spirit teaches that you always meet yourself, and the encounter is holy because you are. The ego teaches that you always encounter your past, and because your dreams were not holy the future cannot be and the present is without meaning. It is evident that the Holy Spirit's perception of time is the exact opposite of the ego's. The reason is equally clear, for they perceive the goal of time as diametrically opposed.

The Holy Spirit interprets time's purpose as rendering the need for it unnecessary. Thus does He regard the function of time as temporary, serving only his teaching function, which is temporary by definition. His emphasis is therefore on the only aspect of time which can extend to the infinite, for now is the closest approximation of eternity which this world offers. It is in the reality of now, without past or future, that the beginning of the appreciation of eternity lies. For only now is here, and it presents the opportunities for the holy encounters in which salvation can be found.

The ego, on the other hand, regards the function of time as one of extending itself in place of eternity, for, like the Holy Spirit, the ego interprets the goal of time as its own. The continuity of past and future, under its direction, is the only purpose the ego perceives in time, and it closes over the present so that no gap in its own continuity can occur. Its continuity, then, would keep you in time, while the Holy Spirit would release you from it. It is His interpretation of the means of salvation which you must learn to accept, if you would share His goal of salvation for you.

You, too, will interpret the function of time as you interpret yours. If you accept your function in the world of time as healing, you will emphasize only the aspect of time in which healing can occur. For healing cannot be accomplished in the past and must be accomplished in the present to release the future. This interpretation ties the future to the present and extends the present rather than the past. But if you interpret your function as destruction, you will lose sight of the present and hold on to the past to ensure a destructive future. And time will be as you interpret it, for of itself it is nothing.

We have said that you have but two emotions, love and fear. One is changeless but continually exchanged, being offered by the eternal to the eternal. In this exchange it is extended, for it increases as it is given. The other has many forms, for the content of individual illusions differs greatly. Yet they have one thing in common; they are all insane. They are made of sights which are not seen and sounds which are not heard. They make up a private world which cannot be shared. For they are meaningful only to their maker, and so they have no meaning at all. In this world their maker moves alone, for only he perceives them.

Each one peoples his world with figures from his individual past, and it is because of this that private worlds do differ. Yet the figures that he sees were never real, for they are made up only of His reactions to his brothers, and do not include their reactions to Him. Therefore he does not see that he made them, and that they are not whole. For these figures have no witnesses, being perceived in one separate mind only.

It is through these strange and shadowy figures that the insane relate to their insane world. For they see only those who remind them of these images, and it is to them that they relate. Thus do they communicate with those who are not there, and it is they who answer them. And no-one hears their answer save him who called upon them, and he alone believes they answered him. Projection makes perception and you cannot see beyond it.

Again and again have men attacked each other because they saw in them a shadow figure in their own private world. And thus it is that you must attack yourself first, for what you attack is not in others. Its only reality is in your own mind, and by attacking others you are literally attacking what is not there.

The delusional can be very destructive, for they do not recognize that they have condemned themselves. They do not wish to die, yet they will not let condemnation go. And so they separate into their private worlds, where everything is disordered, and where what is within appears to be without. Yet what is within they do not see, for the reality of their brothers they cannot see.

You have but two emotions, yet in your private world you react to each of them as though it were the other. For love cannot abide in a world apart, where when it comes it is not recognized. If you see your own hatred as your brother, you are not seeing Him. Everyone draws nigh unto what he loves, and recoils from what he fears. And you react with fear to love, and draw away from it. Yet fear attracts you, and believing it is love, you call it to yourself. Your private world is filled with the figures of fear you have invited into it, and all the love your brothers offer you, you do not see. As you look with open eyes upon your world, it must occur to you that you have withdrawn into insanity.

You see what is not there, and you hear what is soundless. Your behavioural manifestations of emotions are the opposite of what the emotions are. You communicate with no-one, and you are as isolated from reality as if you were alone in all the universe. In your madness you overlook reality completely, and you see only your own split mind everywhere you look. God calls you and you do not hear, for you are preoccupied with your own voice. And the vision of Christ is not in your sight, for you look upon yourself alone.

Little children, would you offer this to your Father? For if you offer it to yourself you are offering it to Him. And He will not return it, for it is unworthy of you because it is unworthy of Him. Yet He would release you from it and set you free. His sane answer tells you that what you have offered yourself is not true, but His offering to you has never changed. You who know not what you do can learn what insanity is and look beyond it. It is given you to learn how to deny insanity and come forth from your private world in peace.

You will see all that you denied in your brothers because you denied it in yourself. For you will love them, and by drawing nigh unto them you will draw them to yourself, perceiving them as witnesses to your reality which you share with God.

I am with them as I am with you, and we will draw them from their private worlds, for as we are united so would we unite with them. The Father welcomes all of us in gladness, and gladness is what we should offer Him. For every Son of God is given you to whom God gave Himself. And it is God whom you must offer them, to recognize His gift to you.

Vision depends on light, and you cannot see in darkness. Yet in the darkness, in the private world of sleep, you see in dreams although your eyes are closed. And it is here that what you see you made. But let the darkness go and all you made you will no longer see, for sight of it depends upon denying vision. Yet from denying vision it does not follow that you cannot see. But this is what denial does, for by it you accept insanity, believing you can make a private world and rule your own perceptions. Yet for this light must be excluded. Dreams disappear when light has come and you can see.

Do not seek vision through your eyes, for you made your way of seeing that you might see in darkness, and in this you are deceived. beyond this darkness, and yet still within you, is the vision of Christ, Who looks on all in light. Your vision comes from fear, as His from love. And He sees for you as your witness to the real world. He is the Holy Spirit's manifestation, looking always on the real world, and calling forth its witnesses and drawing them unto you. For He loves what He sees within you, and He would extend it. And He will not return unto the Father until He has extended your perception even unto Him. And there perception is no more, for He has returned you to the Father with Him.

You have but two emotions, and one you made and one was given you. Each is a way of seeing, and different worlds arise from their different visions. See through the vision that is given you, for through Christ's vision He beholds Himself. And seeing what He is, He knows His Father. Beyond your darkest dreams He sees God's guiltless Son within you, shining in perfect radiance which is undimmed by your dreams. And this you see as you look with Him, for His vision is His gift of love to you, given Him of the Father for you.

The Holy Spirit is the light in which Christ stands revealed. And all who would behold Him can see Him, for they have asked for light. Nor will they see Him alone, for He is no more alone than they are. Because they saw the son they have risen in Him to the Father. And all this will they understand because they looked within and saw beyond the darkness the Christ in them and recognized Him. In the sanity of His vision they looked upon themselves with love, seeing themselves as the Holy Spirit sees them. And with this vision of the truth in them came all the beauty of the world to shine upon them.

To perceive truly is to be aware of all reality through the awareness of your own. But for this no illusions can rise to meet your sight, for all reality leaves no room for any error. This means that you perceive a brother only as you see him now. His past has no reality in the present, and you cannot see it. Your past reactions to him are also not there, and if it is to them that you react now, you see but an image of him which you made and cherish instead of him. In your questioning of illusions, ask yourself if it is really sane to perceive what was now. If you remember the past as you look upon your brother, you will be unable to perceive the reality that is now.

You consider it "natural" to use your past experience as the reference point from which to judge the present. Yet this is unnatural because it is delusional. When you have learned to look upon everyone with no reference at all to the past, either his or yours as you perceived it, you will be able to learn from what you see now. For the past can cast no shadow to darken the present unless you are afraid of light. And only if you are would you choose to bring this darkness with you, and by holding it in your minds, see it as a dark cloud that shrouds your brothers and conceals their reality from your sight.

This darkness is within you. The Christ revealed to you now has no past for He is changeless, and in HIS changelessness lies your release. For if He is as He was created, there is no guilt in Him. No cloud of guilt has risen to obscure Him, and He stands revealed in everyone you meet because you see Him through himself. To be born again is to let the past go and look without condemnation upon the present. For the cloud which obscures God's Son to you is the past, and if you would have it past and gone, you must not see it now. If you see it now in your delusions it has not gone from you, although it is not there.

Time can release as well as imprison, depending on whose interpretation of it you use. Past, present and future are not continuous unless you force continuity on them. You can perceive them as continuous and make them so for you. But do not be deceived and then believe that this is how it is, for to believe that reality is what you would have it be according to your use for it is delusional. You would destroy time's continuity by breaking it into past, present and future for your own purposes. You would anticipate the future on the basis of your past experience and plan for it accordingly.

Yet by doing so you are aligning past and future, and not allowing the miracle, which could intervene between them, to free you to be born again.

The miracle enables you to see your brother without his past, and so perceive HIM as born again. His errors are all past, and by perceiving him without them you are releasing him. And since his past is yours, you share in this release. Let no dark cloud out of your past obscure him from you, for truth lies only in the present, and you will find it if you seek it there. You have looked for it where it is not, and therefore have not found it. Learn, then, to seek it where it is, and it will dawn on eyes that see. Your past was made in anger, and if you use it to attack the present you will not see the freedom that the present holds. Judgement and condemnation are behind you, and unless you bring them with you, you will see that you are free of them.

Look lovingly upon the present, for it holds the only things that are forever true. All healing lies within it because its continuity is real. It extends to all aspects of consciousness at the same time, and thus enables them to reach each other. The present is before time was and will be when time is no more. In it is everything that is eternal, and they are one. Their continuity is timeless and their communication is unbroken, for they are not separated by the past. Only the past can separate and it is nowhere.

The present offers you your brothers in the light that would unite you with them and free you from the past. Would you, then, hold the past against them? For if you do, you are choosing to remain in the darkness that is not there and refusing to accept the light that is offered you. For the light of perfect vision is freely given as it is freely received and can be accepted only without limit. In this one, still dimension of time, which does not change and where there is no sight of what you were, you look at Christ and call His witnesses to shine on you because you called them forth. And they will not deny the truth in you because you looked for it in them and found it there.

Now is the time of salvation, for now is the release from time. Reach out to all your brothers, and touch them with the touch of Christ. In timeless union with them is your continuity, unbroken because it is wholly shared. God's guiltless Son is only light. There is no darkness in him anywhere, for he is whole. Call all your brothers to witness to his wholeness, as I am calling you to join with me. Every voice has a part in the song of redemption, the hymn of gladness and thanksgiving for the light to the Creator of light. The holy light that shines forth from God's Son is the witness that his light is of his Father.

Shine on your brothers in remembrance of your Creator, for you will remember Him as you call forth the witnesses to His creation. Those whom you heal bear witness to your healing, for in their wholeness you will see your own. And as your hymns of praise and gladness rise to your Creator, He will return your thanks in His clear answer to your call. For it can never be that His Son called upon Him and remained unanswered. His call to you is but your call to Him. And in Him you are answered by His peace.

Children of Light, you know not that the light is in you. Yet you will find it through its witnesses, for having given light to them they will return it. Everyone you see in light brings your light closer to your own awareness. Love always leads to love. The sick, who ask for love, are grateful for it, and in their joy they shine with holy thanks. And this they offer you who gave them joy. They are your guides to joy, for having received it of you they would keep it. You have established them as guides to peace, for you have made it manifest in them. And seeing it, its beauty calls you home.

There is a light which this world cannot give. Yet you can give it, as it was given you. And as you give it, it shines forth to call you from the world and follow it. For this light will attract you as nothing in this world can do. And you will lay aside the world and find another. This other world is bright with love which you have given it. And here will everything remind you of your Father and his Holy Son. Light is unlimited, and spreads across this world in quiet joy. All those you brought with you will shine on you, and you will shine on them in gratitude because they brought you here. Your light will join with theirs in power so compelling that it will draw the others out of darkness as you look on them.

Awakening unto Christ is following the laws of love of your free will, and out of quiet recognition of the truth in them. The attraction of light must draw you willingly, and willingness is signified by giving. Those who accept love of you become your willing witnesses to the love you gave them, and it is they who hold it out to you. In sleep you are alone, and your awareness is narrowed to yourself. And that is why the nightmares come. You dream of isolation because your eyes are closed. You do not see your brothers, and in the darkness you cannot look upon the light you gave to them.

And yet the laws of love are not suspended because you sleep. And you have followed them through all your nightmares, and have been faithful in your giving, for you were not alone. Even in sleep has Christ protected you, ensuring the real world for you when you wake. In your name He has given for you and given you the gifts He gave. God's Son is still as loving as his Father.

Continuous with his Father, he has no past apart from Him. So he has never ceased to be his Father's witness and his own. Although he slept, Christ's vision did not leave him. And so it is that he can call unto himself the witnesses that teach him that he never slept.

Sit quietly and look upon the world you see and tell yourself,

"The real world is not like this. It has no buildings, and there are no streets where people walk alone and separate. There are no stores where people buy an endless list of things they do not need. It is not lit with artificial light, and night comes not upon it. There is no day that brightens and grows dim. There is no loss. Nothing is there but shines and shines forever."

The world you see must be denied, for sight of it is costing you a different kind of vision. You cannot see both worlds, for each of them involves a different kind of seeing and depends on what you cherish. The sight of one is possible because you have denied the other. Both are not true, yet either one will seem as real to you as the amount to which you hold it dear. And yet their power is not the same because their real attraction to you is unequal.

You do not really want the world you see, for it has disappointed you since time began. The homes you built have never sheltered you. The roads you made have led you nowhere, and no city that you built has withstood the crumbling assault of time. Nothing you made but has the mark of death upon it. Hold it not dear, for it is old and tired, and ready to return to dust even as you made it. This aching world has not the power to touch the living world at all. You could not give it that, and so although you turn in sadness from it, you cannot find in it the road that leads away from it into another world.

Yet the real world has the power to touch you even here because you love it. And what you call with love will come to you. Love always answers, being unable to deny a call for help, or not to hear the cries of pain that rise to it from every part of this strange world you made but do not want. The only effort you need make to give this world away in glad exchange for what you did not make is willingness to learn the one you made is false.

You have been wrong about the world because you have misjudged yourself. From such a twisted reference point what could you see? All vision starts with the perceiver, who judges what is true and what is false. And what he judges false he does not see. You who would judge reality cannot see it, for whenever judgement enters reality has slipped away. The out of mind is out of sight because what is denied is there but is not recognize it.

Christ is still there, although you know Him not. His Being does not depend upon your recognition. He lives within you in the quiet present and waits for you to leave the past behind and enter into the world He holds out to you in love.

No-one in this distracted world but has seen some glimpses of the other world about him. Yet while he still lays value on his own, he will deny the vision of the other world, maintaining that he loves what he loves not, and following not the road that love points out. Love leads so gladly! And as you follow Him, you will rejoice that you have found His company, and learned of Him the joyful journey home. You wait but for yourself. To give this sad world over and exchange your errors for the peace of God is but your will. And Christ will always offer you the Will of God, in recognition that you share it with Him.

It is God's Will that nothing touch His Son except Himself, and nothing else comes nigh unto him. He is as safe from pain as God Himself, Who watches over him in everything. The world about him shines with love because God placed him in Himself where pain is not, and love surrounds him without end or flaw. Disturbance of his peace can never be. In perfect sanity he looks on love, for it is all about him and within him. He must deny the world of pain the instant he perceives the arms of love around him. And from this point of safety he looks quietly about him and recognizes that the world is one with him.

The peace of God passeth your understanding only in the past. Yet here it is, and you can understand it now. God loves His Son forever, and His Son returns his Father's Love forever. The real world is the way that leads you to remembrance of this one thing that is wholly true and wholly yours. For all else you have lent yourself in time and it will fade. But this one thing is always yours, being the gift of God unto His Son. Your one reality was given you, and by it God created you as one with Him.

You will first dream of peace, and then awaken to it. Your first exchange of what you made for what you want is the exchange of nightmares for the happy dreams of love. In these lie your true perceptions, for the Holy Spirit corrects the world of dreams where all perception is. Knowledge needs no correction. Yet the dreams of love lead unto knowledge. In them you see nothing fearful, and because of this they are the welcome that you offer knowledge. Love waits on welcome, not on time and the real world is but your welcome of what always was. Therefore the call of joy is in it, and your glad response is your awakening to what you have not lost. Praise, then, the Father for the perfect sanity of His most holy Son.

Your Father knoweth that you have need of nothing. In Heaven this is so, for what could you need in eternity? In your world you do need things because it is a world of scarcity in which you find yourself because you are lacking. Yet can you find yourself in such a world? Without the Holy Spirit the answer would be no. Yet because of Him the answer is a joyous yes! As Mediator between the two worlds, He knows what you have need of and what will not hurt you. Ownership is a dangerous concept if it is left to you. The ego wants to have things for salvation, for possession is its law. Possession for its own sake is the ego's fundamental creed, a basic cornerstone in the churches that it builds unto itself. And at its altar it demands you lay all of the things it bids you get, leaving you no joy in them.

Everything that the ego tells you that you need will hurt you. For although the ego urges you again and again to get, it leaves you nothing, for what you get it will demand of you. And even from the very hands that grasped it, it will be wrenched and hurled into the dust. For where the ego sees salvation it sees separation, and so you lose whatever you have gotten in its name. Therefore ask not of yourselves what you need, for you do not know, and your advice unto yourself will hurt you. For what you think you need will merely serve to tighten up your world against the light, and render you unwilling to question the value that this world can really hold for you.

Only the Holy Spirit knows what you need. For He will give you all things that do not block the way to light. And what else could you need? In time, He gives you all the things that you need have and will renew them as long as you have need of them. He will take nothing from you as long as you have any need of it. And yet He knows that everything you need is temporary and will but last until you step aside from all your needs and learn that all of them have been fulfilled. Therefore He has no investment in the things that He supplies except to make certain that you will not use them on behalf of lingering in time. He knows that you are not at home there, and He wills no delay to wait upon your joyous homecoming.

Leave, then, your needs to Him. He will supply them with no emphasis at all upon them. What comes to you of Him comes safely, for He will ensure it never can become a dark spot, hidden in your mind, and kept to hurt you. Under His guidance you will travel light and journey lightly, for His sight is ever on the journey's end, which is His goal. God's Son is not a traveller through outer worlds. However holy his perception may become, no world outside himself holds his inheritance.

Within himself he has no needs, for light needs nothing but to shine in peace, and from itself to let the rays extend in quiet to infinity.

Whenever you are tempted to undertake a foolish journey that would lead away from light, remember what you really want, and say,

"The Holy Spirit leads me unto Christ, and where else would I go? What need have I but to awake in Him?"

Then follow Him in joy, with faith that He will lead you safely through all dangers to your peace of mind that this world sets before you. Kneel not before the altars to sacrifice and seek not what you will surely lose. Content yourselves with what you will as surely keep, and be not restless, for you undertake a quiet journey to the peace of God, where He would have you be in quietness.

In me you have already overcome every temptation that would hold you back. We walk together on the way to quietness that is the gift of God. Hold me dear, for what except your brothers can you need? We will restore to you the peace of mind that we must find together. The Holy Spirit will teach you to awaken unto us and to yourself. This is the only real need to be fulfilled in time. Salvation from the world lies only here. My peace I give you. Take it of me in glad exchange for all the world has offered but to take away. And we will spread it like a veil of light across the world's sad face, in which we hide our brothers from the world, and it from them.

We cannot sing redemption's hymn alone. My task is not completed until I have lifted every voice with mine. And yet it is not mine, for as it is my gift to you, so was it the Father's gift to me, given me through His Spirit. The sound of it will banish sorrow from the mind of God's most holy Son, where it cannot abide. Healing in time is needed, for joy cannot establish its eternal reign where sorrow dwells. You dwell not here, but in eternity. You travel but in dreams while safe at home. Give thanks to every part of you that you have taught how to remember you. Thus does the Son of God give thanks unto his Father for his purity.

All therapy is release from the past. That is why the Holy Spirit is the only therapist. He teaches that the past does not exist, a fact which belongs to the sphere of knowledge, and which therefore no one in the world knows. It would indeed be impossible to be in the world with this knowledge. For the mind that knows this unequivocally knows also that it dwells in eternity and utilizes no perception at all. It therefore does not consider where it is, because the concept "where" does not mean anything to it.

It knows that it is everywhere, just as it has everything, and forever.

The very real difference between perception and knowledge becomes quite apparent if you consider this: There is nothing partial about knowledge. Every aspect is whole, and therefore no aspect is separate. You are an aspect of knowledge, being in the Mind of God, Who knows you. All knowledge must be yours, for in you is all knowledge. Perception, at its loftiest, is never complete. Even the perception of the Holy Spirit, as perfect as perception can be, is without meaning in Heaven. Perception can reach everywhere under His guidance, for the vision of Christ beholds everything in light. Yet no perception, however holy, will last forever.

Perfect perception, then, has many elements in common with knowledge, making transfer to it possible. Yet the last step must be taken by God, because the last step in your redemption, which seems to be in the future, was accomplished by God in your creation. The separation has not interrupted it. Creation cannot be interrupted. The separation is merely a faulty formulation of reality, with no effect at all. The miracle, without a function in Heaven, is needful here. Aspects of reality can still be seen, and they will replace aspects of unreality. Aspects of reality can be seen in everything and everywhere. Yet only God can gather them together by crowning them as one with the final gift of eternity.

Apart from the Father and the Son, the Holy Spirit has no function. He is not separate from either, being in the mind of both and knowing that Mind is one. He is a Thought of God, and God has given Him to you because He has no Thoughts He does not share. His message speaks of timelessness in time, and that is why Christ's vision looks on everything with love. Yet even Christ's vision is not His reality. The golden aspects of reality which spring to light under His loving gaze are partial glimpses of the Heaven that lies beyond them.

This is the miracle of creation; that it is one forever. Every miracle you offer to the Son of God is but the true perception of one aspect of the whole. Though every aspect is the whole, you cannot know this until you see that every aspect is the same, perceived in the same light and therefore one. Everyone seen without the past thus brings you nearer to the end of time by bringing healed and healing sight into the darkness and enabling the world to see. For light must come into the darkened world to make Christ's vision possible even here. Help Him to give His gift of light to all who think they wander in the darkness and let Him gather them into His quiet sight that makes them one.

They are all the same; all beautiful and equal in their holiness. And He will offer them unto His Father as they were offered unto Him. There is one miracle, as there is one reality. And every miracle you do contains them all, as every aspect of reality you see blends quietly into the One Reality of God. The only miracle that was is God's most holy Son, created in the One Reality that is his Father. Christ's vision is His gift to you. His Being is His Father's gift to Him.

Be you content with healing, for Christ's gift you can bestow, and your Father's gift you cannot lose. Offer Christ's gift to everyone and everywhere, for miracles, offered the Son of God through the Holy Spirit, attune you to reality. The Holy Spirit knows your part in the redemption, and who are seeking you and where to find them. Knowledge is far beyond your individual concern. You who are part of it and all of it need only realize that it is of the Father, not of you. Your role in the redemption leads you to it by re-establishing its oneness in your minds.

When you have seen your brothers as yourself you will be released to knowledge, having learned to free yourself of Him Who knows of freedom. Unite with me under the holy banner of His teaching, and as we grow in strength the power of God's Son will move in us, and we will leave no-one untouched and no-one left alone. And suddenly time will be over, and we will all unite in the eternity of God the Father. The holy light you saw outside yourself, in every miracle you offered to your brothers, will be returned to you. And knowing that the light is in you, your creations will be there with you, as you are in your Father.

As miracles in this world join you to your brothers, so do your creations establish your fatherhood in Heaven. You are the witnesses to the Fatherhood of God, and He has given you the power to create the witnesses to your fatherhood in Heaven. The miracle which God created is perfect, as are the miracles which you created in His Name. They need no healing, nor do you, when you know them.

Yet in this world your perfection is unwitnessed. God knows it but you do not, and so you do not share His witness to it. Nor do you witness unto Him, for reality is witnessed to as one. God waits your witness to His Son and to Himself. The miracles you do on earth are lifted up to Heaven and to Him. They witness to what you do not know, and as they reach the gates of Heaven God will open them. For never would He leave His own beloved Son outside them and beyond Himself.

Guilt remains the only thing that hides the Father, for guilt is the attack upon His Son. The guilty always condemn and having done so they will condemn, linking the future to the past as is the ego's law. Fidelity unto this law lets no light in, for it demands fidelity to darkness and forbids awakening. The ego's laws are strict, and breaches are severely punished. Therefore give no obedience to its laws, for they are laws of punishment. And those who follow them believe that they are guilty and so they must condemn. Between the future and the past the laws of God must intervene, if you would free yourselves. Atonement stands between them, like a lamp that shines so brightly that the chain of darkness in which you bound yourselves will disappear.

Release from guilt is the ego's whole undoing. Make no one fearful, for his guilt is yours, and by obeying the ego's harsh commandments you bring its condemnation of yourself, and you will not escape the punishment it offers those who obey it. The ego rewards fidelity to it with pain, for faith in it is pain. And faith can be rewarded only in terms of the belief in which the faith was placed. Faith makes the power of belief, and where it is invested determines its reward. For faith is always given what is treasured, and what is treasured is returned to you.

The world can give you only what you gave it, for being nothing but your own projection, it has no meaning apart from what you found in it and placed your faith in. Be faithful unto darkness and you will not see, because your faith will be rewarded as you gave it. You will accept your treasure, and if you place your faith in the past the future be like it. Whatever you hold as dear you think is yours. The power of your valuing will make it so.

Atonement brings a re-evaluation of everything you cherish, for it is the means by which the Holy Spirit can separate the false and the true, which you have accepted into your minds without distinction. Therefore, you cannot value one without the other, and guilt has become as true for you as innocence. You do not believe the Son of God is guiltless because you see the past and see Him not. When you condemn a brother, you are saying, "I who was guilty choose to remain so." You have denied His freedom, and by so doing you have denied the witness unto yours. You could as easily have freed him from the past and lifted from his mind the cloud of guilt that binds him to it. And in His freedom would have been your own.

Lay not his guilt upon him, for his guilt lies in his secret that he thinks that he has done this unto you. Would you, then, teach him that he is right in his delusion? The idea that the guiltless Son of God can attack himself and make himself guilty is insane. In any form, in anyone, believe this not. For sin and condemnation are the same, and the belief in one is faith in the other, calling for punishment instead of love. Nothing can justify insanity, and to call for punishment upon yourself must be insane.

See no-one, then, as guilty, and you will affirm the truth of guiltlessness unto yourself. In every condemnation that you offer the Son of God lies the conviction of your own guilt. If you would have the Holy Spirit make you free of it, accept His offer of Atonement for all your brothers. For so you learn that it is true for you. Remember always that it is impossible to condemn the Son of God in part. Those whom you see as guilty become the witnesses to guilt in you, and you will see it there, for it is there until it is undone. Guilt is always in your own mind, which has condemned itself. Project it not, for while you do it cannot be undone. With everyone whom you release from guilt great is the joy in Heaven, where the witnesses to your fatherhood rejoice.

Guilt makes you blind, for while you see one spot of guilt within you, you will not see the light. And by projecting it the world seems dark and shrouded in your guilt. You throw a dark veil over it and cannot see it because you cannot look within. You are afraid of what you would see there, but it is not there. The thing you fear is gone. If you would look within you would see only the Atonement, shining in quiet and in peace upon the altar to your Father.

Do not be afraid to look within. The ego tells you all is black with guilt within you, and bids you not to look. Instead, it bids you look upon your brothers and see the guilt in them. Yet this you cannot do without remaining blind. For those who see their brothers in the dark, and guilty in the dark in which they shroud them are too afraid to look upon the light within. Within you is not what you believe is there and what you put your faith in.

Within you is the holy sign of perfect faith your Father has in you. He does not value you as you do. He knows Himself and knows the truth in you. He knows there is no difference, for He knows not of differences. Can you see guilt where God knows there is perfect innocence? You can deny His knowledge, but you cannot change it. Look, then, upon the light He placed within you, and learn that what you feared was there has been replaced with love.

You are accustomed to the notion that the mind can see the source of pain where it is not. The doubtful service of displacement is to hide the real source of your guilt and keep from your awareness the full perception that it is insane. Displacement always is maintained by the illusion that the source, from which attention is diverted, must be true and must be fearful, or you would not have displaced the guilt onto what you believed to be less fearful. You are therefore willing, with little opposition, to look upon all sorts of "sources" underneath awareness, provided that they are not the deeper source to which they bear no real relationship at all.

Insane ideas have no real relationships, for that is why they are insane. No real relationship can rest on guilt, or even hold one spot of it to mar its purity. For all relationships which guilt has touched are used but to avoid the person and the guilt. What strange relationships you have made for this strange purpose! And you forgot that real relationships are holy and cannot be used by you at all. They are used only by the Holy Spirit, and it is that which makes them pure. For by pre-empting for your own ends what you should have given to Him, he cannot use them unto your release. No-one who would unite in any way with anyone for his own salvation will find it in that strange relationship. It is not shared and so it is not real.

In any union with a brother in which you seek to lay your guilt upon him, or share it with him, or perceive his own, you will feel guilty. Nor will you find satisfaction and peace with him because your union with him is not real. You will see guilt in that relationship because you put it there. It is inevitable that those who suffer guilt will attempt to displace it because they do believe in it. Yet, though they suffer, they will not look within and let it go. They cannot know they love and cannot understand what loving is. Their main concern is to perceive the source of guilt outside themselves, beyond their own control.

When you maintain that you are guilty but the source lies in the past, you are not looking inward. The past is not in you. Your weird associations to it have no meaning in the present. Yet you let them stand between you and your brothers, with whom you find no real relationships at all. Can you expect to use your brothers as a means to "solve" the past, and still to see them as they really are? Salvation is not found by those who use their brothers to resolve problems which are not there. You wanted not salvation in the past. Would you impose your idle wishes on the present, and hope to find salvation now?

Determine, then, to be not as you were. Use no relationship to hold you to the past, but with each one each day be born again. A minute, even less, will be enough to free you from the past, and give your mind in peace over to the Atonement. When everyone is welcome to you as you would have yourself be welcome to your Father, you will see no guilt in you. For you will have accepted the Atonement, which shone within you all the while you dreamed of guilt and would not look within and see it.

As long as you believe that guilt is justified in any way, in anyone, whatever he may do, you will not look within, where you would always find Atonement. The end of guilt will never come as long as you believe there is a reason for it. For you must learn that guilt is always totally insane and has no reason. The Holy Spirit seeks not to dispel reality. If guilt were real atonement would not be. The purpose of Atonement is to dispel illusions, not to establish them as real and then forgive them.

The Holy Spirit does not keep illusions in your mind to frighten you and show them to you fearfully to demonstrate what He has saved you from. What He has saved you from is gone. Give no reality to guilt and see no reason for it. The Holy Spirit does what God would have Him do and has always done so. He has seen separation but knows of union. He teaches healing but He also knows of creation. He would have you see and teach as He does, and through Him. Yet what He knows you do not know, though it is yours.

Now it is given you to heal and teach, to make what will be now. As yet it is not now. The Son of God believes that he is lost in guilt, alone in a dark world where pain is pressing everywhere upon him from without. When he has looked within and seen the radiance there, he will remember how much his Father loves him. And it will seem incredible that he has ever thought his Father loved him not and looked upon him as condemned. The moment that you realize guilt is insane, wholly unjustified and wholly without reason, you will not fear to look upon the Atonement and accept it wholly.

You who have been unmerciful unto yourselves do not remember your Father's Love. And looking without mercy upon your brothers, you do not remember how much You love Him. Yet it is forever true. In shining peace within you is the perfect purity in which you were created. Fear not to look upon the lovely truth in you. Look through the cloud of guilt that dims your vision and look past darkness to the holy place where you will see the light. The altar to your Father is as pure as He Who raised it to Himself. Nothing can keep from you what Christ would have you see. His will is like His Father's and He offers mercy to every Child of God, as He would have you do.

Release from guilt as you would be released. There is no other way to look within and see the light of love shining as steadily and as surely as God Himself has always loved His Son. And as his son loves Him. There is no fear in love, for love is guiltless. You who have always loved your Father can have no fear, for any reason, to look within and see your holiness. You cannot be as you believed you were. Your guilt is without reason because it is not in the Mind of God, where you are. And this is reason, which the Holy Spirit would restore to you. He would remove only illusions. All else He would have you see. And in Christ's vision He would show you the perfect purity that is forever within God's Son.

You cannot enter into real relationships with any of God's Sons unless you love them all and equally. Love is not special. If you single out part of the Sonship for your love, you are imposing guilt on all your relationships, and making them unreal. You can love only as God loves. Seek not to love unlike Him, for there is no love apart from His. Until you recognize that this is true you will have no idea what love is like. No-one who condemns a brother can see himself as guiltless in the peace of God. If he is guiltless and in peace and sees it not, he is delusional, and has not looked upon himself.

To him I say,

"Behold the Son of God and look upon his purity and be still. In quiet look upon his holiness and offer thanks unto his Father that no guilt has ever touched him."

No illusion that you have ever held against him has touched his innocence in any way. His shining purity, wholly untouched by guilt and wholly loving, is bright within you. Let us look upon him together and love him. For in our love of him is your guiltlessness. But look upon yourself, and gladness and appreciation for what you see will banish guilt forever. I thank You, Father, for the purity of Your most holy Son, whom You have created guiltless forever.

Like you my faith and my belief are centred on what I treasure. The difference is that I love only what God loves with me, and because of this, I treasure you beyond the value that you set on yourselves, even unto the worth that God has placed upon you. Love all that He created and all my faith and my belief I offer unto it. My faith in you is strong as all the love I give my Father. My trust in you is without limit, and without the fear that you will hear me not. I thank the Father for your loveliness, and for the many gifts that you will let me offer to the Kingdom in honour of its wholeness which is of God.

Praise be unto you who make the Father One with His Own Son. Alone we are all lowly, but together we shine with brightness so intense that none of us alone can even think on it. Before the glorious radiance of the Kingdom guilt melts away, and transformed into kindness, will never more be what it was. Every reaction that you experience will be so purified that it is fitting as a hymn of praise unto your Father. See only praise of Him in what He has created, for He will never cease His praise of you. United in this praise we stand before the gates of Heaven, where we will surely enter in our blamelessness. God loves you. Could I, then, lack faith in you and love Him perfectly?

Forgetfulness and sleep and even death become the ego's best advice for how to deal with the perceived and harsh intrusion of guilt on peace. Yet no-one sees himself in conflict, and ravaged by a cruel war, unless he believes that both opponents in the war are real. Believing this he must escape, for such a war would surely end his peace of mind and so destroy him. Yet if he could but realize the war is between forces that are real and unreal powers, he could look upon himself and see his freedom. No-one finds himself ravaged and torn in endless battles which he Himself perceives as wholly without meaning.

God would not have His Son embattled, and so His Son's imagined "enemy," which he made, is totally unreal. You are but trying to escape a bitter war from which you have escaped. The war is gone. For you have heard the hymn of freedom rising unto Heaven. Gladness and joy belong to God for your release because you made it not. Yet as you made not freedom, so you made not a war that could endanger freedom. Nothing destructive ever was or will be. The war, the guilt, the past are gone as one into the unreality from which they came.

When we are all united in Heaven, you will value nothing that you value here. For nothing that you value here you value wholly, and so you do not value it at all. Value is where God placed it and the value of what God esteems cannot be judged, for it has been established. It is wholly of value. It can merely be appreciated or not. To value it partially is not to know its value. In Heaven is everything God valued, and nothing else. Heaven is perfectly unambiguous. Everything is clear and bright and calls forth one response. There is no darkness, and there is no contrast. There is no variation. There is no interruption. There is a sense of peace so deep that no dream in this world has ever brought even a dim imagining of what it is.

Nothing in this world can give this peace, for nothing in this world is wholly shared. Perfect perception can merely show you what is capable of being wholly shared. It can also show you the results of sharing, while you still remember the results of not sharing. The Holy Spirit points quietly to the contrast, knowing that you will finally let Him judge the difference for you, allowing Him to demonstrate which must be true. He has perfect faith in your final judgement because He knows that He will make it for you. To doubt this would be to doubt that His mission will be fulfilled. How is this possible, when His mission is of God?

You whose minds are darkened by doubt and guilt, remember this: God gave the Holy Spirit to you, and gave Him the mission to remove all doubt and every trace of guilt that His dear Son has laid upon himself. It is impossible that this mission fail. Nothing can prevent what God would have accomplished from accomplishment. Whatever your reactions to the Holy Spirit's Voice may be, whatever voice you choose to listen to, whatever strange thoughts may occur to you, God's Will is done. You will find the peace in which He has established you because He does not change His Mind. He is invariable as the peace in which you dwell, and of which the Holy Spirit reminds you.

You will not remember change and shift in Heaven. You have need of contrast only here. Contrast and differences are necessary teaching aids, for by them you learn what to avoid and what to seek. When you have learned this you will find the answer that makes the need for any differences disappear. Truth comes of its own will unto its own. When you have learned that you belong to truth, it will flow lightly over you without a difference of any kind. For you will need no contrast to help you realize that this is what you want, and only this. Fear not the Holy Spirit will fail in what your Father has given Him to do. The Will of God can fail in nothing.

Have faith in only this one thing, and it will be sufficient: God wills you be in Heaven, and nothing can keep you from it or it from you. Your wildest misperceptions, your weird imaginings, your blackest nightmares all mean nothing. They will not prevail against the peace God wills for you. The Holy Spirit will restore your sanity because insanity is not the Will of God. If that suffices Him, it is enough for you. You will not keep what God would have removed because it breaks communication with you with whom He would communicate. His voice will be heard.

The communication link which God Himself placed within you, joining your minds with His, cannot be broken. You may believe you want it broken and this belief does interfere with the deep peace in which the sweet and constant communication which God would share with you is known. Yet His channels of reaching out cannot be wholly closed and separated from Him. Peace will be yours because His peace still flows to you from Him Whose Will is peace. You have it now. The Holy Spirit will teach you how to use it and by projecting it to learn that it is in you.

God willed you Heaven and will always will you nothing else. The Holy Spirit knows only of His Will. There is no chance that Heaven will not be yours, for God is sure, and what He wills is sure as He is. You will learn salvation because you will learn how to save. It will not be possible to exempt yourself from what the Holy Spirit wills to teach you. Salvation is as sure as God. His certainty suffices. Learn that even the darkest nightmare that disturbed the mind of God's sleeping Son holds no power over him. He will learn the lesson of awaking. God watches over him and light surrounds him.

Can God's Son lose himself in dreams when God has placed within him the glad call to waken and be glad? He cannot separate himself from what is in him. His sleep will not withstand the call to wake. The mission of redemption will be fulfilled as surely as the creation will remain unchanged throughout eternity. You do not have to know that Heaven is yours to make it so. It is so. Yet the Will of God must be accepted as your will, to know it.

The Holy Spirit cannot fail to undo for you everything you have learned that teaches you what is not true must be reconciled with truth. This is the reconciliation which the ego would substitute for your reconciliation unto sanity and unto peace. The Holy Spirit has a very different kind of reconciliation in His Mind for you, and one which He will effect as surely as the ego will not effect what it attempts.

Failure is of the ego, not of God. From Him you cannot wander and there is no possibility that the plan the Holy Spirit offers to everyone, for the salvation of everyone, will not be perfectly accomplished. You will be released, and you will not remember anything you made that was not created for you and by you in return. For how can you remember what was never true, or not remember what has always been? It is this reconciliation with truth, and only truth, in which the peace of Heaven lies.

Yes, you are blessed indeed. Yet in this world you do not know it. But you have the means for learning it and seeing it quite clearly. The Holy Spirit uses logic as easily and as well as does the ego, except that His conclusions are not insane. They take a direction exactly opposite, pointing as clearly to Heaven as the ego points to darkness and to death. We have followed much of the ego's logic, and have seen its logical conclusions. And having seen them, we have realized that they cannot be seen but in illusions, for there alone their seeming clearness seems to be clearly seen. Let us now turn away from them and follow the simple logic by which the Holy Spirit teaches you the simple conclusions that speak for truth, and only truth.

If you are blessed and do not know it, you need to learn it must be so. The knowledge is not taught, but its conditions must be acquired, for it is they that have been thrown away. You can learn to bless and cannot give what you have not. If, then, you offer blessing, it must have come first to yourself. And you must also have accepted it as yours, for how else could you give it away? That is why your miracles offer you the testimony that you are blessed. If what you offer is complete forgiveness, you must have let guilt go, accepting the Atonement for yourself and learning you are guiltless. How could you learn what has been done for you, but which you do not know, unless you do what you would have to do if it had been done unto you? Indirect proof of truth is needed in a world made of denial and without direction. You will perceive the need for this if you will realize that to deny is the decision not to know. The logic of the world must therefore lead to nothing, for its Goal is nothing.

If you decide to have and give and be nothing except a dream, you must direct your thoughts unto oblivion. And if you have and give and are everything, and all this has been denied, your thought system is closed off, and wholly separated from the truth. This is an insane world, and do not underestimate the actual extent of its insanity. There is no area of your perception that it has not touched, and your dream is sacred to you. That is why God placed the Holy Spirit in you, where you placed the dream.

Seeing is always outwards. Were your thoughts wholly of you, the thought system which you made would be forever dark. The thoughts which the mind of God's Son projects have all the power that he gives to them. The thoughts he shares with God are beyond his belief, but those he made are his beliefs. And it is these, and not the truth, that he has chosen to defend and love.

They will not be taken from him. But they can be given up by him, for the Source of their undoing is in him. There is nothing in the world to teach him that the logic of the world is totally insane and leads to nothing. Yet in him who made this insane logic there is One Who knows it leads to nothing, for He knows everything.

Any direction which will lead you where the Holy Spirit leads you not goes nowhere. Anything you deny which He knows to be true you have denied yourself and He must therefore teach you not to deny it. Undoing is indirect, as doing is. You were created only to create, neither to see not do. These are but indirect expressions of the will to live, which has been blocked by the capricious and unholy whim of death and murder that your Father shared not with you. You have set yourselves the task of sharing what cannot be shared. And while you think it possible to learn to do this, you will not believe all that is possible to learn to do.

The Holy Spirit, therefore, must begin His teaching by showing you what you can never learn. His message is not indirect, but He must introduce the simple truth into a thought system which has become so twisted and so complex that you cannot see that it means nothing. He merely looks at its foundation and dismisses it. But you who cannot undo what you have made cannot see through it. It deceives you because you chose to deceive yourselves. Those who choose to be deceived will merely attack direct approaches, which would seem but to encroach upon deception and strike at it.

The Holy Spirit needs a happy learner, in whom His mission can be happily accomplished. You who are steadfastly devoted to misery must first recognize that you are miserable and not happy. The Holy Spirit cannot teach without this contrast, for you believe that misery is happiness. This has is confused you that you have undertaken to learn to do what you can never do, believing that unless you learn it, you will not be happy. You do not realize that the foundation on which this most peculiar learning goal depends means absolutely nothing. It does make sense to you.

Have faith in nothing, and you will find the "treasure" that you sought. Yet you will add another burden to your mind, already burdened or you would not have sought another. You will believe that nothing is of value and will value it. A little piece of glass, a speck of dust, a body or a war are one to you. For if you value nothing made of nothing, you have believed that nothing can be precious, and that you can learn how to make the untrue true.

The Holy Spirit, seeing where you are but know you are elsewhere, begins His lesson in simplicity with the fundamental teaching that truth is true. This is the hardest lesson you will ever learn, and in the end the O one. Simplicity is very difficult for twisted minds. Consider all the distortions you have made of nothing; all the strange forms and feelings and actions and reactions that you have woven out of it. Nothing is so alien to you as the simple truth, and nothing are you less inclined to listen to. The contrast between what is true and what is not is perfectly apparent, yet you do not see it.

The simple and the obvious are not apparent to those who would make palaces and royal robes of nothing, believing they are kings with golden crowns because of them. All this the Holy Spirit sees, and teaches, simply, that all this is not true. To these unhappy learners who would teach themselves nothing and delude themselves into believing that it is not nothing, the Holy Spirit says, with steadfast quietness:

> "The truth is true. Nothing else matters, nothing else is real and everything beside it is not there. Let Me make the one distinction for you which you cannot make but need to learn. Your faith in nothing is deceiving you. Offer your faith to Me and I will place it gently in the holy place where it belongs. You will find no deception there but only the simple truth and you will love it because you will understand it."

Like you, the Holy Spirit did not make truth. Like God, He knows it to be true. He brings the light of truth into the darkness, and lets it shine on you. And as it shines, your brothers see it, and realizing that this light is not what you have made, they see in you more than you see. They will be happy learners of the lesson which this light brings to them because it teaches them release from nothing and from all the works of nothing. The heavy chains which seem to bind them unto despair they do not see as nothing until you bring the light to them. And then they see the chains have disappeared, and so they must have been nothing. And you will see it with them. Because you taught them gladness and release, they will become your teachers in release and gladness.

When you teach anyone that truth is true, you learn it with him. And so you learn that what seemed hardest was the easiest. Learn to be happy learners. You will never learn how to make nothing everything. Yet see that this has been your goal and recognize how foolish it has been. Be glad it is undone, for when you look at it in simple honesty, it id undone. We said before, "Be not content with nothing," for you have believed that nothing could content you. It is not so.

If you would be a happy learner, you must give everything that you have learned over to the Holy Spirit to be unlearned for you. And then begin to learn the joyous lessons that come quickly on the firm foundation that truth is true. For what is builded there is true and built on truth. The universe of learning will open up before you in all its gracious simplicity. With truth before you, you will not look back.

The happy learner meets the conditions of learning here, as he also meets the conditions of knowledge in the Kingdom. All this lies in the Holy Spirit's plan to free you from the past and open up the way to freedom for you. For truth is true. What else could ever be, or ever was? This simple lesson holds the key to the dark door which you believe is locked forever. You made this door of nothing, and behind it is nothing. The key is only the light which shines away the shapes and forms and fears of nothing. Accept this key to freedom from the hands of Christ Who gives it to you, that you may join Him in the holy task of bringing light to darkness. For, like your brothers, you do not realize the light has come, and freed you from the sleep of darkness.

Behold your brothers in their freedom and learn of them how to be free of darkness. The light in you will waken them, and they will not leave you asleep. The vision of Christ is given the very instant that it is perceived. Where everything is clear it is all holy. The quietness of its simplicity is so compelling that you will realize it is impossible to deny the simple truth. For there is nothing else. God is everywhere, and His Son is in Him with everything. Can he sing the dirge of sorrow when this is true?

Learning will be commensurate with motivation, and the interference in your motivation for learning is exactly the same as that which interferes with all your thinking. The happy learner cannot feel guilty about learning. This is so essential to learning that it should never be forgotten. The guiltless learner learns so easily because his thoughts are free. Yet this entails the recognition that guilt is interference, not salvation, and serves no useful function at all.

You are accustomed to using guiltlessness merely to offset the pain of guilt, and do not look upon it as having value in itself. You believe that guilt and guiltlessness are both of value, each representing an escape from what the other does not offer you. You do not want either alone, for without both you do not see yourselves as whole and therefore happy. Yet you are whole only in your guiltlessness, and only in your guiltlessness can you be happy. There is no conflict here. To wish for guilt in any way, in any form, will lose appreciation of the value of your guiltlessness, and push it from your sight.

There is no compromise that you can make with guilt and escape the pain which only guiltlessness allays. Learning is living here, as creating is Being in Heaven. Whenever the pain of guilt seems to attract you, remember that, if you yield to it, you are deciding against your happiness, and will not learn how to be happy. Say, therefore, to yourself, gently, but with the conviction born of the love of God and of His Son,

> "What I experience I will make manifest.
> If I am guiltless I have nothing to fear.
> I choose to testify to my acceptance of the Atonement, not for its rejection.
> I would accept my guiltlessness by making it manifest and sharing it.
> Let me bring peace to God's Son from his Father."

Each day, each hour and minute, even every second, you are deciding between the crucifixion and the resurrection; between the ego and the Holy Spirit. The ego is the choice for guilt; the Holy Spirit the decision for guiltlessness. The power of decision is all that is yours. What you can decide between is fixed, because there are no alternatives except truth and illusion. And there is no overlap between them, because they are opposites which cannot be reconciled, and cannot both be true. You are guilty or guiltless, bound or free, happy or unhappy.

The miracle teaches you that you have chosen guiltlessness, freedom and joy. It is not a cause, but an effect. It is the natural result of choosing right, attesting to your happiness that comes from choosing to be free of guilt. Everyone you offer healing to returns it. Everyone you attack keeps it and cherishes it by holding it against you. Whether he does this or does it not will make no difference; you will think he does. It is impossible to offer what you do not want without this penalty. The cost of giving is receiving.

Either it is a penalty from which you suffer, or the happy purchase of a treasure to hold dear.

No penalty is ever asked of God's Son except by himself and of himself. Every chance given him to heal is another opportunity to replace darkness with light and fear with love. If he refuses it, he binds himself to darkness because he did not choose to free his brother and enter light with him. By giving power to nothing, he threw away the joyous opportunity to learn that nothing HAS no power. And by not dispelling darkness he became afraid of darkness and of light. The joy of learning that darkness has no power over the Son of God is the happy lesson the Holy Spirit teaches and would have you teach with Him. It is his joy to teach it, as it will be yours.

The way to teach this simple lesson is merely this: Guiltlessness is invulnerability. Therefore, make your invulnerability manifest to everyone, and teach him that, whatever he may try to do to you, your perfect freedom from the belief that you can be harmed shows him He is guiltless. He can do nothing that can hurt you, and by refusing to allow him to think he can, you teach him that the Atonement, which you have accepted for yourself, is also His. There is nothing to forgive. No-one can hurt the Son of God. His guilt is wholly without cause and being without cause cannot exist.

God is the only Cause, and guilt is not of Him. Teach no-one he has hurt you, for if you do, you teach yourself that what is not of God has power over you. The causeless cannot be. Do not attest to it, and do not foster belief in it in any mind. Remember always that mind is one and cause is one. You will learn communication with this oneness only when you learn to deny the causeless and accept the Cause of God as yours. The power that God has given to His Son is his, and nothing else can His Son see or choose to look upon without imposing on himself the penalty of guilt in place of all the happy teaching the Holy Spirit would gladly offer him.

Whenever you decide to make decisions for yourself, you are thinking destructively, and the decision will be wrong. It will hurt you because of the concept of decision which led to it. It is not true that you can make decisions by yourself or for yourself alone. No thought of God's Son can be separate or isolated in its effects. Every decision is made for the whole Sonship, directed in and out, and influencing a constellation larger than anything you ever dreamed of. Those who accept the Atonement are invulnerable.

But those who believe they are guilty will respond to guilt, because they think it is salvation and will not refuse to see it and side with it. And they will fail to understand the simple fact that what they do not want must hurt them.

All this arises because they do not believe that what they want is good. Yet will was given them because it is holy, and will bring to them all that they need, coming as naturally as peace that knows no limits. There is nothing their wills will not provide that offers them anything of value. Yet because they do not understand their will, the Holy Spirit quietly understands it for them, and gives them what they will without effort, strain, or the impossible burden of deciding what they want and need alone.

It will never happen that you will have to make decisions for yourself. You are not bereft of help and Help that knows the answer. Would you be content with little, which is all that you alone can offer yourself, when He Who gives you everything will simply offer it to you? He will never ask what you have done to make you worthy of the gift of God. Ask it not therefore of yourselves. Instead, accept His answer, for He knows that you are worthy of everything God wills for you. Do not try to escape the gift of God which He so freely and so gladly offers you. He offers you but what God gave Him for you. You need not decide whether or not you are deserving of it. God knows you are.

Would you deny the truth of God's decision, and place your pitiful appraisal of yourself in place of His calm and unswerving value of His Son? Nothing can shake God's conviction of the perfect purity of everything that He created, for it is wholly pure. Do not decide against it, for being of Him it must be true. Peace abides in every mind that quietly accepts the plan which God has set for his Atonement, relinquishing his own. You know not of salvation, for you do not understand it. Make no decisions about what it is or where it lies, but ask of the Holy Spirit everything, and leave all decisions to His gentle counsel.

The One Who knows the plan of God which God would have you follow can teach you what it is. Only His wisdom is capable of guiding you to follow it. Every decision you undertake alone but signifies that you would define what salvation is, and what you could be saved from. The Holy Spirit knows that all salvation is escape from guilt. You have no other "enemy," and against this strange distortion of the purity of the Son of God the Holy Spirit is your only friend. He is the strong protector of your innocence which sets you free. And it is His decision to undo everything that would obscure your innocence from your unclouded mind.

Let Him, therefore, be the only Guide that you would follow to salvation. He knows the way and leads you gladly on it. With Him you will not fail to learn what God wills for you is your will. Without His guidance you will think you know alone and will decide against your peace as surely as you made the wrong decision in ever thinking that salvation lay in you alone. Salvation is of Him to Whom God gave it for you. He has not forgotten it. Forget Him not, and He will make every decision for you, for your salvation and the peace of God in you.

Seek not to appraise the worth of God's Son whom He created holy, for to do so is to evaluate his Father, and judge against Him. And you will feel guilty for this imagined crime, which no one in this world or Heaven could possibly commit. God's Spirit teaches only that the "sin" of self-replacement on the throne of God is not a source of guilt. What cannot happen can have no effects to fear. Be quiet in your faith in Him Who loves you and would lead you out of insanity. Madness may be your choice, but not your reality. Never forget the Love of God, Who has remembered you. For it is quite impossible that He could ever let His Son drop from His Loving Mind wherein he was created, and where his abode was fixed in perfect peace forever.

Say to the Holy Spirit only "Decide for me," and it is done. For His decisions are reflections of what God knows about you, and in this light error of any kind becomes impossible. Why would you struggle so frantically to anticipate all that you cannot know when all knowledge lies behind every decision which the Holy Spirit makes for you? Learn of His wisdom and His love and teach His answer to everyone who struggles in the dark. For you decide for them and for yourself.

How gracious is it to decide all things through Him Whose equal love is given equally to all alike! He leaves you no-one outside yourself, alone without you. And so He gives you what is yours because your Father would have you share it with Him. In everything be led by Him and do not reconsider. Trust Him to answer quickly, surely, and with love for everyone who will be touched in any way by the decision. And everyone will be. Would you take unto yourself the sole responsibility for deciding what can bring only good to everyone? Would you know this?

You taught yourselves the most unnatural habit of not communicating with your Creator. Yet you remain in close communication with Him, and with everything that is within Him, as it is within yourself. Unlearn isolation through His loving guidance and learn of all the happy communication that you have thrown away but could not lose. Whenever you are in doubt what you should do, think of His Presence in you and tell yourself this and only this:

> "He leadeth me and knows the way which I know not. Yet He will never keep from me what He would have me learn. And so I trust Him to communicate to me all that He knows for me."

Then let Him teach you quietly how to perceive your guiltlessness which is already there.

When you accept a brother's guiltlessness, you will see the Atonement in him. For by proclaiming it in him you make it yours and you will see what you sought. You will not see the symbol of your brother's guiltlessness shining within him while you still believe it is not there. His guiltlessness is your Atonement. Grant it to him, and you will see the truth of what you have acknowledged. Yet truth is offered first to be received even as God gave it first to His Son. The first in time means nothing but the First in eternity is God the Father, Who is both First and One. Beyond the First there is no other, for there is no order, no second or third, and nothing but the First.

You who belong to the First Cause, created by Him like unto Himself and part of Him, are more than merely guiltless. The state of guiltlessness is only the condition in which what is not there has been removed from the disordered mind that thought it was. This state, and only this, must you attain with God beside you. For until you do, you will still think that you are separate from Him. You can feel His Presence next to you but cannot know that you are one with Him. This need not be taught. Learning applies only to the condition in which it happens of itself.

When you have let all that obscured the truth in your most holy mind be undone for you and stand in grace before your Father, He will give Himself to you as He has always done. Giving Himself is all He knows, and so it is all knowledge. For what He knows not cannot be, and therefore cannot be given. Ask not to be forgiven, for this has already been accomplished. Ask, rather, to learn how to forgive, and restore what always was to your unforgiving mind. Atonement becomes real and visible to them that use it. On earth this is your only function, and you must learn that it is all you want to learn.

You will feel guilty till you learn this. For, in the end, whatever form it takes, your guilt arises from your failure to fulfil your function in God's Mind with all of yours. Can you escape this guilt by failing to fulfil your function here? You need not understand creation to do what must be done before that knowledge would be meaningful to you. God breaks no barriers; neither did He make them. When you release them they are gone. God will not fail, nor ever has in anything.

Decide that God is right and you are wrong about yourself. He created you out of Himself, but still within Him. He knows what you are. Remember that there is no second to Him. There cannot, therefore, be anyone without His Holiness, nor anyone unworthy of His perfect Love. Fail not in your function of loving in a loveless place made out of darkness and deceit, for thus are darkness and deceit undone. Fail not yourself, but instead, offer to God and you His blameless Son. For this small gift of appreciation for His Love, God will Himself exchange your gift for His.

Before you make any decisions for yourself, remember that you have decided against your function in Heaven, and consider carefully whether you want to make decisions here. Your function here is only to decide against deciding what you want, in recognition that you do not know. How, then, can you decide what you should do? Leave all decisions to the One Who speaks for God, and for your function as He knows it. So will He teach you to remove the awful burden you have laid upon yourself by loving not the Son of God, and trying to teach him guilt instead of love. Give up this frantic and insane attempt, which cheats you of the joy of living with your God and Father and awaking gladly to His Love and Holiness which join together as the truth in you, making you One with Him.

When you have learned how to decide with God, all decisions become as easy and as right as breathing. There is no effort, and you will be led as gently as if you were being carried along a quiet path in summer. Only your own volition seems to make deciding hard. The Holy Spirit will not delay at all in answering your every question what to do. He knows. And He will tell you and then do it for you. You who are tired might consider whether this is not more restful than sleep. For you can bring your guilt into sleeping, but not into this.

Unless you are guiltless you cannot know God, Whose Will is that you know Him. Therefore, you must be guiltless. Yet if you do not accept the necessary conditions for knowing Him you have denied Him, and do not recognize Him, though He is all around you. He cannot be known without His Son, whose guiltlessness is the condition for knowing Him. Accepting His Son as guilty is denial of the Father so complete that knowledge is swept away from recognition in the very mind where God Himself has placed it. If you would but listen and learn how impossible this is! Do not endow Him with attributes You understand. You made Him not and anything you understand is not of Him.

Your task is not to make reality. It is here without your making, but not without you. You who have thrown your selves away and valued God so little, hear me speak for Him and for yourselves. You cannot understand how much your Father loves you, for there is no parallel in your experience of the world to help you understand it. There is nothing on earth with which it can compare, and nothing you have ever felt, apart from Him, that resembles it ever so faintly. You cannot even give a blessing in perfect gentleness. Would you know of One Who gives forever, and Who knows of nothing except giving?

The Children of Heaven live in the light of the blessing of their Father, because they know that they are sinless. The Atonement was established as the means of restoring guiltlessness to the mind which has denied it, and thus denied Heaven to Itself. Atonement teaches you the true condition of the Son of God. It does not teach you what you are, or what your Father is. The Holy Spirit, Who remembers this for you, merely teaches you how to remove the blocks that stand between you and what you know. His memory is yours. If you remember what you have made, you are remembering nothing. Remembrance of reality is in Him, and therefore in you.

The guiltless and the guilty are totally incapable of understanding one another. Each perceives the other as like himself, making them unable to communicate because each sees the other unlike the way he sees himself. God can communicate only to the Holy Spirit in your mind because only He shares the knowledge of what you are with God. And only the Holy Spirit can answer God for you, for only He knows what God is. Everything else that you have placed within your mind cannot exist, for what is not in communication with the Mind of God has never been. Communication with God is life. Nothing without it is at all.

The only part of your mind that has reality is the part which links you still with God. Would you have all of it transformed into a radiant message of God's Love, to share with all the lonely ones who denied Him with you? God makes this possible. Would you deny His yearning to be known? You yearn for Him as He for you. This is forever changeless. Accept, then, the immutable. Leave the world of death behind and return quietly to Heaven. There is nothing of value here, and everything of value there. Listen to the Holy Spirit, and to God through Him. He speaks of you to you. There is no guilt in you, for God is blessed in His Son as the Son is blessed in Him.

Each one of you has a special part to play in the Atonement, but the message given to each to share is always the same; God's son is guiltless. Each one teaches the message differently and learns it differently. Yet until he teaches it and learns it, he will suffer the pain of dim awareness that his true function remains unfulfilled in him.

The burden of guilt is heavy, but God would not have you bound by it. His plan for your awaking is as perfect as yours is fallible. You know not what you do, but He Who knows is with you. His gentleness is yours, and all the love you share with God He holds in trust for you. He would teach you nothing except how to be happy.

Blessed Son of a wholly blessing Father, joy was created for you. Who can condemn whom God has blessed? There is nothing in the Mind of God that does not share his shining innocence. Creation is the natural extension of perfect purity. Your only calling here is to devote yourself, with active willingness, to the denial of guilt in all its forms. To accuse is not to understand. The happy learners of the Atonement become the teachers of the innocence that is the right of all that God created. Deny them not what is their due, for you will not withhold it from them alone.

The inheritance of the Kingdom is the right of God's Son, given him in his creation. Do not try to steal it from him, or you will ask for guilt and will experience it. Protect his purity from every thought that would steal it away and keep it from his sight. Bring innocence to light, in answer to the call of the Atonement. Never allow purity to remain hidden but shine away the heavy veils of guilt within which the Son of God has hidden himself from his own sight. We are all joined in the Atonement here, and nothing else can unite us in this world. So will the world of separation slip away, and full communication be restored between the Father and the Son.

The miracle acknowledges the guiltlessness which must have been denied to produce need of healing. Do not withhold this glad acknowledgment, for hope of happiness and release from suffering of every kind lie in it. Who is there but wishes to be free of pain? He may not yet have learned how to exchange his guilt for innocence, nor realize that only in this exchange can freedom from pain be his. Yet those who have failed to learn need teaching, not attack. To attack those who have need of teaching is to fail to learn from them.

Teachers of innocence, each in his own way, have joined together, taking their part in the unified curriculum of the Atonement. There is no unity of learning goals apart from this. There is no conflict t in this curriculum, which has one aim however it is taught. Each effort made on its behalf is offered for the single purpose of release from guilt, to the eternal glory of God and His creation. And every teaching that points to this points straight to Heaven, and to the peace of God. There is no pain, no trial, no fear that teaching this can fail to overcome. The power of God Himself supports this teaching and guarantees its limitless results.

Join your own efforts to the power that cannot fail and must result in peace. No-one can be untouched by teaching such as this. You will not see yourself beyond the power of God if you teach only this. You will not be exempt from the effects of this most holy lesson, which seeks but to restore what is the right of God's creation. From everyone whom you accord release from guilt you will inevitably learn your innocence. The circle of Atonement has no end. And you will find ever-increasing confidence in your safe inclusion in what is for all in everyone you bring within its safety and its perfect peace.

Peace, then, be unto everyone who becomes a teacher of peace. For peace is the acknowledgment of perfect purity from which no one is excluded. Within its holy circle is everyone whom God created as His Son. Joy is its unifying attribute, with no-one left outside to suffer guilt alone. The power of God draws everyone to its safe embrace of love and union. Stand quietly within this circle and attract all tortured minds to join with you in the safety of its peace and holiness. Abide with me within it, as teachers of Atonement, not of guilt.

Blessed are you who teach with me. Our power comes not of us, but of our Father. In guiltlessness we know Him, as He knows us guiltless. I stand within the circle, calling you to peace. Teach peace with me, and stand with me on holy ground. Remember for everyone your Father's power that He has given him. Believe not that you cannot teach His perfect peace. Stand not outside but join with me within.

Fail not the only purpose to which my teaching calls you. Restore to God His Son as He created him by teaching him his innocence.

The crucifixion has no part in the Atonement. Only the resurrection became my part in it. That is the symbol of the release from guilt by guiltlessness. Whom you perceive as guilty you would crucify. Yet you restore guiltlessness to whomever you see as guiltless. Crucifixion is always the ego's aim. It sees as guilty, and by its condemnation it would kill. The Holy Spirit sees only guiltlessness, and in His gentleness, He would release from fear, and re-establish the reign of love. The power of love is in His gentleness, which is of God and therefore cannot crucify nor suffer crucifixion. The temple you restore becomes your altar, for it was re-built through you. And everything you give to God us yours. Thus He creates, and thus must you restore.

Each one you see you place within the holy circle of Atonement or leave outside, judging him fit for crucifixion or for redemption. If you bring him into the circle of purity, you will rest there with him. If you leave him without, you join him there. Judge not except in quietness which is not of you. Refuse to accept anyone as without the blessing of Atonement and bring him into it by blessing him. Holiness must be shared, for therein lies everything that makes it holy. Come gladly to the holy circle and look out in peace on all who think they are outside. Cast no one out, for this is what he seeks along with you. Come, let us join him in the holy place of peace, which is for all of us, united as one within the Cause of peace.

The journey that we undertake together is the exchange of dark for light, of ignorance for understanding. Nothing you understand is fearful. It is only in darkness and in ignorance that you perceive the frightening, and you shrink away from it to further darkness. And yet it is only the hidden that can terrify, not for what it is, but for its hiddenness. The obscure is frightening because you do not understand its meaning. If you did, it would be clear and you would be no longer in the dark. Nothing has hidden value, for what is hidden cannot be shared, and so its value is unknown. The hidden is kept apart, but value always lies in joint appreciation. What is concealed cannot be loved, and so it must be feared.

The quiet light in which the Holy Spirit dwells within you is merely perfect openness, in which nothing is hidden, and therefore nothing is fearful. Attack will always yield to love if it is brought to love, not hidden from it. There is no darkness that the light of love will not dispel, unless it is concealed from love's beneficence. What is kept apart from love cannot share its healing power because it has been separated off and kept in darkness. The sentinels of darkness watch over it carefully and you who made these guardians of illusion out of nothing are now afraid of them.

Would you continue to give imagined power to these strange ideas of safety? They are neither safe nor unsafe. They do not protect; neither do they attack. They do nothing at all, being nothing at all. As guardians of darkness and of ignorance, look to them only for fear, for what they keep obscure is fearful. But let them go, and what was fearful will be so no longer. Without protection of obscurity only the light of love remains, for only this has meaning and can live in light. Everything else must disappear.

Death yields to life simply because destruction is not true. The light of guiltlessness shines guilt away because, when they are brought together, the truth of one must make the falsity of its opposite perfectly clear. Keep not guilt and guiltlessness apart, for your belief that you can have them both is meaningless. All you have done by keeping them apart is lose their meaning by confusing them with each other. And so you do not realize that only one means anything and the other is wholly without sense of any kind.

You have interpreted the separation as a means which you have made for breaking your communication with your Father. The Holy Spirit re-interprets it as a means of re-establishing what has not been broken but has been made obscure. All things you made have use to Him, for His most holy purpose. He knows you are not separate from God, but He perceives much in your mind that lets you think you are. All this, and nothing else, would He separate from you. The power of decision, which you made in place of the power of creation, He would teach you how to use on your behalf. You who made it to crucify yourselves must learn of Him how to apply it to the holy cause of restoration.

You who speak in dark and devious symbols do not understand the language you have made. It has no meaning, for its purpose is not communication, but rather, the distribution of communication. If the purpose of language is communication, how can this tongue mean anything? Yet even this strange and twisted effort to communicate through not communicating holds enough of love to make it meaningful, if its interpreter is not its maker.

You who made it are but expressing conflict, from which the Holy Spirit would release you. Leave what you would communicate to Him. He will interpret it to you with perfect clarity, for He knows with Whom you are in perfect communication.

You know not what you say, and so you know not what is said to you. Yet your Interpreter perceives the meaning in your alien language. He will not attempt to communicate the meaningless. But He will separate out all that has meaning, dropping off the rest and offering your true communication to those who would communicate as truly with you. You speak two languages at once, and this must lead to unintelligibility. Yet if one means nothing and the other everything, only that one is possible for purposes of communication.

The other but interferes with it. The Holy Spirit's function is entirely communication. He therefore must remove whatever interferes with it in order to restore it. Therefore, keep no source of interference from His sight, for He will not attack your sentinels. But bring them to Him, and let His gentleness teach you that, in the light, they are not fearful, and cannot serve to guard the dark doors behind which nothing at all is carefully concealed. We must open all doors and let the light come streaming through. There are no hidden chambers in God's temple. Its gates are open wide to greet His Son. No-one can fail to come where God has called him if he close not the door himself upon his Father's welcome.

What do you want? Light or darkness, knowledge or ignorance are yours, but not both. Opposites must be brought together, and not kept apart. For their separation is only in your mind, and they are reconciled by union as you are. In union, everything that is not real must disappear, for truth is union. As darkness disappears in light, so ignorance fades away when knowledge dawns. Perception is the medium by which ignorance is brought to knowledge. Yet the perception must be without deceit, for otherwise it becomes the messenger of ignorance rather than a helper in the search for truth.

The search for truth is but the honest searching out of everything that interferes with truth. Truth is. It can be neither lost nor sought nor found. It is there, wherever you are, being within you. Yet it can be recognized or unrecognized, real or false to you. If you hide it, it becomes unreal to you because you hid it and surrounded it with fear. Under each cornerstone of fear on which you have erected your insane system of belief the truth lies hidden. Yet you cannot know this, for by hiding truth in fear you see no reason to believe the more you look at fear the less you see it, and the clearer what it conceals becomes.

It is not possible to convince the unknowing that they know. From their point of view, it is not true. Yet it is true because God knows it. These are clearly opposite viewpoints of what the "unknowing" are. To God unknowing is impossible. It is therefore not a point of view at all, but merely a belief in something that does not exist. It is only this belief that the unknowing have and by it they are wrong about themselves. They have defined themselves as they were not created. Their creation was not a point of view, but rather a certainty. Uncertainty brought to certainty does not retain any conviction of reality.

You must have noticed that the emphasis has been on bringing what is undesirable to the desirable; what you do not want to what you do. You will realize that salvation must come to you this way if you consider what dissociation is. Dissociation is a distorted process of thinking whereby two systems of belief which cannot coexist are both maintained. It has been recognized that, if they were brought together, their joint acceptance would become impossible. But if one is kept in darkness from the other, their separation seems to keep them both alive, and equal in their reality.

Their joining thus becomes the source of fear, for if they meet, acceptance must be withdrawn from one of them. You cannot have them both, for each denies the other. Apart, this fact is lost from sight, for each in a separate place can be endowed with firm belief. Bring them together and the fact of their complete incompatibility is instantly apparent. One will go because the other is seen in the same place. Light cannot enter darkness when a mind believes in darkness and will not let it go.

Truth does not struggle against ignorance, and love does not attack fear. What needs no protection does not defend itself. Defence is of your making. God knows it not. The Holy Spirit uses defences on behalf of truth only because you made them against it. His perception of them, according to His purpose, merely changes them into a call for what you have attacked with them.

Defences, like everything you made, must be gently turned to your own good, translated by the Holy Spirit from means of self destruction to means of preservation and release. His task is mighty, but the power of God is with Him. Therefore, to Him, it is so easy that it was accomplished the instant it was given Him for you. Do not delay yourselves in your return to peace by wondering how He can fulfil what God has given Him to do. Leave that to Him Who knows.

You are not asked to do mighty tasks yourself. You are merely asked to do the little He suggests you do, trusting Him only to the small extent of believing that, if He asks it, you can do it. You will see how easily all that He asks can be accomplished.

The Holy Spirit asks of you but this; bring to Him every secret you have locked away from Him. Open every door to Him and bid Him enter the darkness and lighten it away. At your request He enters gladly. He brings the light to darkness if you make the darkness open to Him. But what you hide He cannot look upon. For He sees for you, and unless you look with Him He cannot see. The vision of Christ is not for Him alone, but for Him with you. Bring, therefore, all your dark and secret thoughts to Him, and look upon them with Him. He holds the light, and you the darkness. They cannot coexist when both of you together look on them. His judgement must prevail, and He will give it to you as you join your perception to His. Joining with Him in seeing is the way in which you learn to share with Him the interpretation of perception that leads to knowledge.

You cannot see alone. Sharing perception with Him Whom God has given you teaches you how to recognize what you see. It is the recognition that nothing you see means anything alone. Seeing with Him will show you that all meaning, including yours, comes not from double vision, but from the gentle fusing of everything into one meaning, one emotion and one purpose.

God has One Purpose which He shares with you. The single vision which the Holy Spirit offers you will bring this Oneness to your mind with clarity and brightness so intense you could not wish, for all the world, not to accept what God would have you have. Behold your will, accepting it as His, with all His Love as yours. All honour to you through Him and through Him unto God.

In the darkness you have obscured the glory God gave you and the power He bestowed upon His guiltless Son. All this lies hidden in every darkened place shrouded in guilt, and in the dark denial of innocence. Behind the dark doors which you have closed lies nothing, because nothing can obscure the gift of God. It is the closing of the doors that interferes with recognition of the power of God that shines in you. Banish not power from your mind but let all that would hide your glory be brought to the judgement of the Holy Spirit and there undone. Whom He would save for glory is saved for it. He has promised the Father that through Him you would be released from littleness to glory. To what He promised God He is wholly faithful, for He shared with God the promise that was given Him to share with you.

He shares it still, for you. Everything that promises otherwise, great or small, however much or little valued, He will replace with the one promise given unto Him to lay upon the altar to your Father and His Son. No altar stands to God without His Son. And nothing brought there that is not equally worthy of both but will be replaced by gifts wholly acceptable to Father and to Son. Can you offer guilt to God? You cannot, then, offer it to His Son. For they are not apart and gifts to one are offered to the other.

You know not God because you know not this. And yet you do know God and also this. All this is safe within you, where the Holy Spirit shines. He shines not in division, but in the meeting place where God, united with His Son, speaks to His Son through Him. Communication between what cannot be divided cannot cease. The holy meeting place of the unseparated Father and His Son lies in the Holy Spirit and in you. All interference in the communication that God Himself wills with His Son is quite impossible here. Unbroken and uninterrupted love flows constantly between the Father and the Son, as both would have it be. And so it is.

Let your minds wander not through darkened corridors, away from light's centre. You may choose to lead yourselves astray, but you can only be brought together by the Guide appointed for you. He will surely lead you to where God and His Son await your recognition. They are joined in giving you the gift of oneness, before which all separation vanishes. Unite with what you are. You cannot join with anything except reality. God's glory and His Son's belong to you in truth. They have no opposite, and nothing else can you bestow upon yourselves.

There is no substitute for truth. And truth will make this plain to you as you are brought into the place where you must meet with truth. And there you must be led, through gentle understanding which can lead you nowhere else. Where God is, there are you. Such is the truth. Nothing can change the knowledge given you by God into unknowingness. Everything God created knows its Creator. For this is how creation is accomplished by the Creator and by His creations. In the holy meeting place are joined the Father and His creations, and the creations of His Son with Them together. There is one link which joins them all together, holding them in the Oneness out of which creation happens.

The link with which the Father joins Himself to those He gives the power to create like Him can never be dissolved. Heaven itself is union with all of creation, and with its One Creator. And Heaven remains the Will of God for you. Lay no gifts other than this upon your altars, for nothing can coexist beside it. Here your meagre offerings are brought together with the gift of God, and only what is worthy of the Father will be accepted by the Son, for whom it was intended. To whom God gives Himself He is given. Your little gifts will vanish on the altar where He has placed His Own.

The Atonement does not make holy. You were created holy. It merely brings unholiness to holiness; or what you made to what you are. The bringing together of truth and illusion, of the ego to God, is the Holy Spirit's only function. Keep not your making from your Father, for hiding it has cost you knowledge of Him and of yourselves. The knowledge is safe, but wherein is YOUR safety apart from it? The making of time to take the place of timelessness lay in the decision to be not as you were. Thus, truth was made past, and the present was dedicated to illusion. And the past, too, was changed and interposed between what always was and now. The past which you remember never was and represents only the denial of what always was.

Bringing the ego to God is but to bring error to truth, where it stands corrected because it is the opposite of what it meets and is undone because the contradiction can no longer stand. How long can contradiction stand when its impossible nature is clearly revealed? What disappears in light is not attacked. It merely vanishes because it is not true. Different realities are meaningless, for reality must be one. It cannot change with time or mood or chance. Its changelessness is what makes it real. This cannot be undone. Undoing is for unreality. And this reality will do for you.

Merely by being what it is does truth release you from everything that it is not. The Atonement is so gentle you need but whisper to it, and all its power will rush to your assistance and support. You are not frail with God beside you. Yet without Him you are nothing. The Atonement offers you God. The gift which you refused is held by Him in you. His Spirit holds it there for you. God has not left His altar, though His worshippers placed other gods upon it. The temple still is holy, for the Presence that dwells within it is holiness.

In the temple holiness waits quietly for the return of them that love it. The Presence knows they will return to purity and to grace. The graciousness of God will take them gently in and cover all their sense of pain and loss with the immortal assurance of their Father's Love. There, fear of death will be replaced with joy of living.

For God is Life, and they abide in Life. The Presence of holiness lives in everything that lives, for holiness created life, and leaves not what It created holy as Itself.

In this world you can become a spotless mirror, in which the holiness of your Creator shines forth from you to all around you. You can reflect Heaven here. Yet no reflections of the images of other gods must dim the mirror that would hold God's reflection in it. Earth can reflect Heaven or hell; God or the ego. You need but leave the mirror clean and clear of all the images of hidden darkness you have drawn upon it. God will shine upon it of Himself. Only the clear reflection of Himself can be perceived upon it. Reflections are seen in light. In darkness they are obscure, and their meaning seems to lie only in shifting interpretations, rather than in themselves.

The reflection of God needs no interpretation. It is clear. Clean but the mirror, and the message which shines forth from what the mirror holds out for everyone to see no-one can fail to understand. It is the message that the Holy Spirit is holding to the mirror that is in him. He recognizes it because he has been taught his need for it, but knows not where to look to find it. Let him, then, see it in you and share it with you.

Could you but realize, for a single instant, the power of healing that the reflection of God, shining in you, can bring to all the world, you could not wait to make the mirror of your mind clean to receive the image of the holiness that heals the world. The image of holiness which shines in your mind is not obscure, and will not change. Its meaning to those who look upon it is not obscure, for everyone perceives it as the same. All bring their different problems to its healing light, but all their problems are met only with healing there.

The response of holiness to any form of error is always the same. There is no contradiction in what holiness calls forth. Its one response is healing, without regard for what is brought to it. Those who have learned to offer only healing because of the reflection of holiness in them are ready at last for Heaven. There, holiness is not a reflection, but rather the actual condition of what was but reflected to them here. God is no image, and His creations, as part of Him, hold Him in them in truth. They do not merely reflect truth, for they are truth.

When no perception stands between God and His creations, or between His Children and their own, the knowledge of creation must continue forever. The reflections which you accept into the mirror of your minds in time but bring eternity nearer or farther.

But eternity itself is beyond all time. Reach out of time and touch it, with the help of its reflection in you. And you will turn from time to holiness as surely as the reflection of holiness calls everyone to lay all guilt aside. Reflect the peace of Heaven here and bring this world to Heaven. For the reflection of truth draws everyone to truth and as they enter into it they leave all reflections behind.

In Heaven reality is shared, and not reflected. By sharing its reflection here, its truth becomes the only perception the Son of God accepts. And thus, remembrance of his Father dawns on him, and he can no longer be satisfied with anything but his own reality. You on earth have no conception of limitlessness, for the world you seem to live in is a world of limits. In this world, it is not true that anything without order of difficulty can occur. The miracle, therefore, has a unique function, and is motivated by a unique Teacher, Who brings the laws of another world to this one. The miracle is the one thing you can do that transcends order, being based not on differences, but on equality.

Miracles are not in competition, and the number of them that you can do is limitless. They can be simultaneous and legion. This is not difficult to understand, once you conceive of them as possible at all. What is more difficult to grasp is the lack of order of difficulty which stamps the miracle as something that must come from elsewhere, not from here. From the world's viewpoint, this is impossible. You have experienced lack of competition among your thoughts, which, even though they may conflict, can occur to you together and in great numbers. You are so used to this that it can cause you little surprise.

Yet you are also used to classifying some of your thoughts as more important, larger or better, wiser or more productive and valuable than others. And this is true about the thoughts which cross the mind of those who think they live apart. For some are reflections of Heaven, while others are motivated by the ego, which but seems to think. The result is a weaving, changing pattern which never rests, and is never still. It shifts unceasingly across the mirror of your mind, and the reflections of Heaven last but a moment, and grow dim as darkness blots them out. Where there was light darkness removes it in an instant and alternating patterns of light and darkness sweep constantly across your minds.

The little sanity which still remains is held together by a sense of order which you establish. Yet the very fact that you can do this and bring any order into chaos shows you that you are not an ego, and that more than an ego must be in you.

For the ego is chaos, and if it were all of you no order at all would be possible. Yet though the order which you impose upon your minds limits the ego, it also limits you. To order is to judge, and to arrange by judgement. It will seem difficult for you to learn that you have no basis at all for ordering your thoughts. This lesson the Holy Spirit teaches by giving you shining examples to show you that your way of ordering is wrong, but that a better way is offered you.

The miracle offers exactly the same response to every call for help. It does not judge the call. It merely recognizes what it is, and answers accordingly. It does not consider which call is louder or greater or more important. You may wonder how you who are still bound to judgement can be asked to do that which requires no judgement of your own. The answer is very simple. The power of God, and not of you, engenders miracles. The miracle itself is but the witness that you have the power of God in you. That is the reason why the miracle gives equal blessing to all who share in it, and that is also why everyone shares in it. The power of God is limitless. And being always maximal, it offers everything to every call from anyone. There is no order of difficulty here. A call for help is given help.

The only judgement involved at all is the Holy Spirit's one division into two categories; one of love, and the other the call for love. You cannot safely make this division, for you are much too confused either to recognize love, or to believe that everything else is nothing but a need for love. You are too bound to form, and not to content. What you consider content is not content at all. It is merely form, and nothing else. For you do not respond to what a brother really offers you, but only to the particular perception of his offering by which the ego judges it.

The ego is incapable of understanding content and is totally unconcerned with it. To the ego, if the form is acceptable the content must be. Otherwise, it will attack the form. You who believe you understand something of the dynamics of the mind, let me assure you that you know nothing of it at all. For of yourselves you could not know of it. The study of the ego is not the study of the mind.

In fact, the ego enjoys the study of itself, and thoroughly approves the undertakings of students who would analyse it, approving its importance. Yet they but study form with meaningless content. For their teacher is senseless though careful to conceal this fact behind a lot of words which sound impressive, but which lack any consistent sense when they are put together.

This is characteristic of the ego's judgements. Separately, they seem to hold, but put them together, and the system of thought which arises from joining them is incoherent and utterly chaotic. For form is not enough for meaning and the underlying lack of content makes a cohesive system impossible. Separation therefore remains the ego's chosen condition. For no-one alone can judge the ego truly. Yet when two or more join together in searching for truth, the ego can no longer defend its lack of content. The fact of union tells them it is not true.

It is impossible to remember God in secret and alone. For remembering Him means you are not alone, and willing to remember it. Take no thought for yourself, for no thought you hold is for yourself. If you would remember your Father, let the Holy Spirit order your thoughts, and give only the answer with which He answers you. Everyone seeks for love as you do and knows it not unless he joins with you in seeking it. If you undertake the search together, you bring with you a light so powerful that what you see is given meaning. The lonely journey fails because it has excluded what it would find.

As God communicates to the Holy Spirit in you, so does the Holy Spirit translate His communications through you so you can understand them. God has no secret communications, for everything of Him is perfectly open and freely accessible to all, being for all. Nothing lives in secret, and what you would hide from the Holy Spirit is nothing. Every interpretation you would lay upon a brother is senseless. Let the Holy Spirit show him to you and teach you both his love and need for love. Neither his mind nor yours holds more than these two orders of thought.

The miracle is the recognition that this is true. Where there is love, your brother must give it to you because of what it is. But where there is need for love, you must give it because of what you are. Long ago we said this course will teach you what you are, restoring to you your identity. We have already learned that this identity is shared. The miracle becomes the means of sharing it. By supplying your identity wherever it is not recognized, you will recognize it. And God Himself, Who wills to be with His Son forever, will bless each recognition of His Son with all the love He holds for him. Nor will the power of all His Love be absent from any miracle you offer to His Son. How, then, can there be any order of difficulty among them?

Yet the essential thing is learning that you do not know. Knowledge is power, and all power is of God. You who have tried to keep power for yourselves have lost it. You still have the power, but you have interposed so much between it and your awareness of it that you cannot use it. Everything you have taught yourselves has made your power more and more obscure to you. You know not what it is nor where. You have made a semblance of power and a show of strength so pitiful that it must fail you. For power is not a seeming strength, and truth is beyond semblance of any kind. Yet all that stands between you and the power of God in you is but your learning of the false, and your attempts to undo the true.

Be willing, then, for all of it to be undone, and be glad that you are not bound to it forever. For you have taught yourselves how to imprison the Son of God, a lesson so unthinkable that only the insane, in deepest sleep, could even dream of it. Can God learn how not to be God? And can His Son, given all power by Him, learn to be powerless? What have you taught yourselves that you can possibly prefer to keep, in place of what you have and what you are?

Atonement teaches you how to escape forever from everything that you have taught yourselves in the past by showing you only what you are now. Learning has been accomplished before its effects are manifest. Learning is therefore in the past, but its influence determines the present by giving it whatever meaning it holds for you. Your learning gives the present no meaning at all. Nothing you have ever learned can help you understand the present or teach you how to undo the past. Your past is what you have taught yourselves.

Let it all go. Do not attempt to understand any event, or anything, or anyone in its light, for the light of darkness by which you try to see can only obscure.

Put no confidence at all in darkness to illuminate your understanding, for if you do you contradict the light, and thereby think you see the darkness. Yet darkness cannot be seen, for it is nothing more than a condition in which seeing becomes impossible. You who have not yet brought all of the darkness you have taught yourselves unto the light in you can hardly judge the truth and value of this course. Yet God did not abandon you. And so you have another lesson sent from Him, already learned for every Child of light by Him to Whom God gave it. This lesson shines with God's glory, for in it lies His power, which He shares so gladly with His Son.

Learn of His happiness, which is yours. But to accomplish this, all your dark lessons must be brought willingly to truth, and joyously laid down by hands open to receive, not closed to take. Every dark lesson that you bring to Him Who teaches light He will accept from you, because you do not want it. And He will gladly exchange each one for the bright lesson He has learned for you. Never believe that any lesson you have learned apart from Him means anything.

You have one test, as sure as God, by which to recognize if what you learned is true. If you are wholly free of fear of any kind and if all those who meet, or even think of you, share in your perfect peace, then you can be sure that you have learned God's lesson, and not yours. Unless all this is true there are dark lessons in your minds which hurt and hinder you and everyone around you. The absence of perfect peace means but one thing: You think you do not will for God's Son what His Father wills for him. Every dark lesson teaches this, in one form or another. And each bright lesson, with which the Holy Spirit will replace the dark ones you do not accept and hide, teaches you that you will with the Father unto His Son.

Do not be concerned how you can learn a lesson so completely different from everything you have taught yourselves. How would you know? Your part is very simple. You need only recognize that everything you learned you do not want. Ask to be taught and do not use your experiences to confirm what you have learned.

When your peace is threatened, or disturbed in any way, say to yourself,

> "I do not know what anything, including this, means.
> And so I do not know how to respond to it.
> And I will not use my own past learning as the light to guide me now."

By this refusal to attempt to teach yourself what you do not know, the Guide Whom God has given you will speak to you. He will take His rightful place in your awareness the instant you abandon it and offer it to Him.

You cannot be your guide to miracles, for it is you who made them necessary. And because you did, the means on which you can depend for miracles has been provided for you. God's Son can make no needs His Father will not meet, if he but turn to Him ever so little. Yet He cannot compel His Son to turn to Him and remain Himself. It is impossible that God lose His Identity, for if He did, you would lose yours. And being yours, He cannot change Himself, for your Identity is changeless.

The miracle acknowledges His changelessness by seeing His Son as he always was, and not as he would make himself. The miracle brings the effects which only guiltlessness can bring, and thus establishes the fact that guiltlessness must be.

How can you, so firmly bound to guilt and committed so to remain, establish for yourself your guiltlessness? That is impossible. But be sure that you are willing to acknowledge that it is impossible. It is only because you think that you can run some little part or deal with certain aspects of your lives alone, that the guidance of the Holy Spirit is limited. Thus would you make Him undependable, and use this fancied undependability as an excuse for keeping certain dark lessons from Him. And by so limiting the guidance that you would accept, you are unable to depend on miracles to answer all your problems for you.

Do you think that what the Holy Spirit would have you give He would withhold from you? You have no problems which He cannot solve by offering you a miracle. Miracles are for you. And every fear or pain or trial you have has been undone. He has brought all of them to light, having accepted them instead of you, and recognized they never were. There are no dark lessons He has not already lightened for you. The lessons you would teach yourselves He has corrected already. They do not exist in His Mind at all. For the past binds Him not and therefore binds not you. He does not see time as you do. And each miracle He offers you corrects your use of time and makes it His.

He Who has freed you from the past would teach you are free of it. He would but have you accept His accomplishments as yours because He did them for you. And because He did, they are yours. He has made you free of what you made. You can deny Him, but you cannot call on Him in vain. He always gives what He has made in place of you. He would establish His bright teaching so firmly in your mind that no dark lessons of guilt can abide in what He has established as holy by His Presence. Thank God that He is there and works through you. And all His works are yours. He offers you a miracle with everyone you let Him do through you.

God's Son will always be indivisible. As we are held as one in God, so do we learn as one in Him. God's Teacher is as like to His Creator as is His Son, and through His Teacher does God proclaim His Oneness and His Son's. Listen in silence and do not raise your voice against Him. For He teaches the miracle of oneness and before His lesson division disappears. Teach like Him here, and you will remember that you have always created like your Father.

The miracle of creation has never ceased, having the holy stamp of immortality upon it. This is the Will of God for all creation, and all creation joins in willing this.

Those who remember always that they know nothing, but who have become willing to learn everything, will learn it. But whenever they trust themselves, they will not learn. They have destroyed their motivation for learning by thinking they already know. Think not you understand anything until you pass the test of perfect peace, for peace and understanding go together, and never can be found alone. Each brings the other with it, for it is the law of God they be not separate. They are cause and effect, each to the other, so where one is absent the other cannot be.

Only those who see they cannot know unless the effects of understanding are with them can really learn at all. And for this, it must be peace they want, and nothing else. Whenever you think you know, peace will depart from you because you have abandoned the Teacher of Peace. Whenever you fully realize that you know not peace will return, for you will have invited Him to do so by abandoning the ego on behalf of Him. Call not upon the ego for anything. It is only this that you need do. The Holy Spirit will, of Himself, fill every mind that so makes room for Him.

If you want peace you must abandon the teacher of attack. The Teacher of peace will never abandon you. You can desert Him, but He will never reciprocate, for His faith in you is His understanding. It is as firm as is His faith in His Creator, and He knows that faith in His Creator must encompass faith in His creation. In this consistency lies His holiness, which He cannot abandon, for it is not His Will to do so. With your perfection ever in His sight, He gives the gift of peace to everyone who perceives the need for peace, and who would have it. Make way for peace, and it will come. For understanding is in you, and from it peace must come.

The power of God, from which they both arise, is yours as surely as it is His. You think you know Him not only because, alone, it is impossible to know Him. Yet see the mighty works that He will do through you, and you must be convinced you did them through Him. It is impossible to deny the Source of effects so powerful they could not be of you. Leave room for Him, and you will find yourself so filled with power that nothing will prevail against your peace. And this will be the test by which you recognize that you have understood.

Can you imagine what it means to have no cares, no worries, no anxieties, but merely to be perfectly calm and quiet all the time? Yet that is what time is for; to learn just that and nothing more. God's Teacher cannot be satisfied with His teaching until it constitutes all your learning. He has not fulfilled His teaching function until you have become such a consistent learner that you learn only of Him. When this has happened, you will no longer need a teacher or time in which to learn.

One source of perceived discouragement from which you suffer is your belief that this takes time, and that the results of the Holy Spirit's teaching are far in the future. This is not so. For the Holy Spirit uses time in His Own way and is not bound by it. And all the waste that time seems to bring with it is due but to your identification with the ego, which uses time to support its belief in destruction. The ego, like the Holy Spirit, uses time to convince you of the inevitability of the goal and end of teaching. To the ego the goal is death, which is its end. But to the Holy Spirit the goal is life, which has no end.

The ego is an ally of time, but not a friend. For it is as mistrustful of death as it is of life, and what it wants for you it cannot tolerate. The ego wants you dead, but not itself. The outcome of its strange religion must therefore be the conviction that it can pursue you beyond the grave. And out of its unwillingness for you to find peace even in the death it wants for you, it offers you immortality in hell. It speaks to you of Heaven but assures you that Heaven is not for you. How can the guilty hope for Heaven? The belief in hell is inescapable to those who identify with the ego. Their nightmares and their fears are all associated with it.

The ego teaches that hell is in the future, for this is what all its teaching is directed to. Hell is its goal. For, although the ego aims at death and dissolution as an end, it does not believe it. The goal of death, which it craves for you, leaves it unsatisfied. No-one who follows the ego's teaching is without the fear of death. Yet if death were thought of merely as an end to pain, would it be feared? We have seen this strange paradox in the ego's thought system before, but never so clearly as here. For the ego must seem to keep fear from you to keep your allegiance. Yet it must engender fear in order to maintain itself.

Again the ego tries, and all too frequently succeeds, in doing both, by using dissociation for holding its contradictory aims together so that they seem to be reconciled. The ego teaches thus: Death is the end as far as hope of Heaven goes.

Yet because you and itself cannot be separated, and because it cannot conceive of its own death, it will pursue you still, because guilt is eternal. Such is the ego's version of immortality. And it is this the ego's version of time supports.

The ego teaches that Heaven is here and now because the future is hell. Even when it attacks so savagely that it tries to take the life of someone who hears it temporarily as the only voice, it speaks of hell even to him. For it tells him hell is here, and bids him leap from hell into oblivion. The only time the ego allows anyone to look upon with some amount of equanimity is the past. And even there, its only value is that it is no more.

How bleak and despairing is the ego's use of time! And how terrifying! For underneath its fanatical insistence that the past and future be the same is hidden a far more insidious threat to peace. The ego does not advertise its final threat, for it would have its worshippers still believe that it can offer the escape from it. But the belief in guilt must lead to the belief in hell, and always does. The only way in which the ego allows the fear of hell to be experienced is to bring hell here, but always as a foretaste of the future. For no-one who considers himself as deserving hell can believe that punishment will end in peace.

The Holy Spirit teaches thus: There is no hell. Hell is only what the ego has made of the present. The belief in hell is what prevents you from understanding the present, because you are afraid of it. The Holy Spirit leads as steadily to Heaven as the ego drives to hell. For the Holy Spirit, Who knows only the present, uses it to undo the fear by which the ego would make the present useless. There is no escape from fear in the ego's use of time. For time, according to its teaching, is nothing but a teaching device for compounding guilt until it becomes all-encompassing and demands vengeance forever.

The Holy Spirit would undo all of this now. Fear is not of the present but only of the past and future, which do not exist. There is no fear in the present when each instant stands clear and separated from the past, without its shadow reaching out into the future. Each instant is a clean, untarnished birth, in which the Son of God emerges from the past into the present. And the present extends forever. It is so beautiful and so clean and free of guilt that nothing but happiness is there. No darkness is remembered, and immortality and joy are now.

This lesson takes no time. For what is time without a past and future? It has taken time to misguide you so completely, but it takes no time at all to be what you. Begin to practice the Holy Spirit's use of time as a teaching aid to happiness and peace.

Take this very instant, now, and think of it as all there is of time. Nothing can reach you here out of the past, and it is here that you are completely absolved, completely free, and wholly without condemnation. From this holy instant wherein holiness was born again you will go forth in time without fear and with no sense of change with time.

Time is inconceivable without change, yet holiness does not change. Learn from this instant more than merely hell does not exist. In this redeeming instant lies Heaven. And Heaven will not change, for the birth into the holy present is salvation from change. Change is an illusion, taught by those who could not see themselves as guiltless. There is no change in Heaven because there is no change in God. In the holy instant in which you see yourself as bright with freedom, you will remember God. For remembering Him is to remember freedom.

Whenever you are tempted to be dispirited by the thought of how long it would take to change your mind so completely, ask yourself, "How long is an instant?" Could you not give so short a time to the Holy Spirit for your salvation? He asks no more, for He has no need of more. It takes far longer to teach you how to be willing to give Him this than for Him to use this tiny instant to offer you the whole of Heaven. In exchange for this instant, He stands ready to give you the remembrance of eternity.

You will never give this holy instant to the Holy Spirit on behalf of your release while you are unwilling to give it to your brothers on behalf of theirs. For the instant of holiness is shared and cannot be yours alone. Remember, then, when you are tempted to attack a brother, that His instant of release is yours. Miracles are the instants of release you offer and will receive. They attest to your willingness to be released, and to offer time to the Holy Spirit for His use of it. How long is an instant? It is as short for your brother as it is for you. Practice giving this blessed instant of freedom to all who are enslaved by time, and thus make time their friend for them. The Holy Spirit gives their blessed instant to you through your giving it. As you give it, He offers it to you.

Be not unwilling to give what you would receive of Him, for you join with Him in giving. In the crystal cleanness of the release you give is your instantaneous escape from guilt. You must be holy if you offer holiness. How long is an instant? As long as it takes to re-establish perfect sanity, perfect peace, and perfect love for everyone, for God, and for yourself. As long as it takes to remember immortality, and your immortal creations who share it with you.

As long as it takes to exchange hell for Heaven. Long enough to transcend all of the ego's making and ascend unto your Father.

Time is your friend, if you leave it to the Holy Spirit to use. He needs but very little to restore God's whole power to you. He Who transcends time for you understands what time is for. Holiness lies not in time, but in eternity. There never was an instant in which God's Son could lose his purity. His changeless state is beyond time, for his purity remains forever beyond attack and without variability. Time stands still in his holiness, and changes not. And so it is no longer time at all. For, caught in the single instant of the eternal sanctity of God's creation, it is transformed into forever. Give the eternal instant, that eternity may be remembered for you, in that shining instant of perfect release. Offer the miracle of the holy instant through the Holy Spirit and leave His giving it to you to Him.

The Atonement is in time, but not for time. Being in you, it is eternal. What holds remembrance of God cannot be bound by time. No more are you. For unless God is bound, you cannot be. An instant offered to the Holy Spirit is offered to God on your behalf, and in that instant you will awaken gently in Him. In the blessed instant, you will let go all your past learning and the Holy Spirit will quickly offer you the whole lesson of peace. What can take time, when all the obstacles to learning it have been removed? Truth is so far beyond time that all of it happens at once. For as it was created one, so its oneness depends not on time at all.

Do not be concerned with time, and fear not the instant of holiness which will remove all fear. For the instant of peace is eternal because it is wholly without fear. It will come, being the lesson God gives you, through the Teacher He has appointed to translate time into eternity. Blessed is God's Teacher, Whose joy it is to teach God's holy Son his holiness. His joy is not contained in time. His teaching is for you because His joy is yours. Through Him you stand before God's altar, where He gently translates hell into Heaven. For it is only in Heaven that God would have you be.

How long can it take to be where God would have you? For you are where you have forever been and will forever be. All that you have, you have forever. The blessed instant reaches out to encompass time, as God extends Himself to encompass you. You who have spent days, hours, and even years in chaining your brothers to your egos in an attempt to support it, and uphold its weakness, do not perceive the Source of strength. In the holy instant you will unchain all your brothers and refuse to support either their weakness or your own.

You do not realize how much you have misused your brothers by seeing them as sources of ego support. As a result, they witness to the ego in your perception, and seem to provide reasons for not letting it go. Yet they are far stronger and much more compelling witnesses for the Holy Spirit. And they support His strength. It is, therefore, your choice whether they support the ego or the Holy Spirit in you. And you will know which you have chosen by their reactions. A Son of God who has been released through the Holy Spirit in a brother, if the release is complete, is always recognized. He cannot be denied. As long as you remain uncertain, it can be only because you have not given complete release. And because of this, you have not given one single instant completely to the Holy Spirit. For when you have, you will be sure you have. You will be sure because the witness to Him will speak so clearly of Him that you will hear and understand.

You will doubt until you hear one witness whom you have wholly released through the Holy Spirit. And then you will doubt no more. The holy instant has not yet happened to you. Yet it will, and you will recognize it with perfect certainty. No gift of God is recognized in any other way. You can practice the mechanics of the holy instant and will learn much from doing so. Yet its shining and glittering brilliance, which will literally blind you to this world by its own vision, you cannot supply. And here it is, all in this instant, complete, accomplished, and given wholly.

Start now to practice your little part in separating out the holy instant. You will receive very specific instructions as you go along. To learn to separate out this single second, and begin to experience it as timeless, is to begin to experience yourself as not separate. Fear not that you will not be given help in this. God's Teacher and His lesson will support your strength. It is only your weakness that will depart from you in this practice, for it is the practice of the power of God in you. Use it but for one instant, and you will never deny it again. Who can deny the Presence of what the universe bows to, in appreciation and gladness? Before the recognition of the universe which witnesses to It, your doubts must disappear.

Be not content with littleness but be sure you understand what littleness is and why you could never be content with it. Littleness is the offering you gave yourself. You offered this in place of magnitude, and you accepted it. Everything in this world is little because it is a world made out of littleness, in the strange belief that littleness can content you.

When you strive for anything in this world with the belief that it will bring you peace, you are belittling yourself, and blinding yourself to glory. Littleness and glory are the choices open to your striving and your vigilance. You will always choose one at the expense of the other.

Yet what you do not realize, each time you choose, is that your choice is your evaluation of yourself. Choose littleness and you will not have peace, for you will have judged yourself unworthy of it. And whatever you offer as a substitute is much too poor a gift to satisfy you. It is essential that you accept the fact and accept it gladly, that there is no form of littleness that can ever content you. You are free to try as many as you wish, but all you will be doing is to delay your homecoming. For you will be content only in magnitude, which is your home.

There is a deep responsibility you owe yourself and one which you must learn to remember all the time. The lesson will seem hard at first, but you will learn to love it when you realize that it is true and constitutes a tribute to your power. You who have sought and found littleness, remember this: Every decision which you make stems from what you think you are, and represents the value that you put upon yourself. Believe the little can content you, and by limiting yourself, you will not be satisfied. For your function is not little and it is only by finding your function and fulfilling it that you can escape from littleness.

There is no doubt about what your function is, for the Holy Spirit knows what it is. There is no doubt about its magnitude, for it reaches you through Him from Magnitude. You do not have to strive for it, because you have it. All your striving must be directed against littleness, for it does require vigilance to protect your magnitude in this world. To hold your magnitude in perfect awareness in a world of littleness is a task the little cannot undertake.

Yet it is asked of you, in tribute to your magnitude and not your littleness. Nor is it asked of you alone. The power of God will support every effort you make on behalf of His dear Son. Search for the little, and you deny yourself His power. God is not willing that His Son be content with less than everything. For He is not content without His Son, and His Son cannot be content with less than His Father has given him. We asked you once before, "Would you be hostage to the ego or host to God?" Let this question be asked you by the Holy Spirit in you every time you make a decision. For every decision you make does answer this and invites sorrow or joy accordingly.

When God gave Himself to you in your creation, He established you as host to Him forever. He has not left you, and you have not left Him. All your attempts to deny His magnitude, and make His Son hostage to the ego, cannot make little whom God has joined with Him. Every decision you make is for Heaven or for hell and will bring you awareness of what you decided for. The Holy Spirit can hold your magnitude, clean of all littleness, clearly and in perfect safety in your minds, untouched by every little gift the world of littleness would offer you. But for this, you cannot side against Him in what He wills for you.

Decide for God through Him. For littleness, and the belief that you can be content with littleness, are the decisions you have made about yourself. The power and the glory that lie in you from God are for all who, like you, perceive themselves as little, and have deceived themselves into believing that littleness can be blown up by them into a sense of magnitude that can content them. Neither give littleness, nor accept it. All honour is due the host of God. Your littleness deceives you, but your magnitude is of Him Who dwells in you, and in Whom you dwell. Touch no-one, then, with littleness in the Name of Christ, eternal Host unto His Father.

In this season (Christmas), which celebrates the birth of holiness into this world, join with me who decided for holiness for you. It is our task together to restore the awareness of magnitude to the host whom God appointed for Himself. It is beyond all your littleness to give the gift of God, but not beyond you. For God would give Himself through you. He reaches from you to everyone and beyond everyone to His Son's creations, but without leaving you. Far beyond your little world, but still in you, He extends forever. Yet He brings all his extensions to you, as host to Him.

Is it a sacrifice to leave littleness behind and wander not in vain? It is not sacrifice to wake to glory. But it is a sacrifice to accept anything less than glory. Learn that you must be worthy of the Prince of Peace, born in you in honour of Him Whose host you are. You know not what love means because you have sought to purchase it with little gifts, thus valuing it too little to be able to understand its magnitude. Love is not little, and love dwells in you, for you are host to Him. Before the greatness that lives in you, your poor appreciation of yourself and all the little offerings you have given slip into nothingness. Holy Child of God, when will you learn that only holiness can content you and give you peace?

Remember that you learn not for yourself alone, no more than I did. It is because I learned for you that you can learn of me. I would but teach you what is yours, so that together we can replace the shabby littleness that binds the host of God to guilt and weakness with the glad awareness of the glory that is in him. My birth in you is your awakening to grandeur. Welcome me not into a manger, but into the altar to holiness, where holiness abides in perfect peace.

My Kingdom is not of this world because it is in you. And you are of your Father. Let us join in honouring you, who must remain forever beyond littleness.

Decide with me, who have decided to abide with you. I will as my Father wills, knowing His Will is constant, and at peace forever with Itself. You will be content with nothing but His Will. Accept no less, remembering that everything I learned is yours. What my Father loves I love as He does and I can no more accept it as what it is not than He can. And no more can you. When you have learned to accept what you are, you will make no more gifts to offer to yourselves, for you will know you are complete, in need of nothing, and unable to accept anything for yourself. But you will gladly give, having received. The host of God needs not seek to find anything.

If you are wholly willing to leave salvation to the plan of God, and unwilling to attempt to grasp for peace yourself, salvation will be given you. Yet think not you can substitute your plan for His. Rather, join with me in His, that we may release all those who would be bound, proclaiming together that the Son of God is host to Him. Thus will we let no-one forget what you would remember. And thus will you remember it.

Call forth in everyone only the remembrance of God, and of the Heaven that is in him. For where you would help your brother be, there will you think you are. Hear not his call for hell and littleness, but only his call for Heaven and greatness. Forget not that his call is yours and answer him with me. God's power is forever on the side of His host, for it protects only the peace in which He dwells. Lay not littleness before His holy altar, which rises above the stars and reaches even to Heaven because of what is given it.

This course is not beyond immediate learning, unless you prefer to believe that what God wills takes time. And this means only that you would rather delay the recognition that His Will is so. The holy instant is this one and everyone. The one you want it to be it is. The one you would not have it be is lost to you. You must decide on when it is. Delay it not. For beyond the past and future, in which you will not find it, it stands in shimmering readiness for your acceptance. Yet you cannot bring it into glad awareness while you do not want it, for it holds the whole release from littleness.

Your practice must therefore rest upon your willingness to let all littleness go. The instant in which magnitude will dawn upon you is but as far away as your desire for it. As long as you desire it not, and cherish littleness instead, by so much is it far from you. By so much as you want it will you bring it nearer. Think not that you can find salvation in your own way and have it. Give over every plan that you have made for your salvation in exchange for God's. His will content you, and there is nothing else that can bring you peace. For peace is of God, and of no-one beside Him.

Be humble before Him, and yet great in Him. And value no plan of the ego before the plan of God. For you leave empty your place in His plan, which you must fulfil if you would join with me, by your decision to join in any plan but His. I call you to fulfil your holy part in the plan that He has given to the world for its release from littleness. God would have His host abide in perfect freedom. Every allegiance to a plan of salvation that is apart from Him diminishes the value of His Will for you in your own minds. And yet it is your mind that is the host to Him.

Would you learn how perfect and immaculate is the holy altar on which your Father has placed Himself? This you will recognize in the holy instant in which you willingly and gladly give over every plan but His. For there lies peace, perfectly clear because you have been willing to meet its conditions. You can claim the holy instant anytime and anywhere you want it. In your practice, try to give over every plan you have accepted for finding magnitude in littleness. It is not there. Use the holy instant only to recognize that you alone cannot know where it is and can only deceive yourself.

I stand within the holy instant, as clear as you would have me. And the extent to which you learn to be willing to accept me is the measure of the time in which the holy instant will be yours. I call to you to make the holy instant yours at once, for the release from littleness in the mind of the host of God depends on willingness and not on time.

The reason why this course is simple is that truth is simple. Complexity is of the ego and is nothing more than the ego's attempt to obscure the obvious.

You could live forever in the holy instant, beginning now and reaching to eternity, but for a very simple reason. Do not obscure the simplicity of this reason, for if you do, it will be only because you prefer not to recognize it, and not to let it go. The simple reason, simply stated, is this: The holy instant is a time in which you receive and give perfect communication. This means, however, that it is a time in which your mind is open, both to receive and give. It is the recognition that all minds are in communication. It therefore seeks to change nothing, but merely to accept everything.

How can you do this when you would prefer to have private thoughts, and keep them? The only way you could do that is to deny the perfect communication that makes the holy instant what it is. You believe that it is possible to harbor thoughts you would not share, and that salvation lies in keeping your thoughts to yourself alone. For in private thoughts, known only to yourself, you think you find a way to keep what you would have alone, and share what you would share. And then you wonder why it is that you are not in full communication with those around you, and with God Who surrounds all of you together.

Every thought you would keep hidden shuts communication off because you would have it so. It is impossible to recognize perfect communication while breaking communication holds value to you. Ask yourselves honestly, "Would I want to have perfect communication, and am I wholly willing to let everything that interferes with it go forever?" If the answer is no, then the Holy Spirit's readiness to give it to you is not enough to make it yours, for you are not ready to share it with Him. And it cannot come into a mind that has decided to oppose it. For the holy instant is given and received with equal willingness, being the acceptance of the single Will that governs all thought.

The necessary condition for the holy instant does not require that you have no thoughts which are not pure. But it does require that you have none that you would keep. Innocence is not of your making. It is given you the instant you would have it. Yet it would not be Atonement if there were no need for Atonement. You will not be able to accept perfect communication as long as you would hide it from yourself. For what you would hide is hidden from you.

In your practice, then, try only to be vigilant against deception, and seek not to protect the thoughts you would keep unto yourself. Let the Holy Spirit's purity shine them away and bring all your awareness to the readiness for purity He offers you. Thus will He make you ready to acknowledge that you are host to God, and hostage to no-one and nothing.

The holy instant is the Holy Spirit's most useful learning device for teaching you love's meaning. For its purpose is to suspend judgement entirely. Judgement always rests on the past, for past experience is the basis on which you judge. Judgement becomes impossible without the past, for without it you do not understand anything. You would make no attempt to judge, because it would be quite apparent to you that you do not know what anything means. You are afraid of this because you believe that, without the ego, all would be chaos. Yet I assure you that, without the ego, all would be love.

The past is the ego's chief learning device, for it is in the past that you learned to define your own needs and acquired methods for meeting them on your own terms. We said before that to limit love to part of the Sonship is to bring guilt into your relationships and thus make them unreal. If you seek to separate out certain aspects of the totality, and look to them to meet your imagined needs, you are attempting to use separation to save you. How, then, could guilt not enter? For separation is the source of guilt and to appeal to it for salvation is to believe you are alone. To be alone is to be guilty. For to experience yourself as alone is to deny the Oneness of the Father and His Son and thus to attack reality.

You cannot love parts of reality and understand what love means. If you would love unlike to God, Who knows no special love, how can you understand it? To believe that special relationships, with special love, can offer you salvation is the belief that separation is salvation. For it is the complete equality of the Atonement in which salvation lies. How can you decide that special aspects of the Sonship can give you more than others? The past has taught you this. Yet the holy instant teaches you it is not so.

Because of guilt, all special relationships have some elements of fear in them. And this is why they shift and change so frequently. They are not based on changeless love alone. And love, where fear has entered, cannot be depended on because it is not perfect. In His function as Interpreter of what you have made, the Holy Spirit uses special relationships, which you have chosen to support the ego, as a learning experience which points to truth. Under His teaching, every relationship becomes a lesson in love.

The Holy Spirit knows no-one is special. Yet He also perceives that you have made special relationships, which He would purify, and not let you destroy. However unholy the reason why you made them may be, He can translate them into holiness by removing as much fear as you will let Him. You can place any relationship under His care, and be sure that it will not result in pain, if you offer Him your willingness to have it serve no need but His. All the guilt in it arises from your use of it. All the love from His. Do not, then, be afraid to let go your imagined needs, which would destroy the relationship. Your only need is His.

Any relationship which you would substitute for another has not been offered to the Holy Spirit for His use. There is no substitute for love. If you would attempt to substitute one aspect of love for another, you have placed less value on one and more on the other. You have not only separated them, but you have also judged against both. Yet you had judged against yourself first, or you would never have imagined that you needed them as they were not. Unless you had seen yourself as without love, you could not have judged them so like you in lack.

The ego's use of relationships is so fragmented that it frequently goes even farther; one part of one aspect suits its purposes, while it prefers different parts of another aspect. Thus does it assemble reality to its own capricious liking, offering for your seeking a picture whose likeness does not exist. For there is nothing in Heaven or earth that it resembles, and so, however much you seek for its reality, you cannot find it because it is not real.

Everyone on earth has formed special relationships, and although this is not so in Heaven, the Holy Spirit knows how to bring a touch of Heaven to them here. In the holy instant no-one is special, for your personal needs intrude on no-one to make them different. Without the values from the past you would see them all the same, and like yourself. Nor would you see any separation between yourself and them. In the holy instant, you see in each relationship what it will be when you perceive only the present.

God knows you now. He remembers nothing, having always known you exactly as He knows you now. The holy instant parallels His knowing by bringing all perception out of the past, thus removing the frame of reference you have built by which to judge your brothers. Once this is gone, the Holy Spirit substitutes His frame of reference for it. His frame of reference is simply God. The Holy Spirit's timelessness lies only here. For in the holy instant, free of the past, you see that love is in you, and you have no need to look without and snatch it guiltily from where you thought it was.

All your relationships are blessed in the holy instant, because the blessing is not limited. In the holy instant, the Sonship gains as one. And united in your blessing, it becomes one to you. The meaning of love is the meaning God gave to it. Give to it any meaning apart from His, and it is impossible to understand it. Every brother God loves as He loves you; neither less nor more. He needs them all equally, and so do you. In time, you have been told to offer miracles as Christ directs, and let the Holy Spirit bring to you those who are seeking you. Yet in the holy instant, you unite directly with God and all your brothers join in Christ. Those who are joined in Christ are in no way separate. For Christ is the Self the Sonship shares, as God shares His Self with Christ.

Think you that you can judge the Self of God? God has created It beyond judgement, out of His need to extend His Love. With Love in you, you have no need except to extend it. In the holy instant there is no conflict of needs, for there is only one. For the holy instant reaches to eternity, and to the Mind of God. And it is only there love has meaning and only there can it be understood.

It is impossible to use one relationship at the expense of another, and not suffer guilt. And it is equally impossible to condemn part of a relationship and find peace within it. Under the Holy Spirit's teaching, all relationships are seen as total commitments, yet they do not conflict with one another in any way. Perfect faith in each one, for its ability to satisfy you completely, arises only from perfect faith in yourself. And this you cannot have, while guilt remains. And there will be guilt as long as you accept the possibility, and cherish it, that you can make a brother what he is not because you would have him so.

You have so little faith in yourself because you are unwilling to accept the fact that perfect love is in you. And so you seek without for what you cannot find without. I offer you my perfect faith in you, in place of all your doubt. But forget not that my faith must be as perfect in all your brothers as it is in you, or it would be a limited gift to you. In the holy instant, we share our faith in God's Son because we recognize, together, that he is wholly worthy of it, and in our appreciation of his worth, we cannot doubt his holiness. And so we love him.

All separation vanishes as holiness is shared. For holiness is power, and by sharing it, it gains in strength. If you seek for satisfaction in gratifying your needs as you perceive them, you must believe that strength comes from another, and what you gain He loses. Someone must always lose, if you perceive yourself as weak. Yet there is another interpretation of relationships which transcends the concept of loss of power completely. You do not find it difficult to believe that, when another calls on

God for love, your call remains as strong. Nor do you think that, by God's answer to him, your hope of answer is diminished. On the contrary, you are far more inclined to regard his success as witness to the possibility of yours. That is because you recognize, however dimly, that God is an idea, and so your faith in Him is strengthened by sharing. What you find difficult to accept is the fact that, like your Father, you are an idea. And like Him, you can give yourself completely, wholly without loss and only with gain.

Herein lies peace, for here there is no conflict. In the world of scarcity love has no meaning, and peace is impossible. For gain and loss are both accepted, and so no-one is aware that perfect love is in him. In the holy instant, you recognize the idea of love in you, and unite this idea with the Mind that thought It and could not relinquish it. By holding it within Itself, there was no loss. The holy instant thus becomes a lesson in how to hold all of your brothers in your mind, experiencing not loss, but completion. From this, it follows you can only give. And this is love, for this alone is natural, under the laws of God.

In the holy instant the laws of God prevail, and only they have meaning. The laws of this world cease to hold any meaning at all. When the Son of God accepts the laws of God as what he gladly wills, it is impossible that he be bound, or limited in any way. In this instant, he is as free as God would have him be. For the instant he refuses to be bound, he is not bound.

In the holy instant, nothing happens that has not always been. Only the veil that has been drawn across reality is lifted. Nothing has changed. Yet the awareness of changelessness comes swiftly as the veil of time is pushed aside. No-one who has not yet experienced the lifting of the veil and felt himself drawn irresistibly into the light behind it, can have faith in love without fear. Yet the Holy Spirit gives you this faith, because He offered it to me and I accepted it. Fear not the holy instant will be denied you, for I denied it not. And through me the Holy Spirit gave it unto you, as you will give it. Let no need that you perceive obscure your need of this.

For in the holy instant, you will recognize the only need the aspects of the Son of God share equally, and by this recognition you will join with me in offering what is needed.

It is through is that peace will come. Join me in the idea of peace, for in ideas minds can communicate. If you would give yourself as your Father gives His Self, you will learn to understand Selfhood. And therein is love's meaning understood. But remember that understanding is of the mind, and only of the mind. Knowledge is therefore of the mind, and its conditions are in the mind with it. If you were not only an idea and nothing else, you could not be in full communication with all that ever was. Yet as long as you prefer to be something else or would attempt to be nothing else and something else together, the language of communication, which you know perfectly, you will not remember.

In the holy instant God is remembered, and the language of communication with all your brothers is remembered with Him. For communication is remembered together, as is truth. There is no exclusion in the holy instant because the past is gone, and with it goes the whole basis for exclusion. Without its source exclusion vanishes. And this permits your Source, and that of all your brothers, to replace it in your awareness. God and the power of God will take their rightful place in you and you will experience the full communication of ideas with ideas. Through your ability to do this you will learn what you must be for you will begin to understand what your Creator is and what His creation is along with Him.

Beyond the poor attraction of the special love relationship, and always obscured by it, is the powerful attraction of the Father for His Son. There is no other love that can satisfy you, because there is no other love. This is the only love that is fully given and fully returned. Being complete, it asks nothing. Being wholly pure, everyone joined in it has everything. This is not the basis for any relationship in which the ego enters. For every relationship on which the ego embarks is special. The ego establishes relationships only to get something. And it would keep the giver bound to itself through guilt.

It is impossible for the ego to enter into any relationship without anger, for the ego believes that anger makes friends. This is not its statement, but it is its purpose. For the ego really believes that it can get and keep by making guilty. This is its one attraction; an attraction so weak that it would have no hold at all, except that no-one recognises it. For the ego always seems to attract through love and has no attraction at all to anyone who perceives that it attracts through guilt.

The sick attraction of guilt must be recognized for what it is. For having been made real to you, it is essential to look at it clearly, and by withdrawing your investment in it, to learn to let it go. No-one would choose to let go what he believes has value. Yet the attraction of guilt has value to you only because you have not looked at what it is and have judged it completely in the dark. As we bring it to light, your only question will be why it was you ever wanted it. You have nothing to lose by looking open-eyed at this, for ugliness such as this belongs not in your holy mind. The host of God can have no real investment here.

We said before that the ego attempts to maintain and increase guilt, but in such a way that you do not recognize what it would do to you. For it is the ego's fundamental doctrine that what you do to others you have escaped. The ego wishes no one well. Yet its survival depends on your belief that you are exempt from its evil intentions. It counsels, therefore, that if you are host to it, it will enable you to direct the anger that it holds outward, thus protecting you. And thus it embarks on an endless, unrewarding chain of special relationships, forged out of anger, and dedicated to but one insane belief; that the more anger you invest outside yourself, the safer you become.

It is this chain that binds the Son of God to guilt, and it is this chain the Holy Spirit would remove from his holy mind. For the chain of savagery belongs not around the chosen host of God, who cannot make himself host to the ego. In the name of his release, and in the Name of Him Who would release him, let us look more closely at the relationships which the ego contrives and let the Holy Spirit judge them truly. For it is certain that, if you will look at them, you will offer them gladly to Him. What He can make of them you do not know, but you will become willing to find out, if you are willing, first, to perceive what you have made of them.

In one way or another, every relationship which the ego makes is based on the idea that by sacrificing itself, it becomes bigger. The "sacrifice," which it regards as purification, is actually the root of its bitter resentment. For it would much prefer to attack directly and avoid delaying what it really wants. Yet the ego acknowledges "reality" as it sees it and recognizes that no-one could interpret direct attack as love. Yet to make guilty is direct attack but does not seem to be. For the guilty except attack and having asked for it, they are attracted to it.

In these insane relationships, the attraction of what you do not want seems to be much stronger than the attraction of what you do. For each one thinks that he has sacrificed something to the other, and hates him for it. Yet this is what he thinks he wants. He is not in love with the other at all. He merely believes he is in love with sacrifice. And for this sacrifice, which he demanded of himself, he demands the other accept the guilt, and sacrifice himself as well. Forgiveness becomes impossible, for the ego believes that to forgive another is to lose him. For it is only by attack without forgiveness that the ego can ensure the guilt which holds all its relationships together.

Yet they only seem to be together. For relationships, to the ego, mean only that bodies are together. It is always physical closeness that the ego demands, and it does not object where the mind goes or what it thinks, for this seems unimportant. As long as the body is there to receive its sacrifice, it is content. To the ego, the mind is private, and only the body can be shared. Ideas are basically of no concern, except as they draw the body of another closer or farther. And it is in these terms that it evaluates ideas as good or bad. What makes another guilty and hold him through guilt is "good". What release him from guilt is "bad," because he would no longer believe that bodies communicate, and so he would be "gone."

Suffering and sacrifice are the gifts with which the ego would "bless" all unions. And those who are united at its altar accept suffering and sacrifice as the price of union. In their angry alliances, born of the fear of loneliness and yet dedicated to the continuance of loneliness, they seek relief from guilt by increasing it in the other. For they believe that this decreases it in them. The other seems always to be attacking and wounding them, perhaps in little ways, perhaps "unconsciously," yet never without demand of sacrifice. The fury of those joined at the ego's altar far exceeds your awareness of it. For what the ego really wants you do not realize.

Whenever you are angry, you can be sure that you have formed a special relationship which the ego has "blessed," for anger IS its blessing. Anger takes many forms, but it cannot long deceive those who will learn that love brings no guilt at all, and what brings guilt cannot be love, and must be anger. All anger is nothing more than an attempt to make someone feel guilty, and this attempt is the only basis which the ego accepts for special relationships. Guilt is the only need the ego has, and as long as you identify with it, guilt will remain attractive to you.

Yet remember this; to be with a body is not communication. And if you think it is, you will feel guilty about communication, and will be afraid to hear the Holy Spirit, recognizing in His Voice your own need to communicate. The Holy Spirit cannot teach through fear. And how can He communicate with you, while you believe that to communicate is to make yourself alone? It is clearly insane to believe that by communicating you will be abandoned. And yet you do believe it. For you think that your minds must be kept private or you will lose them, and if your bodies are together your minds remain your own. The union of bodies thus becomes the way in which you would keep minds apart. For bodies cannot forgive. They can only do as the mind directs.

The illusion of the autonomy of the body and its ability to overcome loneliness is but the working of the ego's plan to establish its own autonomy. As long as you believe that to be with a body is companionship, you will be compelled to attempt to keep your brother in his body, held there by guilt. And you will see safety in guilt and danger in communication. For the ego will always teach that loneliness is solved by guilt and that communication is the cause of loneliness. And despite the evident insanity of this lesson, you have learned it.

Forgiveness lies in communication as surely as damnation lies in guilt. It is the Holy Spirit's teaching function to instruct those who believe that communication is damnation that communication is salvation. And He will do so, for the power of God in Him and you is joined in real relationship, so holy and so strong that it can overcome even this without fear. It is through the holy instant that what seems impossible is accomplished, making it evident that it is not impossible. In the holy instant guilt holds no attraction, since communication has been restored. And guilt, whose only purpose is to disrupt communication, has no function here.

Here there is no concealment, and no private thoughts. The willingness to communicate attracts communication to it and overcomes loneliness completely. There is complete forgiveness here, for there is no desire to exclude anyone from your completion, in sudden recognition of the value of his part in it. In the protection of your wholeness, all are invited and made welcome. And you understand that your completion is God's, whose only need is to have you be complete. For your completion makes you His in your awareness. And here it is that you experience yourself as you were created and as you are.

The holy instant does not replace the need for learning, for the Holy Spirit must not leave you as your Teacher until the holy instant has extended far beyond time. For a teaching assignment such as His, He must use everything in this world for your release. He must side with every sign or token of your willingness to learn of Him what the truth must be. He is swift to utilize whatever you offer Him on behalf of this. His concern and care for you are limitless. In the face of your fear of forgiveness, which He perceives as clearly as He knows forgiveness is released, He will teach you to remember that forgiveness is not loss, but your salvation. And that in complete forgiveness, in which you recognize that there is nothing to forgive, you are absolved completely.

Hear him gladly and learn of Him that you have need of no special relationships at all. You but seek in them what you have thrown away. And through them you will never learn the value of what you have cast aside, but what you still desire with all your hearts. Let us join together in making the holy instant all that there is, by desiring that it be all that there is. God's Son has such great need of your willingness to strive for this that you cannot conceive of need so great. Behold the only need that God and His Son share and will to meet together. You are not alone in this. The will of your creations call to you, to share your will with them. Turn, then, in peace from guilt to God and them.

Relate only with what will never leave you, and what you can never leave. The loneliness of God's Son is the loneliness of his Father. Refuse not the awareness of your completion and seek not to restore it to yourselves. Fear not to give redemption over to your Redeemer's Love. He will not fail you, for He comes from One Who cannot fail. Accept your sense of failure as nothing more than a mistake in who you are. For the holy host of God is beyond failure, and nothing that he wills can be denied. You are forever in a relationship so holy that it calls to everyone to escape from loneliness and join you in your love. And where you are must everyone seek and find you there.

Think but an instant on this: God gave the Sonship to you, to ensure your perfect creation. This was His Gift, for as He withheld Himself not from you, He withheld not His creation. Nothing that ever was created but is yours. Your relationships are with the universe. And this universe, being of God, is far beyond the petty sum of all the separate bodies you perceive. For all its parts are joined in God through Christ, where they become like to their Father. For Christ knows of no separation from His Father, Who is His One relationship, in which He gives as His Father gives to Him.

The Holy Spirit is God's attempt to free you of what He does not understand. And because of the Source of the attempt, it will succeed. The Holy Spirit asks you to respond as God does, for He would teach you what you do not understand. God would respond to every need, whatever form it takes. And so He has kept this channel open to receive His communication to you, and yours to Him. God does not understand your problem in communication, for He does not share it with you. It is only you who believe that it is understandable.

The Holy Spirit knows that it is not understandable and yet He understands it because you have made it. In Him alone lies the awareness of what God cannot know, and what you do not understand. It is His holy function to accept them both, and by removing every element of disagreement, to join them into one. He will do this because it is His function. Leave, then, what seems to you to be impossible to Him Who knows it must be possible because it is the Will of God. And let Him Whose teaching is only of God teach you the only meaning of relationships. For God created the only relationship which has meaning, and that is His relationship with you.

As the ego would limit your perception of your brothers to the body, so would the Holy Spirit release your vision and let you see the great rays shining from them, so unlimited that they reach to God. It is this shift in vision which is accomplished in the holy instant. Yet it is needful for you to learn just what this shift entails, so you will become willing to make it permanent. Given this willingness It will not leave you, for it is permanent. For once you have accepted it as the only perception you want, it is translated into knowledge by the part which God Himself plays in the Atonement, for it is the only step in it He understands. Therefore, in this there will be no delay when you are ready for it. God is ready now, but you are not.

Our task is but to continue, as fast as possible, the necessary process of looking straight at all the interference and seeing it exactly as it is. For it is impossible to recognize as wholly without gratification what you think you want. The body is the symbol of the ego, as the ego is the symbol of the separation. And both are nothing more than attempts to limit communication, and thereby to make it impossible. For communication must be unlimited in order to have meaning and deprived of meaning it will not satisfy you completely. Yet it remains the only means by which you can establish real relationships.

Real relationships have no limits, having been established by God. In the holy instant, where the great rays replace the body in awareness, the recognition of relationships without limits is given you. But to see this, it is necessary to give up every use the ego has for the body, and to accept the fact that the ego has no purpose you would share with it. For the ego would limit everyone to a body for its purposes, and while you think it has a purpose, you will choose to utilize the means by which it tries to turn its purpose into accomplishment. This will never be accomplished. Yet you have surely recognized that the ego, whose goals are altogether unattainable, will strive for them with all its might, and will do so with the strength which you have given it.

It is impossible to divide your strength between Heaven and hell, God and the ego, and release your power unto creation, which is the only purpose for which it was given you. Love would always give increase. Limits are demanded by the ego, representing its demands to make little and ineffectual. Limit your vision of a brother to his body, which you will do as long as you would not release him from it, and you have denied his gift to you. His body cannot give it. And seek it not through you. Yet your minds are already continuous, and their union need only be accepted, and the loneliness in Heaven is gone.

If you would but let the Holy Spirit tell you of the Love of God for you, and the need your creations have to be with you forever, you would experience the attraction of the eternal. No-one can hear Him speak of this and long remain willing to linger here. For it is your will to be in Heaven, where you are complete and quiet, in such sure and loving relationships that any limit is impossible. Would you not exchange your little relationships for this? For the body is little and limited, and only those whom you would see without the limits the ego would impose on them can offer you the gift of freedom.

You have no conception of the limits you have placed on your perception, and no idea of all the loveliness that you could see. But this you must remember; the attraction of guilt opposes the attraction of God. His attraction for you remains unlimited, but because your power, being His, is as great as His, you can turn away from love. What you invest in guilt you withdraw from God. And your sight grows weak and dim and limited, for you have attempted to separate the Father from the Son and limit their communication. Seek not Atonement in further separation. And limit not your vision of God's Son to what interferes with his release and what the Holy Spirit must undo to set him free. For his belief in limits has imprisoned him.

When the body ceases to attract you, and when you place no value on it as a means for getting anything, then there will be no interference in communication, and your thoughts will be as free as God's. As you let the Holy Spirit teach you how to use the body only for purposes of communication and renounce its use for separation and attack which the ego sees in it, you will learn you have no need of a body at all. In the holy instant there are no bodies, and you experience only the attraction of God. Accepting it as undivided you join Him wholly, in an instant. The reality of this relationship becomes the only truth that you could ever want. All truth is here.

It is in your power, in time, to delay the perfect union of the Father and the Son. For in this world, the attraction of guilt does stand between them. Neither time nor season means anything in eternity. But here, it is the Holy Spirit's function to use them both, though not as the ego uses them. This is the season when you would celebrate my birth into the world. Yet you know not how to do it. Let the Holy Spirit teach you and let me celebrate your birth through Him. The only gift I can accept of you is the gift I gave to you. Release ME as I will your release. The time of Christ we celebrate together, for it has no meaning if we are apart.

The holy instant is truly the time of Christ. For in this liberating instant no guilt is laid upon the Son of God and his unlimited power is thus restored to him. What other gift can you offer me, when only this I will to offer you? And to see me is to see me in everyone and offer everyone the gift you offer me. I am as incapable of receiving sacrifice as God is, and every sacrifice you ask of yourself you ask of me. Learn now that sacrifice of any kind is nothing but a limitation imposed on giving. And by this limitation you have limited acceptance of the gift I offer you.

We who are one cannot give separately. When you are willing to accept our relationship as real, guilt will hold no attraction for you. For in our union you will accept all of our brothers. The gift of union is the only gift that I was born to give. Give it to me, that you may have it. The time of Christ is the time appointed for the gift of freedom, offered to everyone. And by your acceptance of it, you have offered it to everyone. It is in your power to make this season holy, for it is in your power to make the time of Christ be now.

It is possible to do this all at once because there is but one shift in perception that is necessary, for you made but one mistake. It seems like many, but it is all the same. For though the ego takes many forms, it is always the same idea.

What is not love is always fear, and nothing else. It is not necessary to follow fear through all the circuitous routes by which it burrows underground and hides in darkness, to emerge in forms quite different from what it is. Yet it is necessary to examine each one as long as you would retain the principle which governs all of them. When you are willing to regard them, not as separate, but as different manifestations of the same idea, and one you do not want, they go together. The idea is simply this; you believe that it is possible to be host to the ego or hostage to God. This is the choice you think you have, and the decision which you believe that you must make.

You see no other alternatives, for you cannot accept the fact that sacrifice gets nothing. Sacrifice is so essential to your thought system that salvation apart from sacrifice means nothing to you. Your confusion of sacrifice and love is so profound that you cannot conceive of love without sacrifice. And it is this that you must look upon; sacrifice is attack, not love. If you would accept but this one idea, your fear of love would vanish. Guilt cannot last when the idea of sacrifice has been removed. For if there is sacrifice, as you are convinced, someone must pay and someone must get. And the only question which remains to be decided is how much is the price for getting what.

As host to the ego, you believe that you can give all your guilt away whatever you think, and purchase peace. And the payment does not seem to be yours. While it is obvious that the ego does demand payment, it never seems to be demanding it of you. For you are unwilling to recognize that the ego, which you invited, is treacherous only to those who think they are its host. The ego will never let you perceive this, since this recognition would make it homeless. For when this recognition dawns clearly, you will not be deceived by any form the ego takes to protect itself from your sight.

Each form will be recognized as but a cover for the one idea that hides behind them all; that love demands sacrifice, and is therefore inseparable from attack and fear. And that guilt is the price of love, which must be paid by fear. How fearful, then, has God become to you, and how great a sacrifice do you believe His Love demands!

For total love would demand total sacrifice. And so the ego seems to demand less of you than God, and of the two is judged as the lesser of two evils, one to be feared a little, but the other to be destroyed. For you see love as destructive, and your only question is who is to be destroyed, you or another?

You seek to answer this question in your special relationships, in which you are both destroyer and destroyed in part, but with the idea of being able to be neither completely. And this you think saves you from God, Whose total Love would completely destroy you.

You think that everyone outside yourself demands your sacrifice, but you do not see that only you demand sacrifice, and only of yourself. Yet the demand of sacrifice is so savage and so fearful that you cannot accept it where it is. But the real price of not accepting this has been so great that you have given God away rather than look at it. For if God would demand total sacrifice of you, you thought it safer to project Him outward and away from you, and not be host to Him. To Him you ascribed the ego's treachery, inviting it to take His place to protect you from Him. And you do not recognize that it is what you invited in that would destroy you and does demand total sacrifice of you. No partial sacrifice will appease this savage guest, for it is an invader who but seems to offer kindness, but always to make the sacrifice complete.

You will not succeed in being partial hostage to the ego, for it keeps no bargains, and would leave you nothing. You will have to choose between total freedom and total bondage, for there are no alternatives but these. You have tried many compromises in the attempt to avoid recognizing the one decision which must be made. And yet it is the recognition of the decision, just as it is, that makes the decision so easy! Salvation is simple being of God, and therefore very easy to understand. Do not try to project it from you and see it outside yourself. In you are both the question and the answer; the demand for sacrifice and the peace of God.

Fear not to recognize the whole idea of sacrifice as soley of your making. And seek not safety by attempting to protect yourself from where it is not. Your brothers and your Father have become very fearful to you. And you would bargain with them for a few special relationships in which you think you see some scraps of safety. Do not try longer to keep apart your thoughts and the Thought that has been given you. When they are brought together and perceived where they are, the choice between them is nothing more than a gentle awakening, and as simple as opening your eyes to daylight when you have no more need of sleep.

The sign of Christmas is a star, a light in darkness. See it not outside yourself, but shining in the Heaven within, and accept it as the sign the time of Christ has come. He comes demanding nothing. No sacrifice of any kind, of anyone, is asked by Him. In His Presence, the whole idea of sacrifice loses all meaning.

For He is Host to God. And you need but invite Him in Who is there already, by recognizing that His Host is One, and no thought alien to His Oneness can abide with Him there. Love must be total to give Him welcome, for the Presence of holiness creates the holiness which surrounds it. No fear can touch the Host Who cradles God in the time of Christ, for the Host is as holy as the Perfect Innocence which He protects, and Whose power protects Him.

This Christmas, give the Holy Spirit everything that would hurt you. Let yourself be healed completely that you may join with Him in healing and let us celebrate our release together by releasing everyone with us. Leave nothing behind, for release is total, and when you have accepted it with me you will give it with me. All pain and sacrifice and littleness will disappear in our relationship, which is as innocent as our relationship with our Father, and as powerful. Pain will be brought to us and disappear in our presence, and without pain there can be no sacrifice. And without sacrifice there love must be.

You who believe that sacrifice is love must learn that sacrifice is separation from love. For sacrifice brings guilt as surely as love brings peace. Guilt is the condition of sacrifice, as peace is the condition for the awareness of your relationship with God. Through guilt you exclude your Father and your brothers from yourself. Through peace you invite them back and realize that they are where your invitation bids them be. What you excluded from yourself seems fearful, for you endowed it with fear and tried to cast it out, though it was part of you. Who can perceive part of himself as loathsome, and live within himself in peace? And who can try to resolve the perceived conflict of Heaven and hell in him by casting Heaven out and giving it the attributes of hell, without experiencing himself as incomplete and lonely?

As long as you perceive the body as your reality, so long will you perceive yourself as lonely and deprived. And so long will you also perceive yourself as a victim of sacrifice, justified in sacrificing others. For who could thrust Heaven and its Creator aside without a sense of sacrifice and loss? And who can suffer sacrifice and loss without attempting to restore himself? Yet how could you accomplish this yourselves, when the basis of your attempts is the belief in the reality of the deprivation? For deprivation breeds attack, being the belief that attack is justified. And as long as you would retain the deprivation, attack becomes salvation and sacrifice becomes love.

So is it that, in all your seeking for love, you seek for sacrifice and find it. Yet you find not love. It is impossible to deny what love is, and still recognize it. The meaning of love lies in what you have cast outside yourself and it has no meaning at all apart from you. It is what you preferred to keep that has no meaning. While all that you would keep away holds all the meaning of the universe and holds the universe together in its meaning. For unless the universe were joined in you it would be apart from God and to be without Him is to be without meaning.

In the holy instant the condition of love is met, for minds are joined without the body's interference, and where there is communication, there is peace. The Prince of Peace was born to re-establish the condition of love by teaching that communication remains unbroken even if the body is destroyed, provided that you see not the body as the necessary means of communication. And if you understand this lesson, you will realize that to sacrifice the body is to sacrifice nothing and communication, which must be of the mind, cannot be sacrificed. Where, then, is sacrifice?

The lesson I was born to teach, and still would teach to all my brothers, is that sacrifice is nowhere, and love is everywhere. For communication embraces everything and in the peace, it re-establishes love comes of itself. Let no despair darken the joy of Christmas, for the time of Christ is meaningless apart from joy. Let us join in celebrating peace by demanding no sacrifice of anyone, for so will you offer me the love I offer you. What can be more joyous than to perceive we are deprived of nothing? Such is the message of the time of Christ, which I give you that you may give it, and return it to the Father, who gave it to me. For in the time of Christ communication is restored, and He joins us in the celebration of His Son's creation. God offers thanks to the holy host who would receive Him and let Him enter and abide where He would be. And by your welcome does He welcome you into Himself, for what is contained in you who welcome Him is returned to Him. And we but celebrate His Wholeness as we welcome Him into ourselves. Those who receive the Father are One with Him, being host to Him Who created them. And by allowing Him to enter, the remembrance of the Father enters with Him, and with Him they remember the only relationship they ever had, and ever want to have.

This is the weekend in which a new year will be born from the time of Christ. I have perfect faith in you to do all that you would accomplish. Nothing will be lacking, and you will make complete, and not destroy. Say and understand this:

> "I give you to the Holy Spirit as part of
> myself. I know that you will be released,
> unless I want to use you to imprison myself.
> In the name of my freedom I will your release,
> Because I recognize that we will be released together."

So will the year begin in joy and freedom. There is much to do, and we have been long delayed. Accept the holy instant as this year is born, and take your place, so long left unfulfilled, in the Great Awakening. Make this year different by making it all the same. And let all your relationships be made holy for you. This is our will. Amen.

To empathize does not mean to join in suffering, for that is what you must refuse to understand. That is the ego's interpretation of empathy and is always used to form a special relationship in which the suffering is shared. The capacity to empathize is very useful to the Holy Spirit, provided you let Him use it in His way. He does not understand suffering and would have you teach it is not understandable. When He relates through you, He does not relate through the ego to another ego. He does not join in pain, knowing that healing pain is not accomplished by delusional attempts to enter into it, and lighten it by sharing the delusion.

The clearest proof that empathy as the ego uses it is destructive lies in the fact that it is applied only to certain types of problems, and in certain people. These it selects out and joins with. And it never joins except to strengthen itself. Make no mistake about this manoeuvre; the ego always empathizes to weaken and to weaken is always to attack. If you do not know why remember this; you do not know what you're empathizing with. Of this you may be sure; if you will merely sit quietly by and let the Holy Spirit relate through you, you will empathize with strength, and both of you will gain in strength, and not in weakness.

You value to come of the relationship. You will neither to hurt it nor to heal it in your own way. You do not know what healing is. All you have learned of empathy is from the past. And there is nothing from the past that you would share, for there is nothing there that you would keep. Do not use empathy to make the past real, and so perpetuate it. Step gently aside and let the healing be done for you. Keep but one thought in mind, and do not lose sight of it, however tempted you may be to judge any situation, and to determine your response by judging it. Focus your mind only on this:

"I am not alone and I would not intrude the past upon my Guest. I have invited Him and He is here. I need do nothing except not to interfere".

True empathy is of Him Who knows what it is. You will learn His interpretation of it if you let Him use your capacity for strength and not for weakness. He will not desert you but be sure that you desert not Him. Humility is strength in this sense only; to recognize and accept the fact that you do not know is to recognize and accept the fact that He does know. You are not sure that He will do His part because you have never yet done yours completely. You will not know how to respond to what you do not understand. Be tempted not in this and yield not to the ego's triumphant use of empathy for its glory.

The triumph of weakness is not what you would offer to a brother. And yet you know no triumph but this. This is not knowledge and the form of empathy that would bring this about is so distorted that it would imprison what it would release. The unredeemed cannot redeem, yet they have a Redeemer. Attempt to teach Him not. You are the learner; He the Teacher. Do not confuse your role with His, for this will never bring peace to anyone. Offer your empathy to Him, for it is His perception and His strength that you would share. And let Him offer you His strength and His perception, to be shared through you.

The meaning of love is lost in any relationship which looks to weakness and hopes to find love there. The power of love, which is its meaning, lies in the strength of God, which hovers over it and blesses it silently by enveloping it in healing wings. Let this be and do not try to substitute your "miracle" for this. We once said that if a brother asks a foolish thing of you to do it. But be certain that this does not mean to do a foolish thing that would hurt either him or you, for what would hurt one will hurt the other. Foolish requests are foolish for the simple reason that they conflict, because they contain an element of specialness. Only the Holy Spirit recognizes foolish needs as well as real ones. And He will teach you how to meet both without losing either.

You will attempt to do this only in secrecy. And you will think that, by meeting the needs of one you do not jeopardize another because you keep them separate, and secret from each other. That is not the way, for it leads not to light and truth. No needs will long be left unmet if you leave them all to Him Whose function is to meet them. That is his function, and not yours. He will not meet them secretly, for He would share everything you give through Him. And that is why He gives it.

What you give through Him is for the whole Sonship, not for part of it. Leave Him His function, for He will fulfil it if you but ask Him to enter your relationships and bless them for you.

You still think holiness is difficult because you cannot see how it can be extended to include everyone. And you have learned that it must include everyone to be holy. Concern yourselves not with the extension of holiness, for the nature of miracles you do not understand. Nor do you do them. It is their extension, far beyond the limits you perceive, that demonstrates you did not do them. Why should you worry how the miracle extends to all the Sonship when you do not understand the miracle itself? One attribute is no more difficult to understand than is the whole. If miracles are at all, their attributes would have to be miraculous, being part of them.

There is a tendency to fragment and then to be concerned about the truth of just a little part of the whole. And this is but a way of avoiding, or looking away from the whole, to what you think you might be better able to understand. For this is but another way in which you would still try to keep understanding to yourself. A better and far more helpful way to think of miracles is this: You do not understand them, either in part or whole. Yet you have done them. Therefore, your understanding cannot be necessary. Yet it is still impossible to accomplish what you do not understand. And so there must be something in you that does understand.

To you the miracle cannot seem natural because what you have done to hurt your minds has made them so unnatural that they do not remember what is natural to them. And when you are told about it, you cannot understand it. The recognition of the part as whole and of the whole in every part, is perfectly natural. For it is the way God thinks, and what is natural to Him is natural to you. Wholly natural perception would show you instantly that order of difficulty in miracles is quite impossible, for it involves a contradiction of what miracles mean. And if you could understand their meaning, their attributes could hardly cause you perplexity.

You have done miracles, but it is quite apparent that you have not done them alone. You have succeeded whenever you have reached another mind and joined with it. When two minds join as one and share one idea equally, the first link in the awareness of the Sonship as one has been made.

When you have made this joining, as the Holy Spirit bids you, and have offered it to Him to use as He knows how, His natural perception of your gift enables Him to understand it, and you to use His understanding on your behalf. It is impossible to convince you of the reality of what has clearly been accomplished through your willingness as long as you believe that you must understand it, or else it is not real.

You think your lack of understanding is a loss to you, and so you are unwilling to believe that what has happened is true. But can you really believe that all that has happened, even though you do not understand it, has not happened? Yet this is your position. You would have perfect faith in the Holy Spirit and in the effects of His teaching, if you were not afraid to acknowledge what He taught you. For this acknowledgement means that what has happened you do not understand, but that you are willing to accept it because it has happened.

How can faith in reality be yours while you are bent on making it unreal? And are you really safer in maintaining the unreality of what has happened than you would be in joyously accepting it for what it is, and giving thanks for it? Honour the truth that has been given you and be glad you do not understand it. Miracles are natural to God, and to the One Who speaks for Him. For His task is to translate the miracle into the knowledge which it represents, and which is lost to you. Let His understanding of the miracle be enough for you, and do not turn away from all the witnesses that He has given you to His reality.

No evidence will convince you of the truth of what you do not want. Yet your relationship with Him is real and has been demonstrated. Regard this not with fear, but with rejoicing. The One you called upon is with you. Bid Him welcome and honour His witnesses, who bring you the glad tidings He has come. It is true, just as you fear, that to acknowledge Him is to deny all that you think you know. But it was never true. What gain is there to you in clinging to it, and denying the evidence for truth? For you have come too near to truth to renounce it now, and you will yield to its compelling attraction. You can delay this now but only a little while. The host of God has called to you, and you have heard. Never again will you be wholly willing not to listen.

This is a year of joy, in which your listening will increase, and peace will grow with its increase. The power of holiness and the weakness of attack have both been brought into awareness. And this has been accomplished in minds firmly convinced that holiness is weakness, and attack is power.

Should not this be a sufficient miracle to teach you that your Teacher is not of you? But remember also that, whenever you have listened to His interpretation, the results have brought you joy. Would you prefer the results of your interpretation, considering honestly what they have been? God wills you better. Could you not look with greater charity on whom God loves with perfect love?

Do not interpret against God's Love, for you have many witnesses which speak of It so clearly that only the blind and deaf could fail to see and hear them. This year, determine not to deny what has been given you by God, for that is the only reason He has called to you. His Voice has spoken clearly, and yet you have so little faith in what you heard because you have preferred to place still greater faith in the disaster you have made. Today, let us resolve together to accept the joyful tidings that disaster is not real and that reality is not disaster.

Reality is safe and sure, and wholly kind to everyone and everything. There is no greater love than to accept this and be glad. For love asks only that you be happy and will give you everything that makes for happiness. You have never given any problem to the Holy Spirit He has not solved for you, nor will you ever do so. You have never tried to solve anything yourself and been successful. Is it not time you brought these facts together and made sense of them?

This is the year for the application of the ideas which have been given you. For the ideas are mighty forces, to be used and not held idly by. They have already proved their power sufficiently for you to place your faith in them, and not in their denial. This year invest in truth, and let it work in peace. Have faith in what has faith in you. Think what you have really seen and heard and recognise it. Can you be alone with witnesses like these?

You have taught well and yet you have not learned how to accept the comfort of your teaching. If you will consider what you have taught, and how alien it is to what you thought you knew, you will be compelled to recognize that your Teacher came from beyond your thought system, and so could look upon it fairly, and perceive it was untrue. And He must have done so from the basis of a very different thought system, and one with nothing in common with yours. For certainly what He has taught and what you have taught through Him, have nothing in common with what you taught before He came. And the results have been to bring peace where there was pain, and suffering has disappeared, to be replaced by joy.

You have taught freedom, but you have not learned how to be free. We once said, "By their fruits ye shall know them, and they shall know themselves". For it is certain that you judge yourself according to your teaching. The ego's teaching produces immediate results because its decisions are immediately accepted as your choice. And this acceptance means that you are willing to judge yourself accordingly. Cause and effect are very clear in the ego's thought system because all your learning has been directed towards establishing the relationship between them. And would you not have faith in what you have so diligently taught yourself to believe? Yet remember how much care you have exerted in choosing its witnesses, and in avoiding those which spoke for the cause of truth and its effects.

Does not the fact that you have not learned what you have taught show you that you do not perceive the Sonship as one? And does it not also show you that you do not regard yourself as one? For it is impossible to teach successfully wholly without conviction, and it is equally impossible that conviction be outside of you. You could never have taught freedom unless you did believe in it. And it must be that what you taught came from yourself. And yet, this Self you clearly do not know, and do not recognize It even though It functions. What functions must be there. And it is only if you deny what it has done that you could possibly deny its presence.

This is a course in how to know yourself. You have taught what you are but have not let what you are teach you. You have been very careful to avoid the obvious, and not to see the real cause and effect relationship that is perfectly apparent. Yet within you is everything you taught. What can it be that has not learned it? It must be this that is really outside yourself, not by your own projection, but in truth. And it is this that you have taken in that is not you. What you accept into your minds does not really change them. Illusions are but beliefs in what is not there. And the seeming conflict between truth and illusion can only be resolved by separating yourself from the illusion, and not from truth.

Your teaching has already done this, for the Holy Spirit is part of you. Created by God, He left neither God nor His creation. He is both God and you, as you are God and Him together. For God's answer to the separation added more to you than you tried to take away. He protected both your creations and you together, keeping one with you what you would exclude. And they will take the place of what you took in to replace them.

They are quite real, as part of the Self you do not know. And they communicate to you through the Holy Spirit, and their power and gratitude to you for their creation they offer gladly to your teaching of yourself, who is their home. You who are host to God are also host to them. For nothing real has ever left the mind of its creator. And what is not real was never there.

You are not two selves in conflict. What is beyond God? If you who hold Him and whom He holds are the universe, all else must be outside, where nothing is. You have taught this and from far off in the universe, yet not beyond yourself, the witnesses to your teaching have gathered to help you learn. Their gratitude has joined with yours and God's to strengthen your faith in what you taught. For what you taught is true. Alone, you stand outside your teaching and apart from it. But with them you must learn that you but taught yourself and learned from the conviction you shared with them.

This year you will begin to learn and make learning commensurate with teaching. You have chosen this by your own willingness to teach. Though you seemed to suffer for it, the joy of teaching will yet be yours. For the joy of teaching is in the learner, who offers it to the teacher in gratitude, and shares it with him. As you learn, your gratitude to your Self, Who teaches you what He is, will grow and help you honour Him. And you will learn His power and strength and purity and love Him as His Father does. His Kingdom has no limits and no end and there is nothing in Him that is not perfect and eternal. All this is you and nothing outside of this is you.

To your most holy Self all praise is due for what you are and for what He is Who created you as you are. Sooner or later must everyone bridge the gap which he imagines exists between his selves. Each one builds this bridge, which carries him across the gap as soon as he is willing to expend some little effort on behalf of bridging it. His little efforts are powerfully supplemented by the strength of Heaven, and by the united will of all who make Heaven what it is, being joined within it. And so, the one who would cross over is literally transported there.

Your bridge is builded stronger than you think, and your foot is planted firmly on it. Have no fear that the attraction of those who stand on the other side and wait for you will not draw you safely across. For you will come where you would be, and where your Self awaits you.

Be not afraid to look upon the special hate relationship, for freedom lies in looking at it. It would be impossible not to know the meaning of love, except for this. For the special love relationship, in which the meaning of love is lost, is undertaken solely to offset the hate, but not to let it go. Your salvation will rise clearly before your open eyes as you look on this. You cannot limit hate. The special love relationship will not offset it but will merely drive it underground and out of sight. It is essential to bring it into sight, and to make no attempt to hide it. For it is the attempt to balance hate with love that makes love meaningless to you. The extent of the split that lies in this you do not realize. And until you do, the split will remain unrecognized, and therefore unhealed.

The symbols of hate against the symbols of love play out a conflict which does not exist. For symbols stand for something else, and the symbol of love is without meaning if love is everything. You will go through this last undoing quite unharmed and will at last emerge as yourself. This is the last step in the readiness for God. Be not unwilling now, you are too near, and you will cross the bridge in perfect safety, translated quietly from war to peace. For the illusion of love will never satisfy, but its reality, which awaits you on the other side, will give you everything.

The special love relationship is an attempt to limit the destructive effects of hate by finding a haven in the storm of guilt. It makes no attempt to rise above the storm, into the sunlight. On the contrary, it emphasizes guilt outside the haven by attempting to build barricades against it and keep within them. The special love relationship is not perceived as a value in itself, but as a place of safety from which hatred is split off and kept apart. The special love partner is acceptable only as long as he serves this purpose. Hatred can enter, and indeed is welcome in some aspects of the relationship, but it is still held together by the illusion of love. If the illusion goes, the relationship is broken or becomes unsatisfying on the grounds of disillusionment.

Love is not an illusion. It is a fact. Where disillusionment is possible, there was not love but hate. For hate IS an illusion, and what can change was never love. It is certain that those who select certain ones as partners in any aspect of living and use them for any purpose which they would not share with others are trying to live with guilt rather than die of it. This is the choice they see. And love, to them, is only an escape from death. They seek it desperately, but not in the peace in which it would gladly come quietly to them. And when they find the fear of death is still upon them, the love relationship loses the illusion that it is what it is not.

For then the barricades against it are broken, fear rushes in and hatred triumphs.

There are no triumphs of love. Only hate is concerned with the "triumph of love" at all. The illusion of love can triumph over the illusion of hate, but always at the price of making both illusions. As long as the illusion of hatred lasts, so long will love be an illusion to you. And then the only choice which remains possible is which illusion you prefer. There is no conflict in the choice between truth and illusion. Seen in these terms, no one would hesitate. But conflict enters the instant the choice seems to be one between illusions, for this choice does not matter. Where one choice is as dangerous as the other, the decision must be one of despair.

Your task is not to seek for love, but merely to seek and find all of the barriers within yourself which you have built against it. It is not necessary to seek for what is true, but it is necessary to seek for what is false. Every illusion is one of fear, whatever form it takes. And the attempt to escape from one illusion into another must fail. If you seek love outside yourself, you can be certain that you perceive hatred within and are afraid of it. Yet peace will never come from the illusion of love, but only from its reality.

Recognize this, for it is true and truth must be recognized if it is to be distinguished from illusion: The special love relationship is an attempt to bring love into fear and make it real in fear. In fundamental violation of love's condition, the special love relationship would accomplish the impossible. How but in illusion could this be done? It is essential that we look very closely at exactly what it is you think you can do to solve the dilemma which seems very real to you, but which does not exist. You have come very close to truth and only this stands between you and the bridge that leads you into it.

Heaven waits silently and your creations are holding out their hands to help you cross and welcome them. For it is they you seek. You seek but for your own completion, and it is they who render you complete. The special love relationship is but a shabby substitute for what makes you whole in truth, not in illusion. Your relationship with them is without guilt, and this enables you to look on all your brothers with gratitude, because your creations were created in union with them. Acceptance of your creations is the acceptance of the oneness of creation, without which you could never be complete. No specialness can offer you what God has given, and what you are joined with Him in giving.

Across the bridge is your completion, for you will be wholly in God, willing for nothing special, but only to be wholly like unto Him, completing Him by your completion. Fear not to cross to the abode of peace and perfect holiness. Only there is the completion of God and of His Son established forever. Seek not for this in the bleak world of illusion, where nothing is certain, and where everything fails to satisfy. In the Name of God, be wholly willing to abandon all illusions. In any relationship in which you are wholly willing to accept completion, and only this, there is God completed, and His Son with Him.

The bridge that leads to union in yourself must lead to knowledge, for it was built with God beside you, and will lead you straight to Him, where your completion rests, wholly compatible with His. Every illusion which you accept into your mind by judging it to be attainable removes your own sense of completion, and thus denies the Wholeness of your Father. Every fantasy, be it of love or hate, deprives you of knowledge, for fantasies are the veil behind which truth is hidden. To lift the veil which seems so dark and heavy, it is only needful to value truth beyond all fantasy, and to be entirely unwilling to settle for illusion in place of truth.

Would you not go through fear to love? For such the journey seems to be. Love calls, but hate would have you stay. Hear not the call of hate and see no fantasies. See in the call of hate, and in every fantasy that rises to delay you, but the call for help which rises ceaselessly from you to your Creator. Would He not answer you whose completion is His? He loves you, wholly without illusion, as you must love. For love is wholly without illusion, and therefore wholly without fear. Whom God remembers must be whole. And God has never forgotten what makes Him whole. In your completion lies the memory of His Wholeness, and His gratitude to you for His completion. In His link with you lie both His inability to forget and your ability to remember. In Him are joined your willingness to love, and all the Love of God, Who forgot you not.

Your Father can no more forget the truth in you than you can fail to remember it. The Holy Spirit is the bridge to Him, made from your willingness to unite with Him and created by His joy in union with you. The journey that seemed to be endless is almost complete, for what is endless is very near. You have almost recognized it. Turn with me firmly away from all illusions now and let nothing stand in the way of truth. We will take the last foolish journey away from truth together, and then together we go straight to God, in joyous answer to His call for His completion.

If special relationships of any kind would hinder God's completion, can they have value to you? What would interfere with God must interfere with you. Only in time does interference in God's completion seem to be possible. The bridge that He would carry you across lifts you from time into eternity. Waken from time and answer fearlessly the call of Him Who gave eternity to you in your creation. On this side of the bridge to timelessness you understand nothing. But as you step lightly across it, upheld by timelessness, you are directed straight to the Heart of God. At Its centre, and only there, you are safe forever, because you are complete forever. There is no veil the Love of God in us together cannot lift. The way to truth is open. Follow it with me.

In looking at the special relationship, it is necessary first to realize that it involves a great amount of pain. Anxiety, despair, guilt and attack all enter into it, broken into by periods in which they seem to be gone. All these must be understood for what they are. Whatever form they take, they are always an attack on the self to make the other guilty. We have spoken of this before, but there are some aspects of what is really being attempted that we have not touched upon.

Very simply, the attempt to make guilty is always directed against God. For the ego would have you see Him, and Him alone, as guilty, leaving the Sonship open to attack, and unprotected from it. The special love relationship is the ego's chief weapon for keeping you from Heaven. It does not appear to be a weapon, but if you consider how you value it and why, you will realize what it must be. The special love relationship is the ego's most boasted gift, and one which has the most appeal to those unwilling to relinquish guilt. The "dynamics" of the ego are clearest here, for counting on the attraction of this offering, the fantasies which centre around it are often quite open. Here they are usually judged to be acceptable, and even natural. No one considers it bizarre to love and hate together, and even those who believe that hate is sin merely feel guilty, and do not correct it.

This is the "natural" condition of the separation, and those who learn that it is not natural at all seem to be the unnatural ones. For this world is the opposite of Heaven, being made to be its opposite, and everything here takes a direction exactly opposite of what is true. In Heaven, where the meaning of love is known, love is the same as union. Here, where the illusion of love is accepted in love's place, love is perceived as separation and exclusion.

It is in the special relationship, born of the hidden wish for special love from God, that the ego's hatred triumphs.

For the special relationship is the renunciation of the love of God, and the attempt to secure for the self the specialness which He denied. It is essential to the preservation of the ego that you believe this specialness is not hell, but Heaven. For the ego would never have you see that separation can only be loss, being the one condition in which Heaven cannot be.

To everyone Heaven is completion. There can be no disagreement on this, because both the ego and the Holy Spirit accept it. They are, however, in complete disagreement on what completion is, and how it is accomplished. The Holy Spirit knows that completion lies first in union, and then in the extension of union. To the ego, completion lies in triumph, and in the extension of the "victory" even to the final triumph over God. In this it sees the ultimate freedom of the self, for nothing would remain to interfere with it. This is its idea of Heaven. From this it follows that union, which is a condition in which the ego cannot interfere, must be hell.

The special relationship is a strange and unnatural ego device for joining hell and Heaven and making them indistinguishable. And the attempt to find the imagined "best" of both worlds has merely led to fantasies of both and to the inability to perceive either one as it is. The special relationship is the triumph of this confusion. It is a kind of union from which union is excluded and the basis for the attempt at union rests on exclusion. What better example could there be of the ego's maxim, "Seek but do not find"?

Most curious of all is the concept of the self which the ego fosters in the special relationship. This "self" seeks the relationship to make itself complete. Yet when it finds the special relationship in which it thinks it can accomplish this, it gives itself away and tries to "trade" itself for the self of another. This is not union, for there is no increase and no extension. Each partner tries to sacrifice the self he does not want for one he thinks he would prefer. And he feels guilty for the "sin" of taking, and of giving nothing of value in return. For how much value can he place upon a self that he would give away to get a better one?

The "better" self the ego seeks is always one that is more special. And whoever seems to possess a special self is "loved" for what can be taken from him. Where both partners see this special self in each other, the ego sees "a union made in Heaven." For neither one will recognize that he has asked for hell, and so he will not interfere with the ego's illusion of Heaven, which it offered him to interfere with Heaven.

Yet if all illusions are of fear, and they can be of nothing else, the illusion of Heaven is nothing more than an "attractive" form of fear, in which the guilt is buried deep, and rises in the form of "love."

The appeal of hell lies only in the terrible attraction of guilt, which the ego holds out to those who place their faith in littleness. The conviction of littleness lies in every special relationship, for only the deprived could value specialness. The demand for specialness, and the perception of the giving of specialness as an act of love, would make love hateful. And the real purpose of the special relationship, in strict accordance with the ego's goals, is to destroy reality and substitute illusion. For the ego is itself an illusion and only illusions can be the witnesses to its "reality."

If you perceived the special relationship as a triumph over God, would you want it? Let us not think of its fearful nature, nor of the guilt it must entail, nor of the sadness and the loneliness. For these are only attributes of the whole religion of the separation, and of the total context in which it is thought to occur. The central theme in its litany to sacrifice is that God must die so you can live. And it is this theme which is acted out in the special relationship. Through the death of your self, you think you can attack another self, and snatch it from the other to replace the self which you despise. And you despise it because you do not think it offers the specialness which you demand. And hating it, you have made it little and unworthy because you are afraid of it.

How can you grant unlimited power to what you think you have attacked? So fearful has the truth become to you that unless it is weak and little, you would not dare to look upon it. You think it safer to endow the little self which you have made with power you wrested from truth, triumphing over it and leaving it helpless. See how exactly is this ritual enacted in the special relationship. An altar is erected in between two separate people on which each seeks to kill his self, and on his body raise another self which takes its power from his death. Over and over and over this ritual is enacted. And it is never completed, nor ever will be completed. For the ritual of completion cannot complete, and life arises not from death, nor Heaven from hell.

Whenever any form of special relationship tempts you to seek for love in ritual, remember love is content and not form of any kind. The special relationship is a ritual of form, aimed at the raising of the form to take the place of God at the expense of content. There is no meaning in the form, and there will never be.

The special relationship must be recognized for what it is; a senseless ritual, in which strength is extracted from the death of God and invested in His killer as the sign that form has triumphed over content, and love has lost its meaning. Would you want this to be possible, even apart from its evident impossibility? For if it were possible, you would have made yourself helpless. God is not angry. He merely could not let this happen. You cannot change His Mind.

No rituals that you have set up, in which the dance of death delights you, can bring death to the eternal. Nor can your chosen substitute for the Wholeness of God have any influence at all upon It. See in the special relationship nothing more than a meaningless attempt to raise other gods before Him and by worshipping them, to obscure their tininess and His greatness. In the name of your completion, you do not want this. For every idol which you raise to place before Him stands before you, in place of what you are.

Salvation lies in the simple fact that illusions are not fearful because they are not true. They but seem to be fearful to the extent to which you fail to recognize them for what they are and you will fail to do this to the extent to which you want them to be true. And to the same extent you are denying truth, and so are making yourself unable to make the simple choice between truth and illusion; God and fantasy. Remember this, and you will have no difficulty in perceiving the decision as just what it is and nothing more.

The core of the separation delusion lies simply in the fantasy of destruction of love's meaning. And unless love's meaning is restored to you, you cannot know yourself who share its meaning. Separation is only the decision not to know yourself. Its whole thought system is a carefully contrived learning experience, designed to lead away from truth and into fantasy. Yet for every learning that would hurt you, God offers you correction and complete escape from all its consequences. The decision whether or not to listen to this course and follow it is but the choice between truth and illusion. For here is truth, separated from illusion, and not confused with it at all.

How simple does this choice become when it is perceived as only what it is. For only fantasies made confusion in choosing possible, and they are totally unreal. This year is thus the time to make the easiest decision that ever confronted you and also the only one. You will cross the bridge into reality simply because you will recognize that God is on the other side and nothing at all is here. It is impossible not to make the natural decision as this is realized.

The search for the special relationship is the sign that you equate yourself with the ego and not with God. For the special relationship has value only to the ego. To the ego unless a relationship has special value it has no meaning, and it perceives all love as special. Yet this cannot be natural, for it is unlike the relationship of God and His Son, and all relationships that are unlike this One must be unnatural. For God created love as He would have it be, and gave it as it is. Love has no meaning except as its Creator defined it by His Will. It is impossible to define it otherwise and understand it.

Love is freedom. To look for it by placing yourself in bondage is to separate yourself from it. For the love of God, no longer seek for union in separation, nor for freedom in bondage! As you release, so will you be released. Forget this not, or love will be unable to find you and comfort you. There is a way in which the Holy Spirit asks your help, if you would have His. The holy instant is His most helpful tool in protecting you from the attraction of guilt, the real lure in the special relationship. You do not recognize that this is its real appeal, for the ego has taught you that freedom lies in it. Yet the closer you look at the special relationship, the more apparent it becomes that it must foster guilt and therefore must imprison.

The special relationship is totally without meaning without a body. And if you value it, you must also value the body. And what you value you will keep. The special relationship is a device for limiting your self to a body, and for limiting your perception of others to theirs. The great rays would establish the total lack of value of the special relationship, if they were seen. For in seeing them, the body would disappear because its value would be lost. And so your whole investment in seeing it would be withdrawn from it. You see the world you value.

On this side of the bridge, you see the world of separate bodies, seeking to join each other in separate unions, and to become one by losing. When two individuals seek to become one, they are trying to decrease their magnitude. Each would deny his power, for the separate union excludes the universe. Far more is left outside than would be taken in. For God is left without, and nothing taken in. If one such union were made in perfect faith, the universe would enter into it. Yet the special relationship which the ego seeks does not include even one whole individual. For the ego wants but part of him and sees only this part and nothing else.

Across the bridge, it is so different! For a time the body is still seen, but not exclusively, as it is seen here. For the little spark which holds the great rays within it is also visible and this spark cannot be limited long to littleness. Once you have crossed the bridge, the value of the body is so diminished in your sight, that you will see no need at all to magnify it. For you will realize that the only value which the body has is to enable you to bring your brothers to the bridge with you and to be released together there.

The bridge itself is nothing more than a transition in your perspective of reality. On this side, everything you see is grossly distorted and completely out of perspective. What is little and insignificant is magnified and what is strong and powerful cut down to littleness. In the transition there is a period of confusion, in which a sense of actual disorientation seems to occur. But fear it not, for it means nothing more than that you have been willing to let go your hold on the distorted frame of reference which seemed to hold your world together. This frame of reference is built around the special relationship. Without this illusion, there can be no meaning you would still seek here.

Fear not that you will be abruptly lifted up and hurled into reality. Time is kind, and if you use if for reality, it will keep gentle pace with you in your transition. The urgency is only in dislodging your minds from their fixed position here. This will not leave you homeless, and without a frame of reference. The period of disorientation, which precedes the actual transition, is far shorter than the time it took to fix your minds so firmly on illusions. Delay will hurt you now more than before, only because you realize it is delay and that escape from pain is really possible. Find hope and comfort, rather than despair, in this: You could no longer find even the illusion of love in any special relationship here. For you are no longer wholly insane and you would recognize the guilt of self-betrayal for what it is.

Nothing you seek to strengthen in the special relationship is really part of you. And you cannot keep part of the thought system which taught you it was real and understand the Thought that really knows what you are. You have allowed the Thought of your reality to enter your minds, and because you invited it, it will abide with you. Your love for it will not allow you to betray yourself, and you could not enter into a relationship where it could not go with you, for you would not be apart from it.

Be glad you have escaped the mockery of salvation which the ego offered you and look not back with longing on the travesty it made of your relationships. Now no-one need suffer, for you have come too far to yield to the illusion of the beauty and holiness of guilt. Only the wholly insane could look on death and suffering, sickness and despair, and see it thus. What guilt has wrought is ugly, fearful and very dangerous. See no illusion of truth and beauty there. And be you thankful that there is a place where truth and beauty wait for you. Go on to meet them gladly and learn how much awaits you for the simple willingness to give up nothing because it is nothing.

The new perspective you will gain from crossing over will be the understanding of where Heaven is. From here, it seems to be outside and across the bridge. Yet as you cross to join it, it will join with you and become one with you. And you will think, in glad astonishment, that for all this you gave up nothing! The joy of Heaven, which has no limit, is increased with each light that returns to take its rightful place within it. Wait no longer, for the love of God and you. And may the holy instant speed you on the way, as it will surely do if you but let it come to you.

The Holy Spirit asks only this little help of you. Whenever your thoughts wander to a special relationship which still attracts you, enter with Him into a holy instant, and there let Him release you. He needs only your willingness to share His perspective to give it to you completely. And your willingness need not be complete because His is perfect. It is His task to atone for your unwillingness by His perfect faith, and it is His faith you share with Him there. Out of your recognition of your unwillingness for your release, His perfect willingness is given you. Call upon Him, for Heaven is at His call. And let Him call on Heaven for you.

It is impossible to let the past go without relinquishing the special relationship. For the special relationship is an attempt to re-enact the past and change it. Imagined slights, remembered pain, past disappointments, perceived injustices and deprivations all enter into the special relationship, which becomes a way in which you seek to restore your wounded self-esteem. What basis would you have for choosing a special partner without the past? Every such choice is made because of something "evil" in the past, to which you cling, and for which must someone else atone.

The special relationship takes vengeance on the past. By seeking to remove suffering in the past, it overlooks the present in its preoccupation with the past and its total commitment to it. No special relationship is experienced in the present. Shades of the past envelop it and make it what it is. It has no meaning in the present, and if it means nothing now, it cannot have any real meaning at all. How can you change the past except in fantasy? And who can give you what you think the past deprived you of? The past is nothing. Do not seek to lay the blame for deprivation on it, for the past is gone. You cannot really not let go what has already gone. It must be, therefore, that you are maintaining the illusion that it has not gone because you think it serves some purpose that you want fulfilled. And it must also be that this purpose could not be fulfilled in the present, but ONLY in the past.

Do not underestimate the intensity of the ego's drive for vengeance on the past. It is completely savage and completely insane. For the ego remembers everything that you have done which offended it and seeks retribution of you. The fantasies it brings to the special relationships it chooses in which to act out its hate are fantasies of your destruction. For the ego holds the past against you and in your escape from the past, it sees itself deprived of the vengeance it believes that you so justly merit. Yet without your alliance in your own destruction, the ego could not hold you to the past.

In the special relationship, you are allowing your destruction to be. That this is insane is obvious. But what is less obvious to you is that the present is useless to you while you pursue the ego's goal as its ally. The past is gone; seek not to preserve it in the special relationship which binds you to it, and would teach you that salvation is past, and that you must return to the past to find salvation. There is no fantasy which does not contain the dream of retribution for the past. Would you act out the dream, or let it go?

In the special relationship, it does not seem to be an acting out of vengeance which you seek. And even when the hatred and the savagery break briefly through into awareness, the illusion of love is not profoundly shaken. Yet the one thing which the ego never allows to reach awareness is that the special relationship is the acting out of vengeance on yourself. But what else could it be? In seeking the special relationship, you look not for glory in yourself. You have denied that it is there and the relationship becomes your substitute for it. And vengeance becomes your substitute for Atonement, and the escape from vengeance becomes your loss.

Against the ego's insane notion of salvation, the Holy Spirit gently lays the holy instant. We said before that the Holy Spirit must teach through comparisons and uses opposites to point to truth. The holy instant is the opposite of the ego's fixed belief in salvation through vengeance for the past. In the holy instant, it is accepted that the past is gone, and with its passing the drive for vengeance has been uprooted and has disappeared. The stillness and the peace of now enfolds you in perfect gentleness. Everything is gone except the truth.

For a time, you may attempt to bring illusions into the holy instant to hinder your full awareness of the complete difference, in all respects, between your experience of truth and illusion. Yet you will not attempt this long. In the holy instant, the power of the Holy Spirit will prevail because you joined Him. The illusions you bring with you will weaken the experience of Him for a while and will prevent you from keeping the experience in your mind. Yet the holy instant is eternal, and your illusions of time will not prevent the timeless from being what it is, nor you from experiencing it as it is. What God has given you is truly given and will be truly received.

For God's gifts have no reality apart from your receiving them. your receiving completes His giving. You will receive because it is His Will to give. He gave the holy instant to be given you, and it is impossible that you receive it not because He gave it. When He willed that His Son be free, His Son was free. In the holy instant is His reminder that His Son will always be exactly as he was created. And everything the Holy Spirit teaches you is to remind you that you have received what God has given you.

There is nothing you can hold against reality. All that must be forgiven are the illusions you have held against your brothers. Their reality has no past, and only illusions can be forgiven. God holds nothing against anyone, for He is incapable of illusions of any kind. Release your brothers from the slavery of their illusions by forgiving them for the illusions which you perceive in them. Thus, will you learn that you have been forgiven, for it is you who offered them illusions. In the holy instant this is done for you in time, to bring to you the true condition of Heaven.

Remember that you always choose between truth and illusion; between the real Atonement which would heal and the ego's "atonement" which would destroy. The power of God and all His Love, without limit, will support you as you seek only your place in the plan of Atonement arising from His Love. Be an ally of God and not the ego in seeking how Atonement can come to you. His help suffices, for His Messenger understands how to restore the Kingdom to you, and to place all your investment in salvation in your relationship with Him.

Seek and find His message in the holy instant, where all illusions are forgiven. From there the miracle extends to bless everyone and to resolve all problems, be they perceived as great or small, possible or impossible. There is nothing that will not give place to Him and to His majesty. To join in close relationship with Him is to accept relationships as real and through their reality to give over all illusions for the reality of your relationship with God. Praise be to your relationship with Him, and to no other. The truth lies here and nowhere else. You choose this or nothing.

"Forgive us our illusions, Father and help us to accept our true relationship with You, in which there are no illusions and where none can ever enter. Our holiness is Yours. What can there be in us that needs forgiveness when Yours is perfect? The sleep of forgetfulness is only the unwillingness to remember Your forgiveness and Your Love. Let us not wander into temptation, for the temptation of the Son of God is not Your Will. And let us receive only what you have given and accept but this into the minds which You created and which You love. Amen."

The betrayal of the Son of God lies only in illusions, and all his "sins" are but his own imagining. His reality is forever sinless. He need not be forgiven but awakened. In his dreams he has betrayed himself, his brothers and his God. Yet what is done in dreams has not been really done. It is impossible to convince the dreamer that this is so, for dreams are what they are because of their illusion of reality. Only in waking is the full release from them, for only then does it become perfectly apparent that they had no effect on reality at all and did not change it. Fantasies change reality. That is their purpose.

They cannot do so in reality, but they can do so in the mind that would have reality different. It is, then, only your wish to change reality that is fearful, because by your wish you think you have accomplished what you wish. This strange position, in a sense, acknowledges your power. Yet by distorting it, and devoting it to "evil," it also makes it unreal. You cannot be faithful to two masters who ask of you conflicting things. What you use in fantasy you deny to truth. Yet what you give to truth to use for you is safe from fantasy.

When you maintain that there must be order of difficulty in miracles, all you mean is that there are some things you would withhold from truth. You believe that truth cannot deal with them only because you would keep them from truth. Very simply, your lack of faith in the power that heals all pain arises from your wish to retain some aspects of reality for fantasy. If you but realized what this must do to your appreciation of the whole! What you reserve unto yourself, you take away from Him Who would release you. Unless you give it back, it is inevitable that your perspective on reality be warped and uncorrected.

As long as you would have it so, so long will the illusion of order of difficulty in miracles remain with you. For you have established this order in reality by giving some of it to one teacher, and some to another. And so you learn to deal with part of truth in one way, and in another way the other part. To fragment truth is to destroy it by rendering it meaningless. Orders of reality is a perspective without understanding, a frame of reference for reality to which it cannot really be compared at all.

Think you that you can bring truth to fantasy, and learn what truth means from the perspective of illusions? Truth has no meaning in illusion. The frame of reference for its meaning must be itself. When you try to bring truth to illusions, you are trying to make illusions real and keep them by justifying your belief in them. But to give illusions to truth is to enable truth to teach that the illusions are unreal, and thus enable you to escape from them. Reserve not one idea aside from truth, or you establish orders of reality which must imprison you. There is no order in reality because everything there is true.

Be willing, then, to give all you have held outside the truth to Him Who knows the truth, and in Whom all is brought to truth. Be not concerned with anything except your willingness to have this be accomplished. He will accomplish it; not you. But forget not this: When you become disturbed and lose your peace of mind because another is attempting to solve his problems through fantasy, you are refusing to forgive yourself for just this same attempt. And you are holding both of you away from truth and from salvation. As you forgive him, you restore to truth what was denied by both of you. And you will see forgiveness where you have given it.

Can you imagine how beautiful those you forgive will look to you? In no fantasy have you ever seen anything so lovely. Nothing you see here, sleeping or waking, comes near to such loveliness. And nothing will you value like unto this, nor hold so dear. Nothing that you remember that made your heart seem to sing with joy has ever brought you even a little part of the happiness this sight will bring you. For you will see the Son of God. You will behold the beauty which the Holy Spirit loves to look upon, and which He thanks the Father for. He was created to see this for you, until you learn to see it for yourself. And all His teaching leads to seeing it and giving thanks with Him.

This loveliness is not a fantasy. It is the real world, bright and clean and new, with everything sparkling under the open sun. Nothing is hidden here, for everything has been forgiven, and there are no fantasies to hide the truth. The bridge between that world and this is so little and so easy to cross that you could not believe it is the meeting place of worlds so different. Yet this little bridge is the strongest thing that touches on this world at all. This little step, so small it has escaped your notice, is a stride through time into eternity, and beyond all ugliness into beauty that will enchant you and will never cease to cause you wonderment at its perfection.

This step, the smallest ever taken by anything, is still the greatest accomplishment of all in God's plan of Atonement. All else is learned, but this is given, complete and wholly perfect. No-one but Him Who planned salvation could complete it thus. The real world, in its loveliness, you learn to reach. Fantasies are all undone, and no-one and nothing remains still bound by them, and by your own forgiveness you are free to see. Yet what you see is only what you have made, with the blessing of your forgiveness on it. And with this final blessing of God's Son upon Himself, the real perception, born of the new perspective he has learned, has served its purpose.

The stars will disappear in light, and the sun which opened up the world to beauty will vanish. Perception will be meaningless when it has been perfected, for everything that has been used for learning will have no function. Nothing will ever change; no shifts nor shadings, no differences, no variations which made perception possible will occur. The perception of the real world will be so short that you will barely have time to thank God for it. For God will take the last step swiftly when you have reached the real world and have been made ready for Him.

The real world is attained simply by the complete forgiveness of the old, the world you see without forgiveness. The Great Transformer of perception will undertake with you the careful searching of the mind that made this world and uncover to you the seeming reasons for your making it. In the light of the real reason which He brings, as you follow Him, He will show you that there is no reason here at all. Each spot His reason touches grows alive with beauty, and what seemed ugly in the darkness of your lack of reason is suddenly released to loveliness. Not even what the Son of God made in insanity could be without a hidden spark of beauty which gentleness could release.

All this beauty will rise to bless your sight as you look upon the world with forgiving eyes. For forgiveness literally transforms vision, and lets you see the real world reaching quietly and gently across chaos and removing all illusions which had twisted your perception and fixed it on the past. The smallest leaf becomes a thing of wonder, and a blade of grass a sign of God's perfection. From the forgiven world, the Son of God is lifted easily into his home. And there he knows that he has always rested there in peace. Even salvation will become a dream and vanish from his mind. For salvation is the end of dreams, and with the closing of the dream will have no meaning. Who, awake in Heaven, could dream that there could ever be need of salvation?

How much do you want salvation? It will give you the real world, trembling with readiness to be given you. The eagerness of the Holy Spirit to give you this is so intense He would not wait, although He waits in patience. Meet His patience with your impatience at delay in meeting Him. Go out in gladness to meet with your Redeemer and walk with him in trust out of this world and into the real world of beauty and forgiveness.

To forgive is merely to remember only the loving thoughts you gave in the past, and those that were given you. All the rest must be forgotten. Forgiveness is a selective remembering, based not on your selection. For the shadow figures you would make immortal are "enemies" of reality. Be willing to forgive the Son of God for what he did not do. The shadow figures are the witnesses you bring with you to demonstrate he did what he did not. Because you brought them, you will hear them. And you who kept them by your own selection do not understand how they came into your minds, and what their purpose is.

They represent the evil that you think was done to you. You bring them with you only that you may return evil for evil, hoping that their witness will enable you to think guiltily of another and not harm yourself. They speak so clearly for the separation that no one not obsessed with keeping separation could hear them. They offer you the "reasons" why you should enter into unholy alliances which support the ego's goals and make your relationships the witness to its power. It is these shadow figures which would make the ego holy in your sight and teach you what you do to keep it safe is really love.

The shadow figures always speak for vengeance, and all relationships into which they enter are totally insane. Without exception, these relationships have, as their purpose, the exclusion of the truth about the other, and of yourself. This is why you see in both what is not there and make of both the slaves of vengeance. And why whatever reminds you of your past grievances, no matter how distorted the associations by which you arrive at the remembrance may be, attracts you, and seems to you to go by the name of love. And finally, why all such relationships become the attempt at union through the body, for only bodies can be seen as means for vengeance. That bodies are central to all unholy relationships is evident. Your own experience has taught you this. But what you do not realize are all the reasons which go to make the relationship unholy. For unholiness seeks to reinforce itself, as holiness does, by gathering to itself what it perceives as like itself.

In the unholy relationship, it is not the body of the other with which union is attempted, but the bodies of those who are not there. Even the body of the other, already a severely limited perception of him, is not the central focus as it is, or in entirety. What can be used for fantasies of vengeance and what can be most readily associated with those on whom vengeance is really sought, are centred on and separated off, as being the only parts of value.

Every step taken in the making, the maintaining and the breaking off of the unholy relationship is a move toward further fragmentation and unreality. The shadow figures enter more and more and the one in whom they seem to be decreases in importance.

Time is indeed unkind to the unholy relationship. For time is cruel in the ego's hands, as it is kind when used for gentleness. The attraction of the unholy relationship begins to fade and to be questioned almost at once. Once it is formed, doubt must enter in because its purpose is impossible. The only such relationships which retain the fantasies that centre on them are those which have been dreamed of but have not been made at all. Where no reality has entered, there is nothing to intrude upon the dream of happiness. Yet consider what this means; the more reality that enters into the unholy relationship, the less satisfying it becomes. And the more the fantasy can encompass, the greater the satisfaction seems to be.

The "ideal" of the unholy relationship thus becomes one in which the reality of the other does not enter at all to "spoil" the dream. And the less the other really brings to it, the "better" it becomes. Thus, the attempt at union becomes a way of excluding even the one with whom the union was sought. For it was formed to get him out of it, and join with fantasies in uninterrupted "bliss." How can the Holy Spirit bring His interpretation of the body as a means of communication into relationships whose only purpose is separation from reality? What forgiveness is enables Him to do so.

If all but loving thoughts has been forgotten, what remains is eternal. And the transformed past is made like the present. No longer does the past conflict with now. This continuity extends the present by increasing its reality and its value in your perception of it.

In these loving thoughts is the spark of beauty hidden in the ugliness of the unholy relationship in which the hatred is remembered, yet there to come alive as the relationship is given to Him Who gives it life and beauty. That is why Atonement centres on the past, which is the source of separation, and where it must be undone. For separation must be corrected where it was made. The ego seeks to "resolve" its problems, not at their source, but where they were not made. And thus it seeks to guarantee there will be no solution.

The Holy Spirit wills only to make His resolutions complete and perfect, and so He seeks and finds the source of problems where it is, and there undoes it. And with each step in His undoing is the separation more and more undone, and union brought closer. He is not at all confused by any "reasons" for separation. All He perceives in separation is that it must be undone. Let Him uncover the hidden spark of beauty in your relationships and show it to you. Its loveliness will so attract you that you will be unwilling ever to lose the sight of it again. And you will let it transform the relationship, so you can see it more and more. For you will want it more and more and become increasingly unwilling to let it be hidden from you. And you will learn to seek for, and establish, conditions in which this beauty can be seen.

All this you will do gladly, if you but let Him hold the spark before you, to light your way and make it clear to you. God's Son is one. Whom God has joined as one, the ego cannot break apart. The spark of holiness must be safe, however hidden it may be, in every relationship. For the Creator of the one relationship has left no part of it without Himself.

This is the only part of the relationship the Holy Spirit sees because He knows that only this is true. You have made the relationship unreal, and therefore unholy, by seeing it where it is not and as it is not. Give the past to Him Who can change your mind about it for you. But first, be sure you fully realize what you have made the past to represent, and why.

In brief, the past is now your justification for entering into a continuing, unholy alliance with the ego against the present. For the present is forgiveness. Therefore, the relationships which the unholy alliance dictates are not perceived nor felt as now. Yet the frame of reference to which the present is referred for meaning is an illusion of the past, in which those elements which fit the purpose of the unholy alliance are retained and all the rest let go. And what is thus let go is all the truth the past could ever offer to the present as witnesses for its reality, while what is kept but witnesses to the reality of dreams.

It is still up to you to choose to be willing to join with truth or illusion. But remember that to choose one is to let the other go. Which one you choose, you will endow with beauty and reality because the choice depends on which you value more. The spark of beauty or the veil of ugliness, the real world or the world of guilt and fear, truth or illusion, freedom or slavery, – it is all the same.

For you can never choose except between God and the ego. Thought systems are but true or false and all their attributes come simply from what they are. Only the Thoughts of God are true. And all that follows from Them comes from what They are and is as true as is the holy Source from which They came.

My holy brothers, I would enter into all your relationships, and step between you and your fantasies. Let my relationship to you be real to you and let me bring reality to your perception of your brothers. They were not created to enable you to hurt yourselves through them. They were created to create with you. This is the truth that I would interpose between you and your goal of madness. Be not separate from me and let not the holy purpose of Atonement be lost to you in dreams of vengeance. Relationships in which such dreams are cherished have excluded me. Let me enter in the Name of God and bring you peace that you may offer peace to me.

God established His relationship with you to make you happy, and nothing you do which does not share His purpose can be real. The purpose God ascribed to anything is its only function. Because of His reason for creating His relationship with you, the function of relationships became forever "to make happy." And nothing else. To fulfil this function, you relate to your creations as God to His. For nothing God created is apart from happiness, and nothing God created but would extend happiness as its Creator did. Whatever fulfils this function not cannot be real.

In this world, it is impossible to create. Yet it is possible to make happy. We have said, repeatedly, that the Holy Spirit would not deprive you of your special relationships but would transform them. And by that all that is meant is that He will restore to them the function given them by God. The function you have given them is clearly not to make happy. But the holy relationship shares God's purpose, rather than aiming to make a substitute for it. Every special relationship which you have made is a substitute for God's Will and glorifies yours instead of His because of the delusion that they are different.

You have made very real relationships even in this world which you do not recognize, simply because you have raised their substitutes to such predominance that, when truth calls to you, as it does constantly, you answer with a substitute. Every special relationship which you have ever undertaken has, as its fundamental purpose, the aim of occupying your minds so completely that you will not hear the call of truth. In a sense, the special relationship was the ego's answer to the creation of the Holy Spirit, Who was God's answer to the separation.

For although the ego did not understand what had been created, it was aware of threat.

The whole defence system which the ego evolved to protect the separation from the Holy Spirit was in response to the gift with which God blessed it, and by His blessing enabled it to be healed. This blessing holds, within itself, the truth about everything. And the truth is that the Holy Spirit is in close relationship with you because, in Him, is your relationship with God restored to you. The relationship with Him has never been broken, because the Holy Spirit has not been separate from anyone since the separation. And through Him have all your holy relationships been carefully preserved, to serve God's purpose for you.

The ego is hyperalert to threat, and the part of your mind into which the ego was accepted is very anxious to preserve its reason, as it sees it. It does not realize that it is totally insane. And you must realize just what this means, if you would be restored to sanity. The insane protect their thought systems, but they do so insanely. And all their defences are as insane as what they are supposed to protect. The separation has nothing in it, no part, no "reason," and no attribute that is not insane. And its "protection" is part of it, as insane as the whole. The special relationship, which is its chief defence, must therefore be insane.

You have but little difficulty now in realizing that the thought system which the special relationship protects is but a system of delusions. You recognize, at least in general terms, that the ego is insane. Yet the special relationship still seems to you somehow to be "different." Yet we have looked at it far closer than at many other aspects of the ego's thought system which you have been more willing to let go. While this one remains, you will not let the others go. For this one is not different. Retain this one and you have retained the whole.

It is essential to realize that all defences do what they would defend. The underlying basis for their effectiveness is that they offer what they defend. What they defend is placed in them for safe-keeping, and as they operate, they bring it to you. Every defence operates by giving gifts and the gift is always a miniature of the thought system the defence protects, set in a golden frame. The frame is very elaborate, all set with jewels and deeply carved and polished. Its purpose is to be of value in itself and to divert your attention from what it encloses. But the frame without the picture, you cannot have. Defences operate to make you think you can.

The special relationship has the most imposing and deceptive frame of all the defences the ego uses. It's thought system is offered here, surrounded by a frame so heavy and so elaborate that the picture is almost obliterated by its imposing structure. Into the frame are woven all sorts of fanciful and fragmented illusions of love, set with dreams of sacrifice and self-aggrandizement, and interlaced with gilded threads of self-destruction. The glitter of blood shines like rubies and the tears are faceted like diamonds and gleam in the dim light in which the offering is made.

Look at the picture. Do not let the frame distract you. This gift is given you for your damnation and if you take it you will believe that you are damned. You cannot have the frame without the picture. What you value is the frame, for there you see no conflict. Yet the frame is only the wrapping for the gift of conflict. The frame is not the gift. Be not deceived by the most superficial aspects of this thought system, for these aspects enclose the whole, complete in every aspect. Death lies in this glittering gift. Let not your gaze dwell on the hypnotic gleaming of the frame. Look at the picture and realize that death is offered you.

That is why the holy instant is so important in the defence of truth. The truth itself needs no defence, but you do need defence against your own acceptance of the gift of death. When you who are truth accept an idea so dangerous to truth, you threaten truth with destruction. And your defence must now be undertaken, to keep truth whole. The power of Heaven, the Love of God, the tears of Christ and the joy of His eternal Spirit are marshalled to defend you from your own attack. For you attack Them, being part of Them, and They must save you, for They love Themselves.

The holy instant is a miniature of Heaven, sent you from Heaven. It is a picture, too, set in a frame. Yet if you accept this gift, you will not see the frame at all, because the gift can only be accepted through your willingness to focus all your attention on the picture. The holy instant is a miniature of eternity. It is a picture of timelessness, set in a frame of time. If you focus on the picture, you will realize that it was only the frame that made you think it WAS a picture. Without the frame, the picture is seen as what it represents. For as the whole thought system of the ego lies in its gifts, so the whole of Heaven lies in this instant, borrowed from eternity, and set in time for you.

Two gifts are offered you. Each is complete and cannot be partially accepted. Each is a picture of all that you can have, seen very differently. You cannot compare their value by comparing a picture to a frame. It must be the pictures only that you compare, or the comparison is wholly without meaning. Remember that it is the picture that is the gift. And only on this basis are you really free to choose. Look at the pictures. Both of them. One is a tiny picture, hard to see at all beneath the heavy shadows of its enormous and disproportionate enclosure. The other is lightly framed and hung in light, lovely to look upon for what it is.

You who have tried so hard, and are still trying, to fit the better picture into the wrong frame and so combine what cannot be combined, accept this and be glad: These pictures are each framed perfectly for what they represent. One is framed to be out of focus, and not seen. The other is framed for perfect clarity. The picture of darkness and of death grows less convincing as you search it out amid its wrappings. As each senseless stone which seems to shine in darkness from the frame is exposed to light, it becomes dull and lifeless, and ceases to distract you from the picture. And finally, you look upon the picture itself, seeing at last that, unprotected by the frame, it has no meaning.

The other picture is lightly framed, for time cannot contain eternity. There is no distraction here. The picture of Heaven and eternity grows more convincing as you look at it. And now, by real comparison, a transformation of both pictures can at last occur. And each is given its rightful place, when both are seen in relation to each other. The dark picture, brought to light, is not perceived as fearful, but the fact that it is just a picture is brought home at last. And what you see there you will recognize as what it is; a picture of what you thought was real, and nothing more. For beyond this picture, you will see nothing.

The picture of light, in clear cut and unmistakable contrast, is transformed into what lies beyond the picture. As you look on this, you realize that it is not a picture, but a reality. This is no figured representation of a thought system, but the Thought Itself. What it represents is there. The frame fades gently, and God rises to your remembrance, offering you the whole of creation in exchange for your little picture, wholly without value and entirely deprived of meaning.

As God ascends into His rightful place and you to yours, you will experience again the meaning of relationship and know it to be true. Let us ascend in peace together to the Father, by giving Him ascendance in our minds. We will gain everything by giving Him the power and the glory and keeping no illusions of where they are. They are in us, through His ascendance. What He has given is His. It shines in every part of Him, as in the whole. The whole reality of your relationship with Him lies in our relationship to one another. The holy instant shines alike on all relationships, for in it they are one. For here is only healing, already complete and perfect. For here is God, and where He is only the perfect and complete can be.

The holy relationship is the expression of the holy instant in living in this world. Like everything about salvation, the holy instant is a practical device, witnessed to by its results. The holy instant never fails. The experience of it is always felt. Yet without expression, it is not remembered. The holy relationship is a constant reminder of the experience in which the relationship became what it is. And as the unholy relationship is a continuing hymn of hate in praise of its maker, so is the holy relationship a happy song of praise to the

The holy relationship, a major step toward the perception of the real world, is learned. It is the old, unholy relationship, transformed and seen anew. The holy relationship is a phenomenal teaching accomplishment. In all its aspects, as it begins, develops and becomes accomplished, it represents the reversal of the unholy relationship. Be comforted in this; the only difficult phase is the beginning. For here, the goal of the relationship is abruptly shifted to the exact opposite of what it was. This is the first result of offering the relationship to the Holy Spirit, to use for His purposes.

This invitation is accepted immediately, and the Holy Spirit wastes no time in introducing the practical results of asking Him to enter. At once His goal replaces yours. This is accomplished very rapidly, but it makes the relationship seem disturbed, disjunctive and even quite distressing. The reason is quite clear. For the relationship as it is out of line with its own goal, and clearly unsuited to the purpose which has been accepted for it. In its unholy condition, your goal was all that seemed to give it meaning. Now it seems to make no sense. Many relationships have been broken off at this point, and the pursuit of the old goal re-established in another relationship. For once the unholy relationship has accepted the goal of holiness, it can never again be what it was.

The temptation of the ego becomes extremely intense with this shift in goals. For the relationship has not, as yet, been changed sufficiently to make its former goal completely without attraction, and its structure is "threatened" by the recognition of its inappropriateness for meeting its new purpose. The conflict between the goal and the structure of the relationship is so apparent that they cannot co-exist. Yet now, the goal will not be changed. Set firmly in the unholy relationship, there IS no course except to change the relationship to fit the goal. Until this happy solution is seen and accepted as the only way out of the conflict, the relationship seems to be severely strained.

It would not be kinder to shift the goal more slowly, for the contrast would be obscured, and the ego given time to re-interpret each slow step according to its liking. Only a radical shift in purpose could induce a complete change of mind about what the whole relationship is for. As this change develops and is finally accomplished, it grows increasingly beneficent and joyous. But at the beginning, the situation is experienced as very precarious. A relationship, undertaken by two individuals for their unholy purposes, suddenly has holiness for its goal. As these two contemplate their relationship from the point of view of this new purpose, they are inevitably appalled. Their perception of the relationship may even become quite disorganized. And yet, the former organization of their perception no longer serves the purpose they have agreed to meet.

This is the time for faith. You let this goal be set for you. That was an act of faith. Do not abandon faith, now that the rewards of faith are being introduced. If you believed the Holy Spirit was there to accept the relationship, why would you now not still believe that He is there to purify what He has taken under His guidance? Have faith in each other in what but seems to be a trying time. The goal is set. And your relationship has sanity as its purpose. For now you find yourselves in an insane relationship, recognised as such in the light of its goal.

Now the ego counsels thus; substitute for this another relationship to which your former goal was quite appropriate. You can escape from your distress only by getting rid of each other. You need not part entirely if you choose not to do so. But you must exclude major areas of fantasy from each other, to save your sanity. Hear not this now! Have faith in Him Who answered you. He heard. Has He not been very explicit in His answer? You are not now wholly insane.

Can you deny that He has given you a most explicit statement? Now He asks for faith a little longer, even in bewilderment. For this will go, and you will see the justification for your faith emerge, to bring you shining conviction. Abandon Him not now, nor each other. This relationship has been reborn as holy.

Accept with gladness what you do not understand, and let it be explained to you as you perceive its purpose work in it to make it holy. You will find many opportunities to blame each other for the "failure" of your relationship, for it will seem, at times, to have no purpose. A sense of aimlessness will come to haunt you, and to remind you of all the ways you once sought for satisfaction, and thought you found it. Forget not now the misery you really found, and do not now breathe life into your failing egos. For your relationship has not been disrupted. It has been saved.

You are very new in the ways of salvation and think you have lost your way. Your way is lost but think not this is loss. In your newness, remember that you have started again, together. And take each other's hand, to walk together along a road far more familiar than you now believe. Is it not certain that you will remember a goal unchanged throughout eternity? For you have chosen but the goal of God, from which your true intent was never absent.

Throughout the Sonship is the song of freedom heard, in joyous echo of your choice. You have joined with many in the holy instant, and they have joined with you. Think not your choice will leave you comfortless, for God Himself has blessed your holy relationship. Join in His blessing and withhold not yours upon it. For all it needs now is your blessing, that you may see that in it rests salvation. Condemn salvation not, for it has come to you. And welcome it together, for it has come to join you together in a relationship in which all the Sonship is together blessed.

You undertook, together, to invite the Holy Spirit into your relationship. He could not have entered otherwise. Although you may have made many mistakes since then, you have also made enormous efforts to help Him do His work. And He has not been lacking in appreciation for all you have done for Him. Nor does He see the mistakes at all. Have you been similarly grateful to each other? Have you consistently appreciated the good efforts, and overlooked mistakes? Or has your appreciation flickered and grown dim in what seemed to be the light of the mistakes? You are now entering upon a campaign to blame each other for the discomfort of the situation in which you find yourselves. And by this lack of thanks and gratitude, you make yourselves unable to express the holy instant and thus you lose sight of it.

The experience of an instant, however compelling it may be, is easily forgotten if you allow time to close over it. It must be kept shining and gracious in your awareness of time, but not concealed within it. The instant remains. But where are you? To give thanks to each other is to appreciate the holy instant and thus enable its results to be accepted and shared. To attack each other is not to lose the instant, but to make it powerless in its effects. You have received the holy instant, but you have established a condition in which you cannot use it. As a result, you do not realize that it is with you still. And by cutting yourself off from its expression, you have denied yourself its benefit. You reinforce this every time you attack each other, for the attack must blind you to yourself. And it is impossible to deny yourself and recognize what has been given and received by you.

You stand together in the holy presence of truth itself. Here is the goal, together with you. Think you not the goal itself will gladly arrange the means for its accomplishment? It is just this same discrepancy between the purpose that has been accepted and the means as they stand now which seems to make you suffer, but which makes Heaven glad. If Heaven were outside you, you could not share in its gladness. Yet because it is within, the gladness, too, is yours. You are joined in purpose but remain still separate and divided on the means.

Yet the goal is fixed, firm and unalterable, and the means will surely fall in place because the goal is sure. And you will share the gladness of the Sonship that it is so. As you begin to recognize and accept the gifts you have so freely given to each other, you will also accept the effects of the holy instant and use them to correct all your mistakes and free you from their results. And learning this, you will have also learned how to release all the Sonship and offer it in gladness and thanksgiving to Him Who gave you your release and Who would extend it through you.

The practical application of the Holy Spirit's purpose is extremely simple, but it is unequivocal. In fact, in order to be simple, it must be unequivocal. The simple is merely what is easily understood, and for this it is apparent that it must be clear. The setting of the Holy Spirit's goal is general. Now He will work with you to make it specific. There are certain very specific guidelines He provides for any situation but remember that you do not yet realize their universal application.

Therefore, it is essential, at this point, to use them in each situation separately, until you can more safely look beyond each situation, in an understanding far broader than you now possess.

In any situation in which you are uncertain, the first thing to consider, very simply, is, "What do I want to come of this? What is it for?" The clarification of the goal belongs at the beginning, for it is this which will determine the outcome. In the ego's procedure, this is reversed. The situation becomes the determiner of the outcome, which can be anything. The reason for this disorganized approach is evident. The ego does not know what it wants to come of it. It is aware of what it does not want, but only that. It has no positive goal at all.

Without a clear cut, positive goal, set at the outset, the situation just seems to happen, and makes no sense until it has already happened. Then you look back at it, and try to piece together what it must have meant. And you will be wrong. Not only is your judgement in the past, but you have no idea what should happen. No goal was set with which to bring the means in line. And now the only judgement left to make is whether or not the ego likes it; is it acceptable, or does it call for vengeance? The absence of a criterion for outcome, set in advance, makes understanding doubtful and evaluation impossible.

The value of deciding in advance what you want to happen is simply that you will perceive the situation as a means to make it happen. You will therefore make every effort to overlook what interferes with the accomplishment of your objective and concentrate on everything which helps you meet it. It is quite noticeable that this approach has brought you closer to the Holy Spirit's sorting out of truth and falsity. The true becomes what can be used to meet the goal. The false becomes the useless from this point of view. The situation now has meaning, but only because the goal has made it meaningful.

The goal of truth has further practical advantages. If the situation is used for truth and sanity, its outcome must be peace. And this is quite apart from what the outcome is. If peace is the condition of truth and sanity, and cannot be without them, where peace is they must be. Truth comes of itself. If you experience peace, it is because the truth has come to you, and you will see the outcome truly, for deception cannot prevail against you. And you will recognize the outcome because you are at peace. Here again, you see the opposite of the ego's way of looking, for the ego believes the situation brings the experience.

The Holy Spirit knows that the situation is as the goal determines it and is experienced according to the goal.

The goal of truth requires faith. Faith is implicit in the acceptance of the Holy Spirit's purpose and this faith is all-inclusive. Where the goal of truth is set, there faith must be. The Holy Spirit sees the situation as a whole. The goal establishes the fact that everyone involved in it will play his part in its accomplishment. This is inevitable. No-one will fail in anything. This seems to ask for faith beyond you, and beyond what you can give. Yet this is so only from the viewpoint of the ego, for the ego believes in "solving" conflict through fragmentation and does not perceive the situation as a whole. Therefore, it seeks to split off segments of the situation and deal with them separately, for it has faith in separation, and not in wholeness.

Confronted with any aspect of the situation which seems to be difficult, the ego will attempt to take this aspect elsewhere, and resolve it there. And it will seem to be successful, except that this attempt conflicts with unity, and must obscure the goal of truth. And peace will not be experienced except in fantasy. Truth has not come, because faith has been denied, being withheld from where it rightfully belonged. Thus do you lose the understanding of the situation the goal of truth would bring. For fantasy solutions bring but the illusion of experience, and the illusion of peace is not the condition in which the truth can enter.

The substitutes for aspects of the situation are the witnesses to your lack of faith. They demonstrate that you did not believe that the situation and the problem were in the same place. The problem was the lack of faith, and it is this you demonstrate when you remove it from its source and place it elsewhere. As a result, you do not see the problem. Had you not lacked the faith it could be solved, the problem would be gone. And the situation would have been meaningful to you, because the interference in the way of understanding would have been removed. To remove the problem elsewhere is to keep it. For you remove yourself from it and make it unsolvable.

There is no problem in any situation that faith will not solve. There is no shift in any aspect of the problem but will make solution impossible. For if you shift part of the problem elsewhere, the meaning of the problem must be lost, and the solution to the problem is inherent in its meaning. Is it not possible that all your problems have been solved, but you have removed yourself from the solution? Yet faith must be where something has been done, and where you see it done.

A situation is a relationship, being the joining of thoughts. If problems are perceived, it is because the thoughts are judged to be in conflict. But if the goal is truth, this is impossible. Some idea of bodies must have entered, for minds cannot attack.

The thought of bodies is the sign of faithlessness, for bodies cannot solve anything. And it is their intrusion on the relationship, an error in your thoughts about the situation, which then becomes the justification for your lack of faith. You will make this error but be not at all concerned with that. The error does not matter. Faithlessness brought to faith will never interfere with truth. But faithlessness used against truth will always destroy faith. If you lack faith, ask that it be restored where it was lost and seek not to have it made up to you elsewhere, as if you had been unjustly deprived of it.

Only what you have not given can be lacking in any situation. But remember this; the goal of holiness was set for your relationship, and not by you. You did not set it because holiness cannot be seen except through faith, and your relationship was not holy because your faith in one another was so limited and little. Your faith must grow to meet the goal that has been set. The goal's reality will call this forth, for you will see that peace and faith will not come separately. What situation can you be in without faith, and remain faithful to each other?

Every situation in which you find yourself is but a means to meet the purpose set for your relationship. See it as something else, and you are faithless. Use not your faithlessness. Let it enter and look upon it calmly, but do not use it. Faithlessness is the servant of illusion and wholly faithful to its master. Use it and it will carry you straight to illusions. Be tempted not by what it offers you. It interferes, not with the goal, but with the value of the goal to you. Accept not the illusion of peace it offers but look upon its offering and recognize it is illusion.

The goal of illusion is as closely tied to faithlessness as faith to truth. If you lack faith in anyone to fulfil, and perfectly, his part in any situation dedicated in advance to truth, your dedication is divided. And so you have been faithless to each other, and used your faithlessness against each other. No relationship is holy unless its holiness goes with it everywhere. As holiness and faith go hand in hand, so must its faith go everywhere with it. The goal's reality will call forth and accomplish every miracle needed for its fulfillment. Nothing too small or too enormous, too weak or too compelling, but will be gently turned to its use and purpose. The universe will serve it gladly, as it serves the universe. But do not interfere.

The power set in you in whom the Holy Spirit's goal has been established is so far beyond your little conception of the infinite that you have no idea how great the strength that goes with you. And you can use this in perfect safety. Yet for all its might, so great it reaches past the stars and to the universe that lies beyond them, your little faithlessness can make it useless, if you would use the faithlessness instead.

Yet think on this and learn the causes of faithlessness: You think you hold against the other what he has done to you. But what you really blame him for is what you did to Him. It is not His past but yours you hold against him. And you lack faith in him because of what you were. Yet you are as innocent of what you were as he is. What never was is causeless and is not there to interfere with truth.

There is no cause for faithlessness, but there is a Cause for faith. That Cause has entered any situation which shares Its purpose. The light of truth shines from the centre of the situation, and touches everyone to whom the situation's purpose calls. It calls to everyone. There is no situation which does not involve your whole relationship, in every aspect and complete in every part. You can leave nothing of yourself outside it and keep the situation holy. For it shares the purpose of your whole relationship and derives its meaning from it.

Enter each situation with the faith that you give to each other, or you are faithless to your own relationship. Your faith will call the others to share your purpose, as this same purpose called forth the faith in you. And you will see the means you once employed to lead you to illusions transformed to means for truth. When the Holy Spirit changed the purpose of your relationship by exchanging yours for His, the goal He placed there was extended to every situation in which you enter or will ever enter. And every situation was thus made free of the past, which would have made it purposeless.

You call for faith because of Him Who walks with you in every situation. You are no longer wholly insane, nor no longer alone. For loneliness in God must be a dream. You whose relationship shares the Holy Spirit's goal are set apart from loneliness because the truth has come. Its call for faith is strong. Use not your faithlessness against it, for it calls you to salvation and to peace.

The holy instant is nothing more than a special case, or an extreme example, of what every situation is meant to be. The meaning which the Holy Spirit's purpose has given it is also given to every situation. It calls forth just the same suspension of faithlessness, withheld and left unused, that faith might answer to the call of truth. The holy instant is the shining example, the clear and unequivocal demonstration of the meaning of every relationship and every situation, seen as a whole. Faith has accepted every aspect of the situation, and faithlessness has not forced any exclusion on it. It is a situation of perfect peace simply because you have let it be what it is.

This simple courtesy is all the Holy Spirit asks of you. Let truth be what it is. Do not intrude upon it, do not attack it, do not interrupt its coming. Let it encompass every situation and bring you peace. Not even faith is asked of you, for truth asks nothing. Let it enter, and it will call forth and secure for you the faith you need for peace. But rise you not against it, for against your opposition it cannot come.

Would you not want to make a holy instant of every situation? For such is the gift of faith, freely given wherever faithlessness is laid aside, unused. And then the power of the Holy Spirit's purpose is free to use instead. This power instantly transforms all situations into one sure and continuous means for establishing His purpose and demonstrating its reality. What has been demonstrated has called for faith and has been given it. Now it becomes a fact, from which faith can no longer be withheld. The strain of refusing faith to truth is enormous, and far greater than you realize. But to answer truth with faith entails no strain at all.

To you who have acknowledged the call of your Redeemer, the strain of not responding to His call seems to be greater than before. This is not so. Before, the strain was there but you attributed it to something else, believing that the "something else" produced it. This was never true. For what the "something else" produced was sorrow and depression, sickness and pain, darkness and dim imaginings of terror, cold fantasies of fear and fiery dreams of hell. And it was nothing but the intolerable strain of refusing to give faith to truth and see its evident reality.

Such was the crucifixion of the Son of God. His faithlessness did this to him. Think carefully before you let yourself use faithlessness against him. For he is risen, and you have accepted the cause of his awakening as yours. You have assumed your part in his redemption, and you are now fully responsible to him. Fail him not now, for it has been given you to realize what your lack of faith in him must mean to you. His salvation is your only purpose. See only this in every situation and it will be a means for bringing only this.

When you accepted truth as the goal for your relationship, you became givers of peace as surely as your Father gave peace to you. For the goal of peace cannot be accepted apart from its conditions, and you had faith in it, for no-one accepts what he does not believe is real. Your purpose has not changed, and will not change, for you accepted what can never change. And nothing that it needs to be forever changeless can you now withhold from it. Your release is certain. Give as you have received. And demonstrate that you have risen far beyond any situation that could hold you back, and keep you separate from Him Whose call you answered.

To substitute is to accept instead. If you would but consider exactly what this entails, you would perceive at once how much at variance this is with the goal the Holy Spirit has given you and would accomplish for you. To substitute is to choose between, renouncing one in favour of the other. For this special purpose, one is judged more valuable and the other is replaced by him. The relationship in which the substitution occurred is thus fragmented, and its purpose split accordingly. To fragment is to exclude, and substitution is the strongest defence the ego has for separation.

The Holy Spirit never uses substitutes. Where the ego perceives one person as a replacement for another, the Holy Spirit sees them joined and indivisible. He does not judge between them, knowing they are one. Being united, they are one because they are the same. Substitution is clearly a process in which they are perceived as different. One would unite; the other separate. Nothing can come between what God has joined and what the Holy Spirit sees as one. But everything seems to come between the fragmented relationships the ego sponsors to destroy.

The one emotion in which substitution is impossible is love. Fear involves substitution by definition, for it is love's replacement. Fear is both a fragmented and a fragmenting emotion. It seems to take many forms, and each seems to require a different form of acting out for satisfaction. While this appears to introduce quite variable behaviour, a far more serious effect lies in the fragmented perception from which the behaviour stems. No-one is seen complete. The body is emphasized, with special emphasis on certain parts, and used as the standard for comparison for either acceptance or rejection of suitability for acting out a special form of fear.

You who believe that God is fear made but one substitution. It has taken many forms, because it was the substitution of illusion for truth; of fragmentation for wholeness. It has become so splintered and subdivided and divided again, over and over, that it is now almost impossible to perceive it once was one, and still is what it was. That one error, which brought truth to illusion, infinity to time, and life to death, was all you ever made. Your whole world rests upon it. Everything you see reflects it, and every special relationship which you have ever made is part of it.

You have expressed surprise at hearing how very different is reality from what you see. You do not realize the magnitude of that one error. It was so vast and so completely incredible that from it a world of total unreality had to emerge. What else could come of it? Its fragmented aspects are fearful enough, as you begin to look at them. But nothing you have seen begins to show you the enormity of the original error, which seemed to cast you out of Heaven, to shatter knowledge into meaningless bits of disunited perceptions, and to force you to further substitutions.

That was the first projection of error outward. The world arose to hide it and became the screen on which it was projected and drawn between you and the truth. For truth extends inward, where the idea of loss is meaningless, and only increase is conceivable. Do you really think it strange that a world in which everything is backwards and upside-down arose from this? For truth brought to this could only remain within in quiet and take no part in all the mad projection by which this world was made. Call it not sin but madness, for such it was, and so it still remains. Invest it not with guilt, for guilt implies it was accomplished in reality. And above all, be not afraid of it. When you seem to see some twisted form of the original error rise to frighten you, say only, "God is not fear but love" and it will disappear.

The truth will save you. It has not left you, to go out into the mad world and so depart from you. Inward is sanity; insanity is outside you. You but believe it is the other way; that truth is outside and error and guilt within. Your little, senseless substitutions, touched with insanity and swirling lightly off on a mad course like feathers dancing insanely in the wind, have no substance. They fuse and merge and separate, in shifting and totally meaningless patterns which need not be judged at all. To judge them individually is pointless. Their tiny differences in form are no real differences at all. None of them matters. That they have in common, and nothing else. Yet what else is necessary to make them all the same?

Let them all go, dancing in the wind, dipping and turning till they disappear from sight, far, far outside you. And turn you to the stately calm within, where in holy stillness dwells the living God you never left and Who never left you. The Holy Spirit takes you gently by the hand, and retraces with you your mad journey outside yourself, leading you gently back to the truth and safety within. He brings all your insane projections and your wild substitutions which you have placed outside you to the truth. Thus He reverses the course of insanity and restores you to reason.

In your relationship, where He has taken charge of everything at your request, He has set the course inward, to the truth you share. In the mad world outside you, nothing can be shared but only substituted and sharing and substituting have nothing in common in reality. Within yourselves you love each other with a perfect love. Here is holy ground, in which no substitution can enter, and where only the truth about each other can abide. Here you are joined in God, as much together as you are with Him. The original error has not entered here, nor ever will. Here is the radiant truth, to which the Holy Spirit has committed your relationship. Let Him bring it here, where you would have it be. Give Him but a little faith in each other, to help him show you that no substitute you made for Heaven can keep you from it. In you there is no separation, and no substitute can keep you from each other. Your reality was God's creation and has no substitute.

You are so firmly joined in truth that only God is there. And He would never accept something else instead of you. He loves you both, equally and as one. And as He loves you, so you are. You are not joined together in illusions, but in the Thought so holy and so perfect that illusions cannot remain to darken the holy place in which you stand together. God is with you, my brothers. Let us join in Him in peace and gratitude and accept His gift as our most holy and perfect reality, which we share in Him.

Heaven is restored to all the Sonship through your relationship, for in it lies the Sonship, whole and beautiful, safe in your love. Heaven has entered quietly, for all illusions have been gently brought unto the truth in you, and love has shined upon you, blessing your relationship with truth. God and His whole creation have entered it together. How lovely and how holy is your relationship, with the truth shining upon it! Heaven beholds it and rejoices that you have let it come to you. The universe within you stands with you, together. And Heaven looks with love on what is joined in it, along with its Creator.

Whom God has called should hear no substitutes. Their call is but an echo of the original error which shattered Heaven. And what became of peace in those who heard? Return with me to Heaven, walking together out of this world and through another to the loveliness and joy the other holds within it. Would you still further weaken and break apart what is already broken and hopeless? Is it here that you would look for happiness? Or would you not prefer to heal what has been broken, and join in making whole what has been ravaged by separation and disease?

You have been called, together, to the most holy function that this world contains. It is the only one which has no limits and reaches out to every broken fragment of the Sonship with healing and uniting comfort. This is offered you, in your holy relationship. Accept it here, and you will give as you have accepted. The peace of God is given you with the glowing purpose in which you join. The holy light that brought you together must extend, as you accepted it.

Does not a world that seems quite real arise in dreams? Yet think what this world is. It is clearly not the world you saw before you slept. Rather, it is a distortion of the world, planned solely around what you would have preferred. Here, you are "free" to make over whatever seemed to attack you, and change it into a tribute to your ego, which was outraged by the "attack." This would not be your wish unless you saw yourself as one with the ego, which always looks upon itself, and therefore on you, as under attack and highly vulnerable to it.

Dreams are chaotic because they are governed by your conflicting wishes, and therefore they have no concern with what is true. They are the best example you could have of how perception can be utilized to substitute illusions for truth. You do not take them seriously on awaking because the fact that reality is so outrageously violated in them becomes apparent. Yet they are a way of looking at the world and changing it to suit the ego better. They provide striking examples, both of the ego's inability to tolerate reality and your willingness to change reality on its behalf.

You do not find the differences between what you see in sleep and on awaking disturbing. You recognize that what you see on waking is blotted out in dreams. Yet on awakening, you do not expect it to be gone. In dreams, you arrange everything. People become what you would have them be, and what they do you order. No limits on substitution is laid upon you. For a time, it seems as if the world were given you, to make it what you will. You do not realize that you are attacking it, trying to triumph over it and make it serve you.

Dreams are perceptual temper tantrums, in which you literally scream, "I want it thus!" And thus it seems to be. And yet, the dream cannot escape its origin. Anger and fear pervade it, and in an instant, the illusion of satisfaction is invaded by the illusion of terror. For the dream of your ability to control reality by substituting a world which you prefer is terrifying. Your attempts to blot out reality are very fearful, but this you are not willing to accept. And so you substitute the fantasy that reality is fearful, not what you would do to it. And thus is guilt made real.

Dreams show you that you have the power to make a world as you would have it be, and that because you want it you see it. And while you see it, you do not doubt that it is real. Yet here is a world, clearly within your mind, that seems to be outside. You do not respond to it as though you made it, nor do you realize that the emotions which the dream produce must come from you. It is the figures in the dream and what they do that seem to make the dream. You do not realize that you are making them act out for you, for if you did, the guilt would not be theirs, and the illusion of satisfaction would be gone. In dreams these features are not obscure. You seem to waken, and the dream is gone. Yet what you fail to recognize is that what caused the dream has not gone with it.

Your wish to make another world that is not real remains with you. And what you seem to wake to is but another form of this same world you see in dreams. All your time is spent in dreaming. Your sleeping and your waking dreams have different forms, and that is all. Their content is the same. They are your protest against reality, and your fixed and insane idea that you can change it. In your waking dreams, the special relationship is your determination to keep your hold on unreality, and to prevent yourself from waking. And while you see more value in sleeping than in waking, you will not let go of it.

The Holy Spirit, ever practical in His wisdom, accepts your dreams, and uses them as means for waking. You would have used them to remain asleep. We once said that the first change, before dreams disappear, is that your dreams of fear are changed to happy dreams. That is what the Holy Spirit does in your special relationship. He does not destroy it, nor snatch it away from you. Your special relationship will remain, not as a source of pain and guilt, but as a source of joy and freedom. It will not be for you alone, for therein lay its misery. As its unholiness kept it a thing apart, its holiness will become an offering to everyone.

Your special relationship will be a means for undoing guilt in everyone blessed through your holy relationship. It will be a happy dream, and one which you will share with all who come within your sight. Through it, the blessing which the Holy Spirit has laid upon it will be extended. Think not that He has forgotten anyone in the purpose He has given you. And think not that He has forgotten you to whom He gave the gift. He uses everyone who calls on Him as means for the salvation of everyone. And He will waken everyone through you who offered your relationship to Him. If you but recognized His gratitude! Or mine through His! For we are joined as in one purpose, being of one mind with Him.

Let not the dream take hold to close your eyes. It is not strange that dreams can make a world that is unreal. The wish to make it is incredible. Your relationship has become one in which the wish has been removed, because its purpose has been changed from one of dreams to one of truth. You are not sure of this because you think it may be this that is the dream. You are so used to choosing between dreams you do not see that you have made, at last, the choice between the truth and all illusions.

Yet Heaven is sure. This is no dream. It's coming means that you have chosen truth and it has come because you have been willing to let your special relationship meet its conditions. In your relationship, the Holy Spirit has gently laid the real world; the world of happy dreams, from which awaking is so easy and so natural. For as your sleeping and your waking dreams represent the same wishes in your mind, so do the real world and the truth of Heaven join in the Will of God. The dream of waking is easily transferred to its reality. For this dream comes from your will joined with the Will of God. And what this Will would have accomplished has never not been done.

You who have spent your lives in bringing truth to illusion, reality to fantasy, have walked the way of dreams. For you have gone from waking to sleeping and on and on to a yet deeper sleep. Each dream has led to other dreams, and every fantasy which seemed to bring a light into the darkness but made the darkness deeper. Your goal was darkness, in which no ray of light could enter. And you sought a blackness so complete that you could hide from truth forever, in complete insanity. What you forgot was simply that God cannot destroy Himself. The light is in you. Darkness can cover it, but cannot put it out.

As the light comes nearer you will rush to darkness, shrinking from the truth, sometimes retreating to the lesser forms of fear, and sometimes to stark terror. But you will advance because your goal IS the advance from fear to truth. You know this. The goal which you accepted is the goal of knowledge, for which you signified your willingness. Fear seems to live in darkness, and when you are afraid you have stepped back. Let us then join quickly in an instant of light, and it will be enough to remind you that your goal is light.

Truth has rushed to meet you since you called upon it. If you knew Who walks beside you on this way which you have chosen, fear would be impossible. You do not know because the journey into darkness has been long and cruel, and you have gone deep into it. A little flicker of your eyelids, closed so long, has not yet been sufficient to give you confidence in yourselves, so long despised. You go toward love still hating it, and terribly afraid of its judgement upon you. And you do not realize that you are not afraid of love, but only of what you have made of it. You are advancing to love's meaning, and away from all illusions in which you have surrounded it. When you retreat to the illusion your fear increases, for there is little doubt that what you think it means is fearful. Yet what is that to us who travel surely and very swiftly away from fear?

You who hold each other's hand also hold mine, for when you joined each other you were not alone. Do you believe that I would leave you in the darkness you agreed to leave with me? In your relationship is this world's light. And fear must disappear before you now. Be tempted not to snatch away the gift of faith you offered to each other. You will succeed only in frightening yourselves. The gift is given forever, for God Himself received it. You cannot take it back. You have accepted God. The holiness of your relationship is established in Heaven. You do not understand what you accepted but remember that your understanding is not necessary. All that was necessary was merely the wish to understand. That wish was the desire to be holy. The will of God is granted you. For you desire the only thing you ever had, or ever were.

Each instant that we spend together will teach you that this goal is possible and will strengthen your desire to reach it. And in your desire lies its accomplishment. Your desire is now in complete accord with all the power of the Holy Spirit's Will. No little, faltering footsteps that you may take can separate your desire from His Will and from His strength. I hold your hand as surely as you agreed to take each other's. You will not separate for I stand with you and walk with you in your advance to truth. And where we go we carry God with us.

In your relationship, you have joined with me in bringing Heaven to the Son of God, who hid in darkness. You have been willing to bring the darkness to light, and this willingness has given strength to everyone who would remain in darkness. Those who would see will see. And they will join with me in carrying their light into the darkness, when the darkness in them is offered to the light and is removed forever. My need for you, joined with me in the holy light of your relationship, is your need for salvation. Would I not give you what you gave to me? For when you joined each other, you answered me.

You who are now the bringers of salvation have the function of bringing light to darkness. The darkness in you has been brought to light. Carry it back to darkness, from the holy instant to which you brought it. We are made whole in our desire to make whole. Let not time worry you, for all the fear that you experience is really past. Time has been re-adjusted to help us do, together, what your separate pasts would hinder. You have gone past fear, for no two minds can join in the desire for love without love's joining them.

Not one light in Heaven but goes with you. Not one ray that shines forever in the Mind of God but shines on you. Heaven is joined with you in your advance to Heaven. When such great light has joined with you to give the little spark of your desire the power of God Himself, can you remain in darkness? You are coming home together, after a long and meaningless journey which you undertook apart, and which led nowhere. You have found each other and will light each other's way. And from this light will the great rays extend back into darkness and forward unto God, to shine away the past and so make room for His Eternal Presence, in Which everything is radiant in the light.

The holy instant is the result of your determination to be holy. It is the answer. The desire and the willingness to let it come precedes its coming. You prepare your minds for it only to the extent of recognizing that you want it above all else. It is not necessary that you do more; indeed, it is necessary that you realize that you cannot do more. Do not attempt to give the Holy Spirit what He does not ask, or you will add the ego unto Him, and confuse the two. He asks but little. It is he Who adds the greatness and the might. He joins with you to make the holy instant far greater than you can understand. It is your realization that you need do so little that enables Him to give so much.

Trust not your good intentions. They are not enough. But trust implicitly your willingness, whatever else may enter. Concentrate only on this and be not disturbed that shadows surround it. That is why you came. If you could come without them, you would not need the holy instant. Come to it not in arrogance, assuming that you must achieve the state its coming brings with it. The miracle of the holy instant lies in your willingness to let it be what it is. And in your willingness for this lies also your acceptance of yourself as you were meant to be.

Humility will never ask that you remain content with littleness. But it does require that you be not content with less than greatness which comes not of you. Your difficulty with the holy instant arises from your fixed conviction that you are not worthy of it. And what is this but the determination to be as you would make yourself? God did not create His dwelling-place unworthy of Him. And if you believe He cannot enter where He wills to be, you must be interfering with His Will. You do not need the strength of willingness to come from you, but only from His Will.

The holy instant does not come from your little willingness alone. It is always the result of your small willingness combined with the unlimited power of God's Will. You have been wrong in thinking that it is needful to prepare yourself for Him. It is impossible to make arrogant preparations for holiness, and not believe that it is up to you to establish the conditions for peace. God has established them. They do not wait upon your willingness for what they are. Your willingness is needed only to make it possible to teach you what they are. If you maintain you are unworthy of learning this, you are interfering with the lesson by believing that you make the learner different. You did not make the learner, nor can you make him different. Would you first make a miracle yourself, and then expect one to be made for you?

You merely ask the question. The answer is given. Seek not to answer it, but merely receive the answer as it is given. In preparing for the holy instant, do not attempt to make yourself holy to be ready to receive it. That is but to confuse your role with God's. Atonement cannot come to those who think that they must first atone, but only to those who offer it nothing more than simple willingness to make way for it. Purification is of God alone, and therefore for you. Rather than seek to prepare yourself for Him, try to think thus:

> "I who am host to God am worthy of Him.
> He Who established His dwelling-place in me created
> it as He would have it be.
> It is not needful that I make it ready for Him,
> But only that I do not interfere with His plan to restore to me
> my own awareness of my readiness, which is eternal.
> I need add nothing to His plan.
> But to receive it, I must be willing not to substitute my own
> in place of it."

And that is all. Add more and you will merely take away the little that is asked. Remember you made guilt and that your plan for the escape from guilt has been to bring Atonement to it and make salvation fearful. And it is only fear that you will add, if you prepare yourself for love. The preparation for the holy instant belongs to Him Who gives it. Release yourselves to Him Whose function is release. Do not assume His function for Him. Give Him but what He asks, that you may learn how little is your part and how great is His.

It is this that makes the holy instant so easy and so natural. You make it difficult, because you insist there must be more that you need do. And it is very hard for you to realize that it is not personally insulting that your contribution and the Holy Spirit's are so extremely disproportionate. You are still convinced your understanding is a powerful contribution to the truth, and makes it what it is. Yet we have emphasized that you need understand nothing. Salvation is easy just because it asks nothing that you cannot give right now.

Forget not that it has been your decision to make everything that is natural and easy for you impossible. What you believe to be impossible will be, if God so wills it, but you will remain quite unaware of it. If you believe the holy instant is difficult for you, it is because you have become the arbiter of what is possible and remain unwilling to give place to One Who knows. The whole belief in orders of difficulty in miracles is centred on this. Everything God wills is not only possible but has already happened.

And that is why the past has gone. It never happened in reality. Only in your minds, which thought it did, is its undoing needful.

Prepare you now for the undoing of what never was. If you already understood the difference between truth and illusion, the Atonement would have no meaning. The holy instant, your holy relationship, the Holy Spirit's teaching, and all the means by which salvation is accomplished, would have no purpose. For they are all but aspects of the plan to change your dreams of fear to happy dreams, from which you waken easily to knowledge. Put yourself not in charge of this, for you cannot distinguish between advance and retreat. Some of your greatest advances you have judged as failures, and some of your deepest retreats you have evaluated as success.

Never approach the holy instant after you have tried to remove all fear and hatred from your mind. That is its function. Never attempt to overlook your guilt before you ask the Holy Spirit's help. That is His function. Your part is only to offer Him a little willingness to let Him remove all fear and hatred, and to be forgiven. On your little faith, joined with His understanding, He will build your part in the Atonement, and make sure that you fulfil it easily. And with Him, you will build a ladder planted in the solid rock of faith and rising even to Heaven. Nor will you use it to ascend to Heaven alone.

Through your holy relationship, reborn and blessed in every holy instant which you do not arrange, thousands will rise to Heaven with you. Can you plan for this? Or could you prepare yourselves for such a function? Yet it is possible, because God wills it. Nor will He change His Mind about it. The means and purpose both belong to Him. You have accepted one; the other will be provided. A purpose such as this, without the means, is inconceivable. He will provide the means to anyone who shares His purpose.

Happy dreams come true, not because they are dreams, but only because they are happy. And so they must be loving. Their message is, "Thy Will be done," and not, "I want it otherwise." The alignment of means and purpose is an undertaking impossible for you to understand. You do not even realize you have accepted the Holy Spirit's purpose as your own, and you would merely bring unholy means to its accomplishment. The little faith it needed to change the purpose is all that is required to receive the means and use them.

It is no dream to love your brother as yourself. Nor is your holy relationship a dream. All that remains of dreams within it is that it is still a special relationship. Yet it is very useful to the Holy Spirit, Who has a special function here. It will become the happy dream through which He can spread joy to thousands on thousands who believe that love is fear, not happiness. Let Him fulfil the function that He gave to your relationship by accepting it for you, and nothing will be wanting that would make of it what He would have it be.

When you feel the holiness of your relationship is threatened by anything, stop instantly and offer the Holy Spirit your willingness, in spite of fear, to let Him exchange this instant for the holy one which you would rather have. He will never fail in this. But forget not that your relationship is one, and so it must be that whatever threatens the peace of one is an equal threat to the other. The power of joining and its blessing lie in the fact that it is now impossible for either of you to experience fear alone, or to attempt to deal with it alone. Never believe that this is necessary, or even possible. Yet just as this is impossible, so is it equally impossible that the holy instant comes to either of you without the other. And it will come to both at the request of either.

Whichever is saner at the time when the threat is perceived should remember how deep is his indebtedness to the other, and how much gratitude is due him and be glad that he can pay his debt by bringing happiness to both. Let him remember this and say:

> "I desire this holy instant for myself
> That I may share it with my brother, whom I love.
> It is not possible that I can have it without him, or he without me.
> Yet it is wholly possible for us to share it now.
> And so I choose this instant as the one to offer to the Holy Spirit,
> That His blessing may descend on us and keep us both in peace."

There is nothing outside you. That is what you must ultimately learn, for it is the realization that the Kingdom of Heaven is restored to you. For God created only this and He did not depart from it, nor leave it separate from Himself. The Kingdom of Heaven is the dwelling-place of the Son of God, who left not his Father and dwells not apart from Him. Heaven is not a place nor a condition. It is merely an awareness of perfect Oneness and the knowledge that there is nothing else; nothing outside this Oneness and nothing else within.

What could God give but knowledge of Himself? What else is there to give? The belief that you could give and get something else, something outside yourself, has cost you the awareness of Heaven, and the loss of your identity. And you have done a stranger thing than you yet realize. You have displaced your guilt to your bodies from your minds. Yet a body cannot be guilty, for it can do nothing of itself. You who think you hate your bodies deceive yourselves. You hate your minds, for guilt has entered into them, and they would remain separate, which they cannot do.

Minds are joined; bodies are not. Only by assigning to the mind the properties of the body does separation seem to be possible. And it is mind that seems to be fragmented and private and alone. Its guilt, which keeps it separate, is projected to the body, which suffers and dies because it is attacked to hold the separation in the mind, and let it not know its identity. Mind cannot attack, but it can make fantasies and direct the body to act them out. Yet it is never what the body does that seems to satisfy. Unless the mind believes the body is actually acting out its fantasies, it will attack the body by increasing the projection of its guilt upon it.

In this, the mind is clearly delusional. It cannot attack, but it maintains it can and uses what it does to hurt the body to prove it can. The mind cannot attack, but it can deceive itself. And this is all it does when it believes it has attacked the body. It can project its guilt, but it will not lose it through projection. And though it clearly can misperceive the function of the body, it cannot change its function from what the Holy Spirit establishes it to be. The body was not made by love. Yet love does not condemn it, and can use it lovingly, respecting what the Son of God has made, and using it to save him from illusions.

Would you not have the instruments of separation reinterpreted as means for salvation, and used for purposes of love? Would you not welcome and support the shift from fantasies of vengeance to release from them? Your perception of the body can clearly be sick, but project not this upon the body.

For your wish to make destructive what cannot destroy can have no real effect at all. And what God created is only what He would have it be, being His Will. You cannot make His Will destructive. You can make fantasies in which your will conflicts with His, but that is all.

It is insane to use the body as the scapegoat for guilt, directing its attack and blaming it for what you wished it to do. It is impossible to act out fantasies. For it is still the fantasies you want and they have nothing to do with what the body does. It does not dream of them and they but make it a liability where it could be an asset. For fantasies have made your body your "enemy," weak, vulnerable and treacherous, worthy of the hate which you invest in it. How has this served you? You have identified with this thing you hate, the instrument of vengeance and the perceived source of your guilt. You have done this to a thing that has no meaning, proclaiming it to be the dwelling-place of the Son of God, and turning it against him.

This is the host of God that you have made. And neither God nor His most holy Son can enter an abode which harbors hate, and where you have sown the seeds of vengeance, violence and death. This thing you made to serve your guilt stands between you and other minds. The minds are joined, but you do not identify with them. You see yourself locked in a separate prison, removed and unreachable, incapable of reaching out as being reached. You hate this prison you have made and would destroy it. But you would not escape from it, leaving it unharmed, without your guilt upon it.

Yet only thus can you escape. The home of vengeance is not yours; the place you set aside to house your hate is not a prison, but an illusion of yourself. The body is a limit imposed on the universal communication which is an eternal property of mind. But the communication is internal. Mind reaches to itself. It does not go out. Within itself it has no limits, and there is nothing outside it. It encompasses you entirely; you within it, and it within you. There is nothing else, anywhere or ever.

The body is outside you, and but seems to surround you, shutting you off from others, and keeping you apart from them. It is not there. There is no barrier between God and His Son, nor can His Son be separated from himself except in illusions. This is not his reality, though he believes it is. Yet this could only be if God were wrong. God would have had to create differently, and to have separated Himself from His Son to make this possible. He would have had to create different things, and to establish different orders of reality, only some of which were love. Yet love must be forever like itself, changeless forever, and forever without alternative. \

And so, it is. You cannot put a barrier around yourself because God placed none between Himself and you.

You can stretch out your hand and reach to Heaven. You whose hands are joined have begun to reach beyond the body, but not outside yourselves, to reach your shared identity together. Could this be outside you? Where God is not? Is He a body, and did He create you as He is not, and where He cannot be? You are surrounded only by Him. What limit can there be on you whom He encompasses? Everyone has experienced what he would call a sense of being transported beyond himself. This feeling of liberation far exceeds the dream of freedom sometimes experienced in special relationships. It is a sense of actual escape from limitations.

If you will consider what this "transportation" really entails, you will realize that it is a sudden unawareness of the body, and a joining of yourself and something else in which your mind enlarges to encompass it. It becomes part of you, as you unite with it. And both become whole, as neither is perceived as separate. What really happens is that you have given up the illusion of a limited awareness and lost your fear of union. The love that instantly replaces it extends to what has freed you and unites with it. And while this lasts, you are not uncertain of your identity, and would not limit it. You have escaped from fear to peace, asking no questions of reality, but merely accepting it. You have accepted this instead of the body and have let yourself be one with something beyond it, simply by not letting your mind be limited by it.

This can occur regardless of the physical distance which seems to be between you and what you join; of your respective positions in space; and of your differences in size and seeming quality. Time is not relevant; it can occur with something past, present or anticipated. The "something" can be anything and anywhere; a sound, a sight, a thought, a memory, and even a general idea without specific reference. Yet in every case, you joined it without reservation because you love it and would be with it. And so you rush to meet it, letting your limits melt away, suspending all the "laws" your body obeys and gently setting them aside.

There is no violence at all in this escape. The body is not attacked, but simply properly perceived. It does not limit you, merely because you would not have it so. You are not really "lifted out" of it; it cannot contain you.

You go where you would be, gaining, not losing, a sense of self. In these instants of release from physical restrictions, you experience much of what happens in the holy instant; the lifting of the barriers of time and space, the sudden experience of peace and joy, and, above all, the lack of awareness of the body and of the questioning whether or not all this is possible.

It is possible because you want it. The sudden expansion of the self which takes place with your desire for it is the irresistible appeal the holy instant holds. It calls to you to be yourself, within its safe embrace. There are the laws of limit lifted for you, to welcome you to openness of mind and freedom. Come to this place of refuge, where you can be yourself in peace. Not through destruction, not through a "breaking out," but merely by a quiet "melting in." For peace will join you there simply because you have been willing to let go the limits you have placed upon love, and joined it where it is and where it led you, in answer to its gentle call to be at peace. "I need do nothing."

You still have too much faith in the body as a source of strength. What plans do you make that do not involve its comfort or protection or enjoyment in some way? This makes it an end and not a means in your interpretation, and this always means you still find sin attractive. No-one accepts Atonement for himself who still accepts sin as his goal. You have thus not met your one responsibility. Atonement is not welcomed by those who prefer pain and destruction.

You have made much progress and are really trying to make still more, but there is one thing you have never done; not for one instant have you utterly forgotten the body. It has faded at times from your sight, but it has not yet completely disappeared. You are not asked to let this happen for more than an instant, yet it is in this instant that the miracle of Atonement happens. Afterwards, you will see the body again, but never quite the same. And every instant that you spend without awareness of it gives you a different view of it when you return.

At no single instant does the body exist at all. It is always remembered or anticipated, but never experienced just now. Only its past and future make it seem real. Time controls it entirely, for sin is never present. In any single instant, the attraction of guilt would be experienced as pain and nothing else and would be avoided. It has no attraction now. Its whole attraction is imaginary, and therefore must be thought of in the past or in the future.
It is impossible to accept the holy instant without reservation unless, just for an instant, you are willing to see no past or future. You cannot prepare for it without placing it in the future.

Release is given you the instant you desire it. Many have spent a lifetime in preparation and have indeed achieved their instants of success.

This course does not attempt to teach more than they learned in time, but it does aim at saving time. You are attempting to follow a very long road to the goal you have accepted. It is extremely difficult to reach Atonement by fighting against sin. Nor is a lifetime of contemplation and long periods of meditation aimed at detachment from the body necessary. All such attempts will ultimately succeed because of their purpose. Yet the means are tedious and very time consuming, for all of them look to the future for release from a state of present unworthiness and inadequacy.

Your way will be different, not in purpose, but in means. A holy relationship is a means of saving time. One instant spent together restores the universe to both of you. You are prepared. Now you need but to remember you need do nothing. It would be far more profitable now merely to concentrate on this than to consider what you should do. When peace comes at last to those who wrestle with temptation and fight against the giving in to sin; when the light comes at last into the mind given to contemplation, or when the goal is finally achieved by anyone, it always comes with just one happy realization; "I need do nothing."

Here is the ultimate release which everyone will one day find in his own way, at his own time. We do not need this time. Time has been saved for you because you are together. This is the special means this course is using to save you time. You are not making use of the course if you insist on using means which have served others well, neglecting what was made for you. Save time for me by only this one preparation and practice doing nothing else. "I need do nothing" is a statement of allegiance, a truly undivided loyalty. Believe it for just one instant and you will accomplish more than is given to a century of contemplation, or of struggle against temptation.

To do anything involves the body. And if you recognize you need do nothing, you have withdrawn the body's value from your mind. Here is the quick and open door through which you slip past centuries of effort and escape from time. This is the way in which sin loses all attraction right now. For here is time denied, and past and future gone. Who need do nothing has no need for time. To do nothing is to rest and make a place within you where the activity of the body ceases to demand attention. Into this place the Holy Spirit comes, and there abides. He will remain when you forget, and the body's activities return to occupy your conscious mind.

Yet there will always be this place of rest to which you can return. And you will be more aware of this quiet centre of the storm than all its raging activity. This quiet centre, in which you do nothing, will remain with you, giving you rest in the midst of every busy doing on which you are sent. For from this centre will you be directed how to use the body sinlessly. It is this centre, from which the body is absent, that will keep it so in your awareness of it.

It is only the awareness of the body that makes love seem limited. For the body is a limit on love. The belief in limited love was its origin, and it was made to limit the unlimited. Think not that this is merely allegorical, for it was made to limit you. Can you who see yourselves within a body know yourself as an idea? Everything you recognize you identify with externals, something outside itself. You cannot even think of God without a body, or some form you think you recognize.

The body cannot know. And while you limit your awareness to its tiny senses, you will not see the grandeur which surrounds you. God cannot come into a body, nor can you join Him there. Limits on love will always seem to shut Him out, and to keep you apart from Him. The body is a tiny fence around a little part of a glorious and complete idea. It draws a circle, infinitely small, around a very little segment of Heaven splintered from the whole, proclaiming that within it is your kingdom, where God can enter not.

Within this kingdom the ego rules, and cruelly. And to defend this little speck of dust, it bids you fight against the universe. This fragment of your mind is such a tiny part of it that, could you but appreciate the whole, you would see instantly that it is like the smallest sunbeam to the sun, or like the faintest ripple on the surface of the ocean. In its amazing arrogance, this tiny sunbeam has decided it IS the sun; this almost imperceptible ripple hails itself as the ocean. Think how alone and frightened is this little thought, this infinitesimal illusion, holding itself apart against the universe.

The sun becomes the sunbeam's "enemy" which would devour it, and the ocean terrifies the little ripple and wants to swallow it. Yet neither sun nor ocean is even aware of all this strange and meaningless activity. They merely continue, unaware that they are feared and hated by a tiny segment of themselves. Even that segment is not lost to them, for it could not survive apart from them. And what it thinks it is in no way changes its total dependence on them for its being. Its whole existence still remains in them.

Without the sun the sunbeam would be gone; the ripple without the ocean is inconceivable.

Such is the strange position in which those in a world inhabited by bodies seem to be. Each body seems to house a separate mind, a disconnected thought, living alone and in no way joined to the Thought by which it was created. Each tiny fragment seems to be self-contained, needing each other for some things, but by no means totally dependent on their one Creator for everything, and needing the whole to give them any meaning, for by themselves they do mean nothing. Nor have they any life apart and by themselves.

Like to the sun and ocean your Self continues, unmindful that this tiny part regards itself as you. It is not missing; it could not exist if it were separate, nor would the whole be whole without it. It is not a separate kingdom, ruled by an idea of separation from the rest. Nor does a fence surround it, preventing it from joining with the rest, and keeping it apart from its Creator. This little aspect is no different from the whole, being continuous with it and at one with it. It leads no separate life because its life is the oneness in which its being was created.

Do not accept this little, fenced-off aspect as yourself. The sun and ocean are as nothing beside what you are. The sunbeam sparkles only in the sunlight and the ripple dances as it rests upon the ocean. Yet in neither sun nor ocean is the power that rests in you. Would you remain within your tiny kingdom, a sorry king, a bitter ruler of all he surveys, who looks on nothing, yet who would still die to defend it? This little self is not your kingdom. Arched high above it and surrounding it with love is the glorious whole, which offers all its happiness and deep content to every part. The little aspect which you think you set apart is no exception.

Love knows no bodies and reaches to everything created like itself. Its total lack of limit is its meaning. It is completely impartial in its giving, encompassing only to preserve and keep complete what it would give. In your tiny kingdom you have so little! Should it not, then, be there that you would call on love to enter? Look at the desert, dry and unproductive, scorched and joyless, which makes up your little kingdom. And realize the life and joy which love would bring to it from where it comes, and where it would return with you.

The Thought of God surrounds your little kingdom, waiting at the barrier you built to come inside and shine upon the barren ground. See how life springs up everywhere! The desert becomes a garden, green and deep and quiet, offering rest to those who lost their way and wander in the dust.

Give them a place of refuge, prepared by love for them where once a desert was. And everyone you welcome will bring love with him from Heaven for you. They enter one by one into this holy place, but they will not depart as they had come, alone. The love they brought with them will stay with them, as it will stay with you. And under its beneficence, your little garden will expand, and reach out to everyone who thirsts for living water but has grown too weary to go on alone.

Go out and find them, for they bring your Self with them. And lead them gently to your quiet garden and receive their blessing there. So will it grow and stretch across the desert, leaving no lonely little kingdoms locked away from love, and leaving you inside. And you will recognize yourself, and see your little garden gently transformed into the Kingdom of Heaven, with all the love of its Creator shining upon it. The holy instant is your invitation to love, to enter into your bleak and joyless kingdom, and to transform it into a garden of peace and welcome.

Love's answer is inevitable. It will come because you came without the body and interposed no barriers which would interfere with its glad coming. In the holy instant, you ask of love only what it offers everyone, neither less nor more. Asking for everything, you will receive it. And your shining Self will lift the tiny aspect which you tried to hide from Heaven straight into Heaven. No part of love calls on the whole in vain. No Son of God remains outside His Fatherhood.

Be sure of this; love has entered your special relationship and entered fully at your weak request. You do not recognize that love has come because you have not yet let go of all the barriers you hold against each other. And you will not be able to give love welcome separately. You could no more know God alone than He knows you without your brother. But, together, you could no more be unaware of love than love could know you not or fail to recognize itself in you.

You have reached the end of an ancient journey, not realizing yet that it is over. You are still worn and tired and the desert's dust still seems to cloud your eyes and keep you sightless. Yet He Whom you welcomed has come to you and would welcome you. He has waited long to give you this. Receive it now of Him, for He would have you know Him. Only a little wall of dust still stands between you. Blow on it lightly and with happy laughter and it will fall away and walk into the garden love has prepared for both of you.

You have been told to bring the darkness to the light, and guilt to holiness. And you have also been told that error must be corrected at its source. Therefore, it is the tiny part of yourself, the little thought that seems split off and separate, which the Holy Spirit needs. The rest is fully in God's keeping and needs no guide. Yet this wild and delusional thought needs help because, in its delusions, it thinks it is the Son of God, whole and omnipotent, sole ruler of the kingdom it set apart to tyrannize by madness into obedience and slavery.

This is the little part of you, you think you stole from Heaven. Give it back to Heaven. Heaven has not lost it, but you have lost sight of Heaven. Let the Holy Spirit remove it from the withered kingdom in which you set it off, surrounded by darkness, guarded by attack, and reinforced by hate. Within its barricades is still a tiny segment of the Son of God, complete and holy, serene and unaware of what you think surrounds it. Be you not separate, for the One Who does surround it has brought union to you, returning your little offering of darkness to the eternal Light.

How is this done? It is extremely simple, being based on what this little kingdom really is. The barren sands, the darkness and the lifelessness are seen only through the body's eyes. Its vision is distorted and the messages it transmits to you who made it to limit your awareness are little and limited, and so fragmented they are meaningless. From the world of bodies, made by insanity, insane messages seem to be returned to the mind which made it. And these messages bear witness to this world, pronouncing it as true. For you sent forth these messengers to bring this back to you.

Everything these messages relay to you is quite external. There are no messages which speak of what lies underneath, for it is not the body that could speak of this. Its eyes perceive it not; its senses remain quite unaware of it; its tongue cannot relay its messages. Yet God can bring you there, if you are willing to follow the Holy Spirit through seeming terror, trusting Him not to abandon you and leave you there. For it is not His purpose to frighten you, but only yours. You are severely tempted to abandon Him at the outside ring of fear, but He would lead you safely through and far beyond.

The circle of fear lies just below the level the body sees and seems to be the whole foundation on which the world is based. Here are all the illusions, all the twisted thoughts, all the insane attacks, the fury, vengeance and betrayal that were made to keep the guilt in place, so that the world could rise from it and keep it hidden.

Its shadow rises to the surface, enough to hold its most external manifestations in darkness, and to bring despair and loneliness to it and keep it joyless. Yet its intensity is veiled by its heavy coverings and kept apart from what was made to keep it hidden. The body cannot see this, for the body arose from this for its protection, which must always depend on keeping it not seen. The body's eyes will never look on it. Yet they will see what it dictates.

The body will remain guilt's messenger and will act as it directs as long as you believe that guilt is real. For the reality of guilt is the illusion which seems to make it heavy and opaque, impenetrable, and a real foundation for the ego's thought system. Its thinness and transparency are not apparent until you see the light behind it. And then you see it as a fragile veil before the light.

This heavy-seeming barrier, this artificial floor which looks like rock, is like a bank of low dark clouds that seems to be a solid wall before the sun. Its impenetrable appearance is wholly an illusion. It gives way softly to the mountain tops which rise above it and has no power at all to hold back anyone willing to climb above it and see the sun. It is not strong enough to stop a button's fall, nor hold a feather. Try but to touch it and it disappears; attempt to grasp it and your hands hold nothing.

Yet in this cloud bank it is easy to see a whole world rising. A solid mountain range, a lake, a city, all rise in your imagination, and from the clouds the messengers of your perception return to you, assuring you that it is all there. Figures stand out and move about, actions seem real, and forms appear and shift from loveliness to the grotesque. And back and forth they go, as long as you would play the game of children's make believe. Yet however long you play it, and regardless of how much imagination you bring to it, you do not confuse it with the world below, nor seek to make it real.

So should it be with the dark clouds of guilt, no more impenetrable and no more substantial. You will not bruise yourself against them in traveling through. Let your Guide teach you their unsubstantial nature as He leads you past them, for beneath them is a world of light whereon they cast no shadows. Their shadows lie upon the world beyond them, still further from the light. Yet from them to the light their shadows cannot fall.

This world of light, this circle of brightness, is the real world where guilt meets with forgiveness. Here, the world outside is seen anew, without the shadow of guilt upon it. Here are you forgiven, for here you have forgiven everyone. Here is the new perception, where everything is bright and shining with innocence, washed in the waters of forgiveness and cleansed of every evil thought you had laid upon it. Here there is no attack upon the Son of God, and you are welcome. Here is your innocence, waiting to clothe you and protect you, and make you ready for the final step in the journey inward. Here are the dark and heavy garments of guilt laid by, and gently replaced by purity and love.

Yet even forgiveness is not the end. Forgiveness does make lovely, but it does not create. It is the source of healing, but it is the messenger of love, and not its Source. Here you are led that God Himself can take the final step unhindered, for here does nothing interfere with love, letting it be itself. A step beyond this holy place, a step still further inward but the one you cannot take, transports you to something completely different. Here is the Source of light; nothing perceived, forgiven nor transformed. But merely known.

This course will lead to knowledge, but knowledge itself is still beyond the scope of our curriculum. Nor is there any need for us to try to speak of what must forever lie beyond words. We need remember only that whoever attains the real world, beyond which learning cannot go, will go beyond it, but in a different way. Where learning ends there God begins, for learning ends before Him Who is complete where He begins, and where there is no end. It is not for us to dwell on what cannot be attained. There is too much to learn.    The readiness for knowledge still must be attained. Love is not learned. Its meaning lies in itself. And learning ends when you have recognized all it is not. That is the interference; that is what needs to be undone. Love is not learned because there never was a time in which you knew it not. Learning is useless in the Presence of your Creator, Whose acknowledgement of you and yours of Him so far transcend all learning that everything you learned is meaningless, replaced forever by the knowledge of love and its one meaning.

Your relationship has been uprooted from the world of shadows, and its unholy purpose has been safely brought through the barriers of guilt, washed with forgiveness, and set shining and firmly rooted in the world of light. From there, it calls you to follow the course it took, lifted high above the darkness, and gently placed before the gates of Heaven.

The holy instant in which you were united is but the messenger of love, sent from beyond forgiveness to remind you of all that lies beyond it. Yet it is through forgiveness that it will be remembered.

And when the memory of God has come to you in the holy place of forgiveness, you will remember nothing else, and memory will be as useless as learning, for your only purpose will be creating. Yet this you cannot know until every perception has been cleansed and purified, and finally removed forever. Forgiveness removes only the untrue, lifting the shadows from the world, and carrying it, safe and sure within its gentleness, to the bright world of new and clean perception. There is your purpose now. And it is there that peace awaits you.

We said before that, when a situation has been dedicated wholly to truth, peace is inevitable. Its attainment is the criterion by which the wholeness of the dedication can be safely assumed. Yet we also said that peace without faith will never be attained, for what is wholly dedicated to truth as its only goal is brought to truth BY faith. This faith encompasses everyone involved, for only thus the situation is perceived as meaningful and as a whole. And everyone must be involved in it, or else your faith is limited, and your dedication incomplete.

Every situation, properly perceived, becomes an opportunity to heal the Son of God. And he is healed because you offered faith to him, giving him to the Holy Spirit and releasing him from every demand your ego would make of him. Thus do you see him free, and in this vision does the Holy Spirit share. And since He shares it He has given it, and so He heals through you. It is this joining Him in a united purpose which makes this purpose real because you make it whole. And this is healing. The body is healed, because you came without it and joined the Mind in which all healing rests.

The body cannot heal, because it cannot make itself sick. It needs no healing. Its health or sickness depends entirely on how the mind perceives it, and the purpose which the mind would use it for. And it is obvious that a segment of the mind can see itself as separated from the Universal Purpose. When this occurs, the body becomes its weapon, used against this Purpose to demonstrate the "fact" that separation has occurred. The body thus becomes the instrument of illusion, acting accordingly; seeing what is not there, hearing what truth has never said, and behaving insanely, being imprisoned be insanity.

Do not overlook our earlier statement that faithlessness leads straight to illusions. For faithlessness is the perception of a brother as a body, and the body cannot be used for purposes of union. If, then, you see your brother as a body, you have established a condition in which uniting with him becomes impossible. Your faithlessness to him has separated you from him and kept you both apart from being healed. Your faithlessness has thus opposed the Holy Spirit's purpose, and brought illusions, centred on the body, to stand between you. And the body will seem to be sick, for you have made of it an "enemy" of healing, and the opposite of truth.

It cannot be difficult to realize that faith must be the opposite of faithlessness. Yet the difference in how they operate is less apparent, though it follows directly from the fundamental difference in what they are. Faithlessness would always limit and attack; faith would remove all limitations and make whole. Faithlessness would interpose illusions between the Son of God and his Creator; faith would remove all obstacles that seem to rise between them. Faithlessness is wholly dedicated to illusions; faith wholly to truth. Partial dedication is impossible. Truth is the absence of illusion; illusion the absence of truth.

Both cannot be together, nor perceived in the same place. To dedicate yourself to both is to set up a goal forever impossible to attain, for part of it is sought through the body, thought of as a means for seeking out reality through attack, while the other part would heal, and therefore calls upon the mind and not the body. The inevitable compromise is the belief that the body must be healed, and not the mind. For this divided goal has given both an equal reality, which could be possible only if the mind is limited to the body, and divided into little parts of seeming wholeness, but without connection. This will not harm the body, but it will keep the delusional thought system in the mind.

Here, then, is healing needed. And it is here that healing is. For God gave healing not apart from sickness, nor established remedy where sickness cannot be. They are together and when they are seen together, all attempts to keep both truth and illusion in the mind, where both must be, are recognized as dedication to illusion; and given up when brought to truth, and seen as totally unreconcilable with truth, in any respect or in any way.

Truth and illusion have no connection. This will remain forever true, however much you seek to connect them. But illusions are always connected, as is truth. Each is united, a complete thought system, but totally disconnected to each other. Where there is no overlap, there separation must be complete. And to perceive this is to recognize where separation is and where it must be healed. The result of an idea is never separate from its source. The idea of separation produced the body and remains connected to it, making it sick because of its identification with it. You think you are protecting the body by hiding this connection, for this concealment seems to keep your identification safe from the "attack" of truth.

If you but understood how much this strange concealment has hurt your mind, and how confused your own identification has become because of it! You do not see how great the devastation wrought by your faithlessness. For faithlessness is an attack which seems to be justified by its results. For by withholding faith, you see what is unworthy of it, and cannot look beyond the barrier to what is joined with you.

To have faith is to heal. It is the sign that you have accepted the Atonement for yourself and would therefore share it. By faith, you offer the gift of freedom from the past, which you received. You do not use anything your brother has done before to condemn him now. You freely choose to overlook his errors, looking past all barriers between your self and his, and seeing them as one. And in that one you see your faith is fully justified. There is no justification for faithlessness, but faith is always justified.

Faith is the opposite of fear, as much a part of love as fear is of attack. Faith is the acknowledgment of union. It is the gracious acknowledgment of everyone as a Son of your most loving Father, loved by Him like you, and therefore loved by you as yourself. It is His Love that joins you, and for His Love you would keep no-one separate from yours. Each one appears just as he is perceived in the holy instant, united in your purpose to be released from guilt. You saw the Christ in him, and he was healed because you looked on what makes faith forever justified in everyone.

Faith is the gift of God, through Him Whom God has given you. Faithlessness looks upon the Son of God and judges him unworthy of forgiveness. But through the eyes of faith, the Son of God is seen already forgiven, free of all the guilt he laid upon himself. Faith sees him only now because it looks not to the past to judge him, but would see in him only what it would see in you. It sees not through the body's eyes, nor looks to bodies for its justification.

It is the messenger of the new perception, sent forth to gather witnesses unto its coming, and to return their messages to you. Faith is as easily exchanged for knowledge as is the real world. For faith arises from the Holy Spirit's perception and is the sign you share it with Him. Faith is a gift you offer to the Son of God through Him, and wholly acceptable to his Father as to him. And therefore offered you.

Your holy relationship, with its new purpose, offers you faith to give unto each other. Your faithlessness had driven you apart, and so you did not recognize salvation in each other. Yet faith unites you in the holiness you see, not through the body's eyes, but in the sight of Him Who joined you, and in Whom you are united. Grace is not given to a body, but to a mind. And the mind that receives it looks instantly beyond the body and sees the holy place where it was healed. There is the altar where the grace was given, in which it stands. Do you, then, offer grace and blessing to each other, for you stand at the same altar, where grace was laid for both of you. And be you healed by grace together, that you may heal through faith.

In the holy instant, you stand before the altar God has raised unto Himself and both of you. Lay faithlessness aside and come to it together. There will you see the miracle of your relationship as it was made again through faith. And there it is that you will realize that there is nothing faith cannot forgive. No error interferes with its calm sight, which brings the miracle of healing with equal ease to all of them. For what the messengers of love are sent to do they do, returning the glad tidings that it was done to you who stand together before the altar from which they were sent forth.

As faithlessness will keep your little kingdoms barren and separate, so will faith help the Holy Spirit prepare the ground for the most holy garden which He would make of it. For faith brings peace, and so it calls on truth to enter and make lovely what has already been prepared for loveliness. Truth follows faith and peace, completing the process of making lovely which they begin. For faith is still a learning goal, no longer needed when the lesson has been learned. Yet truth will stay forever.

Let, then, your dedication be to the eternal and learn how not to interfere with it and make it slave to time. For what you think you do to the eternal you do to you. Whom God created as His Son is slave to nothing, being lord of all along with his Creator. You can enslave a body, but an idea is free, incapable of being kept in prison, or limited in any way except by the mind that thought it. For it remains joined to its source, which is its jailor or its liberator, according to which it chooses as its purpose for itself.

It is essential that error be not confused with "sin," and it is this distinction which makes salvation possible. For error can be corrected and the wrong made right. But sin, were it possible, would be irreversible. The belief in sin is necessarily based on the firm conviction that minds, not bodies, can attack. And thus the mind is guilty and will forever so remain, unless a mind not part of it can give it absolution. Sin calls for punishment, as error for correction. And the belief that punishment is correction is clearly insane.

Sin is not an error, for sin entails an arrogance which the idea of error lacks. To sin would be to violate reality and to SUCCEED. Sin is the proclamation that attack is real and guilt is justified. It assumes the Son of God is guilty and has thus succeeded in losing his innocence and making himself what God created not. Thus is creation seen as not eternal and the Will of God open to opposition and defeat. Sin is the "grand illusion" underlying all the ego's grandiosity. For by it, God Himself is changed and rendered incomplete.

The Son of God can be mistaken; he can deceive himself; he can even turn the power of his mind against himself. But he cannot sin. There is nothing he can do that would really change his reality in any way, nor make him really guilty. That is what sin would do, for such is its purpose. Yet for all the wild insanity inherent in the whole idea of sin, it is impossible. For the wages of sin is death, and how can the immortal die?

A major tenet in the ego's insane religion is that sin is not error but truth, and it is innocence that would deceive. Purity is seen as arrogance, and the acceptance of the self as sinful is perceived as holiness. And it is this doctrine which replaces the reality of the Son of God as his Father created him and willed that he be forever. Is this humility? Or is it, rather, an attempt to wrest creation away from truth, and keep it separate?

Any attempt to re-interpret sin as error is always indefensible to the ego. The idea of sin is wholly sacrosanct to its thought system, and quite unapproachable except through reverence and awe. It is the most "holy" concept in the ego's system; lovely and powerful, wholly true, and necessarily protected with every defence at its disposal. For here lies its "best" defence, which all the others serve. Here is its armour, its protection, and the fundamental purpose of the special relationship in its interpretation.

It can indeed be said the ego made its world on sin. Only in such a world could everything be upside-down. This is the strange illusion which makes the clouds of guilt seem heavy and impenetrable. The solidness this world's foundation seems to have is found in this. For sin has changed creation from an Idea of God to an ideal the ego wants; a world it rules, made up of bodies, mindless and capable of complete corruption and decay. If this is a mistake, it can be undone easily by truth. Any mistake can be corrected, if truth be left to judge it. But if the mistake is given the status of truth, to what can it be brought? The "holiness" of sin is kept in place by just this strange device. As truth it is inviolate, and everything is brought to it for judgement. As a mistake, it must be brought to truth. It is impossible to have faith in sin, for sin is faithlessness. Yet it is possible to have faith that a mistake can be corrected.

There is no stone in all the ego's embattled citadel more heavily defended than the idea that sin is real; the natural expression of what the Son of God has made himself to be, and what he is. To the ego, this is no mistake. For this is its reality; this is the "truth" from which escape will always be impossible. This is his past, his present and his future. For he has somehow managed to corrupt his Father and changed His Mind completely. Mourn, then, the death of God, Whom sin has killed! And this would be the ego's wish, which in its madness it thinks it has accomplished.

Would you not rather that all this be nothing more than a mistake, entirely correctable, and so easily escaped from that its whole correction is like walking through a mist into the sun? For that is all it is. Perhaps you would be tempted to agree with the ego that it is far better to be sinful than mistaken. Yet think you carefully before you allow yourself to make this choice. Approach it not lightly, for it is the choice of hell or Heaven.

The attraction of guilt is found in sin, not error. Sin will be repeated because of this attraction. Fear can become so acute that the sin is denied the acting out, but while the guilt remains attractive the mind will suffer, and not let go of the idea of sin. For guilt still calls to it, and the mind hears it and yearns for it, making itself a willing captive to its sick appeal. Sin is an idea of evil that cannot be corrected and will be forever desirable. As an essential part of what the ego thinks you are, you will always want it. And only an avenger, with a mind unlike your own, could stamp it out through fear.

The ego does not think it possible that love, not fear, is really called upon by sin, and always answers. For the ego brings sin to fear, demanding punishment. Yet punishment is but another form of guilt's protection for what is deserving punishment must have been really done. Punishment is always the great preserver of sin; treating it with respect and honouring its enormity. For what you think is real you want and will not let it go. An error, on the other hand, is not attractive. What you see clearly as a mistake you want corrected.

Sometimes a sin can be repeated over and over, with obviously distressing results, but without the loss of its appeal. And suddenly, you change its status from a sin to a mistake. Now you will not repeat it; you will merely stop and let it go, unless the guilt remains. For then you will but change the form of sin, granting that it was an error, but keeping it uncorrectable. This is not really a change in your perception, for it is sin that calls for punishment, not error. The Holy Spirit cannot punish sin. Mistakes He recognizes and would correct them all as God entrusted Him to do. But sin He knows not, nor can He recognize mistakes which cannot be corrected. For a mistake which cannot be corrected is meaningless to Him.

Mistakes are for correction, and they call for nothing else. What calls for punishment must call for nothing. Every mistake must be a call for love. What, then, is sin? What could it be but a mistake you would keep hidden; a call for help that you would keep unheard and thus unanswered? In time, the Holy Spirit clearly sees the Son of God can make mistakes. On this you share His vision. Yet you do not share His recognition of the difference between time and eternity. And when correction is completed, time is eternity.

Time is like a downward spiral which seems to travel down from a long, unbroken line along another plane, but which in no way breaks the line, or interferes with its smooth continuousness. Along the spiral, it seems as if the line must have been broken. Yet at the line, its wholeness is apparent. Everything seen from the spiral is misperceived, but as you approach the line, you realize that it was not affected by the drop into another plane at all. Yet from the plane, the line seems discontinuous. And this is but an error in perception, which can be easily corrected in the mind, although the body's eyes will see no change. The eyes see many things the mind corrects, and you respond, not to the eyes' illusions, but to the mind's corrections.

You see the line as broken, and as you shift to different aspects of the spiral, the line looks different. Yet in your mind is One Who knows it is unbroken, and forever changeless. This One can teach you how to look on time differently and see beyond it, but not while you believe in sin. In error, yes, for this can be corrected by the mind. But sin is the belief that your perception is unchangeable, and that the mind must accept as true what it is told through it. If it does not obey, the mind is judged insane. The only power which could change perception is thus kept impotent, held to the body by the fear of changed perception which its Teacher, Who is one with it, would bring.

When you are tempted to believe that sin is real, remember this: If sin is real, both God and you are not. If creation is extension, the Creator must have extended Himself and it is impossible that what is part of Him is totally unlike the rest. If sin is real, God must be at war with Himself. He must be split and torn between good and evil; partly sane and partially insane. For He must have created what wills to destroy Him and has the power to do so. Is it not easier to believe that you have been mistaken than to believe in this?

While you believe that your reality or your brother's is bounded by a body, you will believe in sin. While you believe that bodies can unite, you will find guilt attractive, and believe that sin is precious. For the belief that bodies limit mind leads to a perception of the world in which the proof of separation seems to be everywhere. And God and His creations seem to be split apart and overthrown. For sin would prove what God created holy could not prevail against it, nor remain itself before the power of sin. Sin is perceived as mightier than God, before which God Himself must bow, and offer

His creation to its conqueror. Is this humility or madness? If sin were real, it would forever be beyond the hope of healing. For there would be a power beyond God's, capable of making another will which could attack His Will and overcome It; and give His Son a will apart from His and stronger. And each part of God's fragmented creation would have a different will, opposed to His, and in eternal opposition to Him and to each other. Your holy relationship has, as its purpose now, the goal of proving this is impossible. Heaven has smiled upon it and the belief in sin has been uprooted in its smile of love. You see it still because you do not realize that its foundation has gone. Its source has been removed and so it can be cherished but a little while before it vanishes. Only the habit of looking for it still remains.

And yet you look with Heaven's smile upon your lips, and Heaven's blessing on your sight. You will not see it long. For in the new perception, the mind corrects it when it seems to be seen and it becomes invisible. And errors are quickly recognized and quickly given to correction, to be healed, not hidden. You will be healed of sin and all its ravages the instant that you give it no power over each other. And you will help each other overcome mistakes by joyously releasing one another from the belief in sin.

In the holy instant, you will see the smile of Heaven shining on both of you. And you will shine upon each other, in glad acknowledgment of the grace that has been given you. For sin will not prevail against a union Heaven has smiled upon. Your perception was healed in the holy instant Heaven gave you. Forget what you have seen, and raise your eyes in faith to what you now can see. The barriers to Heaven will disappear before your holy sight, for you who were sightless have been given vision, and you can see. Look not for what has been removed, but for the glory that has been restored for you to see.

Look upon your Redeemer, and behold what He would show you in each other, and let not sin arise again to blind your eyes. For sin would keep you separate, but your Redeemer would have you look upon each other as yourself. Your relationship is now a temple of healing; a place where all the weary ones can come and find rest. Here is the rest that waits for all, after the journey. And it is brought nearer to all by your relationship.

As this peace extends from deep inside yourselves to embrace all the Sonship and give it rest, it will encounter many obstacles. Some of them you will try to impose. Others will seem to arise from elsewhere; from your brothers, and from various aspects of the world outside. Yet peace will gently cover them, extending past completely unhindered. The extension of the Holy Spirit's purpose from your relationship to others, to bring them gently in, will quietly extend to every aspect of your lives, surrounding both of you with glowing happiness and the calm awareness of complete protection. And you will carry its message of love and safety and freedom to everyone who draws nigh unto your temple, where healing waits for him.

You will not wait to give him this, for you will call to him and he will answer you, recognizing in your call the Call of God. And you will draw him in and give him rest, as it was given you. All this will you do. Yet the peace which already lies deeply within must first expand, and flow across the obstacles you placed before it. This will you do, for nothing undertaken with the Holy Spirit remains unfinished. You can indeed be sure of nothing you see outside you, but of this you can be sure: The Holy Spirit asks that you offer Him a resting-place where you will rest in Him. He answered you and entered your relationship. Would you not now return His graciousness and enter into a relationship with Him? For it is He Who offered your relationship the gift of holiness, without which it would have been forever impossible to appreciate each other. The gratitude you owe to Him He asks but that you receive for Him. And when you look with gentle graciousness upon each other, you are beholding Him. For you are looking where He is, and not apart from Him. You cannot see the Holy Spirit, but you can see your brothers truly. And the light in them will show you all that you need to see. When the peace in you has been extended to encompass everyone, the Holy Spirit's function here will be accomplished. What need is there for seeing, then? When God has taken the last step Himself, the Holy Spirit will gather all your thanks and gratitude which you have offered Him and lay them gently before His Creator in the name of His most holy Son. And the Father will accept them in His Name. What need is there of seeing, in the presence of His gratitude?

The first obstacle that peace must flow across is your desire to get rid of it. For it cannot extend unless you keep it. You are the centre from which it radiates outward, to call the others in. You are its home; its tranquil dwelling-place, from which it gently reaches out, but never leaving you. If you would make it homeless, how can it abide within the Son of God? If it would spread across the whole creation, it must begin with you, and from you reach to everyone who calls and bring him rest by joining you.

Why would you want peace homeless? What do you think that it must dispossess, to dwell with you? What seems to be the cost you are so unwilling to pay? The little barrier of sand still stands between you. Would you reinforce it now? You are not asked to let it go for yourselves alone. Christ asks it of you for Himself. He would bring peace to everyone, and how can He do this except through you? Would you let a little bank of sand, a wall of dust, a tiny seeming barrier, stand between your brothers and salvation?

And yet, it is this little remnant of attack you cherish still against each other that is the first obstacle the peace in you encounters in its going forth. This little wall of hatred would still oppose the Will of God, and keep It limited.

The Holy Spirit's purpose rests in peace within you. Yet you are still unwilling to let it join you wholly. You still oppose the Will of God, just by a little. And that little is a limit you would place upon the whole. God's Will is One, not many. It has no opposition, for there is none beside It. What you would still contain behind your little barrier and keep separate from each other seems mightier than the universe, for it would hold back the universe and its Creator. This little wall would hide the purpose of Heaven and keep it from Heaven.

Would you thrust salvation away from the giver of salvation? For such have you become. Peace could no more depart from you than from God. Fear not this little obstacle. It cannot contain the Will of God. Peace will flow across it and join you without hindrance. Salvation cannot be withheld from you. It is your purpose. You cannot will apart from this. You have no purpose apart from each other, nor apart from the one you asked the Holy Spirit to share with you. The little wall will fall away so quietly beneath the wings of peace! For peace will send its messengers from you to all the world. And barriers will fall away before their coming as easily as those which you would interpose will be surmounted.

To overcome the world is no more difficult than to surmount your little wall. For in the miracle of your relationship, without this barrier, is every miracle contained. There is no order of difficulty in miracles, for they are all the same. Each is a gentle winning over from the appeal of guilt to the appeal of love. How can this fail to be accomplished, wherever it is undertaken? Guilt can raise no real barriers against it. And all that seems to stand between you must fall away because of the appeal you answered. For from you who answered, He Who answered you would call. His home is in your holy relationship. Do not attempt to stand between Him and His holy purpose, for it is yours. But let Him quietly extend the miracle of your relationship to everyone contained in it as it was given.

There is a hush in Heaven, a happy expectancy, a little pause of gladness in acknowledgment of the journey's end. For Heaven knows you well, as you know Heaven. No illusions stand between you now. Look not upon the little wall of shadows. The sun has risen over it. How can a shadow keep you from the sun? No more can you be kept by shadows from the light in which illusions end. Every miracle is but the end of an illusion.

Such was the journey; such its ending. And in the goal of truth which you accepted must all illusions end.

The little, insane wish to get rid of Him Who you invited in and push Him out must produce conflict. As you look upon the world, this little wish, uprooted and floating aimlessly, can land and settle briefly upon anything, for it has no purpose now. Before the Holy Spirit entered to abide with you, it seemed to have a mighty purpose; the fixed and unchangeable dedication to sin and its results. Now it is aimless, wandering pointlessly, causing no more than tiny interruptions in love's appeal.

This feather of a wish, this tiny illusion, this microscopic remnant of the belief in sin, is all that remains of what once seemed to be the world. It is no longer an unrelenting barrier to peace. Its pointless wandering makes its results appear to be more erratic and unpredictable than before. Yet what could be more unstable than a tightly-organized delusional system? Its seeming stability is its pervasive weakness, which extends to everything. The variability which the little remnant induces merely indicates its limited results.

How mighty can a little feather be before the great wings of truth? Can it oppose an eagle's flight, or hinder the advance of summer? Can it interfere with the effects of summer's sun upon a garden covered by the snow? See but how easily this little whisp is lifted up and carried away, never to return, and part with it in gladness, not regret. For it is nothing in itself, and stood for nothing when you had greater faith in its protection. Would you not rather greet the summer sun than fix your gaze upon a disappearing snowflake and shiver in remembrance of the winter's cold?

The attraction of guilt produces fear of love, for love would never look on guilt at all. It is the nature of love to look upon only the truth, for there it sees itself, with which it would unite in holy union and completion. As love must look past fear, so must fear see love not.

For love contains the end of guilt, as surely as fear depends on it. Overlooking guilt completely, it sees no fear. Being wholly without attack, it could not be afraid. Fear is attracted to what love sees not, and each believes that what the other looks upon does not exist. Fear looks on guilt with just the same devotion that love looks on itself. And each has messengers which they send forth, and which return to them with messages written in the language in which their going forth was asked.

Love's messengers are gently sent and return with messages of love and gentleness. The messengers of fear are harshly ordered to seek out guilt and cherish every scrap of evil and of sin which they can find, losing none of them on pain of death, and laying them respectfully before their lord and master. Perception cannot obey two masters, each asking for messages of different things in different languages. What fear would feed upon, love overlooks. What fear demands, love cannot even see.

The fierce attraction which guilt holds for fear is wholly absent from love's gentle perception. What love would look upon is meaningless to fear, and quite invisible. Relationships in this world are the result of how the world is seen. And this depends on which emotion was called on to send its messengers to look upon it and return with word of what they saw. Fear's messengers are trained through terror, and they tremble when their master calls upon them to serve him. For fear is merciless even to its friends. Its messengers steal guiltily away in hungry search of guilt, for they are kept cold and starving, and made very vicious by their master, who allows them to feast only upon what they return to him. No little shred of guilt escapes their hungry eyes. And in their savage search for sin, they pounce on any living thing they see, and carry it screaming to their master, to be devoured.

Send not these savage messengers into the world, to feast upon it, and to prey upon reality. For they will bring you word of bones and skin and flesh. They have been taught to seek for the corruptible, and to return with gorges filled with things decayed and rotted. To them such things are beautiful because they seem to allay their savage pangs of hunger. For they are frantic with the pain of fear and would avert the punishment of him who sends them forth by offering him what they hold dear.

The Holy Spirit has given you love's messengers to send instead of those you trained through fear. They are as eager to return to you what they hold dear as are the others. If you send them forth, they will see only the blameless and the beautiful, the gentle and the kind. They will be as careful to let no little act of charity, no tiny expression of forgiveness, no little breath of love escapes their notice. And they will return with all the happy things they found, to share them lovingly with you. Be not afraid of them. They offer you salvation. Theirs are the messages of safety, for they see the world as kind.

If you send forth only the messengers the Holy Spirit gives you, wanting no messages but theirs, you will see fear no more. The world will be transformed before your sight, cleansed of all guilt and softly brushed with beauty. The world contains no fear which you laid not upon it. And none you cannot ask love's messengers to remove from it and see it still. The Holy Spirit has given you His messengers to send to each other and return to each with what love sees. They have been given to replace the hungry dogs of fear you sent instead. And they go forth to signify the end of fear.

Love, too, would set a feast before you, on a table covered with a spotless cloth, set in a quiet garden where no sound but singing and a softly joyous whispering is ever heard. This is a feast which honours your holy relationship, and at which everyone is welcomed as an honoured guest. And in a holy instant grace is said by everyone together, as they join in gentleness before the table of communion. And I will join you there, as long ago I promised and promise still. For in your new relationship am I made welcome. And where I am made welcome, there I am.

I am made welcome in the state of grace, which means you have at last forgiven me. For I became the symbol of your sin and so I had to die instead of you. To the ego sin means death and so Atonement is achieved through murder. Salvation is looked upon as a way by which the Son of God was killed instead of you. Yet would I offer you my body, you whom I love, knowing its littleness? Or would I teach that bodies cannot keep us apart? Mine was no greater value than yours; no better means for communication of salvation, but not its Source. No-one can die for anyone, and death does not atone for sin. Yet you can live to show it is not real. The body does appear to be the symbol of sin, while you believe that it can get you what you want. While you believe that it can give you pleasure, you will also believe that it can bring you pain.

To think you could be satisfied and happy with so little is to hurt yourself, and to limit the happiness that you would have, calls upon pain to fill your meagre store and make your lives complete. This is completion, as the ego sees it. For guilt creeps in where happiness has been removed, and substitutes for it. Communion is another kind of completion, which goes beyond guilt, because it goes beyond the body.

We said that peace must first surmount the obstacle of your desire to get rid of it. Where the attraction of guilt holds sway, peace is not wanted. The second obstacle that peace must flow across, and closely related to the first, is the belief that the body is valuable for what it offers. For here is the attraction of guilt made manifest in the body and seen in it.

This the value that you think peace would rob you of. This is what you believe that it would dispossess and leave you homeless. And it is this for which you would deny a home to peace. This "sacrifice" you feel to be too great to make, too much to ask of you. Is it a sacrifice, or a release? What has the body really given you that justifies your strange belief that in it lies salvation? Do you not see that this is the belief in death? Here is the focus of the perception of Atonement as murder. Here is the source of the idea that love is fear. The Holy Spirit's messengers are sent far beyond the body, calling the mind to join in holy communion and be at peace. Such is the message that I gave them for you.

It is only the messengers of fear that see the body, for they look for what can suffer. Is it a sacrifice to be removed from what can suffer? The Holy Spirit does not demand you sacrifice the hope of the body's pleasure; it has no hope of pleasure. But neither can it bring you fear of pain. Pain is the only "sacrifice" the Holy Spirit asks and this He would remove.

Peace is extended from you only to the eternal, and it reaches out from the eternal in you. It flows across all else. The second obstacle is no more solid than the first. For you will neither to get rid of peace nor limit it. What are these obstacles which you would interpose between peace and its going forth but barriers you place between your will and its accomplishment? You want communion, not the feast of fear. You want salvation, not the pain of guilt. And you want your Father, not a little mound of clay, to be your home. In your holy relationship is your Father's Son. He has not lost communion with Him, nor with himself. When you agreed to join each other, you acknowledged this is so. This has no cost, but it has release from cost.

You have paid very dearly for your illusions, and nothing you have paid for brought you peace. Are you not glad that Heaven cannot be sacrificed, and sacrifice cannot be asked of you? There is no obstacle which you can place before our union, for in your holy relationship I am there already. We will surmount all obstacles together, for we stand within the gates, and not outside. How easily the gates are opened from within, to let peace through to bless the tired world!

Can it be difficult for us to walk past barriers together, when you have joined the limitless? The end of guilt is in your hands to give. Would you stop now to look for guilt in each other?

Let me be to you the symbol of the end of guilt and look upon each other as you would look on me. Forgive me all the sins you think the Son of God committed. And in the light of your forgiveness, he will remember who he is and forget what never was. I ask for your forgiveness, for if you are guilty, so must I be. But if I surmounted guilt and overcame the world, you were with me. Would you see in me the symbol of guilt, or of the end of guilt, remembering that what I signify to you, you see within yourself? From your holy relationship truth proclaims the truth and love looks on itself. Salvation flows from deep within the home you offered to my Father and to me. And we are there together, in the quiet communion in which the Father and the Son are joined. Oh come ye faithful to the holy union of the Father and Son in you! And keep you not apart from what is offered you, in gratitude for giving peace its home in Heaven. Send forth to all the world the joyous message of the end of guilt, and all the world will answer. Think of your happiness as everyone offers you witness of the end of sin and shows you that its power is gone forever. Where can guilt be, when the belief in sin is gone? And where is death, when its great advocate is heard no more?

Forgive me your illusions and release me from punishment for what I have not done. So will you learn the freedom that I taught by teaching freedom to each other, and so releasing me. I am within your holy relationship, yet you would imprison me behind the obstacles you raise to freedom, and bar my way to you. Yet it is not possible to keep away One Who is there already. And in Him it is possible that our communion, where we are joined already, will be the focus of the new perception that will bring light to all the world, contained in you.

Your little part is but to give the Holy Spirit the whole idea of sacrifice. And to accept the peace He gave instead, without the limits which would hold its extension back, and so would limit your awareness of it. For what He gives must be extended, if you would have its limitless power, and use it for the Son of God's release. It is not this you would be rid of and having it you cannot limit it. If peace is homeless, so are you and so am I. And He Who is our home is homeless with us. Is this your will? Would you forever be a wanderer in search of peace? Would you invest your hope of peace and happiness in what must fail?

Faith in the eternal is always justified, for the eternal is forever kind, infinite in its patience, and wholly loving. It will accept you wholly and give you peace. Yet it can unite only with what already is at peace in you, immortal as itself. The body can bring you neither peace nor turmoil; neither pain nor joy. It is a means, and not an end. It has no purpose of itself, but only what is given to it. The body will seem to be whatever is the means for reaching the goal that you assign to it. Peace and guilt are both conditions of the mind, to be attained. And these conditions are the home of the emotion which called them forth, and therefore is compatible with them. But think you which it is that is compatible with you.

Here is your choice, and it is free. But all that lies in it will come with it and what you think you are can never be apart from it. The body is the great seeming betrayer of faith. In it lies disillusionment and the seeds of faithlessness, but only if you ask of it what it cannot give. Can your mistake be reasonable grounds for depression and disillusionment and for retaliative attack on what you think has failed you? Use not your error as the justification for your faithlessness. You have not sinned, but you have been mistaken in what is faithful. And the correction of your mistake will give you grounds for faith.

It is impossible to seek for pleasure through the body and not find pain. It is essential that this relationship be understood, for it is one the ego sees as proof of sin. It is not really punitive at all. It is but the inevitable result of equating yourself with the body, which is the invitation to pain. For it invites fear to enter and become your purpose. The attraction of guilt must enter with it, and whatever fear directs the body to do is therefore painful. It will share the pain of all illusions, and the illusion of pleasure will be the same as pain.

Is not this inevitable? Under fear's orders, the body will pursue guilt, serving its master whose attraction to guilt maintains the whole illusion of its existence. This, then, is the attraction of pain. Ruled by this perception, the body becomes the servant of pain, seeking it dutifully and obeying the idea that pain is pleasure. It is this idea that underlies all of the ego's heavy investment in the body. And it is this insane relationship which it keeps hidden, and yet feeds upon. To you it teaches that the body's pleasure is happiness. Yet to itself it whispers, "It is death."

Why should the body be anything to you? Certainly what it is made of is not precious. And just as certainly, it has no feeling. It transmits to you the feelings that you want. Like any communication medium, the body receives and sends the messages that it is given. It has no feeling for them. All of the feeling with which they are invested is given by the sender and the receiver. The ego and the Holy Spirit both recognize this and both also recognize that here the sender and receiver are the same. The Holy Spirit tells you this with joy. The ego hides it, for it would keep you unaware of it. Who would send messages of hatred and attack if he but understood he sends them to himself? Who would accuse, make guilty and condemn himself?

The ego's messages are always sent away from you, in the belief that for your message of attack and guilt will someone other than yourself suffer. And even if you suffer, yet someone else will suffer more. The great deceiver recognizes that this is not so, but as the "enemy" of peace, it urges you to send out all your messages of hate and free yourself. And to convince you this is possible, it bids the body search for pain in attack upon another, calling it pleasure and offering it to you as freedom from attack.

Hear not its madness and believe not the impossible is true. Forget not that the ego has dedicated the body to the goal of sin, and places in it all its faith that this can be accomplished. Its sad disciples chant the body's praise continually, in solemn celebration of the ego's rule. Not one but must believe that yielding to the attraction of guilt is the escape from pain. Not one but must regard the body as himself, without which he would die, and yet within which is his death equally inevitable.

It is not given to the ego's disciples to realize that they have dedicated themselves to death. Freedom is offered them, but they have not accepted it, and what is offered must also be received, to be truly given. For the Holy Spirit, too, is a communication medium, receiving from the Father and offering His messages unto the Son. Like the ego, the Holy Spirit is both the sender and the receiver. For what is sent through Him returns to Him, seeking itself along the way, and finding what it seeks. So does the ego find the death it seeks, returning it to you.

To you, in whose special relationship the Holy Spirit entered, it is given to release and be released from the dedication to death. For it was offered you, and you accepted. Yet you must learn still more about this strange devotion, for it contains the third of the obstacles which peace must flow across. No-one can die unless he chooses death. What seems to be the fear of death is really its attraction. Guilt, too, is feared and fearful. Yet it could have no hold at all except on those who are attracted to it and seek it out. And so it is with death. Made by the ego, its dark shadow falls across all living things, because the ego is the "enemy" of life.

And yet a shadow cannot kill. What is a shadow to the living? They but walk past and it is gone. But what of those whose dedication it is not to live; the black-draped "sinners," the ego's mournful chorus, plodding so heavily away from life, dragging their chains and marching in the slow procession which honours their grim master, lord of death? Touch any one of them with the gentle hands of forgiveness, and watch the chains fall away, along with yours. See him throw aside the black robe he was wearing to his funeral and hear him laugh at death. The sentence sin would lay upon him he can escape through your forgiveness.

This is no arrogance. It is the Will of God. What is impossible to you who chose His Will as yours? What is death to you? Your dedication is not to death, nor to its master. When you accepted the Holy Spirit's purpose in place of the ego's, you renounced death, exchanging it for life. We know that an idea leaves not its source. And death is the result of the thought we call the ego, as surely as life is the result of the Thought of God.

From the ego came sin and guilt and death, in opposition to life and innocence, and to the Will of God Himself. Where can such opposition lie but in the sick minds of the insane, dedicated to madness and set against the peace of Heaven. One thing is sure; God, Who created neither sin nor death, wills not that you be bound by them. He knows of neither sin nor its results. The shrouded figures in the funeral procession march not in honour of their Creator, Whose Will it is they live. They are not following It; they are opposing It.

And what is the black-draped body they would bury? A body which they dedicated to death, a symbol of corruption, a sacrifice to sin, offered to sin to feed upon and keep itself alive; a thing condemned, damned by its maker, and lamented by every mourner who looks upon it as himself. You who believe you have condemned the Son of God to this are arrogant. But you who would release him are but honouring the Will of his Creator.

The arrogance of sin, the pride of guilt, the sepulchre of separation, all are part of your unrecognized dedication to death. The glitter of guilt you laid upon the body would kill it. For what the ego loves it kills for its obedience. But what obeys it not it cannot kill.

You have another dedication which would keep the body incorruptible and perfect as long as it is useful for your holy purpose. The body no more dies than it can feel. It does nothing. Of itself, it is neither corruptible nor incorruptible. It IS nothing. It is the result of a tiny, mad idea of corruption which can be corrected. For God has answered this insane idea with His Own, an answer which left Him not, and therefore brings the Creator to the awareness of every mind which heard His answer and accepted it.

You who are dedicated to the incorruptible have been given, through your acceptance, the power to release from corruption. What better way to teach the first and fundamental principle in a course on miracles than by showing you the one which seems to be the hardest can be accomplished first? The body can but serve your purpose. As you look upon it, so will it seem to be. Death, were it true, would be the final and complete disruption of communication which is the ego's goal.

Those who fear death see not how often and how loudly they call to it, and bid it come to save them from communication. For death is seen as safety, the great dark saviour from the light of truth, the answer to the Answer, the silencer of the Voice that speaks for God. Yet the retreat to death is not the end of conflict. Only God's answer is its end. The obstacle of your seeming love for death that peace must flow across seems to be very great. For in it lies hidden all the ego's secrets, all its strange devices for deception, all its sick ideas and weird imaginings. Here is the final end of union, the triumph of the ego's making over creation, the victory of lifelessness on Life Itself.

Under the dusty edge of its distorted world the ego would lay the Son of God, slain by its orders, proof in his decay that God Himself is powerless before the ego's might, unable to protect the life that He created against the ego's savage wish to kill. My brothers, Children of our Father, this is a dream of death. There is no funeral, no dark altars, no grim commandments nor twisted rituals of condemnation to which the body leads you. Ask not release of it.

But free it from the merciless and unrelenting orders you laid upon it and forgive it what you ordered it to do. In its exaltation you commanded it to die, for only death could conquer life. And what but insanity could look upon the defeat of God and think it real?

The fear of death will go as its appeal is yielded to love's real attraction. The end of sin, which nestles quietly in the safety of your relationship, protected by your union, ready to grow into a mighty force for God, is very near. The infancy of salvation is carefully guarded by love, preserved from every thought that would attack it, and quietly made ready to fulfil the mighty task for which it was given you. Your newborn purpose is nursed by angels, cherished by the Holy Spirit, and protected by God Himself. It needs not your protection; it is yours. For it is deathless and within it lies the end of death.

What danger can assail the wholly innocent? What can attack the guiltless? What fear can enter and disturb the peace of sinlessness?

What has been given you, even in its infancy, is in full communication with God and you. In its tiny hands it holds, in perfect safety, every miracle you will perform, held out to you. The miracle of life is ageless, born in time but nourished in eternity. Behold this infant, to whom you gave a resting-place by your forgiveness of each other and see in it the Will of God. Here is the babe of Bethlehem reborn. And everyone who gives him shelter will follow him, not to the cross, but to the Resurrection and the Life. When anything seems to you to be a source of fear, when any situation strikes you with terror and makes your body tremble and the cold sweat of fear comes over it, remember it is always for one reason; the ego has perceived it as a symbol of fear, a sign of sin and death. Remember, then, that neither sign nor symbol should be confused with source, for they must stand for something other than themselves. Their meaning cannot lie in them but must be sought in what they represent. And they may thus mean everything or nothing, according to the truth or falsity of the idea which they reflect. Confronted with such seeming uncertainty of meaning, judge it not. Remember the holy presence of the One given to you to be the Source of judgement. Give it to Him to judge for you, and say:

> "Take this from me and look upon it, judging it for me.
> Let me not see it as a sign of sin and death, nor use it for destruction.
> Teach me how not to make of it an obstacle to peace,
> But let You use it for me, to facilitate its coming."

What would you see without the fear of death? What would you feel and think if death held no attraction for you? Very simply, you would remember your Father. The Creator of life, the Source of everything that lives, the Father of the universe and of the universe of universes, and of everything that lies even beyond them would you remember. And as this memory rises in your mind, peace must still surmount a final obstacle, after which is salvation completed and the Son of God entirely restored to sanity. For here your world does end.

The fourth obstacle to be surmounted hangs like a heavy veil before the face of Christ. Yet as His face rises beyond it, shining with joy because He is in His Father's Love, peace will lightly brush the veil aside and run to meet Him and to join with Him at last. For this dark veil, which seems to make the face of Christ Himself like to a leper's, and the bright rays of His Father's Love which light His face with glory appear as streams of blood, fades in the blazing light beyond it when the fear of death is gone.

This is the darkest veil, upheld by the belief in death, and protected by its attraction. The dedication to death and to its sovereignty is but the solemn vow, the promise made in secret to the ego never to lift this veil, not to approach it, nor even to suspect that it is there. This is the secret bargain made with the ego to keep what lies beyond the veil forever blotted out and unremembered. Here is your promise never to allow union to call you out of separation; the great amnesia in which the memory of God seems quite forgotten; the cleavage of your Self from you; – the fear of God, the final step in your dissociation.

See how the belief in death would seem to "save" you. For if this is gone, what can you fear but life? It is the attraction of death that makes life seem to be ugly, cruel and tyrannical. You are no more afraid of death than of the ego. These are your chosen friends. For in your secret alliance with them, you have agreed never to let the fear of God be lifted, so you could look upon the face of Christ and join Him in His Father.

Every obstacle that peace must flow across is surmounted in just the same way; the fear that raised it yields to the love beneath and so the fear is gone. And so it is with this. The desire to get rid of peace and drive the Holy Spirit from you fades in the presence of the quiet recognition that you love Him. The exaltation of the body is given up in favour of the Spirit, which you love as you could never love the body. And the appeal of death is lost forever as love's attraction stirs and calls to you.

From beyond each of the obstacles to love, Love Itself has called, and each has been surmounted by the power of the attraction of what lies beyond. Your wanting fear seemed to be holding them in place. Yet when you heard the voice of love beyond them, you answered and they disappeared.

And now you stand in terror before what you swore never to look upon. Your eyes look down, remembering your promise to your "friends." The "loveliness" of sin, the delicate appeal of guilt, the "holy" waxen image of death, and the fear of vengeance of the ego you swore in blood not to desert, all rise and bid you not to raise your eyes. For you realize that if you look on this and let the veil be lifted, they will be gone forever. All of your "friends," your "protectors" and your "home" will vanish. Nothing that you remember now will you remember.

It seems to you the world will utterly abandon you if you but raise your eyes. Yet all that will occur is you will leave the world forever. This is the re-establishment of your will. Look upon it, open-eyed and you will never more believe that you are at the mercy of things beyond you, forces you cannot control, and thoughts that come to you against your will. It is your will to look on this. No mad desire, no trivial impulse to forget again, no stab of fear nor the cold sweat of seeming death can stand against your will. For what attracts you from beyond the veil is also deep within you, unseparated from it and completely One.

Forget not that you came this far together. And it was surely not the ego that led you here. No obstacle to peace can be surmounted through its help. It does not open up its secrets, and bid you look on them and go beyond them. It would not have you see its weakness, and learn it has no power to keep you from the truth. The Guide Who brought you here remains with you, and when you raise your eyes, you will be ready to look on terror with no fear at all. But first, lift up your eyes and look upon each other in innocence born of complete forgiveness of each other's illusions, and through the eyes of faith, which sees them not.

No-one can look upon the fear of God unterrified unless he has accepted the Atonement, and learned illusions are not real. No one can stand before this obstacle alone, for he could not have reached thus far unless his brother walked beside him. And no one would dare to look on it without complete forgiveness of his brother in his heart. Stand you here a while, and tremble not. You will be ready. Let us join together in a holy instant, here in this place where the purpose given in a holy instant has led you.

And let us join in faith that He Who brought us here together will offer you the innocence you need, and that you will accept it for my love and His.

Nor is it possible to look on this too soon. This is the place to which everyone must come when he is ready. Once he has found his brother he is ready. Yet merely to reach the place is not enough. A journey without a purpose is still meaningless, and even when it is over it seems to make no sense. How can you know that it is over unless you realize its purpose is accomplished? Here, with the journey's end before you, you see its purpose. And it is here you choose whether to look upon it or wander on, only to return and make the choice again.

To look upon the fear of God does need some preparation. Only the sane can look on stark insanity and raving madness with pity and compassion, but not with fear. For only if they share in it does it seem fearful, and you do share in it until you look upon each other with perfect faith and love and tenderness. Before complete forgiveness you still stand unforgiving. You are afraid of God because you fear each other. Those you do not forgive you fear. And no-one reaches love with fear beside him.

This brother who stands beside you still seems to be a stranger. You do not know him and your interpretation of him is very fearful. And you attack him still, to keep what seems to be yourself unharmed. Yet in his hands is your salvation. You see his madness, which you hate because you share it. And all the pity and forgiveness that would heal it gives way to fear. Brothers, you need forgiveness of each other, for you will share in madness or in Heaven together. And you will raise your eyes in faith together, or not at all.

Beside each of you is one who offers you the chalice of Atonement, for the Holy Spirit is in him. Would you hold his sins against him, or accept his gift to you? Is this giver of salvation your friend or enemy? Choose which he is, remembering that you will receive of him according to your choice. He has in him the power to forgive your sins, as you for him. Neither can give it to himself alone. And yet your Saviour stands beside each one. Let him be what he is and seek not to make of love an enemy.

Behold your Friend, the Christ Who stands beside you. How holy and how beautiful He is! You thought He sinned because you cast the veil of sin upon Him to hide His loveliness. Yet still He holds forgiveness out to you, to share His holiness. This "enemy," this "stranger" still offers you salvation as His Friend. The "enemies" of Christ, the worshippers of sin, know not Whom they attack.

This is your brother, crucified by sin, and waiting for release from pain. Would you not offer him forgiveness, when only he can offer it to you? For his redemption he will give you yours as surely as God created every living thing and loves it. And he will give it truly, for it will be both offered and received.

There is no grace of Heaven that you cannot offer to each other and receive from your most holy Friend. Let him withhold it not, for by receiving it you offer it to him. Redemption has been given you to give each other and thus receive it. Whom you forgive is free, and what you give you share. Forgive the sins your brother thinks he has committed and all the guilt you think you see in him.

Here is the holy place of resurrection, to which we come again; to which we will return until redemption is accomplished and received. Think who your brother is, before you would condemn him. And offer thanks to God that he is holy and has been given the gift of holiness for you. Join him in gladness and remove all trace of guilt from his disturbed and tortured mind. Help him to lift the heavy burden of sin you laid upon him and he accepted as his own and toss it lightly and with happy laughter away from him. Press it not like thorns against his brow, nor nail him to it unredeemed and hopeless.

Give each other faith, for faith and hope and mercy are yours to give. Into the hands that give the gift is given. Look on your brother and see in him the gift of God you would receive. It is almost Easter, the time of resurrection. Let us give redemption to each other and share in it, that we may rise as one in resurrection, and not separate in death. Behold the gift of freedom that I gave the Holy Spirit for both of you. And be you free together, as you offer to the Holy Spirit this same gift. And giving it receive it of Him in return for what you gave. He leadeth you and me together, that we might meet here in this holy place, and make the same decision.

Free your brother here, as I freed you. Give him the self same gift, nor look upon him with condemnation of any kind. See him as guiltless as I look on you and overlook the sins he thinks he sees within himself. Offer each other freedom and complete release from sin, here in the garden of seeming agony and death. So will we prepare together the way unto the resurrection of God's Son, and let him rise again to glad remembrance of his Father, Who knows no sin, no death, but only life eternal.

Together we will disappear into the Presence beyond the veil, not to be lost but found; not to be seen but known. And knowing, nothing in the plan God has established for salvation will be left undone. This is the journey's purpose, without which is the journey meaningless. Here is the peace of God, given to you eternally by Him. Here is the rest and quiet that you seek, the reason for the journey from its beginning. Heaven is the gift you owe each other, the debt of gratitude you offer to the Son of God in thanks for what he is, and what his Father created him to be.

Think carefully how you would look upon the giver of this gift, for as you look on him, so will the gift itself appear to be. As he is seen as either the giver of guilt or of salvation, so will his offering be seen, and so received. The crucified give pain because they are in pain. But the redeemed give joy because they have been healed of pain. Everyone gives as he receives, but he must choose what it will be that he receives. And he will recognize his choice by what he gives, and what is given him. Nor is it given anything in hell or Heaven to interfere with his decision.

You came this far because the journey was your choice. And no-one undertakes to do what he believes is meaningless. What you had faith in still is faithful and watches over you in faith so gentle yet so strong that it would lift you far beyond the veil and place the Son of God safely within the sure protection of his Father. Here is the only purpose that gives this world and the long journey through this world whatever meaning lies in them. Beyond this, they are meaningless. You stand together, still without conviction they have a purpose. Yet it is given you to see this purpose in your holy Friend, and recognize it is your own.

This is Palm Sunday, the celebration of victory and the acceptance of the truth. Let us not spend this holy week brooding on the crucifixion of God's Son, but happily in the celebration of his release. For Easter is the sign of peace, not pain. A slain Christ has no meaning. But a risen Christ becomes the symbol of the Son of God's forgiveness on himself; the sign he looks upon himself as healed and whole.

This week begins with palms and ends with lilies, the white and holy sign the Son of God is innocent. Let no dark sign of crucifixion intervene between the journey and its purpose; between the acceptance of the truth and its expression. This week we celebrate life, not death. And we honour the perfect purity of the Son of God, and not his sins. Offer each other the gift of lilies, not the crown of thorns; the gift of love and not the "gift" of fear. You stand beside each other, thorns in one hand and lilies in the other, uncertain which to give. Join now with me and throw away the thorns, offering the lilies to replace them. This Easter, I would have the gift of your forgiveness offered by you to me, and returned by me to you.

We cannot be united in crucifixion and in death. Nor can the resurrection be complete till your forgiveness rests on Christ along with mine. A week is short, and yet this holy week is the symbol of the whole journey the Son of God has undertaken. He started with the sign of victory, the promise of the resurrection, already given him. Let him not wander into the temptation of crucifixion and delay him there. Help him to go in peace beyond it, with the light of his own innocence lighting his way to his redemption and release. Hold him not back with thorns and nails, when his redemption is so near. But let the whiteness of your shining gift of lilies speed him on his way to resurrection.

If you see glimpses of the face of Christ behind the veil, looking between the snow-white petals of the lilies you have received and given as your gift, you will behold each other's face and recognise it. I was a stranger and you took me in, not knowing who I was. Yet for your gift of lilies you will know. In your forgiveness of this stranger, alien to you and yet your ancient Friend, lie his release and your redemption with him. The time of Easter is a time of joy, and not of mourning. Look on your risen Friend and celebrate his holiness along with me. For Easter is the time of your salvation, along with mine.

Look upon all the trinkets made to hang upon the body, or to cover it, or for its use. See all the useless things made for its eyes to see. Think on the many offerings made for its pleasure and remember all these were made to make seem lovely what you hate. Would you employ this hated thing to draw your brother to you, and to attract his body's eyes? Learn you but offer him a crown of thorns, not recognizing it for what it is, and trying to justify your own interpretation of its value by his acceptance. Yet still the gift proclaims his worthlessness to you, as his acceptance and delight acknowledges the lack of value he places on himself.

    Gifts are not made through bodies, if they be truly given and received. For bodies can neither offer nor accept; hold out nor take. Only the mind can value, and only the mind decides on what it would receive and give. And every gift it offers depends on what it wants. It will adorn its chosen home most carefully, making it ready to receive the gifts it wants by offering them to those who come unto its chosen home, or those it would attract to it. And there they will exchange their gifts, offering and receiving what their minds judge to be worthy of them.

    Each gift is an evaluation of the receiver and the giver. No one but sees his chosen home an altar to himself. No-one but seeks to draw to it the worshippers of what he placed upon it, making it worthy of their devotion. And each has set a light upon his altar, that they may see what he has placed upon it, and take it for their own. Here is the value that you lay upon your brother and on yourself. Here is your gift to both; your judgement on the Son of God for what he is. Forget not that it is your Saviour to whom the gift is offered. Offer him thorns and you are crucified. Offer him lilies and it is yourself you free.

    I have great need for lilies, for the Son of God has not forgiven me. And can I offer him forgiveness, when he offers thorns to me? For he who offers thorns to anyone is against me still, and who is whole without him? Be you his friend for me, that I may be forgiven, and you may look upon the Son of God as whole. But look you first upon the altar in your chosen home and see what you have laid upon it to offer me. If it be thorns whose points gleam sharply in a blood-red light, the body is your chosen home, and it is separation that you offer me. And yet the thorns are gone. Look you still closer at them now, and you will see your altar is no longer what it was.

You look still with the body's eyes, and they can see but thorns. Yet you have asked for and received another sight. Those who accept the Holy Spirit's purpose as their own share also His vision. And what enables Him to see His purpose shine forth from every altar now is yours as well as His. He sees no strangers, only dearly loved and loving friends. He sees no thorns but only lilies, gleaming in the gentle glow of peace that shines on everything He looks upon and loves.

This Easter, look with different eyes upon each other. You have forgiven me. And yet I cannot use your gift of lilies while you see them not. Nor can you use what I have given unless you share it. The Holy Spirit's vision is no idle gift, no plaything to be tossed about a while, and laid aside. Listen and hear this carefully, nor think it but a dream; a careless thought to play with, or a toy you would pick up from time to time and then put by. For if you do, so will it be to you:

You have the vision now to look past all illusions. It has been given you to see no thorns, no strangers, and no obstacles to peace. The fear of God is nothing to you now. Who is afraid to look upon illusions, knowing his Saviour stands beside him? With him, your vision has become the greatest power for the undoing of illusion that God Himself could give. For what God gave the Holy Spirit, you have received. The Son of God looks unto you for his release. For you have asked for, and been given, the strength to look upon this final obstacle and see no thorns nor nails to crucify the Son of God, and crown him king of death. Your chosen home is on the other side, beyond the veil. It has been carefully prepared for you and it is ready to receive you now. You will not see it with the body's eyes. Yet all you need you have.

Your home has called to you since time began, nor have you ever failed entirely to hear. You heard, but knew not how to look, nor where. And now you know. In you the knowledge lies, ready to be unveiled and freed from all the terror that kept it hidden. There is no fear in love. The song of Easter is the glad refrain the Son of God was never crucified. Let us lift up our eyes together, not in fear, but faith. And there will be no fear in us, for in our vision will be no illusions; only a pathway to the open door of Heaven, the home we share in quietness, and where we live in gentleness and peace, as one together.

Would you not have your holy brother lead you there? His innocence will light your way, offering you its guiding light and sure protection, and shining from the holy altar within him where you laid the lilies of forgiveness. Let him be to you the Saviour from illusions and look on him with the new vision that looks upon the lilies and brings you joy. We go beyond the veil of fear, lighting each other's way. The holiness that leads us is within us, as is our home. So will we find what we were meant to find by Him Who leads us.

This is the way to Heaven and to the peace of Easter, in which we join in glad awareness that the Son of God is risen from the past and has awakened to the present. Now is he free, unlimited in his communion with all that is within him. Now are the lilies of his innocence untouched by guilt, and perfectly protected from the cold chill of fear and withering blight of sin alike. Your gift has saved him from the thorns and nails, and his strong arm is free to guide you safely through them, and beyond. Walk with him now rejoicing, for the Saviour from illusions has come to greet you and lead you home with him.

Here is your Saviour and your Friend, released from crucifixion through your vision, and free to lead you now where He would be. He will not leave you, nor forsake the Saviour from his pain. And gladly will you walk the way of innocence together, singing as you behold the open door of Heaven, and recognize the home that called to you. Give joyously to one another the freedom and the strength to lead you there. And come before each other's holy altar where the strength and freedom wait, to offer and receive the bright awareness that leads you home. The lamp is lit in both of you for one another. And by the hands that gave it to each other shall both of you be led past fear to love.

The belief in sin is an adjust. And an adjustment is a change; a shift in perception, or a belief that what was so before has been made different. Every adjustment is therefore a distortion and calls upon defences to uphold it against reality. Knowledge requires no adjustment, and, in fact, is lost if any shift or change is undertaken. For this reduces it at once to mere perception; a way of looking in which certainty is lost, and doubt has entered. To this impaired condition are adjustments necessary, because they are not true. Who need adjust to truth, which calls on only what he is, to understand?

Adjustments of any kind are of the ego. For it is the ego's fixed belief that all relationships depend upon adjustments to make of them what it would have them be. Direct relationships, in which there are no interferences, are always seen as dangerous. The ego is the self-appointed mediator of all relationships, making whatever adjustments it deems necessary, and interposing them between those who would meet, to keep them separate and prevent their union. It is this studied interference which makes it difficult of r you to recognize your holy relationship for what it is.

The holy do not interfere with truth. They are not afraid of it, for it is within the truth they recognized their holiness and rejoiced at what they saw. They looked on it directly, without attempting to adjust themselves to it, or it to them. And so they saw that it was in them, not deciding first where they would have it be. Their looking merely asked a question, and it was what they saw that answered them. You make the world and then adjust to it, and it to you. Nor is there any difference between yourself and it in your perception, which made them both.

A simple question yet remains and needs an answer. Do you like what you have made? – a world of murder and attack, through which you thread your timid way through constant dangers, alone and frightened, hoping at most that death will wait a little longer before it overtakes you and you disappear? You made this up. It is a picture of what you think you are; of how you see yourself. A murderer is frightened, and those who kill fear death. All these are but the fearful thoughts of those who would adjust themselves to a world made fearful by their adjustments. And they look out in sorrow from what is sad within and see the sadness there.

Have you not wondered what the world is really like; how it would look through happy eyes? The world you see is but a judgement on yourself. It is not there at all. Yet judgement lays a sentence on it, justifies it, and makes it real. Such is the world you see; a judgement on yourself and made by you. This sickly picture of yourself is carefully preserved by the ego, whose image it is and which it loves and placed outside you in the world. And to this world must you adjust, as long as you believe this picture is outside and has you at its mercy. This world is merciless and were it outside you, you should indeed be fearful. Yet it was you who made it merciless, and now if mercilessness seems to look back at you, it can be corrected.

Who in a holy relationship can long remain unholy? The world the holy see is one with them, just as the world the ego looks upon is like itself. The world the holy see is beautiful because they see their innocence in it. They did not tell it what it was; they did not make adjustments to fit their orders. They gently questioned it and whispered, "What are you?" And He Who watches over all perception answered. Take not the judgement of the world as answer to the question, "What am I?"

The world believes in sin, but the belief that made it as you see it is not outside you. Seek not to make the Son of God adjust to his insanity. There is a stranger in him, who wandered carelessly into the home of truth, and who will wander off. He came without a purpose, but he will not remain before the shining light the Holy Spirit offered, and you accepted. For there the stranger is made homeless and you are welcome.

Ask not this transient stranger, "What am I?" He is the only thing in all the universe that does not know. Yet it is he you asked, and it is to his answer that you would adjust. This one wild thought, fierce in its arrogance, and yet so tiny and so meaningless it slips unnoticed through the universe of truth, becomes your guide. To it you turn to ask the meaning of the universe. And of the one blind thing in all the seeing universe of truth you ask, "How shall I look upon the Son of God?"

Does one ask judgement of what is totally bereft of judgement? And if you have, would you believe the answer, and adjust to it as if it were the truth? The world you look on is the answer that it gave you, and you have given it power to adjust the world to make its answer true. You asked this puff of madness for the meaning of your unholy relationship and adjusted it according to its insane answer. How happy did it make you? Did you meet with joy, to bless the Son of God, and give him thanks for all the happiness which he held out to you? Did you recognize each other as the eternal gift of God to you? Did you see the holiness that shone in both of you, to bless the other? That is the purpose of your holy relationship. Ask not the means of its attainment of the one thing that still would have it be unholy. Give it no power to adjust the means and end.

Prisoners bound with heavy chains for years, starved and emaciated, weak and exhausted, and with eyes so long cast down in darkness they remember not the light, do not leap up in joy the instant they are made free. It takes a while for them to understand what freedom is. You groped but feebly in the dust and found each other's hand, uncertain whether to let it go, or to take hold on life so long forgotten. Strengthen your hold, and raise your eyes unto your strong companion, in whom the meaning of your freedom lies. He seemed to be crucified beside you. And yet his holiness remained untouched and perfect, and with him beside you, you shall this day enter with him to Paradise and know the peace of God.

Such is my will for both of you, and for each of you for one another, and for himself. Here there is only holiness and joining without limit. For what is Heaven but union, direct and perfect, and without the veil of fear upon it? Here are we one, looking with perfect gentleness upon each other, and on ourselves. Here all thoughts of any separation between us becomes impossible. You who were prisoners in separation are now made free in Paradise. And here would I unite with you, my friends, my brothers and my Self. Your gift unto each other has given me the certainty our union will be soon.

Share, then, this faith with me, and know that it is justified. There is no fear in perfect love because it knows no sin, and it must look on others as on itself. Looking with charity within, what can it fear without The innocent see safety and the pure in heart see God within His Son and look unto the Son to lead them to the Father. And where else would they go but where they will to be? Each of you now will lead the other to the Father as surely as God created His Son holy and kept him so. In your brother is the light of God's eternal promise of your immortality. See HIM as sinless, and there can be no fear in you.

Nothing can hurt you unless you give it the power to do so. For you give power as the laws of this world interpret giving; as you give you lose. It is not up to you to give power at all. Power is of God, given by Him and re-awakened by the Holy Spirit, Who knows that as you give you gain. He gives no power to sin, and therefore it has none; nor to its results as this world sees them, – sickness and death and misery and pain. These things have not occurred because the Holy Spirit sees them not and gives no power to their seeming source. Thus would He keep you free of them. Being without illusion of what you are, the Holy Spirit merely gives everything to God, Who has already given and received all that is true. The untrue He has neither received nor given.

Sin has no place in Heaven, where its results are alien, and can no more enter than can their source. And therein lies your need to see your brother sinless. In him is Heaven. See sin in him instead, and Heaven is lost to you. But see him as he is, and what is yours shines from him to you. Your Saviour gives you only love, but what you would receive of him is up to you. It lies in him to overlook all your mistakes, and therein lies his own salvation. And so it is with yours. It is the re-awakening of the laws of God in minds that have established other laws and given them power to enforce what God created not.

Your insane laws were made to guarantee that you would make mistakes and give them power over you by accepting their results as your just due. What could this be but madness? And is it this that you would see within your Saviour from insanity? He is as free from this as you are, and in the freedom that you see in him, you see your own. For this you share. What God has given follows His laws, and His alone. Nor is it possible for those who follow them to suffer the results of any other source.

Those who choose freedom will experience only its results. Their power is of God, and they will give it only to what God has given, to share with them. Nothing but this can touch them, for they see only this, sharing their power according to the Will of God. And thus their freedom is established and maintained. It is upheld through all temptation to imprison and to be imprisoned. It is of them who learned of freedom that you should ask what freedom is. Ask not the sparrow how the eagle soars, for those with little wings have not accepted for themselves the power to share with you. The sinless give as they received. See, then, the power of sinlessness within your brother, and share with him the power of the release from sin you offered him. To each who walks this earth in seeming solitude is a Saviour given, whose special function here is to release him, and so to free himself. In the world of separation each is appointed separately, though they are all the same. Yet those who know that they are all the same need not salvation. And each one finds his Saviour when he is ready to look upon the face of Christ and see Him sinless.

The plan is not of you, nor need you be concerned with anything except the part that has been given you to learn. For He Who knows the rest will see to it without your help. But think not that He does not need your part to help Him with the rest. For in your part lies all of it, without which is no part complete, nor is the whole completed without your part. The ark of peace is entered two by two, yet the beginning of another world goes with them. Each holy relationship must enter here, to learn its special function in the Holy Spirit's plan, now that it shares His purpose. And as this purpose is fulfilled, a new world rises in which sin can enter not and where the Son of God can enter without fear, and where he rests a while, to forget imprisonment and to remember freedom. How can he enter, to rest and to remember, without you? Except you be there, he is not complete. And it is his completion that he remembers there.

This is the purpose given you. Think not that your forgiveness of each other serves but you two alone. For the whole new world rests in the hands of every two who enter here to rest. And as they rest, the face of Christ shines on them, and they remember the laws of God, forgetting all the rest, and yearning only to have His laws perfectly fulfilled in them and all their brothers. Think you when this has been achieved that you will rest without them? You could no more leave one of them outside than I could leave you and forget part of myself.

You may wonder how you can be at peace when, while you are in time, there is so much that must be done before the way to peace is open. Perhaps this seems impossible to you. But ask yourself if it is possible that God would have a plan for your salvation that does not work. Once you accept His plan as the one function that you would fulfil, there will be nothing else the Holy Spirit will not arrange for you without your effort.

He will go before you making straight your path and leaving in your way no stones to trip on, and no obstacles to bar your way. Nothing you need will be denied you. Not one seeming difficulty but will melt away before you reach it. You need take thought for nothing, careless of everything except the only purpose that you would fulfil. As that was given you, so will its fulfillment be. God's guarantee will hold against all obstacles, for it rests on certainty and not contingency. It rests on you. And what can be more certain than a Son of God?

In this world, God's Son comes closest to himself in a holy relationship. There he begins to find the certainty his Father has in him. And there he finds his function of restoring his Father's laws to what was held outside them, and finding what was lost. Only in time can anything be lost, and never lost forever. So do the parts of God's Son gradually join in time, and with each joining is the end of time brought nearer. Each miracle of joining is a mighty herald of eternity. No-one who has a single purpose, unified and sure, can be afraid. No-one who shares his purpose with him cannot be one with him.

Each herald of eternity sings of the end of sin and fear. Each speaks in time of what is far beyond it. Two voices raised together call to the hearts of everyone and let them beat as one. And in that single heart beat is the unity of love proclaimed and given welcome. Peace to your holy relationship, which has the power to hold the unity of the Son of God together. You give to one another for everyone, and in your gift is everyone made glad. Forget not Who has given you the gifts you give, and through you're not forgetting this will you remember Who gave the gifts to Him to give to you. It is impossible to overestimate your brother's value. Only the ego does this, but all it means is that it wants the other for itself, and therefore values him too little. What is inestimable clearly cannot be evaluated. Do you recognize the fear that rises from the meaningless attempt to judge what lies so far beyond your judgement you cannot even see it? Judge not what is invisible to you or you will never see it, but wait in patience for its coming. It will be given you to see your brother's worth when all you want for him is peace. And what you want for him you will receive.

How can you estimate the worth of him who offers peace to you? What would you want except his offering? His worth has been established by his Father, and you will recognize it as you receive his Father's gift through him. What is in him will shine so brightly in your grateful vision that you will merely love him and be glad. You will not think to judge him, for who would see the face of Christ and yet insist that judgement still has meaning? For this insistence is of those who do not see. Vision or judgement is your choice, but never both of these.

Your brother's body is as little use to you as it is to him. When it is used only as the Holy Spirit teaches it has no function, for minds need not the body to communicate. The sight that sees the body has no use which serves the purpose of a holy relationship. And while you look upon each other thus, the means and end have not been brought in line. Why should it take so many holy instants to let this be accomplished, when one would do? There is but one. The little breath of eternity that runs through time like golden light is all the same; nothing before it, nothing afterwards.

You look upon each holy instant as a different point in time. It never changes. All that it ever held, or will ever hold, is here right now. The past takes nothing from it, and the future will add no more. Here, then, is everything. Here is the loveliness of your relationship, with means and end in perfect harmony already. Here is the perfect faith that you will one day offer to each other already offered you. And here the limitless forgiveness you will give each other already given; the face of Christ you yet will look upon already seen.

Can you evaluate the giver of a gift like this? Would you exchange this gift for any other? This gift returns the laws of God to your remembrance. And merely by remembering them, the laws that held you prisoner to pain and death must be forgotten. This is no gift your brother's body offers you. The veil that hides the gift hides him as well. He is the gift and yet he knows it not. No more do you. And yet, have faith that He Who sees the gift in both of you will offer and receive it for you both. And through His vision will you see it, and through His understanding recognize it and love it as your own.

Be comforted, and feel the Holy Spirit watching over you in love and perfect confidence in what He sees. He knows the Son of God and shares his Father's certainty the universe rests in his gentle hands in safety and in peace. Let us consider now what he must learn, to share his Father's confidence in him. What is he, that the Creator of the universe should offer it to him, and know it rests in safety? He looks upon himself not as his Father knows him. And yet it is impossible the confidence of God should be misplaced.

The meaning of the Son of God lies solely in his relationship with his Creator. If it were elsewhere it would rest upon contingency, but there IS nothing else. And this is wholly loving and forever. Yet has the Son of God invented an unholy relationship between him and his Father. His real relationship is one of perfect union and unbroken continuity.

The one he made is partial, self-centred, broken into fragments and full of fear. The one created by his Father is wholly self-encompassing and self-extending. The one he made is wholly self-destructive and self-limiting.

Nothing can show the contrast better than the experience of both a holy and an unholy relationship. The first is based on love, and rests on it serene and undisturbed. The body does not intrude upon it. Any relationship in which the body enters is based not on love, but on idolatry. Love wishes to be known, completely understood and shared. It has no secrets; nothing that it would keep apart and hide. It walks in sunlight, open-eyed and calm, in smiling welcome and in sincerity so simple and so obvious it cannot be misunderstood. But idols do not share.

Idols accept, but never make return. They can be loved but cannot love. They do not understand what they are offered, and any relationship in which they enter has lost its meaning. They live in secrecy, hating the sunlight and happy in the body's darkness, where they can hide and keep their secrets hidden along with them. And they have no relationships, for no-one else is welcome there. They smile on no-one, and those who smile on them they do not see.

Love has no darkened temples where mysteries are kept obscure and hidden from the sun. It does not seek for power, but for relationships. The body is the ego's chosen weapon for seeking power through relationships. And its relationships must be unholy, for what they are it does not even see. It wants them solely for the offerings on which its idols thrive. The rest it merely throws away, for all that it could offer is seen as valueless. Homeless, the ego seeks as many bodies as it can collect to place its idols in, and so establish them as temples to itself.

The Holy Spirit's temple is not a body, but a relationship. The body is an isolated speck of darkness; a hidden secret room, a tiny spot of senseless mystery, a meaningless enclosure carefully protected, yet hiding nothing. Here the unholy relationship escapes reality and seeks for crumbs to keep itself alive. Here it would drag its brothers, holding them here in its idolatry. Here it is "safe," for here love cannot enter. The Holy Spirit does not build His temples where love can never be. Would He Who sees the face of Christ choose as His home the only place in all the universe where it cannot be seen?

You cannot make the body the Holy Spirit's temple, and it will never be the seat of love. It is the home of the idolater and of love's condemnation. For here is love made fearful and hope abandoned.

Even the idols that are worshipped here are shrouded in mystery and kept apart from those who worship them. This is the temple dedicated to no relationships and no return. Here is the "mystery" of separation perceived in awe and held in reverence. What God would have not be is here kept "safe" from Him. But what you do not realize is what you fear within your brother, and would not see in him, is what makes God seem fearful to you, and kept unknown. Idolaters will always be afraid of love, for nothing so severely threatens them as love's approach. Let love draw near them and overlook the body, as it will surely do and they retreat in fear, feeling the seeming firm foundation of their temple begin to shake and loosen. Brothers, you tremble with them. Yet what you fear is but the herald of escape. This place of darkness is not your home. Your temple is not threatened. You are idolaters no longer. The Holy Spirit's purpose lies safe in your relationship, and not your bodies.

You have escape the body. Where you are the body cannot enter, for the Holy Spirit has set His temple there. There is no order in relationships. They either are or not. An unholy relationship is no relationship. It is a state of isolation, which seems to be what it is not. No more than that. The instant that the mad idea of making your relationship with God unholy seemed to be possible, all your relationships were made meaningless. In that unholy instant time was born, and bodies made to house the mad idea, and give it the illusion of reality. And so it seemed to have a home that held together for a little while in time, and vanished. For what could house this mad idea against reality but for an instant?

Idols must disappear and leave no trace behind their going. The unholy instant of their seeming power is frail as is a snowflake, but without its loveliness. Is this the substitute you want for the eternal blessing of the holy instant and its unlimited beneficence? Is the malevolence of the unholy relationship, so seeming powerful and so bitterly misunderstood, and so invested in a false attraction, your preference to the holy instant, which offers you peace and understanding? Then lay aside the body and quietly transcend it, rising to welcome what you really want. And from His holy temple, look you not back on what you have awakened from. For no illusions can attract the minds that have transcended them and left them far behind.

The holy relationship reflects the true relationship the Son of God has with his Father in reality. The Holy Spirit rests within it in the certainty it will endure forever. Its firm foundation is eternally upheld by truth, and love shines on it with the gentle smile and tender blessing it offers to its own. Here the unholy instant is exchanged in gladness for the holy one of safe return. Here is the way to true relationships held gently open, through which you walk together, leaving the body thankfully behind, and resting in the Everlasting Arms. Love's arms are open to receive you and give you peace forever.

The body is the ego's idol; the belief in sin made flesh and then projected outward. This produces what seems to be a wall of flesh around the mind, keeping it prisoner in a tiny spot of space and time, beholden unto death, and given but an instant in which to sigh and grieve and die in honour of its master. And this unholy instant seems to be life; an instant of despair, a tiny island of dry sand, bereft of water and set uncertainly upon oblivion. Here does the Son of God stop briefly by, to offer his devotion to death's idols, and then pass on. And here he is more dead than living. Yet it is also here he makes his choice again between idolatry and love.

Here it is given him to choose to spend this instant paying tribute to the body or let himself be given freedom from it. Here he can accept the holy instant, offered him to replace the unholy one he chose before. And here can he learn relationships are his salvation, and not his doom. You who are learning this may still be fearful, but you are not immobilized. The holy instant is of greater value now to you than its unholy seeming counterpart, and you have learned you really want but one. This is no time for sadness. Perhaps confusion, but hardly discouragement.

You have a real relationship, and it has meaning. It is as like your real relationship with God as equal things are like unto each other. Idolatry is past and meaningless. Perhaps you fear each other a little yet; perhaps a shadow of the fear of God remains with you. Yet what is that to those who have been given one true relationship beyond the body? Can they be long held back from looking on the face of Christ? And can they long withhold the memory of their relationship with their Father from themselves, and keep remembrance of His Love apart from their awareness?

We have said much about discrepancies of means and end, and how these must be brought in line before your holy relationship can bring you only joy. But we have also said the means to meet the Holy Spirit's goal will come from the same Source as does His purpose. Being so simple and direct, this course has nothing in it that is not consistent. The seeming inconsistencies, or parts you find more difficult than others, are merely indications of areas where means and end are still discrepant. And this produces great discomfort. This need not be. This course requires almost nothing of you. It is impossible to imagine one that asks so little or could offer more.

The period of discomfort that follows the sudden change in a relationship from sin to holiness should now be almost over. To the extent you still experience it, you are refusing to leave the means to Him Who changed the purpose. You recognize you want the goal. Are you not also willing to accept the means? If you are not, let us admit that you are inconsistent. A purpose is attained by means, and if you want a purpose, you must be willing to want the means as well. How can one be sincere and say, "I want this above all else, and yet I do not want to learn the means to get it?"

To obtain the goal, the Holy Spirit indeed asks little. He asks no more to give the means as well. The means are second to the goal. And when you hesitate, it is because the purpose frightens you, and not the means. Remember this, for otherwise you will make the error of believing the means are difficult. Yet how can they be difficult if they are merely given you? They guarantee the goal, and they are perfectly in line with it. Before we look at them a little closer, remember that if you think they are impossible, your wanting of the purpose has been shaken. For if a goal is possible to reach, the means to do so must be possible as well.

It is impossible to see your brother as sinless, and yet to look upon him as a body. Is this not perfectly consistent with the goal of holiness? For holiness is merely the result of letting the effects of sin be lifted, so what was always true is recognized. To see a sinless body is impossible, for holiness is positive, and the body is merely neutral. It is not sinful, but neither is it sinless. As nothing, which it is, the body cannot meaningfully be invested with attributes of Christ or of the ego. Either must be an error, for both would place the attributes where they cannot be. And both must be undone for purposes of truth.

The body is the means by which the ego tries to make the unholy relationship seem real. The unholy instant IS the time of bodies. But the purpose here is sin. It cannot be attained but in illusion, and so the illusion of a brother as a body is quite in keeping with the purpose of unholiness. Because of this consistency, the means remain unquestioned while the end is cherished. Vision adapts to wish, for sight is always secondary to desire. And if you see the body, you have chosen judgement and not vision. For vision, like relationships, has no order. You either see or not. Who sees a brother's body has laid a judgement on him and sees him not. He does not really see him as sinful; he does not see him at all. In the darkness of sin, he is invisible. He can but be imagined in the darkness, and it is here that the illusions you hold about him are not held up to his reality. Here are illusions and reality kept separated. Here are illusions never brought to truth, and always hidden from it. And here, in darkness, is your brother's reality imagined as a body, in unholy relationships with other bodies, serving the cause of sin an instant before he dies.

There is indeed a difference between this vain imagining and vision. The difference lies not in them, but in their purpose. Both are but means, each one appropriate to the end for which it is employed. Neither can serve the purpose of the other, for each one is a choice of purpose, employed on its behalf. Either is meaningless without the end for which it was intended, nor is it valued as a separate thing apart from the intention. The means seem real because the goal is valued. And judgement has no value unless the goal is sin.

The body cannot be looked upon except through judgement. To see the body is the sign that you lack vision and have denied the means the Holy Spirit offers you to serve His purpose. How can a holy relationship achieve its purpose through the means of sin? Judgement you taught yourself; vision is learned from Him Who would undo your teaching. His vision cannot see the body because it cannot look on sin. And thus it leads you to reality. Your holy brother, sight of whom is your release, is no illusion. Attempt to see him not in darkness, for your imaginings about him will seem real there. You closed your eyes to shut him out. Such was your purpose, and while this purpose seems to have any meaning, the means for its attainment will be evaluated as worth the seeing and so you will not see.

Your question should not be, "How can I see my brother without the body?" Ask only, "Do I really wish to see him sinless?" And as you ask, forget not that his sinlessness is your escape from fear. Salvation is the Holy Spirit's goal. The means is vision. For what the seeing look upon is sinless. No-one who loves can judge, and what he sees is free of condemnation. And what he sees he did not make, for it was given him to see, as was the vision which made his seeing possible.

Vision will come to you at first in glimpses, but they will be enough to show you what is given you who see your brother sinless. Truth is restored to you through your desire, as it was lost to you through your desire for something else. Open the holy place which you closed off by valuing the "something else", and what was never lost will quietly return. It has been saved for you. Vision would not be necessary had judgement not been made. Desire now its whole undoing and it is done for you.

Do you not want to know your own identity? Would you not happily exchange your doubts for certainty? Would you not willingly be free of misery and learn again of joy? Your holy relationship offers all this to you. As it was given you, so will be its effects. And as its holy purpose was not made by you, the means by which its happy end is yours is also not of you. Rejoice in what is yours but for the asking and think not that you need make either means or end. All this is given you who would but see your brother sinless. All this is given, waiting on your desire but to receive it. Vision is freely given to those who ask to see.

Your brother's sinlessness is given you in shining light, to look on with the Holy Spirit's vision, and to rejoice in along with Him. For peace will come to all who ask for it with real desire and sincerity of purpose, shared with the Holy Spirit and at one with Him on what salvation is. Be willing, then, to see your brother sinless, that Christ may rise before your vision and give you joy. And place no value on your brother's body, which holds him to illusions of what he is. It is HIS desire to see his sinlessness, as it is yours. And bless the Son of God in your relationship, nor see in him what you have made of him.

The Holy Spirit guarantees that what God willed and gave you shall be yours. This is your purpose now, and the vision that makes it yours is ready to be given. You have the vision which enables each one to see the body not. And as you look upon each other, you will see an altar to your Father, holy as Heaven, glowing with radiant purity and sparkling with the shining lilies you laid upon it. What can you value more than this? Why do you think the body is a better home, a safer shelter for God's Son? Why would you rather look on it than on the truth? How can the engine of destruction be preferred, and chosen to replace the holy home the Holy Spirit offers, where He will dwell with you?

The body is the sign of weakness, vulnerability and loss of power. Can such a saviour help you? Would you turn in your distress and need for help unto the helpless? Is the pitifully little the perfect choice to call upon for strength? Judgement will seem to make your Saviour weak. Yet it is you who need his strength. There is no problem, no event or situation, no perplexity that vision will not solve. All is redeemed when looked upon with vision. For this is not your sight and brings with it the laws beloved of Him Whose sight it is.

Everything looked upon with vision falls gently into place, according to the laws brought to it by His calm and certain sight. The end for everything He looks upon is always sure. For it will meet His purpose, seen in unadjusted form, and suited perfectly to meet it. Destructiveness becomes benign, and sin is turned to blessing under His gentle gaze. What can the body's eyes perceive, with power to correct? Its eyes adjust to sin, unable to overlook it in any form and seeing it everywhere, in everything. Look through its eyes, and everything will stand condemned before you. All that could save you, you will never see. Your holy relationship, the source of your salvation, will be deprived of meaning, and its most holy purpose bereft of means for its accomplishment.

Judgement is but a toy, a whim, the senseless means to play the idle game of death in your imagination. But vision sets all things right, bringing them gently within the kindly sway of Heaven's laws. What if you recognized this world is a hallucination? What if you really understood you made it up? What if you realized that those who seem to walk about in it, to sin and die, attack and murder and destroy themselves, are wholly unreal? Could you have faith in what you see, if you accepted this? And would you see it?

Hallucinations disappear when they are recognized for what they are. This is the healing and the remedy. Believe them not and they are gone. And all you need to do is recognize you did this. Once you accept this simple fact, and take unto yourself the power you gave them, you are released from them. One thing is sure; hallucinations serve a purpose, and when that purpose is no longer held, they disappear. Therefore, the question never is whether you want them, but always, do you want the purpose which they serve? This world seems to hold out many purposes, each different and with different values. Yet they are all the same. Again, there is no order, but a seeming hierarchy of values.

Only two purposes are possible. And one is sin, the other holiness. Nothing is in between, and which you choose determines what you see. For what you see is merely how you elect to meet your goal. Hallucinations serve to meet the goal of madness. They are the means by which the outside world, projected from within, adjusts to sin and seems to witness to its reality. It still is true that nothing is without. Yet upon nothing are all projections made. For it is the projection which gives the "nothing" all the meaning that it holds.

What has no meaning cannot be perceived. And meaning always looks within to find itself, and then looks out. All meaning that you give the world outside must thus reflect the sight you saw within; or better, if you saw at all or merely judged against. Vision is the means by which the Holy Spirit translates your nightmares into happy dreams; your wild hallucinations that show you all the fearful outcomes of imagined sin, into the calm and reassuring sights with which He would replace them. These gentle sights and sounds are looked on happily and heard with joy. They are His substitutes for all the terrifying sights and screaming sounds the ego's purpose brought to your horrified awareness. They step away from sin, reminding you that it is not reality which frightens you, and that the errors which you made can be corrected.

When you have looked on what seemed terrifying, and seen it change to sights of loveliness and peace; when you have looked on scenes of violence and death, and watched them change to quiet views of gardens under open skies, with clear, life-giving water running happily beside them in dancing brooks that never waste away; who need persuade you to accept the gift of vision? And after vision, who is there who could refuse what must come after? Think but an instant just on this; you can behold the holiness God gave His Son. And never need you think that there is something else for you to see.

Projection makes perception. The world you see is what you gave it, nothing more than that. But though it is no more than that, it is not less. Therefore, to you it is important. It is the witness to your state of mind, the outside picture of an inward condition. As a man thinketh, so does he perceive. Therefore, seek not to change the world, but will to change your mind about the world. Perception is a result, not a cause. And that is why order of difficulty in miracles is meaningless. Everything looked upon with vision is healed and holy. Nothing perceived without it means anything. And where there is no meaning, there is chaos.

Damnation is your judgement on yourself, and this you will project upon the world. See it as damned, and all you see is what you did to hurt the Son of God. If you behold disaster and catastrophe, you tried to crucify him. If you see holiness and hope, you joined the Will of God to set him free. There is no choice that lies between these two decisions. And you will see the witness to the choice you made and learn from this to recognise which one you chose.

Never forget the world the sightless "see" must be imagined, for what it really looks like is unknown to them. They must infer what could be seen from evidence forever indirect; and reconstruct their inferences as they stumble and fall because of what they did not recognize or walk unharmed through open doorways which they thought were closed. And so it is with you. You do not see. Your cues for inference are wrong, and so you stumble and fall down upon the stones you did not recognize but fail to be aware you can go through the doors you thought were closed, but which stand open before unseeing eyes, waiting to welcome you.

How foolish it is to attempt to judge what could be seen instead. It is not necessary to imagine what the world must look like. It must be seen, before you recognize it for what it is. You can be shown which doors are open, and you can see where safety lies; and which way leads to darkness, which to light. Judgement will always give you false directions, but vision shows you where to go. Why should you guess?

There is no need to learn through pain. And gentle lessons are acquired joyously and are remembered gladly. What gives you happiness you want to learn and not forget. It is not this you would deny. Your question is whether the means by which this course is learned will bring to you the joy it promises. If you believed it would, the learning of it would be no problem. You are not happy learners yet because you still remain uncertain that vision gives you more than judgement does, and you have learned that both you cannot have.

The blind become accustomed to their world by their adjustments to it. They think they know their way about in it. They learned it, not through joyous lessons, but through the stern necessity of limits they believed they could not overcome. And still believing this, they hold those lessons dear, and cling to them because they cannot see. They do not understand the lessons keep them blind. This they do not believe. And so they keep the world they learned to "see" in their imagination, believing that their choice is that or nothing. They hate the world they learned through pain.

And everything they think is in it serves to remind them that they are incomplete and bitterly deprived.

Thus they define their life and where they live, adjusting to it as they think they must, afraid to lose the little that they have. And so it is with all who see the body as all they have and all their brothers have. They try to reach each other, and they fail, and fail again. And they adjust to loneliness, believing that to keep the body is to save the little that they have. Listen, and try to think if you remember what we will speak of now.

Listen, — perhaps you catch a hint of an ancient state not quite forgotten; dim, perhaps and yet not altogether unfamiliar, like a song whose name is long forgotten, and the circumstances in which you heard completely unremembered. Not the whole song has stayed with you, but just a little whisp of melody, attached not to a person or a place or anything particular. But you remember, from just this little part, how lovely was the song, how wonderful the setting where you heard it, and how you loved those who were there and listened with you.

The notes are nothing. Yet you have kept them with you, not for themselves, but as a soft reminder of what would make you weep if you remembered how dear it was to you. You could remember, yet you are afraid, believing you would lose the world you learned since then. And yet you know that nothing in the world you learned is half so dear as this. Listen, and see if you remember an ancient song you knew so long ago and held more dear than any melody you taught yourself to cherish since.

Beyond the body, beyond the sun and stars, past everything you see and yet somehow familiar, is an arc of golden light that stretches as you look into a great and shining circle. And all the circle fills with light before your eyes. The edges of the circle disappear, and what is in it is no longer contained at all. The light expands and covers everything, extending to infinity forever shining, and with no break or limit anywhere. Within it everything is joined in perfect continuity. Nor is it possible to imagine that anything could be outside, for there is nowhere that this light is not.

This is the vision of the Son of God, whom you know well. Here is the sight of him who knows his Father. Here is the memory of what you are; a part of this, with all of it within, and joined to all as surely as all is joined in you. Accept the vision which can show you this, and not the body. You know the ancient song and know it well. Nothing will ever be as dear to you as is this ancient hymn the Son of God sings to his Father still.

And now the blind can see, for that same song they sing in honour of their Creator gives praise to them as well. The blindness which they made will not withstand the memory of this song. And they will look upon the vision of the Son of God, remembering who he is they sing of. What is a miracle but this remembering? And who is there in whom this memory lies not? The light in one awakens it in all. And when you see it in each other, you are remembering for everyone.

We have repeated how little is asked of you to learn this course. It is the same small willingness you need to have your whole relationship transformed to joy; the little gift you offer to the Holy Spirit for which He gives you everything; the very little on which salvation rests; the tiny change of mind by which the crucifixion is changed to resurrection. And being true, it is so simple that it cannot fail to be completely understood. Rejected yes, but not ambiguous. And if you choose against it now, it will not be because it is obscure, but rather that this little cost seemed, in your judgement, to be too much to pay for peace.

This is the only thing that you need do for vision, happiness, release from pain and the complete escape from sin, all to be given you. Say only this, but mean it with no reservations, for here the power of salvation lies:

"I am responsible for what I see.
I chose the feelings I experience, and I decided on the goal I would achieve.
And everything that seems to happen to me
I asked for and received as I had asked."

Deceive yourself no longer that you are helpless in the face of what is done to you. Acknowledge but that you have been mistaken and all effects of your mistakes will disappear. It is impossible the Son of God be merely driven by events outside of him. It is impossible that the happenings that come to him were not his choice. His power of decision is the determiner of every situation in which he seems to find himself by chance or accident. No accident nor chance is possible within the universe as God created it, outside of which is nothing. Suffer, and you decided sin was your goal. Be happy and you gave the power of decision to Him Who must decide for God for you. This is the little gift you offer to the Holy Spirit and even this He gave to you to give yourself. For by this gift is given you the power to release your Saviour, that he may give salvation unto you.

Begrudge not then this little offering. Withhold it and you keep the world as now you see it. Give it away, and everything you see goes with it. Never was so much given for so little. In the holy instant is this exchange effected and maintained. Here is the world you do not want brought to the one you do. And here the one you do is given you because you want it. Yet for this, the power of your wanting must first be recognized. You must accept its strength, and not its weakness. You must perceive that what is strong enough to make a world can let it go and can accept correction if it is willing to see that it was wrong.

The world you see is but the idle witness that you were right. This witness is insane. You trained it in its testimony and as it gave it back to you, you listened and convinced yourself that what it saw was true. You did this to yourself. See only this, and you will also see how circular the reasoning on which your "seeing" rests. This was not given you. This was your gift to you and to your brother. Be willing, then, to have it taken from him and be replaced with truth. And as you look upon the change in him, it will be given you to see it in yourself.

Perhaps you do not see the need for you to give this little offering. Look closer, then, at what it is. And, very simply, see in it the whole exchange of separation for salvation. All that the ego is, is an idea that it is possible that things should happen to the Son of God without his will; and thus without the Will of his Creator, Whose Will cannot be separate from his own.

This is the Son of God's replacement for his will, a mad revolt against what must forever be. This is the statement that he has the power to make God powerless, and so to take it for himself, and leave himself without what God has willed for him. This is the mad idea you have enshrined upon your altars, and which you worship. And anything which threatens this seems to attack your faith, for here is it invested. Think not that you are faithless, for your belief and trust in this is strong indeed.

The Holy Spirit can give you faith in holiness and vision to see it easily enough. But you have not left open and unoccupied the altar where the gifts belong. Where they should be, you have set up your idols to something else. This other will, which seems to tell you what must happen, you gave reality. And what would show you otherwise must therefore seem unreal. All that is asked of you is to make room for truth. You are not asked to make or do what lies beyond your understanding. All you are asked to do is let it in; only to stop your interference with what will happen of itself; simply to recognize again the presence of what you thought you gave away.

Be willing, for an instant, to leave your altars free of what you placed upon them, and what is really there you cannot fail to see. The holy instant is not an instant of creation, but of recognition. For recognition comes of vision and suspended judgement. Then only it is possible to look within and see what must be there, plainly in sight, and wholly independent of inference and judgement. Undoing is not your task, but it is up to you to welcome it or not. Faith and desire go hand in hand, for everyone believes in what he wants.

We have already said that wishful thinking is how the ego deals with what it wants, to make it so. There is no better demonstration of the power of wanting, and therefore of faith, to make its goals seem real and possible. Faith in the unreal leads to adjustments of reality to make it fit the goal of madness. The goal of sin induces the perception of a fearful world to justify its purpose. What you desire you will see. And if its reality is false, you will uphold it by not realizing all the adjustments you have introduced, to make it so.

When vision is denied, confusion of cause and effect becomes inevitable. The purpose now becomes to keep obscure the cause of the effect, and make effect appear to be a cause. This seeming independence of effect enables it to be regarded as standing by itself, and capable of serving as a cause of the events and feelings its maker thinks it causes. Long ago, we spoke of your desire to create your own Creator and be father and not son to Him. This is the same desire. The Son is the effect, whose cause he would deny. And so he seems to be the cause, producing real effects. Nothing can have effects without a cause, and to confuse the two is merely to fail to understand them both.

It is as needful that you recognize you made the world you see as that you recognize that you did not create yourself. They are the same mistake. Nothing created not by your Creator has any influence over you. And if you think what you have made can tell you what you see and feel and place your faith in its ability to do so, you are denying your Creator and believing that you made yourself. For if you think the world you made has power to make you what it wills, you are confusing Son and Father; effect and Source.

The Son's creations are like his Father's. Yet in creating them, the Son does not delude himself that he is independent of his Source. His union with It is the Source of his creating. Apart from this he has no power to create and what he makes is meaningless. It changes nothing in creation, depends entirely upon the madness of its maker, and cannot serve to justify the madness. Your brother thinks he made the world with you. Thus he denies creation.

With you, he thinks the world he made, made him. Thus he denies he made it.

Yet the truth is you were both created by a loving Father, Who created you together and as one. See what "proves" otherwise, and you deny your whole reality. But grant that everything which seems to stand between you, keeping you from each other and separate from your Father, you made in secret, and the instant of release has come to you. All its effects are gone because its source has been uncovered. It is its seeming independence of its source that kept you prisoner. This is the same delusion that you are independent of the Source by which you were created and have never left.

All special relationships have sin as their goal. For they are bargains with reality, toward which the seeming union is adjusted. Forget not this; to bargain is to set a limit and any brother with whom you have a limited relationship you hate. You may attempt to keep the bargain in the name of "fairness," sometimes demanding payment of yourself, perhaps more often of the other. Thus in the "fairness" you attempt to ease the guilt that comes from the accepted purpose of the relationship. And that is why the Holy Spirit must change its purpose to make it useful to Him and harmless unto you.

If you accept this change, you have accepted the idea of making room for truth. The source of sin is gone. You may imagine that you still experience its effects, but it is not your purpose, and you no longer want it. No-one allows a purpose to be replaced while he desires it, for nothing is so cherished and protected as is a goal the mind accepts. This it will follow, grimly or happily, but always with faith and with the persistence that faith inevitably brings. The power of faith is never recognized if it is placed in sin. But it is always recognized if it is placed in love.

Why is it strange to you that faith can move mountains? This is indeed a little feat for such a power. For faith can keep the Son of God in chains as long as he believes he is in chains. And when he is released from them, it will be simply because he no longer believes in them, withdrawing faith that they can hold him, and placing it in his freedom instead. It is impossible to place equal faith in opposite directions. What faith you give to sin you take away from holiness.

And what you offer holiness has been removed from sin. Faith and belief and vision are the means by which the goal of holiness is reached. Through them the Holy Spirit leads you to the real world, and away from all illusions where your faith was laid. This is His direction, the only one He ever sees.

And when you wander, He reminds you there is but one. His faith and His belief and vision are all for you. And when you have accepted them completely instead of yours, you will have need of them no longer. For faith and vision and belief are meaningful only before the state of certainty is reached. In Heaven they are unknown. Yet Heaven is reached through them.

It is impossible that the Son of God lack faith, but he can choose where he would have it be. Faithlessness in not a lack of faith, but faith in nothing. Faith given to illusions does not lack power, for by it does the Son of God believe that he is powerless. Thus is he faithless to himself, but strong in faith in his illusions about himself. For faith, perception and belief you made as means for losing certainty and finding sin. This mad direction was your choice, and by your faith in what you chose, you made what you desired.

The Holy Spirit has a use for all the means for sin by which you sought to find it. But as He uses them, they lead away from sin, because His purpose lies in the opposite direction. He sees the means you use, but not the purpose for which you made them. He would not take them from you, for He sees their value as a means for what He wills for you. You made perception that you might choose among your brothers and seek for sin with them. The Holy Spirit sees perception as a means to teach you that the vision of a holy relationship is all you want to see. Then will you give your faith to holiness, desiring and believing in it because of your desire.

Faith and belief become attached to vision, as all the means that once served sin are redirected now toward holiness. For what you think is sin is limitation and whom you try to limit to the body you hate because you fear. In your refusal to forgive him, you would condemn him to the body because the means for sin are dear to you. And so the body has your faith and your belief. But holiness would set your brother free, removing hatred by removing fear, not as a symptom, but at its source.

Those who would free their brothers from the body can have no fear. They have renounced the means for sin by choosing to let all limitations be removed. Desiring to look upon their brothers in holiness, the power of belief and faith goes far beyond the body, supporting vision, not obstructing it. But first they chose to recognize how much their faith had limited their understanding of the world, desiring to place its power elsewhere should another point of view be given them. The miracles which follow this decision are also born of faith. For all who choose to look away from sin are given vision and are led to holiness.

Those who believe in sin must think the Holy Spirit asks for sacrifice, for this is how they think their purpose is accomplished. Brothers, the Holy Spirit knows that sacrifice brings nothing. He makes no bargains. And if you seek to limit Him, you will hate Him because you are afraid. The gift that He has given you is more than anything that stands this side of Heaven. The instant for its recognition is at hand. Join your awareness to what has been already joined. The faith you give each other can accomplish this. For He Who loves the world is seeing it for you, without one spot of sin upon it, and in the innocence, which makes the sight of it as beautiful as Heaven.

Your faith in sacrifice has given it great power in your sight; except you do not realize you cannot see because of it. For sacrifice must be exacted of a body, and by another body. The mind could neither ask it nor receive it of itself. And no more could the body. The intention is in the mind, which tries to use the body to carry out the means for sin in which the mind believes. Thus is the joining of mind and body an inescapable belief of those who value sin. And so is sacrifice invariably a means for limitation, and thus for hate.

Think you the Holy Spirit is concerned with this? He gives not what it is His purpose to lead you from. You think He would deprive you for your good. But "good" and "deprivation" are opposites and cannot meaningfully join in any way. It is like saying that the moon and sun are one because they come with night and day, and so they must be joined. Yet sight of one is but the sign the other has disappeared from sight. Nor is it possible that what gives light be one with what depends on darkness to be seen. Neither demands the sacrifice of the other. Yet on the absence of the other does each depend.

The body was made to be a sacrifice to sin, and in the darkness so it still is seen. Yet in the light of vision it is looked upon quite differently. You can have faith in it to serve the Holy Spirit's goal and give it power to serve as means to help the blind to see. But in their seeing they look past it, as do you. The faith and the belief you gave it belongs beyond. You gave perception and belief and faith from mind to body. Let them now be given back to what produced them and can use them still to save itself from what it made.

The Holy Spirit will never teach you that you are sinful. Errors He will correct, but this makes no-one fearful. You are indeed afraid to look within and see the sin you think is there. This you would not be fearful to admit. Fear in association with sin the ego deems quite appropriate and smiles approvingly. It has no fear to let you feel ashamed. It doubts not your belief and faith in sin. Its temples do not shake because of this. Your faith that sin is there but witnesses to your desire that it be there to see. This merely seems to be the source of fear.

Remember that the ego is not alone. Its rule is tempered, and its unknown "enemy," Whom it cannot even see, it fears. Loudly the ego tells you not to look inward, for if you do your eyes will light on sin, and God will strike you blind. This you believe, and so you do not look. Yet this is not the ego's hidden fear, nor yours who serve it. Loudly indeed the ego claims it is; too loudly and too often. For underneath this constant shout and frantic proclamation, the ego is not certain it is so. Beneath your fear to look within because of sin is yet another fear and one which makes the ego tremble.

What if you looked within and saw no sin? This "fearful" question is one the ego never asks. And you who ask it now are threatening the ego's whole defensive system too seriously for it to bother to pretend it is your friend. Those who have joined their brothers have detached themselves from their belief that their identity lies in the ego. A holy relationship is one in which you join with what is part of you in truth. And your belief in sin has been already shaken, nor are you now entirely unwilling to look within and see it not.

Your liberation still is only partial; still limited and incomplete yet born within you. Not wholly mad, you have been willing to look on much of your insanity and recognize its madness. Your faith is moving inward, past insanity and on to reason. And what your reason tells you now, the ego would not hear. The Holy Spirit's purpose was accepted by the part of your mind the ego knows not of. No more did you. And yet this part, with which you now identify, is not afraid to look upon itself. It knows no sin. How, otherwise, could it have been willing to see the Holy Spirit's purpose as its own?

This part has seen your brother and recognized him perfectly since time began. And it desired nothing but to join with him and to be free again, as once it was. It has been waiting for the birth of freedom; the acceptance of release to come to you. And now you recognize that it was not the ego that joined the Holy Spirit's purpose and so there must be something else.

Think not that this is madness. For this your reason tells you, and it follows perfectly from what you have already learned.

There is no inconsistency in what the Holy Spirit teaches. This is the reasoning of the sane. You have perceived the ego's madness and not been made afraid because you did not choose to share in it. At times it still deceives you. Yet in your saner moments, its ranting strikes no terror in your hearts. For you have realized that all the gifts it would withdraw from you, in rage at your "presumptuous" wish to look within, you do not want. A few remaining trinkets still seem to shine and catch your eye. Yet you would not "sell" Heaven to have them.

And now the ego is afraid. Yet what it hears in terror, the other part hears as the sweetest music; the song it longed to hear since first the ego came into your minds. The ego's weakness is its strength. The song of freedom, which sings the praises of another world, brings to it hope of peace. For it remembers Heaven, and now it sees that Heaven has come to earth at last, from which the ego's rule has kept it out so long. Heaven has come because it found a home in your relationship on earth. And earth can hold no longer what has been given Heaven as its own.

Look gently on each other and remember the ego's weakness is revealed in both your sight. What it would keep apart has met and joined and looks upon the ego unafraid. Little children, innocent of sin, follow in gladness the way to certainty. Be not held back by fear's insane insistence that sureness lies in doubt. This has no meaning. What matters it to you how loudly it is proclaimed? The senseless is not made meaningful by repetition and by clamour. The quiet way is open. Follow it happily, and question not what must be so.

Perception selects and makes the world you see. It literally picks it out as the mind directs. The laws of size and shape and brightness would hold, perhaps, if other things were equal. They are not equal. For what you look for you are far more likely to discover than what you would prefer to overlook. The still small Voice for God is not drowned out by all the ego's raucous screams and senseless ravings to those who want to hear it. Perception is a choice, and not a fact. But on this choice depends far more than you may realize as yet. For on the voice you choose to hear, and on the sights you choose to see, depends entirely your whole belief in what you are. Perception is a witness but to this, and never to reality. Yet it can show you the conditions in which awareness of reality is possible, or those where it could never be.

Reality needs no cooperation from you to be itself. But your awareness of it needs your help because it is your choice. Listen to what the ego says and see what it directs you see, and it is sure that you will see yourself as tiny, vulnerable and afraid. You will experience depression, a sense of worthlessness, and feelings of impermanence and unreality. You will believe that you are helpless prey to forces far beyond your own control, and far more powerful than you. And you will think the world you made directs your destiny. For this will be your faith. But never believe because it is your faith it makes reality.

There is another vision and another Voice in which your freedom lies, awaiting but your choice. And if you place your faith in them, you will perceive another Self in you. This other Self sees miracles as natural. They are as simple and natural to It as breathing to the body. They are the obvious response to calls for help, the only one It makes. Miracles seem unnatural to the ego because it does not understand how separate minds can influence each other. Nor could they do so. But minds cannot be separate. This other Self is perfectly aware of this. And thus It recognizes that miracles do not affect another's mind, only Its Own. There is no other.

You do not realize the whole extent to which the idea of separation has interfered with reason. Reason lies in the other Self you have cut off from your awareness. And nothing you have allowed to stay in it is capable of reason. How can the segment of the mind devoid of reason understand what reason is, or grasp the information it would give? All sorts of questions may arise in it, but if the basic question stems from reason, it will not ask it. Like all that stems from reason, the basic question is obvious, simple, and remains unasked. But think not reason could not answer it.

God's plan for your salvation could not have been established without your will and your consent. It must have been accepted by the Son of God, for what God wills for him he must receive. For God wills not apart from him, nor does the Will of God wait upon time to be accomplished. Therefore, what joined the Will of God must be in you now, being eternal. You must have set aside a place in which the Holy Spirit can abide and where He is. He must have been there since the need for Him arose and was fulfilled in the same instant. Such would your reason tell you, if you listened. Yet such is clearly not the ego's "reasoning." Its alien nature to the ego is proof you will not find the answer there. Yet if it must be so, it must exist. And if it exists for you, and has your freedom as the purpose given it, you must be free to find it.

God's plan is simple; never circular and never self-defeating. He has no Thoughts except the self-extending and in this your will must be included. Thus, there must be a part of you that knows His Will and shares It. It is not meaningful to ask if what must be is so. But it is meaningful to ask why you are unaware of what is so, for this must have an answer if the plan of God for your salvation is complete. And it must be complete because its Source knows not of incompletion. Where would the answer be but in the Source? And where are you but there, where this same answer is? Your identity, as much a true effect of this same Source as is the answer, must therefore be together and the same.

Oh yes, you know this, and more than this alone. Yet any part of knowledge threatens dissociation as much as all of it. And all of it will come with any part. Here is the part you can accept. What reason points to you can see because the witnesses on its behalf are clear. Only the totally insane can disregard them, and you have gone past this. Reason is a means which serves the Holy Spirit's purpose in its own right. It is not re-interpreted and re-directed from the goal of sin, as are the others. For reason is beyond the ego's range of means.

Faith and perception and belief can be misplaced and serve the great deceiver's needs as well as truth. But reason has no place at all in madness, nor can it be adjusted to fit its end. Faith and belief are strong in madness, guiding perception toward what the mind has valued. But reason enters not at all in this. For the perception would fall away at once, if reason were applied. There is no reason in insanity, for it depends entirely on reason's absence. The ego never uses it because it does not realize that it exists. The partially insane have access to it, and only they have need of it. Knowledge does not depend on it, and madness keeps it out.

The part of mind where reason lies was dedicated, by your will in union with your Father's, to the undoing of insanity. Here was the Holy Spirit's purpose accepted and accomplished, both at once. Reason is alien to insanity, and those who use it have gained a means which cannot be applied to sin. Knowledge is far beyond attainment of any kind. But reason can serve to open doors you closed against it.

You have come very close to this. Faith and belief have shifted, and you have asked the question which the ego will never ask. Does not your reason tell you now the question must have come from something that you do not know, but must belong to you? Faith and belief, upheld by reason, cannot fail to lead to changed perception. And in this change is room made way for vision.

Vision extends beyond itself, as does the purpose which it serves and all the means for its accomplishment.

Reason cannot see sin but can see errors and leads to their correction. It does not value them, but their correction. Reason will also tell you when you think you sin, you call for help. Yet if you will not accept the help you call for, you will not believe that it is yours to give. And so you will not give it, thus maintaining the belief. For uncorrected error of any kind deceives you about the power that is in you to make correction. If it can correct and you allow it not to do so, you deny it to yourself and to your brother. And if he shares this same belief, you both will think that you are damned. This you could spare him and yourself. For reason would not make way for correction in you alone.

Correction cannot be accepted or refused by you without your brother. Sin would maintain it can. Yet reason tells you that you cannot see your brother or yourself as sinful, and still perceive the other innocent. Who looks upon himself as guilty and sees a sinless world? And who can see a sinful world and look upon himself apart from it? Sin would maintain you must be separate. But reason tells you that this must be wrong. If you are joined, how could it be that you have private thoughts? And how could thoughts that enter into what but seems like yours alone have no effect at all on what is yours? If minds are joined, this is impossible.

No-one can think but for himself, as God thinks not without His Son. Only were both in bodies could this be. Nor could one mind think only for itself unless the body were the mind. For only bodies can be separate, and therefore unreal. The home of madness cannot be the home of reason. Yet it is easy to leave the home of madness if you see reason. You do not leave insanity by going somewhere else. You leave it simply by accepting reason where madness was. Madness and reason see the same things, but it is certain that they look upon them differently.

Madness is an attack on reason that drives it out of mind and takes its place. Reason does not attack, but takes the place of madness quietly, replacing madness if it be the will of the insane to listen to it. But the insane know not their will. For they believe they see the body, and let their madness tell them it is real. Reason would be incapable of this. And if you would defend the body against your reason, you will not understand the body or yourself.

The body does not separate you from your brother, and if you think it does, you are insane. But madness has a purpose, and believes it also has the means to make its purpose real. To see the body as a barrier between what reason tells you must be joined must be insane. Nor could you see it, if you heard the voice of reason. What can there be that stands between what is continuous? And if there is nothing in between, how can what enters part be kept away from other parts? Reason would tell you this. But think what you must recognize, if it be so.

If you choose sin instead of healing, you would condemn the Son of God to what can never be corrected. You tell him, by your choice, that he is damned; separate from you and from his Father forever, and without a hope of safe return. You teach him this, and you will learn of him exactly what you taught. For you can teach him only that he is as you would have him, and what you choose he be is but your choice for you. Yet think not this is fearful. That you are joined to him is but a fact, not an interpretation. How can a fact be fearful unless it disagrees with what you hold more dear than truth? Reason will tell you that this fact is your release. Neither your brother nor yourself can be attacked alone. But neither can accept a miracle instead without the other being blessed by it and healed of pain.

Reason, like love, would reassure you, and seeks not to frighten you. The power to heal the Son of God is given you because he must be one with you. You are responsible for how he sees himself. And reason tells you it is given you to change his whole mind, which is one with you, in just an instant. And any instant serves to bring complete correction of his errors and make him whole. The instant that you choose to let yourself be healed, in that same instant is his whole salvation seen as complete with yours. Reason is given you to understand that this is so. For reason, kind as is the purpose for which it is the means, leads steadily away from madness toward the goal of truth. And here you will lay down the burden of denying truth. This is the burden that is terrible and not the truth.

That you are joined is your salvation; the gift of Heaven, not the gift of fear. Does Heaven seem to be a burden to you? In madness, yes. And yet what madness sees must be dispelled by reason. Reason assures you Heaven is what you want and all you want. Listen to Him Who speaks with reason and brings your reason into line with His. Be willing to let reason be the means by which He would direct you how to leave insanity behind. Hide not behind insanity, in order to escape from reason.

What madness would conceal, the Holy Spirit still holds out for everyone to look upon with gladness.

You are your brother's Saviour. He is yours. Reason speaks happily indeed of this. This gracious plan was given love by Love. And what Love plans is like Itself in this: Being united, It would have you learn what you must be. And being one with It, it must be given you to give what It has given and gives still. Spend but an instant in the glad acceptance of what is given you to give your brother and learn with him what has been given both of you. To give is no more blessed than to receive. But neither is it less.

The Son of God is always blessed as one. And as his gratitude goes out to you who blessed him, reason will tell you that it cannot be you stand apart from blessing. The gratitude he offers you reminds you of the thanks your Father gives you for completing Him. And here alone does reason tell you that you can understand what you must be. Your Father is as close to you as is your brother. Yet what is there that could be nearer you than is your Self?

The power that you have over the Son of God is not a threat to his reality. It but attests to it. Where could his freedom lie but in himself, if he be free already? And who could bind him but himself, if he deny his freedom? God is not mocked; no more His Son can be imprisoned save by his own desire. And it is by his own desire that he is freed. Such is his strength, and not his weakness. He is at his own mercy. And where he chooses to be merciful, there is he free. But where he chooses to condemn instead, there is he held a prisoner, waiting in chains his pardon on himself to set him free.

Do you not see that all your misery comes from the strange belief that you are powerless? Being helpless is the cost of sin. Helplessness is sin's condition; the one requirement that it demands to be believed. Only the helpless could believe in it. Enormity has no appeal save to the little. And only those who first believe that they are little could see attraction there. Treachery to the Son of God is the defence of those who do not identify with him. And you are for him or against him; either you love him or attack him, protect his unity or see him shattered and slain by your attack.

No-one believes the Son of God is powerless. And those who see themselves as helpless must believe that they are not the Son of God. What can they be except his enemy? And what can they do but envy him his power, and by their envy make themselves afraid of it? These are the dark ones, silent and afraid, alone and not communicating, fearful the power of the Son of God will strike them dead and raising up their helplessness against him.

They join the army of the powerless, to wage their war of vengeance, bitterness and spite on him, to make him one with them. Because they do not know that they are one with him, they know not whom they hate.

They are indeed a sorry army, each one as likely to attack his brother or turn upon himself as to remember they thought they had a common cause.

Frantic and loud and strong the dark ones seem to be. Yet they know not their enemy, except they hate him. In hatred they have come together but have not joined each other. For had they done so, hatred would be impossible. The army of the powerless must be disbanded in the presence of strength. Those who are strong are never treacherous, because they have no need to dream of power and to act out their dream. How would an army act in dreams? Any way at all. It could be seen attacking anyone with anything. Dreams have no reason in them. A flower turns into a poisoned spear, a child becomes a giant and a mouse roars like a lion. And love is turned to hate as easily. This is no army, but a madhouse. What seems to be a planned attack is bedlam.

The army of the powerless is weak indeed. It has no weapons and it has no enemy. Yes, it can overrun the world and seek an enemy. But it can never find what is not there. Yes, it can dream it found an enemy, but this will shift even as it attacks, so that it runs at once to find another, and never comes to rest in victory. And as it runs, it turns against itself, thinking it caught a glimpse of the great enemy which always eludes its murderous attack by turning into something else. How treacherous does this enemy appear, who changes so it is impossible even to recognize him!

Yet hate must have a target. There can be no faith in sin without an enemy. Who that believes in sin would dare believe he has no enemy? Could he admit that no-one made him powerless? Reason would surely bid him seek no longer what is not there to find. Yet first he must be willing to perceive a world where it is not. It is not necessary that he understand how he can see it. Nor should he try. For if he focuses on what he cannot understand, he will but emphasize his helplessness, and let sin tell him that his enemy must be himself. But let him only ask himself these questions, which he must decide to have it done for him:

"Do I desire a world I rule instead of one which rules me?"
"Do I desire a world where I am powerful instead of helpless?"
"Do I desire a world in which I have no enemies and cannot sin?"
"And do I want to see what I denied because it is the truth?"

You have already answered the first three questions, but not yet the last. For this one still seems fearful, and unlike the others. Yet reason would assure you they are all the same. We said this year would emphasize the sameness of things that are the same. This final question, which is indeed the last you need decide, still seems to hold a threat the rest have lost for you. And this imagined difference attests to your belief that truth may be the enemy you yet may find. Here, then, would seem to be the last remaining hope of finding sin, and not accepting power.

Forget not that the choice of truth or sin, power or helplessness, is the choice of whether to attack or heal. For healing comes of power, and attack of helplessness. Whom you attack you cannot want to heal. And whom you would have healed must be the one you chose to be protected from attack. And what is this decision but the choice whether to see him through the body's eyes, or let him be revealed to you through vision? How this decision leads to its effects is not your problem. But what you want to see must be your choice. This is a course in cause, and not effect.

Consider carefully your answer to the last question you have left unanswered still. And let your reason tell you that it must be answered and is answered in the other three. And then it will be clear to you that, as you look on the effects of sin in any form, all you need do is simply ask yourself,

"Is this what I would see? Do I want this?"

This is your one decision; this the condition for what occurs. It is irrelevant to how it happens, but not to why. You have control of this. And if you choose to see a world without an enemy, in which you are not helpless, the means to see it will be given you. Why is the final question so important? Reason will tell you why. It is the same as are the other three except in time. The others are decisions which can be made and then unmade and made again. But truth is constant, and implies a state where vacillations are impossible. You can desire a world you rule which rules you not and change your mind. You can desire to exchange your helplessness for power and lose this same desire as a little glint of sin attracts you. And you can want to see a sinless world and let an "enemy" tempt you to use the body's eyes and change what you desire.

In content all the questions are the same. For each one asks if you are willing to exchange the world of sin for what the Holy Spirit sees, since it is this the world of sin denies. And therefore those who look on sin are seeing the denial of the real world. Yet the last question adds the wish for constancy in your desire to see the real world, so the desire becomes the only one you have. By answering the final question "yes," you add sincerity to the decisions you have already made to all the rest. For only then have you renounced the option to change your mind again. When it is this you do not want, the rest are wholly answered.

Why do you think you are unsure the others have been answered? Could it be necessary they be asked so often, if they had? Until the last decision has been made, the answer is both "yes" and "no." For you have answered "yes" without perceiving that "yes" must mean "not no." No-one decides against his happiness, but he may do so if he does not see he does it. And if he sees his happiness as ever changing, now this, now that, and now an elusive shadow attached to nothing, he does decide against it.

Elusive happiness, or happiness in changing form that shifts with time and place, is an illusion which has no meaning. Happiness must be constant, because it is attained by giving up the wish for the inconstant. Joy cannot be perceived except through constant vision. And constant vision can be given only those who wish for constancy. The power of the Son of God's desire remains the proof that he is wrong who sees himself as helpless. Desire what you will, and you will look on it and think it real. No thought but has the power to release or kill. And none can leave the thinker's mind or leave him unaffected.

Are thoughts, then, dangerous? To bodies, yes! The thoughts that seem to kill are those which teach the thinker that he can be killed. And so he dies because of what he learned. He goes from life to death, the final proof he valued the inconstant more than constancy. Surely he thought he wanted happiness. Yet he did not desire it because it was the truth and therefore must be constant.

The constancy of joy is a condition quite alien to your understanding. Yet if you could even imagine what it must be, you would desire it, although you understand it not. The constancy of happiness has no exceptions; no change of any kind. It is unshakable as is the Love of God for His creation. Sure in its vision as its Creator is in what He knows, it looks on everything and sees it is the same. It sees not the ephemeral, for it desires that everything be like itself and sees it so. Nothing has power to confound its constancy because its own desire cannot be shaken.

It comes as surely unto those who see the final question is necessary to the rest, as peace must come to those who choose to heal and not to judge.
Reason will tell you that you cannot ask for happiness inconstantly.

For if what you desire you receive, and happiness is constant, then you need ask for it but once to have it always. And if you do not have it always, being what it is, you did not ask for it. For no-one fails to ask for his desire of something he believes holds out some promise of the power of giving it. He may be wrong in what he asks, where, and of what. Yet he will ask because desire is a request, an asking for, and made by one whom God Himself will never fail to answer. God has already given him all that he really wants. Yet what he is uncertain of, God cannot give. For he does not desire it while he remains uncertain, and God's giving must be incomplete unless it is received.

You who complete God's Will and are His happiness, whose will is powerful as His, a power that is not lost in your illusions, think carefully why it should be you have not yet decided how you would answer the final question. Your answer to the others has made it possible to help you be but partially insane. And yet it is the final one that really asks if you are willing to be wholly sane.

What is the holy instant but God's appeal to you to recognize what He has given you? Here is the great appeal to reason; the awareness of what is always there to see, the happiness that could be always yours. Here is the constant peace you could experience forever. Here is what denial has denied revealed to you. For here the final question is already answered, and what you ask for given. Here is the future now, for time is powerless because of your desire for what will never change. For you have asked that nothing stand between the holiness of your relationship and your awareness of its holiness.

Take pity on yourselves, so long enslaved. Rejoice whom God hath joined have come together and need no longer look on sin apart. No two can look on sin together, for they could never see it in the same place and time. Sin is a strictly individual perception, seen in the other, yet believed by each to be within himself. And each one seems to make a different error, and one the other cannot understand. Brothers, it is the same, made by the same, and forgiven for its maker in the same way.

The holiness of your relationship forgives you both, undoing the effects of what you both believed and saw. And with their going is the need for sin gone with them. Who has need for sin? Only the lonely and alone, who see their brothers different from themselves. It is this difference, seen but not real, that makes the need for sin, not real but seen, seem justified. And all this would be real, if sin were so. For an unholy relationship is based on differences, where each one thinks the other has what he has not. They come together, each to complete himself and rob the other. They stay until they think there's nothing left to steal, and then move on. And so they wander through a world of strangers, unlike themselves, living with their bodies perhaps under a common roof that shelters neither; in the same room and yet a world apart.

A holy relationship starts from a different premise. Each one has looked within and seen no lack. Accepting his completion, he would extend it by joining with another, whole as himself. He sees no difference between these selves, for differences are only of the body. Therefore, he looks on nothing he would take. He denies not his own reality because it is the truth. Just under Heaven does he stand, but close enough not to return to earth. For this relationship has Heaven's holiness. How far from home can a relationship so like to Heaven be?

Think what a holy relationship can teach! Here is belief in differences undone. Here is the faith in differences shifted to sameness. And reason now can lead you to the logical conclusion of your union. It must extend, as you extended when you joined. It must reach out beyond itself, as you reached out beyond the body to let yourselves be joined. And now the sameness which you saw extends, and finally removes all sense of differences, so that the sameness that lies beneath them all becomes apparent. Here is the golden circle where you recognize the Son of God. For what is born into a holy relationship can never end.

Let reason take another step. If you attack whom God would heal and hate the one He loves, then you and your Creator have a different will. Yet if you are His Will, what you must then believe is that you are not yourself. You can indeed believe this, and you do. And you have faith in this and see much evidence on its behalf. And where, you wonder, does your strange uneasiness, your sense of being disconnected, and your haunting fear of lack of meaning in yourself arise? It is as though you wandered in without a plan of any kind except to wander off, for only that seems certain.

Yet we have heard a very similar description earlier, but it was not of you. And yet this strange idea which it does accurately describe, you think is you. Reason would tell you that the world you see through eyes which are not yours must make no sense to you.

To whom would vision such as this send back its messages? Surely not you, whose sight is wholly independent of the eyes which look upon the world. If this is not your vision, what can it show to you? The brain cannot interpret what your vision sees. This you would understand. The brain interprets to the body, of which it is a part. But what it says you cannot understand. Yet you have listened to it. And long and hard you tried to understand its messages. You did not realize it is impossible to understand what fails entirely to reach you.

You have received no messages at all you understand. For you have listened to what can never communicate at all. Think, then, what happened. Denying what you are and firm in faith that you are something else, this "something else" which you have made to be yourself became your sight. Yet it must be the "something else" which sees, and as not you, explains its sight to you. Your vision would, of course, render this quite unnecessary. Yet if your eyes are closed and you have called upon this thing to lead you, asking it to explain to you the world it sees, you have no reason not to listen, nor to suspect that what it tells you is not true. Reason would tell you it cannot be true because you do not understand it. God has no secrets. He does not lead you through a world of misery, waiting to tell you, at the journey's end, why He did this to you.

What could be secret from God's Will? Yet you believe that you have secrets. What could your secrets be except another will that is your own, apart from His? Reason would tell you that this is no secret that need be hidden as a sin. But a mistake indeed! Let not your fear of sin protect it from correction, for the attraction of guilt is only fear. Here is the one emotion that you made, whatever it may seem to be. This is the emotion of secrecy, of private thoughts, and of the body. This is the one emotion that opposes love, and always leads to sight of differences and loss of sameness. Here is the one emotion that keeps you blind, dependent on the self you think you made to lead you through the world it made for you.

Your sight was given you, along with everything that you can understand. You will perceive no difficulty in understanding what this vision tells you, for everyone sees only what he thinks he is. And what your sight would show you, you will understand because it is the truth. Only your vision can convey to you what you can see. It reaches you directly, without a need to be interpreted to you. What needs interpretation must be alien. Nor will it ever be made understandable by an interpreter you cannot understand.

Of all the messages you have received and failed to understand, this course alone is open to your understanding and can be understood. This is your language. You do not understand it yet only because your whole communication is like a baby's. The sounds a baby makes and what he hears are highly unreliable, meaning different things to him at different times. Neither the sounds he hears nor sights he sees are stable yet. But what he hears and does not understand will be his native tongue, through which he will communicate with those around him, and they with him. And the strange, shifting ones he sees about him will become to him his comforters, and he will recognize his home, and see them there with him.

So in each holy relationship is the ability to communicate instead of separate reborn. Yet a holy relationship, so recently reborn itself from an unholy relationship and yet more ancient than the old illusion that it has replaced, is like a baby now in its rebirth. Yet in this infant is your vision returned to you, and he will speak the language both of you can understand. He is not nurtured by the "something else" you thought was you. He was not given there, nor was received by anything except yourself. For no two people can unite except through Christ, Whose vision sees them one.

Think what is given you, my holy brothers. This child will teach you what you do not understand, and make it plain. For his will be no alien tongue. He will need no interpreter to you, for it was you who taught him what he knows because you knew it. He could not come to anyone but you, never to "something else." Where Christ has entered no-one is alone, for never could He find a home in separate ones. Yet must He be reborn into His ancient home, so seeming new and yet as old as He, a tiny newcomer, dependent on the holiness of your relationship to let Him live.

Be certain God did not entrust His Son to the unworthy. Nothing but what is part of Him is worthy of being joined. Nor is it possible that anything not part of Him can join. Communication must have been restored to those that join, for this they could not do through bodies. What, then, has joined them? Reason will tell you that they must have seen each other through a vision not of the body and communicated in a language the body does not speak. Nor could it be a fearful sight or sound that drew them gently into one. Rather, in each the other saw a perfect shelter where his Self could be reborn in safety and in peace. Such did his reason tell him; such he believed because it was the truth.

Here is the first direct perception that you have made. You made it through awareness older than perception and yet reborn in just an instant. For what is time to what was always so? Think what that instant brought; the recognition that the "something else" you thought was you is an illusion. And truth came instantly to show you where your Self must be. It is denial of illusions that calls on truth, for to deny illusions is to recognize that fear is meaningless. Into the holy home where fear is powerless love enters thankfully, grateful that it is one with you who joined to let it enter.

Christ comes to what is like Himself; the same, not different. For He is always drawn unto Himself. What is as like Him as a holy relationship? And what draws you together draws Him to you. Here are His sweetness and His gentle innocence protected from attack. And here can He return in confidence, for faith in one another is always faith in Him. You are indeed correct in looking on each other as His chosen home, for here you will with Him and with His Father. This is your Father's Will for you, and yours with His. And who is drawn to Christ is drawn to God as surely as both are drawn to every holy relationship, the home prepared for them as earth is turned to Heaven.

The opposite of illusions is not disillusionment, but truth. Only to the ego, to which truth is meaningless, do they appear to be the only alternatives and different from each other. In truth they are the same. Both bring the same amount of misery, though each one seems to be the way to lose the misery the other brings. Every illusion carries pain and suffering in the dark folds of the heavy garments with which it hides its nothingness. Yet in these dark and heavy garments are those who seek illusions covered and hidden from the joy of truth.

Truth is the opposite of illusions because it offers joy. What else but joy could be the opposite of misery? To leave one kind of misery and seek another is hardly an escape. To change illusions is to make no change. The search for joy in misery is senseless, for how could joy be found in misery? All that is possible in the dark world of misery is to select some aspects out of it, see them as different, and define the difference as joy. Yet to perceive a difference where none exists will surely fail to make a difference.

Illusions carry only guilt and suffering, sickness and death, to their believers. The form in which they are accepted is irrelevant. No form of misery, in reason's eyes, can be confused with joy. Joy is eternal.

You can be sure indeed that any seeming happiness that does not last is really fear. Joy does not turn to sorrow, for the eternal cannot change. But sorrow can be turned to joy, for time gives way to the eternal. Only the timeless must remain unchanged, but everything in time can change with time. Yet if the change be real and not imagined, illusions must give way to truth, and not to other dreams that are but equally unreal. This is no difference.

Reason will tell you that the only way to escape from misery is to recognize it and go the other way. Truth is the same and misery the same, but they are different from each other in every way, in every instance, and without exception. To believe that one exception can exist is to confuse what is the same with what is different. One illusion cherished and defended against the truth makes all truth meaningless, and all illusions real. Such is the power of belief. It cannot compromise. And faith in innocence is faith in sin if the belief excludes one living thing, and holds it out, apart from its forgiveness.

Both reason and the ego will tell you this, but what they make of it is not the same. The ego will assure you now that it is impossible for you to see no guilt in anyone. And if this vision is the only means by which escape from guilt can be attained, then the belief in sin must be eternal. Yet reason looks on this another way, for reason sees the source of an idea as what will make it true or false. This must be so, if the idea is like its source. Therefore, says reason, if escape from guilt was given to the Holy Spirit as His purpose, and by One to Whom nothing He wills can be impossible, the means for its attainment are more than possible. They must be there, and you must have them.

This is a crucial period in this course, for here the separation of you and the ego must be made complete. For if you have the means to let the Holy Spirit's purpose be accomplished, they can be used. And through their use will you gain faith in them. Yet to the ego this must be impossible and no-one undertakes to do what holds no hope of ever being done. You know what your Creator wills is possible, but what you made believes it is not so. Now must you choose between yourself and an illusion of yourself. Not both, but one. There is no point in trying to avoid this one decision. It must be made. Faith and belief can fall to either side, but reason tells you that misery lies only on one side and joy upon the other.

Forsake not now each other. For you who are the same will not decide alone nor differently. Either you give each other life or death; either you are each other's Saviour or his judge, offering him sanctuary or condemnation. This course will be believed entirely or not at all. For it is wholly true or wholly false and cannot be but partially believed. And you will either escape from misery entirely or not at all. Reason will tell you that there is no middle ground where you can pause uncertainly, waiting to choose between the joy of Heaven and the misery of hell. Until you choose Heaven, you are in hell and misery.

There is no part of Heaven you can take and weave into illusions. Nor is there one illusion you can enter Heaven with. A Saviour cannot be a judge, nor mercy condemnation. And vision cannot damn, but only bless. Whose function is to save, will save. how He will do it is beyond your understanding, but when must be your choice. For time you made, and time you can command. You are no more a slave to time than to the world you made.

Let us look closer at the whole illusion that what you made has power to enslave its maker. This is the same belief that caused the separation. It is the meaningless idea that thoughts can leave the thinker's mind, be different from it and in opposition to it. If this were true, thoughts would not be the mind's extensions, but its enemies. And here we see again another form of the same fundamental illusion we have seen many times before. Only if it were possible the Son of God could leave his Father's Mind, make himself different, and oppose His Will, would it be possible that the self he made and all it made, should be his master.

Behold the great projection but look on it with the decision that it must be healed, and not with fear. Nothing you made has any power over you unless you still would be apart from your Creator, and with a will opposed to His. For only if you would believe His Son could be His enemy does it seem possible that what you made is yours. You would condemn His joy to misery and make Him different. And all the misery you made has been your own. Are you not glad to learn it is not true? Is it not welcome news to hear not one of the illusions that you made replaced the truth?

Only your thoughts have been impossible. Salvation cannot be. It IS impossible to look upon your Saviour as your enemy and recognize him. Yet it is possible to recognize him for what he is, if God would have it so. What God has given to your holy relationship is there. For what He gave the Holy Spirit to give to you he gave. Would you not look upon the Saviour that has been given you? And would you not exchange, in gratitude, the function of an executioner you gave him for the one he has in truth? Receive of him what God has given him for you, not what you tried to give yourself.

Beyond the bodies that you interposed between you and shining in the golden light which reaches it from the bright, endless circle that extends forever, is your holy relationship, beloved of God Himself. How still it rests, in time and yet beyond, immortal yet on earth. How great the power that lies in it? Time waits upon its will, and earth will be as it would have it be. Here is no separate will, nor the desire that anything be separate. Its will has no exceptions, and what it wills is true. Every illusion brought to its forgiveness is gently overlooked and disappears. For at its centre Christ has been reborn, to light His home with vision that overlooks the world. Would you not have this holy home be yours as well? No misery is here, but only joy.

All you need do to dwell in quiet here with Christ is share His vision. Quickly and gladly is His vision given to anyone who is but willing to see his brother sinless. And no-one can remain beyond this willingness, if you would be released entirely from all effects of sin. Would you have partial forgiveness for yourself? Can you reach Heaven while a single sin still tempts you to remain in misery? Heaven is the home of perfect purity, and God created it for you. Look on your holy brother, sinless as yourself and let him lead you there.

The introduction of reason into the ego's thought system is the beginning of its undoing. For reason and the ego are contradictory. Nor is it possible for them to co-exist in your awareness. And reason's goal is to make plain and therefore obvious. You can see reason. This is not a play on words, for here is the beginning of a vision that has meaning. Vision is sense, quite literally. If it is not the body's sight, it must be understood. For it is plain, and what is obvious is not ambiguous. It can be understood. And here do reason and the ego separate, to go their different ways.

The ego's whole continuance depends on its belief you cannot learn this course. Share this belief, and reason will be unable to see your errors and make way for their correction. For reason sees through errors, telling you what you thought was real is not. Reason can see the difference between sin and mistakes because it wants correction. Therefore, it tells you what you thought was uncorrectable can be corrected, and thus it must have been an error. The ego's opposition to correction leads to its fixed belief in sin, and disregard of errors. It looks on nothing that can be corrected. Thus does the ego damn and reason save.

Reason is not salvation in itself, but it makes way for peace and brings you to a state of mind in which salvation can be given you. Sin is a block, set like a heavy gate, locked and without a key, across the road to peace. No-one who looks on it without the help of reason would try to pass it. The body's eyes behold it as solid granite, so thick it would be madness to attempt to pass it. Yet reason sees through it easily because it is an error. The form it takes cannot conceal its emptiness from reason's eyes.

Only the form of error attracts the ego. Meaning it does not recognize and does not know if it is there or not. Everything which the body's eyes can see is a mistake an error in perception, a distorted fragment of the whole, without the meaning that the whole would give. And yet mistakes, regardless of their form, can be corrected. Sin is but error in a special form the ego venerates. It would preserve all errors and make them sins. For here is its own stability, its heavy anchor in the shifting world it made; the rock on which its church is built, and where its worshippers are bound to bodies, and believe the body's freedom is their own.

Reason will tell you that the form of error is not what makes it a mistake. If what the form conceals is a mistake, the form cannot prevent correction. The body's eyes see only form. They cannot see beyond what they were made to see. And they were made to look on error, and not see past it. Theirs is indeed a strange perception, for they can see only illusions, unable to look beyond the granite block of sin, and stopping at the outside form of nothing. To this distorted form of vision, the outside of everything, the wall that stands between you and the truth, is wholly true. Yet how can sight which stops at nothingness, as if it were a solid wall, see truly? It is held back by form, having been made to guarantee that nothing else but form will be perceived.

These eyes, made not to see, will never see. For the idea they represent left not its maker, and it is their maker that sees through them. What was its maker's goal but not to see? For this the body's eyes are perfect means, but not for seeing. See how the body's eyes rest on externals and cannot go beyond. Watch how they stop at nothingness, unable to go beyond the form to meaning. Nothing so blinding as perception of form. For sight of form means understanding has been obscured.

Only mistakes have different forms, and so they can deceive. You can change form because it is not true. It could not be reality because it can be changed. Reason will tell you that if form is not reality, it must be an illusion, and is not there to see. And if you see it you must be mistaken, for you are seeing what cannot be real as if it were. What cannot see beyond what is not there must be distorted perception, and must perceive illusions as the truth. Could it, then, recognise the truth?

Let not the form of his mistakes keep you from him whose holiness is yours. Let not the vision of his holiness, the sight of which would show you your forgiveness, be kept from you by what the body's eyes can see. Let your awareness of your brother not be blocked by your perception of his sins, and of his body. What is there in him that you would attack except what you associate with his body, which you believe can sin? Beyond his errors is His holiness and your salvation. You gave him not his holiness but tried to see your sins in him to save yourself. And yet, his holiness is your forgiveness. Can you be saved by making sinful the one whose holiness is your salvation?

A holy relationship, however newly born, must value holiness above all else. Unholy values will produce confusion, and in awareness. In an unholy relationship, each one is valued because he seems to justify the other's sin. He sees within the other what impels him to sin against his will. And thus he lays his sins upon the other, and is attracted to him to perpetuate his sins. And so it must become impossible for each to see himself as causing sin by his desire to have sin real. Yet reason sees a holy relationship as what it is; a common state of mind, where both give errors gladly to correction that both may happily be healed as one.

When you come to the place where the branch in the road is quite apparent, you cannot go ahead. You must go either one way or the other. For now if you go straight ahead, the way you went before you reached the branch, you will go nowhere. The whole purpose of coming this far was to decide which branch you will take now. The way you came no longer matters. It can no longer serve. No-one who reaches this far can make the wrong decision, but he can delay. And there is no part of the journey that seems more hopeless and futile than standing where the road branches, and not deciding on which way to go.

It is but the first few steps along the right way that seem hard, for you have chosen, although you still may think you can go back and make the other choice. This is not so. A choice made with the power of Heaven to uphold it cannot be undone. Your way is decided. There will be nothing you will not be told, if you acknowledge this.

And so you stand, here in this holy place, before the veil of sin that hangs between you and the face of Christ. Let it be lifted! Raise it together, for it is but a veil that stands between you. Either alone will see it as a solid block, nor realize how thin the drapery that separates you now. Yet it is almost over in your awareness, and peace has reached you even here, before the veil. Think what will happen after! The love of Christ will light your faces, and shine from them into a darkened world that needs the light. And from this holy place He will return with you, not leaving it nor you. You will become His messengers, returning Him unto Himself.

Think of the loveliness that you will see, who walk with Him! And think how beautiful will each of you look to the other! How happy you will be to be together, after such a long and lonely journey where you walked alone. The gates of Heaven, open now for you, will you now open to the sorrowful. And none who looks upon the Christ in you but will rejoice.

How beautiful the sight you saw beyond the veil, which you will bring to light the tired eyes of those as weary now as once you were. How thankful will they be to see you come among them, offering Christ's forgiveness to dispel their faith in sin.

Every mistake you make the other will gently have corrected for you, for in his sight your loveliness is his salvation, which he would protect from harm. And each will be the other's strong protector from everything that seems to rise between you. So shall you walk the world with me, whose message has not yet been given to everyone. For you are here to let it be received. God's offer still is open, yet it waits acceptance. From you who have accepted it is it received. Into your joined hands is it safely given, for you who share it have become its willing guardians and protectors.

To all who share the Love of God the grace is given to be the givers of what they have received. And so they learn that it is theirs forever. All barriers disappear before their coming, as every obstacle was finally surmounted which seemed to rise and block their way before. This veil you lift together opens the way to truth to more than you. Those who would let illusions be lifted from their minds are this world's Saviours, walking the world with their Redeemer, and carrying His message of hope and freedom and release from suffering to everyone who needs a miracle to save him.

How easy is it to offer this miracle to everyone! No-one who has received it for himself could find it difficult. For by receiving it, he learned it was not given him alone. Such is the function of a holy relationship; to receive together and give as you received. Standing before the veil, it still seems difficult. But hold out your joined hands and touch this heavy-seeming block, and you will learn how easily your fingers slip through its nothingness. It is no solid wall. And only an illusion stands between you and the holy Self you share.

How does one overcome illusions? Surely not by force or anger, nor by opposing them in any way. Merely by letting reason tell you that they contradict reality. They go against what must be true. The opposition comes from them, and not reality. Reality opposes nothing. What merely is needs no defence and offers none. Only illusions need defence because of weakness. And how can it be difficult to walk the way of truth, when only weakness interferes?

You are the strong ones in this seeming conflict. And you need no defence. Everything that needs defence you do not want, for anything that needs defence will weaken you. Consider what the ego wants defences for. Always to justify what goes against the truth, flies in the face of reason and makes no sense. Can this be justified? What can this be except an invitation to insanity, to save you from the truth? And what would you be saved from but what you fear? Belief in sin needs great defence, and at enormous cost.

All that the Holy Spirit offers must be defended against and sacrificed. For sin is carved into a block out of your peace and laid between you and its return. Yet how can peace be so fragmented? It is still whole and nothing has been taken from it.

See how the means and the material of evil dreams are nothing. In truth you stand together, with nothing in between. God holds your hands and what can separate whom He has joined as one with Him? It is your Father Whom you would defend against. Yet it remains impossible to keep love out. God rests with you in quiet, undefended and wholly undefending, for in this quiet state alone is strength and power. Here can no weakness enter, for here is no attack, and therefore no illusions. Love rests in certainty. Only uncertainty can be defensive. And all uncertainty is doubt about yourself.

How weak is fear; how little and how meaningless! How insignificant before the quiet strength of those whom love has joined! This is your "enemy," – a frightened mouse that would attack the universe. How likely is it that it will succeed? Can it be difficult to disregard its feeble squeaks that tell of its omnipotence, and would drown out the hymn of praise to its Creator which every heart throughout the universe forever sings as one? Which is the stronger? Is it this tiny mouse or everything that God created? You are not joined together by this mouse, but by the Will of God. And can a mouse betray whom God has joined?

If you but recognized how little stands between you and your awareness of your union! Be not deceived by the illusions it presents of size and thickness, weight, solidity and firmness of foundation. Yes, to the body's eyes it looks like an enormous solid body, immovable as is a mountain. Yet within you there is a Force which no illusions can resist. This body only seems to be immovable; this Force is irresistible in truth. What, then, must happen when they come together? Can the illusion of immovability be long defended from what is quietly passed through and gone beyond?

Forget not, when you feel the need arise to be defensive about anything, you have identified yourself with an illusion. And therefore feel that you are weak because you are alone. This is the cost of all illusions. Not one but rests on the belief that you are separate. Not one that does not seem to stand, heavy and solid and immovable, between you and your brother. And not one that truth cannot pass over lightly, and so easily that you must be convinced, in spite of what you thought it was, that it is nothing. If you forgive each other, this must happen. For it is your unwillingness to overlook what seems to stand between you that makes it look impenetrable and defends the illusion of its immovability.

Do you want freedom of the body or of the mind? For both you cannot have. Which do you value? Which is your goal? For one you see as means; the other, end. And one must serve the other and lead to its predominance, increasing its importance by diminishing its own. Means serve the end, and as the end is reached the value of the means decreases, eclipsed entirely when they are recognized as functionless. No-one but yearns for freedom and tries to find it. Yet he will seek for it where he believes it is, and can be found. He will believe it possible of mind or body and he will make the other serve his choice as means to find it.

Where freedom of the body has been chosen, the mind is used as means whose value lies in its ability to contrive ways to achieve the body's freedom. Yet freedom of the body has no meaning and so the mind is dedicated to serve illusions. This is a situation so contradictory and so impossible that anyone who chooses this has no idea of what is valuable. Yet even in this confusion, so profound it cannot be described, the Holy Spirit waits in gentle patience, as certain of the outcome as He is sure of His Creator's Love. He knows this mad decision was made by one as dear to His Creator as love is to itself.

Be not disturbed at all to think how He can change the role of means and end so easily in what God loves and would have free forever. But be you rather grateful that you can be the means to serve His end. This is the only service which leads to freedom. To serve this end, the body must be perceived as sinless, because the goal is sinlessness. The lack of contradiction makes the soft transition from means to end as easy as is the shift from hate to gratitude before forgiving eyes. You will be sanctified by one another, using your bodies only to serve the sinless. And it will be impossible for you to hate what serves what you would heal.

This holy relationship, lovely in its innocence, mighty in strength, and blazing with a light far brighter than the sun which lights the sky you see, is chosen of your Father as a means for His Own plan. Be thankful that it serves yours not at all. Nothing entrusted to it can be misused and nothing given it but will be used. This holy relationship has the power to heal all pain, regardless of its form. Neither of you alone can serve at all. Only in your joint will does healing lie. For here your healing is and here will you accept Atonement. And in your healing is the Sonship healed because your wills are joined.

Before a holy relationship there is no sin. The form of error is no longer seen, and reason, joined with love, looks quietly on all confusion, observing merely, "This was a mistake." And then the same Atonement you accepted in your relationship corrects the error and lays a part of Heaven in its place. How blessed are you who let this gift be given! Each part of Heaven that you bring is given you. And every empty place in Heaven that you fill again with the Eternal Light you bring shines now on you. The means of sinlessness can know no fear because they carry only love with them.

Children of peace, the light has come to you. The light you bring you do not recognize, and yet you will remember. Who can deny himself the vision that he brings to others? And who would fail to recognize a gift he let be laid in Heaven through himself? The gentle service that you give the Holy Spirit is service to yourself. You who are now His means must love all that He loves. And what you bring is your remembrance of everything that is eternal. No trace of anything in time can long remain in minds that serve the timeless. And no illusion can disturb the peace of a relationship which has become the means of peace.

When you have looked upon each other with complete forgiveness, from which no error is excluded and nothing kept hidden, what mistake can there be anywhere you cannot overlook? What form of suffering could block your sight, preventing you from seeing past it? And what illusion could there be you will not recognize as a mistake; a shadow through which you walk completely undismayed? God would let nothing interfere with those whose wills are His and serve it willingly. And could remembrance of what they are be long delayed?

You will see your value through each other's eyes, and each one is released as he beholds his Saviour in place of the attacker who he thought was there. Through this releasing is the world released. This is your part in bringing peace. For you have asked what is your function here, and have been answered. Seek not to change it, nor to substitute another goal. Accept this one and serve it willingly, for what the Holy Spirit does with the gifts you give each other, to whom He offers them, and where and when, is up to Him. He will bestow them where they are received and welcomed. He will use every one of them for peace. Nor will one little smile or willingness to overlook the tiniest mistake be lost to anyone.

What can it be but universal blessing to look on what your Father loves with charity? Extension of forgiveness is the Holy Spirit's function. Leave this to Him. Let your concern be only that you give to Him that which can be extended. Save no dark secrets that He cannot use but offer Him the tiny gifts He can extend forever. He will take each one and make of it a potent force for peace. He will withhold no blessing from it or limit it in any way. He will join to it all the power that God has given Him, to make each little gift of love a source of healing for everyone. Each little gift you offer to the other lights up the world. Be not concerned with darkness; look away from it, and toward each other. And let the darkness be dispelled by Him Who knows the light and lays it gently in each quiet smile of faith and confidence with which you bless each other.

On your learning depends the welfare of the world. And it is only arrogance that would deny the power of your will. Think you the Will of God is powerless? Is this humility? You do not see what this belief has done. You see yourself as vulnerable, frail and easily destroyed, and at the mercy of countless attackers more powerful than you. Let us look straight at how this error came about, for here lies buried the heavy anchor that seems to keep the fear of God in place, unmovable and solid as a rock. While this remains, so will it seem to be.

Who can attack the Son of God and not attack his Father? How can God's Son be weak and frail and easily destroyed unless his Father is? You do not see that every sin and every condemnation which you perceive and justify is an attack upon your Father. And that is why it has not happened, nor could be real. You do not see that this is your attempt because you think the Father and the Son are separate. And you must think that they are separate, because of fear. For it seems safer to attack another or yourself than to attack the great Creator of the universe, Whose power you know.

If you were one with God and recognised this oneness, you would know His power is yours. But you will not remember this while you believe attack of any kind means anything. It is unjustified in any form because it has no meaning. The only way it could be justified is if each one of you were separate from the other, and all were separate from your Creator. For only then would it be possible to attack a part of the creation without the whole, the Son without the Father; and to attack another without yourself or hurt yourself without the other feeling pain. And this belief you want. Yet wherein lies its value except in the desire to attack in safety? Attack is neither safe nor dangerous. It is impossible. And this is so because the universe is one. You would not choose attack on its reality if it were not essential to attack to see it separated from its maker. And thus it seems as if love could attack, and become fearful.

Only the different can attack. So you conclude because you can attack you must be different. Yet does the Holy Spirit explain this differently. Because you are not different, you cannot attack. Either position is a logical conclusion, if only the different can attack. Either could be maintained, but never both. The only question to be answered to decide which must be true is whether you are different. From the position of what you understand, you seem to be, and therefore can attack. Of the alternatives, this seems more natural and more in line with your experience. And therefore it is necessary that you have other experiences, more in line with truth, to teach you what is natural and true.

This is the function of your holy relationship. For what one thinks the other will experience with him. What can this mean except your minds are one? Look not with fear upon this happy fact and think not that it lays a heavy burden on you. For when you have accepted it with gladness, you will realize that your relationship is a reflection of the union of the Creator and His Son. From loving minds there is no separation. And every thought in one brings gladness to the other because they are the same. Joy is unlimited because each shining thought of love extends its being and creates more of itself. There is no difference anywhere in it, for every thought is like itself.

The light that joins you shines throughout the universe, and because it joins you, so it makes you one with your Creator. And in Him is all creation joined. Would you regret you cannot fear alone, when your relationship can also teach the power of love is there, which makes all fear impossible? Do not attempt to keep a little of the ego with this gift. For it was given you to be used, and not obscured. What teaches you, you cannot separate denies the ego.

Let truth decide if you be different or the same and teach you which is true.

Do you not see the opposite of frailty and weakness is sinlessness? Innocence is strength, and nothing else is strong. The sinless cannot fear, for sin of any kind is weakness. The show of strength attack would use to cover frailty conceals it not, for how can the unreal be hidden? No-one is strong who has an enemy, and no-one can attack unless he thinks he has. Belief in enemies is therefore the belief in weakness, and what is weak is not the Will of God. Being opposed to It, it is Its "enemy." And God is feared as an opposing will.

How strange indeed becomes this war against yourself! You will believe that everything you use for sin can hurt you and become your enemy. And you will fight against it and try to weaken it because of this; and you will think that you succeeded, and attack again. It is as certain you will fear what you attack as it is sure that you will love what you perceive as sinless. He walks in peace who travels sinlessly along the way love shows him. For love walks with him there, protecting him from fear. And he will see only the sinless, who cannot attack.

Walk you in glory, with your head held high, and fear no evil. The innocent are safe because they share their innocence. Nothing they see is harmful, for their awareness of the truth releases everything from the illusion of harmfulness. And what seemed harmful now stands shining in their innocence, released from sin and fear, and happily returned to love. They share the strength of love because they looked on innocence. And every error disappeared because they saw it not. Who looks for glory finds it where it is. Where could it be but in the innocent?

Let not the little interferers pull you to littleness. There can be no attraction of guilt in innocence. Think what a happy world you walk, with truth beside you! Do not give up this world of freedom for a little sigh of seeming sin, nor for a tiny stirring of guilt's attraction. Would you, for all these meaningless distractions, lay Heaven aside? Your destiny and purpose are far beyond them, in the clean place where littleness does not exist. Your purpose is at variance with littleness of any kind. And so it is at variance with sin.

Let us not let littleness lead God's Son into temptation. His glory is beyond it, measureless and timeless as eternity. Do not let time intrude upon your sight of him. Leave him not frightened and alone in his temptation but help him rise above it and perceive the light of which he is a part. Your innocence will light the way to his, and so is yours protected, and kept in your awareness.

For who can know his glory, and perceive the little and the weak about him? Who can walk trembling in a fearful world, and realize that Heaven's glory shines on him?

Nothing around you but is part of you. Look on it lovingly and see the light of Heaven in it. So will you come to understand all that is given you. In kind forgiveness will the world sparkle and shine, and everything you once thought sinful now will be re-interpreted as part of Heaven. How beautiful it is to walk, clean and redeemed and happy, through a world in bitter need of the redemption that your innocence bestows upon it! What can you value more than this? For here is your salvation and your freedom. And it must be complete if you would recognize it.

The memory of God comes to the quiet mind. It cannot come where there is conflict, for a mind at war against itself remembers not eternal gentleness. The means of war are not the means of peace, and what the warlike would remember is not love. War is impossible unless belief in victory is cherished. Conflict within you must imply that you believe the ego has the power to be victorious. Why else would you identify with it? Surely you realize the ego is at war with God. Certain it is it has no enemy. Yet just as certain is its fixed belief it has an enemy that it must overcome and will succeed.

Do you not realize a war against yourself would be a war on God? Is victory conceivable? And if it were, is this a victory that you would want? The death of God, if it were possible, would be your death. Is this a victory? The ego always marches to defeat, because it thinks that triumph over you is possible. And God thinks otherwise. This is no war; only the mad belief the Will of God can be attacked and overthrown. You may identify with this belief, but never will it be more than madness. And fear will reign in madness and will seem to have replaced love there. This is the conflict's purpose. And to those who think that it is possible, the means seem real.

Be certain that it is impossible God and the ego or yourself and it, will ever meet. You seem to meet and make your strange alliances on grounds that have no meaning. For your beliefs converge upon the body, the ego's chosen home, which you believe is yours. You meet at a mistake; an error in your self-appraisal. The ego joins with an illusion of yourself you share with it. And yet illusions cannot join. They are the same, and they are nothing. Their joining lies in nothingness; two are as meaningless as one, or as a thousand. The ego joins with nothing, being nothing. The victory it seeks is meaningless as is itself.

Brothers, the war against yourself is almost over. The journey's end is at the place of peace. Would you not now accept the peace offered you here? This "enemy" you fought as an intruder on your peace is here transformed, before your sight, into the giver of your peace. Your "enemy" was God Himself, to Whom all conflict, triumph and attack of any kind are all unknown. He loves you perfectly, completely and eternally. The Son of God at war with his Creator is a condition as ridiculous as nature roaring at the wind in anger and proclaiming that it is part of itself no more.

Could nature possibly establish this and make it true? Nor is it up to you to say what shall be part of you and what is kept apart. The war against yourself was undertaken to teach the Son of God that he is not himself, and not his Father's Son. For this, the memory of his Father must be forgotten. It is forgotten in the body's life, and if you think you are a body, you will believe you have forgotten it. Yet truth can never be forgotten by itself and you have not forgotten what you are. Only a strange illusion of yourself, a wish to triumph over what you are, remembers not.

The war against yourself is but the battle of two illusions, struggling to make them different from each other, in the belief the one which conquers will be true. There is no conflict between them and the truth. Nor are they different from each other. Both are not true. And so it matters not what form they take. What made them is insane, and they remain part of what made them. Madness holds out no menace to reality and has no influence upon it. Illusions cannot triumph over truth, nor can they threaten it in any way. And the reality which they deny is not a part of them.

What you remember is a part of you. For you must be as God created you. Truth does not fight against illusions, nor do illusions fight against the truth. Illusions battle only with themselves. Being fragmented, they fragment. But truth is indivisible, and far beyond their little reach. You will remember what you know when you have learned you cannot be in conflict. One illusion about yourself can battle with another, yet the war of two illusions is a state where nothing happens. There is no victor and there is no victory. And truth stands radiant, apart from conflict, untouched and quiet in the peace of God.

Conflict must be between two forces. It cannot exist between one power and nothingness. There is nothing you could attack that is not part of you. And by attacking it, you make two illusions of yourself, in conflict with each other. And this occurs whenever you look on anything that God created with anything but love. Conflict is fearful, for it is the birth of fear. Yet what is born of nothing cannot win reality through battle. Why would you fill your world with conflicts with yourself? Let all this madness be undone for you, and turn in peace to the remembrance of God, still shining in your quiet mind.

See how the conflict of illusions disappears when it is brought to truth! For it seems real only as long as it is seen as war between conflicting truths, the conqueror to be the truer, the more real, and vanquisher of the illusion that was less real, made an illusion by defeat. Thus, conflict is the choice between illusions, one to be crowned as real, the other vanquished and despised. Here will the Father never be remembered. Yet no illusion can invade His home, and drive Him out of what He loves forever. And what He loves must be forever quiet and at peace because it is His home. And you who are beloved of Him are no illusions, being as true and holy as Himself.

The stillness of your certainty of Him and of yourself is home to both of you, who dwell as one and not apart. Open the door of His most holy home and let forgiveness sweep away all trace of the belief in sin that keeps God homeless and His Son with Him. You are not strangers in the house of God. Welcome your brother to the home where God has set him in serenity and peace, and dwells with him. Illusions have no place where love abides, protecting you from everything that is not true. You dwell in peace as limitless as its Creator, and everything is given those who would remember Him. Over His home the Holy Spirit watches, sure that its peace can never be disturbed.

How can the resting-place of God turn on itself, and seek to overcome the One Who dwells there? And think what happens when the house of God perceives itself divided. The altar disappears, the light grows dim, the temple of the Holy One becomes a house of sin. And nothing is remembered except illusions. Illusions can conflict because their forms are different. And they do battle only to establish which form is true.

Illusion meets illusion; truth, itself. The meeting of illusions leads to war. Peace, looking on itself, extends itself. War is the condition in which fear is born, and grows, and seeks to dominate. Peace is the state where love abides, and seeks to share itself.

Conflict and peace are opposites. Where one abides the other cannot be; where either goes the other disappears. So is the memory of God obscured in minds that have become illusion's battle ground. Yet far beyond this senseless war it shines, ready to be remembered when you side with peace.

The "laws" of chaos can be brought to light, though never understood. Chaotic laws are hardly meaningful, and therefore out of reason's sphere. Yet they appear to constitute an obstacle to reason and to truth. Let us, then, look upon them calmly, that we may look beyond them, understanding what they are, not what they would maintain. It is essential it be understood what they are for, because it is their purpose to make meaningless, and to attack the truth. Here are the laws that rule the world you made. And yet they govern nothing and need not be broken; merely looked upon and gone beyond.

The first chaotic law is that the truth is different for everyone. Like all these principles, this one maintains that each is separate, and has a different set of thoughts which set him off from others. This principle evolves from the belief there is a hierarchy of illusions; some are more valuable, and therefore true. Each one establishes this for himself and makes it true by his attack on what another values. And this is justified because the values differ, and those who hold them seem to be unlike, and therefore enemies.

Think how this seems to interfere with the first principle of miracles. For this establishes degrees of truth among illusions, making it appear that some of them are harder to overcome than others. If it were realized that they are all the same and equally untrue, it would be easy, then, to understand that miracles apply to all of them. Errors of any kind can be corrected because they are untrue. When brought to truth instead of to each other, they merely disappear. No part of nothing can be more resistant to the truth than can another.

The second law of chaos, dear indeed to every worshipper of sin, is that each one must sin, and therefore deserves attack and death. This principle, closely related to the first, is the demand that errors call for punishment, and not correction. For the destruction of the one who makes the error places him beyond correction, and beyond forgiveness. What he has done is thus interpreted as an irrevocable sentence upon himself, which God Himself is powerless to overcome. Sin cannot be remitted, being the belief, the Son of God can make mistakes for which his own destruction becomes inevitable.

Think what this seems to do to the relationship between the Father and the Son. Now it appears that they can never be one again. For one must always be condemned, and by the other. Now are they different, and enemies. And their relationship is one of opposition, just as the separate aspects of the Son meet only to conflict, but not to join. One becomes weak, the other strong by his defeat. And fear of God and of each other now appears as sensible, made real by what the Son of God has done both to himself and his Creator. The arrogance on which the laws of chaos stand could not be more apparent than emerges here.

Here is a principle which would define what the Creator of reality must be; what He must think and what He must believe; and how He must respond, believing it. It is not seen as even necessary that He be asked about the truth of what has been established for His belief. His Son can tell Him this and He has but the choice whether to take his word for it or be mistaken. This leads directly to the third preposterous belief that seems to make chaos eternal. For if God cannot be mistaken, then He must accept his Son's belief in what he is and hate him for it.

See how the fear of God is reinforced by this third principle. Now it becomes impossible to turn to Him for help in misery. For now He has become the "enemy" Who caused it, and to Whom appeal is useless. Nor can salvation lie within the Son, whose every aspect seems to be at war with Him and justified in its attack. And now is conflict made inevitable, and beyond the help of God. And now salvation must remain impossible, because the Saviour has become the enemy.

There can be no release and no escape. Atonement thus becomes a myth, and vengeance, not forgiveness, is the Will of God. From where all this begins, there is no sight of help that can succeed. Only destruction can be the outcome. And God Himself seems to be siding with it, to overcome His Son. Think not the ego will enable you to find escape from what it wants. That is the function of this course, which does not value what the ego cherishes.

The ego values only what it takes. This leads to the fourth law of chaos, which, if the others are accepted, must be true. This seeming law is the belief you have what you have taken. By this, another's loss becomes your gain, and thus it fails to recognize that you can never take away save from yourself. Yet all the other laws must lead to this. For enemies do not give willingly to one another, nor would they seek to share the things they value. And what your enemies would keep from you must be worth having, just because they keep it hidden from your sight.

All of the mechanisms of madness are seen emerging here: The "enemy," made strong by keeping hidden the valuable inheritance which should be yours; your justified position, and attack for what has been withheld; and the inevitable loss the enemy must suffer, to save yourself. Thus do the guilty ones protest their "innocence." Were they not forced into this foul attack by the unscrupulous behaviour of the enemy, they would respond with only kindness. But in a savage world the kind cannot survive, so they must take or else be taken from.

And now there is a vague unanswered question, not yet "explained." What is this precious thing, this priceless pearl, this hidden secret treasure, to be wrested in righteous wrath from this most treacherous and cunning enemy? It must be what you want but never found. And now you "understand" the reason why you found it not. For it was taken from you by this enemy and hidden where you would not think to look. He hid it in his body, making it the cover for his guilt, the hiding place for what belongs to you. Now must his body be destroyed and sacrificed, that you may have that which belongs to you. His treachery demands his death, that you may live. And you attack only in self-defence.

But what is it you want that needs his death? Can you be sure your murderous attack is justified unless you know what it is for? And here a final principle of chaos comes to the rescue. It holds there is a substitute for love. This is the "magic" that will cure all of your pain; the missing factor in your madness that makes it "sane." This is the reason why you must attack. Here is what makes your vengeance justified. Behold, unveiled, the ego's secret gift, torn from your brother's body, hidden there in malice and in hatred for the one to whom the gift belongs. He would deprive you of the secret ingredient which would give meaning to your life. The substitute for love, born of your enmity to one another, must be salvation. It has no substitute, and there is only one. And all your relationships have but the purpose of seizing it and making it your own.

Never is your possession made complete. And never will your brother cease his attack on you for what you stole. Nor will God end His vengeance upon both, for in His madness He must have this substitute for love and kill you both. You who believe you walk in sanity, with feet on solid ground, and through a world where meaning can be found, consider this: These are the principles which make the ground beneath your feet seem solid. And it is here you look for meaning. These are the laws you made for your salvation.

They hold in place the substitute for Heaven which you prefer. This is their purpose; they were made for this. There is no point in asking what they mean. That is apparent. The means of madness must be insane. Are you as certain that you realize the GOAL is madness?

No-one wants madness, nor does anyone cling to his madness if he sees that this is what it is. What protects madness is the belief that it is true. It is the function of insanity to take the place of truth. It must be seen as truth to be believed. And if it is the truth, then must its opposite, which was the truth before, be madness now. Such a reversal, completely turned around, with madness sanity, illusions true, attack a kindness, hatred love and murder benediction, is the goal the laws of chaos serve. These are the means by which the laws of God appear to be reversed. Here do the laws of sin appear to hold love captive and let sin go free.

These do not seem to be the goals of chaos, for by the great reversal, they appear to be the laws of order. How could it not be so? Chaos is lawlessness and has no laws. To be believed, its seeming laws must be perceived as real. Their goal of madness must be seen as sanity. And fear, with ashen lips and sightless eyes, blinded and terrible to look upon, is lifted to the throne of love, its dying conqueror, its substitute, the saviour from salvation. How lovely do the laws of fear make death appear! Give thanks unto the hero on love's throne, who saved the Son of God for fear and death!

And yet, how can it be that laws like these can be believed? There is a strange device that makes it possible. Nor is it unfamiliar; we have seen how it appears to function many times before. In truth it does not function, yet in dreams, where only shadows play the major roles, it seems most powerful. No law of chaos could compel belief but for the emphasis on form and disregard of content. No-one who thinks that one of them is true sees what it says. Some forms it takes seem to have meaning, and that is all.

How can some forms of murder not mean death? Can an attack in any form be love? What form of condemnation is a blessing? Who makes his Saviour powerless and finds salvation? Let not the form of the attack on him deceive you. You cannot seek to harm him and be saved. Who can find safety from attack by turning on himself? How can it matter what the form this madness takes? It is a judgement that defeats itself, condemning what it says it wants to save. Be not deceived when madness takes a form you think is lovely. What is intent on your destruction is not your friend.

You would maintain, and think it true, that you do not believe these senseless laws, nor act upon them. And when you look at what they say, they cannot be believed. Brothers, you do believe them. For how else could you perceive the form they take, with content such as this? Can any form of this be tenable? Yet you believe them for the form they take, and do not recognised the content. It never changes. Can you paint rosy lips upon a skeleton, dress it in loveliness, pet it and pamper it, and make it live? And can you be content with an illusion that you are living?

There is not life outside of Heaven. Where God created life, there life must be. In any state apart from Heaven, life is illusion. At best, it seems like life; at worst, like death. Yet both are judgements on what is not life, equal in their inaccuracy and lack of meaning. Life not in Heaven is impossible, and what is not in Heaven is not anywhere. Outside of Heaven, only the conflict of illusions stands; senseless, impossible and beyond all reason, and yet perceived as an eternal barrier to Heaven. Illusions are but forms. Their content is never true.

The laws of chaos govern all illusions. Their forms conflict, making it seem quite possible to value some above the others. Yet each one rests as surely on the belief the laws of chaos are the laws of order as do the others. Each one upholds these laws completely, offering a certain witness that these laws are true. The seeming gentler forms of the attack are no less certain in their witnessing, or their results. Certain it is illusions will bring fear because of the beliefs that they imply, not for their form. And lack of faith in love, in any form, attests to chaos as reality.

From the belief in sin, the faith in chaos must follow. It is because it follows that it seems to be a logical conclusion; a valid step in ordered thought. The steps to chaos do follow neatly from their starting point. Each is a different form in the progression of truth's reversal, leading still deeper into terror, and away from truth. Think not one step is smaller than another, nor that return from one is easier. The whole descent from Heaven lies in each one. And where your thinking starts, there must it end.

Brothers, take not one step in the descent to hell. For having taken one, you will not recognize the rest for what they are. And they will follow. Attack in any form has placed your foot upon the twisted stairway that leads from Heaven. Yet any instant it is possible to have all this undone. How can you know whether you chose the stairs to Heaven or the way to hell? Quite easily. How do you feel? Is peace in your awareness? Are you certain which way you go? And are you sure the goal of Heaven can be reached?

If not, you walk alone. Ask, then, your Friend to join with you, and give you certainty of where you go.

Is it not true you do not recognize some of the forms attack can take? If it is true attack in any form will hurt you and will do so just as much as in another form which you do recognize, then it must follow that you do not always recognize the source of pain. Attack in any form is equally destructive. Its purpose does not change. Its sole intent is murder, and what form of murder serves to cover the massive guilt and frantic fear of punishment the murderer must feel? He may deny he is a murderer and justify his savagery with smiles as he attacks. Yet he will suffer and will look on his intent in nightmares where the smiles are gone, and where the purpose rises to meet his horrified awareness and pursue him still. For no-one thinks of murder and escapes the guilt the thought entails. If the intent is death, what matter the form it takes?

Is death in any form, however lovely and charitable it may seem to be, a blessing and a sign the Voice for God speaks through you to your brother? The wrapping does not make the gift you give. An empty box, however beautiful and gently given, still contains nothing. And neither the receiver nor the giver is long deceived. Withhold forgiveness from your brother, and you attack him. You give him nothing and receive of him but what you gave.

Salvation is no compromise of any kind. To compromise is to accept but part of what you want; to take a little and give up the rest. Salvation gives up nothing. It is complete for everyone. Let the idea of compromise but enter, and the awareness of salvation's purpose is lost, because it is not recognized. It is denied where compromise has been accepted for compromise is the belief salvation is impossible. It would maintain you can attack a little, love a little, and know the difference. Thus it would teach a little of the same can still be different, and yet the same remain intact, as one. Does this make sense? Can it be understood?

This course is easy just because it makes no compromise. Yet it seems difficult to those who still believe that compromise is possible. They do not see that, if it is, salvation is attack. Yet it is certain the belief that salvation is impossible cannot uphold a quiet, calm assurance it has come. Forgiveness cannot be withheld a little. Nor is it possible to attack for this and love for that and understand forgiveness. Would you not want to recognize assault upon your peace in any form, if only thus does it become impossible that you lose sight of it? It can be kept shining before your vision, forever clear and never out of sight, if you defend it not.

Those who believe that peace can be defended, and that attack is justified on its behalf, cannot perceive it lies within them. How could they know? Could they accept forgiveness side by side with the belief that murder takes some forms by which their peace is saved? Would they be willing to accept the fact their savage purpose is directed against themselves? No-one unites with enemies, nor is at one with them in purpose. And no-one compromises with an enemy but hates him still, for what he kept from him.

Mistake not truce for peace, nor compromise for the escape from conflict. To be released from conflict means that it is over. The door is open; you have left the battleground. You have not lingered there in cowering hope, because the guns are still an instant, and the fear that haunts the place of death is not apparent, that it will not return. There is no safety in a battle ground. You can look down on it in safety from above, and not be touched. But from within it, you can find no safety. Not one tree left standing still will shelter you. Not one illusion of protection stands against the faith in murder. Here stands the body, torn between the natural desire to communicate and the unnatural intent to murder and to die. Think you the form that murder takes can offer safety? Can guilt be absent from a battlefield?

The fear of God is fear of life and not of death. Yet He remains the only place of safety. In Him is no attack and no illusion in any form stalks Heaven. Heaven is wholly true. No difference enters and what is all the same cannot conflict. You are not asked to fight against your wish to murder. But you are asked to realize the form it takes conceals the same intent. And it is this you fear, and not the form. What is not love is murder. What is not loving must be an attack. Every illusion is an assault on truth, and everyone does violence to the idea of love because it seems to be of equal truth.

What can be equal to the truth, yet different? Murder and love are incompatible. Yet if they both are true, then must they be the same, and indistinguishable from one another. So will they be to those who see God's Son a body. For it is not the body that is like the Son's Creator. And what is lifeless cannot be the Son of Life. How can a body be extended to hold the universe? Can it create, and be what it creates? And can it offer its creations all that it is, and never suffer loss?

God does not share His function with a body. He gave the function to create unto His Son because it is His Own. It is not sinful to believe the function of the Son is murder, but it is insanity. What is the same can have no different function. Creation is the means for God's extension and what is His must be His Son's as well. Either the Father and the Son are murderers, or neither is. Life makes not death, creating like itself.

The lovely light of your relationship is like the love of God. It cannot yet assume the holy function God gave His Son, for your forgiveness of one another is not complete as yet and so it cannot be extended to all creation. Each form of murder and attack that still attracts you, and that you do not recognize for what it is, limits the healing and the miracles you have the power to extend to all. Yet does the Holy Spirit understand how to increase your little gifts, and make them mighty. Also He understands how your relationship is raised above the battleground, in it no more. This is your part; to realize that murder in any form is not your will. The overlooking of the battleground is now your purpose.

Be lifted up, and from a higher place look down upon it. From there will your perspective be quite different. Here in the midst of it, it does seem real. Here you have chosen to be part of it. Here murder is your choice. Yet from above, the choice is miracles instead of murder. And the perspective coming from this choice shows you the battle is not real, and easily escaped. Bodies may battle, but the clash of forms is meaningless. And it is over when you realize that it never was begun. How can a battle be perceived as nothingness when you engage in it? How can the truth of miracles be recognized if murder is your choice?

When the temptation to attack rises to make your mind darkened and murderous, remember you can see the battle from above. Even in forms you do not recognize, the signs you know. There is a stab of pain, a twinge of guilt, and above all, a loss of peace. This you know well. When it occurs, leave not your place on high, but quickly choose a miracle instead of murder. And God Himself and all the lights of Heaven will gently lean to you and hold you up. For you have chosen to remain where He would have you, and no illusion can attack the peace of God together with His Son.

See no-one from the battleground, for there you look on him from nowhere. You have no reference-point from where to look, where meaning can be given what you see. For only bodies could attack and murder, and if this is your purpose, then you must be one with them. Only a purpose unifies, and those who share a purpose have a mind as one. The body has no purpose and must be solitary. From below, it cannot be surmounted. From above, the limits it exerts on those in battle still are gone, and not perceived. The body stands between the Father and the Heaven He created for His Son because it has no purpose.

Think what is given those who share their Father's purpose and who know that it is theirs! They want for nothing. Sorrow of any kind is inconceivable. Only the light they love is in awareness, and only love shines upon them forever. It is their past, their present and their future; always the same, eternally complete and wholly shared. They know it is impossible their happiness could ever suffer change of any kind. Perhaps you think the battleground can offer something that you can win. Can it be anything that offers you a perfect calmness, and a sense of love so deep and quiet that no touch of doubt can ever mar your certainty? And that will last forever?

Those with the strength of God in their awareness could never think of battle. What could they gain but loss of their perfection? For everything fought for on the battleground is of the body; something it seems to offer or to own. No-one who knows that he has everything could seek for limitation, nor could he value the body's offerings. The senselessness of conquest is quite apparent from the quiet sphere above the battleground. What can conflict with everything? And what is there that offers less yet could be wanted more? Who with the Love of God upholding him could find the choice of miracles or murder hard to make?

Forget not that the motivation for this course is the attainment and the keeping of the state of peace. Given this state the mind is quiet, and the condition in which God is remembered is attained. It is not necessary to tell Him what to do. He will not fail. Where He can enter, there He is already. And can it be He cannot enter where He wills to be? Peace will be yours because it is His Will. Can you believe a shadow can hold back the Will that holds the universe secure? God does not wait upon illusions to let Him be Himself. No more His Son. They are. And what illusion that idly seems to drift between them has the power to defeat what is Their Will?

To learn this course requires willingness to question every value that you hold. Not one can be kept hidden and obscure, but it will jeopardize your learning. No belief is neutral. Everyone has the power to dictate each decision you make. For a decision is a conclusion based on everything that you believe. It is the outcome of belief and follows it as surely as does suffering follow guilt and freedom sinlessness. There is no substitute for peace. What God creates has no alternative. The truth arises from what He knows. And your decisions come from your beliefs as certainly as all creation rose in His Mind because of what He knows.

Love is extension. To withhold the smallest gift is not to know love's purpose. Love offers everything forever. Hold back but one belief, one offering and love is gone, because you asked a substitute to take its place. And now must war, the substitute for peace, come with the one alternative that you can choose for love. Your choosing it has given it all the reality it seems to have.

Beliefs will never openly attack each other, because conflicting outcomes are impossible. But an unrecognized belief is a decision to war in secret, where the results of conflict are kept unknown and never brought to reason, to be considered sensible or not. And many senseless outcomes have been reached, and meaningless decisions have been made and kept hidden, to become beliefs now given power to direct all subsequent decisions. Mistake you not the power of these hidden warriors to disrupt your peace. For it is at their mercy while you decide to leave it there. The secret enemies of peace, your least decision to choose attack instead of love, unrecognized and swift to challenge you to combat and to violence far more inclusive than you think, are there by your election. Do not deny their presence nor their terrible results. All that can be denied is their reality, but not their outcome.

All that is ever cherished as a hidden belief, to be defended though unrecognized, is faith in specialness. This takes many forms, but always clashes with the reality of God's creation, and with the grandeur which He gave His Son. What else could justify attack? For who could hate someone whose Self is his, and whom He knows? Only the special could have enemies, for they are different and not the same. And difference of any kind imposes orders of reality, and a need to judge that cannot be escaped.

What God created cannot be attacked, for there is nothing in the universe unlike itself. But what is different calls for judgement, and this must come from someone "better," someone incapable of being like what he condemns, "above" it, sinless by comparison with it. And thus does specialness become a means and end at once.

For specialness not only sets apart but serves as grounds from which attack on those who seem "beneath" the special one is "natural" and "just." The special ones feel weak and frail because of differences, for what would make them special is their enemy. Yet they protect its enmity and call it "friend." On its behalf they fight against the universe, for nothing in the world they value more.

Specialness is the great dictator of the wrong decisions. Here is the grand illusion of what you are, and what your brother is. And here is what must make the body dear, and worth preserving. Specialness must be defended. Illusions can attack it, and they do. For what your brother must become to keep your specialness IS an illusion. He who is "worse" than you must be attacked, so that your specialness can live on his defeat. For specialness is triumph, and its victory is his defeat and shame. How can he live, with all your sins upon him? And who must be his conqueror but you?

Would it be possible for you to hate your brother if you were like him? Could you attack him if you realized you journey with him, to a goal that is the same? Would you not help him reach it, in every way you could, if his attainment of it were perceived as yours? You are his enemy in specialness; his friend in a shared purpose. Specialness can never share, for it depends on goals that you alone can reach. And he must never reach them, or your goal is jeopardized. Can love have meaning where the goal is triumph? And what decision can be made for this that will not hurt you? Your brother is your friend because his Father created him like you.

There is no difference. You have been given to each other that love might be extended, not cut off from one another. What you keep is lost to you. God gave you both Himself, and to remember this is now the only purpose that you share. And so it is the only one you have. Could you attack each other if you chose to see no specialness of any kind between you? Look fairly at whatever makes you give each other only partial welcome or would let you think that you are better off apart. Is it not always your belief your specialness is limited by your relationship? And is not this the "enemy" that makes you both illusions to each other?

The fear of God, and of each other, comes from each unrecognized belief in specialness. For each demands the other bow to it against his will. And God Himself must honour it or suffer vengeance. Every twinge of malice, or stab of hate, or wish to separate arises here. For here the purpose which you share becomes obscured from both of you. You would oppose this course because it teaches you, you are alike. You have no purpose that is not the same, and none your Father does not share with you. For your relationship has been made clean of special goals. And would you now defeat the goal of holiness that Heaven gave it? What perspective can the special have that does not change with every seeming blow, each slight, or fancied judgement on itself?

Those who are special must defend illusions against the truth. For what is specialness but an attack upon the Will of God? You love your brother not while it is this you would defend against him. This is what He attacks, and you protect. Here is the ground of battle which you wage against him. Here must he be your enemy, and not your friend. Never can there be peace among the different. He is your friend because you are the same.

Comparison must be an ego device, for love makes none. Specialness always makes comparisons. It is established by a lack seen in another and maintained by searching for and keeping clear in sight, all lacks it can perceive. This does it seek and this it looks upon. And always whom it thus diminishes would be your Saviour, had you not chosen to make of him a tiny measure of your specialness instead. Against the littleness you see in him you stand as tall and stately, clean and honest, pure and unsullied, by comparison with what you see. Nor do you understand it is yourself that you diminish thus.

Pursuit of specialness is always at the cost of peace. Who can attack his Saviour and cut him down, yet recognised his strong support? Who can detract from his omnipotence, yet share his power? And who can use him as the gauge of littleness, and be released from limits? You have a function in salvation. Its pursuit will bring you joy. But the pursuit of specialness must bring you pain. Here is a goal that would defeat salvation and thus run counter to the Will of God. To value specialness is to esteem an alien will to which illusions of yourself are dearer than the truth.

Specialness is the idea of sin made real. Sin is impossible even to imagine without this base. For sin arose from it, out of nothingness; an evil flower with no roots at all. Here is the self-made "saviour," the "creator" who creates unlike the Father and which made His Son like to itself and not like unto Him.

His "special" sons are many, never one, each one in exile from himself, and Him of Whom they are a part. Nor do they love the Oneness Which created them as one with Him. They chose their specialness instead of Heaven and instead of peace, and wrapped it carefully in sin, to keep it "safe" from truth.

You are not special. If you think you are, and would defend your specialness against the truth of what you really are, how can you know the truth? What answer that the Holy Spirit gives can reach you, when it is your specialness to which you listen, and which asks and answers? Its tiny answer, soundless in the melody which pours from God to you eternally in loving praise of what you are, is all you listen to. And that vast song of honour and of love for what you are seems silent and unheard before its "mightiness." You strain your ears to hear its soundless voice, and yet the Call of God Himself is soundless to you.

You can defend your specialness, but never will you hear the Voice for God beside it. They speak a different language and they fall on different ears. To every special one a different message, and one with different meaning, is the truth. Yet how can truth be different to each one? The special messages the special hear convince them they are different and apart; each in his special sins and "safe" from love, which does not see his specialness at all. Christ's vision is their "enemy," for it sees not what they would look upon, and it would show them that the specialness they think they see is an illusion. What would they see instead?

The shining radiance of the Son of God, so like his Father that the memory of Him springs instantly to mind. And with this memory, the Son remembers his own creations, as like to him as he is to his Father. And all the world he made, and all his specialness, and all the sins he held in its defence against himself, will vanish as his mind accepts the truth about himself, as it returns to take their place. This is the only "cost" of truth: You will no longer see what never was, nor hear what makes no sound. Is it a sacrifice to give up nothing, and to receive the Love of God forever?

You who have chained your Saviour to your specialness, and given it his place, remember this: He has not lost the power to forgive you all the sins you think you placed between him and the function of salvation given him for you. Nor will you change his function, any more than you can change the truth in him and in yourself. But be you certain that the truth is just the same in both. It gives no different messages and has one meaning. And it is one you both can understand, and one which brings release to both of you.

Here stands your brother, with the key to Heaven in his hand, held out to you. Let not the dream of specialness remain between you. What is one is joined in truth.

Think of the loveliness that you will see within yourself, when you have looked on him as on a friend. He IS the enemy of specialness, but only friend to what is real in you. Not one attack you thought you made on him has taken from him the gift that God would have him give to you. His need to give it is as great as yours to have it. Let him forgive you all your specialness and make you whole in mind and one with him. He waits for your forgiveness only that he may return it unto you. It is not God Who has condemned His Son. But only you, to save his specialness and kill his Self.

You have come far along the way of truth; too far to falter now. Just one step more, and every vestige of the fear of God will melt away in love. Your brother's specialness and yours are enemies and bound in hate to kill each other and deny they are the same. Yet it is not illusions which have reached this final obstacle that seems to make God and His Heaven so remote that they cannot be reached. Here in this holy place does truth stand waiting to receive you both in silent blessing, and in peace so real and so encompassing that nothing stands outside. Leave all illusions of yourself outside this place, to which you come in hope and honesty.

Here is your Saviour from your specialness. He is in need of your acceptance of himself as part of you, as you for his. You are alike to God as God is to Himself. He is not special, for He would not keep one part of what He is unto Himself, not given to His Son but kept for Him alone. And it is this you fear, for if He is not special, then He willed His Son be like Him, and your brother is like you. Not special but possessed of everything including you.

Give him but what he has, remembering God gave Himself to both of you in equal love, that both might share the universe with Him Who chose that love could never be divided, and kept separate from what it is and must forever be. You are your brother's; part of love was not denied to him. But can it be that you have lost because he is complete? What has been given him makes you complete, as it does him. God's Love gave you to him and him to you because He gave Himself. What is the same as God is one with Him. And only specialness could make the truth of God and you as one seems anything but Heaven, and the hope of peace at last in sight.

Specialness is the seal of treachery upon the gift of love. Whatever serves its purpose must be given to kill. No gift that bears its seal but offers treachery to giver and receiver. Not one glance from eyes it veils but looks on sight of death. Not one believer in its potency but seeks for bargains and for compromise that would establish sin love's substitute and serve it faithfully. And no relationship that holds its purpose dear but clings to murder as safety's weapon, and the great defender of all illusions from the "threat" of love.

The hope of specialness makes it seem possible God made the body as the prison-house which keeps His Son from Him. For it demands a special place God cannot enter, and a hiding-place where none is welcome but your tiny self. Nothing is sacred here but unto you, and you alone, apart and separate from all your brothers; safe from all intrusions of sanity upon illusions; safe from God, and safe for conflict everlasting. Here are the gates of hell you closed upon yourself, to rule in madness and in loneliness your special kingdom, apart from God, away from truth and from salvation.

The key you threw away God gave your brother, whose holy hands would offer it to you when you were ready to accept His plan for your salvation in place of yours. How could this readiness be reached save through the sight of all your misery, and the awareness that your plan has failed, and will forever fail to bring you peace and joy of any kind? Through this despair you travel now, yet it is but illusion of despair. The death of specialness is not your death, but your awaking into life eternal. You but emerge from an illusion of what you are to the acceptance of yourself as God created you.

Forgiveness is the end of specialness. Only illusions can be forgiven, and then they disappear. Forgiveness is release from ALL illusions, and that is why it is impossible but partly to forgive. No-one who clings to one illusion can see himself as sinless, for he holds one error to himself as lovely still. And so he calls it "unforgiveable," and makes it sin. How can he then GIVE his forgiveness wholly, when he would not receive it for himself? For it is sure he would receive it wholly the instant that he gave it so. And thus his secret guilt would disappear, forgiven by himself.

Whatever form of specialness you cherish, you have made sin. Inviolate it stands, strongly defended with all your puny might against the Will of God. And thus it stands against yourself; your enemy, not God's. So does it seem to split you off from God, and make you separate from Him as its defender.

You would protect what God created not. And yet, this idol that seems to give you power has taken it away. For you have given your brother's birthright to it, leaving him alone and unforgiven, and yourself in sin beside him, both in misery, before the idol that can save you not.

It is not you that is so vulnerable and open to attack that just a word, a little whisper that you do not like, a circumstance that suits you not, or an event that you did not anticipate upsets your world, and hurls it into chaos. Truth is not frail. Illusions leave it perfectly unmoved. But specialness is not the truth in you. It can be thrown off balance by anything. What rests on nothing never can be stable. However large and overblown it seems to be, it still must rock and turn and whirl about with every breeze.

Without foundation nothing is secure. Would God have left His Son in such a state, where safety has no meaning? No, His Son is safe, resting on Him. It is your specialness that is attacked by everything that walks and breathes, or creeps or crawls, or even lives at all. Nothing is safe from its attack, and it is safe from nothing. It will forever more be unforgiving, for that is what it is; a secret vow that what God wants for you will never be and that you will oppose His Will forever. Nor is it possible the two can ever be the same while specialness stands like a flaming sword of death between them and makes them "enemies."

God asks for your forgiveness. He would have no separation, like an alien will, rise between what He wills for you and what you will. They are the same, for neither one wills specialness. How could they will the death of love itself? Yet they are powerless to make attack upon illusions. They are not bodies; as one Mind they wait for all illusions to be brought to them and left behind. Salvation challenges not even death. And God Himself, Who knows that death is not your will, must say, "Thy will be done" because you think it is.

Forgive the great Creator of the universe, the Source of life, of love and holiness, the perfect Father of a perfect Son, for your illusions of your specialness. Here is the hell you chose to be your home. He chose not this for you. Ask not He enter this. The way is barred to love and to salvation. Yet if you would release your brother from the depths of hell, you have forgiven Him Whose Will it is you rest forever in the arms of peace, in perfect safety, and without the heat and malice of one thought of specialness to mar your rest. Forgive the Holy One the specialness He could not give, and which you made instead.

The special ones are all asleep, surrounded by a world of loveliness they do not see. Freedom and peace and joy stand there, beside the bier on which they sleep, and call them to come forth and waken from their dream of death. Yet they hear nothing. They are lost in dreams of specialness. They hate the call that would awaken them, and they curse God because He did not make their dream reality. Curse God and die, but not by Him Who made not death; but only in the dream. Open your eyes a little; see the Saviour God gave to you that you might look on him and give him back his birthright. It is yours.

The slaves of specialness will yet be free. Such is the Will of God, and of His Son. Would God condemn himself to hell and to damnation? And do you will that this be done unto your Saviour? God calls to you from him to join His Will to save you both from hell. Look on the print of nails upon his hands that he holds out for your forgiveness. God asks your mercy on His Son and on Himself. Deny them not. They ask of you but that your will be done. They seek your love that you may love yourself. Love not your specialness instead of them. The print of nails are on your hands as well. Forgive your Father it was not His Will that you be crucified.

Specialness is a lack of trust in anyone except yourself. Faith is invested in yourself alone. Everything else becomes your enemy; feared and attacked, deadly and dangerous, hated and worthy only of destruction. Whatever gentleness it offers is but deception, but its hate is real. In danger of destruction it must kill, and you are drawn to it to kill it first. And such is guilt's attraction. Here is death enthroned as saviour; crucifixion is now redemption and salvation can only mean destruction of the world, except yourself.

What could the purpose of the body be but specialness? And it is this that makes it frail and helpless in its own defence. It was conceived to make you frail and helpless. The goal of separation is its curse. Yet bodies have no goal. Purpose is of the mind. And minds can change as they desire. What they are, and all their attributes, they cannot change. But what they hold as purpose can be changed and body states must shift accordingly. Of itself the body can do nothing. See it as means to hurt and it is hurt. See it as means to heal and it is healed.

You can but hurt yourself. This has been oft repeated but is difficult to grasp as yet. To minds intent on specialness it is impossible. Yet to those who wish to heal and not attack it is quite obvious. The purpose of attack is in the mind and its effects are felt but where it is. Nor is mind limited; so must it be that harmful purpose hurts the mind as one.

Nothing could make less sense to specialness. Nothing could make more sense to miracles. For miracles are merely change of purpose from hurt to healing.

This shift in purpose does "endanger" specialness, but only in the sense that all illusions are "threatened" by the truth. They will not stand before it. Yet what comfort has ever been in them, that you would keep the gift your Father asks from Him and give it there instead? Given to Him, the universe is yours. Offered to them, no gifts can be returned. What you have given specialness has left you bankrupt, and your treasure house barren and empty, with an open door inviting everything that would disturb your peace to enter and destroy.

Long ago we said consider not the means by which salvation is attained, nor how to reach it. But do consider, and consider well, whether it is your wish that you might see your brother sinless. To specialness the answer must be "no." A sinless brother is its enemy, while sin, if it were possible, would be its friend. Your brother's sins would justify itself, and give it meaning that the truth denies. All that is real proclaims his sinlessness. All that is false proclaims his sins as real. If He is sinful, then is your reality not real, but just a dream of specialness which lasts an instant, crumbling into dust.

Do not defend this senseless dream, in which God is bereft of what He loves, and you remain beyond salvation. Only this is certain in this shifting world which has no meaning in reality: When peace is not with you entirely, and when you suffer pain of any kind, you have beheld some sin within your brother, and have rejoiced at what you thought was there. Your specialness seemed safe because of it. And thus you saved what you appointed to be your saviour, and crucified the one whom God has given you instead. So are you bound with him, for you are one. And so is specialness his "enemy," and yours as well.

The Christ in you is very still. He looks on what He loves and knows it as Himself. And thus does He rejoice at what He sees, because He knows that it is one with Him and with His Father. Specialness, too, takes joy in what it sees, although it is not true. Yet what you seek for is a source of joy as you conceive it. What you wish is true for you. Nor is it possible that you can wish for something and lack faith that it is so. Wishing makes real, as surely as does will create. The power of a wish upholds illusions as strongly as does love extend itself. Except that one deludes; the other heals.

There is no dream of specialness, however hidden or disguised the form, however lovely it may seem to be, however much it delicately offers the hope of peace and the escape from pain, in which you suffer not your condemnation. In dreams, effect and cause are interchanged, for here the maker of the dream believes that what he made is happening to him. He does not realize he picked a thread from here, a scrap from there, and wove a picture out of nothing. For the parts do not belong together, and the whole contributes nothing to the parts to give them meaning.

Where could your peace arise but from forgiveness? The Christ in you looks only on the truth and sees no condemnation that could need forgiveness. He is at peace because He sees no sin. Identify with Him, and what has He that you have not? He is your eyes, your ears, your hands, your feet. How gentle are the sights He sees, the sounds He hears? How beautiful His hand that holds His brother's and how lovingly He walks beside him, showing him what can be seen and heard and where he will see nothing and there is no sound to hear.

Yet let your specialness direct his way and you will follow. And both will walk in danger, each intent, in the dark forest of the sightless, unlit but by the shifting tiny gleams that spark an instant from the fireflies of sin and then go out, to lead the other to a nameless precipice, and hurl him over it. For what can specialness delight in but to kill? What does it seek for but the sight of death? Where does it lead but to destruction? Yet think not that it looked upon your brother first, nor hated him before it hated you. The sin its eyes behold in him and love to look upon it saw in you and looks on still with joy. Yet is it joy to look upon decay and madness, and believe this crumbling thing, with flesh already loosened from the bone and sightless holes for eyes, is like yourself?

Rejoice you have no eyes with which to see; no ears to listen, and no hands to hold nor feet to guide. Be glad that only Christ can lend you His, while you have need of them. They are illusions, too, as much as yours. And yet because they serve a different purpose, the strength their purpose holds is given them. And what they see and hear and hold and lead is given light, that you may lead as you were led.

The Christ in you is very still. He knows where you are going, and He leads you there in gentleness and blessing all the way. His love for God replaces all the fear you thought you saw within yourself. His holiness shows you Himself in him whose hand you hold, and whom you lead to Him. And what you see is like yourself.

For what but Christ is there to see and hear and love and follow home? He looked upon you first but recognized that you were not complete. And so He sought for your completion in each living thing that He beholds and loves. And seeks it still, that each might offer you the Love of God.

Yet is He quiet, for He knows that love is in you now and safely held in you by that same hand that holds your brother's in your own. Christ's hand holds all His brothers in Himself. He gives them vision for their sightless eyes, and sings to them of Heaven, that their ears may hear no more the sound of battle and of death. He reaches through them, holding out His hand, that everyone may bless all living things, and see their holiness. And He rejoices that these sights are yours, to look upon with Him and share His joy. His perfect lack of specialness He offers you, that you may save all living things from death, receiving from each one the gift of life that your forgiveness offers to your Self. The sight of Christ is all there is to see. The song of Christ is all there is to hear. The hand of Christ is all there is to hold. There is no journey but to walk with Him.

You who would be content with specialness, and seek salvation in a war with love, consider this: The holy Lord of Heaven has Himself come down to you, to offer you your own completion. What is His is yours because in your completion is His Own. He Who willed not to be without His Son could never will that you be brotherless. And would He give a brother unto you except he be as perfect as yourself, and just as like to Him in holiness as you must be?

There must be doubt before there can be conflict. And every doubt must be about yourself. Christ has no doubt, and from His certainty His quiet comes. He will exchange His certainty for all your doubts, if you agree that He is one with you, and that this Oneness is endless, timeless, and within your grasp because your hands are His. He is within you, yet He walks beside you and before, leading the way that He must go to find Himself complete. His quietness becomes your certainty. And where is doubt when certainty has come?

Before your brother's holiness the world is still, and peace descends on it in gentleness and blessing so complete that not one trace of conflict still remains to haunt you in the darkness of the night. He is your Saviour from the dreams of fear. He is the healing of your sense of sacrifice, and fear that what you have will scatter with the wind and turn to dust. In him is your assurance God is here, and with you now. While he is what he is, you can be sure that God is knowable, and will be known to you. For He could never leave His own creation. And the sign that this is so lies in your brother, offered you that all your doubts about yourself may disappear before his holiness.

See in him God's creation. For in him, his Father waits for your acknowledgment that He created you as part of Him. Without you there would be a lack in God, a Heaven incomplete, a Son without a Father. There could be no universe and no reality. For what God wills is whole and part of Him because His Will is One. Nothing alive that is not part of Him, and nothing IS but is alive in Him. Your brother's holiness shows you that God is One with him and you; that what he has is yours because you are not separate from him nor from his Father.

Nothing is lost to you in all the universe. Nothing that God created has He failed to lay before you lovingly, as yours forever. And no thought within His Mind is absent from your own. It is His Will you share His Love for you and look upon yourself as lovingly as He conceived of you before the world began and as He knows you still. God changes not His Mind about His Son with passing circumstance which has no meaning in eternity where He abides, and you with Him. Your brother is as He created him. And it is this that saves you from a world that He created not.

Forget not that the healing of God's Son is all the world is for. That is the only purpose the Holy Spirit sees in it and thus the only one it has. Until you see the healing of the Son as all you wish to be accomplished by the world, by time and all appearances, you will not know the Father nor yourself. For you will use the world for what is not its purpose and will not escape its laws of violence and death. Yet it is given you to be beyond its laws in all respects, in every way and every circumstance; in all temptation to perceive what is not there, and all belief God's Son can suffer pain because he sees himself as he is not.

Look on your brother and behold in him the whole reversal of the laws that seem to rule this world. See in his freedom yours, for such it is. Let not his specialness obscure the truth in him, for not one law of death you bind him to will you escape. And not one sin you see in him but keeps you both in hell. Yet will his perfect sinlessness release you both, for holiness is quite impartial, with one judgement made for all it looks upon. And that is made, not of itself, but through the Voice that speaks for God in everything that lives and shares His Being.

It is His sinlessness that eyes which see can look upon. It is His loveliness they see in everything. And it is He they look for everywhere and find no sight nor place nor time where He is not. Within your brother's holiness, the perfect frame for your salvation and the world's, is set the shining memory of Him in Whom your brother lives, and you along with him.

Let not your eyes be blinded by the veil of specialness that hides the face of Christ from him, and you as well. And let the fear of God no longer hold the vision you were meant to see from you. Your brother's body shows not Christ to you. He is set forth within his holiness.

Choose, then, his body or his holiness as what you want to see, and which you choose is yours to look upon. Yet will you choose in countless situations, and through time which seems to have no end, until the truth be your decision. For eternity is not regained by still one more denial of Christ in him. And where is your salvation, if he is but a body? Where is your peace but in his holiness? And where is God Himself but in that part of Him He set forever in your brother's holiness, that you might see the truth about yourself, set forth at last in terms you recognized and understood?

Your brother's holiness is sacrament and benediction unto you. His errors cannot withhold God's blessing from himself, nor you who see him truly. His mistakes can cause delay, which it is given you to take from him, that both may end a journey that has never been begun and needs no end. What never was is not a part of you. Yet you will think it is until you realize that it is not a part of him who stands beside you. He is the mirror of yourself, wherein you see the judgement you have laid on both of you. The Christ in you beholds his holiness. Your specialness looks on his body and beholds him not.

See him as what he is, that your deliverance may not be long. A senseless wandering, without a purpose and without accomplishment of any kind, is all the other choice can offer you. Futility of function not fulfilled will haunt you while your brother lies asleep, till what has been assigned to you is done, and he is risen from the past. He who condemned himself, and you as well, is given you to save from condemnation, along with you. And both shall see God's glory in His Son, whom you mistook as flesh, and bound to laws that have no power over him at all.

Would you not gladly realize these laws are not for you? Then see him not as prisoner to them. It cannot be what governs part of God holds not for all the rest. You place yourself under the laws you see as ruling him. Think, then, how great the Love of God for you must be, that He has given you a part of Him to save from pain and give you happiness. And never doubt but that your specialness will disappear before the Will of God, Who loves each part of Him with equal love. The Christ in you can see your brother truly. Would you decide against the holiness He sees?

Specialness is the function which you gave yourself. It stands for you alone, as self-created, self-maintained, in need of nothing, and unjoined with anything beyond the body. In its eyes, you are a separate universe, with all the power to hold itself complete within itself, with every entry shut against intrusion, and every window barred against the light. Always attacked and always furious, with anger always fully justified, you have pursued this goal with vigilance you never thought to yield, and effort that you never thought to cease. And all this grim determination was for this; you wanted specialness to be the truth.

Now you are merely asked that you pursue another goal with far less vigilance; with little effort and with little time, and with the power of God maintaining it and promising success. Yet of the two, it is this one you find more difficult. The "sacrifice" of self you understand, nor do you deem this cost too heavy. But a tiny willingness, a nod to God, a greeting to the Christ in you, you find a burden wearisome and tedious, too heavy to be borne. Yet to the dedication to the truth as God established it no sacrifice is asked, no strain called forth, and all the power of Heaven and the might of truth itself is given to provide the means and guarantee the goal's accomplishment.

You who believe it easier to see your brother's body than his holiness, be sure you understand what made this judgement. Here is the voice of specialness heard clearly, judging against the Christ, and setting forth for you the purpose that you can attain, and what you cannot do. Forget not that this judgement must apply to what you do with it as your ally. For what you do through Christ it does not know. To Him this judgement makes no sense at all, for only what His Father wills is possible, and there is no alternative for Him to see. Out of His lack of conflict comes your peace. And from His purpose comes the means for effortless accomplishment and rest.

How bitterly does everyone tied to this world defend the specialness he wants to be the truth! His wish is law unto him, and he obeys. Nothing his specialness demands does he withhold. Nothing it needs does he deny to what he loves. And while it calls to him he hears no other Voice. No effort is too great, no cost too much, no price too dear to save his specialness from the least slight, the tiniest attack, the whispered doubt, the hint of threat, or anything but deepest reverence. This is your son, beloved of you as you are to your Father. Yet it stands in place of your creations, who are son to you, that you might share the Fatherhood of God, not snatch it from Him. What is this son that you have made to be your strength?

What is this child of earth on whom such love is lavished? What is this parody of God's creation that takes the place of yours? And where are they, now that the host of God has found another son which he prefers to them.

The memory of God shines not alone. What is within your brother still contains all of creation, everything created and creating, born and unborn as yet, still in the future or apparently gone by. What is in him is changeless, and your changelessness is recognized in its acknowledgment. The holiness in you belongs to him. And by your seeing it in him, returns to you. All of the tribute you have given specialness belongs to him, and thus returns to you. All of the love and care, the strong protection, the thought by day and night, the deep concern, the powerful conviction this is you, belong to him. Nothing you gave to specialness but is his due. And nothing due him is not due to you.

How can you know your worth while specialness claims you instead? How can you fail to know it is in his holiness? Seek not to make your specialness the truth, for if it were you would be lost indeed. Be thankful, rather, it is given you to see his holiness because it is the truth. And what is true in him must be as true in you.

Ask yourself this: Can you protect the mind? The body, yes, a little; not from time, but temporarily. And much you think to save, you hurt. What would you save it for For in that choice lie both its health and harm? Save it for show, as bait to catch another fish, to house your specialness in better style, or weave a frame of loveliness around your hate, and you condemn it to decay and death. And if you see this purpose in your brother's, such is your condemnation of your own. Weave, rather, then, a frame of holiness around him, that the truth may shine on him and give you safety from decay.

The Father keeps what He created safe. You cannot touch it with the false ideas you made, because it was created not by you. Let not your foolish fancies frighten you. What is immortal cannot be attacked; what is but temporal has no effect. Only the purpose that you see in it has meaning, and if that is true, its safety rests secure. If not, it has no purpose, and is means for nothing. Whatever is perceived as means for truth shares in its holiness and rests in light as safely as itself. Nor will that light go out when it is gone. Its holy purpose gave it immortality, setting another light in Heaven, where your creations recognize a gift from you, a sign that you have not forgotten them.

The test of everything on earth is simply this; "What is it for?" The answer makes it what it is for you. It has no meaning of itself, yet you can give reality to it, according to the purpose which you serve. Here you are but means, along with it. God is a Means as well as End. In Heaven, means and end are one, and one with him. This is the state of true creation, found not within time, but in eternity. To no one here is this describable. Nor is there any way to learn what this condition means. Not till you go past learning to the Given; not till you make again a holy home for your creations is it understood.

A co-creator with the Father must have a Son. Yet must this Son have been created like Himself. A perfect being, all-encompassing and all-encompassed, nothing to add and nothing taken from; not born of size nor weight nor time, nor held to limits or uncertainties of any kind. Here do the means and end unite as one, nor does this one have any end at all. All this is true, and yet it has no meaning to anyone who still retains one unlearned lesson in his memory, one thought with purpose still uncertain or one wish with a divided aim.

This course makes no attempt to teach what cannot easily be learned. Its scope does not exceed your own, except to say that what is yours will come to you when you are ready. Here are the means and purpose separate because they were so made and so perceived. And therefore, do we deal with them as if they were. It is essential it be kept in mind that all perception still is upside down until its purpose has been understood. Perception does not seem to be a means. And it is this that makes it hard to grasp the whole extent to which it must depend on what you see it for. Perception seems to teach you what you see. Yet it but witnesses to what you taught. It is the outward picture of a wish; an image that you wanted to be true.

Look at yourself, and you will see a body. Look at this body in a different light and it looks different. And without a light it seems that it is gone. Yet you are reassured that it is there because you still can feel it with your hands, and hear it move. Here is an image that you want to be yourself. It is the means to make your wish come true. It gives the eyes with which you look on it, the hands that feel it, and the ears with which you listen to the sounds it makes. It proves its own reality to you.

Thus is the body made a theory of yourself, with no provisions made for evidence beyond itself, and no escape within its sight. Its course is sure, when seen through its own eyes. It grows and withers, flourishes and dies. And you cannot conceive of you apart from it. You brand it sinful, and you hate its acts, judging it evil. Yet your specialness whispers, "Here is my own beloved son, in whom I am well pleased." Thus does the "son" become the means to serve his "father's" purpose. Not identical, not even like, but still a means to offer to the "father" what he wants. Such is the travesty on God's creation. For as His Son's creation gave HIM joy and witness to His Love and shared His purpose, so does the body testify to the idea that made it and speak for its reality and truth.

And thus are two sons made, and both appear to walk this earth without a meeting-place and no encounter. One do you see outside yourself, your own beloved son. The other rests within, His Father's Son, within your brother as he is in you. Their difference does not lie in how they look, nor where they go, nor even what they do. They have a different purpose. It is this that joins them to their like and separates each from all aspects with a different purpose. The Son of God retains His Father's Will. The son of man perceives an alien will, and wishes it were so. And thus does his perception serve his wish by giving it appearances of truth. Yet can perception serve another goal. It is not bound to specialness but by your choice. And it is given you to make a different choice and use perception for a different purpose. And what you see will serve that purpose well and prove its own reality to you. The Christ in you inhabits not a body. Yet He is in you. And thus it must be that you are not within a body. What is within you cannot be outside. And it is certain that you cannot be apart from what is at the very centre of your life.

What gives you life cannot be housed in death. No more can you. Christ is within a frame of holiness whose only purpose is that He may be made manifest to those who know Him not, that He may call to them to come to Him and see Him where they thought their bodies were. Then will their bodies melt away, that they may frame His holiness in them.

No-one who carries Christ in him can fail to recognize Him everywhere. except in bodies. And as long as they believe they are in bodies, where they think they are He cannot be. And so they carry Him unknowingly, and do not make Him manifest. And thus they do not recognize Him where He is. The son of man is not the risen Christ. Yet does the Son of God abide exactly where he is, and walks with him within his holiness, as plain to see as is his specialness set forth within his body.

The body needs no healing. But the mind that thinks it is a body is sick indeed! And it is here that Christ sets forth the remedy. His purpose folds the body in His light and fills it with the holiness that shines from Him. And nothing that the body says or does but makes Him manifest. To those who know Him not it carries Him in gentleness and love, to heal their minds. Such is the mission that your brother has for you. And such it must be that your mission is for him.

It cannot be that it is hard to do the task that Christ appointed you to do, since it is He Who does it. And in the doing of it will you learn the body merely seems to be the means to do it. For the Mind is His. And so it must be yours. His holiness directs the body through the mind at one with Him. And you are manifest unto your holy brother, as he to you. Here is the meeting of the holy Christ unto Himself; nor any differences perceived to stand between the aspects of His holiness, which meet and join and raise Him to His Father, whole and pure and worthy of His Everlasting Love.

How can you manifest the Christ in you except to look on holiness, and see Him there? Perception tells you, you are manifest in what you see. Behold the body, and you will believe that you are there. And everybody that you look upon reminds you of yourself; your sinfulness, your evil, and, above all, your death. And would you not despise the one who tells you this, and seek his death instead? The message and the messenger are one. And you must see your brother as yourself. Framed in his body you will see your sinfulness, wherein you stand condemned. Set in his holiness, the Christ in him proclaims Himself as you.

Perception is a choice of what you want yourself to be; the world you want to live in, and the state in which you think your mind will be content and satisfied. It chooses where you think your safety lies, at your decision. It reveals yourself to you as you would have you be. And always is it faithful to your purpose, from which it never separates, nor gives the slightest witness unto anything the purpose in your mind upholdeth not. Perception is a part of what it is your purpose to behold, for means and end are never separate. And thus you learn what seems to have a life apart has none.

You are the means for God; not separate, nor with a life apart from His. His Life is manifest in you who are His Son. Each aspect of Himself is framed in holiness and perfect purity, in love celestial and so complete it wishes only that it may release all that it looks upon unto itself. Its radiance shines through each body that it looks upon and brushes all its darkness into light merely by looking past it to the light. The veil is lifted through its gentleness, and nothing hides the face of Christ from its beholders. And both of you stand there, before Him now, to let Him draw aside the veil that seems to keep you separate and apart.

Since you believe that you are separate, Heaven presents itself to you as separate, too. Not that it is in truth, but that the link that has been given you to join the truth may reach to you through what you understand. Father and Son and Holy Spirit are as One, as all your brothers join as one in truth. Christ and His Father never have been separate and Christ abides within your understanding, in the part of you that shares His Father's Will. The Holy Spirit links the other part, the tiny mad desire to be separate, different and special, to the Christ, to make the oneness clear to what is really one. In this world, this is not understood, but can be taught.

The Holy Spirit serves Christ's purpose in your mind, so that the aim of specialness can be corrected where the error lies. Because His purpose still is one with both the Father and the Son, He knows the Will of God and what you really will. But this is understood by mind perceived as one, aware that it is one, and so experienced. It is the Holy Spirit's function to teach you how this oneness is experienced, what you must do that it can be experienced, and where you should go to do it.

All this takes note of time and place as if they were discrete, for while you think that part of you is separate, the concept of a oneness joined as one is meaningless. It is apparent that a mind so split could never be the teacher of a Oneness Which unites all things within Itself. And so What IS within this mind, and does unite all things together, must be its Teacher. Yet must It use the language which this mind can understand in the condition in which it thinks it is. And It must use all learning to transfer illusions to the truth, taking all false ideas of what you are, and leading you beyond them to the truth that is beyond them. All this can very simply be reduced to this:

> What is the same cannot be different,
> And what is one cannot have separate parts.

Is it not evident that what the body's eyes perceive fills you with fear? Perhaps you think you find a hope of satisfaction there. Perhaps you fancy to attain some peace and satisfaction in the world as you perceive it. Yet it must be evident the outcome does not change. Despite your hopes and fancies, always does despair result. And there is no exception, nor will there ever be. The only value that the past can hold is that you learn it gave you no rewards which you would want to keep. For only thus will you be willing to relinquish it and have it gone forever.

Is it not strange that you should cherish still some hope of satisfaction from the world you see? In no respect, at any time or place, has anything but fear and guilt been your reward. How long is needed for you to realize the chance of change in this respect is hardly worth delaying change that might result in better outcome? For one thing is sure; the way you see, and long have seen, gives no support to base your future hopes, and no suggestions of success at all. To place your hopes where no hope lies must make you hopeless. Yet is this hopelessness your choice, while you would seek for hope where none is ever found.

Is it not also true that you have found some hope apart from this; some glimmering, inconstant, wavering, yet dimly seen, that hopefulness is warranted on grounds that are not in this world? And yet your hope that they may still be here prevents you still from giving up the hopeless and unrewarding task you set yourself. Can it make sense to hold the fixed belief that there is reason to uphold pursuit of what has always failed on grounds that it will suddenly succeed and bring what it has never brought before?

Its past has failed. Be glad that it is gone within your mind, to darken what is there. Take not the form for content, for the form is but a means for content. And the frame is but a means to hold the picture up, so that it can be seen. A frame that hides the picture has no purpose. It cannot be a frame if it is what you see. Without the picture is the frame without its meaning. Its purpose is to set the picture off and not itself.

Who hangs an empty frame upon a wall, and stands before it, deep in reverence, as if a masterpiece were there to see? Yet if you see your brother as a body, it is but this you do. The masterpiece that God has set within this frame is all there is to see. The body holds it for a while, without obscuring it in any way. Yet what God has created needs no frame, for what He has created He supports, and frames within Himself. His masterpiece He offers you to see. And would you rather see the frame instead of this? And see the picture not at all?

The Holy Spirit is the frame God set around the part of Him that you would see as separate. Yet its frame is joined to its Creator, one with Him and with His masterpiece. This is its purpose, and you do not make the frame into the picture when you choose to see it in its place. The frame that God has given it but serves His purpose, not yours apart from His. It is your separate purpose that obscures the picture and cherishes the frame instead of it. Yet God has set His masterpiece within a frame that will endure forever, when yours has crumbled into dust. But think you not the picture is destroyed in any way. What God creates is safe from all corruption, unchanged and perfect in eternity.

Accept God's frame instead of yours, and you will see the masterpiece. Look at its loveliness, and understand the Mind that thought it, not in flesh and bones, but in a frame as lovely as Itself. Its holiness lights up the sinlessness the frame of darkness hides and casts a veil of light across the picture's face, which but reflects the light that shines from it to its Creator. Think not this face was ever darkened because you saw it in a frame of death. God kept it safe that you might look on it and see the holiness that He has given it.

Within the darkness see the Saviour from the dark and understand your brother as his Father's Mind shows him to you. He will step forth from darkness as you look on him, and you will see the dark no more. The darkness touched him not, nor you who brought him forth for you to look upon. His sinlessness but pictures yours. His gentleness becomes your strength, and both will gladly look within, and see the holiness that must be there because of what you looked upon in him. He is the frame in which your holiness is set, and what God gave him must be given you. However, much he overlooks the masterpiece in him, and sees only a frame of darkness, it is still your only function to behold in him what he sees not. And in this seeing is the vision shared that looks on Christ instead of seeing death.

How could the Lord of Heaven not be glad if you appreciate His masterpiece? What could He do but offer thanks to you who love His Son as He does? Would He not make known to you His Love, if you but share His praise of what He loves? God cherishes creation as the perfect Father that He is. And so His joy is made complete when any part of Him joins in His praise, to share His joy. This brother is His perfect gift to you. And He is glad and thankful when you thank His perfect Son for being what he is. And all His thanks and gladness shine on you who would complete His joy, along with Him.

And thus is yours completed. Not one ray of darkness can be seen by those who will to make their Father's happiness complete and theirs along with His. The gratitude of God Himself is freely offered to everyone who shares His purpose. It is not His Will to be alone. And neither is it yours.

Forgive your brother, and you cannot separate yourself from him, nor from his Father. You need no forgiveness, for the wholly pure have never sinned. Give, then, what He has given you, that you may see His Son as one and thank his Father as He thanks you. Nor believe that all His praise is given not to you. For what you give is His, and giving it, you learn to understand His gift to you. And give the Holy Spirit what He offers unto the Father and the Son alike. Nothing has power over you except His Will and yours, who but extend His Will. It was for this you were created, and your brother with you and at one with you.

You are the same as God Himself is One and not divided in His Will. And you must have one purpose, since He gave the same to both of you. His Will is brought together as you join in will, that you be made complete by offering completion to your brother. See not in him the sinfulness he sees but give him honour that you may esteem yourself and him. To each of you is given the power of salvation, that escape from darkness into light be yours to share; that you may see as one what never has been separate, nor apart from all God's Love as given equally.

To the extent to which you value guilt, to that extent will you perceive a world in which attack is justified. To the extent to which you recognize that guilt is meaningless, to that extent will you perceive attack cannot be justified. This is in strict accord with vision's fundamental law: You see what you believe is there, and you believe it there because you want it there. Perception has no other law than this. The rest but stems from this, to hold it up and offer it support. This is perception's form, adapted to this world, of God's more basic law; that love creates itself, and nothing but itself.

God's laws do not obtain directly to a world perception rules, for such a world could not have been created by the Mind to which perception has no meaning. Yet are His laws reflected everywhere. Not that the world where this reflection is, is real at all. Only because His Son believes it is, and from His Son's belief He could not let Himself be separate entirely. He could not enter His Son's insanity with him, but He could be sure His sanity went there with him, so he could not be lost forever in the madness of his wish.

Perception rests on choosing; knowledge does not. Knowledge has but one law because it has but One Creator. But this world has two who made it, and they do not see it as the same. To each it has a different purpose, and to each it is a perfect means to serve the goal for which it is perceived. For specialness, it is the perfect frame to set it off; the perfect battleground to wage its wars, the perfect shelter for the illusions which it would make real. Not one but it upholds in its perception; not one but can be fully justified.

There is another Maker of the world, the simultaneous Corrector of the mad belief that anything could be established and maintained without some link that kept it still within the laws of God; not as the law itself upholds the universe as God created it, but in some form adapted to the need the Son of God believes he has. Corrected error is the error's end. And thus has God protected still His Son, even in error. There is another purpose in the world that error made, because it has another Maker Who can reconcile its goal with His Creator's purpose. In His perception of the world, nothing is seen but justifies forgiveness and the sight of perfect sinlessness. Nothing arises but is met with instant and complete forgiveness.

Nothing remains an instant, to obscure the sinlessness that shines unchanged, beyond the pitiful attempts of specialness to put it out of mind, where it must be and light the body up instead of it. The lamps of Heaven are not for it to choose to see them where it will. If it elects to see them elsewhere from their home, as if they lit a place where they could never be, and you agree, then must the Maker of the world correct your error, lest you remain in darkness, where the lamps are not. Everyone here has entered darkness, yet no one has entered it alone. For he has come with Heaven's Help within him, ready to lead him out of darkness into light at any time.

The time he chooses can be any time, for help is there, awaiting but his choice. And when he chooses to avail himself of what is given him, then will he see each situation that he thought before was means to justify his anger turned to an event which justifies his love. He will hear plainly that the calls to war he heard before are really calls to peace. He will perceive that where he gave attack is but another altar where he can, with equal ease and far more happiness, bestow forgiveness. And he will reinterpret all temptation as just another chance to bring him joy. How can a misperception be a sin? Let all your brother's errors be to you nothing except a chance for you to see the workings of the Helper given you to see the world He made, instead of yours.

What, then, is justified? What do you want? For these two questions are the same. And when you see them as the same, your choice is made. For it is seeing them as one that brings release from the belief there are two ways to see. This world has much to offer to your peace, and many chances to extend your own forgiveness. Such its purpose is, to those who want to see peace and forgiveness descend on them and offer them the light.

The Maker of the world of gentleness has perfect power to offset the world of violence and hate that seems to stand between you and His gentleness. It is not there in His forgiving eyes. And therefore, it need not be there in yours. Sin is the fixed belief perception cannot change. What has been damned is damned and damned forever, being forever unforgivable. If, then, it IS forgiven, sin's perception must have been wrong. And thus is change made possible. The Holy Spirit, too, sees what He sees as far beyond the chance of change. But on His vision sin cannot encroach, for sin has been corrected by His sight. And thus it must have been an error, not a sin. For what it claimed could never be, has been. Sin is attacked by punishment, and so preserved. But to forgive it is to change its state from error into truth.

The Son of God could never sin, but he can wish for what would hurt him. And he has the power to think he can be hurt. What could this be except a misperception of himself? Is this a sin or a mistake, forgivable or not? Does he need help or condemnation? Is it your purpose that he be saved or damned? Forgetting not that what he is to you will make this choice your future? For you make it now, the instant when all time becomes a means to reach a goal. Make, then, your choice. But recognize that in this choice the purpose of the world you see is chosen and WILL be justified.

Minds that are joined, and recognised they are, can feel no guilt. For they cannot attack, and they rejoice that this is so, seeing their safety in this happy fact. Their joy is in the innocence they see. And thus they seek for it, because it is their purpose to behold it and rejoice. Everyone seeks for what will bring him joy, as he defines it. It is not the aim, as such, that varies. Yet it is the way in which the aim is seen that makes the choice of means inevitable, and beyond the hope of change unless the aim is changed. And then the means are chosen once again, as what will bring rejoicing is defined another way, and sought for differently.

Perception's basic law could thus be said, "You will rejoice at what you see because you see it to rejoice." And while you think that suffering and sin will bring you joy, so long will they be there for you to see. Nothing is harmful or beneficent apart from what you wish. It is your wish that makes it what it is in its effects on you. Because you chose it as a means to gain these same effects, believing them to be the bringers of rejoicing and of joy. Even in Heaven does this law obtain. The Son of God creates to bring him joy, sharing his Father's purpose in his own creation, that his joy might be increased, and God's along with his.

You makers of a world that is not so, take rest and comfort in another world where peace abides. This world you bring with you to all the weary eyes and tired hearts that look on sin and beat its sad refrain. From you can come their rest. From you can rise a world they will rejoice to look upon, and where their hearts are glad. In you there is a vision which extends to all of them and covers them in gentleness and light. And in this widening world of light the darkness that they thought was there is pushed away, until it is but distant shadows, far away, not long to be remembered as the sun shines them to nothingness. And all their "evil" thoughts and "sinful" hopes, their dreams of guilt and merciless revenge and every wish to hurt and kill and die, will disappear before the sun you bring.

Would you not do this for the love of God? And for yourself? For think what it would do for you. Your "evil" thoughts that haunt you now will seem increasingly remote and far away from you. And they go farther and farther off, because the sun in you has risen that they may be pushed away before the light. They linger for a while, a little while, in twisted forms too far away for recognition and are gone forever. And in the sunlight you will stand in quiet, in innocence, and wholly unafraid. And from you will the rest you found extend, so that your peace can never fall away and leave you homeless. Those who offer peace to everyone have found a home in Heaven the world cannot destroy. For it is large enough to hold the world within its peace.

In you is all of Heaven. Every leaf that falls is given life in you. Each bird that ever sang will sing again in you. And every flower that ever bloomed has saved its perfume and its loveliness for you. What aim can supersede the Will of God and of His Son, that Heaven be restored to him for whom it was created as his only home? Nothing before and nothing after it. No other place, no other state nor time. Nothing beyond nor nearer. Nothing else. In any form. This can you bring to all the world and all the thoughts that entered it and were mistaken for a little while.

How better could your own mistakes be brought to truth than by your willingness to bring the light of Heaven with you, as you walk beyond the world of darkness into light?

The state of sinlessness is merely this: The whole desire to attack is gone, and so there is no reason to perceive the Son of God as other than he is. The need for guilt is gone because it has no purpose and is meaningless without the goal of sin. Attack and sin are bound as one illusion, each the cause and aim and justifier of the other. Each is meaningless alone but seems to draw a meaning from the other. Each depends upon the other for whatever sense it seems to have. And no-one could believe in one unless the other were the truth, for each attest the other must be true.

Attack makes Christ your enemy, and God along with Him. Must you not be afraid, with "enemies" like these? And must you not be fearful of yourself? For you have hurt yourself and made your Self your "enemy." And now you must believe you are not you, but something alien to yourself and "something else," a "something" to be feared instead of loved. Who would attack whatever he perceives as wholly innocent? And who, because he wishes to attack, can fail to think it must be guilty to deserve the wish and leave him innocent? And who would see the Son of God as innocent, and wish him dead? Christ stands before you both, each time you look on one another. He has not gone because your eyes are closed. But what is there to see by searching for your Saviour, seeing Him through sightless eyes?

It is not Christ you see by looking thus. It is the "enemy," confused with Christ, you look upon. And hate because there is no sin in him for you to see. Nor do you hear his plaintive call, unchanged in content in whatever form the call is made, that you unite with him, and join with him in innocence and peace. And yet, beneath the ego's senseless shrieks, such IS the call that God has given him, that you might hear in him His Call to you, and answer by returning unto God what is His Own.

The Son of God asks only this of you; that you return to him what is his due, that you may share in it with him. Alone does neither have it. So must it remain useless to both. Together, it will give to each an equal strength to save the other and save himself along with him. Forgiven by you, your Saviour offers you salvation. Condemned by you, he offers death to you. In everyone you see but the reflection of what you chose to have him be to you. If you decide against his proper function, the only one he has in truth, you are depriving him of all the joy he would have found, if he fulfilled the role God gave to him.

But think not Heaven is lost to him alone. Nor can it be regained unless the way is shown to him through you, that you may find it, walking by his side.

It is no sacrifice that he be saved, for by his freedom will you gain your own. To let his function be fulfilled is but the means to let yours be. And so you walk toward Heaven or toward hell, but not alone. How beautiful his sinlessness will be when you perceive it! And how great will be your joy, when he is free to offer you the gift of sight God gave to him for you! He has no need but this; that you allow him freedom to complete the task God gave to him.

Remembering but this; that what he does you do, along with him. And as you see him, so do you define the function he will have for you, until you see him differently and let him be what God appointed that he be to you.

Against the hatred that the Son of God may cherish toward himself is God believed to be without the power to save what He created from the pain of hell. But in the love he shows himself is God made free to let His Will be done. In each of you, you see the picture of your own belief in what the Will of God must be for you. In your forgiveness will you understand His Love for you; through your attack believe He hates you, thinking Heaven must be hell. Look once again upon your brother, not without the understanding that he is the way to Heaven or to hell, as you perceive him. But forget not this; the role you give to him is given you and you will walk the way you pointed out to him because it is your judgement on yourself.

The grace of God rests gently on forgiving eyes and everything they look on speaks of Him to the beholder. He can see no evil; nothing in the world to fear, and no-one who is different from himself. And as he loves them, so he looks upon himself with love and gentleness. He would no more condemn himself for his mistakes than damn another. He is not an arbiter of vengeance, nor a punisher of sin. The kindness of his sight rests on himself with all the tenderness it offers others. For he would only heal and only bless. And being in accord with what God wills, he has the power to heal and bless all those he looks on with the grace of God upon his sight.

Eyes become used to darkness, and the light of brilliant day seems painful to the eyes grown long accustomed to the dim effects perceived at twilight. And they turn away from sunlight, and the clarity it brings to what they look upon. Dimness seems better; easier to see, and better recognized.

Somehow, the vague and more obscure seems easier to look upon; less painful to the eyes than what is wholly clear and unambiguous. Yet this is not what eyes are for.
And who can say that he prefers the darkness, and maintain he wants to see? The wish to see calls down the grace of God upon your eyes and brings the gift of light that makes sight possible.

Will you behold your brother? God is glad to have you look on him. He does not will your Saviour be unrecognized by you. Nor does He will that he remains without the function that He gave to him. Let him no more be lonely, for the lonely ones are those who see no function in the world for them to fill; no place where they are needed, and no aim which only they can perfectly fulfil.

Such is the Holy Spirit's kind perception of specialness; His use of what you made, to heal instead of harm. To each He gives a special function in salvation he alone can fill; a part for only him. Nor is the plan complete until he finds his special function, and fulfils the part assigned to him, to make himself complete within a world where incompletion rules.

Here, where the laws of God do not prevail in perfect form, can he yet do one perfect thing, and make one perfect choice. And by this act of special faithfulness to one perceived as other than himself, he learns the gift was given to himself, and so they must be one. Forgiveness is the only function meaningful in time. It is the means the Holy Spirit uses to translate specialness from sin into salvation. Forgiveness is for all. But when it rests on all it is complete, and every function of this world completed with it. Then is time no more.

Yet while in time, there is still much to do. And each must do what is allotted him, for on his part does all the plan depend. He has a special part in time, for so he chose, and choosing it, he made it for himself. His wish was not denied, but changed in form, to let it serve his brother and himself, and thus become a means to save instead of lose. Salvation is no more than a reminder this world is not your home; its laws are not imposed on you, its values are not yours. And this is seen and understood as each one takes his part in its undoing, as he did in making it. He has the means for either, as he always did. The specialness he chose to hurt himself did God appoint to be the means for his salvation, from the very instant that the choice was made. His special sin was made his special grace. His special hate became his special love.

The Holy Spirit needs your special function, that His may be fulfilled. Think not you lack a special value here. You wanted it and it is given you. All that you made can serve salvation easily and well. The Son of God can make no choice the Holy Spirit cannot employ on his behalf, and not against himself. Only in darkness does your specialness appear to be attack. In light, you see it as your special function in the plan to save the Son of God from all attack and let him understand that he is safe, as he has always been, and will remain in time and in eternity alike. This is the function given each of you for one another. Take it gently, then, from one another's hand, and let salvation be perfectly fulfilled in both of you. Do this one thing, that everything be given you.

And if the Holy Spirit can commute each sentence that you laid upon yourself into a blessing, then it cannot be a sin. Sin is the one thing in all the world that cannot change. It is immutable. And on its changelessness the world depends. The magic of the world can seem to hide the pain of sin from sinners and deceive with glitter and with guile. Yet each one knows the cost of sin is death. And so it is. For sin is a request for death, a wish to make this world's foundation sure as love, dependable as Heaven, and as strong as God Himself. The world is safe from love to everyone who thinks sin possible. Nor will it change. Yet is it possible what God created not should share the attributes of His creation, when it opposes it in every way?

It cannot be the "sinner's" wish for death is just as strong as is God's Will for life. Nor can the basis of a world He did not make be firm and sure as Heaven. How could it be that hell and Heaven are the same? And is it possible that what He did not will cannot be changed? What is immutable besides His Will? And what can share Its attributes except Itself? What wish can rise against His Will, and be immutable? If you could realize nothing is changeless but the Will of God, this course would not be difficult for you. For it is this that you do not believe. Yet there is nothing else you could believe, if you but looked at what it really is.

Let us go back to what we said before and think of it more carefully. It must be so that either God is mad or is this world a place of madness. Not one Thought of His makes any sense at all within this world. And nothing that the world believes as true has any meaning in His Mind at all. What makes no sense and has no meaning is insanity. And what is madness cannot be the truth. If one belief so deeply valued here were true, then every Thought God ever had is an illusion.

And if but one Thought of His is true, then all beliefs the world gives any meaning to are false and make no sense at all. This is the choice you make. Do not attempt to see it differently, nor twist it into something it is not. For only this decision can you make. The rest is up to God, and not to you.

To justify one value that the world upholds is to deny your Father's sanity and yours. For God and His beloved Son do not think differently. And it is the agreement of their thought that makes the Son a co-creator with the Mind Whose Thought created him. And if he chooses to believe one thought opposed to truth, he has decided he is not his Father's Son because the Son is mad, and sanity must lie apart from both the Father and the Son. This you believe. Think not that this belief depends upon the form it takes.

Who thinks the world is sane in any way, is justified in anything it thinks, or is maintained by any form of reason, believes this to be true. Sin is not real because the Father and the Son are not insane. This world is meaningless because it rests on sin. Who could create the changeless, if it does not rest on truth?

The Holy Spirit has the power to change the whole foundation of the world you see to something else; a basis not insane, on which a sane perception can be based, another world perceived. And one in which nothing is contradicted that would lead the Son of God to sanity and joy. Nothing attests to death and cruelty, to separation and to differences. For here is everything perceived as one, and no-one loses that each one may gain.

Test everything that you believe against this one requirement. And understand that everything that meets this one demand is worthy of your faith. But nothing else. What is not love is sin, and either one perceives the other as insane and meaningless. Love is the basis for a world perceived as wholly mad to sinners, who believe theirs is the way to sanity. But sin is equally insane within the sight of love, whose gentle eyes would look beyond the madness, and rest peacefully on truth. Each sees a world immutable, as each defines the changeless and eternal truth of what you are. And each reflects a view of what the Father and the Son must be, to make that viewpoint meaningful and sane.

Your special function is the special form in which the fact that God is not insane appears most sensible and meaningful to you. The content is the same. The form is suited to your special needs, and to the special time and place in which you think you find yourself and where you can be free of place and time, and all that you believe must limit you. The Son of God cannot be bound by time nor place, nor anything God did not will. Yet if His Will is seen as madness, then the form of sanity which makes it most acceptable to those who are insane requires special choice. Nor can this choice be made BY the insane, whose problem is their choices are not free, and made with reason in the light of sense.

It would be madness to entrust salvation to the insane. Because He is not mad has God appointed One as sane as He to raise a saner world to meet the sight of everyone who chose insanity as his salvation. To this One is given the choice of form most suitable to him; one which will not attack the world he sees, but enter into it in quietness, and show him he is mad. This One but points to an alternative, another way of looking at what he has seen before, and recognizes as the world in which he lives, and thought he understood before.

Now must he question this, because the form of the alternative is one which he cannot deny, nor overlook, nor fail completely to perceive at all. To each his special function is designed to be perceived as possible and more and more desired, as it proves to him that it is an alternative he really wants. From this position does his sinfulness and all the sin he sees within the world, offer him less and less. Until he comes to understand it cost him his sanity and stands between him and whatever hope he has of being sane.

Nor is he left without escape from madness, for he has a special part in everyone's escape. He can no more be left outside, without a special function in the hope of peace, than could the Father overlook His Son, and pass him by in careless thoughtlessness. What is dependable except God's Love? And where does sanity abide except in Him? The One Who speaks for Him can show you this, in the alternative He chose especially for you. It is God's Will that you remember this, and so emerge from deepest mourning into perfect joy. Accept the function that has been assigned to you in God's Own plan to show His Sons that hell and Heaven are different, not the same. And that in Heaven they are all the same, without the differences which would have made a hell of Heaven and a heaven of hell, had such insanity been possible.

The whole belief that someone loses but reflects the underlying tenet God must be insane. For in this world it seems that one must gain because another lost. If this were true, then God is mad indeed! But what is this belief except a form of the more basic tenet, "Sin is real, and rules the world"? For every little gain must someone lose and pay exact amount in blood and suffering. For otherwise would evil triumph, and destruction be the total cost of any gain at all. You who believe that God is mad, look carefully at this, and understand that it must be that either God or this must be insane, but hardly both.

Salvation is rebirth of the idea no-one can lose for anyone to gain. And everyone must gain, if anyone would be a gainer. Here is sanity restored. And on this single rock of truth can faith in God's eternal saneness rest in perfect confidence and perfect peace. Reason is satisfied, for all insane beliefs can be corrected here. And sin must be impossible, if this is true. This is the rock on which salvation rests, the vantage point from which the Holy Spirit gives meaning and direction to the plan in which your special function has a part. For here your special function is made whole because it shares the function of the whole.

Remember all temptation is but this; a mad belief that God's insanity would make you sane and give you what you want. That either God or you must lose to madness because your aims can not be reconciled. Death demands life, but life is not maintained at any cost. No-one can suffer for the Will of God to be fulfilled. Salvation is His Will because you share it. Not for you alone, but for the Self which is the Son of God. He cannot lose, for if he could, the loss would be his Father's and in Him no loss is possible. And this is sane because it is the truth.

The Holy Spirit can use all that you give to Him for your salvation. But He cannot use what you withhold, for He cannot take it from you without your willingness. For if He did, you would believe He wrested it from you against your will. And so you would not learn it is your will to be without it. You need not give it to Him wholly willingly, for if you could, you had no need of Him. But this He needs; that you prefer He take it than that you keep it for yourself alone and recognize that what brings loss to no-one you would not know. This much is necessary to add to the idea no-one can lose for you to gain. And nothing more.

Here is the only principle salvation needs. Nor is it necessary that your faith in it be strong, unswerving, and without attack from all beliefs opposed to it. You have no fixed allegiance. But remember salvation is not needed by the saved. You are not called upon to do what one divided still against himself would find impossible. Have little faith that wisdom could be found in such a state of mind. But be you thankful that only little faith is asked of you. What but a little faith remains to those who still believe in sin? What could they know of Heaven and the justice of the saved?

There is a kind of justice in salvation of which the world knows nothing. To the world, justice and vengeance are the same, for sinners see justice only as their punishment, perhaps sustained by someone else, but not escaped. The laws of sin demand a victim. Who it may be makes little difference. But death must be the cost and must be paid. This is not justice, but insanity. Yet how could justice be defined without insanity where love means hate and death is seen as victory and triumph over eternity and timelessness and life?

You who know not of justice still can ask and learn the answer. Justice looks on all in the same way. It is not just that one should lack for what another has. For that is vengeance in whatever form it takes. Justice demands no sacrifice, for any sacrifice is made that sin may be preserved and kept. It is a payment offered for the cost of sin, but not the total cost. The rest is taken from another, to be laid beside your little payment, to "atone" for all that you would keep, and not give up. So is the victim seen as partly you, with someone else by far the greater part. And in the total cost, the greater his the less is yours. And justice, being blind, is satisfied by being paid, it matters not by whom. Can this BE justice? God knows not of this. But justice does He know and knows it well. For He is wholly fair to everyone.

Vengeance is alien to God's Mind because He knows of justice. To be just is to be fair, and not be vengeful. Fairness and vengeance are impossible, for each one contradicts the other and denies that it is real. It is impossible for you to share the Holy Spirit's justice with a mind that can conceive of specialness at all. Yet how could He be just if He condemns a sinner for the crimes he did not do, but thinks he did? And where would justice be if He demanded of the ones obsessed with the idea of punishment that they lay it aside, unaided, and perceive it is not true? It is extremely hard for those who still believe sin meaningful to understand the Holy Spirit's justice.

They must believe He shares their own confusion and cannot avoid the vengeance that their own belief in justice must entail. And so they fear the Holy Spirit, and perceive the "wrath" of God in Him. Nor can they trust Him not to strike them dead with lightning bolts torn from the "fires" of Heaven by God's Own angry hand. They do believe that Heaven is hell and are afraid of love. And deep suspicion and the chill of fear comes over them when they are told that they have never sinned. Their world depends on sin's stability. And they perceive the "threat" of what God knows as justice to be more destructive to themselves and to their world than vengeance, which they understand and love.

So do they think the loss of sin a curse. And flee the Holy Spirit as if He were a messenger from hell, sent from above, in treachery and guile, to work God's vengeance on them in the guise of a deliverer and friend. What could He be to them except a devil dressed to deceive, within an angel's cloak. And what escape has He for them except a door to hell that seems to look like Heaven's gate?

Yet justice cannot punish those who ask for punishment, but have a Judge Who knows that they are wholly innocent in truth. In justice, He is bound to set them free, and give them all the honour they deserve, and have denied themselves because they are not fair, and cannot understand that they are innocent. Love is not understandable to sinners because they think that justice is split off from love and stands for something else.

And thus is love perceived as weak, and vengeance strong. For love has lost when judgement left its side and is too weak to save from punishment. But vengeance without love has gained in strength by being separate and apart from love. And what but vengeance now can help and save, while love stands feebly by, with helpless hands, bereft of justice and vitality, and powerless to save? What can Love asks of you who think that all of this is true? Could He, in justice and in love believe, in your confusion, you have much to give? You are not asked to trust Him far. No further than what you see He offers you and what you recognize you could not give yourself.

In God's Own justice does He recognize all you deserve but understands as well that you cannot accept it for yourself. It is His special function to hold out to you the gifts the innocent deserves. And everyone that you accept brings joy to Him as well as you. He knows that Heaven is richer made by each one you accept. And God rejoices as His Son receives what loving justice knows to be his due. For love and justice are not different.

Because they are the same does mercy stand at God's right Hand and gives the Son of God the power to forgive Himself of sin.

To him who merits everything, how can it be that anything be kept from him? For that would be injustice, and unfair indeed to all the holiness that is in him, however much he recognizes it not. God knows of no injustice. He would not allow His Son be judged by those who seek his death, and could not see his worth at all. What honest witnesses could they call forth, to speak on his behalf? And who would come to plead for him and not against his life? No justice would be given him by you. Yet God ensured that justice would be done unto the Son He loves and would protect from all unfairness you might seek to offer, believing vengeance is his proper due.

As specialness cares not who pays the cost of sin, so it be paid, the Holy Spirit heeds not who looks on innocence at last, provided it is seen and recognized. For just one witness is enough, if he sees truly. Simple justice asks no more. Of each one does the Holy Spirit ask if he will be that one, so justice may return to love, and there be satisfied. Each special function He allots is but for this; that each one learns that love and justice are not separate. And both are strengthened by their union with each other. Without love is justice prejudiced and weak. And love without justice is impossible. For love is fair and cannot chasten without cause. What cause can BE to warrant an attack upon the innocent? In justice, then, does love correct mistakes, but not in vengeance. For that would be unjust to innocence.

You can be perfect witness to the power of love and justice, if you understand it is impossible the Son of God could merit vengeance. You need not perceive, in every circumstance, that this is true. Nor need you look to your experience within the world, which is but shadows of all that is really happening within yourself. The understanding which you need comes not of you, but from a larger Self, so great and holy that He could not doubt His innocence. Your special function is a call to Him, that He may smile on you whose sinlessness He shares. His understanding will be yours. And so the Holy Spirit's special function has been fulfilled. God's Son has found a witness unto his sinlessness, and not his sin. How little need you give the Holy Spirit, that simple justice may be given you!

Without impartiality there is no justice. How can specialness be just? Judge not because you cannot, not because you are a miserable sinner, too. How can the special really understand that justice is the same for everyone?

To take from one to give another must be an injustice to them both, since they are equal in the Holy Spirit's sight. Their Father gave the same inheritance to both. Who would have more or less is not aware that he has everything. He is no judge of what must be another's due, because he thinks He is deprived. And so must he be envious, and try to take away from whom he judges. He is not impartial and cannot fairly see another's rights because his own have been obscured to him.

You have the right to all the universe; to perfect peace, complete deliverance from all effects of sin, and to the life eternal, joyous and complete in every way, as God appointed for His Holy Son. This is the only justice Heaven knows, and all the Holy Spirit brings to earth. Your special function shows you nothing else but perfect justice can prevail for you. And you are safe from vengeance in all forms. The world deceives, but it cannot replace God's justice with a version of its own. For only love is just and can perceive what justice must accord the Son of God. Let love decide and never fear that you, in your unfairness, will deprive yourself of what God's justice has allotted you.

What can it be but arrogance to think your little errors cannot be undone by Heaven's justice? And what could this mean except that they are sins and not mistakes, forever uncorrectable, and to be met with vengeance, not with justice? Are you willing to be released from all effects of sin? You cannot answer this until you see all that the answer must entail. For if you answer "yes," it means you will forego all values of this world, in favour of the peace of Heaven. Not one sin would you retain. And not one doubt that this is possible will you hold dear, that sin be kept in place. You mean that truth has greater value now than all illusions. And you recognize that truth must be revealed to you, because you know not what it is.

To give reluctantly is not to gain the gift, because you are reluctant to accepted it. It is saved for you until reluctance to receive it disappears, and you are willing it be given you. God's justice warrants gratitude, not fear. Nothing you give is lost to you or anyone, but cherished and preserved in Heaven, where all of the treasures given to God's Son are kept for him and offered anyone who but holds out his hand in willingness they be received. Nor is the treasure less as it is given out. Each gift but adds to the supply. For God is fair. He does not fight against His Son's reluctance to perceive salvation as a gift from Him. Yet would His justice not be satisfied until it is received by everyone.

Be certain any answer to a problem the Holy Spirit solves will always be one in which no-one loses. And this must be true, because He asks no sacrifice of anyone. An answer which demands the slightest loss to anyone has not resolved the problem, but has added to it, and made it greater, harder to resolve, and more unfair. It is impossible the Holy Spirit could see unfairness as a resolution. To Him, what is unfair must be corrected because it is unfair. And every error is a perception in which one, at least, is seen unfairly. Thus is justice not accorded to the Son of God. When anyone is seen as losing, he has been condemned. And punishment becomes his due, instead of justice.

The sight of innocence makes punishment impossible, and justice sure. The Holy Spirit's perception leaves no ground for an attack. Only a loss could justify attack, and loss of any kind He cannot see. The world solves problems in another way. It sees a resolution as a state in which it is decided who shall win and who shall lose; how much the one shall take, and how much can the loser still defend.

Yet does the problem still remain unsolved, for only justice can set up a state in which there is no loser; no-one left unfairly treated and deprived, and thus with grounds for vengeance. Problem solving cannot be vengeance, which, at best, can bring another problem added to the first, in which the murder is not obvious. The Holy Spirit's problem solving is the way in which the problem ends. It has been solved because it has been met with justice. Until it has it will recur, because it has not yet been solved. The principle that justice means no-one can lose is crucial to this course. For miracles depends on justice. Not as it is seen through this world's eyes, but as God knows it, and as knowledge is reflected in the sight the Holy Spirit gives.

No-one deserves to lose. And what would be unjust to him cannot occur. Healing must be for everyone because he does not merit an attack of any kind. What order can there be in miracles, unless someone deserves to suffer more, and others less? And is this justice to the wholly innocent? A miracle is justice. It is not a special gift to some, to be withheld from others as less worthy, more condemned, and thus apart from healing. Who is there who can be separate from salvation, if its purpose is the end of specialness? Where is salvation's justice if some errors are unforgivable, and warrant vengeance in place of healing and return of peace?

Salvation cannot seek to help God's Son be more unfair than He has sought to be. If miracles, the Holy Spirit's gift, were given specially to an elect and special group, and kept apart from others as less deserving, then is He ally to specialness. What He cannot perceive He bears no witness to. And everyone is equally entitled to His gift of healing and deliverance and peace. To give a problem to the Holy Spirit to solve for you means that you want it solved. To keep it for yourself to solve without His help is to decide it should remain unsettled, unresolved and lasting in its power of injustice and attack. No-one can be unjust to you, unless you have decided first to be unjust. And then must problems rise to block your way, and peace be scattered by the winds of hate.

Unless you think that all your brothers have an equal right to miracles with you, you will not claim your right to them because you were unjust to one with equal rights. Seek to deny and you will feel denied. Seek to deprive and you have been deprived. A miracle can never be received because another could receive it not. Only forgiveness offers miracles. And pardon must be just to everyone.

The little problems that you keep and hide become your secret sins, because you did not choose to let them be removed for you. And so they gather dust and grow, until they cover everything that you perceive, and leave you fair to no-one. Not one right do you believe you have. And bitterness, with vengeance justified and mercy lost, condemns you as unworthy of forgiveness. The unforgiven have no mercy to bestow upon another. That is why your sole responsibility must be to take forgiveness for yourself. The miracle that you receive, you give. Each one becomes an illustration of the law on which salvation rests; that justice must be done to all, if anyone is to be healed. No-one can lose and everyone must benefit.

Each miracle is an example of what justice can accomplish when it is offered to everyone alike. It is received and given equally. It is awareness that giving and receiving are the same. Because it does not make the same unlike, it sees no differences where none exist. And thus it is the same for everyone, because it sees no differences in them. Its offering is universal and it teaches but one message:

> What is God's belongs to everyone and is his due.

In the "dynamics" of attack is sacrifice a key idea. It is the pivot upon which all compromise, all desperate attempts to strike a bargain, and all conflicts achieve a seeming balance. It is the symbol of the central theme that somebody must lose. Its focus on the body is apparent, for it is always an attempt to limit loss.

The body is itself a sacrifice; a giving up of power in the name of saving just a little for yourself. To see a brother in another body, separate from yours, is the expression of a wish to see a little part of him and sacrifice the rest. Look at the world, and you will see nothing attached to anything beyond itself. All seeming entities can come a little nearer, or go a little farther off, but cannot join.

The world you see is based on "sacrifice" of oneness. It is a picture of a complete disunity and total lack of joining. Around each entity is built a wall so seeming solid that it looks as if what is inside can never reach without, and what is out can never reach and join with what is locked away, within the wall. Each part must sacrifice the other part, to keep itself complete. For if they joined, each one would lose its own identity, and by their separation are their selves maintained.

The little that the body fences off becomes the self, preserved through sacrifice of all the rest. And all the rest must lose this little part, remaining incomplete to keep its own identity intact. In this perception of yourself, the body's loss would be a sacrifice indeed. For sight of bodies becomes the sign that sacrifice is limited, and something still remains for you alone. And for this little to belong to you, are limits placed on everything outside, just as they are on everything you think is yours. For giving and receiving are the same. And to accept the limits of a body is to impose these limits on each brother whom you see. For you must see him as you see yourself.

The body is a loss and can be made to sacrifice. And while you see your brother as a body, apart from you and separate in his cell, you are demanding sacrifice of him and you. What greater sacrifice could be demanded than that God's Son perceive himself without his Father? And his Father be without His Son? Yet every sacrifice demands that they be separate and without the other. The memory of God must be denied if any sacrifice is asked of anyone. What witness to the wholeness of God's Son is seen within a world of separate bodies, however much he witnesses to truth? He is invisible in such a world. Nor can his song of union and of love be heard at all. Yet is it given him to make the world recede before his song and sight of him replace the body's eyes.

Those who would see the witnesses to truth instead of to illusion merely ask that they might see a purpose in the world that gives it sense and makes it meaningful. Without your special function has this world no meaning for you. Yet it can become a treasure house as rich and limitless as Heaven itself. No instant passes here in which your brother's holiness cannot be seen, to add a limitless supply to every meagre scrap and tiny crumb of happiness that you allot yourself.

You can lose sight of oneness but cannot make sacrifice of its reality. Nor can you lose what you would sacrifice, nor keep the Holy Spirit from His task of showing you that it has not been lost. Hear, then, the song your brother sings to you. And let the world recede and take the rest his witness offers on behalf of peace. But judge him not, for you will hear no song of liberation for yourself, nor see what it is given him to witness to, that you may see it and rejoice with him. Make not his holiness a sacrifice to your belief in sin. You sacrifice your innocence with his and die each time you see in him a sin deserving death.

Yet every instant can you be reborn and given life again. His holiness gives life to you, who cannot die because his sinlessness is known to God and can no more be sacrificed by you than can the light in you be blotted out because he sees it not. You who would make a sacrifice of life, and make your eyes and ears bear witness to the death of God and of His Holy Son, think not that you have power to make of them what God willed not they be. In Heaven, God's Son is not imprisoned in a body, nor is sacrificed in solitude to sin.

And as he is in Heaven, so must he be eternally and everywhere. He is the same forever. Born again each instant, untouched by time, and far beyond the reach of any sacrifice of life or death. For neither did he make, and only one was given him, by One Who knows His gifts can never suffer sacrifice and loss. God's justice rests in gentleness upon His Son and keeps him safe from all injustice the world would lay upon him. Could it be that you could make his sins reality, and sacrifice his Father's Will for him?

Condemn him not by seeing him within the rotting prison where he sees himself. It is your special function to ensure the door be opened, that he may come forth to shine on you, and give you back the gift of freedom by receiving it of you. What is the Holy Spirit's special function but to release the holy Son of God from the imprisonment he made to keep himself from justice? Could your function be a task apart and separate from His Own?

It is not difficult to understand the reasons why you do not ask the Holy Spirit to solve all problems for you. He has not greater difficulty in resolving some than others. Every problem is the same to Him, because each one is solved in just the same respect, and through the same approach. The aspects which need solving do not change, whatever form the problem seems to take. A problem can appear in many forms, and it will do so while the problem lasts. It serves no purpose to attempt to solve it in a special form. It will recur and then recur again and yet again, until it has been answered for all time, and will not rise again in any form. And only then are you released from it.

The Holy Spirit offers you release from every problem that you think you have. They are the same to Him because each one, regardless of the form it seems to take, is a demand that someone suffer loss, and make a sacrifice that you might gain. And when the situation is worked out so no-one loses, is the problem gone, because it was an error in perception which now has been corrected. One mistake is not more difficult for Him to bring to truth than is another. For there IS but one mistake; the whole idea that loss is possible and could result in gain for anyone. If this were true, then God would be unfair; sin would be possible, attack be justified, and vengeance fair.

This one mistake, in any form, has one correction. There is no loss; to think there is, is a mistake. You have no problems, though you think you have. And yet you could not think so, if you saw them vanish one by one, without regard to size, complexity, or place and time, or any attribute which you perceive that makes each one seem different from the rest. Think not the limits you impose on what you see can limit God in any way.

The miracle of justice can correct all errors. Every problem is an error. It does injustice to the Son of God, and therefore is not true. The Holy Spirit does not evaluate injustices as great or small or more or less. They have no properties to Him. They are mistakes from which the Son of God is suffering, but needlessly. And so He takes the thorns and nails away. He does not pause to judge whether the hurt be large or little. He makes but one judgement; that to hurt God's Son must be unfair and therefore is not so.

You who believe it safe to give but some mistakes to be corrected while you keep the others to yourself, remember this: Justice is total. There is no such thing as partial justice. If the Son of God is guilty then is he condemned, and he deserves no mercy from the God of justice. But ask not God to punish him because you find him guilty and would have him die.

God offers you the means to see his innocence. Would it be fair to punish him because you will not look at what is there to see? Each time you keep a problem for yourself to solve or judge that it is one which has no resolution, you have made it great, and past the hope of healing. You deny the miracle of justice can be fair.

If God is just, then can there be no problems that justice cannot solve. But you believe that some injustices are fair and good, and necessary to preserve yourself. It is these problems that you think are great and cannot be resolved. For there are those you want to suffer loss, and no-one whom you wish to be preserved from sacrifice entirely. Consider once again your special function. One is given you to see in him his perfect sinlessness. And you will ask no sacrifice of him, because you could not will he suffer loss. The miracle of justice you call forth will rest on you as surely as on him. Nor will the Holy Spirit be content until it is received by everyone. For what you give to Him is everyone's, and by your giving it can.

He ensures that everyone receives it equally. Think, then, how great your own release will be, when you are willing to receive correction for all your problems. You will not keep one, for pain in any form you will not want. And you will see each little hurt resolved before the Holy Spirit's gentle sight. For all of them are little in His sight, and worth no more than just a tiny sigh before they disappear, to be forever undone and unremembered. What seemed once to be a special problem, a mistake without a remedy, or an affliction without a cure, has been transformed into a universal blessing. Sacrifice is gone. And in its place the Love of God can be remembered and will shine away all memory of sacrifice and loss.

God cannot be remembered until justice is loved instead of feared. He cannot be unjust to anyone or anything, because He knows that everything that is belongs to Him and will forever be as He created it. Nothing He loves but must be sinless and beyond attack. Your special function opens wide the door beyond which is the memory of His Love kept perfectly intact and undefiled. And all you need to do is but to wish that Heaven be given you instead of hell, and every bolt and barrier that seems to hold the door securely barred and locked will merely fall away, and disappear. For it is not your Father's Will that you should offer or receive less than He gave, when He created you in perfect love.

Complexity is not of God. How could it be, when all He knows is one? He knows of one creation, one reality, one truth, and but one Son. Nothing conflicts with oneness. How, then, could there be complexity in Him? What is there to decide? For it is conflict that makes choice possible.

The truth is simple; it is one, without an opposite. And how could strife enter in its simple presence and bring complexity where oneness is? The truth makes no decisions, for there is nothing to decide between. And only if there were could choosing be a necessary step in the advance toward oneness. What is everything leaves room for nothing else.

Yet is this magnitude beyond the scope of this curriculum. Nor is it necessary we dwell on anything that cannot be immediately grasped. There is a borderland of thought which stands between this world and Heaven. It is not a place, and when you reach it is apart from time. Here is the meeting-place where thoughts are brought together; where conflicting values meet, and all illusions are laid down beside the truth, where they are judged to be untrue. This borderland is just beyond the gate of Heaven. Here is every thought made pure and wholly simple. Here is sin denied and everything that is received instead.

This is the journey's end. We have referred to it as the real world. And yet there is a contradiction here, in that the words imply a limited reality, a partial truth, a segment of the universe made true. This is because knowledge makes no attack upon perception. They are brought together, and only one continues past the gate where Oneness is. Salvation is a borderland where place and time and choice have meaning still, and yet it can be seen that they are temporary, out of place and every choice has been already made. Nothing the Son of God believes can be destroyed. But what is truth to him must be brought to the last comparison that he will ever make, the last evaluation that will be possible, the final judgement upon this world. It is the judgement of the truth upon illusion, of knowledge on perception; – it has no meaning and does not exist.

This is not your decision. It is but a simple statement of a simple fact. But in this world there are no simple facts, because what is the same and what is different remain unclear. The one essential thing to make a choice at all is this distinction. And herein lies the difference between the worlds. In this one, choice is made impossible. In the real world is choosing simplified.

Salvation stops just short of Heaven, for only perception needs salvation. Heaven was never lost, and so cannot be saved. Yet who can make a choice between the wish for Heaven and the wish for hell unless he recognizes they are not the same? This difference is the learning goal this course has set. It will not go beyond this aim. Its only purpose is to teach what is the same and what is different, leaving room to make the only choice which can be made.

There is no basis for choice in this complex and over complicated world. For no-one understands what is the same and seems to choose where no choice really is. The real world is the area of choice made real, not in the outcome, but in the perception of alternatives for choice. That there is choice is an illusion. Yet within this one lies the undoing of every illusion, not excepting this is not this like your special function, where the separation is undone by change of purpose in what once was specialness, and now is union? All illusions are but one. And in the recognition, this is so, lies the ability to give up all attempts to choose between them, and to make them different. There is no conflict here. No sacrifice is possible in the relinquishment of an illusion recognised as such. Where all reality has been withdrawn from what was never true, can it be hard to give it up, and choose what must be true?

Forgiveness is this world's equivalent of Heaven's justice. It translates the world of sin into a simple world, where justice can be reflected from beyond the gate behind which total lack of limits lies. Nothing in boundless love could need forgiveness. And what is charity within the world gives way to simple justice past the gate that opens into Heaven. No-one forgives unless he has believed in sin, and still believes that he has much to be forgiven. Forgiveness thus becomes the means by which he learns he has done nothing to forgive. Forgiveness always rests upon the one who offers it, until he sees himself as needing it no more. And thus is he returned to his real function of creating, which his forgiveness offers him again.

Forgiveness turns the world of sin into a world of glory, wonderful to see. Each flower shines in light, and every bird sings of the joy of Heaven. There is no sadness and there is no parting here, for everything is totally forgiven. And what has been forgiven must join, for nothing stands between, to keep them separate and apart. The sinless must perceive that they are one, for nothing stands between to push the other off. And in the space which sin left vacant do they join as one, in gladness recognizing what is part of them has not been kept apart and separate.

The holy place on which you stand is but the space that sin has left. And here you see the face of Christ, arising in its place. Who could behold the face of Christ and not recall His Father as He really is? Who could fear love and stand upon the ground where sin has left a place for Heaven's altar to rise and tower far above the world, and reach beyond the universe to touch the heart of all creation? What is Heaven but a song of gratitude and love and praise, by everything created to the Source of its creation?

The holiest of altars is set where once sin was believed to be. And here does every light of heaven come, to be rekindled and increased in joy. For here is what was lost restored to them and all their radiance made whole again.

Forgiveness brings no little miracles to lay before the gate of Heaven. Here the Son of God Himself comes to receive each gift that brings him nearer to his home. Not one is lost, and none is cherished more than any other. Each reminds him of His Father's Love as surely as the rest. And each one teaches him that what he feared he loves the most. What but a miracle could change his mind, so that he understands that love cannot be feared? What other miracle is there but this? And what else need there be to make the space between you disappear?

Where sin once was perceived will rise a world which will become an altar to the truth and you will join the lights of Heaven there and sing their song of gratitude and praise. And as they come to you to be complete, so will you go with them. For no-one hears the song of Heaven and remains without a voice that adds its power to the song and makes it sweeter still. And each one joins the singing at the altar which was raised within the tiny spot that sin proclaimed to be its own. And what was tiny then has soared into a magnitude of song in which the universe has joined with but a single voice. This tiny spot of sin that stands between you still is holding back the happy opening of Heaven's gate. How little is the hindrance which withholds the wealth of Heaven from you! And how great will be the joy in Heaven when you join the mighty chorus to the Love of God!

A little hindrance can seem large indeed to those who do not understand that miracles are all the same. Yet teaching that is what this course is for. This is its only purpose, for only that is all there is to learn. And you can learn it many different ways. All learning is a help or hindrance to the gate of Heaven. Nothing in between is possible. There are two teachers only, who point in different ways. And you will go along the way your chosen teacher leads. There are but two directions you can take, while time remains and choice is meaningful. For never will another road be made except the way to Heaven. You but choose whether to go towards Heaven, or away to nowhere. There is nothing else to choose.

Nothing is ever lost but time, which in the end is meaningless. For it is but a little hindrance to eternity, quite meaningless to the real Teacher of the world. Yet since you do believe in it, why should you waste it going nowhere, when it can be used to reach a goal as high as learning can achieve?

Think not the way to Heaven's gate is difficult at all. Nothing you undertake with certain purpose and high resolve and happy confidence, holding each other's hand and keeping step to Heaven's song, is difficult to do. But it is hard indeed to wander off, alone and miserable, down a road which leads to nothing, and which has no purpose.

God gave His Teacher to replace the one you made, not to conflict with it. And what He would replace has been replaced. Time lasted but an instant in your mind, with no effect upon eternity. And so is all time passed, and everything exactly as it was before the way to nothingness was made. The tiny tick of time in which the first mistake was made, and all of them within that one mistake, held also the correction for that one, and all of them that came within the first. And in that tiny instant time was gone, for that was all it ever was. What God gave answer to is answered and is gone.

To you who still believe you live in time and know not it is gone, the Holy Spirit still guides you through the infinitely small and senseless maze you still perceive in time, though it has long since gone. You think you live in what is past. Each thing you look upon you saw but for an instant, long ago, before its unreality gave way to truth. Not one illusion still remains unanswered in your mind. Uncertainty was brought to certainty so long ago that it is hard indeed to hold it to your heart, as if it were before you still.

The tiny instant you would keep and make eternal, passed away in Heaven too soon for anything to notice it had come. What disappeared too quickly to affect the simple knowledge of the Son of God can hardly still be there, for you to choose to be your teacher. Only in the past, – an ancient past, too short to make a world in answer to creation, – did this world appear to rise. So very long ago, for such a tiny interval of time, that not one note in Heaven's song was missed.

Yet in each unforgiving act or thought, in every judgement and in all belief in sin, is that one instant still called back, as if it could be made again in time. You keep an ancient memory before your eyes. And he who lives in memories alone is unaware of where he is. Is this a hindrance to the place whereon he stands? Is any echo from the past that he may hear a fact in what is there to hear where he is now? And how much can his own delusions about time and place affect a change in where he really is?

The unforgiven is a voice that calls from out a past forever more gone by. And everything which points to it as real is but a wish that what is gone could be made real again and seen as here and now, in place of what is really now and here.

Is this a hindrance to the truth the past is gone, and cannot be returned to you? And do you want that fearful instant kept, when Heaven seemed to disappear, and God was feared and made a symbol of your hate?

Forget the time of terror that has been so long ago corrected and undone. Can sin withstand the Will of God? Can it be up to you to see the past and put it in the present? You cannot go back. And everything that points the way in the direction of the past but sets you on a mission whose accomplishment can only be unreal. Such is the justice your Ever-Loving Father has ensured must come to you. And from your own unfairness to yourself has He protected you. You cannot lose your way because there is no way but His, and nowhere can you go except to Him.

Would God allow His Son to lose his way along a road long since a memory of time gone by? A dreadful instant in a distant past, now perfectly corrected, is of no concern nor value. Let the dead and gone be peacefully forgotten. Resurrection has come to take its place. And now you are a part of resurrection, not of death. No past illusions have the power to keep you in a place of death, a vault God's Son entered an instant, to be instantly restored unto His Father's perfect Love. And how can he be kept in chains long since removed, and gone forever from his mind?

The Son that God created is as free as God created him. He was reborn the instant that he chose to die instead of live. And will you not forgive him now, because he made an error in the past that God remembers not, and is not there? Now are you shifting back and forth between the past and present. Sometimes the past seems real, as if it were the present. Voices from the past are heard, and then are doubted. You are like to one who still hallucinates but lacks conviction in what he perceives. This is the borderland between the worlds, the bridge between the past and present. Here the shadow of the past remains, but still a present light is dimly recognized. Once it is seen, this light can never be forgotten. It must draw you from the past into the present, where you really are.

The shadow voices do not change the laws of time or of eternity. They come from what is past and gone and hinder not the true existence of the here and now. The real world is the second part of the hallucination time and death are real and have existence which can be perceived. This terrible illusion was denied in but the time it took for God to give His answer to illusion for all time and every circumstance. And then it was no more, to be experienced as there.

Each day, and every minute in each day, and every instant that each minute holds, you but relive the single instant when the time of terror was replaced by love. And so you die each day to live again, until you cross the gap between past and present, which is not a gap at all. Such is each life; a seeming interval from birth to death, and on to life again, a repetition of an instant gone by long ago, which cannot be relived. And all of time is but the mad belief that what is over is still here and now.

Forgive the past and let it go, for it is gone. You stand no longer on the ground that lies between the worlds. You have gone on and reached the world that lies at Heaven's gate. There is no hindrance to the Will of God, nor any need that you repeat again a journey that was over long ago. Look gently on each other and behold the world in which perception of your hate has been transformed into a world of love.

Anything in this world that you believe is good and valuable and worth striving for can hurt you and will do so. Not because it has the power to hurt, but just because you have denied it is but an illusion and made it real. And it is real to you. It is not nothing. And through its perceived reality has entered all the world of sick illusions. All belief in sin, in power of attack, in hurt and harm, in sacrifice and death, has come to you. For no-one can make one illusion real and still escape the rest. For who can choose to keep the ones which he prefers, and find the safety that the truth alone can give? Who can believe illusions are the same, and still maintain that even one is best?

Lead not your little lives in solitude, with one illusion as your only friend. This is no friendship worthy of God's Son, nor one with which he could remain content. Yet God has given him a better Friend, in whom all power in earth and Heaven rests. The one illusion that you think is friend obscures His grace and majesty from you and keeps his friendship and forgiveness from your welcoming embrace. Without him you are friendless. Seek not another friend to take his place. There is no other friend. What God appointed has no substitute, for what illusion can replace the truth?

Who dwells with shadows is alone indeed and loneliness is not the Will of God. Would you allow one shadow to usurp the throne that God appointed for your Friend, if you but realized its emptiness has left yours empty and unoccupied?

Make no illusion friend, for if you do, it can but take the place of him whom God has called your Friend. And it is he who is your only Friend in truth. He brings you gifts that are not of this world, and only he to whom they have been given can make sure that you receive them. He will place them on your throne, when you make room for him on his.

This is a course in miracles. And as such, the laws of healing must be understood before the purpose of the course can be accomplished. Let us review the principles that we have covered and arrange them in a way that summarizes all that must occur for healing to be possible. For when it once is possible it must occur. All sickness comes from separation. When the separation is denied, it goes. For it is gone as soon as the idea which brought it has been healed and been replaced by sanity. Sickness and sin are seen as consequence and cause, in a relationship kept hidden from awareness that it may be carefully preserved from reason's light.

Guilt asks for punishment, and its request is granted. Not in truth, but in the world of shadows and illusions built on sin. The Son of God perceives what he would see because perception IS a wish fulfilled. Perception changes, made to take the place of changeless knowledge. Yet is truth unchanged. It cannot be perceived, but only known. What is perceived takes many forms, but none has meaning. Brought to truth, its senselessness is quite apparent. Kept apart from truth, it seems to have a meaning and be real.

Perception's laws are opposite to truth, and what is true of knowledge is not true of anything that is apart from it. Yet has God given answer to the world of sickness, which applies to all its forms. God's answer is eternal, though it operates in time, where it is needed. Yet because it is of God, the laws of time do not affect its workings. It is in this world, but not a part of it. For it is real, and dwells where all reality must be. Ideas leave not their source, and their effects but seem to be apart from them. Ideas are of the mind. What is projected out, and seems to be external to the mind, is not outside at all, but an effect of what is in, and has not left its source.

God's answer lies where the belief in sin must be, for only there can its effects be utterly undone, and without cause. Perception's laws must be reversed because they are reversals of the laws of truth. The laws of truth forever will be true, and cannot be reversed; yet can be seen as upside-down. And this must be corrected where the illusion of reversal lies.

It is impossible that one illusion be less amenable to truth than are the rest. But it is possible that some are given greater value, and less willingly offered to truth for healing and for help. No illusion has any truth in it. Yet it appears some are more true than others, although this clearly makes no sense at all. All that a hierarchy of illusions can show is preference, not reality. What relevance has preference to the truth? Illusions are illusions and are false. Your preference gives them no reality. Not one is true in any way, and all must yield with equal ease to what God gave as answer to them all. God's Will is One. And any wish that seems to go against His Will has no foundation in the truth.

Sin is not error, for it goes beyond correction to impossibility. Yet the belief that it is real has made some errors seem forever past the hope of healing, and the lasting grounds for hell. If this were so, would Heaven be opposed by its own opposite, as real as it. Then would God's Will be split in two and all creation be subjected to the laws of two opposing powers, until God becomes impatient, splits the world apart, and relegates attack unto Himself. Thus has He lost His Mind, proclaiming sin has taken His reality from Him, and brought His Love at last to vengeance' heels. For such an insane picture, an insane defence can be expected, but cannot establish that the picture must be true.

Nothing gives meaning where no meaning is. And truth needs no defence to make it true. Illusions have no witnesses, and no effects. Who looks on them is but deceived. Forgiveness is the only function here and serves to bring the joy this world denies to every aspect of God's Son where sin was thought to rule. Perhaps you do not see the role forgiveness plays in ending death and all beliefs that rise from mists of guilt.

Sins are beliefs which you impose between your brother and yourself. They limit you to time and place, and give a little space to you, another little space to him. This separating off is symbolized, in your perception, by a body which is clearly separate and a thing apart. Yet what this symbol represents is but your wish to be apart and separate. Forgiveness takes away what stands between your brother and yourself. It is the wish that you be joined with him and not apart. We call it "wish" because it still conceives of other choices and has not yet reached beyond the world of choice entirely.

Yet is this wish in line with Heaven's state and not in opposition to God's Will. Although it falls far short of giving you your full inheritance, it does remove the obstacles which you have placed between the Heaven where you are, and recognition of where and what you are. Facts are unchanged. Yet facts can be denied and thus unknown, though they were known before they were denied.

Salvation, perfect and complete, asks but a little wish that what is true be true; a little willingness to overlook what is not there; a little sigh that speaks for Heaven as a preference to this world which death and desolation seem to rule. In joyous answer will creation rise within you, to replace the world you see with Heaven, wholly perfect and complete. What is forgiveness but a willingness that truth be true? What can remain unhealed and broken from a Unity Which holds all things within Itself? There is no sin. And every miracle is possible the instant that the Son of God perceives his wishes and the Will of God are One.

What is the Will of God? He wills His Son have everything. And this He guaranteed when He created him as everything. It is impossible that anything be lost, if what you have is what you are. This is the miracle by which creation became your function, sharing it with God. It is not understood apart from Him, and therefore has no meaning in this world.

Here does the Son of God ask not too much, but far too little. He would sacrifice his own identity with everything, to find a little treasure of his own. And this he cannot do without a sense of isolation, loss and loneliness. This is the treasure he has sought to find. And he could only be afraid of it. Is fear a treasure? Can uncertainty be what you want? Or is it a mistake about your will, and what you really are? Let us consider what the error is, so it can be corrected, not protected.

Sin is belief attack can be projected outside the mind where the belief arose. Here is the firm conviction that ideas can leave their source made real and meaningful. And from this error does the world of sin and sacrifice arise. This world is an attempt to prove your innocence, while cherishing attack. Its failure lies in that you still feel guilty, though without understanding why. Effects are seen as separate from their source and seem to be beyond you to control or to prevent. What is thus kept apart can never join.

Cause and effect are one, not separate. God wills you learn what always has been true; that He created you as part of Him, and this must still be true because ideas leave not their source. Such is creation's law; that each idea the mind conceives but adds to its abundance, never takes away.

This is as true of what is idly wished as what is truly willed, because the mind can wish to be deceived, but cannot make it be what it is not. And to believe ideas can leave their source is to invite illusions to be true, without success. For never will success be possible in trying to deceive the Son of God.

The miracle is possible when cause and consequence are brought together, not kept separate. The healing of effect without the cause can merely shift effects to other forms. And this is not release. God's Son could never be content with less than full salvation, and escape from guilt. For otherwise he still demands that he must make some sacrifice, and thus denies that everything is his, unlimited by loss of any kind. A tiny sacrifice is just the same in its effects as is the whole idea of sacrifice. If loss in any form is possible, then is God's Son made incomplete and not himself. He has foresworn his Father and himself and made them both his enemies in hate.

Illusions serve the purpose they were made to serve. And from their purpose, they derive whatever meaning that they seem to have. God gave to all illusions that were made another purpose that would justify a miracle whatever form they took. In every miracle all healing lies, for God gave answer to them all as one. And what is one to Him must be the same. If you believe what is the same is different you but deceive yourself. What God calls one will be forever one, not separate. His Kingdom is united; thus, it was created and thus will it ever be.

The miracle but calls your ancient name, which you will recognize because the truth is in your memory. And to this name your brother calls for his release and yours. Heaven is shining on the Son of God. Deny him not, that you may be released. Each instant is the Son of God reborn, until he chooses not to die again. In every wish to hurt he chooses death, instead of what his Father wills for him. Yet every instant offers life to him, because his Father wills that he should live.

In crucifixion is redemption laid, for healing is not needed where there is no pain or suffering. Forgiveness is the answer to attack of any kind. So is attack deprived of its effects, and hate is answered in the name of love. To you to whom it has been given to save the Son of God from crucifixion and from hell and death, all glory be forever. For you have power to save the Son of God because his Father willed that it be so. And in your hands does all salvation lie, to be both offered and received as one.

To use the power God has given you as He would have it used is natural. It is not arrogant to be as He created you, or to make use of what He gave to answer all His Son's mistakes and set him free. But it is arrogant to lay aside the power that He gave, and choose a little, senseless wish instead of what He wills. The gift of God to you is limitless. There is no circumstance it cannot answer, and no problem which is not resolved within its gracious light.

Abide in peace, where God would have you be. And be the means whereby your brother finds the peace in which your wishes are fulfilled. Let us unite in bringing blessing to the world of sin and death. For what can save each one of us can save us all. There is no difference among the Sons of God. The Unity that specialness denies will save them all, for what is one can have no specialness. And everything belongs to each of them. No wishes lie between a brother and his own. To get from one is to deprive them all. And yet to bless but one gives blessing to them all as one.

Your ancient name belongs to everyone, as theirs to you. Call on your brother's name and God will answer, for on Him you call. Could He refuse to answer when He has already answered all who call on Him? A miracle can make no change at all. But it can make what always has been true be recognized by those who know it not. And by this little gift of truth but let to be itself; the Son of God allowed to be himself, and all creation freed to call upon the Name of God as one.

The one remaining problem that you have is that you see an interval between the time when you forgive and will receive the benefits of trust. This but reflects the little you would keep between yourselves, that you might be a little separate. For time and space are one illusion, which takes different forms. If it has been projected beyond your minds, you think of it as time. The nearer it is brought to where it is, the more you think of it in terms of space.

There is a distance you would keep apart from one another, and this space you see as time because you still believe you are external to each other. This makes trust impossible. And you cannot believe that trust would settle every problem now. Thus do you think it safer to remain a little careful and a little watchful of interests perceived as separate. From this perception you cannot conceive of gaining what forgiveness offers now. The interval you think lies in between the giving and receiving of the gift seems to be one in which you sacrifice and suffer loss. You see eventual salvation, not immediate results.

Salvation is immediate. Unless you so perceive it, you will be afraid of it, believing that the risk of loss is great between the time its purpose is made yours and its effects will come to you. In this form is the error still obscured that is the source of fear. Salvation would wipe out the space you see between you still, and let you instantly become as one. And it is here you fear the loss would lie. Do not project this fear to time, for time is not the enemy that you perceive. Time is as neutral as the body is, except in terms of what you see it for. If you would keep a little space between you still, you want a little time in which forgiveness is withheld a little while. This makes the interval between the time in which forgiveness is withheld and given seem dangerous, with terror justified.

Yet space between you is apparent now and cannot be perceived in future time. No more can it be overlooked except within the present. Future loss is not your fear. But present joining is your dread. Who can feel desolation except now? A future cause as yet has no effects. And therefore must it be that if you fear, there is a present cause. And it is this that needs correction, not a future state.

The plans you make for safety all are laid within the future, where you cannot plan. No purpose has been given it as yet and what will happen has as yet no cause. Who can predict effects without a cause? And who could fear effects unless he thought they has been caused and judged disastrous now? Belief in sin arouses fear and like its cause, is looking forward; looking back, but overlooking what is here and now. Yet only here and now its cause must be, if its effects already have been judged as fearful. And in overlooking this, is it protected and kept separate from healing. For a miracle is now. It stands already here, in present grace, within the only interval of time which sin and fear have overlooked, but which is all there is to time. The working out of all correction takes no time at all.

Yet the acceptance of the working out can seem to take forever. The change of purpose the Holy Spirit brought to your relationship has in it all effects that you will see. They can be looked at now. Why wait till they unfold in time, and fear they may not come, although already there? You have been told that everything brings good that comes from God. And yet it seems as if this is not so. Good in disaster's form is difficult to credit in advance. Nor is there really sense in this idea.

Why should the good appear in evil's form? And is it not deception if it does? Its cause is here, if it appears at all. Why are not its effects apparent, then? Why in the future? And you seek to be content with sighing, and with "reasoning" you do not understand it now but will someday. And then its meaning will be clear. This is not reason, for it is unjust, and clearly hints at punishment until the time of liberation is at hand. Given a change of purpose for the good, there is no reason for an interval in which disaster strikes, to be perceived as "good" someday, but now in form of pain. This is a sacrifice of now, which could not be the cost the Holy Spirit asks for what he gave without a cost at all.

Yet this illusion has a cause which, though untrue, must be already in your mind. And this illusion is but one effect which it engenders, and one form in which its outcome is perceived. This interval in time, when retribution is perceived to be the form in which the "good" appears is but one aspect of the little space that lies between you, unforgiven still.

Be not content with future happiness. It has no meaning and is not your just reward. For you have cause for freedom now. What profits freedom in a prisoner's form? Why should deliverance be disguised as death? Delay is senseless, and the "reasoning" which would maintain effects of present cause must be delayed until a future time is merely a denial of the fact that consequence and cause must come as one. Look not to time, but to the little space between you still, to be delivered from. And do not let it be disguised as time, and so preserved because its form is changed, and what it is cannot be recognized. The Holy Spirit's purpose now is yours. Should not His happiness be yours as well?

Think but how holy you must be from whom the Voice for God calls lovingly unto your brother, that you may awake in him the Voice that answers to your call! And think how holy he must be when in him sleeps your own salvation, with his freedom joined! However much you wish he be condemned, God is in him. And never will you know He is in you as well while you attack His chosen home, and battle with His host. Regard him gently. Look with loving eyes on him who carries Christ within him, that you may behold His glory, and rejoice that Heaven is not separate from you.

Is it too much to ask a little trust for him who carries Christ to you, that you may be forgiven all your sins, and left without a single one you cherish still? Forget not that a shadow held between your brother and yourself obscures the face of Christ and memory of God. And would you trade Them for an ancient hate?

The ground whereon you stand is holy ground because of Them Who, standing there with you, have blessed it with Their innocence and peace.

The blood of hatred fades to let the grass grow green again and let the flowers be all white and sparkling in the summer sun. What was a place of death has now become a living temple in a world of light.

Because of Them. It is Their Presence which has lifted holiness again to take its ancient place upon an ancient throne. Because of Them have miracles sprung up as grass and flowers on the barren ground which hate had scorched and rendered desolate. What hate has wrought have They undone. And now you stand on ground so holy Heaven leans to join with it and make it like itself. The shadow of an ancient hate has gone, and all the blight and withering have passed forever from the land where They have come.

What is a hundred or a thousand years to Them, or tens of thousands? When They come, time's purpose is fulfilled. What never was passes to nothingness when They have come. What hatred claimed is given up to love and freedom lights up every living thing and lifts it into Heaven, where the lights grow ever brighter as each one comes home. The incomplete is made complete again, and Heaven's joy has been increased because what is its own has been restored to it. The bloodied earth is cleansed, and the insane have shed their garments of insanity, to join Them on the ground whereon you stand.

Heaven is grateful for this gift of what has been withheld so long. For They have come to gather in Their Own. What has been locked is opened; what was held apart from light is given up, that light may shine on it, and leave no space nor distance lingering between the light of Heaven and the world.

The holiest of all the spots on earth is where an ancient hatred has become a present love. And They come quickly to the living temple, where a home for Them has been set up. There is no place in Heaven holier. And They have come to dwell within the temple offered them, to be Their resting-place as well as yours. What hatred has released to love becomes the brightest light in Heaven's radiance. And all the lights in Heaven brighter grow, in gratitude for what has been restored.

Around you angels hover lovingly, to keep away all darkened thoughts of sin, and keep the light where it has entered in. Your footprints lighten up the world, for where you walk forgiveness gladly goes with you.

No-one on earth but offers thanks to one who has restored his home and sheltered him from bitter winter and the freezing cold. And shall the Lord of Heaven and His Son give less in gratitude for so much more?

Now is the temple of the Living God rebuilt as host again to Him by Whom it was created. Where He dwells, His Son dwells with Him, never separate. And They give thanks that They are welcome made at last. Where stood a cross stands now the risen Christ, and ancient scars are healed within His sight. An ancient miracle has come to bless and to replace an ancient enmity that came to kill. In gentle gratitude do God the Father and the Son return to what is Theirs and will forever be. Now is the Holy Spirit's purpose done. For They have come! For They have come at last!

What, then, remains to be undone, for you to realize Their Presence? Only this; you have a differential view of when attack is justified and when you think it is unfair, and not to be allowed. When you perceive it as unfair, you think that a response of anger now is just. And thus you see what is the same as different. Confusion is not limited. If it occurs at all, it will be total. And its presence, in whatever form, will hide Their Presence. They are known with clarity or not at all. Confused perception will block knowledge. It is not a question of the size of the confusion, or how much it interferes. Its simple presence shuts the door to Theirs and keeps Them there unknown.

What does it mean if you perceive attack in certain forms to be unfair to you? It means that there must be some forms in which you think it fair. For otherwise, how could some be evaluated as unfair? Some, then, are given meaning, and perceived as sensible. And only some are seen as meaningless. And this denies the fact that all are senseless; equally without a cause or consequence and cannot have effects of any kind. Their Presence is obscured by any veil which stands between Their shining innocence, and your awareness it is your own, and equally belongs to every living thing along with you. God limits not. And what is limited cannot be Heaven. So it must be hell.

Unfairness and attack are one mistake, so firmly joined that where one is perceived, the other must be seen. You cannot be unfairly treated. The belief you are is but another form of the idea you are deprived by someone not yourself. Projection of the cause of sacrifice is at the root of everything perceived to be unfair, and not your just deserts. Yet it is you who ask this of yourself, in deep injustice to the Son of God. You have no enemy except yourself and you are enemy indeed to him because you do not know him as yourself.

What could be more unjust than that he be deprived of what he is, denied the right to be himself, and asked to sacrifice his Father's Love and yours, as not his due?

Beware of the temptation to perceive yourself unfairly treated. In this view, you seek to find an innocence which is not Theirs but yours alone and at the cost of someone else's guilt. Can innocence be purchased by the giving of your guilt to someone else? And IS this innocence, which your attack on him attempts to get? Is it not retribution for your own attack upon the Son of God you seek? Is it not safer to believe that you are innocent of this, and victimized despite your innocence? Whatever way the game of guilt is played, there must be loss. Someone must lose his innocence that someone else can take it from him, making it his own.

You think your brother is unfair to you because you think that one must be unfair to make the other innocent. And in this game do you perceive one purpose for your whole relationship. And this you seek to add unto the purpose given it. The Holy Spirit's purpose is to let the Presence of your holy Guests be known to you. And to this purpose nothing can be added, for the world is purposeless except for this. To add or take away from this one goal is but to take away all purpose from the world and from yourself. And each unfairness that the world appears to lay upon you, you have laid on it by rendering it purposeless, without the function that the Holy Spirit sees. And simple justice has been thus denied to every living thing upon the earth.

What this injustice does to you who judge unfairly, and who see as you have judged, you cannot calculate. The world grows dim and threatening, and not a trace of all the happy sparkle that salvation brought can you perceive, to lighten up your way. And so you see yourself deprived of light, abandoned to the dark, unfairly left without a purpose in a futile world. The world is fair because the Holy Spirit has brought injustice to the light within, and there has all unfairness been resolved, and been replaced with justice and with love. If you perceive injustice anywhere, you need but say:

> "By this do I deny the Presence of the Father and the
> Son. And I would rather know of Them than see
> injustice, which Their Presence shines away."

The wish to be unfairly treated is a compromise attempt that would combine attack and innocence. Who can combine the wholly incompatible, and make a unity of what can never join? Walk you the gentle way, and you will fear no evil and no shadows in the night.

But place no terror symbols on your path, or you will weave a crown of thorns from which your brother and yourself will not escape. You cannot crucify yourself alone. And if you are unfairly treated, he must suffer the unfairness that you see. You cannot sacrifice yourself alone. For sacrifice is total. If it could occur at all, it would entail the whole of God's creation, and the Father with the sacrifice of his beloved Son.

In your release from sacrifice is his made manifest and shown to be his own. But every pain you suffer do you see as proof that he is guilty of attack. Thus would you make yourself to be the sign that he has lost his innocence, and need but look on you to realize that he has been condemned. And what to you has been unfair will come to him in righteousness. The unjust vengeance that you suffer now belongs to him, and when it rests on him are you set free. Wish not to make yourself a living symbol of his guilt, for you will not escape the death you made for him. But in his innocence, you find your own.

Whenever you consent to suffer pain, to be deprived, unfairly treated or in need of anything, you but accuse your brother of attack upon God's Son. You hold a picture of your crucifixion before his eyes, that he may see his sins are writ in Heaven in your blood and death, and go before him, closing off the gate, and damning him to hell. Yet this is writ in hell and not in Heaven, where you are beyond attack, and prove his innocence. The picture of yourself you offer him you show yourself and give it all your faith. The Holy Spirit offers you, to give to him, a picture of yourself in which there is no pain, and no reproach at all. And what was martyred to his guilt becomes the perfect witness to his innocence.

The power of witness is beyond belief because it brings conviction in its wake. The witness is believed because he points beyond himself to what he represents. A sick and suffering you but represents your brother's guilt; the witness which you send lest he forget the injuries he gave, from which you swear he never will escape. This sick and sorry picture you accept, if only it can serve to punish him. The sick are merciless to everyone, and in contagion do they seek to kill. Death seems an easy price, if they can say, "Behold me, brother, at your hand I die." For sickness is the witness to his guilt, and death would prove his errors must be sins.

Sickness is but a "little" death; a form of vengeance not yet total. Yet it speaks with certainty for what it represents. The bleak and bitter picture you have sent your brother you have looked upon in grief. And everything that it has shown to him have you believed, because it witnessed to the guilt in him, which you perceived and loved.

Now in the hands made gentle by His touch, the Holy Spirit lays a picture of a different you. It is a picture of a body still, for what you really are cannot be seen nor pictured. Yet this one has not been used for purpose of attack, and therefore never suffered pain at all. It witnesses to the eternal truth that you cannot be hurt, and points beyond itself to both your innocence and his.

Show this unto your brother, who will see that every scar is healed, and every tear is wiped away in laughter and in love. And he will look on his forgiveness there, and with healed eyes will look beyond it to the innocence that he beholds in you. Here is the proof that he has never sinned; that nothing which his madness bid him do was ever done, or ever had effects of any kind. That no reproach he laid upon his heart was ever justified, and no attack can ever touch him with the poisoned and relentless sting of fear. Attest his innocence and not his guilt. Your healing is his comfort and his health because it proves illusions are not true.

It is not will for life, but wish for death, that is the motivation for this world. Its only purpose is to prove guilt real. No worldly thought or act or feeling has a motivation other than this one. These are the witnesses that are called forth to be believed and lend conviction to the system they speak for and represent. And each has many voices, speaking to your brother and yourself in different tongues. And yet to both the message is the same. Adornment of the body seeks to show how lovely are the witnesses for guilt. Concerns about the body demonstrate how frail and vulnerable is your life; how easily destroyed is what you love. Depression speaks of death and vanity of real concern with anything at all. The strongest witness to futility, which bolsters all the rest and helps them paint the picture in which sin is justified, is sickness in whatever form it takes.

The sick have reason for each one of their unnatural desires and strange needs. For who could live a life so soon cut short, and not esteem the worth of passing joys? What pleasures could there be that will endure? Are not the frail entitled to believe that every stolen scrap of pleasure is their righteous payment for their little lives? Their death will pay the price for all of them, if they enjoy their benefits or not. The end of life must come, whatever way that life be spent. And so take pleasure in the quickly passing and ephemeral.

These are not sins, but witnesses unto the strange belief that sin and death are real, and innocence and sin will end alike within the termination of the grave. If this were true, there would be reason to remain content to seek for passing joys and cherish little pleasures where you can.

Yet in this picture is the body not perceived as neutral and without a goal inherent in itself. For it becomes the symbol of reproach, the sign of guilt whose consequences still are there to see, so that the cause can never be denied.

Your function is to show your brother sin can have no cause. How futile must it be to see yourself a picture of the proof that what your function is can never be! The Holy Spirit's picture changes not the body into something it is not. It only takes away from it all signs of accusation and of blamefulness. Pictured without a purpose, it is seen as neither sick nor well, nor bad nor good. No grounds are offered that it may be judged in any way at all. It has no life, but neither is it dead. It stands apart from all experience of fear or love. For now, it witnesses to nothing yet, its purpose being open, and the mind made free again to choose what it is for. Now is it not condemned, but waiting for a purpose to be given, that it may fulfil the function that it will receive.

Into this empty space, from which the goal of sin has been removed, is Heaven free to be remembered. Here its peace can come, and perfect healing take the place of death. The body can become a sign of life, a promise of redemption, and a breath of immortality to those grown sick of breathing in the fetid scent of death. Let it have healing as its purpose. Then will it send forth the message it received, and by its health and loveliness proclaim the truth and value that it represents. Let it receive the power to represent an endless life, forever unattacked. And to your brother let its message be, "Behold me, brother, at your hand I live."

The simple way to let this be achieved is merely this; to let the body have no purpose from the past, when you were sure you knew its purpose was to foster guilt. For this insists your crippled picture is a lasting sign of what it represents. This leaves no space in which a different view, another purpose, can be given it. You do not know its purpose. You but gave illusions of a purpose to a thing you made to hide your function from yourself. This thing without a purpose cannot hide the function that the Holy Spirit gave. Let, then, its purpose and your function both be reconciled at last and seen as one.

Is healing frightening? To many, yes. For accusation is a bar to love, and damaged bodies are accusers. They stand firmly in the way of trust and peace, proclaiming that the frail can have no trust, and that the damaged have no grounds for peace. Who has been injured by his brother, and could love and trust him still? He has attacked and will attack again. Protect him not, because your damaged body shows that you must be protected from him.

To forgive may be an act of charity but not his due. He may be pitied for his guilt, but not exonerated. And if you forgive him his transgressions, you but add to all the guilt that he has really earned.

The unhealed cannot pardon. For they are the witnesses that pardon is unfair. They would retain the consequences of the guilt they overlook. Yet no-one can forgive a sin which he believes is real. And what has consequences must be real because what it has done is there to see. Forgiveness is not pity, which but seeks to pardon what it knows to be the truth. Good cannot be returned for evil, for forgiveness does not first establish sin and then forgive it. Who can say and mean, "My brother, you have injured me, and yet, because I am the better of the two, I pardon you my hurt." His pardon and your hurt cannot exist together. One denies the other and must make it false.

To witness sin and yet forgive it is a paradox which reason cannot see. For it maintains what has been done to you deserves no pardon. And by giving it, you grant your brother mercy, but retain the proof he is not really innocent. The sick remain accusers. They cannot forgive their brothers and themselves as well. For no-one in whom true forgiveness reigns can suffer. He holds not the proof of sin before his brother's eyes. And thus he must have overlooked it, and removed it from his own. Forgiveness cannot be for one and not the other. Who forgives is healed. And in his healing lies the proof that he has truly pardoned and retains no trace of condemnation that he still would hold against himself or any living thing.

Forgiveness is not real unless it brings a healing to your brother and yourself. You must attest his sins had no effect on you, to demonstrate they were not real. How else could he be guiltless? And how could his innocence be justified unless his sins have no effect to warrant guilt? Sins are beyond forgiveness just because they would entail effects which cannot be undone and overlooked entirely. In their undoing lies the proof that they were merely errors. let yourself be healed, that you may be forgiving, offering salvation to your brother and yourself. A broken body shows the mind has not been healed. A miracle of healing proves that separation is without effect. What you would prove to him you will believe. The power of witness comes from your belief. And everything you say or do or think but testifies to what you teach to him.

Your body can be means to teach that it has never suffered pain because of him. And in its healing can it offer him mute testimony of his innocence. It is this testimony which can speak with power greater than a thousand tongues. For here is his forgiveness proved to him. A miracle can offer nothing less to him than it has given unto you. So does your healing show your mind is healed, and has forgiven what he did not do. And so is he convinced his innocence was never lost and healed along with you.

Thus does the miracle undo all things the world attests can never be undone. And hopelessness and death must disappear before the ancient clarion call of life. This call has power far beyond the weak and miserable cry of death and guilt. The ancient calling of the Father to His Son, and of the Son unto his own, will yet be the last trumpet that the world will ever hear. Brother, there IS no death. And this you learn when you but wish to show your brother that you had no hurt of him. He thinks your blood is on his hands, and so he stands condemned. Yet it is given you to show him, by your healing, that his guilt is but the fabric of a senseless dream.

How just are miracles! For they bestow an equal gift of full deliverance from guilt upon your brother and yourself. Your healing saves him pain as well as you, and you are healed because you wished him well. This is the law the miracle obeys; that healing sees no specialness at all. It does not come from pity, but from love. And love would prove all suffering is but a vain imagining, a foolish wish, with no effects. Your health is a result of your desire to see your brother with no blood upon his hands, nor guilt upon his heart made heavy with the proof of sin. And what you wish is given you to see.

The "cost" of your serenity is his. This is the "price" the Holy Spirit and the world interpret differently. The world perceives it as a statement of the "fact" that your salvation sacrifices his. The Holy Spirit knows your healing is the witness unto his and cannot be apart from his at all. As long as he consents to suffer, you will be unhealed. Yet you can show him that his suffering is purposeless and wholly without cause. Show him your healing, and he will consent no more to suffer. For his innocence has been established in your sight and his. And laughter will replace your sighs, because God's Son remembered that he IS God's Son.

Who, then, fears healing? Only those to whom their brother's sacrifice and pain are seen to represent their own serenity. Their helplessness and weakness represents the grounds on which they justify his pain. The constant sting of guilt he suffers serves to prove that he is slave, but they are free. The constant pain they suffer demonstrates that they are free because they hold him bound.

And sickness is desired to prevent a shift of balance in the sacrifice. How could the Holy Spirit be deterred an instant, even less, to reason with an argument for sickness such as this? And need your healing be delayed because you pause to listen to insanity?

Consider how this self-perception must extend, and do not overlook the fact that every thought extends because that is its purpose, being what it really is. From an idea of self as two, there comes a necessary view of function split between the two. And what you would correct is only half the error, which you think is all of it. Your brother's sins become the central target for correction, lest your errors and his own be seen as one. Yours are mistakes, but his are sins, and not the same as yours. His merit punishment, while yours, in fairness, should be overlooked.

In this interpretation of correction, your own mistakes you will not even see. The focus of correction has been placed outside yourself, on one who cannot be a part of you while this perception lasts. What is condemned can never be returned to its accuser, who hated it, and hates it still. This is your brother, focus of your hate, unworthy to be part of you and thus outside yourself; the other half, which is denied. And only what is left without his presence is perceived as all of you. To this remaining half the Holy Spirit must represent the other half until you recognize it IS the other half. And this He does by giving both of you a function that is one, not different.

Correction is the function given both, but neither one alone. And when it is fulfilled as shared, it must correct mistakes in both of you. It cannot leave mistakes in one unhealed and set the other free. That is divided purpose, which cannot be shared and so it cannot be the function which the Holy Spirit sees as His. And you can rest assured that He will not fulfil a function He cannot understand and recognize as His. For only thus can he keep yours preserved intact, despite your separate views of what your function is. If He upheld divided function, you were lost indeed. His inability to see His goal divided and distinct for each of you preserves your Self from being made aware of any function other than Its Own. And thus is healing given both of you.

Correction must be left to One Who knows correction and forgiveness are the same. With half a mind, this is not understood. Leave, then, correction to the Mind That is united, functioning as one because It is not split in purpose, and conceives a single function as Its only one.

Here is the function given It conceived to be Its Own, and not apart from that Its Giver keeps because it has been shared. In His acceptance of this function lies the means whereby your mind is unified. His single purpose unifies the halves of you which you perceive as separate. And each forgives the other, that he may accept his other half as part of him.

Power cannot oppose. For opposition would weaken it, and weakened power is a contradiction in ideas. Weak strength is meaningless, and power used to weaken is employed to limit. And therefore it must be limited and weak, because that is its purpose. Power is unopposed, to be itself. No weakness can intrude on it without changing it into something it is not. To weaken is to limit and impose an opposite that contradicts the concept which it attacks. And by this does it join to the idea a something it is not and make it unintelligible. Who can understand a double concept, such as "weakened-power" or as "hateful-love?"

You have decided that your brother is a symbol for a "hateful love," a "weakened-power," and above all, a "living-death." And so he has no meaning to you, for he stands for what is meaningless. He represents a double thought, where half is cancelled out by the remaining half. Yet even this is quickly contradicted by the half it cancelled out, and so they both are gone. And now he stands for nothing. Symbols which but represent ideas that cannot be must stand for empty space and nothingness. Yet nothingness and empty space cannot be interference. What can interfere with the awareness of reality is the belief that there is something there.

The picture of your brother that you see means nothing. There is nothing to attack or to deny; love or hate, or to endow with power or to see as weak. The picture has been wholly cancelled out, because it symbolized a contradiction which cancelled out the thought it represents. And thus the picture has no cause at all. Who can perceive effect without a cause? What can the causeless be but nothingness? The picture of your brother that you see is wholly absent and has never been. Let, then, the empty space it occupies be recognised as vacant, and the time devoted to its seeing be perceived as idly spent, a time unoccupied.

An empty space which is not seen as filled, an unused interval of time not seen as spent and fully occupied, become a silent invitation to the truth to enter and to make itself at home. No preparation can be made that would enhance the invitation's real appeal. For what you leave as vacant God will fill, and where He is, there must the truth abide. Unweakened power, with no opposite, is what creation is. For this there are no symbols.

Nothing points beyond the truth, for what can stand for more than everything? Yet true undoing must be kind. And so the first replacement for your picture is another picture, of another kind.

As nothingness cannot be pictured, so there is no symbol for totality. Reality is ultimately known without a form, unpictured and unseen. Forgiveness is not yet a power known as wholly free of limits. Yet it sets no limits you have chosen to impose. Forgiveness is the means by which the truth is represented temporarily. It lets the Holy Spirit make exchange of pictures possible until the time when aids are meaningless, and learning done. No learning aid has use which can extend beyond the goal of learning. When its aim has been accomplished, it is functionless. Yet in the learning interval it has a use which now you fear, but yet will love.

The picture of your brother given you to occupy the space so lately left unoccupied and vacant will not need defence of any kind. For you will give it overwhelming preference. Nor delay an instant in deciding that it is the only one you want. It does not stand for double concepts. Though it is but half the picture and is incomplete, within itself it is the same. The other half of what it represents remains unknown but is not cancelled out. And thus is God left free to take the final step Himself. And what will ultimately take the place of every learning aid will merely be. Forgiveness vanishes and symbols fade, and nothing which the eyes have ever seen, or ears have heard, remains to be perceived.

A Power wholly limitless has come, not to destroy, but to receive Its Own. There is no choice of function anywhere. The choice you fear to lose you never had. Yet only this appears to interfere with power unlimited and single thoughts, complete and happy, without opposite. You do not know the peace of power which opposes nothing. Yet no other kind can be at all. Give welcome to the Power beyond forgiveness, and beyond the world of symbols and of limitations. He would merely be, and so He merely is.

In quietness are all things answered, and is every problem quietly resolved. In conflict there can be no answer and no resolution, for its purpose is to make no resolution possible, and to ensure no answer will be plain. A problem set in conflict has no answer, for it is seen in different ways. And what would be an answer from one point of view is not an answer in another light. You are in conflict. Thus it must be clear you cannot answer anything at all, for conflict has no limited effects. Yet if God gave an answer, there must be a way in which your problems are resolved, for what He wills already has been done.

Thus it must be that time is not involved, and every problem can be answered now. Yet it must also be that, in your state of mind, solution is impossible. Therefore, God must have given you a way of reaching to another state of mind, in which the answer is already there. Such is the holy instant. It is here that all your problems should be brought and left. Here they belong, for here their answer is. It must be pointless to attempt to solve a problem where the answer cannot be. Yet just as surely it must be resolved, if it is brought to where the answer is.

Attempt to solve no problems but within the holy instant's surety. For there the problem will be answered and resolved. Outside, there will be no solution, for there is no answer there that could be found. Nowhere outside a single, simple question is ever asked. The world can only ask a double question, with many answers, none of which will do.

It does not ask a question to be answered, but only to restate its point of view. All questions asked within this world are but a way of looking, not a question asked. A question asked in hate cannot be answered, because it is an answer in itself. A double question asks and answers, both attesting the same thing in different form.
The world asks but one question. It is this: "Of these illusions, which of them are true? Which ones establish peace and offer joy? And which can bring escape from all the pain of which this world is made?" Whatever form the question takes, its purpose is the same. It asks but to establish sin is real and answers in the form of preference. "Which sin do you prefer? That is the one which you should choose. The others are not true. What can the body get that you would want the most of all? It is your servant and your friend. But tell it what you want, and it will serve you lovingly and well." And this is not a question, for it tells you what you want, and where to go for it. It leaves no room to question its beliefs, except that what it states takes question's form.

A pseudo-question has no answer. It dictates the answer even as it asks. Thus is all questioning within the world a form of propaganda for itself. Just as the body's witnesses are but the senses from within itself, so are the answers to the questions of the world contained within the questions. Where answers represent the questions they add nothing new and nothing has been learned.

An honest question is a learning tool which asks for something that you do not know. It does not set conditions for response, but merely asks what the response should be. But no-one in a conflict state is free to ask this question, for he does not want an honest answer, where the conflict ends.

Only within the holy instant can an honest question honestly be asked. And from the meaning of the question does the meaningfulness of the answer come. Here is it possible to separate your wishes from the answer, so it can be given you and also be received. The answer is provided everywhere. Yet it is only here it can be heard.

An honest answer asks no sacrifice because it answers questions truly asked. The questions of the world but ask of whom is sacrifice demanded, asking not if sacrifice is meaningful at all. And so unless the answer tells "of whom" it will remain unrecognized, unheard, and thus the question is preserved intact because it gave the answer to itself. The holy instant is the interval in which the mind is still enough to hear an answer which is not entailed within the question asked. It offers something new and different from the question. How could it be answered if it but repeats itself?

Therefore, attempt to solve no problems in a world from which the answer has been barred. But bring the problem to the only place which holds the answer lovingly for you. Here are the answers which will solve your problems because they stand apart from them and see what can be answered; what the question is. Within the world the answers merely raise another question, though they leave the first unanswered. In the holy instant, you can bring the question to the answer, and receive the answer that was made for you.

The only way to heal is to be healed. The miracle extends without your help, but you are needed that it can begin. Accept the miracle of healing, and it will go forth because of what it is. It is its nature to extend itself the instant it is born. And it is born the instant it is offered and received. No-one can ask another to be healed. But he can let himself be healed, and thus offer the other what he has received. Who can bestow upon another what he does not have? And who can share what he denies himself? The Holy Spirit speaks to you. He does not speak to someone else. Yet by your listening, His Voice extends because you have accepted what He says.

Health is the witness unto health. As long as it is unattested, it remains without conviction. Only when demonstrated has it been proved and must compel belief. No-one is healed through double messages. If you wish only to be healed, you heal. Your single purpose makes this possible. But if you are afraid of healing, then it cannot come through you. The only thing that is required for a healing is a lack of fear. The fearful are not healed and cannot heal. This does not mean the conflict must be gone forever from your mind. For if it were, there were no need for healing then.

But it does mean, if only for an instant, you love without attack. An instant is sufficient. Miracles wait not on time.

The holy instant is the miracle's abiding-place. From there, each one is born into this world as witness to a state of mind which has transcended conflict and has reached to peace. It carries comfort from the place of peace into the battle-ground and demonstrates that war has no effects. For all the hurt that war has sought to bring, the broken bodies and the shattered limbs, the screaming dying and the silent dead, are gently lifted up and comforted. There is no sadness where a miracle has come to heal. And nothing more than just one instant of your love without attack is necessary, that all this occur. In that one instant are you healed and in that single instant is all healing done.

What stands apart from you, when you accept the blessing that the holy instant brings? Be not afraid of blessing, for the One Who blesses you loves all the world, and leaves nothing within the world that could be feared. But if you shrink from blessing, will the world indeed seem fearful, for you have withheld its peace and comfort, leaving it to die. Would not a world so bitterly bereft be looked on as a condemnation by the one who could have saved it, but stepped back because he was afraid of being healed? The eyes of all the dying bring reproach, and suffering whispers, "What is there to fear?" Consider well its question. It is asked of you on your behalf. A dying world asks only that you rest an instant from attack upon yourself, that it be healed.

Come to the holy instant and be healed, for nothing that is there received is left behind, on your returning to the world. And being blessed, you will bring blessing. Life is given you to give the dying world. And suffering eyes no longer will accuse but shine in thanks to you who blessing gave. The holy instant's radiance will light your eyes, and give them sight to see beyond all suffering, and see Christ's face instead. Healing replaces suffering. Who looks on one cannot perceive the other, for they cannot both be there. And what you see the world will witness and will witness to.

Thus is your healing everything the world requires, that it may be healed. It needs one lesson which has perfectly been learned. And then, when you forget it, will the world remind you gently of what you have taught. No reinforcement will its thanks withhold from you who let yourself be healed that it might live. It will call forth its witnesses to show the face of Christ to you who brought the right to them, by which they witnessed it.

The world of accusation is replaced by one in which all eyes look lovingly upon the Friend who brought them their release. And happily your brother will perceive the many friends he thought were enemies.

Problems are not specific, but they take specific forms, and these specific shapes make up the world. And no-one understands the nature of his problem. If he did, it would be there no more for him to see. Its very nature is that it is not. And thus, while he perceives it, he cannot perceive it as it is. But healing is apparent in specific instances and generalizes to include them all. This is because they really are the same, despite their different forms. All learning aims at transfer, which becomes complete within two situations which are seen as one, for only common elements are there. Yet this can only be attained by One Who does not see the differences you see. The total transfer of your learning is not made by you. But that it has been made in spite of all the differences you see, convinces you that they could not be real.

Your healing will extend and will be brought to problems that you thought were not your own. And it will also be apparent that your many different problems will be solved, as any one of them has been escaped. It cannot be their differences which made this possible, for learning does not jump from situations to their opposites and bring the same results. All healing must proceed in lawful manner, in accord with laws which have been properly perceived, but never violated. Fear you not the way that you perceive them. You are wrong, but there is One within you Who is right.

Leave, then, the transfer of your learning to the One Who really understands its laws, and Who will guarantee that they remain unviolated and unlimited. Your part is merely to apply what He has taught you to yourself, and He will do the rest. And thus the power of your learning will be proved to you by all the many different witnesses it finds. Your brother first among them will be seen, but thousands stand behind him, and beyond each one there are a thousand more. Each one may seem to have a problem which is different from the rest. Yet they are solved together. And their common answer shows the questions could not have been separate.

Peace be to you to whom is healing offered. And you will learn that peace is given you when you accept the healing for yourself. Its total value need not be appraised by you to let you understand that you have benefited from it. What occurred within the instant which love entered in without attack will stay with you forever.

Your healing will be one of its effects, as will your brother's. Everywhere you go will you behold its multiplied effects. Yet all the witnesses that you behold will be far less than all there really are. Infinity cannot be understood by merely counting up its separate parts. God thanks you for your healing, for He knows it is a gift of love unto His Son, and therefore is it given unto Him.

Pain demonstrates the body must be real. It is a loud, obscuring voice whose shrieks would silence what the Holy Spirit says and keep His words from your awareness. Pain compels attention, drawing it away from Him, and focusing upon itself. Its purpose is the same as pleasure, for they both are means to make the body real. What shares a common purpose is the same. This is the law of purpose, which unites all those who share in it within itself. Pleasure and pain are equally unreal, because their purpose cannot BE achieved. Thus are they means for nothing, for they have a goal without a meaning. And they share the lack of meaning which their purpose has.

Sin shifts from pain to pleasure, and again to pain. For either witness is the same and carries but one message: "You are here, within this body and you can be hurt. You can have pleasure, too, but only at the cost of pain." These witnesses are joined by many more. Each one seems different because it has a different name, and so it seems to answer to a different sound. Except for this, the witnesses of sin are all alike. Call pleasure pain, and it will hurt. Call pain a pleasure, and the pain behind the pleasure will be felt no more. Sin's witnesses but shift from name to name, as one steps forward and another back. Yet which is foremost makes no difference. Sin's witnesses hear but the call of death.

This body, purposeless within itself, holds all your memories and all your hopes. You use its eyes to see, its ears to hear, and let it tell you what it is it feels. It does not know. It tells you but the names you gave it to use, when you call forth the witnesses to its reality. You cannot choose among them which are real, for any one you choose is like the rest. This name or that, but nothing more, you choose. You do not make a witness true because you called him by truth's name. The truth is found in him if it is truth he represents. And otherwise he lies, if you should call him by the holy Name of God Himself.

God's Witness sees no witnesses against the body. Neither does He harken to the witnesses by other names which speak in other ways for its reality. He knows it is not real. For nothing could contain what you believe it holds within. Nor could it tell a part of God Himself what it should feel, and what its function is.

Yet must He love whatever you hold dear. And for each witness to the body's death He sends a witness to your life in Him Who knows no death. Each miracle He brings is witness that the body is not real. Its pains and pleasures does He heal alike, for all sin's witnesses do His replace.

The miracle makes no distinctions in the names by which sin's witnesses are called. It merely proves that what they represent has no effects. And this it proves because its own effects have come to take their place. It matters not the name by which you called your suffering. It is no longer there. The One Who brings the miracle perceived them all as one and called by name of fear. As fear is witness unto death, so is the miracle the witness unto life. It is a witness no-one can deny, for it is the effects of life it brings. The dying live, the dead arise, and pain has vanished. Yet a miracle speaks not but for itself, but what it represents.

Love, too, has symbols in a world of sin. The miracle forgives because it stands for what is past forgiveness and is true. How foolish and insane it is to think a miracle is bound by laws which it came solely to undo! The laws of sin have different witnesses, with different strengths. And they attest to different sufferings. Yet to the One Who sends forth miracles to bless the world, a tiny stab of pain, a little worldly pleasure, and the throes of death itself, are but a single sound; a call for healing, and a plaintive cry for help within a world of misery. It is their sameness that the miracle attests. It is their sameness that it proves.

The laws which call them different are dissolved and shown as powerless. The purpose of a miracle is to accomplish this. And God Himself has guaranteed the strength of miracles for what they witness to. Be witnesses unto the miracle, and not the laws of sin. There is no need to suffer anymore. But there is need that you be healed, because the suffering of the world has made it deaf to its salvation and deliverance.

The resurrection of the world awaits your healing and your happiness, that you may demonstrate the healing of the world. The holy instant will replace all sin, if you but carry its effects with you. And no-one will elect to suffer more. What better function could you serve than this? Be healed that you may heal and suffer not the laws of sin to be applied to you. And truth will be revealed to you who chose to let love's symbols take the place of sin.

Suffering is an emphasis upon all that the world has done to injure you. Here is the world's demented version of salvation clearly shown. Like to a dream of punishment, in which the dreamer is unconscious of what brought on the attack against himself, he sees himself attacked unjustly, and by something not himself. He is the victim of this "something else," a thing outside himself, for which he has no reason to be held responsible. He must be innocent because he knows not what he does, but what is done to him. Yet is his own attack upon himself apparent still, for it is he who bears the suffering. And he cannot escape because its source is seen outside himself.

Now you are being shown you can escape. All that is needed is you look upon the problem as it is, and not the way that you have set it up. How could there be another way to solve a problem which is very simple, but has been obscured by heavy clouds of complication, which were made to keep the problem unresolved? Without the clouds, the problem will emerge in all its primitive simplicity. The choice will not be difficult, because the problem is absurd when clearly seen. No-one has difficulty making up his mind to let a simple problem be resolved if it is seen as hurting him and also very easily removed.

The "reasoning" by which the world is made, on which it rests, by which it is maintained, is simply this: "You are the cause of what I do. Your presence justifies my wrath, and you exist and think apart from me. While you attack, I must be innocent. And what I suffer from is your attack." No-one who looks upon this "reasoning" exactly as it is could fail to see it does not follow, and it makes no sense. Yet it seems sensible because it looks as if the world were hurting you. And so it seems as if there is no need to go beyond the obvious in terms of cause.

There is indeed a need. The world's escape from condemnation is a need which those within the world are joined in sharing. Yet they do not recognize their common need. For each one thinks that if he does his part, the condemnation of the world will rest on him. And it is this that he perceives to be his part in its deliverance. Vengeance must have a focus. Otherwise is the avenger's knife in his own hand and pointed to himself. And he must see it in another's hand, if he would be a victim of attack he did not choose. And thus he suffers from the wounds a knife he does not hold has made upon himself. This is the purpose of the world he sees. And looked at thus, the world provides the means by which this purpose seems to be fulfilled.

The means attest the purpose, but are not themselves a cause. Nor will the cause be changed by seeing it apart from its effects. The cause produces the effects, which then bear witness to the cause, and not themselves. Look, then, beyond effects. It is not here the cause of suffering and sin must lie. And dwell not on the suffering and sin, for they are but reflections of their cause.

The part you play in salvaging the world from condemnation is your own escape. Forget not that the witness to the world of evil cannot speak except for what has seen a need for evil in the world. And this is where your guilt was first beheld. In separation from your brother was the first attack upon yourself begun. And it is this the world bears witness to. Seek not another cause, nor look among the mighty legions of its witnesses for its undoing. They support its claim on your allegiance. What conceals the truth is not where you should look to find the truth. The witnesses to sin all stand within one little space. And it is here you find the cause of your perspective on the world.

Once you were unaware of what the cause of everything the world appeared to thrust upon you, uninvited and unasked, must really be. Of one thing you were sure; of all the many causes you perceived as bringing pain and suffering to you, your guilt was not among them. Nor did you, in any way, request them for yourself. This is how all illusions come about. The one who makes them does not see himself as making them, and their reality does not depend on him. Whatever cause they have is something quite apart from him, and what he sees is separate from his mind. He cannot doubt his dreams' reality because he does not see the part he plays in making them and making them seem real.

No-one can waken from a dream the world is dreaming for him. He becomes a part of someone else's dream. He cannot choose to waken from a dream he did not make. Helpless he stands, a victim to a dream conceived and cherished by a separate mind. Careless indeed of him this mind must be, as thoughtless of his peace and happiness as is the weather or the time of day. It loves him not, but casts him as it will, in any role that satisfies its dream. So little is his worth that he is but a dancing shadow, leaping up and down according to a senseless plot conceived within the idle dreaming of the world.

This is the only picture you can see, the one alternative that you can choose, the other possibility of cause, if you be not the dreamer of your dreams. And this is what you choose, if you deny the cause of suffering is in your mind. Be glad indeed it is, for thus are you the one decider of your destiny in time.

The choice is yours to make between a sleeping death and dreams of evil or a happy wakening and joy of life. What could you choose between but life or death, waking or sleeping, peace or war, your dreams or your reality? Yet if the choice is really given you, then you must see the causes of the things you choose between exactly as they are and where they are. What choices can be made between two states, but one of which is clearly recognized? Who could be free to choose between effects, when only one is seen as up to him?

An honest choice could never be perceived as one in which the choice is split between a tiny you and an enormous world, with different dreams about the truth in you. The gap between reality and dreams lies not between the dreaming of the world and what you dream in secret. They are one. The dreaming of the world is but a part of your own dream you gave away and saw as if it were its start and ending, both. Yet was it started by your secret dream, which you do not perceive, although it caused the part you see and do not doubt is real. How could you doubt it while you lie asleep, and dream in secret that its cause is real?

A brother separated from yourself, an ancient enemy, a murderer who stalks you in the night and plots your death yet plans that it be lingering and slow; of this you dream. Yet underneath this dream is yet another, in which you become the murderer, the secret enemy, the scavenger and the destroyer of your brother and the world alike. Here is the cause of suffering, the space between your dreams and your reality. The little gap you do not even see, the birthplace of illusions and of fear, the time of terror and of ancient hate, the instant of disaster, all are here. Here is the cause of unreality. And it is here that it will be undone.

You are the dreamer of the world of dreams. No other cause it has, nor ever will. Nothing more fearful than an idle dream has terrified God's Son and made him think that he has lost his innocence, denied his Father, and made war upon himself. So fearful is the dream, so seeming real, he could not waken to reality without the sweat of terror and a scream of mortal fear, unless a gentler dream preceded his awaking, and allowed his calmer mind to welcome, not to fear, the Voice that calls with love to waken him. God willed he waken gently, and with joy. And gave him means to waken without fear. Accept the dream He gave instead of yours. It is not difficult to change a dream when once the dreamer has been recognized.

Rest in the Holy Spirit and allow His gentle dreams to take the place of those you dreamed in terror, and in fear of death. He brings forgiving dreams, in which the choice is not who is the murderer and who shall be the victim. In the dreams He brings, there is no murder and there is no death. The dream of guilt is fading from your sight, although your eyes are closed. A smile has come to lighten up your sleeping face. The sleep is peaceful now, for these are happy dreams.

Dream softly of your sinless brother, who unites with you in holy innocence. And from this dream, the Lord of Heaven will Himself awaken His beloved Son. Dream of your brother's kindnesses instead of dwelling in your dreams on his mistakes. Select his thoughtfulness to dream about instead of counting up the hurts he gave. Forgive him his illusions and give thanks to him for all the helpfulness he gave. And do not brush aside his many gifts because he is not perfect in your dreams.

He represents his Father, Whom you see as offering both life and death to you. Brother, He gives but life. Yet what you see as gifts your brother offers represent the gifts you dream your Father gives to you. Let all your brother's gifts be seen in light of charity and kindness offered you. And let no pain disturb your dream of deep appreciation for his gifts to you.

The body is the central figure in the dreaming of the world. There is no dream without it, nor does it exist without the dream in which it acts as if it were a person, to be seen and be believed. It takes the central place in every dream, which tells the story of how it was made by other bodies, born into the world outside the body, lives a little while and dies, to be united in the dust with other bodies dying like itself. In the brief time allotted it to live, it seeks for other bodies as its friends and enemies. Its safety is its main concern. Its comfort is its guiding rule. It tries to look for pleasure and avoid the things that would be hurtful. Above all, it tries to teach itself its pains and joys are different and can be told apart.

The dreaming of the world takes many forms, because the body seeks in many ways to prove it is autonomous and real. It puts things on itself which it has bought with little metal discs or paper strips the world proclaims as valuable and good. It works to get them, doing senseless things and tosses them away for senseless things it does not need, and does not even want. It hires other bodies, that they may protect it and collect more senseless things that it can call its own. It looks about for special bodies which can share its dream.

Sometimes it dreams it is a conqueror of bodies weaker than itself. But in some phases of the dream, it is the slave of bodies that would hurt and torture it.

The body's serial adventures, from the time of birth to dying is the theme of every dream the world has ever had. The "hero" of this dream will never change, nor will its purpose. Though the dream itself takes many forms and seems to show a great variety of places and events wherein its "hero" finds itself, the dream has but one purpose, taught in many ways. This single lesson does it try to teach again, and still again, and yet once more; that it is cause and not effect. And you are its effect and cannot be its cause.

Thus are you not the dreamer, but the dream. And so you wander idly in and out of places and events which it contrives. That this is all the body does is true, for it is but a figure in a dream. But who reacts to figures in a dream unless he sees them as if they were real? The instant that he sees them as they are, they have no more effects on him because he understands he gave them their effects by causing them and making them seem real.

How willing are you to escape effects of all the dreams the world has ever had? Is it your wish to let no dream appear to be the cause of what it is you do? Then let us merely look upon the dream's beginning, for the part you see is but the second part, whose cause lies in the first. No-one asleep and dreaming in the world remembers his attack upon himself. No-one believes there really was a time when he knew nothing of a body and could never have conceived this world as real. He would have seen at once that these ideas are one illusion, too ridiculous for anything but to be laughed away. How serious they now appear to be! And no-one can remember when they would have met with laughter and with disbelief.

We can remember this, if we but look directly at their cause. And we will see the grounds for laughter, not a cause for fear. Let us return the dream he gave away unto the dreamer, who perceives the dream as separate from himself, and done to him. Into eternity, where all is one, there crept a tiny, mad idea, at which the Son of God remembered not to laugh. In his forgetting did the thought become a serious idea, and possible of both accomplishment and real effects. Together, we can laugh them both away, and understand that time cannot intrude upon eternity. It is a joke to think that time can come to circumvent eternity, which means there is no time.

A timelessness in which is time made real; a part of God which can attack itself; a separate brother as an enemy; a mind within a body, all are forms of circularity, whose ending starts at its beginning, ending at its cause. The world you see depicts exactly what you thought you did. Except that now you think that what you did is being done to you. The guilt for what you thought is being placed outside yourself, and on a guilty world which dreams your dreams and thinks your thoughts instead of you. It brings its vengeance, not your own. It keeps you narrowly confined within a body, which it punishes because of all the sinful things the body does within its dream. You have no power to make the body stop its evil deeds, because you did not make it, and cannot control its actions or its purpose or its fate.

The world but demonstrates an ancient truth; you will believe that others do to you exactly what you think you did to them. But once deluded into blaming them, you will not see the cause of what they do because you want the guilt to rest on them. How childish is this petulant device to keep your innocence by pushing guilt outside yourself, but never letting go! It is not easy to perceive the jest when all around you do your eyes behold its heavy consequences, but without their trifling cause. Without the cause do its effects seem serious and sad indeed. Yet they but follow. And it is their cause which follows nothing and is but a jest.

In gentle laughter does the Holy Spirit perceive the cause and looks not to effects. How else could He correct your error, who have overlooked the cause entirely? He bids you bring each terrible effect to Him, that you may look together on its foolish cause, and laugh with Him a while. You judge effects, but He has judged their cause. And by His judgement are effects removed. Perhaps you come in tears, but hear Him say, "My brother, Holy Son of God, behold your idle dream, in which this could occur," and you will leave the holy instant with your laughter and your brothers joined with His.

The secret of salvation is but this: That you are doing this unto yourself. No matter what the form of the attack, this still is true. Whoever takes the role of enemy and of attacker, still is this the truth. Whatever seems to be the cause of any pain and suffering you feel, this is still true. For you would not react at all to figures in a dream you knew that you were dreaming. Let them be as hateful and as vicious as they may, they could have no effect on you unless you failed to recognize it is your dream. This single lesson learned will set you free from suffering, whatever form it takes.

The Holy Spirit will repeat this one inclusive lesson of deliverance until it has been learned, regardless of the form of suffering that brings you pain. Whatever hurt you bring to Him He will make answer with this very simple truth. For this one answer takes away the cause of every form of sorrow and of pain. The form affects His answer not at all, for He would teach you but the single cause of all of them, no matter what their form. And you will understand that miracles reflect the simple statement,

"I have done this thing, and it is this I would undo."

Bring, then, all forms of suffering to Him Who knows that everyone is like the rest. He sees no differences where none exist, and He will teach you how each one is caused. None has a different cause from all the rest, and all of them are easily undone by but a single lesson truly learned. Salvation is a secret you have kept but from yourself. The universe proclaims it so. Yet to its witnesses you pay no heed at all. For they attest the thing you do not want to know. They seem to keep it secret from you. Yet you need but learn you choose but not to listen, not to see. How differently will you perceive the world when this is recognized! When you forgive the world your guilt, you will be free of it. Its innocence does not demand your guilt, nor does your guiltlessness rest on its sins.

This is the obvious; a secret kept from no-one but yourself. And it is this that has maintained you separate from the world, and kept your brother separate from you. Now need you but to learn that both of you are innocent or guilty. The one thing that is impossible is that you be unlike each other; that they both be true. This is the only secret yet to learn. And it will be no secret you are healed.

The miracle does nothing. All it does is to undo. And thus it cancels out the interference to what has been done. It does not add, but merely takes away. And what it takes away is long since gone, but being kept in memory, appears to have immediate effects. This world was over long ago. The thoughts that made it are no longer in the mind that thought of them and loved them for a little while. The miracle but shows the past is gone, and what has truly gone has no effects. Remembering a cause can but produce illusions of its presence, not effects.

All the effects of guilt are here no more. For guilt is over. In its passing went its consequences, left without a cause. Why would you cling to it in memory if you did not desire its effects?

Remembering is as selective as perception, being its past tense. It is perception of the past as if it were occurring now and still were there to see. Memory, like perception, is a skill made up by you, to take the place of what God gave in your creation. And like all the things you made, it can be used to serve another purpose, and to be the means for something else. It can be used to heal and not to hurt, if you so wish it be.

Nothing employed for healing represents an effort to do anything at all. It is a recognition that you have no needs which mean that something must be done. It is an unselective memory, which is not used to interfere with truth. All things the Holy Spirit can employ for healing have been given Him, without the content and the purposes for which they have been made. They are but skills without an application. They await their use. They have no dedication and no aim.

The Holy Spirit can indeed make use of memory, for God Himself is there. Yet this is not a memory of past events, but only of a present state. You are so long accustomed to believe that memory holds only what is past, that it is hard for you to realize it is a skill that can remember now. The limitations on remembering the world imposes on it are as vast as those you let the world impose on you. There is no link of memory to the past. If you would have it there, then there it is. But only your desire made the link, and only you have held it to a part of time where guilt appears to linger still.

The Holy Spirit's use of memory is quite apart from time. He does not seek to use it as a means to keep the past, but rather as a way to let it go. Memory holds the message it receives and does what it is given it to do. It does not write the message, nor appoint what it is for. Like to the body, it is purposeless within itself. And if it seems to serve to cherish ancient hate, and offers you the pictures of injustices and hurts which you were saving, this is what you asked its message be, and this is what it is. Committed to its vaults, the history of all the body's past is hidden there. All of the strange associations made to keep the past alive, the present dead, are stored within it, waiting your command that they be brought to you, and lived again. And thus do their effects appear to be increased by time, which took away their cause.

Yet time is but another phase of what does nothing. It works hand in hand with all the other attributes with which you seek to keep concealed the truth about yourself. Time neither takes away nor can restore. And yet you make strange use of it, as if the past had caused the present, which is but a consequence in which no change can be made possible, because its cause has gone.

Yet change must have a cause that will endure, or else it will not last. No change can be made in the present, if its cause is past. Only the past is held in memory as you make use of it, and so it is a way to hold the past against the now.

Remember nothing that you taught yourself, for you were badly taught. And who would keep a senseless lesson in his mind, when he can learn and can preserve a better one? When ancient memories of hate appear, remember that their cause is gone. And so you cannot understand what they are for. Let not the cause that you would give them now be what it was which made them what they were or seemed to be. Be glad that it is gone, for this is what you would be pardoned from. And see, instead, the new effects of cause accepted now, with consequences here. They will surprise you with their loveliness. The ancient new ideas they bring will be the happy consequences of a cause so ancient that it far exceeds the span of memory which your perception sees.

This is the Cause the Holy Spirit has remembered for you, when you would forget. It is not past because He let It not be unremembered. It has never changed because there never was a time in which He did not keep It safely in your mind. Its consequences will indeed seem new, because you thought that you remembered not their Cause. Yet was It never absent from your mind, for it was not your Father's Will that He be unremembered by His Son. What you remember never was. It came from causelessness which you confused with cause. It can deserve but laughter, when you learn you have remembered consequences which were causeless and could never be effects. The miracle reminds you of a Cause forever present, perfectly untouched by time and interference. Never changed from what It is. And you are its effects, as changeless and as perfect as Itself. Its memory does not lie in the past, nor waits the future. It is not revealed in miracles. They but remind you that It has not gone. When you forgive It for your sins, It will no longer be denied.

You who have sought to lay a judgement of your own Creator cannot understand it is not He Who laid a judgement on His Son. You would deny Him His effects, yet have they never been denied. There was no time in which His Son could be condemned for what was causeless, and against His Will. What your remembering would witness to is but the fear of God. He has not done the thing you fear. No more have you. And so your innocence has not been lost. You need no healing to be healed. In quietness, see in the miracle a lesson in allowing Cause to have Its own effects, and doing nothing that would interfere.

The miracle comes quietly into the mind that stops an instant and is still. It reaches gently from that quiet time, and from the mind it healed in quiet then, to other minds to share its quietness. And they will join in doing nothing to prevent its radiant extension back into the Mind Which caused all minds to be. Born out of sharing, there can be no pause in time to cause the miracle delay in hastening to all unquiet minds, and bringing them an instant's stillness, when the memory of God returns to them. Their own remembering is quiet now, and what has come to take its place will not be wholly unremembered afterwards.

He to Whom time is given offers thanks for every quiet instant given Him. For in that instant is His memory allowed to offer all its treasures to the Son of God, for whom they have been kept. How gladly does He offer them unto the one for whom He has been given them! And His Creator shares His thanks, because He would not be deprived of His effects. The instant's silence that His Son accepts gives welcome to eternity and Him and lets Them enter where They would abide. For in that instant does the Son of God do nothing that would make himself afraid.

How instantly the memory of God arises in the mind that has no fear to keep the memory away. Its own remembering has gone. There is no past to keep its fearful image in the way of glad awakening to present peace. The trumpets of eternity resound throughout the stillness yet disturb it not. And what is now remembered is not fear, but, rather, is the cause that fear was made to render unremembered and undone. The stillness speaks in gentle sounds of love the Son of God remembers from before his own remembering came in between the present and the past, to shut them out.

Now is the Son of God at last aware of present Cause and Its benign effects. Now does he understand what he has made is causeless, making no effects at all. He has done nothing. And in seeing this, he understands he never had a need for doing anything, and never did. His Cause is Its effects. There never was a cause beside It that could generate a different past or future. Its effects are changelessly eternal, beyond fear, and past the world of sin entirely. What has been lost, to see the causeless not? And where is sacrifice, when memory of God has come to take the place of loss?

What better way to close the little gap between illusions and reality than to allow the memory of God to flow across it, making it a bridge an instant will suffice to reach beyond?

For God has closed it with Himself. His memory has not gone by and left a stranded Son forever on a shore where he can glimpse another shore which he can never reach. His Father wills that he be lifted up, and gently carried over. He has built the bridge and it is He Who will transport His Son across it. Have no fear that He will fail in what He wills. Nor that you be excluded from the Will that is for you.

Without a cause there can be no effects and yet without effects there is no cause. The cause a cause is made by its effects; the Father is a father by His Son. Effects do not create their cause, but they establish its causation. Thus, the Son gives fatherhood to his Creator, and receives the gift that he has given Him. It is because he is God's Son that he must also be a father, who creates as God created him. The circle of creation has no end. Its starting and its ending are the same. But in itself it holds the universe of all creation, without beginning and without an end.

Fatherhood is creation. Love must be extended. Purity is not confined. It is the nature of the innocent to be forever uncontained, without a barrier or limitation. Thus is purity not of the body. Nor can it be found where limitation is. The body can be healed by its effects, which are as limitless as is itself. Yet must all healing come about because the mind is recognized as not within the body and its innocence is quite apart from it, and where all healing is. Where, then, is healing? Only where its cause is given its effects. For sickness is a meaningless attempt to give effects to causelessness and make it be a cause.

Always in sickness does the Son of God attempt to make himself his cause, and not allow himself to be his Father's Son. For this impossible desire, he does not believe that he is Love's effect, and must be cause because of what he is. The cause of healing is the only Cause of everything. It has but one effect. And in that recognition, causelessness is given no effects, and none are seen. A mind within a body and a world of other bodies, each with separate minds, are your "creations," you the "other" mind, creating with effects unlike yourself. And as their "father," you must be like them. Nothing at all has happened but that you have put yourself to sleep and dreamed a dream in which you were an alien to yourself, and but a part of someone else's dream.

The miracle does not awaken you, but merely shows you who the dreamer is. It teaches you there is a choice of dreams while you are still asleep, depending on the purpose of your dreaming. Do you wish for dreams of healing, or for dreams of death?

A dream is like a memory in that it pictures what you wanted shown to you. An empty storehouse, with an open door, holds all your shreds of memories and dreams. Yet if you are the dreamer, you perceive this much at least; that you have caused the dream and can accept another dream as well. But for this change in content of the dream, it must be realized that it is you who dreamed the dreaming that you do not like. It is but an effect which you have caused, and you would not be cause of this effect.

In dreams of murder and attack are you the victim in a dying body slain. But in forgiving dreams is no-one asked to be the victim and the sufferer. These are the happy dreams the miracle exchanges for your own. It does not ask you make another; only that you see you made the one you would exchange for this. This world is causeless, as is every dream that anyone has dreamed within the world. No plans are possible, and no design exists that could be found and understood.

What else could be expected from a thing that has no cause? Yet if it has no cause, it has no purpose. You may cause a dream, but never will you give it real effects. For that would change its cause, and it is this you cannot do. The dreamer of a dream is not awake, but does not know he sleeps. He sees illusions of himself as sick or well, depressed or happy, but without a stable cause with guaranteed effects.

The miracle establishes you dream a dream, and that its content is not true. This is a crucial step in dealing with illusions. No-one is afraid of them when he perceives he made them up. The fear was held in place because he did not see that he was author of the dream, and not a figure in the dream. He gives himself the consequences which he dreams he gave his brother. And it is but this the dream has put together and has offered him, to show him that his wishes have been done. Thus does he fear his own attack, but sees it at another's hands. As victim, he is suffering from its effects, but not their cause. He authored not his own attack, and he is innocent of what he caused. The miracle does nothing but to show him that he has done nothing. What he fears is cause without the consequences which would make it cause. And so it never was.

The separation started with the dream the Father was deprived of His effects, and powerless to keep them, since He was no longer their Creator. In the dream, the dreamer made himself, but what he made has turned against him, taking on the role of its creator, as the dreamer had. And as he hated his Creator, so the figures in the dream have hated him.

His body is their slave, which they abuse because the motives he has given it have they adopted as their own. And hate it for the vengeance it would offer them. It is their vengeance on the body which appears to prove the dreamer could not be the maker of the dream. Effect and cause are first split off, and then reversed, so that effect becomes a cause; the cause, effect.

This is the separation's final step, with which salvation, which proceeds to go the other way, begins. This final step is an effect of what has gone before, appearing as a cause. The miracle is the first step in giving back to cause the function of causation, not effect. For this confusion has produced the dream, and while it lasts, will wakening be feared. Nor will the call to wakening be heard, because it seems to be the call to fear.

Like every lesson which the Holy Spirit requests you learn, the miracle is clear. It demonstrates what He would have you learn and shows you its effects are what you want. In His forgiving dreams are the effects of yours undone, and hated enemies perceived as friends, with merciful intent. Their enmity is seen as causeless now, because they did not make it. And you can accept the role of maker of their hate because you see that it has no effects. Now are you freed from this much of the dream; the world is neutral, and the bodies which still seem to move about as separate things need not be feared. And so they are not sick.

The miracle returns the cause of fear to you who made it. But it also shows that, having no effects it is not cause, because the function of causation is to have effects. And where effects are gone, there is no cause. Thus is the body healed by miracles because they show the mind made sickness, and employed the body to be victim, or effect, of what it made. Yet half the lesson will not teach the whole. The miracle is useless if you learn but that the body can be healed, for this is not the lesson it was sent to teach. The lesson is the mind was sick that thought the body could be sick; projecting out its guilt caused nothing and had no effects.

This world is full of miracles. They stand in shining silence next to every dream of pain and suffering, of sin and guilt. They are the dream's alternative, the choice to be the dreamer, rather than deny the active role in making up the dream. They are the glad effects of taking back the consequence of sickness to its cause. The body is released because the mind acknowledges "this is not done to me, but I am doing this." And thus the mind is free to make another choice instead.

Beginning here, salvation will proceed to change the course of every step in the descent to separation, until all the steps have been retraced, the ladder gone, and all the dreaming of the world undone.

What waits in perfect certainty beyond salvation is not our concern. For you have barely started to allow your first, uncertain steps to be directed up the ladder separation led you down. The miracle alone is your concern at present. Here is where we must begin. And having started, will the way be made serene and simple in the rising up to waking and the ending of the dream. When you accept a miracle, you do not add your dream of fear to one that is already being dreamed. Without support, the dream will fade away without effects. For it is your support that strengthens it.

No mind is sick until another mind agrees that they are separate. And thus it is their joint decision to be sick. If you withhold agreement and accept the part you play in making sickness real, the other mind cannot project its guilt without your aid in letting it perceive itself as separate and apart from you. Thus is the body not perceived as sick by both your minds, from separate points of view. Uniting with a brother's mind prevents the cause of sickness and perceived effects. Healing is the effect of minds which join, as sickness comes from minds which separate.

The miracle does nothing just because the minds are joined and cannot separate. Yet in the dreaming has this been reversed, and separate minds are seen as bodies, which are separated, and which cannot join. Do not allow your brother to be sick, for if he is, have you abandoned him to his own dream by sharing it with him. He has not seen the cause of sickness where it is, and you have overlooked the gap between you, where the sickness has been bred. Thus are you joined in sickness, to preserve the little gap unhealed, where sickness is kept carefully protected, cherished, and upheld by firm belief, lest God should come to bridge the little gap that leads to Him. Fight not His coming with illusions, for it is His coming that you want above all things that seem to glisten in the dream.

The end of dreaming is the end of fear, and love was never in the world of dreams. The gap is little. Yet it holds the seeds of pestilence and every form of ill, because it is a wish to keep apart and not to join. And thus it seems to give a cause to sickness which is not its cause. The purpose of the gap is all the cause that sickness has. For it was made to keep you separated, in a body which you see as if it were the cause of pain.

The cause of pain is separation, not the body, which is only its effect. Yet separation is but empty space, enclosing nothing, doing nothing and as unsubstantial as the empty place between the ripples that a ship has made in passing by. And covered just as fast, as water rushes in to close the gap and as the waves, in joining, cover it. Where is the gap between the waves when they have joined and covered up the space which seemed to keep them separate for a little while? Where are the grounds for sickness when the minds have joined to close the little gap between them where the seeds of sickness seemed to grow?

God builds the bridge, but only in the space left clean and vacant by the miracle. The seeds of sickness and the shame of guilt He cannot bridge, for He cannot destroy the alien will that He created not. Let its effects be gone, and clutch them not with eager hands, to keep them for yourself. The miracle will brush them all aside, and thus make room for Him Who wills to come, and bridge His Son's returning to Himself.

Count, then, the silver miracles and golden dreams of happiness as all the treasures you would keep within the storehouse of the world. The door is open, not to thieves, but to your starving brothers, who mistook for gold the shining of a pebble, and who stored a heap of snow that shone like silver. They have nothing left behind the open door. What is the world except a little gap perceived to tear eternity apart, and break it into days and months and years? And what are you who live within the world except a picture of the Son of God in broken pieces, each concealed within a separate and uncertain bit of clay?

Be not afraid, but let your world be lit by miracles. And where the gap was seen to stand between you, join your brother there. And sickness will be seen without a cause. The dream of healing in forgiveness lies, and gently shows you that you never sinned. The miracle would leave no proof of guilt to bring you witness to what never was. And in your storehouse, it will make a place of welcome for your Father and your Self. The door is open, that all those may come who would no longer starve, and would enjoy the feast of plenty set before them there. And they will meet with your invited Guests the miracle has asked to come to you.

This is a feast unlike indeed to those the dreaming of the world has shown. For here, the more that anyone receives, the more is left for all the rest to share. The Guests have brought unlimited supply with Them. And no-one is deprived or can deprive. Here is a feast the Father lays before His Son and shares it equally with him.

And in Their sharing there can be no gap in which abundance falters and grows thin. Here can the lean years enter not, for time waits not upon this feast, which has no end. For Love has set Its table in the space that seemed to keep your Guests apart from you.

Accepting the Atonement for yourself means not to give support to someone's dream of sickness and of death. It means that you share not his wish to separate and let him turn illusions on himself. Nor do you wish that they be turned, instead, on you. Thus have they no effects. And you are free of dreams of pain because you let him be. Unless you help him, you will suffer pain with him because that is your wish. And you become a figure in his dream of pain, as he in yours. So do you both become illusions and without identity. You could be anyone or anything, depending on whose evil dream you share. You can be sure of just one thing; that you are evil, for you share in dreams of fear.

There is a way of finding certainty right here and now. Refuse to be a part of fearful dreams whatever form they take, for you will lose identity in them. You find yourself by not accepting them as causing you and giving you effects. You stand apart from them, but not apart from him who dreams them. Thus you separate the dreamer from the dream, and join in one, but let the other go. The dream is but illusion in the mind. And with the mind you would unite, but never with the dream. It is the dream you fear, and not the mind. You see them as the same, because you think that you are but a dream. And what is real and what is but illusion in yourself you do not know and cannot tell apart.

Like you, your brother thinks he is a dream. Share not in his illusion of himself, for your identity depends on his reality. Think, rather, of him as a mind in which illusions still persist, but as a mind which brother is to you. He is not brother made by what he dreams, nor is his body, "hero" of the dream, your brother. It is his reality that is your brother, as is yours to him. Your mind and his are joined in brotherhood. His body and his dreams but seem to make a little gap, where yours have joined with his.

And yet, between your minds there is no gap. To join his dreams is thus to meet him not, because his dreams would separate from you. Therefore, release him, merely by your claim on brotherhood, and not on dreams of fear. Let him acknowledge who he is, by not supporting his illusions by your faith, for if you do, you will have faith in yours. With faith in yours, He will not be released, and you are kept in bondage to his dream. And dreams of fear will haunt the little gap, inhabited but by illusions which you have supported in each other's minds.

Be certain, if you do your part, he will do his, for he will join you where you stand. Call not to him to meet you in the gap between you or you must believe that it is your reality, as well as his. You cannot do his part, but this you do when you become a passive figure in his dream, instead of dreamer of your own. Identity in dreams is meaningless because the dreamer and the dream are one. Who shares a dream must be the dream he shares, because by sharing is a cause produced.

You share confusion, and you are confused, for in the gap no stable self exists. What is the same seems different, because what is the same appears to be unlike. His dreams are yours because you let them be. But if you took your own away would he be free of them, and of his own as well. Your dreams are witnesses to his, and his attest the truth of yours. Yet if you see there is no truth in yours, his dreams will go, and he will understand what made the dream.

The Holy Spirit is in both your minds, and He is One because there is no gap that separates His Oneness from Itself. The gap between your bodies matters not, for what is joined in Him is always one. No-one is sick if someone else accepts his union with him. His desire to be a sick and separated mind cannot remain without a witness or a cause. And both are gone if someone wills to be united with him. He has dreams that he was separated from his brother who, by sharing not his dream, has left the space between them vacant. And the Father comes to join His Son the Holy Spirit joined.

The Holy Spirit's function is to take the broken picture of the Son of God and put the pieces into place again. This holy picture, healed entirely, does He hold out to every separate piece that thinks it is a picture in itself. To each he offers his identity, which the whole picture represents, instead of just a little, broken bit which he insisted was himself. And when he sees THIS picture, he will recognize himself. If you share not your brother's evil dream, this IS the picture that the miracle will place within the little gap, left clean of all the seeds of sickness and of sin. And here the Father will receive His Son, because His Son was gracious to himself.

I thank you, Father, knowing you will come to close each little gap that lies between the broken pieces of Your Holy Son. Your holiness, complete and perfect, lies in every one of them. And they are joined, because what is in one is in them all. How holy is the smallest grain of sand, when it is recognized as being part of the completed picture of God's Son! The forms the broken pieces seem to take mean nothing. For the whole is in each one. And every aspect of the Son of God is just the same as every other part.

Join not your brother's dreams, but join with Him, and where you join His Son, the Father is. Who seeks for substitutes when he perceives he has lost nothing? Who would want to have the "benefits" of sickness when he has received the simple happiness of health? What God has given cannot be a loss and what is not of Him has no effects. What, then, would you perceive within the gap?

The seeds of sickness come from the belief that there is joy in separation, and its giving up would be a sacrifice. But miracles are the result, when you do not insist on seeing in the gap what is not there. Your willingness to let illusions go is all the Healer of God's Son requires. He will place the miracle of healing where the seeds of sickness were. And there will be no loss, but only gain.

What is a sense of sickness but a sense of limitation? Of a splitting off and separating from? A gap perceived between yourselves and what is seen as health? The good is seen outside; the evil, in. And thus is sickness separating off the self from good and keeping evil in. God is the alternate to dreams of fear. Who shares in them can never share in Him. But who withdraws his mind from sharing them is sharing Him. There is no other choice. Except you share it, nothing can exist. And you exist because God shared His Will with you, that His creation might create.

It is the sharing of the evil dreams of hate and malice, bitterness and death, of sin and suffering and pain and loss, that makes them real. Unshared, they are perceived as meaningless. The fear is gone from them because you did not give them your support. Where fear has gone there love must come, because there are but these alternatives. Where one appears, the other disappears. And which you share becomes the only one you have. You have the one which you accept, because it is the only one you wish to have. You share no evil dreams if you forgive the dreamer and perceive that he is not the dream he made. And so he cannot be a part of yours, from which you both are free. Forgiveness separates the dreamer from the evil dream and thus releases him.

Remember if you share an evil dream, you will believe you are the dream you share. And fearing it, you will not want to know your own identity, because you think that it is fearful. And you will deny your Self and walk upon an alien ground which your Creator did not make and where you seem to be a something you are not. You will make war upon your Self, which seems to be your enemy; and will attack your brother, as a part of what you hate. There is no compromise. You are your Self or an illusion. What can be between illusion and the truth? A middle ground, where you can be a thing that is not you, must be a dream and cannot be the truth.

You have conceived a little gap between illusions and the truth to be the place where all your safety lies, and where your Self is safely hidden by what you have made. Here is a world established that is sick, and this the world the body's eyes perceive. Here are the sounds it hears; the voices which its ears were made to hear. Yet sights and sounds the body can perceive are meaningless. It cannot see nor hear. It does not know what seeing IS; what listening is for. It is as little able to perceive as it can judge or understand or know. Its eyes are blind; its ears are deaf. It cannot think, and so it cannot have effects.

What is there God created to be sick? And what that He created not can be? Let not your eyes behold a dream; your ears bear witness to illusion. They were made to look upon a world that is not there; to hear the voices that can make no sound. Yet are there other sounds and other sights which can be seen and heard and understood. For eyes and ears are senses without sense, and what they see and hear they but report. It is not they that hear and see, but you, who put together every jagged piece, each senseless scrap and shred of evidence, and make a witness to the world you want. Let not the body's ears and eyes perceive these countless fragments seen within the gap which you imagined and let them not persuade their maker his imaginings are real.

Creation proves reality because it shares the function all creation shares. It is not made of little bits of glass, a piece of wood, a thread or two perhaps, all put together to attest its truth. Reality does not depend on this. There IS no gap which separates the truth from dreams and from illusions. Truth has left no room for them in any place or time. For it fills every place and every time and makes them wholly indivisible.

You who believe there is a little gap between you, do not understand that it is here that you are kept as prisoners in a world perceived to be existing here. The world you see does not exist, because the place where you perceive it is not real. The gap is carefully concealed in fog, and misty pictures rise to cover it with vague, uncertain forms and changing shapes, forever unsubstantial and unsure. Yet in the gap is nothing. And there are no awesome secrets and no darkened tombs where terror rises from the bones of death. Look at the little gap, and you behold the innocence and emptiness of sin that you will see within yourself, when you have lost the fear of recognising love.

Who punishes the body is insane? For here the little gap is seen, and yet it is not here. It has not judged itself, nor made itself to be what it is not. It does not seek to make of pain a joy and look for lasting pleasure in the dust. It does not tell you what its purpose is and cannot understand what it is for. It does not victimize, because it has no will, no preferences and no doubts. It does not wonder what it is. And so it has no need to be competitive. It can be victimized but cannot feel itself as victim. It accepts no role, but does what it is told, without attack.

It is indeed a senseless point of view to hold responsible for sight a thing that cannot see and blame it for the sounds you do not like, although it cannot hear. It suffers not the punishment you give, because it has no feeling. It behaves in ways you want, but never makes the choice. It is not born and does not die. It can but follow aimlessly the path on which it has been set. And if that path is changed, it walks as easily another way. It takes no sides, and judges not the road it travels. It perceives no gap, because it does not hate. It can be used for hate, but it cannot be hateful made thereby.

The thing you hate and fear and loathe and want, the body does not know. You send it forth to seek for separation and to be a separate thing. And then you hate it, not for what it is, but for the uses you have made of it. You shrink from what it sees and what it hears and hate its frailty and littleness. And you despise its acts, but not your own. It sees and acts for you. It hears your voice. And it is frail and little by your wish. It seems to punish you, and thus deserve your hatred for the limitations which it brings to you. Yet you have made of it a symbol for the limitations which you want your mind to have and see and keep.

The body represents the gap between the little bit of mind you call your own, and all the rest of what yours is really. You hate it, yet you think it is yourself, and that, without it, would your self be lost. This is the secret vow which you have made with every brother who would walk apart. This is the secret oath you take again, whenever you perceive yourself attacked. No-one can suffer if he does not see himself attacked and losing by attack. Unstated and unheard in consciousness is every pledge to sickness. Yet it is a promise to another to be hurt by him, and to attack him in return.

Sickness is anger taken out upon the body, so that it will suffer pain. It is the obvious effect of what was made in secret, in agreement with another's secret wish to be apart from you, as you would be apart from him. Unless you both agree that is your wish, it can have no effects. Whoever says,

"There is no gap between my mind and yours" has kept God's promise, not his tiny oath to be forever faithful unto death. And by his healing is his brother healed.

Let this be your agreement with each one; that you be one with him, and not apart. And he will keep the promise that you make with him, because it is the one which he has made to God, as God has made to him. God keeps His promises; His Son keeps his. In his creation did his Father say, "You are beloved of Me and I of you forever. Be you perfect as Myself, for you can never be apart from Me." His Son remembers not that he replied "I will," though in that promise he was born. Yet God reminds him of it every time he does not share a promise to be sick, but lets his mind be healed and unified. His secret vows are powerless before the Will of God, Whose promises he shares. And what he substitutes is not his will, who has made promise of himself to God.

God asks for nothing, and His Son, like Him, need ask for nothing. For there is no lack in him. An empty space, a little gap, would be a lack. And it is only there that he could want for something he has not. A space where God is not, a gap between the Father and the Son is not the Will of either, who have promised to be One. God's promise is a promise to himself and there is no-one who could be untrue to what He wills as part of what He is. The promise that there is no gap between Himself and what He is cannot be false. What will can come between what MUST be One, and in Whose wholeness there can be no gap?

The beautiful relationship you have with all your brothers is a part of you because it is a part of God Himself. Are you not sick, if you deny yourself your wholeness and your health, the Source of help, the Call to healing and the Call to heal? Your Saviour waits for healing and the world waits with him. Nor are you apart from it. For healing will be one or not at all, its oneness being where the healing lies. What could correct for separation but its opposite? There is no middle ground in any aspect of salvation. You accept it wholly or accept it not. What is unseparated must be joined. And what is joined cannot be separate.

Either there is a gap between you and your brother, or you are as one. There is no in between, no other choice and no allegiance to be split between the two. A split allegiance is but faithlessness to both and merely sets you spinning round to grasp uncertainly at any straw that seems to hold some promise of relief. Yet who can build his home upon a straw, and count on it as shelter from the wind? The body can be made a home like this, because it lacks foundation in the truth.

And yet, because it does, it can be seen as not your home, but merely as an aid to help you reach the home where God abides.

With this as purpose is the body healed. It is not used to witness to the dream of separation and disease. Nor is it idly blamed for what it did not do. It serves to help the healing of God's Son and for this purpose it cannot be sick. It will not join a purpose not your own and you have chosen that it not be sick. All miracles are based upon this choice and given you the instant it is made. No forms of sickness are immune, because the choice cannot be made in terms of form. The choice of sickness seems to be a form, yet it is one, as is its opposite. And you are sick or well, accordingly.

But never you alone. This world is but the dream that you can be alone and think without affecting those apart from you. To be alone must mean you are apart, and if you are, you cannot but be sick. This seems to prove that you must be apart. Yet all it means is that you tried to keep a promise to be true to faithlessness. Yet faithlessness is sickness. It is like the house set upon straw. It seems to be quite solid and substantial in itself. Yet its stability cannot be judged apart from its foundation. If it rests on straw, there is no need to bar the door and lock the windows and make fast the bolts. The wind will topple it, and rain will come and carry it into oblivion.

What is the sense in seeking to be safe in what was made for danger and for fear? Why burden it with further locks and chains and heavy anchors, when its weakness lies, not in itself, but in the frailty of the little gap of nothingness whereon it stands? What can be safe which rests upon a shadow? Would you build your home upon what will collapse beneath a feather's weight?

Your home is built upon your brother's health, upon his happiness, his sinlessness, and everything his Father promised him. No secret promise you have made instead has shaken the Foundation of his home. The winds will blow upon it, and the rain will beat against it, but with no effect. The world will wash away, and yet this house will stand forever, for its strength lies not within itself alone. It is an ark of safety, resting on God's promise that His Son is safe forever in Himself. What gap can interpose itself between the safety of this shelter and its Source? From here the body can be seen as what it is, and neither less nor more in worth than the extent to which it can be used to liberate God's Son unto his home. And with this holy purpose, is it made a home of holiness a little while, because it shares your Father's Will with you.

There is no time, no place, no state where God is absent. There is nothing to be feared. There is no way in which a gap could be conceived of in the wholeness that is His. The compromise the least and littlest gap would represent in His eternal Love is quite impossible. For it would mean His Love could harbor just a hint of hate; His gentleness turn sometimes to attack; and His eternal patience sometimes fail. All this do you believe, when you perceive a gap between your brother and yourself. How could you trust Him, then? For He must be deceptive in His Love. Be wary, then; let Him not come too close, and leave a gap between you and His Love, through which you can escape if there be need for you to flee.

Here is the fear of God most plainly seen. For love is treacherous to those who fear, since fear and hate can never be apart. No-one who hates but is afraid of love, and therefore must he be afraid of God. Certain it is he knows not what love means. He fears to love and loves to hate, and so he thinks that love is fearful; hate is love. This is the consequence the little gap must bring to those who cherish it and think that it is their salvation and their hope.

The fear of God! The greatest obstacle that peace must flow across has not yet gone. The rest are past, but this one still remains to block your path, and make the way to light seem dark and fearful, perilous and bleak. You had decided that your brother is your enemy. Sometimes a friend, perhaps, provided that your separate interests made your friendship possible a little while. But not without a gap between you, lest he turn again into an enemy. A cautious friendship, limited in scope and carefully restricted in amount, became the treaty you had made with him. You shared a qualified entente, in which a clause of separation was a point on which you both agreed to keep intact. And violating this was thought to be a breach of treaty not to be allowed.

The gap between you i snot one of space between two separate bodies. This but seems to be dividing off your separate minds. It is the symbol of a promise made to meet when you prefer, and separate until you both elect to meet again. And then your bodies seem to get in touch, and signify a meeting-place to join. But always is it possible to go your separate ways. Conditional upon the "right" to separate will you agree to meet from time to time, and keep apart in intervals of separation, which protect you from the "sacrifice" of love. The body saves you, for it gets away from total sacrifice, and gives you time in which to build again your separate selves, which you believe diminish as you meet.

The body could not separate your minds unless you wanted it to be a cause of separation and of distance seen between you. Thus do you endow it with a power that lies not within itself. And herein lies its power over you. For now you think that it determines when you meet, and limits your ability to make communion with each other's mind. And now it tells you where to go and how to go there, what is feasible for you to undertake, and what you cannot do. It dictates what its health can tolerate, and what will tire it and make it sick. And its "inherent" weaknesses set up the limitations on what you would do, and keep your purpose limited and weak.

The body will accommodate to this, if you would have it so. It will allow but limited indulgences in "love", with intervals of hatred in between. And it will take command of when to "love" and when to shrink more safely into fear. It will be sick because you do not know what loving means. And so you must misuse each circumstance and everyone you meet, and see in them a purpose not your own.

It is not love that asks a sacrifice. But fear demands the sacrifice of love, for in love's presence fear cannot abide. For hate to be maintained love must be feared, and only sometimes present; sometimes gone. Thus is love seen as treacherous, because it seems to come and go uncertainly and offer no stability to you. You do not see how limited and weak is your allegiance and how frequently you have demanded that love go away and leave you quietly alone, in "peace."

The body innocent of any goal is your excuse for variable goals you hold, and force the body to maintain. You do not fear its weakness, but its lack of strength or weakness. Would you recognize that nothing stands between you? Would you know there is no gap behind which you can hide? There is a shock that comes to those who learn their Saviour is their enemy no more. There is a wariness that is aroused by learning that the body is not real. And there are overtones of seeming fear around the happy message "God is love."

Yet all that happens when the gap is gone is peace eternal. Nothing more than that, and nothing less. Without the fear of God, what could induce you to abandon Him? What toys or trinkets in the gap could serve to hold you back an instant from His love? Would you allow the body to say "no" to Heaven's calling, were you not afraid to find a loss of self in finding God? Yet can your Self be lost by being found?

Why would you not perceive it as release from suffering to learn that you are free? Why would you not acclaim the truth, instead of looking on it as an enemy? Why does an easy path, so clearly marked it is impossible to lose the way, seem thorny, rough, and far too difficult for you to follow? Is it not because you see it as the road to hell, instead of looking on it as a simple way, without a sacrifice or any loss, to find yourself in Heaven and in God? Until you realize you give up nothing, until you understand there is no loss, you will have some regrets about the way that you have chosen. And you will not see the many gains your choice has offered you. Yet though you do not see them, they are there. Their cause has been effected, and they must be present where their cause has entered in.

You have accepted healing's cause, and so it must be you are healed. And being healed, the power to heal must also now be yours. The miracle is not a separate thing which happens suddenly, as an effect without a cause. Nor is it, in itself, a cause. But where its cause is must it be. Now is it caused, though not as yet perceived. And its effects are there, though not yet seen. Look inward now, and you will not behold a reason for regret, but cause indeed for glad rejoicing and for hope of peace.

It has been hopeless to attempt to find the hope of peace upon a battleground. It has been futile to demand escape from sin and pain of what was made to serve the function of retaining sin and pain. For pain and sin are one illusion, as are hate and fear, attack and guilt but one. Where they are causeless their effects are gone, and love must come wherever they are not. Why are you not rejoicing? You are free of pain and sickness, misery and loss, and all effects of hatred and attack. No more is pain your friend and guilt your god, and you should welcome the effects of love.

Your Guest has come. You asked Him, and He came. You did not hear Him enter, for you did not wholly welcome Him. And yet His gifts came with Him. He has laid them at your feet and asks you now that you will look on them and take them for your own. He needs your help in giving them to all who walk apart, believing they are separate and alone. They will be healed when you accept your gifts, because your Guest will welcome everyone whose feet have touched the holy ground whereon you stand, and where His gifts for them are laid.

You do not see how much you now can give, because of everything you have received. Yet He Who entered in but waits for you to come where you invited Him to be. There is no other place where He can find His host, nor where His host can meet with Him.

And nowhere else His gifts of peace and joy, and all the happiness His Presence brings, can be obtained. For they are where He is Who brought them with Him, that they might be yours. You cannot see your Guest, but you can see the gifts He brought. And when you look on them, you will believe His Presence must be there. For what you now can do could not be done without the love and grace His Presence holds.

Such is the promise of the loving God; His Son have life and every living thing be part of him, and nothing else have life. What you have given "life" is not alive and symbolizes but your wish to be alive apart from life, alive in death, with death perceived as life and living, death. Confusion follows on confusion here, for on confusion has this world been based, and there is nothing else it rests upon. Its basis does not change, although it seems to be in constant change. Yet what is that except the state confusion really means? Stability to those who are confused is meaningless and shift and change become the law on which they predicate their lives.

The body does not change. It represents the larger dream that change is possible. To change is to attain a state unlike the one in which you found yourself before. There is no change in immortality, and Heaven knows it not. Yet here on earth it has a double purpose, for it can be made to teach opposing things. And they reflect the teacher who is teaching them. The body can appear to change with time, with sickness or with health and with events that seem to alter it. Yet this but means the mind remains unchanged in its belief of what the purpose of the body is.

Sickness is a demand the body be a thing that it is not. Its nothingness is guarantee that it cannot be sick. In your demand that it be more than this lies the idea of sickness. For it asks that God be less than all He really is. What, then, becomes of you, for it is you of whom the sacrifice is asked? For He is told that part of Him belongs to Him no longer. He must sacrifice your self, and in His sacrifice are you made more, and He is lessened by the loss of you. And what is gone from Him becomes your god, protecting you from being part of Him.

The body that is asked to be a god will be attacked, because its nothingness has not been recognized. And so it seems to be a thing with power in itself. As something, it can be perceived and thought to feel and act and hold you in its grasp as prisoner to itself. And it can fail to be what you demanded that it be.

And you will hate it for its littleness unmindful that the failure does not lie in that it is not more than it should be but only in your failure to perceive that it is nothing. Yet its nothingness is your salvation from which you would flee.

As "something" is the body asked to be God's enemy, replacing what He is with littleness and limit and despair. It is His loss you celebrate when you behold the body as a thing you love or look upon it as a thing you hate. For if He be the sum of everything, then what is not in Him does not exist, and His completion IS its nothingness. Your Saviour is not dead, nor does he dwell in what was built as temple unto death. He lives in God, and it is this that makes him Saviour unto you, and only this. His body's nothingness releases yours from sickness and from death. For what is yours cannot be more nor less than what is his.

Condemn your Saviour not because he thinks he is a body. For beyond his dreams is his reality. But he must learn he is a Saviour first, before he can remember what he is. And he must save who would be saved. On saving you depends his happiness. For who is Saviour but the one who gives salvation? Thus he learns it must be his to give. Unless he gives, he will not know he has, for giving is the proof of having. Only those who think that God is lessened by their strength could fail to understand this must be so. For who could give unless he has, and who could lose by giving what must be increased thereby?

Think you the Father lost Himself when He created you? Was He made weak because He shared His love? Was He made incomplete by your perfection? Or are you the proof that He is perfect and complete? Deny Him not His witness in the dream His Son prefers to his reality. He must be Saviour from the dream he made, that he be free of it. He must see someone else as not a body, one with him without the wall the world has built to keep apart all living things who know not that they live. Within the dream of bodies and of death is yet one theme of truth; no more, perhaps, than just a tiny spark, a space of light created in the dark, where God still shines.

You cannot wake yourself. Yet you can let yourself be wakened. You can overlook your brother's dreams. So perfectly can you forgive him his illusions, he becomes your Saviour from your dreams. And as you see him shining in the space of light where God abides within the darkness, you will see that God Himself is where his body is. Before this light the body disappears, as heavy shadows must give way to light. The darkness cannot choose that it remain.

The coming of the light means it is gone. In glory will you see your brother then and understand what really fills the gap so long perceived as keeping you apart.

There, in its place, God's Witness has set forth the gentle way of kindness to God's Son. Whom you forgive is given power to forgive you your illusions. By your gift of freedom is it given unto you. Make way for love, which you did not create, but which you can extend. On earth this means forgive your brother, that the darkness may be lifted from your mind. When light has come to him through your forgiven your face he saw the light that he would keep beside him, as he walks through darkness to the everlasting light.

How holy are you, that the Son of God can be your Saviour in the midst of dreams of desolation and disaster? See how eagerly he comes, and steps aside from heavy shadows that have hidden him, and shines on you in gratitude and love. He is himself, but not himself alone. And as his Father lost not part of Him in your creation, so the light in him is brighter still because you gave your light to him, to save him from the dark. And now the light in you must be as bright as shines in him. This is the spark that shines within the dream; that you can help him waken and be sure his waking eyes will rest on you. And in his glad salvation you are saved.

Do you believe that truth can be but some illusions? They are dreams because they are not true. Their equal lack of truth becomes the basis for the miracle, which means that you have understood that dreams are dreams; and that escape depends, not on the dream, but only on awaking. Could it be some dreams are kept, and others wakened from? The choice is not between which dreams to keep, but only if you want to live in dreams or to awaken from them. Thus it is the miracle does not select some dreams to leave untouched by its beneficence. You cannot dream some dreams and wake from some, for you are either sleeping or awake. And dreaming goes with only one of these.

The dreams you think you like would hold you back as much as those in which the fear is seen. For every dream is but a dream of fear, no matter what the form it seems to take. The fear is seen within, without, or both. Or it can be disguised in pleasant form. But never is it absent from the dream, for fear is the material of dreams from which they all are made. Their form can change, but they cannot be made of something else. The miracle were treacherous indeed if it allowed you still to be afraid because you did not recognise the fear. You would not then be willing to awake, for which the miracle prepares the way.

In simplest form, it can be said attack is a response to function unfulfilled as you perceive the function. It can be in you or someone else, but where it is perceived it will be there it is attacked. Depression or assault must be the theme of every dream, for they are made of fear. The thin disguise of pleasure and of joy in which they may be wrapped but slightly veils the heavy lump of fear which is their core. And it is this the miracle perceives, and not the wrappings in which it is bound.

When you are angry, is it not because someone has failed to fill the function you allotted him? And does not this become the "reason" your attack is justified? The dreams you think you like are those in which the functions you have given have been filled; the needs which you ascribe to you are met. It does not matter if they be fulfilled, or merely wanted. It is the idea that they exist from which the fears arise. Dreams are not wanted more or less. They are desired or not. And each one represents some function which you have assigned; some goal which an event, or body, or a thing should represent, and should achieve for you. If it succeeds, you think you like the dream. If it should fail, you think the dream is sad. But whether it succeeds or fails is not its core, but just the flimsy covering.

How happy would your dreams become if you were not the one who gave the "proper" role to every figure which the dream contains. No-one can fail but your idea of him, and there is no betrayal but of this. The core of dreams the Holy Spirit gives is never one of fear. The coverings may not appear to change, but what they mean has changed, because they cover something else. Perceptions are determined by their purpose, in that they seem to be what they are for. A shadow figure who attacks becomes a brother giving you a chance to help, if this becomes the function of the dream. And dreams of sadness thus are turned to joy.

What is your brother for? You do not know, because your function is obscure to you. Do not ascribe a role to him which you imagine would bring happiness to you. And do not try to hurt him when he fails to take the part which you assigned to him, in what you dream your life was meant to be. He asks for help in every dream he has, and you have help to give him if you see the function of the dream as He perceives its function, Who can utilize all dreams as means to serve the function given Him. Because He loves the dreamer, not the dream, each dream becomes an offering of love. For at its centre is His love for you, which lights whatever form it takes with love.

There is a place in you where this whole world has been forgotten; where no memory of sin and of illusion linger still. There is a place in you which time has left, and echoes of eternity are heard. There is a resting place so still no sound except a hymn to Heaven rises up to gladden God the Father and the Son. Where both abide are They remembered, both. And where They are is Heaven and is peace. Think not that you can change Their dwelling-place. For your Identity abides in Them and where They are, forever must you be.

The changelessness of Heaven is in you, so deep within that nothing in this world but passes by, unnoticed and unseen. The still infinity of endless peace surrounds you gently in its soft embrace, so strong and quiet, tranquil in the might of its Creator, nothing can intrude upon the sacred Son of God within. Here is the role the Holy Spirit gives to you who wait upon the Son of God and would behold him waken and be glad. He is a part of you and you of him, because he is his Father's Son, and not for any purpose you may see in him. Nothing is asked of you but to accept the changeless and eternal that abide in him, for your Identity is there. The peace in you can but be found in him. And every thought of love you offer him but brings you nearer to your wakening to peace eternal and to endless joy.

This sacred Son of God is like yourself; the mirror of his Father's love for you, the soft reminder of his Father's love by which he was created and which still abides in him, as it abides in you. Be very still and hear God's Voice in him, and let It tell you what his function is. He was created that you might be whole, for only the complete can be a part of God's completion, Which created you.

There is no gift the Father asks of you but that you see in all creation but the shining glory of His gift to you. Behold His Son, His perfect gift, in whom his Father shines forever, and to whom is all creation given as his own. Because he has it is it given you, and where it lies in him behold your peace. The quiet that surrounds you dwells in him, and from this quiet come the happy dreams in which your hands are joined in innocence. These are not hands that grasp in dreams of pain. They hold no sword, for they have left their hold on every vain illusion of the world. And being empty, they received, instead, a brother's hand in which completion lay.

If you but knew the glorious goal that lies beyond forgiveness, you would not keep hold on any thought, however light the touch of evil on it may appear to be. For you would understand how great the cost of holding anything God did not give in minds that can direct the hand to bless, and lead God's Son unto his Father's house.

Would you not want to be a friend to him, created by his Father as His home? If God esteems him worthy of Himself, would you attack him with the hands of hate? Who would lay bloody hands on Heaven itself, and hope to find its peace? Your brother thinks he holds the hand of death. Believe him not. But learn, instead, how blessed are you who can release him, just by offering him yours.

A dream is given you in which he is your Saviour, not your enemy in hate. A dream is given you in which you have forgiven him for all his dreams of death; a dream of hope you share with him, instead of dreaming evil separate dreams of hate. Why does it seem so hard to share this dream? Because unless the Holy Spirit gives the dream its function, it was made for hate, and will continue in death's services. Each form it takes in some way calls for death. And those who serve the lord of death have come to worship in a separated world, each with his tiny spear and rusted sword, to keep his ancient promises to die.

Such is the core of fear in every dream that has been kept apart from use by Him Who sees a different function for a dream. When dreams are shared, they lose the function of attack and separation, even though it was for this that every dream was made. Yet nothing in the world of dreams remains without the hope of change and betterment, for here is not where changelessness is found. Let us be glad indeed that this is so and seek not the eternal in this world. Forgiving dreams are means to step aside from dreaming of a world outside yourself. And leading finally beyond all dreams, unto the peace of everlasting life.

How willing are you to forgive your brother? How much do you desire peace instead of endless strife and misery and pain? These questions are the same, in different form. Forgiveness IS your peace, for herein lies the end of separation, and the dream of danger and destruction, sin and death; of madness and of murder, grief and loss. This is the "sacrifice" salvation asks, and gladly offers peace instead of this.

Swear not to die, you holy Son of God! You make a bargain that you cannot keep. The Son of Life cannot be killed. He is immortal as his Father. What he is cannot be changed. He is the only thing in all the universe that must be one. What seems eternal all will have an end. The stars will disappear, and night and day will be no more. All things that come and go, the tides, the seasons, and the lives of man; all things that change with time and bloom and fade, will not return. Where time has set an end is not where the eternal is. God's Son can never change by what man made of him.

He will be as he was and as he is, for time appointed not his destiny, nor set the hour of his birth and death. Forgiveness will not change him. Yet time waits upon forgiveness that the things of time may disappear because they have no use.

Nothing survives its purpose. If it be conceived to die, then die it must unless it does not take this purpose as its own. Change is the only thing that can be made a blessing here, where purpose is not fixed, however changeless it appears to be. Think not that you can set a goal unlike God's purpose for you and establish it as changeless and eternal. You can give yourself a purpose that you do not have. But you cannot remove the power to change your mind and see another purpose there. Change is the greatest gift God gave to all that you would make eternal, to ensure that only Heaven would not pass away. You were not born to die. You cannot change, because your function has been fixed by God. All other goals are set in time and change that time might be preserved, excepting one. Forgiveness does not aim at keeping time, but at its ending, when it has no use. Its purpose ended, it is gone. And where it once held seeming sway is now restored the function God established for His Son in full awareness. Time can set no end to its fulfillment, nor its changelessness. There is no death because the living share the function their Creator gave to them. Life's function cannot be to die. It must be life's extension, that it be as one forever and forever, without end.

This world will bind your feet and tie your hands and kill your body only if you think that it was made to crucify God's Son. For even though it was a dream of death, you need not let it stand for this to you. Let this be changed, and nothing in the world but must be changed as well. For nothing here but is defined as what you see it for. How lovely is the world whose purpose is forgiveness of God's Son! How free from fear, how filled with blessing and with happiness! And what a joyous thing it is to dwell a little while in such a happy place! Nor can it be forgot, in such a world, it IS a little while till timelessness comes quietly to take the place of time.

Seek not outside yourself. For it will fail, and you will weep each time an idol falls. Heaven cannot be found where it is not, and there can be no peace excepting there. Each idol that you worship when God calls will never answer in His place. There IS no other answer you can substitute and find the happiness His answer brings. Seek not outside yourself. For all your pain comes simply from a futile search for what you want, insisting where it must be found. What if it is not there? Do you prefer that you be right or happy?

Be you glad that you are told where happiness abides and seek no longer elsewhere. You will fail. But it is given you to know the truth, and not to seek for it outside yourself.

No-one who comes here but must still have hope, some lingering illusion, or some dream that there is something outside of himself that will bring happiness and peace to him. If everything is in him, this cannot be so. And therefore, by his coming, he denies the truth about himself, and seeks for something more than everything, as if a part of it were separated off, and found where all the rest of it is not. This is the purpose he bestows upon the body; that it seek for what he lacks and give him what would make himself complete. And thus he wanders aimlessly about, in search of something that he cannot find, believing that he is what he is not.

The lingering illusion will impel him to seek out a thousand idols, and to seek beyond them for a thousand more. And each will fail him, all excepting one; for he will die, and does not understand the idol that he seeks is but his death. Its form appears to be outside himself. Yet does he seek to kill God's Son within and prove that he is victor over him. This is the purpose every idol has, for this the role that is assigned to it and this the role that cannot be fulfilled.

Whenever you attempt to reach a goal in which the body's betterment is cast as major beneficiary, you try to bring about your death. For you believe that you can suffer lack, and lack is death. To sacrifice is to give up and thus to be without and to have suffered loss. And by this giving up is life renounced. Seek not outside yourself. The search implies you are not whole within, and fear to look upon your devastation and prefer to seek outside yourself for what you are.

Idols must fall because they have no life and what is lifeless is a sign of death. You came to die, and what would you expect but to perceive the signs of death you seek? No sadness and no suffering proclaims a message other than an idol found that represents a parody of life which, in its lifelessness, is really death, conceived as real and given living form. Yet each must fail and crumble and decay, because a form of death cannot be life and what is sacrificed cannot be whole.

All idols of this world were made to keep the truth within from being known to you; and to maintain allegiance to the dream that you must find what is outside yourself to be complete and happy. It is vain to worship idols in the hope of peace. God dwells within, and your completion lies in Him. No idol takes His place. Look not to idols. Do not seek outside yourself. Let us forget the purpose of the world the past has given it.

For otherwise, the future will be like the past and but a series of depressing dreams, in which all idols fail you, one by one and you see death and disappointment everywhere.

To change all this and open up a road of hope and of release in what appeared to be an endless circle of despair, you need but to decide you do not know the purpose of the world. You give it goals it does not have, and thus do you decide what it is for. You try to see in it a place of idols found outside yourself, with power to make complete what is within by splitting what you are between the two. You choose your dreams, for they are what you wish, perceived as if it had been given you. Your idols do what you would have them do and have the power you ascribe to them. And you pursue them vainly in the dream, because you want their power as your own.

Yet where are dreams, but in a mind asleep? And can a dream succeed in making real the pictures it projects outside itself? Save time, my brothers; learn what time is for. And speed the end of idols in a world made sad and sick by seeing idols there. Your holy minds are altars unto God, and where He is no idols can abide. The fear of God is but the fear of loss of idols. It is not the fear of loss of your reality. But you have made of your reality an idol, which you must protect against the light of truth. And all the world becomes the means by which this idol can be saved. Salvation thus appears to threaten life and offer death.

It is not so. Salvation seeks to prove there is no death, and life only exists. The sacrifice of death is nothing lost. An idol cannot take the place of God. Let Him remind you of His love for you, and do not seek to drown His Voice in chants of deep despair to idols of yourself. Seek not outside your Father for your hope. For hope of happiness is not despair.

What is an idol? Do you think you know? For idols are unrecognized as such, and never seen for what they really are. That is the only power which they have. Their purpose is obscure, and they are feared and worshipped, both, because you do not know what they are for, and why they have been made. An idol is an image of your brother which you would value more than what he is. Idols are made that he may be replaced, no matter what their form. And it is this which never is perceived and recognized. Be it a body or a thing, a place, a situation or a circumstance, an object owned or wanted, or a right demanded or achieved, it is the same.

Let not their form deceive you. Idols are but substitutes for your reality. In some way, you believe they will complete your little self, for safety in a world perceived as dangerous, with forces massed against your confidence and peace of mind.

They have the power to supply your lacks and add the value which you do not have. No-one believes in idols who has not enslaved himself to littleness and loss. And thus must seek beyond his little self for strength to raise his head and stand apart from all the misery the world reflects. This is the penalty for looking not within for certainty and quiet calm which liberates you from the world and lets you stand apart, in quiet and in peace.

An idol is a false impression, or a false belief; some form of antiChrist, which constitutes a gap between the Christ and what you see. An idol is a wish, made tangible and given form, and thus perceived as real, and seen outside the mind. Yet it is still a thought and cannot leave the mind that is its source. Nor is its form apart from the idea it represents. All forms of anti-Christ oppose the Christ. And fall before His face like a dark veil which seems to shut you off from Him, alone in darkness. Yet the light is there. A cloud does not put out the sun. No more a veil can banish what it seems to separate, nor darken by one whit the light itself.

This world of idols is a veil across the face of Christ, because its purpose is to separate your brother from yourself. A dark and fearful purpose, yet a thought without the power to change one blade of grass from something living to a sign of death. Its form is nowhere, for its source abides within your mind, where God abideth not. Where is this place where what is everywhere has been excluded and been kept apart? What hand could be held up to block God's way? Whose voice could make demand He enter not? The "more-than-everything" is not a thing to make you tremble, and to quail in fear. Christ's enemy is nowhere. He can take no form in which he ever will be real.

What is an idol? Nothing! It must be believed before it seems to come to life and given power that it may be feared. Its life and power are its believer's gift, and this is what the miracle restores to what has life and power worthy of the gift of Heaven and eternal peace. The miracle does not restore the truth, the light the veil between has not put out. It merely lifts the veil, and lets the truth shine unencumbered, being what it is. It does not need belief to be itself, for it has been created, so it is. An idol is established by belief, and when it is withdrawn, the idol "dies."

This is the anti-Christ; the strange idea there is a power past omnipotence, a place beyond the infinite, a time transcending the eternal. Here the world of idols has been set by the idea this power and place and time are given form and shape the world where the impossible has happened.

Here the deathless come to die, the all-encompassing to suffer loss, the timeless to be made the slaves of time. Here does the changeless change; the peace of God, forever given to all living things, give way to chaos. And the Son of God, as perfect, sinless and as loving as his Father, come to hate a little while; to suffer pain, and finally to die.

Where is an idol? Nowhere! Can there be a gap in what is infinite, a place where time can interrupt eternity? A place of darkness set where all is light, a dismal alcove separated off from what is endless, has no place to be. An idol is beyond where God has set all things forever and has left no room for anything to be except His Will. Nothing and nowhere must an idol be, while God is everything and everywhere.

What purpose has an idol, then? What is it for? This is the only question which has many answers, each depending on the one of whom the question has been asked. The world believes in idols. No-one comes unless he worshipped them, and still attempts to seek for one that yet might offer him a gift reality does not contain. Each worshipper of idols harbors hope his special deities will give him more than other men possess. It must be more. It does not really matter more of what; more beauty, more intelligence, more wealth, or even more affliction and more pain. But more of something is an idol for. And when one fails another takes its place, with hope of finding more of something else. Be not deceived by forms the "something" takes. An idol is a means for getting more. And it is this that is against God's Will.

God has not many sons, but only One. Who can have more, and who be given less? In Heaven would the Son of God but laugh, if idols could intrude upon his peace. It is for him the Holy Spirit speaks and tells you idols have no purpose here. For more than Heaven can you never have. If Heaven is within, why would you seek for idols which would make of Heaven less, to give you more than God bestowed upon your brother and on you, as one with Him? God gave you all there is. And to be sure you could not lose it, did He also give the same to every living thing as well. And thus is every living thing a part of you, as of Himself. No idol can establish you as more than God. But you will never be content with being less.

The slave of idols is a willing slave. For willing he must be to let himself bow down in worship to what has no life and seek for power in the powerless. What happened to the holy Son of God that this could be his wish; to let himself fall lower than the stones upon the ground, and look to idols that they raise him up?

Hear, then, your story in the dream you made, and ask yourself if it be not the truth that you believe that it is not a dream: A dream of judgement came into the mind that God created perfect as Himself. And in that dream was Heaven changed to hell and God made enemy unto His Son.

How can God's Son awaken from the dream? It is a dream of judgement. So must he judge not, and he will waken. For the dream will seem to last while he is part of it. Judge not, for he who judges WILL have need of idols, which will hold the judgement off from resting on himself. Nor can he know the Self he has condemned. Judge not, because you make yourself a part of evil dreams, where idols are your "true" identity and your salvation from the judgement laid in terror and in guilt upon yourself.

All figures in the dream are idols, made to save you from the dream. Yet they are part of what they have been made to save you from. Thus does an idol keep the dream alive and terrible, for who could wish for one unless he were in terror and despair? And this the idol represents and so its worship is the worship of despair and terror, and the dream from which they come. Judgement is an injustice to God's Son, and it is justice that who judges him will not escape the penalty he laid upon himself within the dream he made. God knows of justice, not of penalty. But in the dream of judgement, you attack and are condemned; and wish to be the slave of idols, which are interposed between your judgement and the penalty it brings.

There can be no salvation in the dream as you are dreaming it. For idols must be part of it, to save you from what you believe you have accomplished, and have done to make you sinful, and put out the Light within you. Little children, It is there. You do but dream, and idols are the toys you dream you play with. Who has need of toys but children? They pretend they rule the world, and give their toys the power to move about, and talk and think and feel, and speak for them. Yet everything their toys appear to do is in the minds of those who play with them. But they are eager to forget that they made up the dream in which their toys are real, nor recognize their wishes are their own.

Nightmares are childish dreams. The toys have turned against the child who thought he made them real. Yet can a dream attack? Or can a toy grow large and dangerous and fierce and wild? This does the child believe, because he fears his thoughts, and gives them to the toys instead. And their reality becomes his own, because they seem to save him from his thoughts.

Yet do they keep his thoughts alive and real, but seen outside himself, where they can turn against him for his treachery to them. He thinks he needs them that he may escape his thoughts, because he thinks the thoughts are real. And so he makes of anything a toy, to make his world remain outside himself, and play that He is but a part of it.

There is a time when childhood should be passed and gone forever. Seek not to retain the toys of children. Put them all away, for you have need of them no more. The dream of judgement is a children's game, in which the child becomes the father, powerful, but with the little wisdom of a child. What hurts him is destroyed; what helps him, blessed. Except he judges this as does a child, who does not know what hurts and what will heal. And bad things seem to happen, and he is afraid of all the chaos in a world he thinks is governed by the laws he made. Yet is the real world unaffected by the world he thinks is real. Nor have its laws been changed because he did not understand.

The real world still is but a dream. Except the figures have been changed. They are not seen as idols which betray. It is a dream in which no-one is used to substitute for something else, nor interposed between the thoughts the mind conceives and what it sees. No-one is used for something he is not, for childish things have all been put away. And what was once a dream of judgement now has changed into a dream where all is joy, because that is the purpose which it has. Only forgiving dreams can enter here, for time is almost over. And the forms which enter in the dream are now perceived as brothers, not in judgement, but in love.

Forgiving dreams have little need to last. They are not made to separate the mind from what it thinks. They do not seek to prove the dream is being dreamed by someone else. And in these dreams a melody is heard which everyone remembers, though he has not heard it since before all time began. Forgiveness, once complete, brings timelessness so close the song of Heaven can be heard, not with the ears, but with the holiness which never left the altar which abides forever deep within the Son of God. And when he hears this song again, he knows he never heard it not. And where is time, when dreams of judgement have been put away?

Whenever you feel fear in any form, – and you are fearful if you do not feel a deep content, a certainty of help, a calm assurance Heaven goes with you, – be sure you made an idol, and believe it will betray you. For beneath your hope that it will save you, lie the guilt and pain of self-betrayal and uncertainty, so deep and bitter that the dream cannot conceal completely all your sense of doom.

Your self betrayal must result in fear, for fear is judgement, leading surely to the frantic search for idols and for death.

Forgiving dreams remind you that you live in safety, and have not attacked yourself. So do your childish terrors melt away, and dreams become a sign that you have made a new beginning, not another try to worship idols, and to keep attack. Forgiving dreams are kind to everyone who figures in the dream. And so they bring the dreamer full release from dreams of fear. He does not fear his judgement, for he has judged no-one, nor has sought to be released through judgement from what judgement must impose. And all the while he is remembering what he forgot when judgement seemed to be the way to save him from its penalty.

The new beginning now becomes the focus of the curriculum. The goal is clear, but now you need specific methods for attaining it. The speed by which it can be reached depends on this one thing alone; your willingness to practice every step. Each one will help a little every time it is attempted. And together will these steps lead you from dreams of judgement to forgiving dreams and out of pain and fear. They are not new to you, but they are more ideas than rules of thought to you as yet. So now we need to practice them awhile, until they are the rules by which you live. We seek to make them habits now, so you will have them ready for whatever need.

Decisions are continuous. You do not always know when you are making them. But with a little practice with the ones you recognize, a set begins to form which sees you through the rest. It is not wise to let yourself become preoccupied with every step you take. The proper set, adopted consciously each time you wake, will put you well ahead. And if you find resistance strong and dedication weak, you are not ready. Do not fight yourself. But think about the kind of day you want, and tell yourself there is a way in which this very day can happen just like that. Then try again to have the day you want.

1. The outlook starts with this:

    "Today I will make no decisions by myself."

    This means that you are choosing not to be the judge of what to do. But it must also mean you will not judge the situations where you will be called upon to make response. For if you judge them, you have set the rules for how you should react to them. And then another answer cannot but produce confusion and uncertainty and fear.

    This is your major problem now. You still make up your mind, and then decide to ask what you should do. And what you hear may not resolve the problem as you saw it first. This leads to fear because it contradicts what you perceive, and so you feel attacked. And therefore angry. There are rules by which this will not happen. But it does occur at first, while you are learning how to hear.

2. Throughout the day, at any time you think of it, and have a quiet moment for reflection, tell yourself again the kind of day you want; the feelings you would have, the things you want to happen to you and the things you would experience and say,
"If I make no decision by myself,
This is the kind of day that will be given me."
These two procedures, practiced well, will serve to let you be directed without fear, for opposition will not first arise and then become a problem in itself.
But there will still be times when you have judged already. Now the answer will provoke attack, unless you quickly straighten out your mind to want an answer that will work. Be certain this has happened if you feel yourself unwilling to sit by and ask to have the answer given you. This means you have decided by yourself, and cannot see the question. Now you need a quick restorative before you ask.

3. Remember once again the day you want and recognize that something has occurred which is not part of it. Then realize that you have asked a question by yourself and must have set an answer in your terms. Then say,
"I have no question. I forgot what to decide."
This cancels out the terms which you have set and lets the answer show you what the question must have really been.
Try to observe this rule without delay, despite your opposition. For you have already gotten angry and your fear of being answered in a different way from what your version of the questions asks will gain momentum, until you believe the day you want is one in which you get your answer to your question. And you will not get it, for it would destroy the day by robbing you of what you really want. This can be very hard to realize, when once you have decided by yourself the rules which promise you a happy day. Yet this decision still can be undone, by simple methods which you can accept.

4. If you are so unwilling to receive you cannot even let your question go, you can begin to change your mind with this:
"At least I can decide I do not like what I feel now."
This much is obvious and paves the way for the next easy step.

5. Having decided that you do not like the way you feel, what could be easier than to continue with,

"And so I hope I have been wrong."

This works against the sense of opposition and reminds you that help is not being thrust upon you but is something that you want and that you need, because you do not like the way you feel. This tiny opening will be enough to let you go ahead with just a few more steps you need to let yourself be helped.

Now you have reached the turning-point, because it has occurred to you that you will gain if what you have decided is not so. Until this point is reached, you will believe your happiness depends on being right. But this much reason have you now attained; you would be better off if you were wrong.

6. This tiny grain of wisdom will suffice to take you further. You are not coerced, but merely hope to get a thing you want. And you can say in perfect honesty,

"I want another way to look at this."

Now you have changed your mind about the day and have remembered what you really want. Its purpose has no longer been obscured by the insane belief you want it for the goal of being right when you are wrong. Thus is the readiness for asking brought to your awareness, for you cannot be in conflict when you ask for what you want, and see that it IS this for which you ask.

7. This final step is but acknowledgment of lack of opposition to be helped. It is a statement of an open mind, not certain yet, but willing to be shown:

"Perhaps there is another way to look at this.
What can I lose by asking?"

Thus you now can ask a question that makes sense, and so the answer will make sense as well. Nor will you fight against it, for you see that it is you who will be helped by it.

It must be clear that it is easier to have a happy day if you prevent unhappiness from entering at all. But this takes practice in the rules which will protect you from the ravages of fear. When this has been achieved, the sorry dream of judgement has forever been undone. But meanwhile, you have need for practicing the rules for its undoing. Let us, then, consider once again the very first of the decisions which are offered here.

We said you can begin a happy day with the determination not to make decisions by yourself. This seems to be a real decision in itself. And yet, you cannot make decisions by yourself. The only question really is with what you choose to make them. That is really all. The first rule, then, is not coercion, but a simple statement of a simple fact. You will not make decisions by yourself whatever you decide. For they are made with idols or with God. And you ask help of Christ or anti-Christ, and which you choose will join with you and tell you what to do.

Your day is not at random. It is set by what you choose to live it with, and how the friend whose counsel you have sought perceives your happiness. You always ask advice before you can decide on anything. Let this be understood, and you can see there cannot be coercion here, nor grounds for opposition that you may be free. There is no freedom from what must occur. And if you think there is, you must be wrong.

The second rule as well is but a fact. For you and your advisor must agree on what you want before it can occur. It is but this agreement which permits all things to happen. Nothing can be caused without some form of union, be it with a dream of judgement or the Voice for God. Decisions cause results because they are not made in isolation. They are made by you and your advisor, for yourself, and for the world as well. The day you want you offer to the world, for it will be what you have asked for, and will reinforce the rules of your advisor in the world. Whose kingdom is the world for you today? What kind of day will you decide to have?

It needs but two who would have happiness this day to promise it to all the world. It needs but two to understand that they cannot decide alone, to guarantee the joy they asked for will be wholly shared. For they have understood the basic law that makes decision powerful and gives it all effects that it will ever have. It needs but two. These two are joined before there can be a decision. Let this be the one reminder that you keep in mind, and you will have the day you want, and give it to the world by having it yourself. Your judgement has been lifted from the world by your decision for a happy day. And as you have received, so must you give.

Do you not understand that to oppose the Holy Spirit is to fight yourself? He tells you but your will; He speaks for you. In His Divinity is but your own. And all He knows is but your knowledge, saved for you that you may do your will through Him. God asks you do your will. He joins with you. He did not set His kingdom up alone. And Heaven itself but represents your will, where everything created is for you. No spark of life but was created with your glad consent, as you would have it be. And not one Thought that God has ever had but waited for your blessing to be born. God is no enemy to you. He asks no more than that He hear you call Him "Friend."

How wonderful it is to do your will! For that is freedom. There is nothing else that ever should be called by freedom's name. Unless you do your will you are not free. And would God leave His Son without what he has chosen for himself? God but ensured that you would never lose your will when He gave you His perfect answer. Hear it now, that you may be reminded of His love and learn your will. God would not have His Son made prisoner to what he does not want. He joins with you in willing you be free. And to oppose Him is to make a choice against yourself and choose that you be bound.

Look once again upon your enemy, the one you chose to hate instead of love. For thus was hatred born into the world and thus the rule of fear established there. Now hear God speak to you through Him Who is His Voice and yours as well, reminding you that It Is not your will to hate, and be a prisoner to fear, a slave to death, a little creature with a little life. Your will is boundless; it is not your will that it be bound. What lies in you has joined with God Himself in all creation's birth. Remember He Who has created you, and through your will created everything. Not one created thing but gives you thanks, for it is by your will that it was born. No light of Heaven shines except for you, for it was set in Heaven by your will.

What cause have you for anger in a world which merely waits your blessing to be free? If you be prisoner, then God Himself could not be free. For what is done to him whom God so loves is done to God Himself. Think not He wills to bind you, Who has made you co-creator of the universe along with Him. He would but keep your will forever and forever limitless.

1. This world awaits the freedom you will give when you have recognized that you are free. But you will not forgive the world until you have forgiven Him Who gave your will to you. For it is by your will the world is given freedom. Nor can you be free apart from Him Whose holy Will you share. God turns to you to ask the world be saved, for by your own salvation it is healed. And no-one walks upon the earth but must depend on your decision, that he learn death has no power over him because he shares your freedom, as he shares your will. It is your will to heal him, and because you have decided with him, he is healed. And now is God forgiven, for you chose to look upon your brother as a friend.

Idols are quite specific. But your will is universal, being limitless. And so it has no form, nor is content for its expression in the terms of form. Idols are limits. They are the belief that there are forms which will bring happiness, and that, BY limiting, is all attained. It is as if you said, "I have no need of everything. This little thing I want, and it will be as everything to me." And this must fail to satisfy, because it is your will that everything be yours. Decide for idols, and you ask for loss. Decide for truth, and everything is yours.

It is not form you seek. What form can be a substitute for God the Father's love? What form can take the place of all the love in the Divinity of God the Son? What idol can make two of what is one? And can the limitless be limited? You do not want an idol. It is not your will to have one. It will not bestow on you the gift you seek. When you decide upon the form of what you want, you lose the understanding of its purpose. So you see your will within the idol, thus reducing it to a specific form. Yet this could never be your will, because what shares in all creation cannot be content with small ideas and little things.

Behind the search for every idol lies the yearning for completion. Wholeness has no form because it is unlimited. To seek a special person or a thing to add to you to make yourself complete can only mean that you believe some form is missing. And by finding this, you will achieve completion in a form you like. This is the purpose of an idol; that you will not look beyond it, to the source of the belief that you are incomplete. Only if you had sinned could this be so. For sin is the idea you are alone and separated off from what is whole. And thus it would be necessary for the search for wholeness to be made beyond the boundaries of limits on yourself.

It never is the idol that you want. But what you think it offers you, you want indeed, and have the right to ask for. Nor could it be possible it be denied. Your will to be complete is but God's will, and this is given you by being His. God knows not form. He cannot answer you in terms which have no meaning. And your will could not be satisfied with empty forms, made but to fill a gap which is not there. It is not this you want. Creation gives no separate person and no separate thing the power to complete the Son of God. What idol can be called upon to give the Son of God what he already has?

Completion is the function of God's Son. He has no need to seek for it at all. Beyond all idols stands his holy will to be but what he is. For more than whole is meaningless. If there were change in him, if he could be reduced to any form and limited to what is not in him, he would not be as God created him. What idol can he need to be himself? For can he give a part of him away? What is not whole cannot make whole. But what is really asked for cannot be denied. Your will is granted. Not in any form that would content you not, but in the whole completely lovely Thought God holds of you.

Nothing that God knows not exists. And what He knows exists forever, changelessly. For thoughts endure as long as does the mind that thought of them. And in the Mind of God there is no ending, nor a time in which His Thoughts were absent, or could suffer change. Thoughts are not born and cannot die. They share the attributes of their creator, nor have they a separate life apart from his. The thoughts you think are in your mind, as you are in the Mind Which thought of you. And so there are no separate parts in what exists within God's Mind. It is forever one, eternally united and at peace.

Thoughts seem to come and go. Yet all this means is that you are sometimes aware of them, and sometimes not. An unremembered thought is born again to you when it returns to your awareness. Yet it did not die when you forgot it. It was always there, but you were unaware of it. The Thought God holds of you is perfectly unchanged by your forgetting. It will always be exactly as it was before the time when you forgot and will be just the same when you remember. And it is the same within the interval when you forgot.

The Thoughts of God are far beyond all change and shine forever. They await not birth. They wait for welcome and remembering. The Thought God holds of you is like a star, unchangeable in an eternal sky. So high in Heaven is it set that those outside of Heaven know not it is there. Yet still and white and lovely will it shine through all eternity.

There was no time it was not there; no instant when its light grew dimmer or less perfect ever was.

Who knows the Father knows this light, for He is the eternal sky which holds it safe, forever lifted up and anchored sure. Its perfect purity does not depend on whether it is seen on earth or not. The sky embraces it, and softly holds it in its perfect place, which is as far from earth as earth from Heaven. It is not the distance nor the time which keeps this star invisible to earth. But those who seek for idols cannot know this star is there.

Beyond all idols is the Thought God holds of you. Completely unaffected by the turmoil and the terror of the world; the dreams of birth and death that here are dreamed; the myriad of forms that fear can take; quite undisturbed, the Thought God holds of you remains exactly as it always was. Surrounded by a stillness so complete no sound of battle comes remotely near, it rests in certainty and perfect peace. Here is your one reality kept safe, completely unaware of all the world that worships idols, and that knows not God. In perfect sureness of its changelessness, and of its rest in its eternal home, the Thought God holds of you has never left the Mind of its Creator, Whom it knows as its Creator knows that it is there.

Where could the Thought God holds of you exist but where you are? Is your reality a thing apart from you, and in a world which your reality knows nothing of? Outside you, there is no eternal sky, no changeless star, and no reality. The Mind of Heaven's Son in Heaven is, for there the Mind of Father and of Son joined in creation which can have no end. You have not two realities, but one. Nor can you be aware of more than one. An idol or the Thought God holds of you is your reality. Forget not, then, that idols must keep hidden what you are, not from the Mind of God, but from your own. The star shines still; the sky has never changed. But you, the holy Son of God Himself, are unaware of your reality.

You will attack what does not satisfy, and thus you will not see you made it up. You always fight illusions. For the truth behind them is so lovely and so still in loving gentleness, were you aware of it you would forget defensiveness entirely, and rush to its embrace. The truth could never be attacked. And this you knew when you made idols. They were made that this might be forgotten. You attack but false ideas, and never truthful ones. All idols are the false ideas you made to fill the gap you think arose between yourself and what is true. And you attack them for the things you think they represent. What lies beyond them cannot be attacked.

The wearying, dissatisfying gods you made are blown-up children's toys. A child is frightened when a wooden head springs up as a closed box is opened suddenly, or when a soft and silent woolly bear begins to squeak as he takes hold of it. The rules he made for boxes and for bears have failed him and have broken his "control" of what surrounds him. And he is afraid because he thought the rules protected him. Now must he learn the boxes and the bears did not deceive him, broke no rules, nor mean his world is made chaotic and unsafe. He was mistaken. He misunderstood what made him safe and thought that it had left.

The gap that is not there is filled with toys in countless forms. And each one seems to break the rules you set for it. It never was the thing you thought. It must appear to break your rules for safety, since the rules were wrong. But you are not endangered. You can laugh at popping heads and squeaking toys, as does the child who learns they are no threat to him. Yet while he likes to play with them, he still perceives them as obeying rules he made for his enjoyment. So there still are rules which they can seem to break and frighten him. Yet is he at the mercy of his toys? And can they represent a threat to him?

Reality observes the laws of God and not the rules you set. It is His laws which guarantee your safety. All illusions that you believe about yourself obey no laws. They seem to dance a little while, according to the rules you set for them. But then they fall and cannot rise again. They are but toys, my children. Do not grieve for them. Their dancing never brought you joy. But neither were they things to frighten you, nor make you safe if they obeyed your rules. They must be neither cherished nor attacked, but merely looked upon as children's toys, without a single meaning of their own. See one in them, and you will see them all. See none in them, and they will touch you not.

Appearances deceive because they are appearances, and not reality. Dwell not on them in any form. They but obscure reality and they bring fear because they hide the truth. Do not attack what you have made to let you be deceived, for thus you prove that you have been deceived. Attack has power to make illusions real. Yet what it makes is nothing. Who could be made fearful by a power that can have no real effects at all? What could it be but an illusion, making things appear like to itself? Look calmly at its toys and understand that they are idols which but dance to vain desires. Give them not your worship, for they are not there.

Yet this is equally forgotten in attack. God's Son needs no defence against his dreams. His idols do not threaten him at all. His one mistake is that he thinks them real. What can the power of illusions do?

Appearances can but deceive the mind that wants to be deceived. And you can make a simple choice that will forever place you far beyond deception. You need not concern yourself with how this will be done, for this you cannot understand. But you will understand that mighty changes have been quickly brought about, when you decide one very simple thing; you do not want whatever you believe an idol gives. For thus the Son of God declares that he is free of idols. And thus is he free.

Salvation is a paradox indeed! What could it be except a happy dream? It asks you but that you forgive all things that no-one ever did; to overlook what is not there; and not to look upon the unreal as reality. You are but asked to let your will be done and seek no longer for the things you do not want. And you are asked to let yourself be free of all the dreams of what you never were and seek no more to substitute the strength of idle wishes for the Will of God. Here does the dream of separation start to fade and disappear. For here the gap that is not there begins to be perceived without the toys of terror that you made. No more than this is asked. Be glad indeed salvation asks so little, not so much. It asks for nothing in reality. And even in illusions it but asks forgiveness be the substitute for fear. Such is the only rule for happy dreams. The gap is emptied of the toys of fear, and then its unreality is plain. Dreams are for nothing. And the Son of God can have no need of them. They offer him no single thing that he could ever want. He is delivered from illusions by his will, and but restored to what he is. What could God's plan for his salvation be, except a means to give him to Himself?

The real world is the state of mind in which the only purpose of the world is seen to be forgiveness. Fear is not its goal, and the escape from guilt becomes its aim. The value of forgiveness is perceived, and takes the place of idols, which are sought no longer, for their "gifts" are not held dear. No rules are idly set, and no demands are made of anyone or anything to twist and fit into the dream of fear. Instead, there is a wish to understand all things created as they really are. And it is recognized that all things must be first forgiven, and then understood.

Here, it is thought that understanding is acquired by attack. There, it is clear that by attack is understanding lost. The folly of pursuing guilt as goal is fully recognized. And idols are not wanted there, for guilt is understood as the sole cause of pain in any form. No one is tempted by its vain appeal, for suffering and death have been perceived as things not wanted, and not striven for. The possibility of freedom has been grasped and welcomed, and the means by which it can be gained can now be understood. The world becomes a place of hope, because its only purpose is to be a place where hope of happiness can be fulfilled. And no-one stands outside this hope, because the world has been united in belief the purpose of the world is one which all must share, if hope be more than just a dream.

Not yet is Heaven quite remembered, for the purpose of forgiveness still remains. Yet everyone is certain he will go beyond forgiveness and he but remains until it is made perfect in himself. He has no wish for anything but this. And fear has dropped away, because he is united in his purpose with himself. There is a hope of happiness in him so sure and constant he can barely stay and wait a little longer with his feet still touching Earth. Yet is he glad to wait till every hand is joined and every heart made ready to arise and go with him. For thus is He made ready for the step in which is all forgiveness left behind.

The final step is God's, because it is but God Who could create a perfect Son and share His Fatherhood with him. No-one outside of Heaven knows how this can be, for understanding this is Heaven itself. Even the real world has a purpose still beneath creation and eternity. But fear is gone, because its purpose is forgiveness, not idolatry. And so is Heaven's Son prepared to be Himself, and to remember that the Son of God knows everything his Father understands and understands it perfectly with Him.

The real world still falls short of this, for this is God's Own purpose; only His, and yet completely shared and perfectly fulfilled. The real world is a state in which the mind has learned how easily do idols go when they are still perceived but wanted not. How willingly the mind can let them go when it has understood that idols are nothing and nowhere and are purposeless. For only then can guilt and sin be seen without a purpose, and as meaningless.

Thus is the real world's purpose gently brought into awareness, to replace the goal of sin and guilt. And all that stood between your image of yourself and what you are, forgiveness washes joyfully away. Yet God need not create His Son again, that what is his be given back to him.

The gap between your brother and yourself was never there. And what the Son of God knew in creation he must know again.

When brothers join in purpose in the world of fear, they stand already at the edge of the real world. Perhaps they still look back, and think they see an idol that they want. Yet has their path been surely set away from idols toward reality. For when they joined their hands, it was Christ's hand they took, and they will look on Him Whose hand they hold. The face of Christ is looked upon before the Father is remembered. For He must be unremembered till His Son has reached beyond forgiveness, to the love of God. Yet is the love of Christ accepted first. And then will come the knowledge They are One.

How light and easy is the step across the narrow boundaries of the world of fear, when you have recognized Whose hand you hold! Within your hand is everything you need to walk with perfect confidence away from fear forever, and to go straight on, and quickly reach the gate of Heaven itself. For He Whose hand you hold was waiting but for you to join Him. Now that you have come, would He delay in showing you the way that He must walk with you? His blessing lies on you as surely as His Father's love rests upon Him. His gratitude to you is past your understanding, for you have enabled Him to rise from chains, and go with you, together, to His Father's house.

An ancient hate is passing from the world. And with it goes all hatred and all fear. Look back no longer, for what lies ahead is all you ever wanted in your hearts. Give up the world! But not to sacrifice. You never wanted it. What happiness have you sought here that did not bring you pain? What moment of content has not been bought at fearful price in coins of suffering? Joy has no cost. It is your sacred right and what you pay for is not happiness. Be speeded on your way by honesty and let not your experiences here deceive in retrospect. They were not free from bitter cost and joyless consequence.

Do not look back except in honesty. And when an idol tempts you, think of this:

"There never was a time an idol brought
You anything except the "gift" of guilt.
Not one was bought except at cost of pain,
Nor was it ever paid by you alone."

Be merciful unto your brother, then. And do not choose an idol thoughtlessly, remembering that he will pay the cost as well as you. For he will be delayed when you look back, and you will not perceive Whose loving hand you hold. Look forward, then, and walk in confidence, with happy hearts that beat in hope and do not pound in fear.

The Will of God forever lies in those whose hands are joined. Until they joined, they thought He was their enemy. But when they joined and shared a purpose, they were free to learn their will is one. And thus the Will of God must reach to their awareness. Nor can they forget for long that it is but their own.

Anger is never justified. Attack has no foundation. It is here escape from fear begins and will be made complete. Here is the real world given in exchange for dreams of terror. For it is on this forgiveness rests and is but natural. You are not asked to offer pardon where attack is due and would be justified. For this would mean that you forgive a sin by overlooking what is really there. This is not pardon. For it would assume that, by responding in a way which is not justified, your pardon will become the answer to attack that has been made. And thus is pardon inappropriate, by being granted where it is not due.

Pardon is always justified. It has a sure foundation. You do not forgive the unforgivable, nor overlook a real attack that calls for punishment. Salvation does not lie in being asked to make unnatural responses which are inappropriate to what is real. Instead, it merely asks that you respond appropriately to what is not real by not perceiving what has not occurred. If pardon were unjustified, you would be asked to sacrifice your rights when you return forgiveness for attack. But you are merely asked to see forgiveness as the natural reaction to distress which rests on error, and thus calls for help. Forgiveness is the only sane response. It keeps your rights from being sacrificed.

This understanding is the only change that lets the real world rise to take the place of dreams of terror. Fear cannot arise unless attack is justified, and if it had a real foundation, pardon would have none. The real world is achieved when you perceive the basis of forgiveness is quite real and fully justified. While you regard it as a gift unwarranted, it must uphold the guilt you would "forgive."

Unjustified forgiveness is attack. And this is all the world can ever give. It pardons "sinners" sometimes but remains aware that they have sinned. And so they do not merit the forgiveness that it gives. This is the false forgiveness which the world employs to keep the sense of sin alive.

And recognizing God is just, it seems impossible His pardon could be real. Thus is the fear of God the sure result of seeing pardon as unmerited. No-one who sees himself as guilty can avoid the fear of God. But he is saved from this dilemma if he can forgive. The mind must think of its Creator as it looks upon itself. If you can see your brother merits pardon, you have learned forgiveness is your right as much as his. Nor will you think that God intends for you a fearful judgement which your brother does not merit. For it is the truth that you can merit neither more nor less than he.

Forgiveness recognized as merited will heal. It gives the miracle its strength to overlook illusions. This is how you learn that you must be forgiven, too. There can be no appearance that cannot be overlooked. For if there were, it would be necessary first there be some sin which stands beyond forgiveness. There would be an error that is more than a mistake; a special form of error which remains unchangeable, eternal, and beyond correction or escape. There would be one mistake which had the power to undo creation, and to make a world which could replace it, and destroy the Will of God. Only if this were possible could there be some appearances which could is this except a simple statement of the truth?

Look on your brother with this hope in you, and you will understand he could not make an error that could change the truth in him. It is not difficult to overlook mistakes that have been given no effects. But what you see as having power to make an idol of the Son of God you will not pardon. For he has become to you a graven image, and a sign of death. Is this your Saviour? Is his Father wrong about His Son? Or have you been deceived in him who has been given you to heal, for your salvation and deliverance?

Would God have left the meaning of the world to your interpretation? If He had, it has no meaning. For it cannot be that meaning changes constantly, and yet is true. The Holy Spirit looks upon the world as with one purpose, changelessly established. And no situation can affect its aim but must be in accord with it. For only if its aim could change with every situation could each one be open to interpretation which is different every time you think of it. You add an element into the script you write for every minute in the day, and all that happens now means something else. You take away another element, and every meaning shifts accordingly.

What do your scripts reflect except your plans for what the day should be? And thus you judge disaster and success, advance, retreat, and gain and loss. These judgements all are made according to the roles the script assigns.

The fact they have no meaning in themselves is demonstrated by the ease with which these labels change with other judgements, made on different aspects of experience. And then, in looking back, you think you see another meaning in what went before. What have you really done, except to show there was no meaning there? But you assigned a meaning in the light of goals that change, with every meaning shifting as they change.

Only a constant purpose can endow events with stable meaning. But it must accord one meaning to them all. If they are given different meanings, it must be that they reflect but different purposes. And this is all the meaning that they have. Can this be meaning? Can confusion be what meaning means? Perception cannot be in constant flux and make allowance for stability of meaning anywhere. Fear is a judgement never justified. Its presence has no meaning but to show you wrote a fearful script and are afraid accordingly. But not because the thing you fear has fearful meaning in itself.

A common purpose is the only means whereby perception can be stabilized, and one interpretation given to the world and all experiences here. In this shared purpose is one judgement shared by everyone and everything you see. You do not have to judge, for you have learned one meaning has been given everything, and you are glad to see it everywhere. It cannot change because you would perceive it everywhere, unchanged by circumstance. And so you offer it to all events and let them offer you stability.

Escape from judgement simply lies in this; all things have but one purpose, which you share with all the world. And nothing in the world can be opposed to it, for it belongs to everything as it belongs to you. In single purpose is the end of all ideas of sacrifice, which must assume a different purpose for the one who gains and him who loses. There could be no thought of sacrifice apart from this idea. And it is this idea of different goals which makes perception shift and meaning change. In one united goal does this become impossible, for your agreement makes interpretation stabilize and last.

How can communication really be established while the symbols which are used mean different things? The Holy Spirit's goal gives one interpretation, meaningful to you and to your brother. Thus can you communicate with him and he with you. In symbols which you both can understand, the sacrifice of meaning is undone. All sacrifice entails the loss of your ability to see relationships among events. And looked at separately, they have no meaning. For there is no light by which they can be seen and understood.

They have no purpose. And what they are for cannot be seen. In any thought of loss, there is no meaning. No-one has agreed with you on what it means. It is a part of a distorted script, which cannot be interpreted with meaning. It must be forever unintelligible.

This is not communication. Your dark dreams are but the senseless, isolated scripts you write in sleep. Look not to separate dreams for meaning. Only dreams of pardon can be shared. They mean the same to both of you.

Do not interpret out of solitude, for what you see means nothing. It will shift in what it stands for, and you will believe the world is an uncertain place, in which you walk in danger and uncertainty. It is but your interpretations which are lacking in stability, for they are not in line with what you really are. This is a state so seemingly unsafe that fear must rise. Do not continue thus, my brothers. We have One Interpreter. And through His use of symbols are we joined, so that they mean the same to all of us. Our common language lets us speak to all our brothers, and to understand with them forgiveness has been given to us all, and thus we can communicate again.

Appearances deceive but can be changed. Reality is changeless. It does not deceive at all, and if you fail to see beyond appearances you are deceived. For everything you see will change, and yet you thought it real before, and now you think it real again. Reality is thus reduced to form, and capable of change. Reality is changeless. It is this that makes it real, and keeps it separate from all appearances. It must transcend all form to be itself. It cannot change.

The miracle is means to demonstrate that all appearances can change because they are appearances and cannot have the changelessness reality entails. The miracle attests salvation from appearances by showing they can change. Your brother has a changelessness in him beyond appearance and deception, both. It is obscured by changing views of him which you perceive as his reality. The happy dream about him takes the form of the appearance of his perfect health, his perfect freedom from all forms of lack, and safety from disaster of all kinds. The miracle is proof he is not bound by loss or suffering in any form, because it can so easily be changed. This demonstrates that it was never real and could not stem from his reality. For that is changeless and has no effects which anything in Heaven or on earth could ever alter. But appearances are shown to be unreal because they change.

What is temptation but a wish to make illusions real? It does not seem to be the wish that no reality be so. Yet it is an assertion that some forms of idols have a powerful appeal which makes them harder to resist than those you would not want to have reality. Temptation, then, is nothing more than this; a prayer the miracle touch not some dreams but keep their unreality obscure and give to them reality instead. And Heaven gives no answer to the prayer, nor can a miracle be given you to heal appearances you do not like. You have established limits. What you ask is given you, but not of God Who knows no limits. You have limited yourself.

Reality is changeless. Miracles but show what you have interposed between reality and your awareness is unreal and does not interfere at all. The cost of the belief there must be some appearances beyond the hope of change is that the miracle cannot come forth from you consistently. For you have asked it be withheld from power to heal all dreams. There is no miracle you cannot have when you desire healing. But there is no miracle that can be given you unless you want it. Choose what you would heal, and He Who gives all miracles has not been given freedom to bestow His gifts upon God's Son. When he is tempted, he denies reality. And he becomes the willing slave of what he chose instead.

Because reality is changeless is a miracle already there to heal all things that change and offer them to you to see in happy form, devoid of fear. It will be given you to look upon your brother thus. But not while you would have it otherwise in some respects. For this but means you would not have him healed and whole. The Christ in him is perfect. Is it this that you would look upon? Then let there be no dreams about him which you would prefer to seeing this. And you will see the Christ in him because you let Him come to you. And when He has appeared to you, you will be certain you are like Him, for He is the changeless in your brother and in you.

This will you look upon when you decide there is not one appearance you would hold in place of what your brother really is. Let no temptation to prefer a dream allow uncertainty to enter here. Be not made guilty and afraid when you are tempted by a dream of what he is. But do not give it power to replace the changeless in him in your sight of him. There is no false appearance but will fade, if you request a miracle instead. There is no pain from which he is not free, if you would have him be but what he is. Why should you fear to see the Christ in him? You but behold yourself in what you see. As he is healed are you made free of guilt, for his appearance is your own to you.

How simple is salvation! All it says is what was never true is not true now, and never will be. The impossible has not occurred and can have no effects. And that is all. Can this be hard to learn by anyone who wants it to be true? Only unwillingness to learn it could make such an easy lesson difficult. How hard is it to see that what is false cannot be true, and what is true cannot be false? You can no longer say that you perceive no differences in false and true. You have been told exactly how to tell one from the other, and just what to do if you become confused. Why, then, do you persist in learning not such simple things?

There is a reason. But confuse it not with difficulty in the simple things salvation asks you learn. It teaches but the very obvious. It merely goes from one apparent lesson to the next, in easy steps which lead you gently from one to another, with no strain at all. This cannot be confusing, yet you are confused. For somehow you believe that what is totally confused is easier to learn and understand. What you have taught yourselves is such a giant learning feat it is indeed incredible. But you accomplished it because you wanted to and did not pause in diligence to judge it hard to learn, or too complex to grasp.

No-one who understands what you have learned, how carefully you have learned it and the pains to which you went to practice and repeat the lessons endlessly, in every form you could conceive of them, could ever doubt the power of your learning skill. There is no greater power in the world. The world was made by it and even now depends on nothing else. The lessons you have taught yourselves have been so overlearned and fixed they rise like heavy curtains to obscure the simple and the obvious. Say not you cannot learn them. For your power to learn is strong enough to teach you that your will is not your own, your thoughts do not belong to you, and even you are someone else.

Who could maintain that lessons such as these are easy? Yet you have learned more than this. You have continued, taking every step, however difficult, without complaint, until a world was built that suited you. And every lesson that makes up the world arises from the first accomplishment of learning; an enormity so great the Holy Spirit's Voice seems small and still before its magnitude. The world began with one strange lesson, powerful enough to render God forgotten and His Son an alien to himself, in exile from the home where God Himself established him. You who have taught yourselves the Son of God is guilty, say not that you cannot learn the simple things salvation teaches you!

Learning is an ability you made and gave yourselves. It was not made to do the Will of God, but to uphold a wish that It could be opposed and that a will apart from It was yet more real than It. And this has learning sought to demonstrate and you have learned what it was made to teach. Now does your ancient overlearning stand implacable before the Voice of truth and teach you that Its lessons are not true; too hard to learn, too difficult to see, and too opposed to what is really true. Yet you will learn them, for their learning is the only purpose for your learning skill the Holy Spirit sees in all the world. His simple lessons in forgiveness have a power mightier than yours, because they call from God and from your Self to you.

Is this a little voice, so small and still It cannot rise above the senseless noise of sounds which have no meaning? God willed not His Son forget Him. And the power of His Will is in the Voice that speaks for Him. Which lesson will you learn? What outcome is inevitable, sure as God, and far beyond all doubt and question? Can it be your little learning, strange in outcome, and incredible in difficulty will withstand the simple lessons being taught to you in every moment of each day, since time began and learning had been made?

The lessons to be learned are only two. Each has its outcome in a different world. And each world follows surely from its source. The certain outcome of the lesson that God's Son is guilty is the world you see. It is a world of terror and despair. Nor is there hope of happiness in it. There is no plan for safety you can make that ever will succeed. There is no joy that you can seek for here, and hope to find. Yet this is not the only outcome which your learning can produce. However much you may have overlearned your chosen task, the lesson which reflects the love of God is stronger still. And you will learn God's Son is innocent and see another world.

The outcome of the lesson that God's Son is guiltless is a world in which there is no fear, and everything is lit with hope, and sparkles with a gentle friendliness. Nothing but calls to you in soft appeal to be your friend, and let it join with you. And never does a call remain unheard, misunderstood, nor left unanswered in the self same tongue in which the call was made. And you will understand it was this call that everyone and everything within the world has always made, but you had not perceived it as it was. And now you see you were mistaken. You had been deceived by forms the call was hidden in. And so you did not hear it, and had lost a friend who always wanted to be part of you.

The soft, eternal calling of each part of God's creation to the whole is heard throughout the world this second lesson brings.

There is no living thing which does not share the universal will that it be whole, and that you do not leave its call unheard. Without your answer is it left to die, as it is saved from death when you have heard its calling as the ancient call to life, and understood that it is but your own. The Christ in you remembers God with all the certainty with which He knows His love. But only if His Son is innocent can He be Love. For God were fear indeed if he whom He created innocent could be a slave to guilt. God's perfect Son remembers his creation. But in guilt he has forgotten what he really is.

The fear of God results as surely from the lesson that His Son is guilty as God's love must be remembered when he learns his innocence. For hate must father fear and look upon its father as itself. How wrong are you who fail to hear the call that echoes past each seeming call to death, that sings behind each murderous attack, and pleads that love restore the dying world! You do not understand Who calls to you beyond each form of hate, each call to war. Yet you will recognize Him as you give Him answer in the language that He calls. He will appear when you have answered Him, and you will know in Him that God is Love.

What is temptation but a wish to make the wrong decision on what you would learn, and have an outcome that you do not want? It is the recognition that it is a state of mind unwanted that becomes the means whereby the choice is reassessed; another outcome seen to be preferred. You are deceived if you believe you want disaster and disunity and pain. Hear not the call for this within yourself. But listen, rather, to the deeper call beyond it, that appeals for peace and joy. And all the world will give you joy and peace. For as you hear, you answer. And behold! Your answer is the proof of what you learned. Its outcome is the world you look upon.

Let us be still an instant and forget all things we ever learned, all thoughts we had, and every preconception which we hold of what things mean, and what their purpose is. Let us remember not our own ideas of what the world is for. We do not know. Let every image held of everyone be loosened from our minds and swept away. Be innocent of judgement, unaware of any thoughts of evil or of good that ever crossed your mind of anyone. Now do we know him not. But you are free to learn of him and learn of him anew. Now is he born again to you, and you are born again to him, without the past that sentenced him to die and you with him.

Now is he free to live, as you are free, because an ancient learning passed away, and left a place for truth to be reborn.

An ancient lesson is not overcome by the opposing of the new and old. It is not vanquished that the truth be known, nor fought against to lose to truth's appeal. There is no battle which must be prepared; no time to be expended and no plans that need be laid for bringing in the new. There is an ancient battle being waged against the truth, but truth does not respond. Who could be hurt in such a war, unless he hurts himself? He has no enemy in truth. And can he be assailed by dreams?

Let us review again what seems to stand between you and the truth of what you are. For there are steps in its relinquishment. The first is a decision that you make. But afterwards, the truth is given you. You would establish truth. And by your wish, you set two choices to be made each time you think you must decide on anything. Neither is true. Nor are they different. Yet must we see them both, before you can look past them, to the one alternative that is a different choice. But not in dreams you made, that this might be obscured to you.

What you would choose between is not a choice, and gives but the illusion it is free, for it will have one outcome either way. Thus is it really not a choice at all. The leader and the follower emerge as separate roles, each seeming to possess advantages you would not want to lose. So in their fusion there appears to be the hope of satisfaction and of peace. You see yourself divided into both these roles, forever split between the two. And every friend or enemy becomes a means to help you save yourself from this.

Perhaps you call it love. Perhaps you think that it is murder justified at last. You hate the one you gave the leader's role when you would have it, and you hate as well his not assuming it. At times you want to let the follower in you arise and give away the role of leadership. And this is what you made your brother for and learned to think that this his purpose is. Unless he serves it, he has not fulfilled the function that was given him by you. And thus he merits death, because he has no purpose and no usefulness to you.

And what of him? What does he want of you? What could he want, but what you want of him? Herein is life as easily as death, for what you choose, you choose as well for him. Two calls you make to him, as he to you. Between these two is choice, because from them there is a different outcome. If he be the leader or the follower to you, it matters not, for you have chosen death. But if he calls for death or calls for life; for hate or for forgiveness and for help, is not the same in outcome.

Hear the one, and you are separate from him, and are lost. But hear the other, and you join with him, and in your answer is salvation found. The voice you hear in him is but your own. What does he ask you for? And listen well! For he is asking what will come to you because you see an image of yourself and hear your voice requesting what you want. Before you answer, pause to think of this:

> "The answer that I give my brother is
> What I am asking for. And what I learn
> Of him is what I learn about myself."

Then let us wait an instant and be still, forgetting everything we thought we heard; remembering how much we do not know. This brother neither leads nor follows us, but walks beside us on the self same road. He is like us, as near or far away from what we want as we will let him be. We make no gains he does not make with us and we fall back if he does not advance. Take not his hand in anger but in love, for in his progress do you count your own. And we go separately along the way unless you keep him safely by your side. Because he is your equal in God's love, you will be saved from all appearances, and answer to the Christ Who calls to you. Be still and listen. Think not ancient thoughts. Forget the dismal lessons that you learned about this Son of God who calls to you. Christ calls to all with equal tenderness, seeing no leaders and no followers, and hearing but one answer to them all. Because He hears one Voice, he cannot hear a different answer from the one He gave when God appointed Him His only Son.

Be very still an instant. Come without all thought of what you ever learned before and put aside all images you made. The old will fall away before the new without your opposition or intent. There will be no attack upon the things you thought were precious and in need of care. There will be no assault upon your wish to hear a call that never has been made. Nothing will hurt you in this holy place, to which you come to listen silently and learn the truth of what you really want. No more than this will you be asked to learn. But as you hear it, you will understand you need but come away without the thoughts you did not want and that were never true.

Forgive your brother all appearances, which are but ancient lessons that you taught yourself about the sinfulness in you. Hear but his call for mercy and release from all the fearful images he holds of what he is, and of what you must be. He is afraid to walk with you, and thinks perhaps a bit behind, a bit ahead, would be a safer place for him to be.

Can you make progress if you think the same, advancing only when he would step back, and falling back when he would go ahead? For so do you forget the journey's goal, which is but to decide to walk with him, so neither leads nor follows. Thus it is a way you go together, not alone. And in this choice is learning's outcome changed, for Christ has been reborn to both of you.

An instant spent without your old ideas of who your great Companion is and what he should be asking for, will be enough to let this happen. And you will perceive his purpose is the same as yours. He asks for what you want and needs the same as you. It takes, perhaps, a different form in him, but it is not the form you answer to. He asks and you receive, for you have come with but one purpose; that you both may learn you love each other with a brother's love. And as a brother, must his Father be the same as yours, as he is like yourself.

Together is your joint inheritance remembered and accepted by you both. Alone it is denied to both of you. Is it not clear that while you still insist on leading or on following, you think you walk alone, with no-one by your side? This is the road to nowhere, for the light cannot be given while you walk alone, and so you cannot see which way you go. And thus there is confusion, and a sense of endless doubting, as you stagger back and forward in the darkness and alone. Yet these are but appearances of what the journey is, and how it must be made. For next to you is One Who holds the light before you, so that every step is made in certainty and sureness of the road. A blindfold can indeed obscure your sight but cannot make the way itself grow dark. And He Who travels with you has the light.

Only the self-accused condemn. As you prepare to make a choice that will result in different outcomes, there is first one thing that must be overlearned. It must become a habit of response so typical of everything you do that it becomes your first response to all temptation and to every situation that occurs. Learn this and learn it well, for it is here delay of happiness is shortened by a span of time you cannot realize. You never hate your brother for his sins, but only for your own. Whatever form his sins appear to take it but obscures the fact that you believe it to be yours, and therefore meriting a "just" attack.

Why should his sins be sins, if you did not believe they could not be forgiven in you? Why are they real in him, if you did not believe that they are your reality? And why do you attack them everywhere except you hate yourself? Are you a sin?

You answer "yes" whenever you attack, for by attack do you assert that you are guilty and must give as you deserve. And what can you deserve but what you are? If you did not believe that you deserved attack, it never would occur to you to give attack to anyone at all. Why should you? What would be the gain to you? What could the outcome be that you would want? And how could murder bring you benefit?

Sins are in bodies. They are not perceived in minds. They are not seen as purposes, but actions. Bodies act, and minds do not. And therefore must the body be at fault for what it does. It is not seen to be a passive thing, obeying your commands and doing nothing of itself at all. If you are sin you are a body, for the mind acts not. And purpose must be in the body, not the mind. The body must act on its own and motivate itself. If you are sin, you lock the mind within the body and you give its purpose to its prison-house, which acts instead of it. A jailer does not follow orders but enforces orders on the prisoner.

Yet is the body prisoner and not the mind. The body thinks no thoughts. It has no power to learn, to pardon, nor enslave. It gives no orders that the mind need serve, nor sets conditions that it must obey. It holds in prison but the willing mind that would abide in it. It sickens at the bidding of the mind that would become its prisoner. And it grows old and dies, because that mind is sick within itself. Learning is all that causes change. And so the body, where no learning can occur, could never change unless the mind preferred the body change in its appearances, to suit the purpose given by the mind. For it can learn and there is all change made.

The mind that thinks it is a sin has but one purpose; that the body be the source of sin and keep it in the prison-house it chose and guards, and hold itself at bay, a sleeping prisoner to the snarling dogs of hate and evil, sickness and attack; of pain and age, of grief and suffering. Here are the thoughts of sacrifice preserved, for here guilt rules, and orders that the world be like itself; a place where nothing can find mercy or survive the ravages of fear except in murder and in death. For here are you made sin, and sin cannot abide the joyous and the free, for they are enemies which sin must kill. In death is sin preserved, and those who think that they are sin must die for what they think they are.

Let us be glad that you will see what you believe, and that it has been given you to change what you believe. The body will but follow. It can never lead you where you would not be. It does not guard your sleep, nor interfere with your awakening.

Release your body from imprisonment, and you will see no-one as prisoner to what you have escaped. You will not want to hold in guilt your chosen enemies, nor keep in chains to the illusion of a changing love the ones you think are friends.

The innocent release in gratitude for their release. And what they see upholds their freedom from imprisonment and death. Open your mind to change, and there will be no ancient penalty exacted from your brother or yourself. For God has said there is no sacrifice that can be asked; there is no sacrifice that can be made.

There is a tendency to think the world can offer consolation and escape from problems which its purpose is to keep. Why should this be? Because it is a place where choice among illusions seems to be the only choice. And you are in control of outcomes of your choosing. Thus you think, within the narrow band from birth to death, a little time is given you to use for you alone; a time when everyone conflicts with you, but you can choose which road will lead you out of conflict, and away from difficulties which concern you not. Yet they are your concern. How, then, can you escape from them by leaving them behind? What must go with you, you will take with you whatever road you choose to walk along.

Real choice is no illusion. But the world has none to offer. All its roads but lead to disappointment, nothingness and death. There is no choice in its alternatives. Seek not escape from problems here. The world was made that problems could not be escaped. Be not deceived by all the different names its roads are given. They have but one end. And each is but the means to gain that end, for it is here that all its roads will lead, however differently they seem to start; however differently they seem to go. Their end is certain, for there is no choice among them. All of them will lead to death. On some you travel gaily for a while, before the bleakness enters. And on some the thorns are felt at once. The choice is not what will the ending be, but when it comes.

There is no choice where every end is sure. Perhaps you would prefer to try them all, before you really learn they are but one. The roads this world can offer seem to be quite large in number, but the time must come when everyone begins to see how like they are to one another. Men have died on seeing this, because they saw no way except the pathways offered by the world. And learning they led nowhere, lost their hope. And yet this was the time they could have learned their greatest lesson. All must reach this point and go beyond it. It is true indeed there is no choice at all within the world. But this is not the lesson in itself. The lesson has a purpose, and in this you come to understand what it is for.

Why would you seek to try another road, another person or another place, when you have learned the way the lesson starts, but do not yet perceive what it is for? Its purpose is the answer to the search that all must undertake who still believe there is another answer to be found. Learn now, without despair, there is no hope of answer in the world. But do not judge the lesson which is but begun with this. Seek not another signpost in the world which seems to point to still another road. No longer look for hope where there is none. Make fast your learning now and understand you but waste time unless you go beyond what you have learned to what is yet to learn. For from this lowest point will learning lead to heights of happiness, in which you see the purpose of the lesson shining clear, and perfectly within your learning grasp.

Who would be willing to be turned away from all the roadways of the world, unless he understood their real futility? Is it not needful that he should begin with this, to seek another way instead? For while he sees a choice where there is none, what power of decision can he use? The great release of power must begin with learning where it really has a use. And what decision has power if it be applied in situations without choice?

The learning that the world can offer but one choice, no matter what its form may be, is the beginning of acceptance that there is a real alternative instead. To fight against this step is to defeat your purpose here. You did not come to learn to find a road the world does not contain. The search for different pathways in the world is but the search for different forms of truth. And this would keep the truth from being reached.

Think not that happiness is ever found by following a road away from it. This makes no sense and cannot be the way. To you who seem to find this course to be too difficult to learn, let me repeat that, to achieve a goal, you must proceed in its direction, not away from it. And every road that leads the other way will not advance the purpose to be found. If this be difficult to understand, then is this course impossible to learn. But only then. For otherwise, it is a simple teaching in the obvious.

There is a choice which you have power to make when you have seen the real alternatives. Until that point is reached you have no choice, and you can but decide how you would choose the better to deceive yourself again. This course attempts to teach no more than that the power of decision cannot lie in choosing different forms of what is still the same illusion and the same mistake.

All choices in the world depend on this; you choose between your brother and yourself, and you will gain as much as he will lose, and what you lose is what is given him. How utterly opposed to truth is this, when what the lesson's purpose is to teach that what your brother loses you have lost, and what he gains is what is given you.

He has not left His Thoughts! But you forgot His Presence and remembered not His love. No pathway in the world can lead to Him, nor any worldly goal is one with His. What road in all the world will lead within, when every road was made to separate the journey from the purpose it must have unless it be but futile wandering? All roads that lead away from what you are will lead you to confusion and despair. Yet has He never left His Thoughts to die, without their Source forever in themselves. He has not left His Thoughts! He could no more depart from them than they could keep Him out. In unity with Him do they abide, and in their Oneness both are kept complete.

There is no road that leads away from Him. A journey from yourself does not exist. How foolish and insane it is to think that there could be a road with such an aim! Where could it go? And how could you be made to travel on it, walking there without your own reality at one with you? Forgive yourself your madness and forget all senseless journeys and all goal-less aims. They have no meaning. You cannot escape from what you are. For God is merciful and did not let His Son abandon Him. For what He is, be thankful, for in that is your escape from madness and from death. Nowhere but where He is can you be found. There is no path that does not lead to Him.

The learning of the world is built upon a concept of the self adjusted to the world's reality. It fits it well. For this an image is that suits a world of shadows and illusions. Here it walks at home, where what it sees is one with it. The building of a concept of the self is what the learning of the world is for. This is its purpose; that you come without a self and make one as you go along. And by the time you reach "maturity," you have perfected it to meet the world on equal terms, at one with its demands.

A concept of the self is made by you. It bears no likeness to yourself at all. It is an idol, made to take the place of your reality as Son of God. The concept of the self the world would teach is not the thing that it appears to be. For it is made to serve two purposes, but one of which the mind can recognize. The first presents the face of innocence, the aspect acted on. It is this face that smiles and charms and even seems to love.

It searches for companions, and it looks, at times with pity, on the suffering, and sometimes offers solace. It believes that it is good, within an evil world.

This aspect can grow angry, for the world is wicked and unable to provide the love and shelter innocence deserves. And so this face is often wet with tears at the injustices the world accords to those who would be generous and good. This aspect never makes the first attack. But every day a hundred little things make small assaults upon its innocence, provoking it to irritation, and at last to open insult and abuse.

The face of innocence the concept of the self so proudly wears can tolerate attack in self-defence, for is it not a well-known fact the world deals harshly with defenceless innocence? No-one who makes a picture of himself omits this face, for he has need of it. The other side, he does not want to see. Yet it is here the learning of the world has set its sights, for it is here the world's "reality" is set, to see to it the idol lasts.

Beneath the face of innocence there is a lesson that the concept of the self was made to teach. It is a lesson in a terrible displacement, and a fear so devastating that the face which smiles above it must forever look away, lest it perceive the treachery it hides. The lesson teaches this; "I am the thing you made of me, and as you look on me you stand condemned, because of what I am." On this conception of the self the world smiles with approval, for it guarantees the pathways of the world are safely kept, and those who walk on them will not escape.

Here is the central lesson that ensures your brother is condemned eternally. For what you are has now become HIS sin. For this is no forgiveness possible. No longer does it matter what he does, for your accusing finger points to him, unwavering and deadly in its aim. It points to you as well, but this is kept still deeper in the mists below the face of innocence. And in these shrouded vaults are all his sins and yours preserved, and kept in darkness, where they cannot be perceived as errors, which the light would surely show. You can be neither blamed for what you are, nor can you change the things it makes you do. And you are each the symbol of your sins to one another, silently, and yet with ceaseless urgency, condemning still your brother for the hated thing you are.

Concepts are learned. They are not natural. Apart from learning they do not exist. They are not given, and they must be made. Not one of them is true, and many come from feverish imaginations, hot with hatred and distortions born of fear. What is a concept but a thought to which its maker gives a meaning of his own? Concepts maintain the world. But they cannot be used to demonstrate the world is real. For all of them are made within the world, born in its shadow, growing in its ways, and finally "maturing" in its thought. They are ideas of idols, painted with the brushes of the world, which cannot make a single picture representing truth.

A concept of the self is meaningless, for no-one here can see what it is for, and therefore cannot picture what it is. Yet is all learning which the world directs begun and ended with the single aim of teaching you this concept of yourself, that you will choose to follow this world's laws, and never seek to go beyond its roads, nor realize the way you see yourself. Now must the Holy Spirit find a way to help you see this concept of the self must be undone, if any peace of mind is to be given you. Nor can it be unlearned except by lessons aimed to teach that you are something else. For otherwise, you would be asked to make exchange of what you now believe for total loss of self and greater terror would arise in you.

Thus are the Holy Spirit's lesson plans arranged in easy steps, that though there be some lack of ease at times and some distress, there is no shattering of what was learned, but just a re-translation of what seems to be the evidence on its behalf. Let us consider, then, what proof there is that you are what your brother made of you. For even though you do not yet perceive that this is what you think, you surely learned by now that you behave as if it were. Does He react for you? And did he know exactly what would happen?

Could he see your future and ordain, before it came, what you should do in every circumstance? He must have made the world as well as you, to have such prescience in the things to come.
That you are what your brother made of you seems most unlikely. Even if he did, who gave the face of innocence to you? Is this your contribution? Who is, then, the "you" who made it? And who is deceived by all your goodness and attacks it so? Let us forget the concept's foolishness and merely think of this; there are two parts to what you think yourself to be. If one was generated by your brother, who was there to make the other? And from whom must something be kept hidden? If the world be evil, there is still no need to hide what you are made of. Who is there to see? And what but is attacked could need defence?

Perhaps the reason why this concept must be kept in darkness is that, in the light, the one who would not think it true is you. And what would happen to the world you know, if all its underpinnings were removed? Your concept of the world depends upon this concept of the self. And both would go, if either one were ever raised to doubt. The Holy Spirit does not seek to throw you into panic. So He merely asks if just a little question might be raised.

There are alternatives about the thing that you must be. You might, for instance, be the thing you chose to have your brother be. This shifts the concept of the self from what is wholly passive, and at least makes way for active choice, and some acknowledgment that interaction must have entered in. There is some understanding that you chose for both of you, and what he represents has meaning that was given it by you. It also shows some glimmering of sight into perception's law that what you see reflects the state of the perceiver's mind. Yet who was it that did the choosing first? If you are what you chose your brother be, alternatives were there to choose among, and someone must have first decided on the one to choose, and let the others go. Although this step has gains, it does not yet approach a basic question. Something must have gone before these concepts of the self. And something must have done the learning which gave rise to them. Nor can this be explained by either view. The main advantage of the shifting to the second from the first is that you somehow entered in the choice by your decision. But this gain is paid in almost equal loss, for now you stand accused of guilt for what your brother is. And you must share his guilt, because you chose it for him in the image of your own. While only he was treacherous before, now must you be condemned along with him.

The concept of the self has always been the great preoccupation of the world. And everyone believes that he must find the answer to the riddle of himself. Salvation can be seen as nothing more than the escape from concepts. It does not concern itself with content of the mind, but with the simple statement that it thinks. And what can think has choice and can be shown that different thoughts have different consequence. So it can learn that everything it thinks reflects the deep confusion that it feels about how it was made, and what it is. And vaguely does the concept of the self appear to answer what it does not know.

Seek not your Self in symbols. There can be no concept that can stand for what you are. What matters it which concept you accept while you perceive a self which interacts with evil, and reacts to wicked things?

Your concept of yourself will still remain quite meaningless. And you will not perceive that you can interact but with yourself. To see a guilty world is but the sign your learning has been guided by the world, and you behold it as you see yourself. The concept of the self embraces all you look upon and nothing is outside of this perception. If you can be hurt by anything, you see a picture of your secret wishes. Nothing more than this. And in your suffering of any kind, you see your own concealed desire to kill.

You will make many concepts of the self as learning goes along. Each one will show the changes in your own relationships, as your perception of yourself is changed. There will be some confusion every time there is a shift but be you thankful that the learning of the world is loosening its grasp upon your mind. And be sure and happy in the confidence that it will go at last and leave your mind at peace. The role of the accuser will appear in many places and in many forms. And each will seem to be accusing you. Yet have no fear it will not be undone.

The world can teach no images of you unless you want to learn them. There will come a time when images have all gone by, and you will see you know not what you are. It is to this unsealed and open mind that truth returns, unhindered and unbound. Where concepts of the self have been laid by is truth revealed exactly as it IS. When every concept has been raised to doubt and question and been recognized as made on no assumptions which would stand the light, then is the truth left free to enter in its sanctuary, clean and free of guilt. There is no statement that the world is more afraid to hear than this:

> "I do not know the thing I am and therefore do not know what I am doing, where I am, or how to look upon the world or on myself."

Yet in this learning is salvation born. And what you are will tell you of Itself.

You see the flesh or recognize the Spirit. There is no compromise between the two. If one is real the other must be false, for what is real denies its opposite. There is no choice in vision but this one. What you decide in this determines all you see and think is real and hold as true. On this one choice does all your world depend, for here have you established what you are, as flesh or Spirit in your own belief.

If you choose flesh, you never will escape the body as your own reality, for you have chosen that you want it so. But choose the Spirit, and all Heaven bends to touch your eyes and bless your holy sight, that you may see the world of flesh no more except to heal and comfort and to bless.

Salvation is undoing. If you choose to see the body, you behold a world of separation, unrelated things, and happenings that make no sense at all. This one appears and disappears in death; that one is doomed to suffering and loss. And no-one is exactly as he was an instant previous, nor will he be the same as he is now an instant hence. Who could have trust where so much change is seen, for who is worthy if he be but dust? Salvation is undoing of all this. And constancy arises in the sight of those whose eyes salvation has released from looking at the cost of keeping guilt, because they chose to let it go instead.

Salvation does not ask that you behold the Spirit and perceive the body not. It merely asks that this should be your choice. For you can see the body without help, but do not understand how to behold a world apart from it. It is your world salvation will undo, and let you see another world your eyes could never find. Be not concerned how this could ever be. You do not understand how what you see arose to meet your sight. For if you did, it would be gone. The veil of ignorance is drawn across the evil and the good, and must be passed that both may disappear, so that perception finds no hiding place. How is this done? It is not done at all. What could there be within the universe which God created that must still be done?

Only in arrogance could you conceive that you must make the way to Heaven plain. The means are given you by which to see the world that will replace the one you made. Your will be done! In Heaven as on earth this is forever true. It matters not where you believe you are, nor what you think the truth about yourself must really be. It makes no difference what you look upon, nor what you choose to feel or think or wish. For God Himself has said, "Your will be done." and it is done to you accordingly.

You who believe that you can choose to see the Son of God as you would have him be, forget not that no concept of yourself will stand against the truth of what you are. Undoing truth would be impossible. But concepts are not difficult to change. One vision, clearly seen, that does not fit the picture as it was perceived before will change the world for eyes that learn to see, because the concept of the self has changed. Are you invulnerable? Then the world is harmless in your sight. Do you forgive?

Then is the world forgiving, for you have forgiven it its trespasses, and so it looks on you with eyes that see as yours. Are you a body? So is all the world perceived as treacherous and out to kill.

Are you a Spirit, deathless, and without the promise of corruption and the stain of sin upon you? So the world is seen as stable, fully worthy of your trust; a happy place to rest in for a while, where nothing need be feared, but only loved. Who is unwelcome to the kind in heart? And what could hurt the truly innocent? Your will be done, you holy Child of God. It does not matter if you think you are in earth or Heaven. What your Father wills for you can never change. The truth in you remains as radiant as a star, as pure as light, as innocent as Love Itself. And you are worthy that your Will be done!

Learning is change. Salvation does not seek to use a means as yet too alien to your thinking to be helpful, nor to make the kinds of change you could not recognize. Concepts are needed while perception lasts and changing concepts is salvation's task. For it must deal in contrasts, not in truth, which has no opposite and cannot change. In this world's concepts are the guilty "bad;" the "good" are innocent. And no-one here but holds a concept of himself in which he counts the "good" to pardon him the "bad." Nor does he trust the "good" in anyone, believing that the "bad" must lurk behind. This concept emphasizes treachery, and trust becomes impossible. Nor could it change while you perceive the "bad" in you.

You could not recognise your "evil" thoughts as long as you see value in attack. You will perceive them sometimes but will not see them as meaningless. And so they come in fearful form, with content still concealed, to shake your sorry concept of yourself, and blacken it with still another "crime." You cannot give yourself your innocence, for you are too confused about yourself. But should one brother dawn upon your sight as wholly worthy of forgiveness, then your concept of yourself is wholly changed. Your "evil" thoughts have been forgiven with his, because you let them all affect you not. No longer did you choose that you should be the sign of evil and of guilt in him. And as you gave your trust to what is good in him, you gave it to the good in you.

In terms of concepts, it is thus you see him more than just a body, for the good is never what the body seems to be. The actions of the body are perceived as coming from the "baser" part of you, and thus of him as well. By focusing upon the good in him, the body grows decreasingly persistent in your sight, and will at length be seen as little more than just a shadow circling round the good.

And this will be your concept of yourself, when you have reached the world beyond the sight your eyes alone can offer you to see. For you will not interpret what you see without the Aid that God has given you. And in His sight there is another world.

You live in that world just as much as this. For both are concepts of yourself, which can be interchanged but never jointly held. The contrast is far greater than you think, for you will love this concept of yourself, because it was not made for you alone. Born as a gift for someone not perceived to be yourself, it has been given you. For your forgiveness, offered unto him, has been accepted now for both of you.

Have faith in him who walks with you, so that your fearful concept of yourself may change. And look upon the good in him, that you may not be frightened by your "evil" thoughts, because they do not cloud your view of him. And all this shift requires is that you be willing that this happy change occur. No more than this is asked. On its behalf, remember what the concept of yourself which now you hold has brought you in its wake, and welcome the glad contrast offered you. Hold out your hand, that you may have the gift of kind forgiveness which you offer one whose need for it is just the same as yours. And let the cruel concept of yourself be changed to one which brings the peace of God.

The concept of yourself which now you hold would guarantee your function here remain forever unaccomplished and undone. And thus it dooms you to a bitter sense of deep depression and futility. Yet it need not be fixed unless you choose to hold it past the hope of change and keep it static and concealed within your mind. Give it instead to Him Who understands the changes that it needs to let it serve the function given you to bring you peace, that you may offer peace to have it yours. Alternatives are in your mind to use, and you can see yourself another way. Would you not rather look upon yourself as needed for salvation of the world, instead of as salvation's enemy?

The concept of the self stands like a shield, a silent barricade before the truth, and hides it from your sight. All things you see are images, because you look on them as through a barrier which dims your sight and warps your vision, so that you behold nothing with clarity. The light is kept from everything you see. At most, you glimpse a shadow of what lies beyond. At least, you merely look on darkness and perceive the terrified imaginings that come from guilty thoughts and concepts born of fear.

And what you see is hell, for fear is hell. All that is given you is for release; the sight, the vision and the inner Guide all lead you out of hell with those you love beside you, and the universe with them.

Behold your role within the universe! To every part of true creation has the Lord of Love and Life entrusted all salvation from the misery of hell. And to each one has He allowed the grace to be a Saviour to the holy ones especially entrusted to his care. And this he learns when first he looks upon one brother as he looks upon himself and sees the mirror of himself in him. Thus is the concept of himself laid by, for nothing stands between his sight and what he looks upon, to judge what he beholds. And in this single vision does he see the face of Christ and understands he looks on everyone as he beholds this One. For there is light where darkness was before, and now the veil is lifted from his sight.

The veil across the face of Christ, the fear of God and of salvation and the love of guilt and death, they all are different names for just one error; that there is a space between you and your brother, kept apart by an illusion of yourself which holds him off from you, and you away from him. The sword of judgement is the weapon which you give to the illusion of yourself, that it may fight to keep the space that holds your brother off unoccupied by love. Yet while you hold this sword, you must perceive the body as yourself, for you are bound to separation from the sight of him who holds the mirror to another view of what he is, and thus what you must be.

What is temptation but the wish to stay in hell and misery? And what could this give rise to but an image of yourself that can be miserable, and remain in hell and torment? Who has learned to see his brother not as this has saved himself, and thus is he a Saviour to the rest. To everyone has God entrusted all, because a partial saviour would be one who is but partly saved. The holy ones whom God has given each of you to save are everyone you meet or look upon, not knowing who they are; all those you saw an instant and forgot, and those you knew a long while since, and those you will yet meet, the unremembered and the not yet born. For God has given you His Son to save from every concept that he ever held.

Yet while you wish to stay in hell, how could you be the Saviour of the Son of God? How would you know his holiness while you see him apart from yours? For holiness is seen through holy eyes that look upon the innocence within, and thus expect to see it everywhere. And so they call it forth in everyone they look upon, that he may be what they expect of him. This is the Saviour's vision; that he see his innocence in all he looks upon, and sees his own salvation everywhere.

He holds no concept of himself between his calm and open eyes and what he sees. He brings the light to what he looks upon, that he may see it as it really is.

Whatever form temptation seems to take, it always but reflects a wish to be a self which you are not. And from that wish a concept rises, teaching that you are the thing you wish to be. It will remain your concept of yourself until the wish that fathered it no longer is held dear. But while you cherish it, you will behold your brother in the likeness of the self whose image has the wish begot of you. For vision can but represent a wish, because it has no power to create. Yet it can look with love or look with hate, depending only on the simple choice of whether you would join with what you see, or keep yourself apart and separate.

The Saviour's vision is as innocent of what your brother is as it is free of any judgement made upon yourself. It sees no past in anyone at all. And thus it serves a wholly open mind, unclouded by old concepts, and prepared to look on only what the present holds. It cannot judge because it does not know. And recognizing this, it merely asks, "What is the meaning of what I behold?" Then is the answer given. And the door held open for the face of Christ to shine upon the one who asks, in innocence, to see beyond the veil of old ideas and ancient concepts held so long and dear against the vision of the Christ in you.

Be vigilant against temptation, then, remembering that it is but a wish, insane and meaningless, to make yourself a thing which you are not. And think as well upon the thing that you would be instead. It is a thing of madness, pain and death; a thing of treachery and black despair, of failing dreams and no remaining hope except to die and end the dream of fear. This is temptation; nothing more than this. Can this be difficult to choose against? Consider what temptation is and see the real alternatives you choose between.

There are but two. Be not deceived by what appears as many choices. There is hell or Heaven and of these you choose but one. Let not the world's light, given unto you, be hidden from the world. It needs the light, for it is dark indeed, and men despair because the Saviour's vision is withheld, and what they see is death. Their Saviour stands, unknowing and unknown, beholding them with eyes unopened. And they cannot see until he looks on them with seeing eyes and offers them forgiveness with his own. Can you to whom God says, "Release My Son!" be tempted not to listen, when you learn that it is you for whom He asks release? And what but this is what this course would teach? And what but this is there for you to learn?

Temptation has one lesson it would teach, in all its forms, wherever it occurs. It would persuade the holy Son of God he is a body, born in what must die, unable to escape its frailty, and bound by what it orders him to feel. It sets the limits on what he can do; its power is the only strength he has; his grasp cannot exceed its tiny reach. Would you be this, if Christ appeared to you in all His glory, asking you but this,

> "Choose once again if you would take your place among the Saviours of the world, or would remain in hell and hold your brothers there."

For He has come and He is asking this. How do you make the choice? How easily is this explained! You always choose between your weakness and the strength of Christ in you. And what you choose is what you think is real. Simply by never using weakness to direct your actions, you have given it no power. And the light of Christ in you is given charge of everything you do. For you have brought your weakness unto Him, and He has given you His strength instead.

Trials are but lessons which you failed to learn presented once again, so where you made a faulty choice before you now can make a better one, and thus escape all pain which what you chose before has brought to you. In every difficulty, all distress and each perplexity Christ calls to you and gently says, "My brother, choose again." He would not leave one source of pain unhealed, nor any image left to veil the truth. He would not leave you comfortless, alone in dreams of hell, but would release your minds from everything that hides His face from you. His holiness is yours because He is the only power that is real in you. His strength is yours because He is the Self that God created as His only Son.

The images you make cannot prevail against what God Himself would have you be. Be never fearful of temptation, then, but see it as it is; another chance to choose again and let Christ's strength prevail in every circumstance and every place you raised an image of yourself before. For what appears to hide the face of Christ is powerless before His majesty and disappears before His holy sight.

The Saviours of the world, who see like Him, are merely those who chose His strength instead of their own weakness, seen apart from Him. They will redeem the world, for they are joined in all the power of the Will of God.

And what they will is only what He wills. Learn, then, the happy habit of response to all temptation to perceive yourself as weak and miserable with these words,

> "I am as God created me. His Son
> can suffer nothing. And I am His
> Son."

Thus is Christ's strength invited to prevail, replacing all your weakness with the strength that comes from God and that can never fail. And thus are miracles as natural as fear and agony appeared to be before the choice for holiness was made. For in that choice are false distinctions gone, illusory alternatives laid by, and nothing left to interfere with truth.

You are as God created you, and so is every living thing you look upon, regardless of the images you see. What you behold as sickness and as pain, as weakness and as suffering and loss, is but temptation to perceive yourself defenceless and in hell. Yield not to this, and you will see all pain, in every form, wherever it occurs, but disappear as mists before the sun. A miracle has come to heal God's Son, and close the door upon his dreams of weakness, opening the way to his salvation and release. Choose once again what you would have him be, remembering that every choice you make establishes your own identity as you will see it and believe it is.

Deny me not the little gift I ask, when in exchange I lay before your feet the peace of God, and power to bring this peace to everyone who wanders in the world uncertain, lonely, and in constant fear. For it is given you to join with him, and through the Christ in you unveil his eyes, and let him look upon the Christ in him. My brothers in salvation, do not fail to hear my voice and listen to my words. I ask for nothing but your own release. There is no place for hell within a world whose loveliness can yet be so intense and so inclusive it is but a step from there to Heaven. To your tired eyes I bring a vision of a different world, so new and clean and fresh you will forget the pain and sorrow that you saw before. Yet this a vision is which you must share with everyone you see, for otherwise you will behold it not. To give this gift is how to make it yours. And God ordained, in loving kindness, that it be for you.

Let us be glad that we can walk the world and find so many chances to perceive another situation where God's gift can once again be recognized as ours! And thus will all the vestiges of hell, the secret "sins" and hidden hates be gone. And all the loveliness which they concealed appear like lawns of Heaven to our sight, to lift us high above the thorny roads we travelled on before the Christ appeared. Hear me, my brothers, hear and join with me. God has ordained I cannot call in vain, and in His certainty I rest content. For you will hear, and you will choose again. And in this choice is everyone made free.

I thank You, Father, for these holy ones who are my brothers as they are Your Sons. My faith in them is Yours. I am as sure that they will come to me as You are sure of what they are and will forever be. They will accept the gift I offer them, because You gave it me on their behalf. And as I would but do Your Holy Will, so will they choose. And I give thanks for them. Salvation's song will echo through the world with every choice they make. For we are one in purpose, and the end of hell is near.

In joyous welcome is my hand outstretched to every brother who would join with me in reaching past temptation, and who looks with fixed determination toward the light that shines beyond in perfect constancy. Give me my own, for they belong to You. And can You fail in what is but Your Will? I give You thanks for what my brothers are. And as each one elects to join with me, the song of thanks from earth to Heaven grows from tiny scattered threads of melody to one inclusive chorus from a world redeemed from hell and giving thanks to You.

And now we say "Amen." For Christ has come to dwell in the abode You set for Him before time was, in calm eternity. The journey closes, ending at the place where it began. No trace of it remains. Not one illusion is accorded faith, and not one spot of darkness still remains to hide the face of Christ from anyone. Thy Will is done, complete and perfectly, and all creation recognizes You, and knows You as the only Source it has. Clear in Your Likeness does the Light shine forth from everything that lives and moves in You. For we have reached where all of us are One, and we are home, where You would have us be.

www.ingramcontent.com/pod-product-compliance
Lightning Source LLC
Chambersburg PA
CBHW051931290426

44110CB00015B/1941